PREDATORY
BUREAUCRACY

PREDATORY BUREAUCRACY

The Extermination

of Wolves and

the Transformation

of the West

Michael J. Robinson

University Press of Colorado

© 2005 by the University Press of Colorado

Published by the University Press of Colorado
5589 Arapahoe Avenue, Suite 206C
Boulder, Colorado 80303

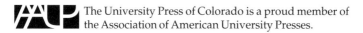 The University Press of Colorado is a proud member of
the Association of American University Presses.

The University Press of Colorado is a cooperative publishing enterprise supported, in part,
by Adams State College, Colorado State University, Fort Lewis College, Mesa State College,
Metropolitan State College of Denver, University of Colorado, University of Northern Colorado, and Western State College of Colorado.

∞ The paper used in this publication meets the minimum requirements of the American
National Standard for Information Sciences—Permanence of Paper for Printed Library Materials. ANSI Z39.48-1992

Library of Congress Cataloging-in-Publication Data

Robinson, Michael J., 1964–
    Predatory bureaucracy : the extermination of wolves and the transformation of the
west / Michael J. Robinson.
        p. cm.
    Includes bibliographical references and index.
        ISBN 0-87081-819-8 (pbk. : alk. paper) — ISBN 0-87081-818-X (hardcover : alk. paper)
        1. Wolves—Control—United States—History. 2. Wolves—Control—West (U.S.)—
History. 3. Wolves—Control—Government policy—United States—History. I. Title.
        SF810.7.W65R63 2005
        639.9′66′0978—dc22

                                                                          2005014130

Design by Daniel Pratt

14   13   12   11   10   09   08   07   06   05   10   9   8   7   6   5   4   3   2   1

This publication was supported in part by the Summerlee Foundation.

For Jennifer L. Sprague

Contents

Contents

Illustrations

PHOTOGRAPHS

MAPS

TABLES

Acknowledgments

The genesis of this book was a term paper on the history of wolves in Colorado written for a 1992 class on the philosophy of environmental law, taught by Charles Wilkinson at the University of Colorado. Charles is a scholar and a gentleman, and I am grateful for his early encouragement.

When it appeared sufficient material existed to write a book on the subject—well before the emergence of the broader topic of predator extermination and control throughout the West—I approached the Summerlee Foundation of Dallas, Texas, for support. The Summerlee Foundation's financial contribution at the outset in 1993 and 1995 and at the conclusion of this endeavor in 2004 served as catalyst, fuel, and landing pad for this book—even as its flight path took unexpected directions.

What I had described to the foundation as a two-year project stretched into a twelve-year epoch. I am grateful not just to the foundation for persevering for so long but especially to Summerlee's program director for animals, Melanie A. Lambert. Thank you, Melanie, for your encouragement, your patience, and your friendship; you have shown me the heart of philanthropy.

Judy Gould, Peter MacAusland, Delia Malone, Julia Portmore, and Jean-Yves Tola also contributed to the research component of this project by donating matching funds to meet the terms of the Summerlee Foundation's initial challenge grant. Lynne M. Butler, when the notion of the book was morphing from improbable idea to far-fetched intent, sponsored my attendance at a workshop to help me learn how to raise money for both this book and my other ventures. John Towner generously contributed to subsequent research expenses—on the condition that others involved in the project not know about his generosity. Thank you, John; please don't be too embarrassed.

I wish to acknowledge my colleagues at Sinapu, the non-profit Colorado wolf reintroduction organization I helped found, between 1992 and 1996 when this book was an organizational project. I especially appreciate the flexibility and support of the Center for Biological Diversity, my employer since 1997. It is a great honor to work with America's foremost protectors of endangered species; I hope *Predatory Bureaucracy* helps foster more of the savvy, informed, and effective advocacy for which the Center for Biological Diversity is renowned.

This story could not have been told in outline form, and the meaning of events decades ago—just as now—accrue in the day-to-day living of them. The remembrances and records of those days, or some of them, are collected in countless journals, correspondence, newspaper articles, government files, and more. Many people dug up a telling detail or three as a favor for me. At the risk of forgetting someone crucial to this research, I acknowledge and thank David E. Brown, Colleen Buchanan, Jasper Carlton, Douglas Caywood, Brendan Cummings, Alexander A. Drummond, Thomas R. Dunlap, Maggie Dwire, Rob Edward, John Ellenberger, Toby Fisher, Dave Foreman, Marc Gaede, Marnie Gaede, Kathy Goodwin, Diana Hadley, Susan Hagood, Hub Hall, Steve Herman, Mary Anne Hitt, Elisabeth A. Jennings, Steve Johnson, Terry B. Johnson, Wendy Keefover-Ring, Kelly Kindscher, Angie Krall, Dave Kreutzer, Dr. Steve Lacy, the late David Lavender, Carsten Lien, John Little, Stephen O. MacDonald, Elizabeth Mills, Jean Ossorio, Peter Ossorio, Julie Palmquist, Brent Plater, Kimberly Riggs, Kirk Robinson, Andrew "Slugthang" Rodman, Monica Romero, Dr. Nicole Rosmarino, Gary Schiffmiller, Morris Snider, Jenny Sprague, Gary Sprung, Keir Sterling, Kieran Suckling, the late T. H. Watkins, Pat Wolff, and Nancy Zierenberg. To the friends who helped me and to the acquaintances and kind strangers who took the time to find answers to bizarre questions about the long ago, your kindness is not forgotten.

Several people with personal connections to the incidents in this book or with familial connections to the principals agreed to be interviewed. Thank you to the Honorable John D. Dingell; the late Peter Edge, son of Rosalie Edge; Dr. H. H. Hall, son of E. Raymond Hall; Bob Hohnholz, son of John Hohnholz; Elisabeth A. Jennings; Doug McKenna; David R. Parsons; Wayne Pettee, M.D.; Inez Prator, daughter of Roy Spangler; and Acker Young, son of Stanley P. Young.

The staffs of not a few libraries also played integral roles in my research. I am grateful to the people who work in the following institutions: the Arizona State University Library (Tempe), the Colorado Historical Society, the Colorado State Archives, the Denver Public Library's Western History Department, the J.

Cloyd Miller Library at Western New Mexico University in Silver City (especially its stellar interlibrary loan department), the Joseph R. Skeen Library at New Mexico Tech (Socorro), the Museum of Vertebrate Zoology at the University of California at Berkeley, the National Archives, the New Mexico State University Library Archives and Special Collections (Las Cruces), Norlin Library at the University of Colorado at Boulder, the Preservation and Access Service Center for Colorado Academic Libraries (Denver), the Silver City Public Library, the Smithsonian Institution Archives, the University of Arizona Library (Tucson), the University of New Mexico Library (Albuquerque), and the U.S. Office of Personnel Management.

My sister, Dvora J. Robinson, herself the coordinator of a small library, contributed far more than the single hour or afternoon helping me track down one or two details. Over a five-year period she checked innumerable facts from far-flung books and journals, and in the last hectic two months she located the owners of most of the photographs depicted to request permission to reprint. Thank you, Dvora; you make me proud. I look forward to making up for the time communicating only through phone and e-mail with some long river trips together.

Pamela A. Uihlein, my colleague at Sinapu and primary researcher for *Predatory Bureacracy*, was part of this project from its inception, initially as coauthor of what was meant to be a simple book about the demise of wolves in a single state. Pam spent weeks tabulating and classifying each of the 38,451 bounty receipts stored in the Colorado State Archives and in various county courthouses in Colorado—allowing me to connect the spread of railroads to the increasing lethality of frontier ranching culture. She scanned and read through tens of thousands of documents at the Smithsonian Institution, the National Archives, and the Denver Public Library, selecting a small but crucial fraction that revealed the telling details of policies and personalities. She traveled to Stanley P. Young's birthplace in Astoria, Oregon, and discovered the essay by Young's sister about their childhood home. When I wondered about Logan B. Crawford, Young's predecessor as predatory animal inspector in the Colorado district of the Bureau of Biological Survey, Pam located his family's locally published booklet describing his life—a typical miracle in her labors. Without Pam's work, this book would have been impossible; and without her enthusiasm and good humor, our adventures fighting for wolf recovery in Colorado would have been much less fun. Most of all, Pam, thank you for being a true friend through all the vagaries of life.

I was fortunate that several comrades, fellow travelers, and wise souls expressed interest in and read portions of the manuscript as it evolved. Thanks to Gary Clauss, Annie Decker, Alex Drummond, Carol Beth Elliot, Scott Greacen, Lisa Jennings, David Kreutzer, Jean Ossorio, Peter Ossorio, Van Perkins, David Petersen, Thomas Powers, Chuck Romaniello, Pam Uihlein, Bethanie Walder, and Charles Wilkinson. Each offered insights that helped reframe my thinking and expression.

Todd Schulke read multiple iterations of the manuscript as I struggled through rewrites, and he commented at each stage, year after year. Thanks, Todd, for the acerbic remarks scrawled across pages and the heartfelt arguments under the box-elder tree. And beyond the advice, you know how much I appreciate your solid (if saturnine) friendship—not to mention your wicked sardonicism.

My father, Ivor Robinson, was the sole person who read every chapter of this book in draft form. I know nobody else as broadly erudite and linguistically rigorous, nobody as keen to nail a cliché or ask the telling question about the meaning of a word. Many a paragraph would read less clearly without his edits, and at least one major misrendering of history (concerning the FDR years) would have slipped in without his perspicacity. Thanks, Dad, not just for your help on this book but for insisting that I take education seriously.

Before I could share draft chapters, they had to be printed, a task that for many years eluded my technological capabilities at home. Sally Smith allowed me to use her computer and printer. Sally's daughter, Elsie Bjornstad, tolerated the sounds of epic conflict as I sought to bind the machines to my will.

I typed the first words of this book at the Kreutzer kitchen table and rechecked my sources at the end of this endeavor at the same table—thanks to the hospitality of Julie and Dave Kreutzer and their son, Bruce (who wasn't around at the onset).

Thanks to Yael Grauer for proofreading the manuscript in a three-day marathon session, to Diane Sylvain for developing the accompanying maps, and to Jenny Sprague for long nights at our kitchen table creating the index.

I also appreciate Joanna Hurley, Thomas Powers, and Stephen Topping for their helpful recommendations on publishing.

Sandy Crooms, Laura Furney, Daniel Pratt, Darrin Pratt, and Ann Wendland of the University Press of Colorado were patient and supportive as this project hit turbulence and delays.

Finally, I am very grateful to the following people and institutions for making photographs available for publication: the Aldo Leopold Foundation; Alliance Communications; Jerry Choate; the Cooper Ornithological Society; the Denver Public Library; Marnie and Marc Gaede, Brant Gaede, and Robin Lodewick for the photo of Irving Brant (Robin's father and Marc and Brant's grandfather); the J. N. "Ding" Darling Foundation; Hawk Mountain Sanctuary Association; Hub Hall; the Humane Society of the United States; Edwin McKee; the Murie Center; the New Mexico State University library; Willard Prator (grandson of Roy Spangler); Nancy Rosi (grandniece of Logan Crawford); Tread of Pioneers Historical Museum; the University of Arizona Library; the University of Kansas Libraries; the U.S. Fish and Wildlife Service; the U.S.G.S. National Museum of Natural History; the U.S. National Archives and Records Administration; the Washington State University Library (Pullman); and the Wildlife Management Institute.

I am, of course, solely responsible for any errors in fact or interpretation.

Prologue: The Last Wolf

Old age made movement more difficult. No longer would the sight of a hare or a deer prompt a burst of unstoppable speed through the pines. Hunger was a frequent companion. And the witless sheep in the forested mountains above southern Colorado's San Luis Valley had proved too tempting.

What role did memory play? We cannot know. Brothers and sisters had disappeared abruptly seventeen years before. Perhaps the flicker of images occasionally returned: the seven more-dominant pack members trotting ahead through sage and rabbit brush, the sharp clang of the first trap and the yelp of terror and pain, then the siblings running off the trail and into the fatal minefield of traps.

We don't even know the last wolf's sex. But it hardly matters: by 1945 no mates of either gender were to be found. Only the dry notations recorded by the U.S. Fish and Wildlife Service, which had set the trap, recall the animal's capture in Colorado's Conejos County. For the previous six years—since another wolf had died high in the southern San Juans a couple of dozen miles to the west or southwest—there had been no other wolf scent in Colorado. Hundreds of miles north, Wyoming's last wolf had been shot five years before, in 1940, and the infrequent lobo crossing from Mexico rarely lived longer than a month.

Another's lupine howl might have sounded odd. Coyotes still offered their sorority of song, and the autumnal whistling bugles of elk spoke to a soundscape of intimate familiarity. But no other wolves. Strychnine had finally quieted the rolling grasslands to the east, and the canyonlands to the west were wolfless as well. The next nearest of its kind after Mexico lived in Canada.

Who can tell how the last hours of freedom were spent? Did the vague smell of man or iron or horse portend danger, or did the trap spring from the earth utterly without warning? Perhaps the bite of steel and then the long wait had been expected. This was the way the others had departed.

PREDATORY
BUREAUCRACY

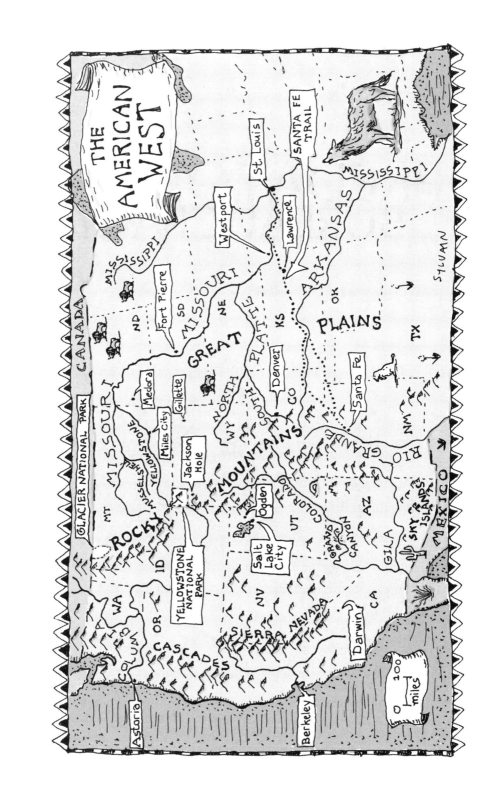

H ow does a civilization exterminate a species, extinguishing a unique evolutionary lineage that trails back like paw prints in the sand for tens of thousands of years? For some species, extermination was a facile and all too quick affair. The passenger pigeon, following a mass migration carved by instinct into each bird's genes (as if etched into the wind itself), succumbed to an anarchistic army of frontier riflemen.

Exterminating the wolf was another matter. Canny, adaptable, and determined to survive and breed, members of the lobo tribe refused to melt away before the fur trappers and poisoners of the frontier, seemed to get the better of the cattle barons, and would not disappear even with high bounties on their hides. The cultural code of the pioneer—to kill what couldn't be dominated, an imperative as ineluctable as DNA—failed against the wolf.

But that same code, divested of its populist frontier context and transplanted into the very system of centralized government that replaced the frontier, eventually accomplished what bounties, ranchers, and fur trappers could not. In fact, exterminating the wolf in the American West proved so challenging that the enterprise brought into being new political institutions and financial relationships—which turned out to be at least as resilient as the wolf itself.

The United States Forest Service began killing wolves as a means of currying favor with its ranching constituency. Then the job was taken over by the U.S. Bureau of Biological Survey, which developed an ever-growing list of species to be wiped out and collected money for that task from states, local governments, and private associations. National Park Service rangers and idealistic young men who were part of Franklin D. Roosevelt's Civilian Conservation Corps distributed millions of poisoned baits to kill not just wolves and coyotes but also the pesky prey animals whose numbers the predators would otherwise have controlled. And the federal Grazing Service, precursor to the Bureau of Land Management, helped funnel part of the fees paid for grazing on the public domain to the extermination campaign.

The master strategist for building this program was Stanley P. Young. Born in 1889 and raised on the romance of the recently tamed frontier, Young joined the Biological Survey in 1917 and quickly became expert at trapping wolves. (He caught the first wolf for the agency in Arizona.) But Young learned another lesson also: that at the height of a world war, home defense agencies along the U.S. border with Mexico might be persuaded to donate their money to kill predators.

Promoted and sent to Colorado, the epicenter of the western livestock industry and of bounties on predators, Young learned how to organize people around funding the survey's salaried hunters instead of bounties and how to use the media to shape public perception. Promoted to positions of increasing responsibility in the nation's capitol, he helped the survey recast extermination as "control" and kept expanding the agency's budget for killing despite fierce opposition from scientists and lovers of nature who had friends in the White House.

Finally, Young installed a protégé to lead the Biological Survey under the new name of the U.S. Fish and Wildlife Service. (Since the agency's inception in 1885 its name has changed nine times.)

While the Bureau of Biological Survey became a powerful federal agency under Young's influence, a handful of lone wolves survived into the 1930s and 1940s. The San Juan mountain chain along the Colorado–New Mexico border was one of the few regions supporting wolves in the entire western United States. But one by one, with unlimited federal resources brought to bear, the wolves were poisoned and trapped. Other wolves periodically crossed into the United States from Mexico and Canada but were targeted as soon as the Fish and Wildlife Service learned they were about.

After passage of the federal Endangered Species Act in 1973, it was those country's populations—in Mexico reduced to just five animals—that served as the seed for wolf reintroduction in the northern Rocky Mountains and the Southwest. But despite the change in policy from extermination to recovery and despite overwhelming public support, reintroduced wolves have run up against the same array of political forces that were behind the original extermination campaign. The future of the gray wolf and its ecosystems is far from secure.

Uncovering the political, social, and biological saga of wolves in the Rocky Mountains, the Great Plains, and the Southwest opens up a map to a little-explored West—a political topography of frontier-era institutions riding strong into the twenty-first century. It explains more fully than any other tale why the group for which wolf extermination was accomplished—the livestock industry—continues to dominate western national parks, forests, and other public lands and still all too often determines the fate of their myriad wildlife.

The Immutable Laws of Progress

G eorge Frederick Ruxton, a British adventurer, made his solo camp on a mountain tributary of Colorado's South Platte River, most likely in the South Park valley. Neither of his two memoirs, *Adventures in Mexico and the Rocky Mountains, 1846–1847* and *Life in the Far West*, specifies the date, but we do know he was twenty-five or twenty-six years old and already a veteran of the 1840 Spanish civil war. Ruxton, destined to die at age twenty-seven from internal injuries sustained in a fall from his mule, delighted in roaming the blank spaces on the world map. Few were as blank as America's undulant grasslands and their flank of mountains steadily releasing snowmelt onto the plains.[1]

The night, once again, was cold and snowy, a wet snow that weighed heavily on the ponderosa pine boughs and forced them downward until the burden became too great, and with a "whoosh" of collapsing snow the branch sprang upward. Ruxton loved such nights. "With a plentiful supply of dry pine-logs on the fire, and its cheerful blaze streaming far up into the sky," he watched the flames illuminate his picketed mules, the white fairyland coming down, and the curvature of the mountains beyond. As Ruxton lit his pipe and sat cross-legged under a makeshift tent of supple willow boughs and stretched deerskins, the blue smoke curling upward would take his thoughts to other nights and the conviviality of hearty companions.[2]

This night, stretching out inside his blanket, Ruxton was satisfied that the great pile of wood on the conflagration would survive until morning. But in the middle of the night the cold awakened him, and turning toward the fire, still burning brightly and cheerfully, he was astonished to see a large gray wolf sitting quietly before it, "his eyes closed and his head nodding in sheer drowsiness."[3]

Seeing a wolf was hardly a surprise. Ruxton and other early travelers across the plains and the mountains glimpsed wolves as frequently as many modern suburbanites notice springtime robins. An avid hunter who counted on the bounty of the wilderness for every repast, he had enjoyed many opportunities to observe wolves at close quarters. "I had frequently seen wolves evince their disregard to fires, by coming within a few feet of them to seize upon any scraps of meat which might be left exposed,"[4] he recalled. And they went even further in seeking sustenance from his camps: "It is a very common thing for these animals to gnaw the straps of a saddle on which your head is reposing for a pillow."[5] On another occasion, as winter subsided into spring on the upper Arkansas River, "the wolves infested the camp to that degree, that I could scarcely leave my saddles for a few minutes on the ground without finding the straps of raw hide gnawed to pieces; and one night the hungry brutes ate up all the ropes which were tied on the necks of the animals and trailed along the ground: they were actually devoured to within a yard of the mules' throats."[6]

But for all that, "I had never seen or heard of one approaching so close as to warm his body, and for that purpose alone. . . . I looked at him for some moments without disturbing the beast, and closed my eyes and went to sleep, leaving him to the quiet enjoyment of the blaze."[7]

Ruxton's pacific attitude toward this canid campmate reflected his sentiment that "[w]olves are so common on the plains and in the mountains, that the hunter never cares to throw away a charge of ammunition upon them."[8] Once a wolf had followed Ruxton and his friends for days as they climbed the Sangre de Cristo Mountains on horseback. "I had him twenty times a-day within reach of my rifle," Ruxton recalled, "but he became such an old friend that I never dreamed of molesting him."[9]

Wolves were common in the American West because their prey was abundant. In summer herds of elk, mule deer, and bighorn sheep roamed the dark forests and the crenellated cliff faces sloping up to the bald alpine peaks of the Rocky Mountains. In fall the crisp weather turned aspen leaves yellow, and the first wisps of snow wafted in like unhurried emissaries from a season the hard, cold ground had never quite forgotten. Then the herds grazed their way downward to broad mountain valleys such as South Park. In the winter most of the animals gathered on the plains and in the sheltered canyons that linked the lowlands with the mountains. Yet at least during some winters sufficient prey stayed in the mountain valleys to provision an occasional wolf.

The Great Plains teemed with even more life, and, unlike in the mountains, the big animals remained year-round. Starting in April 1843, artist and naturalist John James Audubon traveled up the Missouri River from the frontier town of St. Louis to Fort Pierre in Dakota Territory, returning to civilization in October. Traveling on an American Fur Company steamboat that took hunters and trappers into the wilderness, Audubon's aim was to acquire animal specimens to paint for his work-in-progress, "Viviparous Quadrupeds of North America." On May 28, before noon, according to his journal, he viewed more than 2,000 bison (universally known as "buffalo") grazing by the river as the steamship labored upstream.[10] On August 19 he noted, "Wolves howling, and bulls roaring, just like the long-continued roll of a hundred drums. Saw large gangs of Buffaloes walking along the river. . . . Abundance of bear tracks."[11] Seldom a day went by without him seeing wolves, and every day Audubon saw, shot, and meticulously recounted a plethora of mammals and birds constituting a virtual "who's who" of the western panorama. On the morning of June 3, for instance, his hired hunter brought in three prairie dogs he had killed the night before around fifteen miles inland. As the day progressed and they worked their way up the river they saw

> one Goose with a gosling, several Coots, Grebes, Blue Herons, Doves, Magpies, Red-shafted Woodpeckers, etc. On a sand-bar Bell [a companion] counted ten Wolves feeding on some carcass. We also saw three young whelps. This morning we saw a large number of Black-headed Gulls feeding on a dead Buffalo with some Ravens; the Gulls probably were feeding on the worms, or other insects about the carcass. We saw four Elks, and a large gang of Buffaloes. One Wolf was seen crossing the river towards our boat; being fired at, it wheeled round, but turned towards us again, again wheeled round.[12]

Another wolf was successfully shot that day to provide measurements for Audubon's notes, the first of many wolves his associates and he would kill for both sport and art over the next several months on the river and at Fort Pierre. He concluded the day's notes: "We ran this evening till our wood was exhausted, and I do not know how we will manage to-morrow. Good-night. God bless you all."[13] (It is not clear to whom he offered this benediction, for although he had a wife and family they never received these notes, and his grandchildren did not discover and read his journals until the 1880s—over three decades after his death.[14]) One week later and far upstream, the party having managed to find wood to keep the steamship's boilers cranking, Audubon again had a productive day, noting in his journal the presence of elk, bison, bighorn sheep, sharp-tailed grouse, geese, a sparrow hawk, red-shafted woodpeckers, grizzly bears, and wolves. Many of these animals were shot.[15]

But amid the profusion of life, it was the bison that somehow always seized white travelers' imaginations as the puissance of the plains, engraving themselves more permanently into the region's iconography than, as it turned out, they would prove engraved on the landscape itself. In 1541 the chronicler for the expedition of Spanish conquistador Don Francisco Vásquez de Coronado described the bare-backed bison of late spring—when their massive heads and shoulders were even more prominent than usual—as resembling African lions (a comparison echoed over three centuries later by frontiersman and future president Theodore Roosevelt).[16]

The resemblance was precipitated by some of the prairie's smallest denizens, which induced the great beasts to roll on their backs to plaster themselves with a thick layer of insect-repelling mud. In a later bout on its back, the hard cast of mud would come off each animal's torso along with much of its hair, thus creating a full-maned leonine appearance. In the fall the mud-pits in which the bison rolled became pothole lakes twenty to thirty feet across, supporting multitudes of wild ducks and geese[17] and also incubating the mosquitoes and biting flies whose energetic pursuit of the wild bovines led to further formation of their own breeding grounds.[18] In the spring a circle of brilliant flowers offset these wet hollows.[19]

The bison's profound influence on the landscape also reflected their vast numbers, which dominated every early commentary. An estimated 20 to 60 million bison originally occupied the Great Plains in herds that stretched for scores and sometimes hundreds of miles.[20] In 1872 one mass of bison was reported to have taken up to six or seven weeks to cross southeastern Colorado's Arkansas River.[21] Coronado's scribe, calling the bison "cows," described them as "the most monstrous thing in the way of animals which has ever been seen or read about," adding, "[t]here is such a quantity of them that I do not know what to compare them with, except with the fish in the sea."[22]

Coronado might never have seen a single bison except for a quirk. Busy looting the pueblos of the region eventually known as New Mexico, he was convinced by one of his Indian slaves that the seven cities of gold at the heart of Spanish lore lay many days' journey to the east and north. Unbeknown to Coronado, the slave, whom the Spanish called "the Turk," had conspired with the inhabitants of the Rio Grande to send the onerous Europeans on a fool's quest into barren land, in which they would either starve or become so weakened that they could be killed after they returned. "The Turk had said when they left Tiguex [the populated upper Rio Grande around present-day Albuquerque] that they ought not to load the horses with too much provisions, which would tire them," Coronado's chronicler recounted, "so that they could not afterward carry the gold and silver."[23] But the Indians hadn't counted on the Spaniards' ability to survive on bison. During one two-week period in which they labored across the Great Plains, the conquistadors killed more than 500 bulls and received a taste of the bison's defensive abilities when wounded animals charged and fatally gored several of their horses. "There are very great numbers of wolves on these plains which go round with the cows," added Coronado's man. "They have white skins."[24]

Hundreds of miles into the grasslands, having "seen nothing but cows and the sky," the Spaniards were given the bad news by itinerant plains dwellers (perhaps Comanches), whom they compared to Arabs, that no gold-filled cities were to be found. The Turk confessed to his ruse. The Spaniards garroted the would-be savior, erected a forlorn cross to mark the furthest extent of Christianity, and turned back to the settlements on the Rio Grande. Unencumbered by hopes of mineral wealth, upon their return they noted the "large number of animals like squirrels and a great number of their holes"—supplementing the first written mention of wild bison with a similar record of the prairie dogs that rivaled the bison in number.[25]

Just as bison transformed the landscape with their wallowing and trampling and provided food for wolves, so the innumerable prairie dogs created a labyrinth below the earth's surface and supported additional predators. On September 17, 1804, while travelling up the Missouri River, Meriwether Lewis set out before sunrise with six of the best hunters from among the expedition that bears his name and that of Captain William Clark. Already in Dakota Territory, far from civilization, Lewis felt he had been spending too much time confined on their boat and was determined "to devote this day to amuse myself on shore with my gun and view the interior of the country." The interior sported "immense herds of Buffaloe, deer Elk and Antelopes which we saw in every direction feeding on the hills and plains," along with miles of land "intirely occupied by the burrows of the *barking squiril* . . . in infinite numbers." Amid the prairie dogs he also saw "a great number of wolves of the small kind, halks and some pole-cats," referring to coyotes, hawks, and blackfooted ferrets—the latter a weasel-like carnivore adapted specifically to prey on and occupy prairie dogs' tunnels. "I presume that those anamals feed on this squirril," he correctly noted.[26]

Ruxton was also greatly impressed by prairie dogs. "Frequently, when hunting, I have amused myself for hours in watching their frolicsome motions," he wrote,

> On the first approach of such a monster as man, all the dogs which have been scattered over the town scamper to their holes as fast as their little legs will admit, and, concealing all but their heads and tails, bark lustily their displeasure at the intrusion. When they have sufficiently exhibited their daring, every dog dives into his burrow, but two or three who remain as sentinels, chattering in high dudgeon, until the enemy is within a few paces of them, when they take the usual summerset, and the town is silent and deserted. Lying perfectly still for several minutes, I could observe an old fellow raise his head cautiously above his hole, and reconnoitre; and if satisfied that the coast was clear, he would commence a short bark. . . . When this warning has been given, others are soon seen to emerge from their houses, and, assured of their security, play and frisk about. After a longer delay, rattlesnakes issue from the holes, and coil themselves in the sunny side of the hillock, erecting their treacherous heads, and rattling an angry note of warning if, in his play, a thoughtless pup approaches too near; and, lastly, a sober owl appears, and if the sun be low, hops through the town, picking up the lizards and cameleons which everywhere abound. At the first intimation of danger given by the sentinels, all the stragglers hasten to their holes, tumbling over owls and

rattlesnakes, who hiss and rattle angrily at being disturbed. Every one scrambles off to his own domicile, and if, in his hurry, he should mistake his dwelling, or rush for safety into any other than his own, he is quickly made sensible of his error, and without ceremony, ejected.[27]

The real danger came not from Ruxton but from hawks, eagles, coyotes, wolves, and rattlesnakes. "The rattlesnake," said Ruxton, "I fear, is not the welcome guest he reports himself to be; for often I have slain the wily serpent, with a belly too much protuberant to be either healthy or natural, and bearing, in its outline, a very strong resemblance to the figure of a prairie dog."[28]

On an early summer evening in 1846, the same year Ruxton first discovered Colorado's prairies, a wide-eyed twenty-three-year-old Boston-born adventurer named Francis Parkman camped on the banks of the Platte River and reflected on his day's jaunt on horseback:

Several times I passed through villages of prairie-dogs, who sat, each at the mouth of his burrow, holding his paws before him in the supplicating attitude, and yelping away most vehemently, whisking his little tail with every squeaking cry he uttered. Prairie-dogs are not fastidious in their choice of companions; various long checkered snakes were sunning themselves in the midst of the village, and demure little gray owls, with a large white ring around each eye, were perched side by side with the rightful inhabitants. The prairie teemed with life. Again and again I looked toward the crowded hillsides, and was sure I saw horsemen; and riding near, with a mixture of hope and dread, for Indians were abroad, I found them transformed into a group of buffalo. There was nothing in human shape amid all this vast congregation of brute forms.[29]

Parkman's day had started with the exhilaration of a mounted hunt for bison, during which he had become separated from his two companions as each raced off in a different direction after the stampeding beasts. Only after arresting his horse's charge did Parkman, now solitary, slow down sufficiently to observe the extent of what is known today as biological diversity:

When I turned down the buffalo path, the prairie seemed changed; only a wolf or two glided by at intervals, like conscious felons, never looking to the right or left. Being now free from anxiety, I was at leisure to observe minutely the objects around me; and here, for the first time, I noticed insects wholly different from any of the varieties found farther to the eastward. Gaudy butterflies fluttered about my horse's head; strangely formed beetles, glittering with metallic lustre, were crawling upon plants that I had never seen before; multitudes of lizards, too, were darting like lightning over the sand.[30]

Between the microfauna of lizards and butterflies and the iconic presence of bison, many other animals also found an ecological niche, including the continent's swiftest land animal, the pronghorn—known as the "antelope." "The antelope were very numerous," Parkman noted about the terrain through which he rode following his buffalo chase, "and as they are always bold when in the neighborhood of buffalo, they would approach to look at me, gaze intently with their great round eyes, then suddenly leap aside, and stretch lightly away over the prairie, as swiftly as a race-horse. Squalid, ruffian-like wolves sneaked through the hollows and sandy ravines."[31] These wolves may have seemed like curs to the young Brahmin Parkman, who had been born to privilege. But they had their work cut out for them preying on the pronghorns, whose graceful speed appeared to Lewis "reather the rappid flight of birds than the motion of quadrupeds."[32] And for all their flightiness, the pronghorns were surprisingly spirited. "A single antelope will bravely face a single wolf, and successfully beat off his attack, and a herd does not fear the attack of any number of wolves," observed Lieutenant Colonel Richard Irving Dodge, a punctilious West Point officer who reveled in leave from his frontier military posts to take to the hunt. The account in his 1877 book *The Plains of the Great West and Their Inhabitants,* subtitled *Being a Description of the Plains, Game, Indians, &c. of the Great North American Desert,* continued: "Wherever the antelope are numerous there will generally be found plenty of wolves, who lie around the herd at a little distance, watchful and ready to take advantage of any accident in their favor; now pouncing upon one which has strayed from the protection of the herd, and making a prompt meal of any one which should happen to be sick or get injured in any way." An injury could occur at the hands of human hunters. In following an antelope he had just wounded, Dodge "started a pack of six or eight wolves, and, going to the spot, found our antelope, its throat lacerated, its hamstrings cut, its flanks torn open, and half the viscera already devoured."[33]

Even when the hunter got to the prey first, the wolves expected their due. In the vicinity of the Rio Grande valley near Colorado's present-day border with New Mexico, Ruxton observed: "On emerging from the uplands, we entered a level prairie, covered with innumerable herds of antelope. These graceful animals, in bands containing several thousands, trotted up to us, and, with pointed ears and their beautiful eyes staring with eager curiosity, accompanied us for miles, running parallel to our trail within fifty or sixty yards." While butchering some of the pronghorn, Ruxton was surrounded by wolves "so tame, and hungry at the same time, that I thought they would actually have torn the meat from under my knife."[34]

In time such brazenness became the rule rather than the exception, particularly along the Santa Fe Trail, which connected St. Louis to Santa Fe. Although routes on the trail varied, the main branch followed the Arkansas River from today's Kansas, then cut southwest through the tip of southeastern Colorado and across the Oklahoma panhandle toward Santa Fe. This and another route that followed the Arkansas further upstream into Colorado before diverging south over waterless terrain became the primary commercial corridor through the southern Great Plains. Since white travelers sustained themselves through profligate hunting, the wolves quickly learned to associate humans with discarded carcasses. One of the first regular traders in the 1840s, Josiah Gregg, recounted a wolf "guard of honor" that followed him for several hundred miles along the Santa Fe Trail, "at first attracted no doubt by the remains of buffalo which were killed by us upon the high plains." He was not as gentle toward the wolves as Ruxton, noting, "Not a few of them paid the penalty of their lives for their temerity."[35]

By 1846, when Parkman and his friends took their epic trek westward, bison hunting was quickly becoming established as the primary reason—aside from traversing the Oregon Trail to settle in the Pacific Northwest—whites ventured onto the plains. Parkman described hunting bison three different ways: by chasing the animals on horseback, sneaking up on them, or ambushing bison when they approached a water hole to drink. In each case—although he and his companions relied on buffalo for much of their food—most of the animals were killed merely for adventure; they salvaged "the fattest and choicest parts of eight or nine cows" from each two-ton animal, "and the rest abandoned to the wolves." That was not an insignificant amount of food:

> The number of carcasses that by this time were lying about the neighboring prairie summoned the wolves from every quarter; the spot where Shaw and Henry had hunted together soon became their favorite resort, for here about a dozen dead buffalo were fermenting under the hot sun. I used often to go over the river and watch them at their meal. By lying under the bank it was easy to get a full view of them. There were three different kinds: the white wolves and the gray wolves, both very large, and besides these the small prairie wolves, not much bigger than spaniels. They would howl and fight in a crowd around a single carcass, yet they were so watchful, and their senses so acute, that I never was able to crawl within a fair shooting distance; whenever I attempted it, they would all scatter at once and glide silently away through the tall grass.[36]

Similarly, in 1859 Daniel Ellis Conner, a traveler along the same route, described the presence of "wolves of all sizes and species known on the plains"—including, no doubt, coyotes—"as common as the days." They would "collect in little bands and lazily lounge around the prairie around our camps at safe distances," he said.

> There could be seen a convention of them, some standing, and some lying down, almost in any direction and almost any day. All waiting for the camp to be deserted so as to come in and fight with each other and also with the ravens, which were numerous, over the debris of the camp. A raven would alight to pick up a scrap and a wolf would savagely charge on him, while others would charge on one another in succession, until the old campground was thoroughly gleaned. One morning after camping on the river's low bank, I concluded to remain under the brink until the wagon train should get well off from the place, and break up the anticipated picnic of the wolves and ravens. A wolf is monstrous cunning and cautious. The ravens, while sailing around over the campground prospecting, could see me, concealed behind the bank of the creek. And because they didn't alight the wolves were too prudent to come hastily. They kept

me waiting until I became uneasy, for the wagons must have been gone an hour. I peeped cautiously over the bank and fired upon a large grey fellow and shot him through. He turned and snapped his teeth rapidly toward me after delivering a slight half-whine and half-growl in his surprise, then ran away onto the plain with the rest of them, out of reach. I was not content with one shot, but emptied one of my six-shooters after the fleeing wolves.[37]

Conner, in turn, almost paid with his life for his wolf-ambushing delay. In catching up to the main party, he was attacked by mounted Indians and barely made it to the safety of his group. "This was the last time I ever stopped back at old camps to shoot wolves or anything else," he confessed.[38]

Wolves could also become interested in human carcasses. When escapades with Indians or any other cause proved fatal, companions would pile rocks on the decedent's makeshift grave to protect the body from lupine excavation.[39] On the Oregon Trail along the Platte River through present-day Nebraska, Parkman noted cases where immigrant graves were insufficiently protected: "The earth was usually torn up, and covered thickly with wolf-tracks."[40] In June 1843, Audubon discovered dead Assiniboin Indians in simple coffins perched in trees near the confluence of the Yellowstone and Missouri rivers in present-day North Dakota—adequate protection from wolves, although not from the painter, who stole their skulls.[41] But a Pawnee Indian killed in battle, his remains left by his countrymen, became a "well-picked skeleton" within a few days, according to Ruxton.[42] Of course, coyotes, badgers, ravens, vultures, and other scavengers also fed on carcasses.

Although common and occasionally a nuisance, wolves held no particular economic importance, and for that reason early explorers did not often speak of them at length. With wolves no more remarkable than any other wild novelty, some wayfarers mentioned the great canids only to illustrate a point or garnish a literary device. In 1828 a caravan of silver traders, transporting the precious metal along the Santa Fe Trail to St. Louis, was attacked by Comanches in retaliation for a massacre by another group of white traders. With their horses driven off, the group set out on a disastrous pedestrian odyssey of hunger and terror on the western Kansas grasslands. During the trek, one unlucky venture capitalist was allegedly saved at the last moment from wolves he had been fending off with a stick while lying on his back, blind from starvation.[43] Although marginally possible, the incident begs the question of how long wolves accustomed to killing bison, elk, and antelope could have been held off by a weakened man. Most likely the incident was made up to communicate to comfortable easterners the extreme dangers to which western adventurers were exposed.

In a more realistic starvation on the prairie incident, in 1843, deep in the grassland canyons of southeastern Colorado's Purgatoire River, hungry humans ended up killing and eating a wolf.[44] (No account exists of the wolf putting up the same heroic resistance as the erstwhile silver trader had.)

Other early wolf reports indicated their vast numbers, and some of those accounts may speak more to the human propensity to exaggerate than to conditions on the ground. A newcomer to the plains in the 1840s reported 40,000 wolves in one pack crossing the Arkansas River during one night; his traveling companions did not believe him.[45] Parkman evinced a keen eye and ear for detail, and also along the Arkansas River he estimated that he heard several hundred wild canids gathered near an Arapaho Indian camp: "A horrible discord of low mournful wailings, mingled with ferocious howls, arose . . . for several hours after sunset. We could distinctly see the wolves running about the prairie within a few rods of our fire, or bounding over the sand-beds of the river and splashing through the water. There was not the slightest danger from them, for they are the greatest cowards of the prairie."[46] Parkman, like many others, lumped coyotes in as a species of wolf.[47] Since two or three ululating coyotes can easily sound like half a dozen, who knows how many wolves or coyotes he actually heard?

During the last years of the eighteenth century an increasing number of white trappers began to wander the plains and mountains, indirectly bringing wolves into the maw of a colonial economy. Wolves were not their initial target. Rather, an important wolf prey species, the beaver, drew seekers of riches and fugitives from social constraint to the headwaters of the rivers that issued from the Rocky Mountains.

Since 1638, when the English King Charles II mandated use of beaver fur in the manufacture of hats,[48] trappers had pursued the creature whose intricate defense against wolves and other natural predators—constructing dams and underwater lodges—would not suffice against human ingenuity. By the 1820s beavers were largely eradicated from the East, large fur companies dominated trapping in the northern Great Plains and Rocky Mountains, and Mexican authorities had banned Americans from trapping in areas under their control—including present-day New Mexico extending north to the Arkansas River in Colorado. So in 1824 a group of American and French trappers based in the crude Mexican outposts of San Fernandez (later known as Taos) and Santa Fe set out north and northwest with mules and steel traps.[49] Two years later the Frenchman Ceran St. Vrain, holed up in Taos, decided the territory of New Mexico was not only over-trapped but too inconvenient because of patrols by Mexican authorities, and he too set out on a major expedition to the north.[50] Over the next few years the trapping business boomed throughout the West, largely by soliciting Indians to kill animals and barter the furs. By 1831 western trade, including skins and ores, represented half a million dollars worth of goods, an enormous sum at the time.

That year two veteran trappers, the brothers William and Charles Bent, decided they might do better as traders, buying furs from the mountain men and Indians and selling them in the East. In partnership with St. Vrain, the brothers decided to establish a commercial partnership in the wilderness, which ended up as an adobe fort on the north bank of the Arkansas River, just outside

13

Mexican territory. The location acknowledged not only geo-political but also bio-commercial realities: it was located on one of the routes of the Santa Fe Trail, sufficiently close to the mountains for beaver yet squarely on the prairies inhabited by great herds of shaggy bison.

The establishment of the trading company that would eventually own and become known as Bent's Fort marked an ominous portent for the southern Great Plains, which heretofore had witnessed bison-killing forays by whites but no highly organized commercial extractive activity. Charles Bent substituted ox-drawn wagons for mules, thus setting the stage for the cattle industry that flourished four decades later and would prove incompatible with the Great Plains ecosystem. As early as 1839 Bent's Fort could be construed as a ranch—Colorado's first—with surplus oxen grazing by the river and 200 sheep roaming immediately outside the fort's baked-mud walls.[51]

Another inauspicious change was in the works. In 1832, the year after the Bent brothers planned their fort (but before its construction), John Jacob Astor, the vastly wealthy owner of the American Fur Company, noticed British men wearing hats made of silk instead of beaver pelts. Other furs, such as nutria and raccoon, were also gaining favor in the European markets where most American furs ended up. At the same time, foreign nations were exporting furs to the United States duty-free, but tariffs raised the price of American furs abroad. As a result of all these factors, the following year prices for beaver pelts collapsed, and trapping diminished accordingly. An overseas fashion switch probably saved the beaver from extinction in North America, yet helped doom the bison to that fate over almost its entire range.

By the late 1830s, with beaver constituting a distinct minority of the fur trade the species had once defined,[52] the bison holocaust had begun. The price of hides was low, but a host of former beaver trappers was available to kill the unwary beasts. In 1840 the Bent–St. Vrain corporation, consisting of both Bent's Fort and another one north on the St. Vrain River, exported 15,000 buffalo robes to St. Louis (a town that had started as a fur trading post but had long exhausted its wealth of nearby wildlife).[53] With a glut of robes entering the market, fur company executives worked to grow the demand.[54] Meanwhile, in 1843 a powerful Taos priest, Padre Antonio José Martinez, who had a history of enmity toward the Bent brothers, warned Mexican president Santa Ana that the American traders' "constant slaughter" of bison was already diminishing the herds and "will finally result in the extinction of the species in a very short time."[55]

The warning was true, and throughout the vast plains the story was the same. On May 18, 1843, Audubon, who was traveling upstream on the Missouri River, visited cordially with a white trading party from the Dakotas traveling to St. Louis on four barges loaded with 10,000 buffalo robes. His own boat held a hundred hunters and trappers, of whose company he was a guest. On August 5, while on a hunting trip from his base at Fort Pierre, he wrote in his journal: "There is a perceptible difference in the size of the herds. Before many years the Buffalo, like the Great Auk, will have disappeared; surely this should not be permitted." (But perhaps his coda to the statement, pertaining to the subspecies of bighorn sheep that would later bear his name and eventually become extinct from overhunting but that he was having trouble acquiring at the time, reveals more: "I wish I had a couple of Bighorns. God bless you all.")[56]

In 1844 artist George Catlin, who had visited the plains in the 1830s, anticipated the same fate for the bison, imagining "[h]undreds and thousands" of bison "strewed upon the plains—they were flayed, and their reddened carcasses left; and about them bands of wolves, and dogs, and buzzards were seen devouring them."[57] Catlin proposed to save both the bison and the native people who depended upon the bison in a Great Plains national park containing "man and beast in all the wild and freshness of their nature's beauty." His idea went nowhere.[58]

In 1847 Ruxton, who also favored conserving the bison, confirmed the decline among the herds:

> It is a singular fact that within the last two years the prairies, extending from the mountains to a hundred miles or more down the Arkansa, have been entirely abandoned by the buffalo. Indeed, in crossing from the settlements of New Mexico, the boundary of their former range is marked by skulls and bones, which appear fresher as the traveller advances westward and towards the waters of the Platte. As the skulls are said to last only three years on the surface of the ground, that period has consequently seen the gradual disappearance of the buffalo from their former haunts.[59]

The reason was clear: "Upwards of one hundred thousand buffalo robes find their way annually into the United States [from the western territories] and Canada; and these are the skins of *cows* alone, the bull's hide being so thick that it is never dressed."[60] But that hardly stopped the killing of bulls.

In fact, whether the motive was commercial, recreational, or even artistic, killing bison seemed the chief pre-occupation of all who traveled west. Audubon, although atypical in his disinclination to kill what he could not use, did not hesitate to shoot animals every day, whether for food or to secure as models for his paintings. His companions dispensed with Audubon's limited compunctions and self-imposed proscriptions. "These two managed to kill four Buffaloes," the illustrator recounted of a pair of hunters aboard his steamer, who had set out on an overnight pedestrian excursion in May 1843. Audubon continued:

> But one of them was drowned as it took to the river after being shot. Only a few pieces from a young bull, and its tongue, were brought on board, most of the men being too lazy, or too far off, to cut out even the tongues of the others; and thus it is that thousands multiplied by thousands of Buffaloes are murdered in senseless play, and their enormous carcasses are suffered to be the prey of the Wolf, the Raven and the Buzzard.[61]

As party after party of white adventurers made their way west to taste the exhilarating freedom of the plains and avail themselves of the area's seemingly infinite wildlife, they each played out the same role in a drama everyone implicitly understood but not all articulated. One who did so was British investor William Blackmore, who wrote the introduction to Dodge's *The Plains of the Great West and Their Inhabitants*. Appalled at the bison slaughter and at what he described forthrightly as the "extermination" of various Native American tribes, Blackmore nevertheless conceived of a bright side:

> But sad as the fate of the Red Man is, yet, even as philanthropists, we must not forget that, under what appears to be one of the immutable laws of progress, the savage is giving place to a higher and more civilised race. Three hundred thousand Red Men at the present time require the entire occupation of a continent as large as Europe, in order that they may obtain an uncertain and scanty subsistence by the chase. Ought we, then, to regret if in the course of a few generations their wigwams, tepees, and mud lodges, rarely numbering more than one hundred in a village, are replaced by new cities of the West, each equalling, perhaps, in magnificence, in stately structures, and in population (exceeding that of all the Indians), either St. Louis or Chicago? Or if in supplanting less than 300,000 wandering, debased, and half-naked savages we can people the self-same district with a population of many tens of millions of prosperous and highly civilised whites.
>
> The countless herds of buffalo, which formerly ranged the plains, will be superseded by treble their number of improved American cattle; the sparse herds of the smooth-haired antelope will be replaced by countless flocks of woolly sheep; and the barren prairies, now covered with the short buffalo grass, yellow sunflower, and prickly cactus, barely sufficient to support the wild denizens of the Plains, will under cultivation teem with yellow harvests of wheat and corn, providing food for millions; so that in a few years the only reminiscence of the Red Men will be the preservation of the names of some of the extinct tribes and dead chiefs in the nomenclature of the leading cities, counties, and States of the Great West.[62]

American Indians were doomed, in this view, by their reliance on tradition and the hunt. Blackmore's vision, an unquestioned article of faith among Euro-American society, accepted a hierarchy based largely on a self-serving reading of the Christian Bible that placed white men at the top and other races, animals, plants, and, finally, inanimate objects beneath them.

Seen in that light, it was inevitable that the Indians and the buffalo would give way to white ranchers and their cattle. In Blackmore's view, Indians were responsible for their own extinction because of their refusal to change.

In contrast, indigenous people, although they still killed animals for use, regarded them as equals of a sort and were not so quick to jettison tradition for the allure of progress. American Indian stories of the past, often built around lessons learned from animals, structured thought and conduct. And perhaps because wolves operated socially, like humans, to kill the same kinds of animals humans killed, they readily lent themselves to anthropomorphic description. According to Cheyenne legend, one winter a man caught on the plains in a night-time storm was rescued by an enigmatic group of men who sheltered him for four days, instructing him to memorize special dances and ceremonial costumes. When he later discovered his mysterious friends were wolves magically disguised as humans, his appreciation and respect led him to found the Wolf Soldier Society, which incorporated the dances and dress the rescuing wolves had taught him.[63] Another mythic lupine intervention into Cheyenne life involved a woman whose husband had been beating her. She fled from the village and was found by a wolf, who brought her meat, warned her of the approach of a bear, and ultimately saw her home safely. As the wolf left, he asked her to put out a little meat for him each morning. When she returned to her husband, she had incorporated some of the wolf's strength and told him she would kill him if he beat her again—a threat he heeded the rest of his life.[64]

What animates these stories is not, as we commonly believe today, their explanatory or euhemeristic value; people who feed on wild animals can least afford to abandon an empirical approach to understanding their world. Rather, the stories reinforce a sense of reciprocity between human and other and between the past and the future, and thus shaped an ethical universe within and beyond the visible terrain.

But the newcomers to the West understood themselves as instruments in fulfilling Blackmore's redemptive vision of supplanting the natives and the wildlife with the moral superiority of American civilization. In 1872 a Nebraska newspaper couched this sentiment in gay verse:

Behind the Squaw's light birch canoe,
The Steamboat rocks and raves,
And City lots are staked for sale
Above old Indian graves.[65]

Often the pursuit of profits served as the lodestone to those ushering out the old era and ushering in the new. Consider the case of two prairie entrepreneurs who stationed themselves along the Santa Fe Trail just east of the modern Colorado-Kansas state line in the mid-1850s. Since Bent's Fort had increased trade and the accompanying bison killing along the Santa Fe Trail and beyond, the region's wolves had become accustomed to the ready carcasses left by travelers. In the summer the two men sustained themselves by selling knick-knacks to traders and other travelers on the trail. In the winter they holed up in a rough mud "fort" (perhaps a term they used in envy of the more luxurious walled compound maintained by the Bent brothers). Venturing out into the cold, they would periodically kill a bison and use bits of the carcass to bait neighboring wolves—and then poison those that were drawn in.

Deceiving the wolves was not difficult; one morning the pair picked up sixty-four dead wolves within a mile and a half of their camp. That winter they grossed more than $4,000, a hefty sum. At a likely price of about seventy-five cents per pelt, the season's take suggests that the two men probably killed around 6,000 wolves.[66]

The poison used was strychnine, which had recently become available on the frontier. Made of the seed of an East Indian fruit, strychnine attacks its victim's central nervous system around ten to twenty minutes after ingestion, causing severe cramps that intensify rapidly and culminate in violent muscle spasms throughout the entire body. Death results from asphyxiation as a result of continuous convulsions of the respiratory muscles. The convulsions often leave the victim's back arched at death, a condition common to poisoned wolves and humans alike. Death either ensues within minutes or takes much longer, depending on the dose and the amount of food in the victim's stomach. In 1897 an elderly man, recalling for readers of the magazine *Forest and Stream* his poisoning activities four decades previously, described the fate of a red fox, as written in the snow:

> He had taken the bait and apparently stood just long enough to lick his chops and pat himself on the shoulder over his good lunch when grief overtook him. Starting off for a dozen steps on a trot, his pace changed to three or four sidewise jumps developing into a race of 200 yds. in length and in the direction of a half circle, finishing with a few of the most prodigious leaps possible.
>
> His last jump was his longest, and into this he threw all his soul.
>
> This carried him across the road and head first into a big snowdrift, where stretched to his fullest length and buried to his hips, with hindlegs and brush projecting into the open air like the blaze of a camp-fire, we found him frozen solid.[67]

Strychnine had been used occasionally to poison wolves in colonial America. In 1834 a Pennsylvania company began commercial production. As early as the late 1840s or early 1850s, the Missouri River frontier post of Westport—where hunters, trappers, traders, and Indians customarily convened and which was the staging area for Parkman's trek—began to import strychnine in wholesale quantities to kill wolves.[68]

With beaver hats still out of fashion and beaver populations largely depleted throughout the West, wolf pelts began to join bison robes as a substitute commodity in the trans-Atlantic economy, although they were not yet worth much commercially. Whereas some former trappers became robe hunters and killed bison, others substituted strychnine for traps and became "wolfers," sending wolf skins eastward from whence some crossed the Atlantic for eventual use by the Russian army. A contemporary observer described the wolfer's work:

> If it was in the autumn, he moved slowly in the wake of a buffalo herd, making open camp, and shooting down a few of the beasts, and after ripping them open, saturating their warm blood and intestines with from one to three bottles of strychnine to each carcass.

After his line of poisoned buffalo has been put out to his notion, the wolfer makes a camp in a ravine or coulee and prepares for the morrow. With the first glimmer of light in the eastern sky, he rises, makes his fire, and cooks his coffee, then hitches up, if he has a team, or saddles up if with packs, and follows his line to the finish. Around each buffalo carcass will probably be from three to a dozen dead wolves, which he packs off some distance from his baits, and skins them.[69]

This type of poisoning operation also killed other animals. Raccoons, skunks, bears, weasels, blackfooted ferrets, badgers, coyotes, foxes, magpies, crows, and eagles all scavenge carrion and were invariably found scattered around poisoned baits.[70] One poisoned buffalo carcass on the Kansas plains yielded thirteen wolves, fifteen coyotes, and about forty skunks.[71]

For all the growing profit, economic incentives for killing wolves, beaver, and bison do not explain the magnitude of slaughter on the Great Plains. Other possible motivations abound. An underlying fear of the infinite-appearing wild landscape may have provoked the intensity of the killing. Perhaps the sheer magnitude of the plains appeared to diminish each man alone or in small entourages far from the comforts of home. Visitors to such a vast wilderness would quickly sense how little their own exalted life or death impacted the surrounding animals, who might regard a human's prairie demise as the opportunity for a meal. The notion that a safe civilization would eventually replace such a lonely and frightening landscape provided an overarching impetus beyond the immediate profits to be made from animal skins.

As with Native American myths, Euro-American stories about wolves also illuminate broader attitudes toward the world at large. Tales about wolves attacking or eating humans reveal the terrain of terror the western wilderness—peopled by primitive aborigines and their equally vicious animal counterparts—held for the American imagination.[72] In one instance, that terror found creative release in pioneer verses celebrating animal savages devouring their human counterparts. A white traveler comes upon wolves

Gorging and growling o'er carcass and limb,
They were too busy to bark at him.
From a Pani's [Pawnee's] scull [sic] they had stripped the flesh,
As ye peel the fig when the fruit is fresh.[73]

But such graphic images failed to amuse when civilized humanity was their subject. Did the near-constant killing of animals keep such reminiscences at bay? Parkman's group shot at bison, wolves, vultures, prairie dogs, and eagles—virtually anything that moved.[74] Previous prairie explorers evinced the same attitude. In the 1830s Josiah Gregg attacked rattlesnakes with a venom, "determined to let none of them escape."[75] Meriwether Lewis and William Clark reached for their rifles reflexively at the sight of bears, "panthers" (which they encountered far from the mountain habitat we associate with the American lion today), and most other large animals.[76] In 1859 Daniel Ellis Conner, looking skyward while positioning himself to shoot two bald eagles, almost stumbled on a pair of snakes and made them his victims instead. "I was by this time so nervous that I could hardly start back to camp, but I got off at last without waiting to reload my gun," he said to explain why he left the eagles alive.[77]

Francis Parkman's masterful descriptive powers best recall the Great Plains at mid-century. "The vast plain waved with tall rank grass, that swept our horses' bellies," he wrote in *The Oregon Trail.* "It swayed to and fro in billows with the light breeze, and far and near antelope and wolves were moving through it, the hairy backs of the latter alternately appearing and disappearing as they bounded awkwardly along."

Surveying this scene, Parkman's companion, Henry Chatillon, admitted feeling "lonesome." But young Francis allowed himself no such despondency. The breadth of his narrative belies the dearth of his personal insight, and his response perhaps most clearly describes the general motivation behind the violence: "I dismounted, and amused myself with firing at the wolves."[78]

A Howling Wilderness With a Vengeance

In the 1840s the Bent, St. Vrain, & Company established additional ranches in the juniper and pine foothills of the plains in what would eventually become southeastern Colorado, close to the border with New Mexico. Nestled in grassy valleys and overseen by Mexican herdsmen living in lean-tos made of poles, hides, and pine boughs, these ranches constituted some of the pioneering establishments of the cattle empires of thirty years hence.[1] Although the beginnings of ranching were idiosyncratic to different parts of the interior West, the Bent, St. Vrain, & Company's model roughly paralleled those elsewhere; around trading posts, military forts, and evangelical missions, the local depletion of bison and other large animals as a result of hunting led to the establishment of cattle herds.[2] The beef augmented the food supply for those living there, as well as for people who stopped by: professional hunters, trading Indians, adventuring easterners, and families traveling to new settlements.

In the case of Bent's Fort, in the summer of 1846 the company's herds were swelled by around 20,000 horses, mules, and oxen attached to the U.S. Army of the West, recently arrived to engage in the war with Mexico (which resulted in the United States gaining New Mexico). The fort teemed with unaccustomed activity, a constant low level of pandemonium enveloping Charles and William Bent with more customers for their limited stocks of supplies than the traders could have anticipated a few short years before. Visiting Indians were awed by the number of troops—1,700 fervent young volunteers from the frontier state of Missouri. The Arkansas River was lined with tents for miles, and the army's stock was picketed among them.

Notwithstanding the mud-daubed trading post overlooking the river, none of the green recruits mistook the region for civilized. The Santa Fe Trail along which they had marched for hundreds of miles was a thin necklace beaded by caravans of travelers; on either side of the trail lay wilderness stretching beyond the limits of imagination.

If imagination would not suffice, the wilderness imposed itself in forceful reminders. Wolves frightened off the troopers' picketed mules at their camp near the confluence of the Purgatoire River and the larger Arkansas, around a dozen miles downstream of Bent's Fort. Several hundred mules set off running, their panic aggravated by their trailing picket pins. The tumult of dust, smell of frightened animals, ricochet of metal and hooves, and yelling of men may have been accompanied by the occasional glimpse of gray tawny forms in pursuit. Although the wolves are not known to have actually killed any mules in this incident, it probably took hours to retrieve the mules.[3]

The following year produced the first known record of wolves killing livestock in that region of the plains. With the American army still appropriating many of Bent, St. Vrain, & Company's assets and using the company's outlying ranches to graze around a thousand head of beef cattle alongside corporate stock, a combination of wolves and storms killed four mules that were part of a herd being driven on the Santa Fe Trail.[4]

By 1856, livestock figures had not changed significantly; only 1,500 head of cattle grazed on the Arkansas and Purgatoire rivers and their tributaries.[5] Expansions of ranch operations had been stymied largely because of clashes with Indians who were retaliating for the ongoing bison slaughter.[6]

In 1858 William Green Russell from Georgia discovered gold along the edge of the Colorado Rockies—ten years after an equally epochal auriferous discovery in California. With the nation in an economic downturn in the spring of 1859, tens of thousands of people headed west in search of untold riches in the "Pikes Peak" goldfields of what was then Kansas Territory and would soon be called Jefferson Territory (a short-lived name). But mining was not easy work, and riches were not guaranteed. Many new arrivals did not end up knee-deep in icy mountain streams sifting gravel for gold. It is estimated that during the boom every persevering miner may have supported five other people who supplied his physical, economic, and social needs. Within a year the population of "Denver City" (first known as the St. Charles Town Company) reached 4,749, and other towns also appeared—incongruously—like mushrooms springing forth from the uncultivated mountains and plains.[7]

The nascent white settlements also attracted livestock interests searching for new forage. In 1859 cattle were being driven from Indian Territory (Oklahoma) onto the plains of what would later be called Colorado.[8] The next year Colonel Alexander Majors wintered 5,000 head of cattle on the Arkansas River.[9]

Shortly thereafter, John W. Prowers, whose name would later grace a county of the future state, brought a herd from Missouri to the region.[10]

As early as 1860, travelers on the plains north of Denver came upon fifty abandoned cattle carcasses, dead from disease.[11] To wolves grown accustomed to the easy fare left behind by bison hunters, adjusting to this new food source must have come naturally. And cattle not found dead could be pulled down. Although no specific records of predation remain from this early period, it is certain that wolves and other predators, along with weather and disease, took their toll on open-range cattle.

The Civil War (1861–1865) created a hiatus in the rush westward.[12] The military could no longer commit to protecting pioneer settlements from Native Americans.[13] And instead of battling the people and animals of a dangerous wilderness outside the states, many young men left home to fight at Bull Run, Gettysburg, and the other rural landscapes that bespoke a nation unable to reconcile itself. It was not until 1866 that cattle production began in earnest on the plains.[14] British cattle corporations extensively utilized the free range of the West,[15] and the beef was exported not only to the states back East but, as early as 1868, also to England. By 1875, exports to England were becoming common and immensely profitable, and overseas interests owned 500,000 cattle in Colorado.[16] Just as the fur trade had before it, ranching transformed the West's natural bounties into international commodities.

Had livestock been raised primarily for local markets, western ecosystems would have been impacted to a far lesser degree, and an ecologically sustainable society might have been possible. But the railroads linking western ranches to global markets precipitated profound changes on the western landscape and in the relationship between settlers on the frontier and the people they left behind in the East. In 1867 the Union Pacific Railroad Company began building the first transcontinental railroad through the southern part of what would shortly be called Wyoming Territory; two years later it met its counterpart from San Francisco, and the line was completed at Promontory, Utah. In June 1870 a spur line built southward from the Union Pacific at Cheyenne was extended to Denver; two months later another line connected Kansas City to Denver.[17] The Queen City of the Plains, as it began to be known, became a hub of commerce, and additional lines were soon being built outward from Denver. As a result, getting beef to eastern markets became considerably cheaper, creating incentives to further expand ranching and eliminate whatever stood in the way.

The bison contested with cattle for grass. In 1873, on the verge of their final population collapse, bison were still plentiful enough in Colorado's far northeastern corner, near the border with Nebraska and Kansas, to drive cattle away from an open-range ranch near Julesburg.[18] With markets for their cattle quickly accessible by rail, ranchers saw no reason the bison should remain.

In addition, military strategists understood that killing off the bison would destroy the basis for Indian society.[19] Some Indians, with tragic shortsightedness, participated in the slaughter and sold or traded the pelts.[20] Furthermore, sport hunters of the same temperament as Francis Parkman were all too ready to vacation in the West for a comfortably provisioned killing spree.

The railroads that made cattle grazing increasingly profitable furnished the means to kill the bison. The vehicle and proud symbol of nineteenth-century commerce stood ready to accommodate every motive for the slaughter of a beast possessing no instinctive fear of humanity.

A healthy bison, especially one in a herd, can usually stand off a pack of wolves; as a species, bison evolved to either face danger or stampede (and wolves likely preyed mostly on bison that were weakened or very young). But the hundreds of miles of steel rail bisecting the Great Plains proved a far different sort of danger. Shooters from railroad cars could kill one bison after another without alerting the next victim to its fate. In 1870, the year the railroad reached Colorado, Philadelphia hide tanners learned to create a widely marketable bison hide leather.[21] The British army bought hides, industrialists bought them for belting on machines, and craftsmen started using them for a host of luxury items, such as furniture and wall panelings.[22] With available markets and economical means to transport the hides, the slaughter knew no bounds.

Although tourists might not have wanted to leave their railroad cars while hunting, hardy entrepreneurs quickly spread the carnage across the entire landscape. In 1873 the nation's economy took another downturn, again inducing many people to set out for the West seeking their fortunes. By 1874 hundreds of bison-hunting parties roamed the prairies, each systematically divided into killers, skinners, "wagon men," and a cook. Each hunting party heard its neighbors 50-caliber buffalo guns day after day within a few miles' distance throughout the southern plains. The killer would crouch a hundred or more yards from a herd and shoot the closest bison through the lungs. As the victim gasped and blew blood and then collapsed, the other bison would congregate around and sniff at their suffering fellow. One by one, each would be shot until the entire herd of a few dozen or even a hundred animals was dead. Then the skinners would go to work: removing the hides, stretching them on the ground to dry, and loading them onto the wagons. The hunting party then moved on to the next grazing herd.[23] Behind them, the great muscled carcasses would fester, and, as the sun and scavenging beetles broke down the flesh, the buffalo fat would stream through the grass.[24]

Between 1870 and 1874 more than 4 million bison were killed on the southern plains, and by the mid-1870s the great bison herds in Colorado and Kansas were gone. Then the hunters moved south, finishing off almost all the bison in Texas by 1878. Five years later the northern herds in Montana, Dakota Territory, and Canada had been eliminated as well, and in 1883 hunters wandered the empty plains of Montana, unable or unwilling to comprehend that there were essentially no more buffalo left to kill.[25]

Many across the nation wished to save the bison. In 1872 the *Rocky Mountain News* editorialized against the slaughter, particularly against "the firing of guns from the train." That same year Colorado's territorial legislature passed a law forbidding the waste of meat that accompanied killing bison for hides alone. But out on the remote plains the law was ignored.[26] Colorado's territorial representative in Congress, Hiram Bennett, also urged the animals' statutory protection, but although he was joined by representatives and senators from as far afield as California, Arizona, and Massachusetts, this and similar measures failed—in part because they were considered unenforceable.[27]

In 1874, with few bison remaining, Congress finally passed a law prohibiting the killing of any female bison by non-Indians, prohibiting the waste of bison meat, and penalizing violations with a $100 fine for each animal killed. But President Ulysses Grant's secretary of the interior, Columbus Delano, favored the extermination. The previous year he had written "I would not seriously regret the total disappearance of the buffalo from our western prairies, in its effect upon the Indians. I would regard it rather as a means of hastening their sense of dependence upon the products of the soil and their own labors." With this sentiment dominant in his administration, the president pocket-vetoed the legislation, and the bison continued to die.[28]

One of the last bison to survive on Colorado's plains was an old bull sighted by twenty-eight-year-old English rancher R. B. Townshend one spring day in 1874 while he was out looking for stray horses about twenty-five miles east of Colorado Springs. "I came in sight of a solitary black object more than a mile away that at first I took to be nothing less than an Indian sitting bent forward over the neck of his mount," Townshend recounted in his memoir *A Tenderfoot in Colorado,* written in the 1890s after he had settled in Oxford. Upon riding closer he identified the object as a buffalo. The bull, sporting a red gash on his side that had likely resulted from the horn of a rival bull, was shadowed by a "wolf pack lying down in the grass and waiting," Townshend wrote. He wished the bull no harm: "I had robes and meat enough at home already," he recalled. But he was also aware that the wolves might not share his good intentions, and he anticipated their attack on the "old warrior":

> As soon as the pinch of hunger gave them courage to attack, they would make a combined rush at him; the more cunning ones would bay him in front, always avoiding his irresistible charge and the fierce toss of those wicked horns, till at last the boldest of the cowardly lot seizing his opportunity, and springing on the victim from behind, with one tearing snap of his terrible wolfish fangs, would cut the hamstring; and behold the ex-monarch of the prairie crippled and helpless! Last of all, I saw in my vision the fall of the monarch, the disembowelling alive and the gruesome feast of victory.[29]

Taking a notion to save the bison from such a fate, Townshend charged the little group of animals, none of which had perceived his presence behind a hill. The wolves noticed him first, jumping to their feet in alarm. Then the bison saw him coming:

> Away fled the buffalo in the curious rocking gallop of his kind . . . while the hungry wolf pack scattered before me like a frightened covey of partridges before the swoop of a falcon. I wasted half a dozen pistol-shots just for the fun of seeing them stretch themselves, but I could not afford to waste horse-flesh in riding them down, so I presently left them and turned once more to renew the search for my lost stock.[30]

But far from having saved the bison, Townshend had done the opposite. The bull ran straight toward the nearby shack of a fellow English immigrant, the recently arrived Mr. MacTaggart, whose sheep were eating the grass Townshend counted on for his cattle. When MacTaggart saw the animal coming, he loaded his shotgun and set out in pursuit. His first load of buckshot missed, and his mare, unused to such a close blast, plunged and threw him on the ground. The bull turned and charged him, and while still on the ground MacTaggart fired his second barrel, breaking the animal's left front leg and momentarily stopping the charge. When MacTaggart got up, the bull charged him again on three legs. The sheep rancher ran in tight circles, narrowly averting the horns of an animal whose injury limited his ability to turn with agility.

With this drama under way, up rode one of MacTaggart's two hired hands with a revolver and fired six shots into the bull. "The very last shot went into his lungs, and he fell down and bled at the mouth and died," the other hired hand told Townshend.[31]

MacTaggart used the bison's hide to cover his roof, sold the thousand pounds of meat for three cents a pound, and put strychnine in the offal for the wolves. Townshend, having heard this story at the sheep ranch after finding his missing horses, turned toward home. "Dimly through the gathering dusk I saw the hungry grey wolves busy over the poisoned entrails as I passed the spot where the king of the prairie had fallen."[32]

Most other ungulates on the plains met the same fate. Townshend, despite his attempt to succor the last bison in his region, killed all the pronghorn he could and exchanged the meat at a sawmill for boards with which to build his corral and the floor of his six-room house.[33] The railroad had arrived early on southeastern Colorado's plains where he ranched between 1869 and 1874. In 1878 the northeastern corner of Colorado from Greeley to Julesburg "was reported to be alive with antelope," according to a livestock industry historian. But in 1881 a much-anticipated spur line of the Union Pacific Railroad was completed between Denver and Julesburg, precipitating a growth in ranching. Between August 1, 1885, and January 20 of the following year, the local ranching outfit, the Bartholf Brothers, slaughtered almost 1,100 pronghorn, presumably to save forage for stock. Elk, too, were numerous on the Great Plains, but ranchers believed their wild contumacy was contagious to nearby cattle and disposed of them accordingly.[34]

Undoubtedly, many distant consumers of beef would not have countenanced the wildlife slaughter paid for indirectly with their food dollars. But the slaughter did not take place in front of them, and thus the railroad helped foster a psychological distance between urban consumers—whether American or European—and the grounds for their sustenance in the West.[35]

Not only beef consumers but railroad investors also shaped the way in which the livestock industry impacted wildlife. The railroads, like the cattle industry they serviced, were financed largely by private investors from the East (as well as by huge tracts of salable land granted by the federal government and by locally issued municipal bonds).[36] These investors expected returns, and the railroad companies relied on shipping tremendous volumes to help recoup the huge fixed costs of laying down tracks, buying trains, and operating the line. Such economies of scale precluded local idiosyncrasies in production[37] and indirectly eliminated commercial growing of the most predator-resistant cattle breed in the West, the Texas longhorn.

Although wolves could certainly kill longhorns with no greater difficulty than they could bison, their namesake feature made them much less vulnerable than other cattle.[38] Yet the railroads, whose fixed costs and hence shipping charges largely remained the same no matter how many cattle they shipped per car, could fit two times more short-horn cattle in one car than animals of the

Texas breed, with their five-foot-plus span of horns. This factor, along with fear of disease carried by the Texas stock, eliminated almost all longhorns from the western range; by 1890 few were left in Colorado.[39]

The railroad also spawned a new technology—the refrigerated boxcar—that was initially developed for commercial market hunters before it was used to transport the remains of domestic animals.[40] Refrigeration enabled hunters to develop national markets for wild meat—potentially as deadly a development as the tanning industry had been to the bison. As early as 1878 James H. Cook, a cowboy turned market hunter, focused his efforts on areas in northern Colorado and southern Wyoming close to the Union Pacific line, from whence his white-tailed and mule deer, elk, pronghorn, and bighorn sheep were shipped as close as Cheyenne and as far as New York and San Francisco.[41]

A random culinary report of eastern high society gives us a glimpse into the ecological pressures exerted out West. In February 1899 millionaire Randolph Guggenheimer served "Roast Mountain Sheep with Puree of Chestnuts" as one of twenty-one courses for a banquet at New York's old Waldorf-Astoria, according to a history of American culture and society of the period. Bighorn sheep were making their last stand on the plains (by 1905 the subspecies named for John James Audubon would be extirpated from its stronghold in the South Dakota Badlands[42]), so it is not known whether Guggenheimer's entrées, shipped via "fast express in small portable refrigerators," emanated from this doomed population or from the somewhat more robust numbers in the Rocky Mountains.[43]

By the first few years of the twentieth century, Colorado had the most miles of railroad of any western public-land state except California (and far more than California per square mile).[44] This put the greatest strains on wildlife populations in Colorado, since the closer a carcass lay to the railroad, the greater the ease in transport and the less decay before refrigeration. Not surprisingly given the Queen City's centralized rail network, in 1914 Denver was the only far-western town among eight "plague-spots for the sale of wild game" listed by citizen wildlife advocate William T. Hornaday[45] (who will be encountered at length in Chapter 8).

The railroad was commerce, embodying an age determined to overcome any natural boundary or limit. Such a spirit would not be confined to a band of land alongside the tracks. Even far from the tracks, animals were slaughtered both for individual use and simply for pleasure. In 1881, for instance, Gunnison miner William McGinley snowshoed into the mountains for food and, cornering a band of pronghorn antelope in a natural enclave surrounded by deep snow, shot all thirty-two animals—carrying home only a little meat.

Government seemed helpless to stop such behavior. As early as 1867, Colorado's territorial legislature passed the Preserve Game Act, setting seasons delineating when "game" animals could be killed and when they could not. In 1874 and also in 1877, additional provisions banned killing more animals than could be eaten. But with loose definitions, no means of enforcement, and little popular concern for the laws' intent, wildlife received no respite.[46]

In the sagebrush-covered mountain valleys of Colorado, where thousands of pronghorn were reported to have once lived, few could be found by 1905. Informed population estimates for the swift ochre-striped animals dropped from 25,000 in 1898 to 1,200 in 1909. Three years later, scientists with the federal government, looking at such collapses across the species' entire range, predicted the pronghorn's imminent extinction.[47]

All wild ungulates faced the same prospect. In New Mexico and Arizona, Merriam's elk, a subspecies smaller than the Rocky Mountain elk but with larger antlers, was completely exterminated by 1906.[48] By 1909 in Colorado only 600 to 800 elk survived, and they were declining.[49] In 1912 the estimated number of bighorn sheep in Colorado was a healthier 3,500 animals. But since poachers were selling their meat for six cents per pound in the mountains southwest of Denver, their future seemed little more secure than that of the elk.[50] Deer fared no better. In 1912 Colorado's game and fish commissioner warned that unless deer were "carefully protected," they would "meet the fate of the buffalo and become entirely extinct."[51]

Bison had mainly been plains animals, but smaller numbers had also lived in the mountains.[52] A few bison survived in a mountain fastness as late as 1897, in what is today the Lost Creek Wilderness southwest of Denver. That February, however, hunters in league with eager taxidermists killed the last four remaining animals: two bulls, a cow, and a calf.[53]

For millennia, bison and other ungulates had sustained wolves and, at the same time, limited the wolf population to the number that could survive on prey sufficiently old, young, or sick to be taken down. But those constraints dropped away in the mid-1800s. With growing numbers of animal carcasses available, it is likely that wolf litter sizes and the number of surviving pups increased and that by the early 1870s wolf populations on the plains and in adjacent mountain foothills reached unprecedented highs.

When the vast bison herds were gone in the mid-1870s and other wildlife were trending toward the same fate, the unnaturally magnified wolf population needed a food source. Cattle drifting on the open range provided the ready substitute. As early as 1868, the government exploring expedition of Major John Wesley Powell ran across a herd of thirty-five untended stray cattle (one of which they ate) in the wilderness of far northwestern Colorado between the White and Yampa rivers. On his trip back to the region in 1869, Powell found that the sizable valley of Brown's Hole, along the Green River and at the eastern edge of today's Dinosaur National Monument, supported thousands of cattle—better protected than the strays, presumably, since he also ran across cabins.[54] The Great Plains to the east were similarly stocked.

Preying on cattle carried a risk for the wolves. In 1874 E. R. Stark, a rancher on the plains of eastern Colorado, came across a wolf-killed calf while on a corn-buying trip. "I had two bottles of strychnine with me which I put on the carcass. On my return the next morning I found 13 dead gray wolves near the carcass," he recalled fifty-one years later. "Their hides and the bounty on their scalps more than paid for the load of corn."[55]

The bounty was privately financed, likely by an affiliate of the Colorado Stockgrowers Association. Founded in 1867 and organized as a coalition of local chapters, this was the nation's first statewide cattlemen's group.[56] The primary impetus to form the association was to crack down on "maverickers" who rustled cattle on the open range. The association and its affiliates recorded livestock brands to deter the sale of stolen cattle, pushed for stricter and more efficient range law enforcement, and funded bounties to apprehend rustlers. Members regarded wolves as a type of animal rustler, although less threatening.[57] The Bent-Prowers County Cattle and Horse Growers Association on Colorado's southeastern plains—the first such local group to form—was typical, allocating its members' money toward buying poison to kill wolves and toward a $4.50 bounty on wolf scalps.[58]

Observers of the hubbub of western ranching might have viewed it as fulfilling what William Blackmore had termed the immutable laws of progress. It seemed the natural course of such progress that stock companies could report annual dividends as high as 42 percent. To most observers the newly-opened frontier land seemed like oxygen: inexhaustible, a medium that one believed in without seeing it and that one remembered only if reminded. The livestock industry encouraged that view, and the Colorado Stockgrowers Association worked to attract investors from afar.[59] The *Colorado Livestock Record* proclaimed ebulliently that "cattle is one of those investments men cannot pay too much for, since, if left alone, they will multiply, replenish, and grow out of a bad bargain."[60]

Investment and stocking on the open range soared. Back in 1871 a newspaper writer in San Francisco, Henry George, had warned that the nation's population growth would someday make land precious and argued against the policy of disposing of federal lands in the West, in particular against allocating vast swathes to the railroads. In his book *Our Land and Land Policy* he asked, "Does our 450,000,000 acres of available public land seem 'practically inexhaustible' when we turn our faces towards the future and hear in imagination, in the years that are almost on us, the steady tramp of the tens of millions, and of the hundreds of millions, who are coming?"[61] But his was a voice alone and unheeded. In the mid-1870s the bleaching bones of the bison littering the undulating grasses served as mute testimony that humanity would limit nature, not the other way around. By the end of the decade the bones were freighted east to produce fertilizer,[62] and the once-inexhaustible bison herds became symbol alone, incorporated not into the earth but into human imagination.

To those whose struggles against nature were not abstract but the substance of every bone-weary day, this onward rush of progress proved elevating. Where once the buffalo had roamed now rose empires of cattle, and each ill-paid man on horseback, each woman in a sod house remembering the comforts and community of eastern life, felt this remarkable feat to proclaim his and her moral significance. The sense of accomplishment and the thrill of infinite opportunity stretched across continents, and European investment in the great cattle bonanza continued to rise in the 1880s, along with the number of cattle on the open range.[63] As one European promoter of the western livestock industry exuberantly put it, "There is not the slightest element of uncertainty in cattle-raising."[64]

Yet the wolves still killed cattle and other domestic animals. Keeping out of rifle range, they seemed to define the periphery of a man's power. If household hounds attempted to chase them away, the wolves would "tear an old dog to pieces," seemingly "just to see what he's made of."[65] At night, long, drawn-out howls emphasized the meager light a lantern cast against the stark and impersonal panoply of stars.

The stockgrowers didn't just put up their own money to kill predators. Stanley P. Young, who figures prominently in the story of the West's wolves, credited the ranching industry with eliciting societal support for bounties. In his book *The Wolves of North America*, published in 1944, he explained:

> The stock interests of the Western States and Territories took the leading part in fostering county and State bounty legislation, for they felt that, as taxpayers, they were footing a large part of the taxes collected, and bounties were a means of some direct and beneficial aid to them in perpetuating the industry which, in turn, made assessments of taxes a surety, for they held that each head of livestock killed by wolves reduced the number that could be taxed.[66]

Faced with this sort of logic, in 1869, two years after the stockgrowers' genesis, Colorado's territorial legislature enacted a fifty-cent bounty on wolves, giving wolfers extra incentive above local private bounties and the profits to be made from pelts.

Over the next two decades, state after state in the West followed suit, with the Territory of Montana enacting a bounty in 1883, Wyoming doing so in 1893, and the Arizona–New Mexico territorial legislature passing a law in 1893 allowing counties to pay bounties on "predatory wolves, big bears [grizzlies], mountain lions, bobcats and coyotes."[67] Throughout the western states, by 1914 more than a million dollars per year was being paid in government bounties for all kinds of animals, but wolves were the foremost targets. And this sum did not include the substantial private bounties paid by livestock associations.[68]

The turn to bounties reflected that most obvious frontier experience with wildlife: animals whose remains drew a price could be made to disappear rapidly. In the case of wolves and coyotes, however, this truism did not apply. Fertility rates and an ability to raise pups to maturity increase with available food. The killing of some wolves would free up resources for others and result in a greater reproductive rate for the species.

The eventual realization that bounties would not get rid of predators, especially wolves, would provide the rationale, as will be seen, for the growth of a federal agency that would do so. The bounty phenomenon of the late nineteenth and early twentieth centuries serves as a window into the shifting fortunes and aspirations of western ranchers—and into what happened to wolves as livestock replaced native ungulates.

By its legislature's action in 1869, Colorado became the first Rocky Mountain territory to enact a wolf bounty (although in the northeastern states wolf bounties preceded the Declaration of Independence, and Iowa had enacted a bounty in 1858, followed by Kansas in 1864).[69] But although the idea was destined to spread throughout the region, acceptance was hardly universal at first. Fiscal conservatives questioned its worth, and, responding to this sentiment, the legislature cut off bounty appropriations between 1872 and 1875.

In 1876 (the year of statehood), with the bison gone, the Colorado General Assembly reinstated the bounty. Legislators added coyotes as a target species alongside wolves and approved provisions for county treasurers to dispense funds, destroy the wolf and coyote scalps turned in for surety, and keep records. In 1879 the legislature raised the bounty to 75 cents per scalp. Two years later it raised the bounty to $1.50 and added skunks, hawks, and mountain lions to the list of targeted species.[70]

Many of the receipts for scalps turned in and bounties paid are stored at the Colorado State Archives, and some others are stored at county courthouses. They indicate the year and county in which each animal was bountied, collectively providing a numeric outline of wolf and coyote mortality during the period when bison were being eliminated and for several years following.[71]

Although the bounty was reinstated in 1876, no records are available for that year or for 1877. But receipts for the years 1878 through 1885 are available and are broken down by county (see appendixes for detailed figures). Because the data are fragmentary (in part because most county clerks neglected to note whether a wolf or a coyote scalp was turned in), a methodology to estimate the numbers of each species was developed (and is explained in a methodological note preceding the appendixes).

The data indicate that at first the overwhelming majority of wolves turned in for bounties in Colorado came from the Great Plains but that in subsequent years a growing proportion were trapped in the mountains, foothills, and parks (labeled simply as "Mountains" in the table that follows). During this eight-year period an estimated 2,641 wolf scalps were turned in, 1,688 of them killed on the plains and 953 in the mountains.

Estimated Numbers of Wolves Bountied in Colorado, 1869–1885

Year	1869	1870	1871	1878	1879	1880	1881	1882	1883	1884	1885
Plains	?	?	?	126	148	132	107	346	399	357	73
Mountains	?	?	?	4	35	53	59	145	266	360	31
Total	27	57	66	130	183	185	166	491	665	717	104

Even with many lacunae and uncertainties, the data can help illustrate what was happening on the ground. Most significant, the extension of railroad lines can be tied quite closely in some instances to the increase in the killing of wolves and coyotes. For example, around 1874 miners first established settlements in the area in central Colorado's mountains that became Gunnison County. In 1880 only 1,329 beef cattle and no sheep were grazed in the county, and many of those were probably butchered for local use. No records indicate anyone had turned in any wolves or coyotes for bounty. By 1882, local smelting of ores led to railroad access. The railroad shipped out not only precious metals but also livestock.[72] In 1881, before the railroad had arrived, the first bounty record—the only one for that year—was for a single coyote; no wolves were turned in. The following year hunters turned in 36 coyotes, 5 confirmed wolves, and 91 unspecified canids, of which I estimate 7 were wolves.

In another region, the San Luis Valley of southern Colorado, livestock were present long before the railroad, but the laying down of tracks precipitated a change in livestock numbers or husbandry practices or both that led to a dramatic increase in killing predators. The San Luis Valley was in many ways an ideal place to raise stock—because of the same conditions that had made it a high-quality habitat for so many wildlife species. Hemmed in on the west by the San Juans and on the east by the sunset-tinged Sangre de Cristo ("blood of Christ") range, the 150-mile-long valley receives snowmelt from both sides. That abundant moisture not only flows into the Rio Grande but also replenishes subsurface groundwater and creates extensive shallow pools. Willow thickets line the streams in the valley, interspersed with groves of huge, shade-producing cottonwoods. The valley's damp soil, rich with decay, produces abundant grass.[73] Altogether, the valley's wealth of wetlands must have supported large numbers of beaver, whereas the ponderosa-fringed grasslands nurtured bison, elk, deer, bighorn sheep, and antelope.

Colorado's first territorial governor, William Gilpin, always prone to overstatement (and owning vast amounts of land in the San Luis Valley whose value he wanted to promote), described the valley as "the brightest gem of the whole world," according to R. B. Townshend, who shared a stage coach ride from Cheyenne to Denver with the former governor.[74] But Captain Zebulon M. Pike, who favored a more austere lexicon in recording his 1806–1807 journal of exploration, had reached a similar conclusion, calling the valley a "terrestrial paradise."[75]

San Luis Valley culture developed differently from that on the Great Plains. As we have seen, in the 1870s consumers and financiers in Chicago (an important railroad and banking center), the Atlantic seaboard, and England drove the dramatic re-fashioning of the Great Plains' ecology. In satisfying those demands from afar, ranchers on the Great Plains were driven by the same feverish impulse as any gold miner seeking instant wealth. In contrast, ranching in the San Luis Valley had begun decades earlier as an outgrowth of ranching in northern New Mexico. As early as 1821, while trappers pursued beaver in the same regions, Mexican sheepherders had pushed their flocks north into Colorado along the Rio Grande, its tributary the Conejos, and the rivers' headwaters in the San Juan Mountains—where the vast coniferous forests of the southern Rocky Mountains meet the red-rock cliffs of the Southwest. In 1852 sheep ranchers played an instrumental role in founding the village of San Luis in the valley, and by the middle of that decade sheep grazed not only on the San Juan Mountains but also on the Sangre de Cristo range.[76] The first sheep ranchers in the region (as in most of the West) were regionally financed, employed local shearers, and sold wool to local companies or used it and the mutton themselves. Perhaps because local money was more limited, the largest Colorado sheep rancher in the nineteenth century operated on a considerably smaller scale than his counterparts in the cattle industry.[77]

So early sheep ranching was less of a corporate and more of a small-business endeavor. Even though much of the wool would enter the national economy eventually, in general the sheep ranchers owed stronger allegiances to their local communities than did cattle ranchers, whose business relationships extended internationally.

The railroad reached the San Luis Valley in 1878,[78] eight years after reaching Colorado's Great Plains. That year in the San Luis Valley, bounty payments were made to the killers of 1 confirmed coyote and 7 unidentified canids I estimate were also coyotes. In 1879, 9 coyotes were bountied there plus 43 unidentified canids, which I estimate included 3 wolves. Then, in 1880 the numbers jump more dramatically: 4 wolves were confirmed killed, as well as 68 coyotes and 116 unspecified canids, which I estimate included 9 wolves—and those high levels were breached in subsequent years.

San Luis Valley Bounty Payments, 1878–1885[79]

	1878	1879	1880	1881	1882	1883	1884	1885
Confirmed wolves	0	0	4	3	35	77	51	4
Confirmed coyotes	1	9	68	92	109	128	426	216
Unspecified	7	43	116	114	156	151	95	23
Total estimated wolves	0	3	13	12	48	88	58	6
Total estimated coyotes	8	49	175	197	252	268	514	237

What do these numbers indicate? The small number of wolves and coyotes turned in for bounties in the first two years after the railroad arrived may have reflected an economic and cultural anachronism: San Luis Valley ranchers' long-standing willingness to adapt their business operations to local conditions. At least as early as the 1830s and probably long before, sheep ranchers in New Mexico used herders and guard dogs to protect their flocks from wolves.[80] These methods may have worked sufficiently well in the 1870s to obviate the need for mass poisoning.

It could also be that small-scale Mexican ranchers, whose livelihoods did not depend on the vagaries of railroad freight rates and international markets, felt less compulsion to scapegoat predators than did operators who felt close to the bottom rung of an already gargantuan economic ladder.

By 1880, however, two years after the trains' arrival in the San Luis Valley and ten years after the first whistle-stop in Denver, whatever economic or cultural differences allowed predators some respite in the San Luis Valley had disappeared. That year yielded the first county-by-county agricultural statistics for Colorado. For its relatively small size, the San Luis Valley was heavily stocked in 1880, with roughly two sheep for every cow.[81]

Like other regions, data from the San Luis Valley reveal a very rough correlation between livestock production and the number of bountied wolves and coyotes (see Appendixes V and VI). But that correlation indicated a political weakness in areas where ranching was subordinate to the other major early statehood industry—mining—whose employees, investors, and communities had no interest in spending tax money to kill predators. In 1885 the earlier fiscal doubts were revisited, and Colorado governor James Benton Grant declared:

> The state is under no more obligation to clear the farmer's ranch of poisonous weeds, under no more obligation to protect the herdsman's flocks against wolves and lions than it is to pump the water from the silver and lead mines and to free the coal mines from poisonous gasses. These bounty laws represent a species of provincial legislation to those counties whose citizens have displayed such aptitude in scalping wolves and harvesting loco-weed.[82]

Pitting miners against ranchers won the support of the *San Juan Prospector* and proved a winner in the state legislature, which scrapped the bounty that year. Like the *Prospector*, the name of another local newspaper points to its community's interests. The northeastern plains town of Brush responded with alarm. Brush's paper, the *Lariat*, complained of horses and heifers killed by wolves along the South Platte River, pointing to "a pack of twenty grays . . . making their headquarters . . . twenty-six miles south" of the town. "If nothing is done to abate this nuisance the plains will, in a few years, become a howling wilderness with a vengeance," the paper warned.[83]

Last Feast on Wild Meat

D uring the winter of 1885–1886 it seemed the wilderness did return with a vengeance. With the southern Great Plains already stocked with more cattle than the land could support, the stage was set by President Grover Cleveland's order to remove white-owned livestock from Indian Territory, reserved for the Cheyenne and Arapaho in the area now known as Oklahoma. Two hundred thousand cattle were herded into Colorado and Kansas. Then the blizzards hit. Uncommonly cold winds from the north pushed thin, gritty snow ahead of them, quickly covering up what remained of the buffalo grasses. Whereas bison, with their great mat of hair, would have faced the storm and pawed through the snow for grass, cattle were helpless. Some no doubt drifted with the winds, searching out forage that was not there to be found, before succumbing. Others, their fat reserves already depleted, died where they stood. Brief thaws were followed by more blizzards, and where once the openness of the plains had portended unlimited opportunity, now the whiteness of the sky signified a cell block of cold encasing thousands of square miles.

That winter and the subsequent spring, up to 85 percent of the cattle in this region of the plains died. The wolves, adapted to such conditions, perhaps waited out each storm with noses tucked under their tails in the slight shelter of gullies, gulches, or overhangs. Between storms a pack would have broken through the wolf-high snow in single file, searching for sustenance. Even had the manpower existed, there would have been insufficient strychnine in the

West to poison half or even a quarter of the cattle carcasses. Without going far, wolves would have come upon clumps of dead cattle, unseeing heads peering toward the sky, bodies frozen and then blanketed with snow where they fell.

The storms that proved fatal to the cows renewed the wolves. With Colorado's bounty removed the previous year, there was less incentive to try to kill them, even had the weather been conducive. Although wolf pelts could still be sold and large-scale ranchers as well as homesteaders with only a few stock would have liked to have wiped them out, the remaining wolves on the plains enjoyed a reprieve. The banquet of untainted carrion must have rivaled the gastronomic bonanza produced by the bison slaughter a decade earlier. Perhaps as a result of greater fertility among well-fed wolves (and other mammals), ranchers in Wyoming reported a subsequent increase in their numbers.

The next year the same phenomenon occurred in other areas of the West as extreme weather killed off cattle on overstocked ranges. The summer of 1886 proved dry throughout the Great Plains, and poor grass growth left cattle thin at the approach of fall. But stock prices had crashed nationwide. So rather than sell cattle, ranchers prayed for a mild winter, and many southern plains ranchers trailed their herds' survivors north to where grass was presumed to be in better shape. But the northern plains also had been grazed down to dirt, and the incoming herds did not help the situation. That winter, blizzards killed off up to 95 percent of the cattle in some regions of Montana. But as in Colorado, the Montana territorial legislature, with mining interests ascendant over ranching interests, rescinded the bounty law in 1887.[1] Future president Theodore Roosevelt, a usually absentee rancher during this period in the portion of Dakota Territory east of Montana, later recalled that in the late 1880s or early 1890s wolves increased in number there "until they became once more as numerous as ever and infinitely more wary and difficult to kill."[2]

The blizzards and droughts throughout the West, and the resurgence of wolves, upended popular and political perceptions about the proper role of government in taming the wild frontier. For decades, boosters had extolled the natural beneficence of the West's climate and soils. In 1868, in an unforgettable subordination of climatology to frontier theology, scientist Cyrus Thomas had posited that rain follows the plow, rendering previously infertile lands suitable for farming. Others hypothesized that it was the railroad, that monument to the creed of progress, that turned the weather to agriculture's needs, just as it had tamed a hostile terrestrial sphere. In the late 1880s, however, it seemed nature would not bend to human exigencies, and perhaps government would have to aid development. On the federal level western senators, including Colorado's Henry Moore Teller, a former railroad executive, pushed for more substantial government involvement in western settlement, including surveys of land suitable for irrigated agriculture.[3] To aid struggling stockmen, in 1889 the Colorado General Assembly again approved bounties, this time back to $1.50 for each wolf or coyote and $10.00 per bear or mountain lion.

Attached to the new bounty law were provisions to penalize the fraudulent practice of turning in scalps from other states or from animals killed before the bounty was reinstated. These clauses were essentially a secondary bounty attached to the primary one, rewarding the informer with half the fine on the bounty cheater; the other half went to county schools.[4] Cutting down on dishonesty, killing wolves, and building schools seemed part and parcel of progress.

Soon after the 1889 Colorado bounty law was passed, the Colorado Supreme Court declared unconstitutional the provisions dispensing fines to informants and to county schools. This invalidated the entire law and halted state reimbursements to counties. In response, in 1893 the legislature appropriated $6,000 for back bounty payments to counties and passed a new, constitutionally sound bounty law.[5] For the first time, it paid different amounts for wolves and coyotes: $2.00 and $1.00, respectively.[6] The difference may have reflected greater economic losses caused by wolves, their relative scarcity, greater difficulty in capturing them, or a combination of these factors. Bounty fraud, such as the "common practice of substituting scalps from domestic animals, such as dogs, for those of wolves,"[7] remained a misdemeanor, although without incentives for informers.[8]

Another possibility for bounty fraud opened in 1897, when the legislature took a further step and formally enabled counties to impose their own wolf bounties (in addition to the state payments and privately issued bounties, which needed no state sanction).[9] Shortly afterward, Prowers County (which had been carved out of Bent County on the southern plains) provided its own bounty, paying $5.00 per dead wolf. In 1898, perhaps as a result of the greater incentive offered, forty-four wolves were turned in within that county. But there is no way of knowing how many of those wolves had never been in Prowers County while still alive.

Still another form of fraud surfaced in 1900, when the Bent-Prowers County Cattle and Horse Growers Association started paying a bounty of $2.50 for wolf pup scalps and $5.00 for adult scalps. In response, wolfer O. G. Strain tried to collect the larger amount for the scalp of a wolf he had captured as a pup and reared until adulthood. His skullduggery was exposed, and the association awarded him $2.50, apparently not sufficiently troubled to penalize him for the attempted fraud.[10]

Aside from the insight bounty fraud affords into the social interactions of frontier ranching, it also indicates that it was becoming more difficult to kill wolves. The Montana State Legislature addressed bounty fraud in 1883, six years before Colorado did so,[11] and the problem would eventually be recognized as ubiquitous. In previous decades wolfers had simply shot a grazing animal at random, applied a bottle or three of strychnine to its flesh, and returned the next morning to skin the surrounding wolf carcasses. By the 1880s several factors may have made honest wolf-killing a more challenging occupation and turned some bounty seekers to engage in fraud.

First, there were far fewer wolves to kill after decades of poisoning—even accounting for reprieves during particularly severe winters and some let-up when the bounty was suspended. In 1902 *Forest and Stream* magazine reported that wolves were very scarce in northern Colorado and southern Wyoming between 1888 and 1894 and appeared to have increased their numbers only "in the last few years."[12]

Next, there were no bison left to kill on the plains, and other wild grazers, such as antelope and elk, were rare. Although domestic animals could be used, a cow or a horse had a commercial value to be considered.

Lastly, the remaining wolves were more wary of poison, traps, and rifles. One wolf killer speculated in *Forest and Stream* in 1897 that the "half poisoned brutes had a way of influencing other wolves to avoid the poisoned baits."[13] Outdoorsman and naturalist Enos Mills, who spent much of his time from 1890 to 1905 in the backcountry of Colorado and Wyoming and who vigorously tracked down others' wildlife experiences, wrote about an elk killed in Wyoming by hunters who left the animal lying on the ground all night. According to Mills, "Its only protection was a handkerchief tied to one of the horns. Tracks in the snow showed that wolves were about and that they had circled the carcass, but without going close enough to touch it." Mills similarly reported on two ponies that died at different times in the same region on the plains. One pony was shod and the other was not, and wolves—ever suspicious of the smell of iron—ate the unshod animal but would not touch the other one.[14]

Mills also cited a hunter who left a deer out all night and ensured that wolves wouldn't touch it simply by rubbing his hands over the carcass, leaving the danger-associated scent of humanity as a guard.[15] In another instance, Mills "watched a trapper spend several hours in placing more than a hundred traps round the carcass of a cow," but to no avail:

> He [the trapper] avoided touching the carcass. This concealed trap arrangement was as complicated as a barbed-wire entanglement. At one place he set the traps three abreast and five deep. On another probable line of approach he set ten traps, singly, but on a zigzag line. Two fallen logs made a V-shaped chute, which ended close to the carcass. In the narrow end of this chute another cluster of traps was set. Thus the carcass was completely surrounded by numerous concealed traps. It seemed impossible for any animal to walk to the carcass without thrusting a foot into one of the steel jaws of this network of concealed traps. Yet a wolf got through that night and feasted on the carcass![16]

Mills concluded that surviving wolves "must be exceptionally wide-awake and wary."[17]

In 1884, in response to the presence of a pack of eight wolves on northeastern Colorado's plains near Sterling, citizens there added $6.00 to the state bounty (resulting in the retrieval of only one wolf carcass).[18] Such substantial local expenditures reflected both the economic impact of the wolves and their fearsome reputation. A series of articles printed in 1882 and 1883 by a Leadville newspaper described several successive wolf attacks on humans in the region of the upper Arkansas River, all thwarted by the near-victims' incredible luck and skill. A January 5, 1883, column described a man on horseback chased at night by a pack of wolves. In the mad dash for their lives, his horse slipped and fell:

> [A]nd the rider went flying through the air as though thrown from a catapult. . . . He struck in the forks of a pine tree whose stem had divided about twenty feet above the ground. The force of the fall broke his left arm below the elbow and knocked him senseless. He hung there suspended safely above his pursuers, while they glutted their thirst for blood on the helpless horse.[19]

Although this tale sounds contrived, the sentiment behind it added allure to the prosaic business of poisoning wolves. In fact, wolves could on rare occasions prove to be a real hazard. According to an account from the early 1870s, a rabid wolf in western Kansas bit a homesteader's boy, who quickly became sick. Rather than see his child suffer unduly, the stoic father killed his son. The wolf, after biting pets and livestock, was later also killed.[20]

And in the winter of 1890–1891 in the Oklahoma panhandle, wolves are said to have attacked the horse of a missionary traveling at night through a blizzard. The unarmed man, J. H. McQuistion, was walking alongside his weary mount, kicking at wolves that got too close, and in the fray his hand was bitten. According to the story, neither missionary nor horse was seriously injured; the pack's attention was diverted by a herd of cattle, from which they did make a meal.[21]

Certainly, wolves had the potential to hurt humans, yet the mythology of wolf attacks often seems more animated than the wolves themselves. Take, for example, a tale from the plains of Iowa featuring "Fiddlin' Jim," whose violin served in place of a rifle when he was menaced by wolves. When rescuers found him vigorously playing to a seated circle of the dreaded predators, the near-victim declared: "You came in right handy. Them wolves sure meant business, and every time I quit playin', they started movin' up. But I sure got tuned up good."[22]

Regardless of the truth behind each sensational story, wolves had virtually no public defenders on the frontier or back East. Those opposed to the bison slaughter described the big herbivores as "a work of God"[23] and the "finest wild animal in our hemisphere," extolling the bison's harmless and tame disposition and the value of its meat and hides.[24] But wolves remained at the bottom of a moral hierarchy so obvious that it needed no articulation. A wolf in southwestern Kansas seemed to elevate the social status of the black man who gained fame from shooting him. "Dat wolf," the hero was said to have proclaimed as ranchers and local officials sang his praises, "represent Bad."[25]

Ultimately, those who felt that "badness" the keenest were forced to cooperate to address their losses. Whereas the job of pursuing wolves tended to favor individual action in setting traps or poison and returning to the same place to retrieve the proof of one's good works, and although a substantial number of wolfers might be suspected of not putting a premium on honesty, the bounty era also left records of ranchers for whom wolfers worked similarly exhibiting selfish behavior. In 1896 the general manager of the Standard Cattle Company, which owned ranches in several western states, became so disgruntled at his neighbors' lack of cooperation in eradicating wolves that he abandoned civic-mindedness, as well as his previous hope of raising the amount paid per scalp under the Wyoming bounty law:

> [I]t is my expectation, by continuous hunting, to cause the wolves to leave our own part of the country and to drive them onto our neighbors. I have made every possible effort to secure some union of action for the abating of this nuisance, but as in everything else of the kind, I have borne the greater share of the expense and done most of the work, while others are indifferent or careless and reluctant to join in the movement. Any further legislation in the direction of a sufficient bounty is useless, and I shall not attempt it.[26]

Over time, however, ranchers learned to discourage non-cooperation among themselves. Beginning in 1904, the Piceance Creek Stock-Growers Association in northwestern Colorado's sagebrush-covered Rio Blanco County offered $25.00 per wolf scalp, then raised that amount to $50.00 several years later. Although all area ranchers benefited from the killing of wolves, not all ponied up. In 1912, after some association members had consistently refused to pay their share of the bounty, ranchers formed a parallel stock association for the same region—informally known as the Wolf Bounty Association—whose by-laws prohibited anyone in arrears on their bounty assessment from receiving aid from members in the annual round-ups. (With additional money made available, the Wolf Bounty Association later raised the bounty to $100 and finally to $150.)[27]

From early on, wolves represented the antithesis of civilization; their elimination would serve conjoined psychic and economic causes. But killing wolves also served as attempted redress for other problems caused by civilization's westward expansion—most notably the gunning down of their natural prey, which had forced the wolves to turn to domestic stock.

By the turn of the twentieth century around 1.3 million beef cattle occupied Colorado, along with more than 2 million sheep.[28] In 1909 in central Colorado's Gunnison County, the stronghold for the state's remaining elk (supporting a contemporaneously estimated 400 to 500 wapiti), almost 20,000 cattle (and almost 10,000 sheep) grazed, a ratio of at least 40 cows to each elk. In the northwestern counties of Rio Blanco and Routt, where 200 to 300 elk constituted the bulk of the remaining population in the state, more than 120,000 beef cattle (and 20,000 sheep) ranged—at least 400 cattle for each elk.[29] It is not difficult to understand why the surviving wolves preyed on livestock.

The chain of unintended consequences during the passage from frontier to civilization can be seen as the hallmark of the era. Immediately after the bison were killed off in the 1870s, western prairies were ravaged by a plague of grasshoppers, which may have irrupted in the absence of competitors for grass.[30]

Other side effects followed from the introduction of livestock to replace the wild ungulates. In 1901 C. S. Crandall, an official with the Bureau of Forestry (predecessor of the Forest Service), noted extensive soil erosion and "many slopes, saddles, and mountain tops entirely destitute of trees" as a result of both grazing and logging.[31] Enos Mills counted forty-three massive landslides resulting from one storm in the San Juans.[32] Crandall reported that "there is very little of the region that is not grazed to the limit of its ability to support animal life."[33] Similar conditions prevailed almost everywhere in the West.

Some of the animal life impacted would otherwise have thrived even in the face of hunting pressure. As noted, by 1832, when the price of beaver pelts plummeted and beaver trapping had largely ended, beaver in most of the West's waters had been exterminated. But by 1850 the fecund species had rebounded, according to a later authoritative history of the fur trade.[34] Mills reported that when the first white settlers arrived in the upper Arkansas valley near Leadville, Colorado, in the 1870s, as many as fifty beaver dams dotted each linear mile of the river's headwater tributaries. These dams held the water back in a series of swamps and ponds. But by 1904, according to Mills, most of the beaver and their dams were once again gone.

In the intervening three decades, first the forests had been razed to provide wood to prop up mine shafts and to be used as fuel for smelters, while at the same time sheep ate the new shoots of young trees and cattle ate and trampled the streamside willows and cottonwoods on which beaver fed. Mills attributed the rarity of beaver dams in the first years of the new century to deforestation.[35] With insufficient ground cover and vegetation to hold back the rains, and with beaver populations impacted by their declining food base, the dams washed away and were not rebuilt.

The decline of beaver deprived wolves and other predators of a food source (in some regions beaver constitute a third of wolves' diets) and also had secondary impacts on wolves' cuisine. Beaver ponds, after slowly silting in, become wet, grassy meadows used by deer and elk, so the loss of beaver eventually resulted in further decline of ungulate habitats.

Beyond such unthought-of changes in western montane ecosystems resulting from grazing, logging, and mining, more dramatic changes came in the form of cataclysmic floods, often accompanied by loss of human life and disappearance of fertile soil. On July 24, 1896, Bear Creek flooded through Morrison, Colorado, in the foothills southwest of Denver, killing twenty-seven people. In southwestern New Mexico, Silver City lost its Main Street in 1895 and then again in 1903 to twelve-foot walls of water pouring off the denuded Pinos

Altos Mountains to the north. Today, the former boulevard is a tree-lined stream at the bottom of a canyon of its own creation thirty-five feet below the streets that parallel it.[36]

In 1915 the Gila River in southeastern Arizona flooded 2,500 acres in one county alone. Along one of its mountain tributaries, the Blue River, 90 percent of 4,000 cultivated acres were rendered worthless because of floods from upstream overgrazing, according to naturalist Aldo Leopold in an essay titled "Pioneers and Gullies," originally published in 1924. The soil erosion, Leopold noted, led more than two-thirds of the valley's 300 residents to depart and the rest to lose income and a lifestyle whose value cannot be measured: "A stock ranch deprived of its garden patch, orchard, milk cows, and poultry is no fit place to establish a home and raise a family," he wrote. "Regardless of the profit of the business, it is an unsocial institution."[37]

Despite the West's blizzards, droughts, floods, locusts, and wolves—an almost biblical array of curses—the grail of progress shimmered so brightly as to cast restraint into the shadows. Civilization had arrived in the West as a series of appetites to be sated one after another—for gold, game, and ultimately, in the landslides, erosion, and floods, for the ground itself. Almost nobody was immune to the blandishments of the gospel of progress. Frederick Chapin, for example, was a mountaineer with an appreciation of nature more highly developed than that of almost all his contemporaries at the end of the nineteenth century. In the area that later became Rocky Mountain National Park, during an August 1888 outing Chapin and his friends spied a bear (species unrecorded); they immediately pulled their revolvers and left a bullet "lodged in bear meat." The injured animal escaped, and Chapin proceeded to climb a mountain, blithely recounting that the bear "gave us lots of fun for a few minutes."[38]

Although wolves were hardly the only animal that died in the course of taming the plains, they bore the brunt of frontier immigrants' hatred and fear of the wild. President Theodore Roosevelt described wolves in a 1905 article as the "beast of waste and desolation"[39]; and stockmen and others regularly assailed them for their seemingly cruel nature, their "ravenous appetite,"[40] and their general status as one of the most fearful representatives of lands that had not yielded to the gentle touch of domestic improvement.

On January 27, 1898, as the closing feature of the first annual National Live Stock Association convention in Denver, a banquet featuring the bounty of the plains was planned. At noon on that bright winter day an estimated 30,000 people, including visiting stockmen and resident Denverites, were to be treated to 15,000 loaves of bread, 500 pounds of coffee, 300 kegs of beer, 3 barrels of sugar, 10,000 pickles, and 35 barrels of yams—all of which supplemented the 10 beef cattle, 30 sheep, 200 opossums, 15 antelope, 5 bison, 4 elk, and 2 bears laid out for the feast.

Events did not go as planned. The great meal symbolizing civilization's triumph over the wilderness instead became a bacchanalian riot as thousands of people broke down iron fences in a mad rush for what they considered the "last feast on wild meat," according to later reports. When the orgy of eating and drinking was over, one man was dead and the other participants had stolen every dish and item of silverware: 1,000 forks and knives, 2,000 tin cups, and 50 china platters.[41]

Nothing remained.

The Best-Organized Interest in the West

T he first two wolves seen in decades within Denver's city limits cowered at the back corner of their small wooden crate on the morning of January 25, 1899. The night before had been filled with revelry for the thousand-plus delegates to the second annual convention of the National Live Stock Association, and, notwithstanding the previous year's celebratory excess, many had stayed up till 5 A.M. enjoying the Queen City's charms. Now, more than an hour after the day's program was scheduled to begin, the assorted ranchers—about a quarter of whom hailed from Colorado— shuffled into the Tabor Grand Opera House, stopping in the hallway to stoop over the crate and peer at the two "unwilling delegates" recently captured in Wyoming, now securely held by metal chains around their necks. Close by the live wolves, pelts of their kin lay spread out, testimony to the fate of the two frightened animals who had been arranged as props for the morning session.[1]

Wolf extermination headed the day's discussion topics, a fitting follow-up to the convention's opening invocation the previous morning in which the Reverend Dean Martyn Hart had urged the delegates "to subdue the earth" and "use the forces of nature for [their] own benefit."[2] Although western ranchers had not waited for that moment of ecclesiastic assent to eliminate most of the wolves on the plains, the species was still populous in the mountains, and as long as even a few wolves survived, the potential existed for a rebound. In fact, the topic's featured speaker—the bearded, austere, balding cattleman A. J. Bothwell of south-central Wyoming—insisted that the numbers of this "much

"Unwilling delegates from Wyoming." The first two wolves seen for decades within Denver's city limits awaited their fate as props for the wolf extermination agenda item at the second annual convention of the National Live Stock Association, January 25, 1899. (Charles F. Martin, Proceedings of the Second Annual Convention of the National Live Stock Association, *Denver Chamber of Commerce)*

dreaded scourge and devastator of the stock ranges" were growing dramatically and that wolves were now spotted in places they had never been seen before. The problem, he pointed out, lay in "the fact that the public are ever indifferent toward evils through which they are not personally damaged."[3]

Indeed, whatever menace they represented to livestock producers, neither wolves nor their absence affected the overwhelming majority of the West's citizens. The bonanza days for cattlemen had peaked in the 1880s, and by 1899 more people (350) were working in Denver's breweries supplying the livestock association delegates with their ale than there were Colorado delegates at the convention (344 ranchers from the state). Many urban people did depend on the livestock industry, including the 440 employees of the local packing-house and a significant proportion of Denver's 814 railroad workers. Nevertheless, the city's economy as a whole rested primarily on mining, urban construction, and services, not on the cattle and sheep in the hinterlands. For example, smelting employed 1,700 people, carpentry 400, and laundries 850. (By way of contrast, taxidermy only employed 12 people and furriery 14.)[4]

Bothwell knew the stock industry was increasingly irrelevant to ordinary westerners at the turn of the twentieth century, and he warned that "the general feeling of indifference on the part of the public" presented a problem in mobilizing sufficiently vigorous and comprehensive government support for a "final extermination" of wolves. He had a suggestion, however: that the livestock association in each western county direct concerted political pressure toward a single solution. Instead of relying on the vagaries of political tides to finance wolf bounties, whose amounts would always ebb and flow, Bothwell proposed "a uniform and permanent bounty law for all states interested in this problem." Such a bounty "should be large enough to warrant men in following the business of wolf killing," and each legislative session should appropriate enough money "to carry the law into effect from one legislature to another" without respite.[5]

Only such a coordinated effort, he concluded, would make "the warfare against wolves a persistent and effective movement in the West, until the race is finally and completely exterminated." The association approved his motion without debate.[6]

In preparation for such a trans-state effort, at the previous month's Southern Colorado Stock Grower's Association meeting in Pueblo, the association and members of the Colorado Cattle Grower's Association* drafted model bounty legislation, largely based on Colorado's existing bounty law, designed to be grafted into any state's book of statutes.[7] In practice, however, the National Live Stock Association had too many other irons in the fire to devote sufficient resources to make the so-called West-wide bounty system a reality. Although ranchers in Colorado, Utah, Wyoming, Montana, and Minnesota attempted to follow through, according to Stanley P. Young the plan "died 'several natural deaths' for want of unified action."[8] Even had unified action been forthcoming, oddly enough the model Colorado delegates introduced into the convention retained the relatively modest two dollar price tag for a dead wolf (half the amount Bothwell had criticized as inadequate in Wyoming) and the provisions penalizing bounty fraud that had been struck down by the Colorado Supreme Court almost a decade previously.

Such apparent difficulties in adapting their actions to new information transcended the administrative details of the proposed bounty law and kept the ranchers from assessing clearly whether bounties would even work for extermination. The bounty had been effective on the plains largely because it was not the sole motivation to kill wolves. As noted, people killed wolves for

---

*Livestock association names varied considerably over time and places. Thus, *cattle growers, stock growers,* and *wool growers* are variously rendered as one word or two and with or without apostrophes, depending on my sources.

the commercial value of their pelts, to protect livestock, and simply because frontier progress and even frontier religion seemed to demand predator extermination. Most individuals wanted to feel they were participants in the progressive and edifying endeavor that constituted civilization.

The West-wide bounty was one of a series of ideas proposed by turn-of-the-century ranchers to address the inadequacy of individual action against wolves. In 1897 a northern New Mexico rancher, Arthur Tisdall, charging that "[t]he State and county bounties result in very little good," issued the first known suggestions for a federal role in wolf extermination. First, he proposed that "the Government issue to responsible men in every county, poison free of charge, to be by him distributed to the owners of stock, on application." And more dramatically, Tisdall called for "a United States law making wolf scalps legal tender for payment of taxes, at say $10 per head."[9] Both these ideas constituted an ideological bridge (one very typical of this moment preceding the Progressive era) from individual effort to group solutions—the very concept of government. Perhaps foreshadowing the future relationship western ranchers (despite their libertarian and individualist rhetoric) would enjoy with a munificent and bountiful federal government, Tisdall presented his ideas the day after Christmas.

Not only wolf extermination demanded collective action from livestock producers. In fact, much of the business of ranching could hardly be done by one individual. As described, ranchers initially banded together to protect their property from rustlers as well as from wolves. The Colorado Stockgrowers Association also exercised its collective bargaining power to attack the exorbitant freighting rates set by railroad monopolies transporting livestock to eastern markets and to challenge laws governing the shipment and treatment of stock.[10]

Finally, as the once-open range filled in the 1880s with "nesters"—homesteaders seeking not empire but simply a farm with 160 acres, often with no direct access to a stream—ranchers and farmers alike increasingly turned to irrigation to grow forage for livestock and crops for humanity. Irrigation canals, diversion ditches, and small dams to collect water required huge capital outlays, organization of large numbers of laborers, and regional planning beyond the scope of single property owners.[11] These factors together—protection of stock, collective bargaining, and irrigation—encouraged the growth of a cooperative ethic within western ranching culture, reflected in the tightly organized National Live Stock Association.

In spite of both this spirit and government subsidies (the bounty), wolves on the Great Plains had been decimated almost entirely by individual action. Unfettered capitalism, shaped by the growth of immense cattle and railroad corporations, proved inimical to the natural systems that governed life. Once privatized, railroaded, fenced, and fully stocked, the plains offered little refuge from the ubiquitous rifle, strychnine bottle, and steel trap. The state-sponsored bounty only put extra pressure on a population of animals that might have eventually been eliminated, if for no other reason than because their pelts held commercial value.

Nonetheless, capitalism, ecologically devastating though it was, could not exterminate the West's wolves entirely. Rather, a species of socialism shaped by the stock association's organized and cooperative nature vanquished wolves from the mountains. This would take almost half a century to accomplish.

The National Live Stock Association's first plan in 1899 to organize the different states toward a uniform bounty sufficient for the entire West faltered in the face of more pressing concerns. For many western ranchers at the turn of the twentieth century, federal control of forests seemed more threatening than wolves.

It is ironic that the wolves in the mountains, whose forested habitat afforded them considerable natural protection, died in part in the cause of conserving trees. The U.S. Forest Service, a new agency charged with conserving the country's disappearing forests, initiated federal wolf extermination as a means to build political support for its conservation mission. And the stock association that would not devote sufficient organizational resources to enact a uniform West-wide bounty law attacked federal control of forests instead, thus inspiring another federal agency to kill wolves far more efficiently than any individual or even state could have done.

The Forest Service came into being as a result of two and a half decades of nationwide concern about the unchecked deforestation of the country. Colonial clearing of New England's forests had been only the first step. In Colorado, by the early 1870s entire mountainsides were being cleared to provide timber to brace mine shafts open[12] and to fuel smelters, and wilderness homesteaders and city dwellers alike were cutting trees for house construction and home heating. By the late 1880s giant lumber mills in Chicago had chewed up the majority of the white pine forests of northern Wisconsin and Michigan, leaving fire-scarred stump fields in their wake.[13]

The problem was twofold. First, federal frontier laws such as the Free Timber Act, passed in 1878, provided exactly what their names implied throughout the vast federal western domain. At first the Free Timber Act was restricted in its application, but when Colorado senator Henry Moore Teller became secretary of the interior in 1882, he loosened the regulations associated with the act to allow any settler or timber company to cut trees anywhere. Other laws were even looser, granting the title to any part of the public domain to virtually anybody who claimed it. Timber companies ended up with millions of acres of land.

Second, even administrations attempting to restrain deforestation of public lands were thwarted by a general western sense that laws enacted in distant Washington had no bearing on "rights" to use timber for any reason whatsoever. In 1887 one Colorado man was charged with cutting 39,000 cords of wood illegally. But overall, prosecutions were as rare as they were unsuccessful.

In 1904 Senator Thomas Patterson of Colorado estimated that in his state and in Wyoming, "eight acres of land out of ten to which title has been given in the last twenty years have been obtained fraudulently." Even when the executive branch attempted to enforce provisions limiting land giveaways to their intended purpose of promoting settlement, congressional westerners such as Teller (who had moved back to the Senate after his stint as interior secretary) continually subverted it.[14] His reasons seemed commonsensical to many westerners. "Why did the Almighty clothe the hills with timber if it was not that they might be made beneficial to mankind?" Teller asked. "Are not homes better than forests?" His answer was clear: "[T]he Almighty intended these forests to be used."[15]

Not deforestation alone but the general disappearance of wilderness, of wild animals for hunting, and even of wild Indians concerned the nation. In 1893 historian Frederick Jackson Turner posited that America's democratic character had been forged in frontier conditions, which according to the 1890 census no longer existed.[16] A handful of people advocated preserving forests for their sheer naturalness. Among the most prominent were Enos Mills and his paragon, Sierra Nevada naturalist and wilderness prophet John Muir, who founded the Sierra Club in 1892. These two men valued forests for the wildlife they sheltered (regardless of whether the animals could be hunted) and for the spiritual benefits nature provided to humanity.[17]

Although by the mid-1890s such preservationist sentiment enjoyed considerable popular support,[18] a far stronger political movement grew around conserving forests for purely utilitarian reasons, chiefly to prevent downstream flooding and siltation of reservoirs and irrigation canals. As early as 1876, a bill was introduced into Congress to preserve forests near the headwaters of rivers, but it went nowhere. The effort was catching on in Colorado, too. In 1884 civic-minded residents of Denver, Colorado Springs, and Pueblo formed a State Forestry Association to urge the passage of forest conservation laws, both to protect irrigators and to ensure that the state did not run out of the timber needed for development. The next year the American Forestry Congress called for keeping some timbered land in the public domain, and the following year the Colorado State Forest commissioner warned of "desolation" as a result of ongoing deforestation.[19]

With practical more than romantic thoughts foremost, in 1891 the American Forestry Association and President Benjamin Harrison's administration surreptitiously passed a law to grant the president power to set aside "forest reserves," areas exempted from privatization under the various land laws enacted to encourage western settlement. To bypass Teller and other anti-conservation western senators who dominated the public-land committees, conservationist congressmen slipped this sweeping provision into a land-use bill after it had already passed both the House of Representatives and the Senate and was being considered in a conference committee designed to iron out differences between the versions passed by the two bodies. Rushed to a vote in the closing days of the session, the leadership curtailed debate in the House, and the Senate voted for the bill before the new amendment was even printed. Thus the national forest system was inaugurated without the knowledge of almost every member of Congress who approved it and without the support of many westerners who wanted no restrictions on homesteading, timber cutting, or livestock grazing.[20]

Almost immediately, President Harrison started creating forest reserves, beginning with the Yellowstone Park Timberland Reserve (today the Bridger-Teton National Forest), comprising over 1.25 million acres that adjoined Yellowstone National Park in Wyoming.[21] The second withdrawal of land from public disposal, the White River Plateau Reserve, designated in October 1891, encompassed 1.2 million thickly forested acres surrounded by steep cliffs in northwestern Colorado. The following year the president announced the designation of more reserves throughout the West.

Although many western settlers and urban residents approved of the federal reserves, most ranchers strenuously opposed them, particularly after 1894. In that year, largely at the behest of western irrigators, the interior secretary banned livestock from all reserves to protect watersheds. The Interior Department, however, could not enforce its protective edicts, and the secretary of war refused a request to provide troops to evict ranching operations from the reserves. As a result, at no time were the federal forests actually free of cattle and sheep. Despite the lack of enforcement, ranchers, joined by miners and loggers, had the vociferous support of western congressmen—many of whom worked strenuously during the 1890s to undo designation of the reserves or to transfer them to state jurisdiction.[22]

Almost all political pressure in favor of the forest reserves was leveled by people who wanted to regulate use to avoid the adverse economic consequences of wasted timber (through human-ignited forest fires) and denuded watersheds. Gifford Pinchot, who promoted "scientific forestry" in America after returning in 1890 from a study of European methods of forest conservation, believed from the outset in what he called "wise use," not nature preservation. In practice, that entailed selective cutting of trees, replanting the ground afterward, and carefully regulating where and when to log. Pinchot, whose efforts in the field later propelled him to a position as the first chief of the Forest Service, was unequivocal in his goal: "Forestry is Tree Farming . . . handling trees so that one crop follows another. To grow trees as a crop is Forestry." The only thing as bad as unregulated logging, Pinchot held, was no logging at all.[23]

Despite this utilitarian tone within the early forest reserve movement, anti-conservationists routinely painted their opponents as eastern dilettantes and nature lovers who wanted to shut down all development, with no conception of the consequences on the pioneers' already arduous lives. In 1904, for instance, Colorado congressman Herschel Hogg referred to conservationists as "goggle-eyed, bandy-legged dudes from the East and sad-eyed, absent-minded professors and bugologists."[24]

In fact, had there been a strong movement for wilderness and wildlife preservation, the Interior Department and members of Congress might have felt the need to assuage it by pushing for national parks where hunting, logging, and grazing were proscribed. Congress had first designated such a park in the Yellowstone region of northwestern Wyoming, but not for wilderness or wildlife purposes. Rather, preservation of Yellowstone followed an 1871 government research expedition that confirmed earlier fabulous reports of geysers, canyons, and waterfalls. Railroad executives anticipated turning Yellowstone into a tourist draw for which their planned rail lines would serve as the only practical access. Congress was used to passing railroad-friendly legislation and the following year approved a law designating Yellowstone as the world's first national park, to preserve such "natural curiosities" for public enjoyment.[25]

Although not the original intent, the idea of parks as pristine wilderness gained popular appeal in the late nineteenth century, and other such parks were proposed around the West. The differing responses to such proposals, once railroads already provided widespread access, illustrate in part the influence of geography on demographic patterns and thus on the political climates of each state. The coastal, wet states, where ranching was outcompeted by myriad other less land-extensive but more remunerative activities (such as fruit growing and fishing), proved receptive to wilderness protection. In California, Yosemite and Sequoia national parks were designated in 1890, even though Yosemite had been utilized by sheep; ranchers, although locally powerful, were just one interest among many. In similarly situated Washington state, Mt. Rainier National Park was founded in 1899.

In Colorado, ranchers were amassing far more power. Aridity and the concomitant paucity of forage also forced them to utilize extensive tracts of land to raise enough cattle or sheep from which to make a living. From the outset they were disinclined to regard land set-asides with friendly eyes. National parks were proposed in 1877 in the San Juan Mountains near Pagosa Springs, in 1885 around Pikes Peak west of Colorado Springs, the following year at the Mesa Verde cliff dwellings in the Four Corners region, in 1889 in the Flat Tops area of northwestern Colorado, and in 1903 in the Uncompahgre region of the San Juans. Of these early proposals only Mesa Verde eventually became a park (in 1906),[26] reflecting eventual political backing for archaeological protection but less support for wildlife and wilderness, at least early on. Rocky Mountain National Park, whose designation did reflect the preservationist imperative, was not created until 1915.

With limited early backing for preservation in the arid West, the real controversy arose between proponents of utilitarian forestry such as Pinchot, who intended to sustain in perpetuity the extraction of wood from forests, and self-proclaimed anti-conservationists such as Teller, who responded largely to the sentiments of the livestock industry. "I do not believe there is either a moral or any other claim upon me," said the Colorado senator, "to postpone the use of what nature has given me, so that the next generation or generations yet un-born may have an opportunity to get what I myself ought to get."[27]

Under this type of attack, the Interior Department could not hold its ground. Although officials knew livestock damaged the forest,[28] they saw the main culprit of forest abuse as unregulated logging, not grazing. And according to Pinchot, ranchers, especially sheep ranchers, were "the best-organized inter-est in the West."[29] This reality reflected the longtime frontier ranching exigency to cooperate on building fences and irrigation works, exterminating predators, and pushing favorable legislation. "When the protection of the public timber-lands was a live political issue," Pinchot recounted in his memoirs, "we were faced with this simple choice: Shut out all grazing and lose the Forest Reserves, or let stock in under control and save the Reserves for the Nation."[30]

As a result of this choice, in 1897 the Interior Department, guided by a committee on which Pinchot served, once again authorized allowing cattle in the reserves.[31] This acquiescence had the intended result, and, after a hot de-bate, the delegates to the 1899 National Live Stock Association convention approved a resolution supporting the forest reserves and even the exclusion of sheep from them.[32] Three years later, however, the Interior Department bowed to sheep ranchers as well and permitted on the reserves the animals that Muir, a former sheepherder, called "wooly locusts."[33]

Even after the most serious political threats to the existence of the reserves had diminished, the question of their use remained in the first years of the twentieth century. When Vice President Theodore Roosevelt assumed the presi-dency in 1901, following the assassination of President William C. McKinley, he immediately ensconced Pinchot as his foremost adviser on conservation issues. Although Pinchot had acquiesced, with little reluctance, to grazing in the reserves, he felt it was imperative to regulate the livestock. Armed with new authority, he insisted on a system of permits, including a fee for grazing use. But he suspected the Department of Interior could not handle permitting with-out corruption. Much of its history consisted of illegal collusion between mon-eyed logging, grazing, and mining interests and venal officials appointed not on the basis of experience or character but as rewards for political favors. With that in mind, Pinchot and Roosevelt pushed to transfer the forest reserves to the Department of Agriculture, where the business of tree farming could re-ceive scientific and apolitical attention.[34]

By this time many ranchers had come to accept the reserves, but the idea of paying a "grazing tax" infuriated them, and the talk of transfer to a scientific-based administration in the Agriculture Department sounded like a round-about means to enact the earlier attempt to ban livestock.[35] But their fears were groundless. True, nature lovers such as Muir and Mills envisioned preserves for both wildlife and the elevation of the human spirit, and they recognized the incongruity of having livestock in such areas.[36] But their vision, although popu-lar nationwide, as yet lacked a strong organizational voice, especially in the West. Although Pinchot never considered preserving natural areas, to the extent that advocates of unrestrained use could portray such a threat they gained political clout. Colorado congressman John Bell, for instance, urged on by the National Livestock Association ("Live Stock" had been shortened to one word), "declared that the people of his state wanted no buffalo pastures and hunting preserves for rich Easterners."[37]

Shortly after Roosevelt won election to a full term in the fall of 1904, Congress approved the transfer of the forest reserves to the Department of Agriculture, and the president immediately named Pinchot to head the newly created Forest Service within that department. By the end of 1905, acting on guidance from Pinchot, Roosevelt designated new reserves throughout the West (including eleven in Colorado, totaling 8.8 million acres).[38] Pinchot, acting without explicit statutory authority (but not contrary to any law either), enacted a grazing fee.[39]

Ranchers immediately challenged the fee and, more broadly, the Forest Service's regulatory authority, as Pinchot had known they would. In the early 1870s, as seen, Congress had hesitated to pass a bill protecting bison because of the impracticality of enforcement. In many respects, more than three decades later the federal presence in the West was not much stronger; among many others, rancher Fred Light in Pitkin County, Colorado, aimed to keep it that way. In 1906 Light let his 500 cattle wander from his private land up a valley through several miles of unreserved public domain onto the Holy Cross Forest Reserve, as they were accustomed. He stated his intention not to apply for a permit and threatened to resist if anyone attempted to remove his stock. In April 1908 the Forest Service filed charges in the Federal Circuit Court of Colorado, which ruled against Light. But he continued to trespass in defiance of the court. The Colorado General Assembly appropriated funds to pursue his appeal to the U.S. Supreme Court, which heard the case in 1911.[40]

The Supreme Court upheld the Forest Service's authority to regulate grazing as it saw fit. "The United States can prohibit absolutely or fix the terms on which its property may be used," the Court ruled. The government's prior failure to object to the presence of Light's cattle "did not confer any vested right on the complainant, nor did it deprive the United States of the power of recalling any implied license under which the land had been used for private purposes."[41]

Even before this decisive ruling, Pinchot had secured many ranchers' acquiescence to his system of permitting that would ensure that no more than one person's cattle would be allowed on any given tract of land. Although Light's case would take five years to wend its way through the courts after the rancher's initial trespass, and although ranchers would persist over the next 100 years in attempting to reverse in Congress the Supreme Court's decision that graziers had no rights to the federal domain, Pinchot had secured a remarkable victory over the anti-conservationists. That victory was sustained at the outset, as well as decades later, largely because he had chosen to show livestock interests that federally controlled conservation would ultimately redound to their benefit.

But the grazing fee still rankled some. According to Stanley Young, the Forest Service faced a "mounting volume of complaints regarding wolf infestations on many of the newly established western national forests. The stock interests felt, and forcefully expressed that it was unfair to collect a grazing fee for the use of forage on a forest area heavily infested with wolves and other predators, unless some degree of protection from predation was simultaneously afforded."[42]

So in 1905, the first year of its existence, the fledgling Forest Service purchased leghold traps so its rangers could kill wolves on the reserves.[43] It also turned to an obscure federal scientific agency, the Bureau of Biological Survey, also in the Department of Agriculture, to help locate those wolves.

5

Bug Hunters and Gopher Detectives

The Bureau of Biological Survey's 1905 assignment to locate wolves for the Forest Service to kill seemed a natural one for an agency born to science but metamorphosing, by the early years of the twentieth century, into a national clearinghouse for information on wildlife. Formed in 1885 as a federal research arm called the "Office of Economic Ornithology and Mammalogy," the agency was at first literally just an office attached to the Department of Agriculture's Division of Entomology. That division, founded in the wake of the 1873 locust irruption on the Great Plains, researched insect biology and destruction and disseminated its findings to farmers.

Congress had long recognized that insectivorous birds might assist farmers, and in 1862 it had briefly funded the importation and freeing of foreign birds for that purpose.[1] The first appropriation over twenty years later, for $5,000 to create the Office of Economic Ornithology and Mammalogy, provided government backing to a project to track bird migrations run by the private American Ornithologists' Union. The appropriation, sponsored by Senator Warner Miller of New York, followed lobbying by an increasingly prominent member of the Ornithologists' Union, Miller's cousin C. Hart Merriam. Merriam, whose father was also a former congressman, soon became the first head of the new government agency.[2]

C. Hart Merriam had been a hunter and an amateur naturalist since his boyhood in New York state. To accommodate these interests, his father arranged for his early education in taxidermy and also introduced him to the head of the Smithsonian Institution, Spencer F. Baird, the most eminent American scientist of his day. With Hart's skills rapidly growing, in 1872 Baird arranged for the sixteen-year-old to become the official ornithologist for a government-sponsored research expedition to the West.[3] Hart had joined the fraternity of scientists.

That year the wide-eyed boy traveled to Utah, Idaho, Montana, and the Yellowstone region of northwestern Wyoming under the leadership of Ferdinand V. Hayden, whose Yellowstone trip the previous year had resulted in the designation of the world's first national park. Although the 1872 expedition reported on such "beautiful decorations" as hot springs, young Merriam concentrated on a different type of decoration. He brought back the remains of 313 birds, along with 67 nests complete with eggs.[4]

After returning from the expedition Merriam continued his formal education, acquiring a medical degree at age twenty-three. But his fascination with birds (as well as a growing interest in mammals) was stronger than the pull of medicine. In 1883, four years after becoming a physician, he helped found the American Ornithologists' Union, which in seeking to document bird distribution had first come up with the notion of a biological science branch of the government.[5]

Such a government function followed logically from the federal appropriations that had paid for the 1872 Hayden expedition on which Merriam had served. Throughout the 1860s and 1870s, Hayden had secured his funding through strong entreaties to friendly congressmen, and three other explorers received separate appropriations for their own research treks. In the tradition of Lewis and Clark's Corps of Discovery from the early nineteenth century, the government was sending out investigators with all-purpose goals of mapping new lands, identifying new life forms, and, in some cases, investigating the native tribes whose lands were being appropriated by settlers. Economic, imperial, and scientific interests melded almost seamlessly in these surveys, which together can be understood as the scientific arm of the nation's much broader westward impulse and which were impelled by the same giddiness over progress.

Each of the early scientific expeditions was initiated not by the government but by the man leading it, and those men's individual interests and resources dictated the surveys' destinations, personnel, and goals. In 1879, in the interest of efficiency and in the face of long-term rivalries among the principal explorers, Congress had created the U.S. Geological Survey, combining the functions of the three remaining active expeditions. In the same act, Congress also created the U.S. Bureau of Ethnology to record the customs and languages of the native societies that it was expected would soon disappear or be radically transformed.[6]

Six years later, in a similar vein, given the need to understand, utilize, and displace animals, Congress instituted the Office of Economic Ornithology and Mammalogy to assist the ornithological union in "the promotion of economic ornithology, or the study of the interrelation of birds and agriculture." The new office was also charged with investigating "the food, habits, and migration of birds in relation to both insects and plants, and publishing reports thereon."[7]

In retrospect, the newborn agency seems to have been seeded from that point onward with the central controversy of its existence—the tension between pure science and economic interests. And the germ of that conflict was a comma. In 1929 the agency's semi-official historian, working for a nongovernmental think tank later called the Brookings Institution, wrote that the enabling legislation had included a typo: no comma, he claimed, should have separated "food" and "habits."[8] If he was right, the agency would have had no mandate to investigate any bird habits aside from their feeding and travel—both exquisitely practical things to know and, arguably, the only economically pertinent aspects of avian behavior.

But no one at the time paid attention to the comma, least of all legislators. Whether the comma was intended or accidental, Merriam had sold Congress on the idea that the Office of Economic Ornithology and Mammalogy would provide information beneficial to agriculture.[9] His own inclinations, however, tended toward scientific advancement for its own sake, and often he skipped the word *Economic* in the agency's new (1886) name, the Division of Economic Ornithology and Mammalogy. In 1889, in response, Congress obligingly dropped "Economic" from the title.[10]

Not surprisingly, the Division of Ornithology and Mammalogy followed in the footsteps of the Hayden expedition in which Merriam had gotten his start. Federal scientists wandered the country with gun in hand, taking careful measurements of everything they killed and classifying and naming species and subspecies based on their observations. Back in Washington the division forged close ties with museums and universities, accumulating tens of thousands of animal specimens and energetically publishing bulletins of new species identified and new locales for old species. Its investigations, or "biological surveys," covered such far-flung locales as the Hudson Bay region of Canada, California's Mount Shasta, and Texas.[11]

Merriam and the other scientists he hired were naturalists rather than specialists—men as comfortable identifying plants as animals and intuitively grasping to understand the connections between creatures and their habitats.[12] His first two assistants became division stalwarts, but they each also played a key role in turning the agency away from its naturalist roots.

The first was an old friend, Albert K. Fisher, who came on in 1885 shortly after the Office of Economic Ornithology and Mammalogy's inception. Fisher, who shared Merriam's passion for ornithology, had attended medical school and roomed with Merriam when they were in their early twenties. After graduation, broke and unable to pass his exams for certification as an army physician, Fisher was no doubt grateful to Merriam for an appointment that became his career. The two roomed together in the nation's capitol as they started their venture in government science.[13]

Merriam's second assistant, Vernon Bailey, also shared strong personal and professional ties with the founder and also made the newfound government post his life-long work. But Bailey had not grown up in the genteel environment that produced Merriam and Fisher. In fact, he was so rustic he didn't even know what year he had been born (federal administrators finally used an old family Bible to pin down the date: June 21, 1864).[14] Bailey was the product of a Minnesota farm, which consumed so much of his energies that he never finished high school. But his enterprise and curiosity were prodigious. One of his farm chores was to eradicate gophers, and to accomplish this Vernon constructed live-capture traps—thus sparking an early interest in wildlife.

At age eight he had acquired a shotgun and soon was mounting the birds and mammals he killed, but he had few books or other resouces to aid identification. "My father and older brother, like most of the pioneers of that borderland, were hunters and trappers as well as farmers, and knew in a general way much about the game and fur-bearing mammals, the birds, fishes and trees," Bailey recalled in 1935 after he retired. "[B]ut I was ambitious to know them all, even the small birds and tiniest shrews." He first contacted Merriam at age nineteen, two years before the founding of the Office of Economic Ornithology and Mammalogy. "I wrote and offered to send him specimens, if he could tell me the names of them." By 1886, the year the name was changed to Division of Economic Ornithology and Mammalogy, the twenty-two-year-old farmer was already an expert, collecting mammals found around his farm to Merriam's specifications and selling them to the government science branch Merriam headed. That year he earned $268.55 for 495 skins, 575 skulls, and 10 alcohol-preserved carcasses.[15]

But Bailey's real compensation was instruction by Merriam in taxonomy and in collecting and preserving techniques. In May 1887 Bailey was put on the division's payroll as a field agent (when additional field agents were hired, he was upgraded to "chief field naturalist") at a salary of $1,800 per annum, charged (in his own words nine years later) with "collecting and studying the birds and mammals of the U.S." An 1896 memo by Merriam, in which he recommends a raise for Bailey, describes his working conditions: "Mr. Bailey's duties are such that he is obliged to furnish, at his own expense, a wagon and pack outfit with horses or mules or both, and to hire a man as teamster and cook." Merriam added a significant tribute: "Mr. Bailey has filled the position he now holds for a number of years and is universally recognized as the most competent man in America for the place."[16]

Three and a half years later, in December 1899, Bailey married Merriam's younger sister, Florence, an early campaigner for saving imperiled birds and against using their feathers in women's hats. The couple spent most of their time traveling the western United States, and Florence, who specialized in ornithology, eventually joined her husband in the top tier of the nation's naturalists.

When obliged to apply its ornithology and mammalogy to economic problems, the generalist mind-set of the division made it prone to a proto-ecological view. For one of the division's first investigations, Fisher analyzed the stomach contents of over a thousand hawks and owls killed in Pennsylvania and turned in for bounties, and in 1887 he issued a report. Fisher found that without even taking into account the $90,000 the state paid in bounties over a one-and-a-half-year period, each hawk and owl—by eating mice and insects that would have caused $30 in agricultural damage over the same time period—more than covered the 25¢ chickens it killed. He concluded that the $1,875 worth of chickens saved by killing these predators came at the cost of $3,857,130 in rodent and insect damage.[17]

In one respect—the appreciation for predators' role in controlling farm pests—the report represents a brief, ecologically informed period in a long-lasting agency's system of values, almost a window into a primordial innocence. In another respect—its urging that Pennsylvania's bounty on owls, hawks, minks, and weasels should be abolished—the report seems to foreshadow the agency's almost obsessive and even instinctual later hostility to bounties, even as the ostensible reason for that stance changed.

The same year his division urged tolerance of raptors, Merriam called for extermination of the English sparrow, the now-ubiquitous urban bird that at the time was solidifying its tenure in North America. Citing the sparrow's displacement of native birds and the damage it did to agriculture, Merriam called the small brown and gray bird "a curse of such virulence that it ought to be systematically attacked and destroyed."[18] Again, the analysis was largely ecological, but the proposed solution, like the criticism of bounties, would also characterize the Division of Economic Ornithology and Mammalogy throughout its history, even as the agency's name changed repeatedly and its focus turned sharply away from ecology.

As the division juggled pure biological research with studies of the economic impacts of wildlife, its image varied wildly. In 1896 a fawning Oregon newspaper praised Merriam and his assistants' "picturesque, rough-and-ready, frontier appearance" and called the agency's identifications of new wildlife species "results of mammoth significance."[19] Others, however, saw the division as uninterested in the lot of those tilling the soil, and they never compared its scientists to heroic breakers of the frontier. That same year the Department of Agriculture lobbied Congress to appropriate $6,000 to hire a director to coordinate all its scientific branches, including the Division of Biological Survey (as Merriam's agency began to be called that year). In a response reminiscent of the language often applied to the forest conservation movement during the same period, one newspaper called the funding request "absurd, useless, a sham, and a derision" and described the department as composed of "bug hunters and gopher detectives" doing "as much good to agriculture as a frost in June." The paper concluded, "Abolish it [the department] now!"[20]

Four years later, with the Department of Agriculture and its Division of Biological Survey still extant, Congress passed the nation's first comprehensive wildlife law, the Lacey Act, named for its champion, Iowa congressman

John F. Lacey—long a fighter for forest conservation and wildlife preservation (and destined to make his most enduring mark in sponsoring the Antiquities Protection Act under which millions of acres have been designated as national monuments). The Lacey Act put federal teeth into violations of state wildlife statutes by making it a crime to transport across state lines animals killed out of season. The Biological Survey, specializing in the taxonomy of birds and mammals, was the obvious agency choice to determine whether the maker of a woman's fancy hat was using feathers from a grebe or a grouse and from where that bird originated.[21] Thus in 1900, for the first time, the Biological Survey gained a specific mission; before that it could almost have been viewed as a permanent base camp for scientists just returned from a field trip, just about to head out on such a trip, or typing up their field notes with bird in hand to measure wing tips and bill length.

To enforce a law like the Lacey Act, the Biological Survey had to do more than simply identify wildlife. It had to find the people who were illegally killing and transporting animals. To this end, the agency built upon its tradition of relying on local informants and an academic network in locating wildlife and began to work with state wildlife officials, private wildlife protection groups, and furriers and milliners who might use pelts or feathers obtained illegally.[22]

Although Lacey Act enforcement was the survey's most direct congressional mandate, Merriam had little interest in this new responsibility. The clearest way to manage multiple tasks was to assign them to underlings. Among other effects, enforcing the Lacey Act accelerated the bureaucratization of the Biological Survey—literally. In 1905 (the same year the Forest Service was born and began trapping wolves), Congress turned the Division of Biological Survey into the Bureau of Biological Survey, an evolution toward permanence on the political landscape.[23]

Commensurate with its status as a bureau, the following year the Biological Survey's projects were divided into divisions. Lacey Act enforcement and management of game preserves were given to Merriam's third assistant, Theodore S. Palmer, who had joined the survey a year after graduating from the University of California in 1888 (and who had earned a medical degree in 1895).[24] Fisher, with his early focus on stomach contents, led the Division of Economic Investigations. Bailey, who more than anything loved to roam the wilderness and who rivaled Merriam as the nation's foremost expert on mammal taxonomy, was assigned the Division of Geographic Distribution, in charge of conducting a continent-wide survey of plants and animals that Merriam had long regarded as "the fundamental object" of his agency.[25]

Merriam, who headed the entire agency, paid his two primary assistants equally and promoted them together over the next five years of his tenure[26] while he dealt with the daily headaches of meetings, editing reports, and, above all, answering correspondence. He fretted at administrative responsibilities that left so little time for his research, which he considered his real work.

The bureaucracy also represented the maturing of the Department of Agriculture into an agency with real consequences for people's lives and with concomitant political importance. The mood in the legislative branch had changed considerably from the 1880s and early 1890s, when Congress had been happy to allow the survey to elucidate the complexities of the zones of ecological life to Merriam's heart's content.

Starting in 1902, Merriam repeatedly clashed with the chair of the survey's funding committee in the House of Representatives, Representative James Wolcott Wadsworth, who failed to appreciate the value of science for its own sake. Merriam—blunt, humorless, and only slightly more inclined toward politics than his mounted specimens—made few conciliatory gestures to address Wadsworth's concerns. In 1906 Wadsworth expressed dissatisfaction at the disproportionate allocation of work to projects on the Pacific Coast, where the agency was conducting extensive biological investigations, but that work continued in spite of his concerns.

In January 1907 another powerful congressman greeted Merriam's request for funding with sharp questions regarding the usefulness to agriculture of the survey's research on the distribution of species of skunks throughout the country. Wadsworth promptly eliminated the survey's entire annual budget—in effect terminating the bureau. Finally realizing the consequences of bucking those who held his agency's purse strings, Merriam conferred with his old friend President Theodore Roosevelt, an accomplished naturalist, who helped persuade key senators and representatives to restore the survey's funding.[27]

A few years later Congress passed a law "providing for the public printing and binding and the distribution of public documents," requiring the Department of Agriculture to print 500,000 copies of a section of its annual report "specially suited to interest and instruct the farmers of the country." Four hundred and seventy thousand of these copies, according to the law, were to be given to Congress, whose members, presumably, would distribute them to farmers. The department itself was allowed to keep the remaining 30,000 copies to distribute on its own.[28]

These requirements point to the importance legislators attached to the Department of Agriculture's political potential. Not only was the survey to focus on economic issues, but its publications were to be given to those whose household economies were at stake. And who could possibly prove a better messenger for the federal government's helpful missives than local members of congress or the state's U.S. senators?

In March 1906 Vernon Bailey was briefly transferred from the Bureau of Biological Survey to the Forest Service to, in the words of forester Gifford Pinchot, "undertake a study to determine methods for the extermination of wild animals which prey upon live stock in the forest reserves."[29] This assignment resulted in the January 1907 publication of a booklet authored by Bailey illustrating the practical benefits of the survey's biological investigations. *Wolves in Relation to Stock, Game, and the National Forest Reserves*, published by the Forest

Service, was mainly intended "to put in the hands of every hunter, trapper, forest ranger, and ranchman directions for trapping, poisoning, and hunting wolves and finding the dens of young."[30]

Beyond that, however, the thirty-one-page booklet served political aims for both agencies responsible for its creation. First, it intended to address anti-conservationist ranchers who might harbor continuing doubts about the Forest Service. (Annual reports of the Department of Agriculture during this period indicate that many ranchers followed Fred Light's lead by trespassing their stock on the forests without permits, and the agency was cracking down.) To that end, an opening subsection entitled "Wolves Not a Product of Forest Reserves" displayed a map of northwestern Wyoming delineating the boundaries of the Yellowstone Forest Reserve and the locations of litters of wolf pups that had been dug out of their dens. Conveniently for the Forest Service, the map showed almost all the wolves denning at elevations below reserve boundaries. The text, however, admitted such was not the case in New Mexico and Arizona, where the reserves encompassed lower ground. The bottom line, according to the publication, was that "their distribution depends largely on food supply" and that wolves' presence at any given elevation depends on the seasonal availability of prey there, certainly not on any respite provided by the Forest Service.

Wolves in Relation to Stock, Game, and the National Forest Reserves also provided a rationale for the Biological Survey's detailed scientific queries. Notwithstanding that the survey's ongoing inventory of the West's flora and fauna rested on the highest scientific standards of the day, Bailey's treatise on wolves reflected the congressional imperative to find practical—that is, economic—applications for the survey's biological investigations. So additional chapters of the wolf booklet addressed "The Destruction of Stock by Wolves" and "The Destruction of Game by Wolves."

Reflecting the survey's rapid rebound from the political abyss of life zones and skunk research, the text stressed that the animals did indeed affect agriculture. In fact, the survey's technique seemed to count only wolves that preyed on livestock,which were easy to notice. "Over the Central Plains region of the United States wolves in great numbers originally preyed on the buffalo herds," the report intoned. "But the buffalo wolf has now become preeminently the cattle wolf."[31] Wolves in Colorado received a paragraph in the booklet, and those in New Mexico were given a full page—reflecting the collapse of both states' deer, elk, and bison populations and their replacement with cattle and sheep. But in Idaho, where wild ungulates were still abundant, wolves might as well have been extinct for all the attention given them. The Biological Survey was learning quickly that Congress might only fund surveys of animals that affected its constituents' pocketbooks.

Lest anyone doubt the economic toll wolves levied, *Wolves in Relation to Stock, Game, and the National Forest Reserves* gave full voice to ranchers throughout the West who claimed the predators killed up to 20 percent of their cattle.

The wolves of the period, if as potent as credited, could hardly kill less: "The ranchmen in the wolf country maintain that a 'critter' even slightly bitten by a wolf will die of blood poisoning, and many detailed instances seem fully to substantiate this," Bailey reported. "More cattle are therefore killed than are eaten."[32] (Wolves today are not known to poison the blood of the animals they bite.)

Although wolves were seemingly busy killing cattle, Bailey reported that "herded sheep are rarely troubled by wolves, which are kept at a distance by the presence of herders and dogs."[33] Similarly, he could find little evidence that wolves decimated wild ungulates: "Wolves kill far less game in the western United States than either coyotes or mountain lions," he wrote. The animals they did manage to kill, he found, were seldom in their prime: "While wolves are usually found around antelope herds, they are probably able to kill only the sick, crippled, and young."[34] But that was hardly to their credit: "Wherever wolves inhabit timbered country they are destructive to game in proportion to their abundance, to the abundance of game," he concluded, "and to the scarcity of domestic cattle."[35]

There could be only one denouement to a publication describing an animal of such baneful proportions, and the second-to-last chapter did not neglect the most practical and seemingly most economic-related aspect of wolf biology. Succinctly titled "Destruction of Wolves," its subsections addressed "Hunting," "Capture of Wolf Pups," "Poisoning," "Trapping," and "Preservation of Wolf Skins."

Beyond providing technical information to help people kill wolves, the pamphlet criticized the efficacy of the bounty system. "Bounties, even when excessively high, have proved ineffective in keeping down the wolves, and the more intelligent ranchmen are questioning whether the bounty system pays," wrote Bailey, adding:

> In the past ten years Wyoming has paid out in State bounties over $65,000 on wolves alone, and $160,156 on wolves, coyotes, and mountain lions together, and to this must be added still larger sums in local and county bounties on the same animals.
>
> In many cases three bounties are paid on each wolf. In the upper Green River Valley the local stockmen's association pays a bounty of $10 on each wolf pup, $20 on each grown dog wolf, and $40 on each bitch with pup. Fremont County adds $3 to each of these, and the State of Wyoming $3 more. Many of the large ranchers pay a private bounty of $10 to $20 in addition to the county and State bounty. . . .
>
> A floating class of hunters and trappers receive most of the bounty money and drift to the sections where the bounty is highest. If extermination is left to these men it will be a long process. Even some of the small ranch owners support themselves in part from the wolf harvest, and it is not uncommon to hear men boast that they know the location of dens, but are leaving the young to grow up for higher bounty.[36]

The production of *Wolves in Relation to Stock, Game, and the National Forest Reserves* also carried another important political lesson for anyone within the survey who was attentive (although the lesson's enormous potential was likely not imagined then): when trying to juggle expenses in the face of a tight budget, another agency might be induced to pay for a survey employee and share the credit for his work. A decade later the survey instituted a system whose scale and purpose would dwarf its early prototype in Bailey's assignment to the Forest Service.

Bailey followed up *Wolves in Relation to Stock, Game, and the National Forest Reserves* the following year with a briefer circular entitled *Destruction of Wolves and Coyotes: Results Obtained During 1907,* this time published by the survey. In this publication, for the first time, the killing of wolves (which received far more attention than coyotes) was inventoried on a national basis. It was no surprise that Bailey, who had spent considerable time traveling from state to state and talking with forest rangers and many others, found that his previous year's instructions had paid off. In spring 1906 he had shown ranchers in Wyoming's upper Green River valley how to locate and dig out wolf dens. "Much interest in locating the dens was aroused among the ranchmen in the valley, first by personal intercourse and later by the distribution of publications," he explained.

In 1907 the Forest Service had expanded its direct killing of wolves, begun in 1905, by moving from merely purchasing leghold traps for its regular rangers to hiring "a number of expert hunters and trappers . . . in the worst infested regions." That same year Bailey revisited the Green River valley and found his eager students had dug up forty-seven pups from six dens, beating his record in the same area from 1906 and sparing the special Forest Service hunters the work when they arrived a few weeks later: "Although excellent hunters, the rangers could find no more dens."[37]

But Bailey knew it would take a lot of persevering people with that level of enthusiasm to make a difference. "The areas thus protected are but widely separated spots in a vast extent of wolf country," he wrote, "and unless ranchmen and settlers are stimulated to similar efforts permanent results are not to be expected."[38]

The Agriculture Department, overseeing both the Biological Survey and the Forest Service, concluded that the fledgling interagency public and private cooperative program had been a tremendous success in 1907:

Following the adoption of the methods recommended, especially that of destroying the pups in the breeding dens, so many wolves have been killed that the saving of stock this year amounts to at least a million dollars, and it is believed that persistent efforts will result in a permanent reduction of the numbers of these destructive animals, if not their practical extermination in the cattle country. Their absolute and final extermination will probably not be practicable so long as extensive tracts of wild land remain to afford them harborage.[39]

Wolves Killed in Colorado by the U.S. Forest Service, 1907–1914

Fiscal Year	Adults	Pups	Total
1907	58	7	65
1908	?	?	?
1909	1	0	1
1910	6	11	17
1911	31	25	56
1912	4	0	4
1913	1	8	9
1914	0	24	24
TOTAL	101	75	176

Sources: Vernon Bailey, *Destruction of Wolves and Coyotes: Results Obtained During 1907*, U.S. Department of Agriculture Bureau of Biological Survey Circular 63, April 29, 1908; Ora B. Peake, *The Colorado Range Cattle Industry* (Glendale, CA: Arthur H. Clark, 1937), 94.

The Agriculture Department's claim to savings of $1 million reflected an estimate (made by ranchers and parroted by the Biological Survey without any attempts at verification) that each wolf consumed more than $1,000 worth of livestock each year.[40] But these financial savings must be viewed from a political and a bureaucratic perspective. The Forest Service needed to develop a constituency in the West if it were to retain jurisdiction over its recently acquired lands, and the livestock industry, as Pinchot had noted, was strong and getting stronger. The Biological Survey, in turn, needed a clear pragmatic justification for its existence, something more compelling than enforcement of the Lacey Act.[41] "Devising methods to abate the evil" of wolves, as the Agriculture Department phrased it,[42] would at once endear the Forest Service to ranchers and explain to key members of Congress the practical value of an agency largely known for its dedication to pure biological research.

In the same politically pragmatic vein, in 1909 Bailey authored yet another informative publication, *Key to the Animals on Which Wolf and Coyote Bounties Are Paid*.[43] This booklet enabled the Biological Survey to help states, counties, and private livestock associations detect bounty fraud in the form of dogs' and other animals' remains passed off as those of wolves or coyotes. But in so doing, the publication also highlighted the haphazardness of the bounty system and its inherent weakness in exterminating wolves. The new pamphlet implicitly argued that perhaps a more centralized system should replace the state-by-state incentives.

But in the meantime, cooperation between the Forest Service and the Bureau of Biological Survey continued to prove fruitful. And wolves weren't the only victims of this partnership. In 1909 Congress appropriated the survey $25,000 for "experiments and demonstrations in destroying noxious animals."[44] The agency devoted that money to developing poison formulas and baits for killing rodents, which competed with livestock for forage and also damaged crops and tree roots. Saturating grains with strychnine seemed the most promising broad-scale eradication technique.

The appropriations, and the agency's growing interest in the subject, continued year by year. In its annual report for fiscal year 1908, the agency extolled "the usefulness of such servants of man as bats, skunks, weasels, badgers, foxes and moles" to ensure "that their lives may be spared and they be allowed to continue their good work."[45] But in the fiscal year 1911 report the survey reported that, contrary to its assessment just three years before, one of the smallest genera of mammals—moles—were harmful animals, their propensity to eat insects outweighed by their proclivities toward crops. The agency pledged to issue a bulletin defining the mole's economic status and "explaining methods of destroying it when necessary by traps and poisons."[46]

Survey officials were possibly learning more about the federal appropriations process than they were about the culinary habits of moles. In 1910 Merriam retired from the agency he had founded, tired of the losing fight to keep science paramount within the Biological Survey and needing more money than the pittance allocated him by a parsimonious Congress.[47] In 1911 the survey worked with large ranch owners and the Forest Service in several states to find the most efficient means of poisoning ground squirrels and prairie dogs, and officials were casting their eyes about for other animals that needed to be killed. In 1912 Congress directed $3,000 toward combating ground squirrels in California national forests as part of the bureau's larger allocation for such experiments and demonstrations. The next year Congress again targeted ground squirrels in national forests but lifted the restriction limiting such work to California.[48]

These new responsibilities fit within Albert Fisher's bailiwick as head of the Division of Economic Investigations, and Fisher was up for the task. Since the early days of constant field trips, Fisher had increasingly yearned to return to Washington. His instincts and talents tended toward management: he was upbeat and well-organized but willing to cut corners where needed.[49]

In the meantime, Bailey increasingly chafed at being held to Washington supervising the Division of Biological Investigations (the new name, since 1910, for the Division of Geographic Distribution). In 1913 he requested and received a demotion back to chief field naturalist, retaining the same salary of $3,000 per year.[50]

The early years of the agency forged strong bonds among its principals, particularly through their backcountry collecting expeditions. At first glance the federal biologists did not stand out from those around them. In the lightly settled West their accoutrements of firearms and their acquisitive hunger were familiar features. But theirs was an avarice for scientific advancement rather than for personal wealth, and that made them an oddity. When Bailey rode into the southeastern California mining town of Darwin on December 31, 1890, a crowd of twelve to fifteen men asked him if he knew a man on a yellow horse who had ridden in earlier. The man was his colleague, Edward W. Nelson, who was later appointed chief of the survey and who, with Bailey, was part of an expedition cataloging the life of the Death Valley region. Bailey replied that he did know him, and the men asked what was the matter with him. "He is going about poking under sage brush and acting as if he was crazy," Bailey was told, learning also that the men were considering "going out and getting him." He disabused the crowd of that idea by explaining Nelson's and his business.[51]

Division of Ornithology and Mammalogy staff Vernon Bailey, C. Hart Merriam, T. S. Palmer, and Albert K. Fisher (with rifle). Comic pose or serious, Fisher commands the moment for the unfathomable future that his efforts at extermination will dominate. (Biological Survey Unit, USGS, Patuxent Wildlife Research Center, National Museum of Natural History, Washington, D.C.)

The esprit de corps developed amid such social isolation became part of the soul of the agency as it grew into a powerful federal bureau. That camaraderie united the bureau despite the different and potentially conflicting missions of each of its divisions. Decades later, as will be seen, Bailey developed grave doubts about the direction he had helped lead the agency in promoting the killing of wolves. But he kept those doubts to himself.

Almost half a year after Nelson aroused suspicions with his unorthodox activities, in the nearby Owens Valley the Division of Ornithology and Mammalogy's Death Valley expedition posed for a picture. The photographer may have been Nelson, for he is not shown. The picture offers a preview of the agency's future direction and priorities.

In 1891, taking a picture (although less slow and cumbersome than it had been two decades before) was a deliberate act freighted with the gravity of preparing to cheat the passage of time by preserving this very moment. Four men stand in a field: Vernon Bailey, whose scientific reputation would soon rival Merriam's; C. Hart Merriam, accomplished, always energetic, and a driver of his men; Theodore S. Palmer, later head of the survey division that enforced the Lacey Act and protected wildlife in bird and game refuges; and Albert K. Fisher, destined to transform his Division of Economic Investigations into an instrument of extermination and, in so doing, make it the survey's dominant branch.

It is June 13, but all the men are wearing hats, long sleeves, and pants. Bailey on the left, hands in his pockets, insouciant, perhaps reserved, gazes into the camera or over it and beyond. Merriam, next to him and in front, is giving Fisher an almost quizzical sideways look. Palmer is looking at Fisher with a straightforward, friendly benevolence. But Fisher does not return their gaze.

Infamous among the close-knit group for his practical jokes but deadly earnest and efficient when he needed to be, Fisher wears striped pants, brandishes a rifle, and stares intently at the camera. Comic pose or serious, we cannot discern. He peers into the black lens, commanding the moment for the unfathomable future.[52]

One Big Joke With Him

espite its initial successes, the federal government's proficiency in killing wolves was dwarfed by the body count accruing as a result of bounties, inefficient though they were. In addition to the Colorado state bounty, which was up to $2 per wolf and $1 per coyote (and down to $3 per mountain lion), many livestock associations and counties still offered far more generous rewards for killing wolves. In 1907, for example, the $10 wolf bounty offered by the Bent County Stock Growers Association (which had pioneered private wolf bounties in Colorado and throughout the West in the 1870s) was collected on 14 pups in two litters, likely excavated from their dens on the state's southeastern plains.[1]

In 1912 and 1913 William H. Caywood killed 140 wolves, for which he was paid $50 apiece by the Wolf Bounty Association of Rio Blanco County (the group formed to corral reluctant ranchers into paying their bounty dues). During the same period the Forest Service's salaried hunters were only able to bring in 5 adult and 8 juvenile wolves throughout Colorado. Federal hunters (as well as private individuals) throughout northern Colorado and southern Wyoming likely brought their catches to northwestern Colorado and chose to report the wolves as killed there rather than record the wolves' real provenances in the forests to which the hunters were assigned.

It is easy to understand why, from the perspective of enterprising early-twentieth-century ranchers, high bounty payments might appear prudent investments. Joseph N. Neal of the Wolf Bounty Association, a rancher who became a livestock and real estate banker in the Rio Blanco County town of Meeker, recounted that for four or five years, wolf depredations on cattle prevented any increase in his herds: "It was at times the difference between success or failure in the stock business."[2]

Looking back three decades later, Neal estimated that at their heyday wolves killed or injured at least a quarter of all cattle in the region. The injured were often "bobtailed," their tails bitten off by wolves—an offshoot, he explained, of a female wolf's means of teaching her young how to knock down prey. The wolf would grab and pull on the tail of a fleeing cow and then quickly release it, whereupon the cow would lose her balance and fall forward. The mother wolf would then allow her offspring to finish off the downed animal. Many bobtailed cattle not finished off by wolves subsequently died of infection. Wary wolves seldom returned to scavenge strychnine-impregnated carcasses.[3]

The emotional shock of discovering bobtailed and otherwise injured and dying cattle could only exacerbate the sense of frustration at lost economic opportunities. "We noticed it so much in our rides—the cows had calves which had been killed," said Neal. "Cows with distended bags caused by loss [of] the calf."[4]

Even those not engaged in ranching may have sympathized with ranchers' travails. The period from the turn of the twentieth century to U.S. entry into World War I continued the nineteenth century's heady enthusiasm for societal advancement. Yet in 1900, even in the cities, technology could not insulate the average American from the life-and-death world of nature. With only 8,000 automobiles registered in the nation, transportation still overwhelmingly depended on either railroad or horse and buggy. Less than 2 percent of the population owned telephones. Sixteen percent of American babies died before their first birthday, and childbirth was the thirteenth-leading cause of death, just after appendicitis.[5] To urban residents aware of the advantages of having nearby neighbors, doctors, and other trappings of sodality, the western ranching industry seemed the vanguard of civilization's inevitable conquest of wilderness. It deserved all the support society could muster. State-sponsored bounties reflected that support.

Ranchers' positive public image may have stemmed in part from their implicit contrast with the grimy miners emerging from poisonous caverns and industrial furnaces to strike, bomb, and even murder their bosses—as occasionally happened during the first fifteen years of the century. (The mine owners, who included tycoons from Standard Oil Company and the Guggenheim fortune, were backed up by an equally truculent national guard.) By the early 1900s, with memories dimming of the open-range disputes between cattle and sheep owners, ranching seemed a sea of peace. Urban people were easily smitten with men who embodied America's highest virtues—"ranchers with the bluest eyes, like sailors' eyes, used to looking at great distances . . . Uncle Sam as Uncle Sam ought to look without the goatee," in the words of famous New

York actress Ethel Barrymore in 1906. She was describing an Idaho jury in the murder trial of Western Federation of Miners' leader and anarchist William Haywood of Colorado, and the contrast could not have been clearer. The *Denver Post,* reporting on the same twelve men, was similarly struck: "They are frontiersmen, hard-bitten in the life of the frontier . . . men of their hands, sun-baked, hard-gripped, deep-bitten men, small ranch owners mostly, who thought for themselves and believe above everything in the individual freedom of individual Americans."[6] In short, the archetypal rancher (often confused with his employee, the cowboy) was well on his way to becoming America's foremost hero.

Many more people were employed in mining than in ranching, but the miners' political clout did not equal that of the ranchers. Cattle ranchers, despite their subservient position to such dominant institutions as railroads, typically owned a few dozen to a few thousand acres of land on which they lived and grazed stock, in addition to the government land they used. Frontier challenges had ensured that they worked together, and they were becoming used to political organizing within their communities as well. Most miners, in contrast, did not own their mines, and although they lived in company towns, many were itinerants tethered to one place only by the next week's wages.

Whereas ranchers united to fight giant out-of-state railroad companies over shipping rates and reimbursement for cattle killed by trains,[7] miners united to fight giant out-of-state mine companies over working conditions and wages. Both achieved some success, but the ranchers also had political capital and support to garner state funds for bounties. The far more numerous miners had no political capital to spare.

In the heat of the mining fracases in 1902, Coloradans overwhelmingly elected banker James Peabody as governor. As expected, he immediately threw the state's constabulary apparatus squarely behind the mine owners and against the strikers. That same election a ballot issue for an eight-hour work-day in the mines—one of the union's demands—also passed by a landslide. Peabody's triumph represented more anxiety over the anarchistic and social-ist tendencies of the unionized miners than principled opposition to social or economic reform.[8] Coloradans wanted law and order, as did many other Americans faced with anarchistic violence throughout the country (including the assassination of President McKinley the previous year).[9] Opening their newspapers on June 5, 1902, those establishmentarians would have been stirred by sympathy for ranchers and their stock. A Denver policeman visiting the desert grasslands of northwestern Colorado witnessed "a tragedy on the plains" that he could not prevent: "Two gray wolves, gaunt and desperate from hunger, attacked a cow and her calf."[10] Reading about a representative of the law being helpless to avert such a tragedy must have impressed upon urban residents the degree of security they enjoyed next to that of their rural neighbors.

The problem was all around them. That same year wolf depredations were reported on cattle, sheep, and even dogs east and north of Denver.[11] Throughout the West, in spite of the bounties and poisoning, wolf populations seemed cyclical. President Theodore Roosevelt, recalling his own experiences as a cattle rancher in the Dakotas, reported that wolf numbers had risen in the late 1880s and early 1890s. More recently, he wrote in a 1905 article for *Scribner's Magazine* titled "A Wolf Hunt in Oklahoma," citing accounts by frontier friends with whom he maintained contact and newer hunting companions, the numbers were declining again. But this was little consolation to those who regarded the animals as a pestilence. "If any individuals survive at all," he wrote, generalizing from wolves to all wild animals, "the succeeding generations are far more difficult to exterminate than were their ancestors and they cling much more tenaciously to their old homes."[12]

It seemed to many ranchers that while the rest of society moved forward, they were mired in an unacceptable stand-off with an implacable force from the past: wolves. Take the case of Thomas John Payne, who in 1883 had left a teaching career in his native England to begin a new life in the American West. Unlike many other would-be ranchers at the time, Payne had no personal fortune to invest in his new vocation. In early May 1884 he arrived in North Park, Colorado, with 18 cows, grazing them on the open range as the snow slowly melted off the steep sides of the surrounding mountains and gathered in ox-bowed streams on the valley floor. The next year his sweetheart from "the old country" joined him, discovering a land where dinner depended merely on stepping out the front door with a rifle to choose from among the abundant deer, elk, and pronghorn antelope within sight.

Twenty-five years later, North Park was no longer a frontier. The great herds of elk and antelope had been killed, railroad access just across the state line in Wyoming had shrunk the distance for cattle drives (and within a year would service the town of Walden in North Park), and Payne had managed to build his holdings to more than 800 cattle. The hefty, thickly bearded immigrant was a pillar of the community and served as secretary of the North Park Stockgrowers Association.[13]

Payne had struggled against cattle diseases, harsh weather, and rustlers, but he had seldom been troubled by predators, only occasionally losing a colt to mountain lions. But in late December 1909 a pack of wolves began killing the cattle that belonged to Payne and his neighbors while also feeding on a few horses and the area's surviving deer. Payne lost nine cattle to the pack. "They seem to try to isolate an animal from the bunch and then attack it in the hind parts generally above the hocks and they tear the flesh away before the animal is dead," he explained to Colorado naturalist and writer Enos Mills, who had asked Payne about his experiences with wolves. And just as Joseph Neal learned around the same period, Payne's cattle that survived the initial attack subsequently succumbed to infection. "Not all animals are killed, but nearly all die in a very short time no matter how slightly they are wounded," Payne reported, repeating a common myth: "It seems as though the bite of the wolf is poisonous."[14]

The stockgrowers' association hurriedly met and approved a $75 per wolf bounty, but local trappers and hunters failed to capture any. The association sent for the best wolfer in the Colorado-Wyoming region, S. A. McIntyre, better known as "Rattlesnake Jack." The nickname stemmed from an 1891 incident in a Gillette, Wyoming, saloon.[15] Two cowpunchers were making the patrons dance to the accompaniment of six-shooters. McIntyre entered the establishment and was ordered to start dancing. "All right boys," he said, "and we will have a little music," pulling out from under his shirt his two pet rattlers and thus abruptly ending the cowboys' festivities.

Rattlesnake Jack had learned to consort with snakes through his previous career as a snake charmer traveling with a circus. He boasted that only he had worked with fully envenomed snakes. "All other rattlesnake charmers pull their fangs fore they touch 'em," he told Payne's twenty-one-year-old son, Stephen.[16] In the 1880s he quit the circus and took up bounty trapping in Wyoming and Colorado. There he developed a reputation as the best trapper around, but he was not the kind of person always welcome in civilized quarters.

The first sign of Rattlesnake Jack's arrival in January 1910 was his smell. Stephen Payne was returning to the ranch house after hauling hay on a sleigh behind his horse team when, he later recalled, "I knew some stranger was there. Any normal human could smell Rattlesnake Jack a full quarter mile away."[17] This was partly a result of his diet of wild caught meat, including skunk, muskrat, and his namesake serpent. His trademark wolf lure left its pungent aroma on him as well. Between 1894 and 1905 the trapper and his son, "Little Rattle," had tested wolf olfactory lures on six captive wolves. They devised "a scent that the tame wolves went wild over" but that "a tenderfoot when he gets a good smell of it says goodby dinner," according to the younger wolfer.[18] But Rattlesnake Jack's rank effluvium was also attributable to his disdain for soap, which he feared might alert coyotes and wolves to his presence. "Them fools as use soap 'll never catch nothin'," he explained brusquely to Stephen (whose father, contrary to the code of frontier etiquette, could not bring himself to invite the trapper in for dinner when he and Little Rattle arrived).[19]

"He was a heavyset man past middle age with a meaty face and strange, bloodshot, wild-animal eyes, always affected by the dope he could not live without," described the younger Payne. "He used fifty cents worth of morphine each day, which our doctor P. W. Fisher at Walden let him have or the man would have gone nuts. He had sort of scattered whiskers of a nondescript color, neither gray nor brown nor white." His plethoric complexion was rendered more ghoulish by "layers of dirt caked on his skin."[20] Winter or summer, he wore a fur hat festooned with feathers.

Before long, Rattlesnake Jack and his son had trapped five or six wolves—one of which was stolen from their trap and the bounty claimed by the thieves. They managed to shoot two more wolves. Then, in April 1910 their three trained dogs ferreted out a wolf den, and the trappers dug up four pups; the parents escaped, but the depredations ceased.[21]

Less than a year later, on a cold Saturday night in February 1911, Rattlesnake Jack turned his gun on himself, putting a final end to his bibulous meandering from saloons to trails and from enrapturing snakes to killing wolves.[22] Little Rattle, or Albert, who had accompanied him on the trap lines since age six, was twenty-five years old. No records remain of Albert's mother.

The still fresh century promised a dazzling world of electric streetlights in the cities, horseless carriages, and a nation grown smaller by the untiring speed of locomotives. Albert was young enough to make a new start in any booming western town and was even capable of a rudimentary level of reading and writing his father had taught him.

But he chose fealty to his father's métier of killing wolves. Immensely proud of that frontier cachet, he formalized his nickname to "Rattlesnake Jack Junior." He took a job with the Forest Service as a seasonal trapper for $75 a month, and he supplemented that income by selling pelts and collecting bounties from stock associations.

Bounty hunting was not an easy business. A wolf in North Park whose escape from a leghold trap had left him with only three toes on one paw, hence the name Three Toes, seemed to tease the hunters seeking to collect the almost $150 bounty placed on his head. In the winter of 1912–1913, according to Rattlesnake Jack Junior,

> three men the crack shots of Jackson County they would start at daybreak trail him all day at night he would take thery trail back to the ranchs pick up the crombs whear they eat dinner his joke was climb all high peaks and seemed to be one big joke with him yet he was not scared because they was lots of powder burnt at him.[23]

Yet some of that powder might have left a fatal mark, as Three Toes was not seen again after the spring of 1914, perhaps dead from old age or perhaps—as the young bounty hunter conjectured—"someone took a long shot and got [gut] shot him thought they hade missed."[24]

A Good Wolf

$\mathbf{W}$ hether Three Toes escaped the bounty hunters or not, many people thought the bounty system as a whole was missing the mark in exterminating wolves and other predators. In 1909 A. R. Harding, the publisher of the magazine *Hunter Trapper Trader,* echoed the Biological Survey's criticism of bounties. "For many years the state governments of the wolf infested country have been paying bounties on wolves and coyotes," Harding wrote in a how-to book entitled *Wolf and Coyote Trapping,* based largely on information provided in the survey's publications. Harding continued: "It is doubtful, however, whether the bounties offered are sufficient to encourage any, other than the regular trappers, to hunt wolves, and if they are, it [the bounty system] has certainly had no definite results."[1]

That sentiment was becoming ever more common. As Stanley P. Young, a tireless opponent of the bounty system, later explained, "[S]trong sentiment continued to develop to the effect that the National Government should take more of an active part in wolf control because of the vast acreages of wolf-infested national forest and the federal public domian [*sic*]."[2]

As seen, ranchers at the turn of the twentieth century could only envision a predator extermination policy modeled after the state-by-state bounty system, never conceiving of the greater efficiency of a federal agency with interstate authority to exterminate wolves. In the same fashion, the Lacey Act of 1900 largely strengthened existing state wildlife protection laws without outlining any significant new federal policy. The Lacey Act and the earlier suggestion of a West-wide bounty constituted transitional measures between sole state authority and an active federal role in wildlife policy. The hiring of trappers by the Forest Service in 1907 represented another step toward a federal wildlife policy. The idea of interstate wolf extermination was merging gradually with the idea of a federal agency enforcing state policy objectives. But the Forest Service, whose main focus was forestry, was not the most efficient federal entity to handle the killing of wolves. The Biological Survey—smaller, obscure, and politically fragile—was destined to metamorphose into the invincible child of the union of these two policy impulses. That change would ultimately secure the agency's future.

The survey was building a solid reputation among agriculturalists for its demonstrations on how to destroy ground squirrels, prairie dogs, and other rodents. But many ranchers viewed wolves as a greater threat than rodents. The Forest Service was already using the survey's science-based guidance in locating and killing them, and the survey had been experimenting to determine the right amount of strychnine needed to kill wolves— by poisoning different-sized dogs with carefully measured levels of food in their stomachs. These experiments were conducted under the direction of Albert K. Fisher, who in 1906, a year after the Division of Biological Survey became the Bureau of Biological Survey, had taken over the newly created Division of Economic Investigations created within the bureau.[3]

When C. Hart Merriam retired in 1910, Fisher had vied to follow him as chief of the survey. Despite his regular contretemps with members of Congress, Merriam still retained enough clout to be able, in effect, to anoint his own successor. Selecting Fisher might have seemed a slap at Division of Biological Investigations head Vernon Bailey, the other obvious choice. Merriam instead turned to a third old friend and ornithologist, Henry W. Henshaw, who had worked briefly for the agency before moving to Hawaii for ten years. In 1905 Merriam had recruited Henshaw back to the survey and installed him as his number-two man. Five years later, upon Merriam's departure, Henshaw assumed the chieftainship.[4] Fisher, Bailey, and Theodore S. Palmer, who led the Division of Game and Bird Conservation, retained jurisdiction over their respective divisions. Henshaw's ascent represented a transition from an agency dominated by its founder's energy and vision to a more stable institution whose programs and personnel evolved in relative independence of their leadership.

With ever increasing congressional appropriations for his Division of Economic Investigations, Fisher's responsibilities were growing. Henshaw, unlike Merriam, would not let a dream of scientific advancement for its own sake stand in the way of that growth. In 1908, as assistant chief, he had published an article about the survey in *National Geographic Magazine,* conceding that "[t]he pursuit of science solely for its own sake, however commendable it may be, is not the spirit that animates our government in its support of scientific research." He added the obvious: "In its aims and ambitions this is a practical age."[5]

Congress, in its annual Agriculture Department spending bill for fiscal year 1915 (July 1, 1914, through June 30, 1915), for the first time added wolves to the target list for the survey's aid programs. That year $115,000 was approved for "experiments and demonstrations in destroying wolves, prairie dogs, and other animals injurious to agriculture and animal husbandry."[6]

In early 1915 the survey requested $110,000 for the next fiscal year's experiments and demonstrations in animal killing, a $5,000 decrease from the previous year and an indication that it was operating at maximum capacity for the job at hand. But western ranchers had come to understand the federal government's capacity to aid their endeavors beyond merely showing them how to kill animals. A November 1914 article entitled "The Wolf at the Stockman's Door—Sheep and Cattle Killers Breed in the National Reserves," printed in *The Country Gentleman* magazine, asked, "[w]hy have these animals not been eradicated?" The article's author, S. W. McClure, answered his own question: "Simply because the Federal Government has withdrawn from settlement or development millions of acres of land on which carnivorous wild animals breed." He suggested as remedy a direct government appropriation of $100,000 to the Forest Service to kill the animals in the forests and $250,000 to kill them elsewhere. (He did not specify which agency should get the latter sum.)[7]

Two months later the Oregon State Legislature took the same stance, passing a resolution "petitioning the United States government to appropriate $300,000 for suppressing carnivorous wild animals destructive to live stock in the public-land States of the West." Legislators pointed to the money already expended by state, county, and stockmen's bounties and the role of forests and other federally reserved lands, "now withdrawn from settlement in some form or other," as "the principal breeding ground and refuge of these carnivorous wild animals." The Arizona State Legislature followed with a similar resolution.[8]

Western senators serving on the Agriculture Department's funding committee took up the cause in a debate on February 15, 1915. Senators from Wyoming, Montana, North Dakota, New Mexico, and Arizona sought to increase the survey's appropriation for killing animals, emphasizing the federal government's responsibility for the destructive beasts residing and breeding in the national forests—and even suggesting that the forests served as inviolate sanctuaries where hunting of predators was forbidden.[9]

Two other western senators, from Colorado and Kansas, were leery of such an increase and skeptical of the survey's role. If the Forest Service impinged on state prerogatives, Colorado's Charles S. Thomas seemed to feel, then the survey might end up just as bad. "We have just appropriated, or will appropriate in this bill, over five and a half million dollars for the care of our forest reserves," he argued. Thomas continued:

> If it is true, as here asserted, that they have become safety places for the predatory animals of the region, which can not be attacked or extermi-

nated by the State authorities, it is very easy to provide in the bill that the forest rangers and the inspectors and supervisors and assistant supervisors and deputy assistant supervisors and deputy inspectors and the other members and attachés of that army of employees who bask in the sunshine of the civil service be required to devote a part of their valuable time in exterminating these animals.

Thomas worried about "additional agents and representatives of the Government," adding, "[i]f this bill passes, we will have a superintendent of coyote destruction and a supervisor of prairie dogs and a bureau of investigation on fur-bearing animals, together with assistants, deputy assistants, and stenographers."[10]

Clearly, a decade after the establishment of the Forest Service, sensitivities over the withdrawn federal lands and increased federal presence remained acute among western politicians—both those supporting and those opposing the survey's appropriation increase. (In fact, the old resentment toward the withdrawals can be loosely measured by several senators' use of the pre-1905 term—forest reserves—over their official name as national forests; neither the new name nor a new appreciation had rooted in their consciousnesses.)

The debate about excess administrative costs, and the suspiciously abstract sound of the standard funding formulation for "experiments and demonstrations," forced advocates of the increase to articulate how it would solve the problem at hand. Senator Francis E. Warren from Wyoming called the phrase a "technicality" that really referred to "the establishment of a system . . . for destroying the wild animals."[11] Senator Wesley L. Jones from Washington state, sympathetic to that intent but also wary of the growth of a bureaucracy, suggested specifying that point in the legislation. "I am in favor of appropriating money for the destruction of these animals, but I am not in favor of increasing this appropriation by a large sum of money and leaving it to the discretion of these officials to be used under the general terms of this clause," he said. Jones continued: "Those who want predatory animals destroyed ought to provide for their destruction, and we ought to so frame the law that the money will be used for that very purpose."[12]

The committee adopted this idea over the continued objections of Senator Thomas and his colleague from Kansas, Senator William H. Thompson. The bill specified that "not less than $125,000 shall be used on the National forests and the public domain in destroying wolves, coyotes, and other animals injurious to agriculture and animal husbandry." It passed the Senate by a vote of forty-three to fifteen.[13]

Thomas's and Thompson's fiscal and administrative conservatism was not uncommon, but before long western members of Congress rarely applied similar standards to survey funding requests.

Fisher, an efficient administrator, understood that close supervision of hunters could not take place from Washington, D.C. In the fall of 1915, as fiscal year 1916 began, he created nine districts, each supervised by a predatory animal inspector.[14] Fisher selected Logan B. Crawford to supervise the Colorado district.

Crawford had been born in Missouri in 1869, but at age four he moved with his parents to the northwestern Colorado wilderness, where the family established a ranch. Logan spent his childhood hunting mountain lions, bears, and other animals and became sufficiently proficient as a woodsman to begin guiding other hunters when he was still a boy. A six-year stint as manager of Colorado's fish hatchery prepared him for public administration.[15]

For those in Crawford's position, establishing an effective predator killing service entailed hiring people capable of killing the animals. During that fall (1915) the survey hired 300 hunters throughout the West, many of them recommended by the Forest Service. But not all of those who wanted the federal jobs were qualified. One applicant, responding to a question as to how he would clear a region of wolves and coyotes, proposed constructing a ten-foot-long log cabin to secure wolves, accessible only through a tunnel-like trench secured with a one-way trap door. To entice the animals in, he would leave a mile-long trail of blood terminating in "a piece of fresh bloody Meat" placed inside. As a denouement to this comically impractical scheme, the applicant explained that the first wolves captured would be devoured by their packmates.[16] (Simpler versions of such a cabin trap were occasionally used to capture grizzly bears. But even if wolves capable of avoiding all but the most carefully concealed leghold traps would have entered such an elaborate contraption, the labor involved in constructing it compared to the other methods used consigned the idea to the realm of absurdity.)

Those who made the cut as qualified hunters were not always up to the other standards Fisher imposed. One of Crawford's new recruits in Colorado was the orphaned, itinerant, and mephitic Rattlesnake Jack Junior, formally known as Albert McIntyre, based in Jelm, Wyoming, near the Colorado border. McIntyre's most recent stint with the Forest Service had ended in April 1914, when he joined four others seeking to collect an especially high bounty posted for a notorious wolf known as Two Toes. As McIntyre wrote in response to a detailed questionnaire sent by Enos Mills, the wolf was "puting the fear of the saints in Laramie river ranchers hearts."[17]

Two Toes had originally frequented North Park but had moved east and now traversed the forty-odd miles between the Laramie River valley and the rolling, open foothills farther east where the plains meet the mountains near the Wyoming border. The Laramie River is an alder-clogged freshet issuing northward from headwaters in Colorado into Wyoming's high plains. Between its headwaters and the eastern plains lies the 11,000-foot Laramie range, dotted with small lakes amid bluish-green forests of spruce and fir and hillsides of aspen that in winter appeared ghostly alabaster, like careless swipes of a white brush.

An estimated ten years old and a connoisseur of cattle from both sides of the Laramie range, Two Toes was accustomed to human threats, having learned caution the hard way. He had once stepped into a trap and had freed himself by either tearing or biting off the two center toes on his right front foot—thus gaining his moniker. Perhaps from that encounter with steel, he also had a broken upper left canine tooth—a handicap that along with his maimed foot would have made it hard to kill wild prey.

Even had his difficulties not encouraged Two Toes to feed on slow-moving and dim-witted cattle, neither deer nor elk had recovered from past hunting sufficiently to serve as a reliable prey source in the region. Only about 15,000 mule deer lived in Colorado,[18] a good start to recovery from the species' nadir a few years before but still thinly scattered and a minuscule number compared to the state's potential. In any event, Two Toes had killed an estimated 70 cattle in the past two years; with his characteristic track inviting personal enmity from the owners of those stock and a price of $175 on his head, he had not reached the venerable age of ten through carelessness.

McIntyre's prospects, had he followed his competitors' regimen of tracking the animal to get a good shot, were not good: "[O]ne hunter hear swears his legs is 3 inchs shorter than when he started after two toes," McIntyre reported to Mills. "I am no sucker," he added, "traps for me." And he did know trapping: "[F]ather or me never could tell no man how our sets it always seemed a Natural instinkt with us to set a trap for a coyote or wolf ever scracth seems it meant something."[19]

In June 1915, having failed to land Two Toes and laboring at a ranch for $40 a month plus board, McIntyre received a telegram from Washington, D.C., asking him to work as a predatory animal hunter for the Biological Survey. The Biological Survey had gotten his name from the Forest Service, and in the first weeks of the new fiscal year the survey was using Forest Service rangers to supervise the trappers it was hurriedly hiring. Ordered, as he put it in a letter to Mills, to "take my outfit June the 24 and do my level best to get two toes," within days McIntyre had established a camp and had local ranchers show him a recently killed steer and fresh wolf tracks. He quickly renewed his efforts in the Laramie range: "kept his [Two Toes's] main runs full of traps and tryed ever set I could think of."[20]

While riding up the forest paths, trap-and-gear-laden horse behind him, carefully studying each wolf print and meticulously building each trap set, Rattlesnake Jack Junior may have believed he was following in his father's footsteps. But the Biological Survey, in seeking to eliminate wolves, had helped eliminate the frontier universe of the original Rattlesnake Jack. The son soon bumped up against the changing times.

The Forest Service, focused on efficient timber production and on implementing its permit system for range allocation, had paid little attention to supervising its salaried wolf hunters. As long as wolves were being killed, the program's primary purpose of gaining ranchers' support for federal management was met. During McIntyre's term as a Forest Service employee, he sold his pelts and collected bounties where he could. But the Biological Survey had determined that bounties were inefficient for eliminating wolves. Local bounties encouraged localized attempts to kill wolves while ignoring their presence elsewhere—a type of squeeze-the-balloon governance that failed to address the problem systematically. Moreover, the parochial and entrepreneurial nature of the bounty system represented an ideological challenge to the notion of increasing efficiency through professional and centralized government. From the start, survey employees were forbidden to accept bounties and were required to turn in all pelts to the government.

Within the first three months of his tenure with the survey, McIntyre killed two wolves and received $50 for each from the Upper Laramie River Stockmen's Association. Whether he knew the survey forbade this practice for its employees is unclear, but he was accustomed to the prerogative and was unprepared to give it up.

Riding in from the trap line on September 23, 1915, McIntyre ran into his newly hired supervisor, Logan B. Crawford. Crawford, driving from his home in Steamboat Springs to his new base in Denver, was taking advantage of the journey to meet trappers already hired by the survey and to scout potential new recruits.

Crawford had spent two days trying to track the trapper down because McIntyre had established three separate camps to support his far-flung network of trap lines and was spending most of his time away from the camps and in the field. In the course of asking local ranchers whether they knew McIntyre's whereabouts, Crawford was informed about the recent bounty payments. After finding the right camp and waiting four hours for the trapper's return, Crawford was just driving off when the trapper rode up.

The automobile represented a power of mobility, a wealth and sophistication foreign to Rattlesnake Jack Junior; it represented, in short, a class difference. McIntyre, who by his own account had left his camp at three that morning, took offense at what he perceived as his new supervisor's supercilious reprimand for collecting bounties. "[I]f mr mr Logan B Crawford just keeps the gait he started hear he will be the most hated man in Colorado," he gushed by way of an opening to an eight-page protest letter to survey officials in Washington, D.C. "[I]n the 4 hours he was in this county he stirred up more trouble than can be straitend out in a month." To strengthen his case, the trapper methodically listed the expenses he had incurred in building up his professional capacity:

> the last 3 months it hase cost me $40 per month for grain and grub . . .
> have one team worth two hundred dollars in the field Wagon Harness
> saddle pack saddle another Hundred my traps the way they are chained
> stands me colse to three hundred dollars bedding camp outfit tools stands
> me colse to Two Hundred dollars . . . besides this have 23 year experince
> on the trap line nothing but wolves and coyotes know thary habits from a
> to z.[21]

McIntyre's bottom line was that "to do good work cleaning this cournty of predatory animals will have to have the Bounty and Fur overwise I will gladly resign if the man over me is going to keep me in hot water."[22]

The Survey was adamant. Fisher wrote to Crawford:

> We cannot permit one of our men to receive bounties and prevent the others from doing so. Mr. McIntyre should refund the money to the association. If you can furnish me with the name of the live stock association that paid the bounty, a letter will be prepared for the signature of the Secretary [of Agriculture] or the Chief of the Bureau, requesting that in the future not to pay any bounties to our hunters. The sooner we get away from the bounty system and build up an effective corps of hunters, the sooner will stockmen look to us for relief against the damages committed by predacious animals. I believe that McIntyre is a very good trapper and a useful man, and I would hate to lose him, but he must follow our regulations.
>
> At the present state of the fur market he would be very foolish to leave us to do trapping. Even prime furs sell at a ridiculously low price, and do not command more than a third of the amount they did two years ago. Deal with McIntyre gently but firmly and try to make him see the error of his ways. Report the result of your conference.[23]

The survey did arrange to pay $30 a month for expenses connected with the use of McIntyre's two horses plus $10 for his other equipment, thus effectively raising his pay from $75 to $115 a month. In correspondence back and forth between his remote Colorado camps and the nation's capital, McIntyre insisted on a minimum of $125 per month plus a guarantee of steady employment all year (including the unremunerative summer months, when wolves and coyotes lose their thick, lustrous coats), if he were to give up bounty payments and the sale of furs. But by the end of October, having no doubt reached the same conclusion on the state of the fur market as Fisher had, he finally accepted the $115 a month. Fisher, in turn, quietly dropped the demand that McIntyre refund the $100 he had received from the Upper Laramie River Stockmen's Association.[24]

Beyond the monetary issues at stake, Rattlesnake Jack Junior saw the world through the eyes of a scammer. His correspondence is rife with accusations that the survey or Crawford was playing a "game" with him or running a "racket" in which he was the intended dupe. He used the same terms to refer to wolf behavior in seeking to evade his traps. His letters make clear that despite others' wiles, he would not be exploited. He must have thought that his stratagems to maximize the benefits of federal employment were either a legitimate defense against unscrupulous machinations or an admirable racket of his own, or both.

In mid-October 1915, while still negotiating his salary, McIntyre purchased seven old horses to slay and butcher for wolf baits. But a storm blew in, leaving a layer of wet snow that rendered setting traps futile. At the end of the month, the weather having cleared and eight coyotes and two bobcats having stumbled into his traps, he had developed another beef with Crawford. This time his complaint was over the survey's requirement that its trappers clean, retain, and turn in the skulls of their victims—which were needed to study subspeciation and to display for public approbation. "Now I am no hog as it is enoughft to ride all day then have to flesh the hides take care of them without any skull game," McIntyre complained to Fisher. "I thought it was bad enought to have to give up all fur and except no bountys but this skull game is to [sic] much."[25]

Five days later, on November 4, McIntyre quit federal service—retroactively as of November 1. His timing, just as the coats on all mammals in the region were reaching their full winter thickness, also took into account the five coyotes and two badgers he had caught since the beginning of the month. Aside from the growing number of conflicts with Crawford, his departure was probably planned well in advance; indeed, a Forest Service official familiar with McIntyre had predicted to Crawford that the trapper would quit federal service as soon as the furs became prime. In any event, his stint of federal employment had conveniently enabled him to establish and winterize three camps and to scout out wolf signs for his three trap lines—thus drawing a salary for conducting the preparatory work to bringing in furs. (Just two weeks after McIntyre resigned he sent Fisher a respectful and almost penitent letter expressing interest in rejoining the Biological Survey the following March— shortly before furs would again become unmarketable and after he would have wiped out most of the region's marketable mammals. The survey rehired McIntyre late the following spring.)

Meanwhile, as the weather finally began to clear at the end of October, Two Toes turned east to the plains for sustenance, with two of his pups killing a couple of cows. McIntyre had identified Two Toes's standard route over the Laramie range, one that bypassed the steepest and highest mountains and instead skirted north at the juncture of the Colorado National Forest (now the Arapaho-Roosevelt National Forest) and unclaimed public domain (today Bureau of Land Management land). Particularly because of its low elevation and consequent lesser snow accumulation, Two Toes was most likely to travel this way if he returned west during the winter.

The wolf runway followed a six-mile wagon road over the quarter-mile-wide Horse Ranch Pass, set between two low hills just south of the Wyoming border. Two Toes could occasionally take advantage of the road's packed snow from previous travelers to ease his own trek. Along this road McIntyre set 33 of his 212 traps.

But Two Toes avoided all the traps. McIntyre's correspondence, which provides the bulk of what we know of Two Toes's fate, is tantalizingly incomplete. A letter from McIntyre to Mills suggests that Toe Toes stayed east of the Laramie range for months. Other McIntyre letters mention extremely harsh blizzards month after month, which made trapping impossible until mid-

February: "Have done all my own work and been alone all the way through. October and February only caught 4 coyotes," he later wrote the Forest Service and the survey.[26] His eccentric punctuation could mean either that the poor catch occurred in each of those two months or that it occurred through that five month period—thus indicating unpropitious weather conditions.

In mid-February 1916 McIntyre returned to Horse Ranch Pass, checking, re-bedding, and re-scenting the trap line. This time, apparently, he eschewed meat baits and simply applied a dab of his father's custom-concocted wolf lure. On March 2, 3, or 4, Two Toes followed the road westward and caught whiff of the enticing odor. He padded off the road and sunk two toes of his left paw—the remaining good one—into a trap set just short of the olfactory enticement.

Two Toes had been in this predicament before, however, and he knew what to do. After two fruitless days of pulling and yanking and biting at the trap and chain, he started chewing off his toes. With one toe chewed off and working on the next one, Two Toes faced McIntyre riding over a rise. McIntyre got off his horse, tethered it, and took his club to kill Two Toes with blows to the head—a means of avoiding a bullet hole in the hide. But at the first blow the wolf, who McIntyre noted had a more massive than average head and neck, barked sharply and lunged at his attacker. McIntyre, apprehending that only one toe kept the wolf in the trap, returned to his horse, grabbed his thirty-thirty Winchester rifle—which he called "Old Meat in the Pot"—and fatally shot Two Toes. Adapting an old Indian-killers' phrase, McIntyre concluded that now "two toes was a good wolf."[27]

Two Toes left a pregnant mate. It is impossible to be sure when they met. A month later McIntyre thought he glimpsed two separate litters of pups with her, but without their bodies he could not be sure. Perhaps she had borne Two Toes's progeny the previous spring, in 1915. Or a prior mate could have sired pups before succumbing to poison or traps, prompting her hegira and Two Toes's avuncular support for the clan. In undisturbed wolf packs, typically only one pair mates while the other animals help secure food for and "baby-sit" the pups. (Although there is no direct evidence that this female was Two Toes's mate, the geography argues strongly that this was the case. Wolves' rigid territoriality usually keeps family groups separated by many miles. The fact that the den was in the center of Two Toes's range and likely within a mile of where he was killed makes it almost inconceivable that they were not paired.)

At Two Toes's death she was close to giving birth, having dug a den just south of Horse Ranch Pass where Two Toes died. She now had to feed herself and her pups alone.

There is much we cannot know. For two months after Two Toes's demise, the female wolf survived and fed her nursing pups without killing a single known cow or sheep or colt. To McIntyre, the lifelong wolf hunter, this was something new. Did she understand the peril in culling domestic stock? However cognizant she was of human danger, her den site on Bull Mountain at the edge of the high country was ideally suited to whatever deer or elk survived in the region. Those ungulates used the high country for summer cover and the lowlands for winter forage.

On May 1 John Hohnholz, a rancher who had frequently lost cattle to Two Toes, stumbled on the den and dug out four pups, which he killed and skinned. The mother and two other pups escaped. Hohnholz immediately sent word to McIntyre, who arrived at his ranch late the next day as a fresh snow started to fall. The next morning, May 3, the rancher led McIntyre back to Bull Mountain, where they picked up the female wolf's tracks going both directions, carrying something bloody. When they followed the trail back to the den, they found she had been traveling to and fro, ferrying the four fur-less carcasses in her mouth to her remaining pups, secreted elsewhere for safety. McIntyre conjectured she was feeding the hungry survivors their siblings.

The two men followed the plain tracks in the snow. Around noon they jumped the female and eight or twelve pups, who ran into nearby pines. But there they stood, confused, until Hohnholz shot one pup, evidently from the same litter as his previous victims. The rest disappeared.[28] To the rancher's patent dismay, it was evident the Laramie range still harbored wolves. But Rattlesnake Jack Junior, having just collected a bounty that totaled $175 for Two Toes, may have felt optimistic about the continuance of the notorious wolf's mate and progeny in the region.

Manly Sport With the Rifle

When he left federal employment in November 1915, Albert McIntyre, also known as Rattlesnake Jack Junior, may have thought he was up against a capricious supervisor, Logan B. Crawford. But in fact he was battling the Progressive-era legacy of a very different western pioneer, former president Theodore Roosevelt, who had retired from politics at the end of his second term in 1909 and failed in 1912 to win back the presidency from his one-time protégé, William Howard Taft. (Both Roosevelt and Taft lost to Democrat Woodrow Wilson.) More than anyone, it was Roosevelt, a man whose personal instincts were forged in the world of Rattlesnake Jack Senior, who destroyed the possibilities of that world for Rattlesnake Jack Junior.

The nineteenth-century reservoir of wilderness had allowed such societal riffraff as the original Rattlesnake Jack to thrive, whether in the frontier circus entertainment industry, in lawless western saloons, or in the wilderness itself. That atmosphere in the early 1880s in the Badlands of Dakota Territory had allowed the young Roosevelt to flourish as well.

Roosevelt had gone into ranching in the Badlands as a consequence of a September 1883 bison-hunting expedition there. The exhilarating freedom of the hunt likely reinforced his lifelong exaltation of frontier values. Although the great herds in the region had been gunned down only six months previously, a handful of bison—exceedingly wary—still wandered the abrupt and broken plains. The twenty-four-year-old Roosevelt stepped off the train into the collection of shacks that constituted the village of Medora (in the future North Dakota) and started looking for a hunting guide to help him bag a buffalo—wild and dangerous game for a restless New York state assembly-man hungry for physical challenge.

His experiences on the prairie over the next few weeks (which included having his horses frightened off by a prowling wolf) convinced him that virtue flourished in the bracing atmosphere of man against the wild. The future president so strongly trusted his instincts to discriminate between the obvious desperadoes at the edge of civilization and his fellow upstanding frontiersmen that just three weeks after he arrived at the frontier he wrote a $14,000 check to two men he had met just hours before as a down payment on a ranch.

In turning down the offer of a receipt from the men, who had agreed to purchase cattle for him and serve as his ranch managers (the land was owned by an absentee railroad company and the absentee federal government, so no land was bought), Roosevelt declared, "If I didn't trust you men, I wouldn't go into business with you." The young rancher-politician's confidence in his own judgment was likely strengthened two days later when, after three weeks of strenuous but futile effort, he finally killed his bison. As Roosevelt danced a victory jig around the slain bull buffalo, could he have helped but believe, at least for a moment, that his brashness in business and his dogged perseverance in the hunt were but two sides of the same charmed coin?[1]

But although Roosevelt believed in the virtue of individuals and in his own good judgment in distinguishing good men from bad, he did not believe subjective judgment should govern people's rise to positions of governmental authority. His own rise to power was occasioned by campaigns to standardize government conduct and make it accountable to more than a select few powerful individuals—as in his late 1890s battle against New York City's ubiquitous police corruption while serving as president of the city's board of police commissioners. Thus Roosevelt developed a counterweight to his impetuous frontier romanticism: an equally powerful policy idealism. "There is every reason why," the president had proclaimed in 1905, "our executive governmental machinery should be at least as well planned, economical, and efficient as the best machinery of the great business organizations."[2]

By modeling government on the efficiency of a machine, Roosevelt sought to emulate the recent successes of American industries, which had ballooned in size and power through mass automation. Adopting the central motif of the industrial assembly line—the uniformity of raw materials, production methods, and final product—proved similarly effective in expanding government. Roosevelt's method of choice, and his most enduring pre-presidential political reform when he served as civil service commissioner, was beginning to enforce, in 1889, a merit system as standardized as any assembly line: the federal civil service system.[3] Agencies within the Agriculture Department, such as the Biological Survey and the Forest Service, proved particularly adept at building organizational cultures around proper procedures and rigid rules—precisely the type of environment that so irked the son of Rattlesnake Jack. (Although salaried hunters such as Albert McIntyre were not covered by the civil service, predatory animal inspectors like Logan B. Crawford took the exam, as did his boss in Washington, Albert K. Fisher.)

If the culture of government had been changing before and changed even more rapidly during Roosevelt's administration and in the Taft and Wilson administrations to follow, so did everything else. Wilderness was disappearing as fast as a south-facing snow bank on a sunny April afternoon, in the words of Robert Marshall.[4] Wildlife was vanishing just as quickly. People's normal modes of interacting with each other, and many of their assumptions about their own society, were changing too. All of these factors drew unprecedented attention and support to conservationists in the West and throughout the United States. But for various reasons no one opposed the Biological Survey's extermination campaign.

The women's reform movement provided the strongest impetus for conservation, and it was premised largely on repudiating the values of men such as McIntyre. Thus the reformers found themselves in implicit sympathy with the professional agency that supplanted him.

McIntyre's wolf-trapping career reflected his identification with his two-fisted, herpetologically armed, perpetually stoned frontier-era father. Apposing the McIntyres of the West were middle- and upper-class women newly ascendant in a surprisingly vigorous crusade to reform America's spirit.

The urbanization and mechanization of the country had exacerbated the ennui at the heart of the American character. Not only was there no longer an open frontier promising a perpetually new beginning to the footloose, ambitious, or maladjusted, but many peoples' economic and social lives had come apart. With the growth of manufacturing and the advent of assembly-line employment, economic ties were not necessarily personal ties. The transformation of farmers, craftsmen, and small-store owners into employees left more people feeling dispossessed and marginal. Some of those people added to the ranks of civilization's familiar detritus—the homeless, the alcoholic, and the mentally ill.[5]

Others banded together in social clubs that replaced the camaraderie once integral to small-town life. Much of the reform movement's strength stemmed from the creation of such clubs, bringing women together while their husbands convened at the Benevolent and Protective Order of Elks, the Odd Fellows, the Knights of Pythias, and similar entities.

But whereas men generally had multiple outlets in which to exercise power and influence, women in the 1910s did not. Elks club members largely sought to enhance their social (and associated business) relations; distaff groups such as the General Federation of Women's Clubs went a step further. The women used the clubs as a vehicle for political clout, flaunting their moral authority as life-givers and home-makers to address directly the dissipation that led others astray. They campaigned against drinking, gambling, cigarettes, spitting on the streets, pornography, and prostitution; they fought for raising the age of sexual consent, for child labor laws, female labor laws, pure food laws, libraries, world peace, city parks, and national forests, among many other causes.

The purpose of women's clubs and similar social and political organizations could be boiled down to reforming the national culture, or what historian William Allen White termed the "revolt of the American conscience." The bonhomie invigorated members and made their dedication to cleaning up the nation all the more potent an agent of societal change. The time was right for reformers. After all, who could doubt that moral advancement was possible? The crusades sprouted naturally from turn-of-the-century optimism and the concomitant bandwagon of efficiency—the same spirit that animated the young Forest Service and the changing face of the Bureau of Biological Survey. And if institutions could be made to work better, why not human beings? Young men had not yet voyaged across an ocean to fight the war to end all wars. Nor was the cynical, almost nihilistic materialism of the post-war 1920s yet in view. Mass moral improvement seemed achievable.[6]

Such improvement included conservation, and, in fact, to many of America's upper-class women flexing unprecedented public influence and power, conservation was central. As Gertrude Bullen Hollister, president of the Colorado Federation of Women's Clubs, put it in 1910:

> Women's work and conservation are largely the same thing whether by right of citizenship or only by moral suasion. She must stand for the things that mean most to humanity: conservation, life, health, love, happiness, children and home; working for an education that will instill into our youth an active conscience, a clean comprehension of life and its responsibilities, an intelligent understanding and love of nature that counts it a dishonor to take from her without paying tribute and making a just return.[7]

In linking love of nature with the virtues of home life such as education and sobriety, the women's movement sketched a cultural alternative to the lives of frontier men whose respite from rugged outdoor work lay not in a return to the hearthstone but in visits to saloons. Hollister's remarks were not the language one would overhear in a saloon in Gillette, Wyoming, not in 1891 or two decades later. But acting on such sentiments, the Colorado Federation of Women's Clubs, along with the female-led Cliff Dwellers Association, played key roles in the creation of Mesa Verde National Park in 1906. In Colorado and nationally, women's groups provided strong support for national forests, irrigation, and municipal tree planting.[8]

But the source of the women's reform movement's moral and political clout—its base in domestic sentiment—also limited its insight. Although a female-led crusade to protect endangered songbirds had transformed millinery styles and helped pass the landmark Lacey Act in 1900, no such redemptive campaign was conceivable for large predators. In staking moral ground as the antipode of coarseness, the early-twentieth-century movement never evinced concern for a species—the wolf—whose name epitomized excessive carnal appetites.

Ironically, despite the obvious chasm between Mrs. H. L. Hollister (as she was known) and Rattlesnake Jack Junior, together they represented a common American notion of civilization. First, the trapper tames the frontier to ready it for civilization, then the matron of high morals appears as its blossoming flower. (In fact, the link could be seen in the fatuous turn-of-the-century habit of picking huge bouquets of wildflowers, to the detriment of the remaining flora, to "fair adorn," as one poet put it, "the votive vase, the dining hours, blossoms on a maiden's breast, [and] a bridal shower."[9] Behind the flowers' domestic iconography lay an act of violence toward nature not entirely dissimilar to that of the trapper.)

After 1911, the Colorado Federation of Women's Clubs broadened its purview by transforming its Forestry Committee into a Conservation Committee. This reflected a move away from the strict utilitarianism of Theodore Roosevelt and Gifford Pinchot's policies. But even before the committee's name changed, the rhetoric that particularly moved the women focused on the aesthetic qualities of wilderness and the spiritual growth, broadly considered, attending human contact with the wild. Conservationist Enos Mills's most evocative and successful lectures to the women's clubs on behalf of Roosevelt's forest policy emphasized the forests' beauty and grandeur. In keeping with that romantic spirit, in 1913 women's groups nationally allied themselves with John Muir in the unsuccessful fight to preserve Hetch Hetchy Valley in California's Yosemite National Park from inundation by a hydroelectric dam.[10]

Women's salience in western land-use controversies followed the region's leadership in the movement for women's electoral franchise (which likely stemmed from women's greater responsibilities in building the frontier society). In 1893 Colorado became the second state after Wyoming to grant women suffrage, and within the next sixteen years eleven women were elected to the state legislature.[11] By 1920 women could vote in thirteen western and midwestern states but only in two eastern states.[12]

Conservationists of all stripes could find what they wanted in Roosevelt's policies, utilitarian though they were. In 1912 women in states that allowed them to vote largely supported Roosevelt's unsuccessful comeback bid.[13] Although that election predates the use of modern polling and focus groups, it is safe to say that Roosevelt's identity as a conservationist helped attract female support.[14]

Although they were not opposed to the goal of wolf extermination, the reformers viewed men like McIntyre as too wolfish in character. The government, under the general aegis of conservation, was replacing such men, or at least subsuming them into a professional agency—hardly cause for consternation. In the mid-teen years, any awareness members of the General Federation of Women's Clubs might have had of the Biological Survey's predator-killing campaign would not have raised alarm bells. The reformers had no reason to distrust the granting of authority to protect livestock to a federal scientific body, particularly given the inadequate protection provided by the free market and individual states. Such powers were the essence of the reforms Roosevelt's brand of Progressivism had instituted.

Whereas the women's reform movement and its conservation wing by and large lacked a direct connection to the life-and-death arena of predator extermination, contemporaneous conservationists were intimately familiar with America's wildlife and the public policies influencing it. Nevertheless, the leaders of other strands of the conservation movement either advocated predator extermination or ignored the issue.

This orientation reflected at least some of those leaders' roots in the hunting tradition of Theodore Roosevelt, who compensated for his youthful frailty by pursuing dangerous game. Although Roosevelt feared a vitiation of American manhood absent the rigors of pioneer life, it never seemed to occur to him that killing fierce predators could only continue as long as some remained.[15]

Others' myopia might have reflected an excessive tendency to compartmentalize ideas. William Temple Hornaday, one of the most successful conservationists of the period, was an ardent and tireless pugilist for wildlife but perpetually fought yesterday's battles and drew conclusions from his experiences that were too limited. As a young man, Hornaday had traveled the world for sport and wrote about his adventures in such works as *Two Years in the Jungle: The Experiences of a Hunter and Naturalist in India, Ceylon, the Malay Peninsula, and Borneo* (1885).[16] From an early age he subscribed to a code of sportsmanship inimical to the market hunting that decimated the bison during the 1870s. But his code did not stretch to preventing him—like Roosevelt—from doing his part in the extirpation. For Hornaday the rationale was science.

In 1886 the thirty-one-year-old Hornaday was the chief taxidermist for the U.S. National Museum in Washington, D.C. He discovered to his alarm that "the museum was actually without presentable specimens of this most important and interesting mammal," the bison. He hurriedly arranged to head west to rectify the problem, cognizant that the species' rapid extermination meant that even a few weeks' delay might leave the American public no adequate model of what the famous buffalo looked like.[17] Like Roosevelt three years before and about eighty miles to the southwest, in May Hornaday stepped off the train station in Miles City, Montana, eager to ensure that the next few bison to die would contribute to the museum's collection. After almost a month of searching, he managed to kill three bison, but local cowboys told him a herd of around thirty-five lived in the badlands farther north. He "resolved to leave the buffaloes entirely unmolested until autumn, and then, when the robes would be in the finest condition, return for a hunt on a liberal scale."[18]

When he returned in September, he hired three cowboys and set out north for the hunt. After establishing a camp, they began the search through the maze of canyons and buttes that sheltered the animals. After eight weeks they

William T. Hornaday with a bison calf. Hornaday wrote the first book dedicated to saving animals from extinction, published in 1913, and founded the American Bison Society to save and reintroduce the creature that he himself had helped to wipe out. But to curry favor with the Bureau of Biological Survey, he added his voice to those calling for extinction of wolves. (Smithsonian Institution Archives, record unit 95, photo negative number 79-13252)

had managed to kill twenty-six bison. One they could not salvage because they left it overnight, and before morning Indians raided the carcass for the meat and pelt, leaving only yellow and red war paint and a strip of red cloth tied to a horn on the unskinned head.[19] (The natives who left this glowering death mask perhaps did not appreciate that saving bison in the National Museum was more important than saving them on the prairie.)

Back in Washington, Hornaday went to work creating the bison exhibit. Rather than display the specimens in the clinical isolation customary to museums, he grouped the animals as part of a tableau representing their natural habitats. This innovation won popular acclaim, with the Washington *Star* praising it as "a picturesque group—a bit of the wild West . . . real buffalo-grass, real Montana dirt, and real buffaloes." The star-struck writer, affecting a willed ignorance of reality, described the diorama as follows:

> It is as though a little group of buffalo that have come to drink at a pool had been suddenly struck motionless by some magic spell, each in a natural attitude, and then the section of prairie, pool, buffalo, and all had been carefully cut out and brought to the National Museum. . . . In the grass some distance from the pool lie the bleaching skulls of two buffalo who have fallen victims to hunters who have cruelly lain in wait to get a shot.[20]

The reporter's condemnation of the cruel hunters while characterizing Hornaday's hunt as a "magic spell" may have had roots in the bifurcated state of Hornaday's mind. The following year Hornaday wrote a report entitled "The Extermination of the American Bison, With a Sketch of Its Discovery and Life History," published by the National Museum in 1889. Included within was a detailed account of his successful hunt to provision the museum's bison exhibit. The report remains an important piece of scholarship on the bison. It is also a fascinating glimpse into Hornaday's cognitive dissonance about his role in the extermination. Speaking in general terms and about others, he pulled no punches:

> The idea of the frontiersman (the average, at least) has always been to kill as much game as possible before some other fellow gets a chance at it, *and before it is all killed off* [original italics]! So he goes at the game, and as a general thing kills all he can while it lasts, and with it feeds himself and family, his dogs, and even his hogs, to repletion. I knew one Montana man north of Miles City who killed for his own use twenty-six black-tail deer in one season, and had so much more venison than he could consume or give away that a great pile of carcasses lay in his yard until spring and spoiled.
>
> During the existence of the buffalo it was declared by many an impossibility to stop or prevent the slaughter. Such an accusation of weakness and imbecility on the part of the General Government is an insult to our strength and resources.[21]

Several pages further he methodically listed the few remaining bison he had reason to believe survived unprotected in the wild in North America as of January 1, 1889 (excluding the Yellowstone herd of around 200 that was protected as long as it stayed within the national park).

Surviving Bison in North America

Region	Number of Bison
In the Pan-handle of Texas	25
In Colorado	20
In southern Wyoming	26
In Musselshell country, Montana	10
In western Dakota	4
Total number in the United States	85
In Athabasca, Northwest Territory (estimated)	550
Total in all North America	635

Source: William T. Hornaday, "The Extermination of the American Bison, With a Sketch of Its Discovery and Life History." *Report of the U.S. National Museum, 1887.* Washington, D.C., 1889, 525.

Hornaday's concern about the species' potentially imminent extinction was genuine and long-lasting. In December 1905, with President Roosevelt's help, he organized the American Bison Society to reintroduce live bison held in private collections to public reserves.[22] Hornaday served as president, and Roosevelt consented to be the society's honorary president (and later signed legislation creating a National Bison Range in Montana). Yet neither in his 1889 report nor in any subsequent writings did Hornaday express regret over his own role in whittling down the species. To the contrary, exultation permeates his description of the hunt. "After a short chase my horse carried me alongside my buffalo, and as he turned toward me I gave him a shot through the shoulder, breaking the fore leg and bringing him promptly to the ground," he recalled. He then chased a female bison in the herd of three he had stumbled upon, and returning "back to the old bull" he described the conclusion:

> When he saw me coming he got upon his feet and ran a short distance but was easily overtaken. He then stood at bay, and halting within 30 yards of him I enjoyed the rare opportunity of studying a live bull buffalo of the largest size on foot on his native heath. I even made an outline sketch of him in my note-book. Having studied his form and outlines as much as was really necessary, I gave him a final shot through the lungs, which soon ended his career. . . .
> I was delighted with our remarkably good fortune in securing such a prize, for, owing to the rapidity with which the large buffaloes are being found and killed off these days, I had not hoped to capture a really old individual. Nearly every adult bull we took carried old bullets in his body, and from this one we took four of various sizes that had been fired into him on various occasions.[23]

Twenty years later, in 1909, Hornaday published "A Sportsmen's Platform: Fifteen Cardinal Principles Affecting Wild Game and Its Pursuit," which argued for self-restraint in hunting. "The best hunter is the man who finds the most game, kills the least and leaves behind him no wounded animals" was one principle. Another inveighed against killing female hoofed animals "save for special preservation." Hornaday still considered taxidermy an important reason to hunt.[24]

The wiping out of the bison remained Hornaday's object lesson in the failure to abide by a proper code of hunting, and he extended his concern over the consequences of such conduct to a host of other animals. But he remained unable to recognize his own blind spots. In 1913, as director of the New York Zoological Park, he published the first book devoted to arousing opposition to species extinction. *Our Vanishing Wildlife: Its Extermination and Preservation* was a remarkable jeremiad against "an Army of Destruction that now is almost beyond all control."[25] Fiercely didactic and as uncompromising as an Old Testament prophet, the man whose middle name—Temple—evoked the absolute made no apologies for his idée fixe:

> To-day, the thing that stares me in the face every waking hour, like a grisly spectre with bloody fang and claw, is *the extermination of species* [original italics]. To me, that is a horrible thing. It is wholesale murder, no less. It is capital crime, and a black disgrace to the races of civilized mankind. I say "civilized mankind," because savages don't do it![26]

In between such fulminations, *Our Vanishing Wildlife* meticulously documented the unrestrained hunting that had already wiped out six birds native to North America and that threatened to exterminate dozens of other birds and mammals. Hornaday cataloged the status of each North American species known to be in peril or already extinct, creating the first comprehensive endangered species list. His principal solution, the exposition of which required another, even more exhortatory work published the following year, was "*the conversion of every national forest into a national game-preserve* [original italics]."[27] Noting tremendous growth in public concern for wildlife since the turn of the century yet evincing profound skepticism about the states' ability to protect "game," he hoped to arouse a mass movement within a few years that would push Congress to "*enact a law making every national forest a hard-and-fast game preserve, with all hunting forever prohibited, save of predatory animals*" [original italics].[28] Turning the forests into game refuges was not a new idea; in 1903 Representative John F. Lacey (whose name graced the act putting federal teeth into enforcement of state wildlife laws) had introduced a bill to give the president authority to turn individual forest reserves into such refuges, but the bill did not pass. As a result of Hornaday's organizing efforts, a bill known informally as the Hornaday Plan was introduced to establish federal game refuges. Hornaday traveled the nation vigorously promoting his ideas and the bill, but it failed also.[29]

As the wording of his game preserve proposal indicates, "save of predatory animals," Hornaday had another solution to help preserve declining game, singling out wolves for special condemnation:

> At the head of this list of evil-doers stands the big *Gray Wolf or "Timber" Wolf* [original italics], strong of limb and jaw, insatiable in appetite, a master of cunning and the acme of cruelty. The states that still possess gray wolves have done well in placing a high cash bounty, varying from $10 to $25 on the head of this four-footed fiend. At this moment, many a forest ranger west of the great plains is on the alert for signs that will

show the location of the dens of breeding pairs of gray wolves, in order that if possible the parents may be destroyed before the young are born; or, failing that, that the young may be destroyed in the spring before they leave the den.

Ever since the range steer took the place of the American bison, a relentless warfare has been waged against the gray wolf. The hordes of gray marauders that once battened and fattened on the millions of wasted buffalo carcasses have been reduced to scattered fragments. On the plains there is to-day perhaps one gray wolf to every hundred that were there prior to 1885. . . .

Wherever found, the proper course with a wild gray wolf is to kill it as quickly as possible.[30]

Oddly enough for one so preoccupied by the plight of game animals, Hornaday's principal complaint against wolves was not that they killed wild-life but that they killed domestic animals. Although urging what he considered judicious reductions in the numbers of mountain lions, lynxes, and even golden eagles to stem predations on bighorn sheep, he reserved his harshest vituperations for wolves on account of their depredations against livestock.[31] This is the same man who chided the western cattle and sheep industries for overgrazing national forests in the Rocky Mountains to the extent of leaving no forage for elk and deer[32] and who chastised the National Wool Growers Association for its opposition to western game preserves and for the government subsidies it received.[33] (In fact, even though it killed sheep, he supported preserving the Tasmanian wolf, a misnamed Australian marsupial predator not in fact related to wolves.[34])

Hornaday's abomination of gray wolves, and the hackneyed prose he used to describe them, conformed to the intellectual conventions of the period and indeed to those of the English language itself. But his inconsistency in execrating wolves for their effect on ranching, an industry for which he otherwise displayed no sympathy, smacks of another motivation. In his desperate search for political support in his crusade against unlimited hunting, Hornaday found a willing ally in the Bureau of Biological Survey, which at the time managed game preserves that were off-limits to hunters.[35] (These preserves are now called national wildlife refuges and are open to hunting.) And in writing *Our Vanishing Wildlife,* Hornaday drew heavily on information gleaned from the survey, which had first excelled in both bird preservation and predator killing by dint of its network of scientific and lay informants.

In generous reciprocation, *Our Vanishing Wildlife* lavished praise on the survey's assistant chief, Dr. Theodore S. Palmer, naming him the second champion of wildlife after former president Roosevelt and crediting him for making the survey "the recognized special champion of preservation in America." (Palmer, the third scientist hired by C. Hart Merriam, had started and long overseen the survey's Division of Game and Bird Conservation.) The book urged Congress "to enlarge the fighting force of the Biological Survey," which

Hornaday termed "a splendid center of activity and initiative in the preservation of our wild life."[36]

It is no more surprising that Hornaday would accept uncritically the survey's stance favoring wolf extermination (although in the early teen years he was slow to catch on to the fact that the survey was increasingly critical of bounties) than it is that Palmer would take the opportunity to emphasize to a prominent wildlife advocate the threat wolves posed not only to livestock but to wildlife as well. Hornaday had many ties with the survey, including belonging to an elite group of big-game hunters, the Boone and Crocket Club. Founded in 1887 by Theodore Roosevelt, among others, "to promote manly sport with the rifle," the club's constitution limited membership to 100 select invitees, each of whom had shot "in fair chase . . . at least one adult male individual of each of three of the various species of American large game."[37] In 1910 the club's focus expanded to include game preservation, and the next year it urged the creation of national game refuges, "better means of enforcing game laws," and "more effective means for the extermination of natural enemies of all kinds of game." At this time, not coincidentally, it was closely allied with the survey, whose leaders were numbered among the club's associate membership (a secondary tier of belonging).[38] Thus in part because of such social ties, America's most visible activist for endangered species preservation gave his unqualified support to the extermination of one of the country's most endangered species.

To the extent that the Biological Survey basked in Hornaday's encomiums for its role in protecting ungulates and non-predatory fowl, it also accepted game preservation as a rationale—albeit a secondary one after livestock protection—for predator extermination. In August 1917 the survey's national chief, Dr. Edward W. Nelson—who had replaced Henry W. Henshaw that year—speaking at a conference of state game commissioners, explained the broad importance of his agency's efforts: "Everyone is aware that mountain lions, wolves, coyotes and other beasts of prey destroy vast numbers of game animals. For this reason, the destruction of the predatory animals, while primarily to protect live stock, at the same time is helping increase the amount of game."[39]

This argument automatically expanded the survey's constituency to include many civic-minded Americans whose interest in livestock production extended no further than their own palates and to a passing appreciation for the nation's pastoral past but who had been awakened by Hornaday and his allies to the acute plight of game animals. In rapidly urbanizing Colorado, the day had long passed when the ranching industry was central to many people's lives. As far back as eleven years, in 1906, an observer had noted the Queen City's remove from its ranching roots: "Let a cowboy, with chaps, spurs, and his rope at his saddle, ride through the streets of Denver, and he will be stared at as if he were in the streets of New York."[40] By 1920 the nation as a whole consisted of more urban than rural dwellers.[41] To those people capable of recognizing ranching as a business venture distinct from its romantically viewed past and naturally interested in pursuing its parochial economic interest, the disappearance of wildlife loomed as an issue of public concern.

Although Hornaday's books and perorations failed to secure the transformation of national forests into inviolate wildlife preserves, he did alert the nation to the dangerous plight of game. His prescriptions on sportsmanship, first discussed by a few men with the luxury to spend months on safari in Asia, were gradually becoming common wisdom, and the public was losing its laissez-faire attitude toward poaching.

In 1913 the Colorado General Assembly banned the killing of male deer for a five-year span and the killing of male bighorn sheep, pronghorn, and elk for eleven years. (The law already banned killing antlerless ungulates on the grounds that the females were more important to population growth, but evidently the killing of males was also limiting the species.) In 1916 local businessmen collaborated with the Elks Lodge—which at the beginning of the century had been killing elk to acquire their teeth for badges—to reverse the decline of the club's namesake animal. They began importing elk from Jackson Hole, Wyoming (the winter range for the Yellowstone elk herd), and from Montana to Colorado's Front Range where the mountains meet the plains.[42] (The state Game and Fish Department later joined the effort.) That same year only one elk was known to have been killed in Colorado by poachers.[43] Even assuming some undetected illegal hunting, the figure bespeaks a sea change in attitude from the recent era when game laws were chiefly honored in the breach.

Not even the exigencies of war weakened Colorado's resolve to preserve game. Despite national exhortations in 1918 to reduce meat consumption to ensure its availability to soldiers on the front lines,[44] the Colorado General Assembly resisted the temptation to liberalize hunting laws as a stopgap for meat-deprived citizens.[45] Hornaday's crusade played a substantial role in the survival of several species. In 1919 the Forest Service claimed that the number of elk in Colorado's national forests had grown to 5,384 animals, the number of deer to 23,797, and and the number of bighorn to 6,772 animals.[46]

One of those whose interest and concern Hornaday piqued was an avid hunter and manager-on-leave of a national forest in northern New Mexico. Twenty-six-year-old Aldo Leopold, forced into uncharacteristic inactivity by a serious illness, had bought *Our Vanishing Wildlife* for his father, but before giving the gift he read it himself. Hornaday's arguments made a serious impression.[47]

Leopold, a hunter since childhood, readily recognized that even short of extinction, if game failed to rebound, public disapprobation would limit the seasons and places—including national forests—available to hunting. "Advocates of restrictive game laws," he later argued in the newsletter for the American Game Protective Association, expostulate that "the scarcer the game the more restrictions [should be imposed]. Long or even permanent closed seasons on threatened species are a logical corollary of their doctrine."[48]

Such a view "regards the perpetuation of native species as an end in itself, equal if not greater in importance than the perpetuation of 'something to shoot.'"

Although he admitted that this perspective "enjoys the advantage of an ethical as well as of an utilitarian objective,"[49] Leopold nevertheless feared such restrictions on public hunting access would result in game farms—the breeding of animals solely for well-to-do hunters—and the consequent demise of America's frontier-nurtured democracy:

> A wide-open market, almost universal game farming, commercialized shooting privileges, and some incidental overflow shooting for the poor man—is this not the sum and substance of the European system? It is. And the European system of game management is undemocratic, unsocial, and therefore dangerous. I assume that it is not necessary to argue that the development of any undemocratic system in this country is to be avoided at all costs.[50]

Leopold also appreciated, however, the moral imperative behind Hornaday's apocalyptic warnings of a mass extinction crisis. In the fall of 1915 he was greatly inspired to finally meet Hornaday, who was on a speaking and slide show tour throughout the West. Buoyed by Hornaday's fervor, Leopold helped establish the New Mexico Game Protective Association,[51] an affiliate of the American Game Protective Association (which was funded heavily by firearms manufacturers concerned that as game populations fell, their profits would fall too). Shortly afterward, Leopold published a Hornaday-sounding warning that in North America "eleven species have been already exterminated, and twenty-five more are now candidates for oblivion. Nature was a million years, or more, in developing a species. . . . Man, with all his wisdom, has not evolved so much as a ground squirrel, a sparrow, or a clam."[52]

Leopold faced the problem of reconciling his concern for species preservation with his grave misgivings about excessive limitations on public hunting access. Clearly, public hunting could only continue if the number of game rebounded; the trick was to limit public hunting without eliminating it and, in particular, without banning it in the national forests—the solution advocated by Hornaday. In surveying alternative means to increase game, Hornaday's other solution—exterminating predators—seemed, in Leopold's later words, "plain common sense, which nobody will seriously question."[53]

Such a course must have seemed all the more transparent to Leopold because his brother-in-law was president of the New Mexico Wool Growers Association. When it came to predators, Leopold realized, the interests of hunters coincided neatly with those of ranchers: after all, wolves and other varmints would either kill livestock or would have to rely on deer, elk, and other ungulates coveted by sportsmen. "For some unfathomable reason," he began another 1915 essay entitled "The Varmint Question," "there appears to have been a kind of feeling of antagonism between men interested in game protection and between some individuals connected with the stock growing industry." He continued, "It seems never to have occurred to anybody that the very opposite should be the case, and that the stockmen and the game protectionists are mutually and vitally interested in a common problem. This problem is the reduction of predatory animals."[54]

Leopold took the initiative on behalf of the New Mexico Game Protective Association to confer with his brother-in-law, the sheep rancher, and with Stokley Ligon, the Biological Survey's top official in New Mexico, about forming an informal coalition with hunters to persuade Congress to increase the survey's appropriation for predator killing. Both men, not surprisingly, were very receptive.[55] Largely because of Aldo Leopold's strenuous organizing efforts, New Mexico led the nation in hunters' enthusiasm for eliminating carnivores.[56]

In reviewing Leopold's activism for eliminating predators, it is too facile to solely examine the influence of Hornaday, his own family connections, and his overweening drive to make his mark on the world. All of these factors were important, but an incident from several years previous, when Leopold was only twenty-two, probably inclined him toward killing "varmints" at least as strongly as anything else had.

The year was 1909, and Leopold, fresh out of Yale Forestry School and engaged by the nascent Forest Service to inventory timber in the forested canyons of southeastern Arizona, was eating lunch with his crew on a rimrock overlooking a turbulent river:

"The challenge of fang against bullet." In 1909, twenty-two-year-old Aldo Leopold and the other members of his Forest Service timber crew gunned down a female wolf and her pups in southeastern Arizona, and within a few years he was advocating for an organized predator extermination program. (Courtesy, the Aldo Leopold Foundation)

> We saw what we thought was a doe fording the torrent, her breast awash in white water. When she climbed the bank toward us and shook out her tail, we realized our error: it was a wolf. A half dozen others, evidently grown pups, sprang from the willows and all joined in a welcoming mêlée of wagging tails and playful maulings. What was literally a pile of wolves writhed and tumbled in the center of an open flat at the foot of our rimrock.[57]

"In those days we had never heard of passing up a chance to kill a wolf," he wrote decades later. "In a second we were pumping lead into the pack, but with more excitement than accuracy. . . . When our rifles were empty, the old wolf was down, and a pup was dragging a leg into impassable slide-rocks. We reached the old wolf in time to watch a fierce green fire dying in her eyes."[58]

Toward the end of his life, Leopold described that incident as an epiphany that forever changed his attitude toward predators. But in fact it was not until decades after he killed the wolf that the import of the event, imbued with his probing into the meaning of land health, led him to renounce predator extermination. In the meantime, throughout his twenties and beyond, killing a wolf signified solely to Leopold "the challenge of fang against bullet."[59]

There were conservationists who failed to conform to either the civic housekeeping or the fang-against-bullet strands of the movement. These were the rare dissenters against the American faith in the conquest of wilderness, acolytes of John Muir (perhaps the nineteenth century's most anachronistic public figure) who argued strenuously for the sanctity of unblemished wild places. Muir's rationale was nature's intrinsic worth, including the need to shelter "the wild animals, our happy fellow mortals and neighbors."[60] In the ferment of the first fifteen or so years of the twentieth century—from the time Roosevelt began creating forest reserves up until American troops fixed their bayonets and lowered themselves into Europe's sanguinary trenches—a small force of people argued for the preservation of wild places, in part to preserve the animals that lived there.

Enos Mills of Colorado was one such conservationist. Mills was a close observer of the mountains in which he spent so much time, and it was his questions to Albert McIntyre that induced the latter to record the fate of Two Toes. Mills seemed to appreciate wolves as much as he did every other animal, as indicated by his account of wolves at play:

> A tumbleweed in a Wyoming windstorm furnished the plaything in an exciting game for a pack of wolves. I watched the play from the shelter of a ravine. Flying before the wind, the tumbleweed bounded a ridge with a huge wolf after it. Closely pressing him came a pursuing pack of twenty. A lull in the wind and the tumbleweed, colliding with the leading wolf's head, bounded off to one side. Other wolves sprang in the air after it, but the wind carried the tumbleweed along and the entire pack rushed in pursuit.
>
> This big, much-branched, ball-shaped weed was two feet in diameter. When it touched the earth the gale swept it, bounding forward and rolling over and over, across the brown, wide plains. After it came the closely massed wolves. Just as those in the lead were nearing this animated plaything it was caught by a whirlwind and pulled high into the air. Two wolves leaped and tried to seize it. Several sat down and stared after it as though it were gone forever. The tumbleweed commenced to descend, but buoyed up by the air it came down slowly. The pack surged this way and that, as the weed surged in descending, to be beneath it; and while it was still several feet above them a high-leaping fellow struck it head-on and sent it flying to one side. It disappeared in a hollow and the wolves vanished after it.[61]

As this passage suggests, Mills's uncommon observational skills enabled him to break through the clichés about wolves and recount their actual behaviors. In fact, he went out of his way to refute the unearned reputation of wolves, bears, and cougars as threats to humans.[62] But like his mentor Muir, who although personally comfortable around flesh-eating animals never seemed to fully embrace predation as essential to ecological health,[63] Mills disliked predation. He once actually tried to foil a lion attack on a deer.

Mills championed and vigorously campaigned for the creation of a national park on the outskirts of Estes Park, in part to protect wildlife. In 1915, as a result of his efforts, Congress carved out 358 square miles of national forest land in northern Colorado to create Rocky Mountain National Park. The next year, with more than 50,000 people visiting the new park,[64] Congress passed the National Park Service Act, creating an agency and a mission to manage the baker's dozen areas—including Rocky Mountain—that had been set aside for their scenic splendors. Unlike the designation of Yellowstone as the world's first national park in 1872, the 1916 act reflected genuine popular sentiment for landscape preservation. (In fact, to a significant extent the act represented political damage control—if not a mea culpa—for Congress's recent decision, despite many thousands of constituent letters in opposition, to build a hydroelectric dam within Hetch Hetchy Valley in Yosemite National Park.[65]) But even with this political wind at his back, Mills never proposed the park be exempted from the Biological Survey's traps and poisons.[66]

Ultimately, Hollister, Hornaday, Leopold, and Mills—all ardent and thoughtful advocates for the natural world—failed to take up the cause of predators precisely when wolves needed it most. The 1915 congressional appropriation to the Bureau of Biological Survey to systematically destroy wolves, coyotes, and other animals signaled the most organized institutional force yet arrayed against the canny and adaptable but not omnipotent social mammal, the wolf. The four abdicated an aspect of their loftiest ideals, each for his or her own reasons.

Gertrude Hollister, champion of social reform, would not have thought to question a federal agency whose professionalism was supplanting such scrofulous trappers as Rattlesnake Jack Junior. William T. Hornaday, the iconoclastic animal idealist, undercut the heart of his crusade against extinction through a politically expedient alliance with the Biological Survey. Aldo Leopold—still young and land ignorant, committed to ideas yet ambitious to act—was seduced by the congruity of interests between two activities close to his heart, hunting and ranching. And Enos Mills, so taken by the transformative beauty of nature, ultimately ignored the natural predators that resisted the currents of the era's nature aestheticism.

Of the four, only Leopold would eventually recant his stance on predator extermination. But by that time it was too late for the West—or perhaps still too early.

A Certain Faction of the Natives

I n the long, sloping mesas of the far northwestern corner of Colorado, the land holds on to the summer sunlight past its due. As evening falls and deer uncurl from their diurnal beds under twisted junipers, the light still suffuses the grasslands, casting long shadows from each pinyon-pine-studded ridge. As late as 9:00 at night, the higher-elevation aspen stands glow lambently, like the last sentinels of the day protesting the sun's retreat.

By September, with the first snows covering the unnaturally cropped tops of the yellow grasses, grazed through the summer by cattle and sheep, the sunlight burns just as intensely but is vitiated by distance. Only in winter, when clouds darken the sky and the snow parachutes in like a tide filling the grottos of a seashore, does the light appear murky and the time—even at mid-day—always seem crepuscular.

In September 1916 Logan B. Crawford, the Bureau of Biological Survey's predatory animal inspector for the Colorado district, took a field trip to meet ranch owners and some of their cowboys in the vicinity of today's Dinosaur National Monument. The trip was a return to familiar territory for Crawford, who had grown up in Steamboat Springs, a town that had sprung up around his family's ranch (and which his father had served as mayor and represented as a state legislator). In fall 1886, at age seventeen, he had ridden the 150 miles from his home to the region to deliver ballots for the November election. The next year he again had ridden there alone, this time on a quixotic assignment from the state game and fish commissioner to stop the Utes from killing deer for their hides. (He stopped for the night unknowingly at the abode of a local rancher who had been purchasing the hides and who sent a cowboy on a nocturnal ride to the Ute camp to warn them that the "Buckskin Police" were on their trail. Not realizing the Buckskin Police consisted of just one ardent and modestly armed young man, the next day, when Crawford rode up, dozens of Utes fled in a panic.)[1]

In the early fall of 1916, with Crawford just past his forty-seventh birthday, the choppy desert grasslands of far northwestern Colorado had changed little. Although the Utes had been herded onto a reservation in Utah and the land was grazed by livestock and subject to a brief flurry of new (and often short-lived) homesteading settlement, not a single paved road penetrated the region.[2]

Something else hadn't changed, either: the expansive terrain still harbored abundant wolves. In fact, northwest Colorado seemed the state's stronghold for the species, part of a regional population that swept into adjacent Utah and southwestern Wyoming. Although Crawford did not attempt to estimate precise numbers, his counterpart in Utah thought about twenty-five wolves roamed Uintah County directly across the state line, occasionally crossing the border into Colorado.[3]

Even without this intelligence, Crawford knew well that the wolves were out there, in part because on his September 1916 visit he received reports of recent livestock losses. The wolves were active on Douglas Mountain between the Snake and Green rivers, as well as on and around Black Mountain farther east in the Routt National Forest.

It was not as if Crawford had not had a good start on the problem. Despite the conflicts with Albert McIntyre, he had built up a respectable cadre of hunters during the year. In fiscal year 1916, which had ended on June 30, he employed eighteen salaried hunters.[4] These men killed an astounding forty-nine wolves throughout Colorado, the most since the fifty-six killed five years previously.[5] Private individuals and the Forest Service killed thirty-one more.[6] Never again would so many wolves die in the state in one year.

Nevertheless, there were always more requests for his elite force of federal hunters than Crawford could satisfy. The Great War taking place in Europe, although not yet embroiling the United States directly, was beginning to boost demand for American beef. Throughout the West the Forest Service responded by increasing stocking levels beyond what agency officials, never conservative in such matters, admitted the land could support.[7]

By 1920 Colorado supported more than 1.4 million head of cattle (not including 300,000 dairy cows generally confined closer to homesteads and therefore less accessible to wolves).[8] This represented an increase of around 100,000 over the figures from 1910 and meant that for each elk available to wolves (according to the Forest Service's 1919 statewide population estimate of only 5,384 elk), there were more than 250 cows. Similarly, in 1920 there were

1.8 million domestic sheep in Colorado—an increase of half a million over the previous decade.[9] This meant that each deer was still outnumbered by sheep seventy to one. Similar conditions prevailed throughout the West.

The inflated livestock numbers inevitably meant less forage for native ungulates but greater opportunity for wolves to secure livestock. The wolf depredations Crawford learned about in northwestern Colorado were hardly surprising, given the continuation of severe overstocking.

It is highly unlikely that any contemporary framed the issue that way, least of all those with a financial interest in the matter. A horse dealer named Joe Jones from the town of Craig typified local stockmen's sentiment with his pragmatic desire to identify the wolves' locations and eradicate the beasts forthwith. After meeting with Jones, Crawford wrote in a report to Washington, D.C., "The supposition is that it is an old female wolf and her this years [sic] litter of pups with perhaps a couple of old males"—in other words, a family group or pack. Jones requested the survey's help in killing the wolves, but Crawford told him "that my this years [sic] allotment was practically all taken up and that I could not give him any assistance at present." Jones proposed that the area's ranchers suspend bounty payments and contribute what they would have spent on bounties directly to the survey instead. Crawford liked the idea but could not commit: "I told him that I would take it up with the Bureau and see what could be done."[10]

The survey had been born to cooperation between the private American Ornithologists' Union and the federal government. Its early scientific investigators collected information from local inhabitants and shared that information with appropriate authorities—and that method had largely been carried over into enforcement of the Lacey Act. Its early-twentieth-century demonstrations in rodent killing had put the survey in the role of providing technical outreach to private and other public entities. It was fitting to develop the still-new predator-killing system along similar cooperative lines; all that was needed was an accounting method to ensure proper disposition of monies taken in.

Albert K. Fisher, in charge of the Division of Economic Investigations, was not one to hold up a good idea with excessive bureaucracy. Henry W. Henshaw, the bureau's chief, however, might have been so inclined. He had become increasingly rigid and difficult to accommodate in his personal and professional habits, and the next year he would be replaced, destined to spend his last years in a mental hospital for clinical paranoia.[11] (A sign, perhaps, of his incipient mental collapse and unsuitability for his position was his growing disinclination to kill animals, expressed in 1920 after a career built on scientific collecting.[12])

But whatever obstacles Henshaw might have put up, as will be seen, it is likely that the agency was hearing Jones's suggestion to Crawford simultaneously from more than one source. By the next year Crawford had obtained authorization, and by October 1917 the money started coming in. The Western Slope Wool Growers Association was the first entity to contribute directly to the survey in Colorado, earmarking funds for an intensive coyote-poisoning campaign in the west-central county of Montrose.

The success of this endeavor inspired fund-raising for the same purpose among sheep ranchers elsewhere in the state. Local wool grower affiliate groups based in neighboring Delta County contributed, as did the South Park Sheep Growers Association and groups in the San Luis Valley.[13] Recently retired governor Julius C. Gunter, who owned a huge sheep ranch in southeastern Colorado, began organizing among his neighbors.[14]

Pooling its money, first for bounties and then to give to the Biological Survey, fit the livestock industry's habit of cooperation—a trait particularly well-developed in Colorado. As mentioned, the livestock industry's first organizational steps in the nineteenth century consisted of uniting local cattlemen's groups into the Colorado Stockgrowers Association, before ranchers elsewhere created such a group.

The cooperative habit also made for potent politics, and nowhere did ranchers have as much success in shaping government as in Colorado. Ranchers had already built a cohesive and politically potent community based on a variety of common interests: passage of bounty laws, construction of irrigation projects, passage of laws governing water distribution (which quickly became the model for other states), and favorable rates for railroad transport. Frequent advocacy for such causes tended to perpetuate and strengthen a culture of political engagement among ranchers; many problems, they learned, could be solved through government.[15] Colorado stockmen were confident that they had the "best stock laws of any state in the union," as one of them pointed out with satisfaction at a 1922 stockgrowers association meeting.[16]

How did that power play out on the ground? The same fall (1916) in which Crawford was introduced to the idea of private entities helping to fund his government hunters, ranchers in Colorado were parrying a threat that would induce them to flex political muscle in a manner unseen since the joust over grazing in the old forest reserves near the turn of the twentieth century. Ironically, this new battle arose over an electoral initiative that would have had the inadvertent effect of reducing predator kills, obviating much of the basis for exterminating them. Tired of the trespass of free-ranging cattle on their members' lands, the Grange and other farmers' groups sought to use Colorado's recently granted right to citizen initiative to enact a law requiring owners of livestock to ensure that their animals would not encroach on others' property. Colorado and other western states at the time—and most to this day—put the onus of responsibility for preventing livestock trespass on those wishing to keep cattle off their property, not on the owners of the animals.

Because of the prohibitive cost of fencing, in many places passage of this legislation would have entailed hiring herders to keep cattle from straying. Such year-round cowboys—retained beyond the seasonal movement of cattle onto summer ranges and in the fall roundup—would have offered incidental but significant protection from wolves, coyotes, bears, and cougars. This, in turn, would have greatly reduced the economic rationale behind the Biological Survey's rapidly evolving predator extermination campaign.

The Colorado Stockgrowers Association first attempted to prevent people from signing petitions to put the law on the ballot.[17] When that failed, the association mounted a sophisticated political campaign worthy of contemporary electioneering. The association approached every bank in the state, implying (if the arguments are at all similar to contemporary appeals to the financial industry) that ranchers would go bankrupt and be unable to repay outstanding loans if the initiative passed. The group also presented its case to Denver civic and commercial organizations, as well as to the city's mayor. To influence the press, the association contacted more than 270 weekly and daily newspapers and even paid a *Rocky Mountain News* reporter "to cooperate with the publicity agent of the association to prepare articles for the press." Not content with such mediated outreach, the campaign bought prominent billboard space and mailed a packet of information on the issue to every registered Colorado voter.[18]

This impressive display of political muscle had the intended results, and the herding law went down in a landslide. But the stock association, shaken by the challenge to its members' prerogatives, hired a private detective firm to investigate and smear the initiative's proponents. The private investigators duly discovered several petition circulators who had given false addresses or were underage, along with two female petitioners who had solicited signatures under the names of, respectively, their husband and son.[19]

Three years later, with this and other victories behind them, coupled with the fact that private associations were already giving funds directly to the Biological Survey, it made sense for the state's ranchers to duplicate the nineteenth-century experience with bounties. Just as bounties began as private arrangements but soon also drew on state and local government coffers, so went cooperation with the survey. In 1919 Saguache County, comprising the northern San Luis Valley and adjacent areas of the San Juan and Sangre de Cristo ranges, began contributing its own money for the survey to hire two coyote poisoners.[20]

In January 1919 the American National Live Stock Association once again held its annual convention in Denver, its home turf. And once again the convention proved an ideal venue to express public policy preferences. The survey's burgeoning cooperative network of predator hunters was a hit. States had long been paying bounties, so why shouldn't they join counties and private stockmen's groups in contributing to this new and more promising endeavor to achieve what bounties had not? Voting unanimously, the membership passed a motion urging the replacement of state bounty laws with state appropriations "to equal the amounts to be expended by the Federal Government in the different states," adding that "such state appropriations should be expended under the direction of the Biological Survey, to be handled in conjunction with the funds appropriated by Congress." The group also urged Congress "to appropriate the additional sum of $300,000 for immediate use in the extermination of predatory wild animals and range destroying rodents."[21]

Within weeks or perhaps even days, at least one of the people who had approved the resolution acted on it directly. State representative Robert F. Rockwell, later a member of Congress, owned a ranch near the town of Paonia (along the North Fork of the Gunnison River) in Delta County.[22] As a politically active rancher in Colorado, he almost certainly numbered among the conventioneers in Denver. Rockwell introduced a bill "for the eradication of predatory animals" that appropriated $50,000 "or so much thereof as is equivalent to the sum appropriated by the United States government for a like purpose in the State of Colorado." The money was to be delivered directly to the Biological Survey.[23]

Unlike 1885, when the legislature had suspended the state's bounty in a bout of fiscal conservatism, this time the ranchers triumphed. One-third of Colorado's thirty state senators in 1919 listed agriculture as their profession. Rockwell had lined up bipartisan support from fellow ranchers and their supporters hailing from districts that still sustained wolf populations: rancher-representatives William A. Bronaugh and William E. Gardner, both from the San Luis Valley,[24] co-sponsored the bill, as did representatives George Colgate and A. E. Wiklins (occupations unknown), the latter hailing from North Park, also occupied wolf habitat. On March 28, just two and a half months after the stockmen's convention, the Colorado General Assembly approved the measure with only two dissenting votes.[25]

In preparation for passage of the bill, Crawford had recruited and begun to train twenty extra hunters, expecting to receive the state's money in the early summer. But month after month, for reasons he could not understand, the state auditing board held up release of the money, and he was forced to lay off his newly trained recruits. When the money finally arrived in November he was again ready. "With the exception of the two field foremen, [George] Trickel and [John W.] Crook, all hunters formerlly paid by the Goverment will be reimbursed by the State of Colorado as well as aproportionate share of the expenditures for poisons, ammunition etc," wrote Crawford at the end of that month.[26] The next month the state's appropriation paid for nine men—two based in the San Luis Valley, two around Montrose and Delta counties, one on the southern plains (where unspecified wolf depredations had recently been reported), one on the northern plains, two in the San Juan Mountains, and the last in and around Rocky Mountain National Park. "With the exception of one engaged in lion hunting with a pack of trained hounds, the balance were more or less engaged in the distribution of poison baits," reported Crawford.[27]

In Colorado and elsewhere, Biological Survey hunters worked semi-autonomously, responding to local complaints of depredations by all kinds of predators. Wolves, coyotes, bears, cougars, jaguars, and "wildcats" (a category that included bobcats and lynxes) were all at various times and places pulling down cattle, horses, sheep, or poultry. The survey's men set traps for a variety of animals, pursued cougars and bears with dogs, dug out coyote dens, and shot what they could. In Idaho one hunter specialized in tracking wolves by ski and, camouflaged in a white outfit, swooping down at them with rifle blazing.[28] But among the various tools available, poison was the quickest and easiest to use. The survey set up a plant in Albuquerque, New Mexico, to mass-produce strychnine tablets for insertion in one-inch cubes of hog or beef fat.

In the field, hunters perfected two ways to use the baits. The first was simply to drop them along likely wildlife routes such as trails and streams. The second they called "poison bait stations," which entailed leaving an unpoisoned side or quarter of an old horse or another animal slaughtered for the occasion, surrounded by the toxic baits. The idea was that cautious wolves or coyotes might hesitate to consume the large, obvious food source but would not resist the small cubes of fat at its periphery. This approach was elaborated through "pre-baiting," in which unpoisoned cubes of fat were left out for a period to habituate coyotes before poisoned baits made their appearance.

In addition to the full-time poisoners paid for by federal, state, county, and private sources, the survey gave strychnine to the Forest Service and the Park Service for their rangers to distribute. The Park Service (and probably the Forest Service as well) entered into a formal cooperative agreement with the survey and initiated poisoning in Glacier National Park in northwestern Montana during fiscal year 1918. In Colorado the Forest Service received 17,000 poison tabs in 1919. It is not known how many the Park Service planted in Rocky Mountain National Park, but the practice continued there until at least 1922.[29]

The sheer volume and promiscuous distribution of poison during this period duplicated the baiting that had begun on the Great Plains a few decades earlier; and the death toll, although proportionately lower reflecting the tremendous killing that had already taken place, was still heavy. Even Crawford had reservations about the Forest Service's use of the poison. "We, no doubt, killed a considerable number of fur-bearong [sic] animals in this high territory and no particular check was obtained on the number of predatory animals killed," he wrote to Washington in his 1920 annual report, adding, "I will not carry on co-operation with the Forest Service this fall, along the same lines."[30]

In Colorado the poisoning and other efforts were having their intended effect. Whereas in 1917 reports of depredating wolves arrived from across the state,[31] the following year Crawford reported that "[t]he loss by wolves has been somewhat lighter and with the exception of a few localities we receive no reports of their being any seen or or of any damage done by these pests."[32] The next year wolves seemed scarce, with the only depredations reported on the Uncompahgre Plateau and in the southern San Juans. Other predators were also rare, judging from the scarcity of reported depredations in 1919. The following year Crawford estimated 75 to 100 wolves were left under his jurisdiction.[33] (Subsequent killings revealed that the estimate was too high.)

Although wolves were successfully trapped by the survey from the outset of its systematic entry into predator killing, the first wolves known to have

Poisoned coyotes near the carcass that drew them in. The Bureau of Biological Survey scattered one-inch cubes of fat and meat, each impregnated with strychnine, for wary wolves and coyotes that would not feed directly from such carcasses. (Still Photographs, 1920–1980, Records of the Animal and Plant Health Inspection Service, Record Group 463, National Archives and Records Administration—Rocky Mountain Region)

been poisoned by the federal government in Colorado were three animals in the San Juan Mountains near Pagosa Springs in October 1920. (Of course, wolves killed previously by poison might not have been found.) These three were part of a pack of eight, but five were caught in traps. "The last wolf of the pack was poisoned and trailed nearly a mile by [survey employee] Mr. [Hegewa A.] Roberts before he found it," Crawford reported. "Evidence showed that this wolf tarried no time whatsoever around the poison station, but had visited the station practically on the run, taking one bait in so doing. It then continued on its journey until finally taken down with a fit of convulsions eventually resulting in its death." He added: "Since this pack has been taken, there are rumors of one lone wolf still remaining in this locality. It is probable that it is a young wolf pup. Steps have been taken to substantiate these rumors and if found true, measures will be taken for the capture of this remaining wolf."[34]

Among the miscellaneous animals killed during this period were wolverines (although there are no records of the manner of their death). One died in 1919 at the head of the Los Pinos River in today's Weminuche Wilderness in the San Juans. The previous year a family of wolverines had been killed in northwestern Colorado's Moffat County between the towns of Meeker and

The Biological Survey's first predatory animal inspector for the Colorado district, Logan B. Crawford, pictured here cooking over a campfire, had qualms about his agency's inadvertent poisoning of fur-bearing animals in 1920. But that same year he pushed for the extermination of bears despite the growing movement for bruin conservation and the survey's official stance of protecting non-stock-killing bears. (Courtesy, Tread of Pioneers Museum, Steamboat Springs, CO)

Craig,[35] but the San Juans were probably near the southern extent of the range of this rare scavenger and predator. (Today, nobody can be sure whether any wolverines survive in Colorado.[36])

The crashing predator populations allowed sheep ranchers a luxury already enjoyed by cattle ranchers. "It is now possible to allow sheep to go unattended for days and not have a single sheep lost by predatory animals in the Western Slope unit," wrote Crawford in his fiscal year 1919 annual report. He continued, "This is in itself very gratifying to sheepmen, who formerly were obliged to keep a vigilant watch on flocks."[37]

Satisfied members of the Park County Wool Growers Association, one of the converts to funding the survey, estimated that so many coyotes were poisoned that only a third of their carcasses were retrieved.[38] Crawford reported that "[f]or long periods of time after poisoning operations have been stopped in a poison district, we hear of numbers of coyotes being found by interested parties."[39]

But local cattlemen in Delta County were losing their dogs to the poison. Other people complained that poison (possibly intended for prairie dogs) was killing grouse and sage hens. Before long, residents (whom Crawford termed "a certain faction of the natives") were circulating a petition to evict the survey from the region. Crawford tracked down some of the signatories, and, according to his account, "[w]hen the situation was explained to them in its true light," the misguided individuals "promised their cooperation in the future."[40]

Wolves Killed by the Biological Survey in Colorado Under Logan B. Crawford's Supervision

Fiscal Year	Number of Wolves Killed
1916	49
1917	18
1918	11
1919	9
1920	22

Sources: "Number and Species of Animals Taken and Cost Per Month, FY 1916–1917," USDA-APHIS Wildlife Services; "History of Predator and Rodent Control Colorado District," National Archives, Washington, DC, 2.

Other Biological Survey districts also began receiving new infusions of private and public money around the same period as Colorado and similarly spent most of it on poisoning. Counties and stock associations throughout the West funded local poisoning campaigns. State legislators carved out funds from general revenues, often sending the money through game departments but sometimes via odder conduits. In New Mexico the College of Education and Mechanical Arts became (and remains) the funding vehicle. In both Arizona and New Mexico, in 1918 each state's Council of Defense, a war-time institution, chipped in to the survey's killing program coffers—presumably on the basis of guarding the nation's food supply.[41]

Beyond allowing it to put greater numbers of men in the field, the advent of multiple sources of funding heralded important institutional strengths for the survey. From this point on, the agency garnered increasing shares of its extermination campaign funding from various other entities—both private and public. Such arrangements significantly augmented the survey's budget. Even more important for the long term, they tightened professional relationships among the federal agency, its private constituents, and local, state, and other federal agencies. Those relationships, and the sense of investment felt by so many locally powerful people who helped fund the survey, eventually proved crucial when the agency was under attack by budget-cutters.

Although the idea of a direct cash infusion from ranchers had been new to Crawford in 1916, survey officials were likely receiving similar suggestions from many sources. The era seemed conducive to innovative cooperative funding agreements between agricultural interests and government. Most of the time the money went from government to the private sector. That same year, for instance, Congress passed and President Woodrow Wilson signed a bill subsidizing a rural credit system of low-interest loans.[42] And in 1914, the year before Congress began appropriating money for a systematic killing campaign, it voted into existence the Cooperative Extension System run by the Federal Extension Service, a sister agency to the survey within the Department of Agriculture.

The Extension Service fielded county agents to serve as liaisons among the department, federally funded state colleges of agriculture, and farmers and ranchers. The idea was that modern farming technologies developed in the colleges with federal assistance would be disseminated to farmers in the field. But in practice, within a few years the agents were becoming minions of a rapidly growing private organization consisting of local "farm bureaus" (which in 1919 confederated into the tax-exempt American Farm Bureau Federation). With the support of the Farm Bureau, county agents provided the survey with manpower for its rodent-poisoning campaigns.[43] (Whereas trapping and poisoning predators was sufficiently tricky to require specially trained hunters, killing the much less wary rodents was a far more tedious matter of laying out poisoned grain over large areas.) Thus, while Crawford was being introduced to the idea of accepting private funds for the survey's work, the agency was on the verge of joining forces with a ballooning private-public financial network. And in joining together to help fund the survey, other players in this network found themselves working together on yet another front—thus strengthening the network further.

The survey's federal allocations increased dramatically as funds poured in from other sources. Survey officials were quick to trumpet the cooperative system, and members of Congress recognized the support this represented back home. The survey also found a new reason, aside from livestock and game protection, to maintain its killing program: rabies.

Lieutenant Colonel Dodge had recounted in his 1877 book *The Plains of the Great West* a "perfectly authenticated" instance of a rabid wolf that several years earlier had entered an army base in Kansas, attacking three people before being shot. One person died of the disease a month later.[44] Rabies had also been reported in Routt County, Colorado, in 1898.[45] In 1916 the disease was spreading throughout the Pacific Northwest and Nevada. But it had a tendency to pop up unexpectedly anywhere.

In early April 1916, with deep snow still piled on the nearby San Juan Mountains, sheepherder Ma Maguil Revera was herding Lee Parr's sheep on the desert range of the Southern Ute Indian Reservation along Colorado's border with New Mexico. (Sheep in 1916 were still herded for their own protection.) Large tracts of the reservation were (and still are) leased to white ranchers, who, along with their cohorts throughout the West, found willing shepherds among the immigrants from the Basque region of Spain. Revera was probably a Basque. To his astonishment, a wolf ran into the flock and quickly killed three sheep, paying him no heed. According to Crawford, who read Parr's account, the herder, "unarmed with the exception of a large pocket knife," picked up a billet of wood and attempted to chase the animal away as it attacked a fourth sheep. But "the wolf was evidently mad" and instead of fleeing turned on Revera, sank his teeth into the hapless man's arm, and hung on. "Revera[,] unable to disengage the brute, managed to get the knife out of his rear pocket and opened it with his teeth. He sawed the animals [*sic*] throat until he killed it." But infected with the deadly hydrophobia, Revera died three months later.[46] Two months before he was bitten, Congress allocated the survey an extra $75,000 in a special "deficiencies appropriations" law to combat rabies West-wide by killing "wolves, coyotes, and other predatory wild animals" (even though the act acknowledged the disease was being transmitted to wildlife by "stock and other domestic animals," not the other way around). The month after the shepherd died, through the regular annual appropriations cycle Congress gave the survey $125,000 more for that purpose, over and beyond its regularly allocated $125,000 to kill the predators for livestock protection. But it appears that the story of Revera's unhappy fate was never mentioned during these funding requests.[47]

These sums accounted for much of the survey's expenditures during this period. Whereas in fiscal year 1914, before its first appropriation for systematic predator destruction, the agency's entire budget was $170,990, by fiscal year 1916 killing predators for livestock protection and rabies alone accounted for $200,000. By 1917 predator killing was funded in the amount of $250,000.[48]

From the survey's perspective, the only limitation on its ability to enter into cooperative agreements was a chronic shortage of manpower. Initially, skilled hunters were scarce as a result of mobilization for the Great War. "Owing to the scarcity of labor it is almost impossible to find men to carry on the work," complained Crawford in an April 1918 report to Washington. "Men with knowledge of the work are very scarce and it seems that it is up to the Inspector to take on green men and train them or do without help. This runs up the cost of taking predatory animals considerably but seems to be the only solution of the problem at present."[49]

The global influenza pandemic spreading at the same time as the war also contributed to the survey's labor woes. The disease killed thousands of people in Colorado—one of the four hardest-hit states in the union—and among other impacts forced sheep ranchers to tend to their own flocks when their hired herders became infected or had to care for stricken family members. As a result, the ranchers could not work closely with the survey in coordinating the extermination campaign. Realistic fear of contagion, at its worst in the fall of 1918, even kept the healthy from communicating effectively. Crawford noted that this concern "prevented public meetings so necessary for the arranging of definite plans of action in the disbursing of funds for the work."[50]

On the plains, a quarantine to contain the disease briefly delayed the promotion of future survey chief Ira N. Gabrielson, who was taking a vacation from poisoning jackrabbits in South Dakota to visit family in Iowa. When he returned to work he learned of his assignment to supervise the rodent extermination campaign in Oregon.[51] In Arizona the flu almost killed Crawford's colleague, Predatory Animal Inspector Mark E. Musgrave.[52]

After the war and the passing of the epidemic, the survey found it hard to retain people for an entirely different reason. The booming post-war economy of 1919[53] caused fur prices to rise, which in turn attracted skilled trappers to the private sector, according to one of Crawford's reports:

> Trouble in securing suitable men in the past year has been very prominent. It was almost impossible to get men with any ability in hunting and trapping predatory animals, caused mainly by the high prices secured for furs. For instance, men that were real good trappers refused to work for the Survey and went out independent and trapped through the good fur months and made more money in three months than they could have received from the Survey in a year.[54]

Crawford encouraged the development of private trappers, as one of his reports from 1919 indicates:

> The prevelant high price of furs has had an active tendency to start a great number of individual trappers working about the state, and the State Game & Fish Commissioners office has been the recipient of hundreds of applications for trappers permits from all corners of the State this season, which will help materially in cutting down the number of pests. It has been noted however, that as a general rule the average farmer boy or beginner in the trapping game, has knowledge of but one method of setting traps. He depends entirely on some old carcass as a drawing card for his sets, which in most cases fail to help him capture over one or two animals then are shunned by these wiley creatures. After a few unsuccessful visits to his sets, the amateur trapper pulls up his traps and hangs them up in the wood shed. We have many calls for instructions in methods used by the Survey in taking p [sic] predatory animals and endeavor to instruct applicants for enlightenment on subject. Assistant Reid has given personal instruction to many would-be trappers in the eastern section of the state where coyotes prevail in large numbers. A large field is open for this form of promoting the work along this line, and would materially assist not only in decreasing the number of predatory animals, but also in financing many struggling homesteader through the hard winter months.[55]

Presumably, Crawford had some interest in increasing the future pool of potential survey employees; the agency tutoring a farm boy now might hire him after he had developed further skills. But Crawford's openness to the private sector may have led him to be too tolerant of the survey's old ideological nemesis, the bounty system.

Although the survey's success can be marked by the growth in the number of entities contributing money to it, the livestock industry did not abandon bounties entirely. In the Middle Park region, in 1918 survey hunter Bill Caywood killed four wolves, but private bounty hunters digging up a den killed several others, collecting a hefty local $175 reward per wolf. Crawford regarded these efforts as helpful. "This past season has practically cleaned up the wolves there," he noted.[56]

In far northwestern Colorado private individuals cleaned up as well. In the Powder Wash area near the Wyoming border, one rancher killed two adult wolves and a litter of seven pups. Another rancher caught a large female wolf on Blue Mountain, south of Dinosaur National Monument, and seven other wolves were killed on Douglas and Blue mountains.[57] A private individual, using specially trained dogs, chased down and killed one of three wolves in a pack still roaming the southeastern plains.

The survey had criticized bounties as early as 1896 and had strongly reiterated those criticisms in Vernon Bailey's publications in the first decade of the new century.[58] The 1915 mandate and appropriation to destroy wolves and other animals was largely the fruit of the seeds of doubt planted then. Yet during Crawford's tenure, contrary to survey policy, the state game and fish commissioner ruled that a $25 lion bounty offered by *The Denver Post* was payable to a hunter supervised by the survey but officially listed as a Colorado state cooperative hunter—presumably on the basis that his salary was paid by the state and it did not oppose bounties. It is unclear how strongly, if at all, Crawford contested the award.[59]

If Crawford could be faulted for inadequate jealousy over the inroad of bounties into the survey's niche, in another arena he overreached in trying to drum up business for the survey. In January 1920, at the annual convention of the Colorado Stockgrowers Association, he encouraged the assembly to pass a resolution urging his agency to target bears for extinction, along with wolves and other carnivores. "I have letters from the Forest Department and renters [ranchers holding grazing permits] in different forests I think of at least two-thirds of the forests in Colorado," he exclaimed, "asking in the last year for help to exterminate the bear, stating that they were running the stock off the range and killing the stock."[60]

Although many ranchers agreed, state representative Rockwell, who had championed the survey in the previous year's appropriation request, did not: "There are not a great many of them [bears], and I question whether they do very much damage, and there is a good deal of sport in our country in getting them."[61]

Crawford not only crossed a powerful member of the survey's constituency at the meeting, but he also misrepresented the Forest Service's position. Three years previously, in 1917, the Forest Service had urged Colorado's governor to protect bears from extermination. "Although in the past bears have been considered as predatory animals, it appears that they are becoming scarce enough to be classed as game animals and should be protected during the season of the year when their hides and meat are worthless," district forester Smith Riley had written in a letter that was copied to the Biological Survey. Riley continued: "The numerous reports received from Forest officers seem to establish this animal as a game type instead of [a] predatory animal. A few exceptions to this have been noted in the past, but the general observations seem to show that the bear found in this State are, as a whole, scavengers rather than stock-killers."[62]

In suggesting the targeting of bears, Crawford was swimming against the currents of popular opinion, not just the Forest Service's institutional point of

"There was an old bear that was fat and I know she had to be eating beef to be in that shape this time of year so I killed her," according to a survey hunter in the Gila National Forest during spring 1925. Livestock grazing reduced food sources for bears, inducing them to scavenge on or kill domestic animals. New Mexico's last grizzly was killed in the Gila in 1931. (Denver Public Library, Western History Department, J. Stokley Ligon files)

view. In 1909 William H. Wright, a bruin-hunting aficionado who had picked up the camera and put down his gun, published *The Grizzly Bear,* a memoir of his hunting and photography experiences. Dedicated "with the respect, admiration, and affection of the author to the noblest wild animal of North America, the grizzly bear," Wright encouraged the conservation of his disappearing subject. A decade later, in 1919, Enos Mills published *The Grizzly,* a slender book urging the protection of an animal he described—based on his own and associates' encounters—as intelligent, fascinating, and gentle. Across the West the conservation of bears was gaining the support of both hunters and the growing number of national park visitors—a constituency impossible to ignore. In 1920 the survey fired Ben V. Lilly from its rolls in New Mexico, although he was perhaps the most successful lion killer in the West in his day, because he was killing too many bears.[63] By 1922 the survey had officially announced its policy to protect non-stock-killing bears.[64]

On July 1, 1921, the first day of a new fiscal year, Crawford was replaced by his young lieutenant Stanley P. Young, who had arrived in the state from Arizona in December of the previous year. Although Crawford's resignation from the survey was effective on August 31, there seemed nothing left for him to do after Young took over.[65]

Crawford's job performance had not been bad. The agency's chief in Washington had previously noted his skill as a hunter and trapper, particularly of mountain lions. He had succeeded in securing the cooperation of a number of livestock associations and individual ranchers.[66] Nevertheless, his relationships could have been better. "I believe it is the general feeling among the stock interests and sportsmen of Colorado," Crawford wrote in one report, "that they are willing to give the Survey their moral support but do not feel very strong on the financial support in the way of protection of live stock and game."[67]

As Crawford's assistant, then as a predatory animal inspector, and finally as Albert K. Fisher's replacement as head of the Division of Economic Investigations, Young would set a standard for effective organization and cooperation and would display a canny knack for never openly contravening the prevailing currents. These attributes would prove, in the words of biologist David E. Brown, "bad medicine" for the remaining wolves in Colorado, and later throughout the United States, that were savvy enough not to have already eaten poison or stumbled into traps.[68]

Wide Awake and Anxious

T he grasslands of southeastern Colorado are sculpted with surprisingly precipitous canyons that start as barely perceptible vales, then drop into what seem to be ad hoc arroyos, before culminating in a landscape that could almost be mistaken for the canyonlands of southern Utah.

One late spring day in the early 1920s, a herd of pronghorn antelope was feeding on a hillside in Butler Pasture, on a limestone-caprock formation southeast of Pueblo. Suddenly, the antelope looked up and faced two wolves approaching them in a none-too-subtle stalk. The wolves, seeing that they had been discovered, sprawled out on their bellies, watching the prey and assessing the situation.

Although pronghorn antelope were far more difficult to catch than the cattle the wolves encountered almost constantly, the pair of wolves may have sensed the proprietary interest the strange and baleful two-legged species attached to their slow and dopey kine. The wolves had probably witnessed countless kin's demise from poison or traps after making a meal of cattle. It is even likely that they were the two untouched packmates of the wolf run down with hounds in those parts in 1919 and had heard, as they made their escape, the decisive shot that ended the barks, snarls, and yips of their companion's last battle.

Therefore antelope, although much rarer, vastly more alert, and swifter than any domestic animal, seemed safer fare and worth the trouble. In some manner ineffable to humans, the two wolves plotted a strategy for their hunt. Decision reached, the bitch stood up and trotted slowly back in the direction from which they had come. Gradually, however, she veered to swing upslope toward the herd. Moving, she fixed the antelope's attention on herself. They watched her carefully, turning slowly to follow her progress with their eyes.

With their attention distracted, the male wolf sprang up suddenly, running a low, swift streak not at the antelope but for an arroyo whose course began almost exactly at the flank of the herd. Once under the cover of the draw, he could approach the prey unseen. Although he could never outrun a pronghorn in an open race, the element of surprise, coupled with a pincer movement from his mate on the other side of the herd, might yield them both a meal.

But as he neared the arroyo, the dirt under his chest suddenly exploded with a slug, and he heard the explosion of a rifle emanating from the gorge for which he was aiming. Instantly he veered and, with a fear more powerful than any hunger, redoubled his speed to make his escape.

Stanley P. Young stood up, disappointed, and surveyed a landscape bereft of wolves and antelope, with the dust still settling from their retreat. The shot had been close. It was exceedingly rare to surprise a wolf, and had he aimed a few inches higher it would have been another episode in his growing repertoire of professional accomplishments.

Then he started marveling at what he had seen, a demonstration of wolf cunning equal to any he had witnessed. Had he only evinced the same strategic patience possessed by those wolves, he chided himself, had he waited just another few seconds for the male to get closer, Young would have gotten his prey.[1]

Young's near-miss occurred midway in his career rise from hired trapper for the Biological Survey to its highest official in charge of predator and rodent extermination and the unofficial power broker for the entire agency. As he matured, his actions increasingly took their cue from the resourcefulness and sagacity evinced by that hunting pair of wolves.

Having grown up learning wilderness skills and absorbing through a cultural and familial osmosis the outlook of pioneers, Young parlayed his background first into a field job with the survey and eventually into positions from which he could exploit the nation's nostalgia for its lost frontier youth. Through most of the 1920s Young's capacity to organize and inspire reduced the number of Colorado's endangered wolves—which constituted, notwithstanding their precarious status, a potentially recoverable population—to a handful of lone individuals.

Then in 1934, nineteen years after the Biological Survey had started building a predator- and rodent-killing program, Young's political acumen on the national stage would rescue the agency from wildlife advocates of the period and ensure that Franklin D. Roosevelt's administration would not pull the plug on its budget. As a direct result, the remaining wolves in all the contiguous western states—many of whom inhabited the San Juan Mountains along the Colorado–New Mexico border—lost their last opportunity for respite from federal persecution.

Since the destruction of wildlife in the nineteenth century had as much to do with the internal landscape of the American psyche as with any economic rationale, perhaps it is axiomatic that the era inevitably produced individuals such as Albert K. Fisher to institutionalize that destruction and the perfect person, Stanley P. Young, to ensure the institution's perpetuation. Had the survey been required to make do solely with the likes of Logan B. Crawford, it might have gone out of existence as a killing machine in 1934.

But on October 30, 1889, Stanley Paul Young was born in an adjunct room to his father's stately business office in a Victorian mansion on the outskirts of Astoria, Oregon. There Stanley entered the world amid diamond-shaped terracotta tiling on the floor, large framed pictures on the walls, and bright potted flowers in the bay window overlooking a driveway. Stanley would have noted—had he the perspicuity of his mature years—emanating from the office next door the somber beat of the old-fashioned clock his father had had shipped from his boyhood home of Lomma, Sweden. Stanley's mother, Christine, cheered the family house with exotic potted flowers, whereas Stanley's father, Benjamin, treasured his roots, even as he built a business empire in a new land.[2]

The next to last of eight children, Stanley was given his middle name to honor the Apostle Paul.[3] Perhaps the apostle reminded Benjamin of his youth spent wandering a pelagic wilderness. Benjamin apparently had set to sea relatively young, occasionally returning to visit the girl he would later marry and likely also to see his family. Finally, in the late 1860s or early 1870s, he ended up with a proverbial sweet job, one worth staying at for a number of years, at the Sprenkels sugar-refining factory in San Francisco.[4]

Around the same time (1868), another peripatetic native of northern Europe arrived in San Francisco and quickly left for his promised land in the Sierra Nevada. But Scottish-born John Muir, although roughly Benjamin's age, had already suffered his father's Calvinist-tinted imperial dreams in the harsh soil of a Wisconsin farm and would have nothing of riches scraped from a reluctant earth.[5]

Unlike Muir, Benjamin Young was a child of his expansionist era. Benjamin's brother Andrew moved to Astoria, on the Oregon coast, sending word to his brother about the prolific fish swimming up the Columbia River and the industry based on the fish. So in 1874, with his wife and three-month-old daughter in tow, Benjamin left California and moved to Astoria.

By the time Stanley was born, the mission in the wilderness had prospered. The Young mansion was built upon the fruitful canning of millions of would-be spawning Columbia salmon. Benjamin owned one of Astoria's five canneries and one in British Columbia as well. The vision of the promised land surrounding the family must have seemed a happy balance between civilized abundance and sustained natural bounties.

Whereas the mouth of the great Columbia served as a gateway for tides of salmon making their way up to the Rocky Mountains and British Columbia, Astoria had proved a gateway for empires in fur trapping, fishing, and logging. Established in 1811 as a fur-trading post by shipborne employees of John Jacob Astor of New York, the nation's wealthiest fur merchant, the little settlement was sold a year later (without Astor's knowledge) to a British-owned fur company to avoid a hostile takeover by a scavenging British sloop-of-war, the H.M.S. *Raccoon,* during the War of 1812. But regardless of which distant nation claimed it, Astoria prospered because of the surrounding wilderness and the native people who traded the skins of wild animals for industrial goods.

After a brief period of colonial neglect, in the early 1840s overland settlers arrived at Astoria, and in 1847 the first postmaster west of the Rockies was appointed there, recognition that a real community had supplanted a mere trading post. White settlement was undoubtedly eased by a plague that killed hundreds of the native Clatsop and Chinook people during the 1830s. In 1874, when the Young clan arrived, Astoria was a booming town of around 2,500 people, complete with a newspaper, the *Daily Morning Astorian.* By the time Stanley was born, the town had telephones, a telegraph, electric streetlights, established tourist attractions for visitors, the "finest public school building" north of San Francisco, and community pride in the equal treatment and pay women received as teachers alongside men in the three schools. But the town also hosted racial tensions between the dominant whites and a large minority of Chinese immigrants (many employed in the canneries); and news about a thriving nightlife of gambling, booze, prostitution, and muggings filled the *Astorian's* pages.

The three-quarters-of-an-acre Young estate was removed from the tawdry side of town, however, and was also distant from the city's electric lights. The children filled, cleaned, and trimmed the wicks of the coal oil lamps that lit the home. Benjamin traveled occasionally to British Columbia or worked in his office lined with books of adventurous sea tales and Cooper and Dickens novels. Stanley's mother tended roses in the garden. Stanley was free to explore the surrounding landscape upon which the community—and his family's wealth—was founded.[6]

In the 1890s, as noted, President Benjamin Harrison was establishing the nation's first forest reserves, later called national forests. These designations implicitly acknowledged limits to the ability of American lands to support individual enterprises. But in Astoria, at the end of the American continent and the beginning of the vast wilderness of the Pacific Ocean, there were no limits for a boy like Stanley. In addition to standard childhood pursuits such as playing marbles and walking on stilts, Stanley fished and swam in the ocean and streams, live-trapped chipmunks, hunted ducks, and picked berries.

The boy who later made his mark overseeing a department of professional government predator killers had a rocky start with the government's inscriptions on the local topography. One night, while walking along a pier to his favorite crawfish creek, he espied a light and assumed it was the lantern of a competing crawfisher. But the light turned out to be a government marker far out in the harbor, as Stanley found out when he fell fourteen feet off the pier onto rocks below. "Torch went one way, bucket went another, and I didn't get a scratch," he recalled five decades later.[7]

Although government buoys proved little danger, a private sawmill was a different matter. Running from another child during a game of tag, Stanley leaped into the chute of a sawmill. He hit his head, was knocked unconscious, and then was moved 120 feet by cable up a chute toward the blade that transformed coastal Douglas firs into boards for construction. Just before he would have hit the blade, someone grabbed him off the chute. Foreshadowing his adult deftness at linking the prosaic business of killing to civilization's finer aspirations, Stanley recalled his brush with death in unusual terms. While unconscious, he dreamed of a "beautiful soft twilight of roses" and of "his mother asking him for just one more bucket of manure" to nurture those flowers.[8] But although that frightening experience with frontier technology sent him into a fantasy of domestic security, Stanley retained a fascination and admiration for the wild. Meriwether Lewis and William Clark, the adventurous pair who made the trip from St. Louis to the mouth of the Columbia in 1805, became Stanley's lasting icons for the place of his childhood.[9]

Young attended the University of Oregon at Eugene for four years, primarily studying geology. In June 1911, with no degree, he left school and got a job with the Dixie Meadows Mining Company in eastern Oregon.[10] In August 1911 he likely returned to Astoria to visit family and friends during his hometown's greatest week of glory: the centennial celebration. On the second day of the elaborately planned week, close to 10,000 people visited the site of a giant replica of the original Fort Astoria. The event marked the stages of Astoria's history through the popular lens of nineteenth- and early-twentieth-century economic boosters, who confidently asserted that the progress of civilization followed clearly delineated steps from savagery to pastoralism to settled farming and, finally, to urban culture.[11] Visiting members of the Yakima and Nez Perce tribes put on a war dance for the visitors, followed by appearances by the governor of Oregon and a personal representative of President William Howard Taft, the latter of whom expressed the president's "hearty congratulations on the wonderful prosperity that has marked [Astoria's] development."[12] Young, emerging from an academic environment that recorded action according to a geological timeline, might have felt the tug—like a coastal tide heading to sea—of a different mind-set: history as reflected in heroic men's marks on the natural landscape and on national culture.

In September 1911 Young quit the gold mines of eastern Oregon and began wandering. For the next three years he prospected for mica deposits in the Canadian Rockies and took on other jobs on the coast of British Columbia and elsewhere in the Pacific Northwest—occupations he later obliquely referred to as "geological and biological work" and "work in the contracting business" (meaning, presumably, mining jobs and possibly market hunting for mining or logging camps).

In September 1914 Young enrolled in school again, this time at the University of Michigan at Ann Arbor where he acquired a B.S. in geology. He took graduate courses and held an assistantship, but in August 1915 he left the school. (As he became increasingly prominent in later decades, Young fuzzed over his academic history, leading reporters and others to assume he had received his B.S. in Oregon and an M.S. in Michigan and further suggesting that his advanced degree was in biology.[13])

Leaving Michigan in 1915, Young took a train to visit his older brother Arthur, who had a ranch on Turkey Creek in the Canelo Hills of southeastern Arizona. He planned to continue on to the Panama-Pacific Exposition in San Francisco, an affair that celebrated the city's comeback from the devastating 1906 earthquake, as well as the newly dug Panama Canal's opening to commerce. The themes were tinged with imperial grandeur, the crowds were enormous, and the event no doubt glittered in the minds of many a young person.[14]

After the exposition he apparently intended to return to school. Much later, reminiscing on this period, he implied that he had a teaching career waiting for him at a California university, neglecting to mention that he had only one undergraduate degree after five and a half years in two institutions of higher learning. In any event, he stayed in Arizona, never even making it to San Francisco.

In February 1917 (a year and a half after arriving in Arizona) he secured a job as a surveyor for the Coronado National Forest (a position that lasted only two months and that Young, in his later life, invariably implied he assumed shortly after arriving in Arizona and kept for two years until he was hired by the survey). A federal memo recommending his employment that February records that Young "for the past several years has been engaged in mining in Arizona" and "is not engaged in any other line of work."[15] A memo from three and a half years later—when he was working for the survey—approving his transfer and promotion to Colorado, says Young "[h]as had considerable training and experience in this line of work due to his employment as a hunter for a greater part of the time since the fall of 1916."[16]

A biographical article on Young in the Bisbee (Arizona) Daily Review from July 1, 1958—more than four decades later and riddled with errors in chronology—states that after his hiring by the Biological Survey in October 1917 (the correct date) Young "purchased a small ranch near his brother, raised a little stock and did a bit of dry-land farming in his spare time." But given his rapid rise within the survey, he probably had little spare time, and it seems more likely that he purchased the ranch earlier.

Federal forms Young filled out when he began working for the Forest Service and three years later when he was with the survey note that on March 28, 1916, he married Helen Rodgers, the daughter of local Forest Service ranger

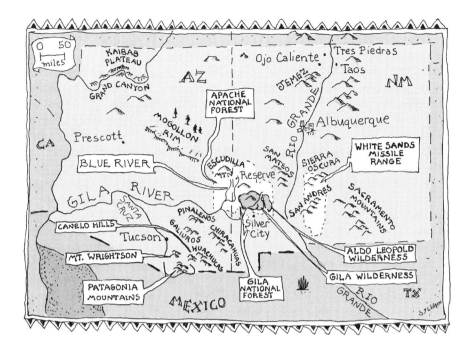

Robert A. Rodgers.[17] But except in these personnel documents, Young never again, so far as can be determined, left a record of the marriage.[18]

For a man who had spent all but a year and a half of his life in the Pacific Northwest, southeastern Arizona may have seemed initially like another planet. Arriving in August 1915, the afternoon monsoon rains would have seemed more drenching and episodic than the gentle and near-constant precipitation of the coast. In the cloudless mornings he would have marveled at the pellucid air and the infinite shades of red, brown, yellow, and green in the distant hills. He would have learned quickly in rides to the desert below not to touch the strange and prickly vegetation. But in the highest reaches of the nearby mountains he would have discovered towering Douglas firs with soft mosses and curlicued ferns at their feet, reminiscent of his home forests.

If Young subscribed to the then-popular boosters' view of history, southeastern Arizona in the teen years of the twentieth century may have seemed societally equivalent to the Oregon of his boyhood. Unlike the native peoples of his coastal homeland, the Apaches of the Southwest had not been considerate enough to succumb to disease and then quietly adapt to white settlement. Rather, for decades leading up to 1886, warriors of that loosely knit nation defended their mountain homelands in a series of armed raids that considerably slowed economic development in the hinterlands. Ranchers thirty years later could still imagine themselves a short step away from savagery, at the cutting edge of an advancing and still tenuous civilization.

Although civilization's inevitable mastery of the wilderness may have seemed inchoate and tenuous from the Young ranch house at the edge of Turkey Creek, ironically, in 1915 the natural ecology of the Canelo Hills had been subject to European influences far longer than that of coastal Oregon. Whereas the accelerating clear-cuts on Oregon's coast and the urbanity of turn-of-the-century Astoria may have struck Stanley as defining marks of long-standing civilization, in fact the livestock grazing in the arid Southwest effected an even greater transformation of the landscape. And Turkey Creek itself offered an excellent perspective on the changes.

The Canelo Hills consist of an undulating oak savanna intermediate in elevation between the forested Huachuca Mountains on the east and desert to the north and west. In this dry region the Canelo Hills are more lush than nearby mountain ranges—a cattlemen's paradise they must have seemed at first, laced with some of the most extensive natural wetlands, termed *cienegas*, in the Southwest. These springs, seeping down hillsides, suffuse swampy acres in which evolved a unique orchid (the Canelo Hills ladies' tress), an endemic amphibian (the Sonoran tiger salamander), and a floating plant in the parsley family (the Huachuca water umbel). The springs feed the San Pedro and Santa Cruz rivers in the desert below, lined with cottonwoods, sycamores, alders, and willows. These rivers, in turn, supported songbirds such as the southwestern willow flycatcher and the yellow-billed cuckoo.

Surrounding the *cienegas* of the Canelo Hills were forests of mesquite trees—shelter from the incessant sun. Beyond the forests rolled a seemingly limitless expanse of knee-high bunchgrasses, maintained by natural or Indian-ignited fires. Where fires failed to burn, the grasses were spotted with pinyon pine, juniper, and oak trees, along with manzanita and mountain mahogany bushes.

In the 1690s Father Eusebio Francisco Kino, an Italian-born missionary, led expeditions north from Mexico to convert lost souls and re-organize Indian society around Jesuit missions. Although Kino's social imprint proved ephemeral, his biological imprint was not: he left behind cattle that quickly became feral. For almost 200 years those cattle thrived on the lush vegetation of the *cienegas*, streams, and rivers of southeastern Arizona, although they were undoubtedly culled by predators.

In the mid- to late-nineteenth century, miners and ranchers arrived. While the miners clear-cut the mesquite forests to provide fuel for copper smelters, the ranchers greatly increased the stock of cattle on the open range. Even when Apaches periodically drove the ranchers out, their stock remained, peaking in the mid- to late-1880s when the last warring Apaches finally surrendered and were shipped off to Florida as prisoners of war. But by that time the natural system had been overwhelmed with too many non-native animals. In 1885 the rains barely came (not an unusual climatic event for the region), and the grasses failed to spring up from the trampled and compacted soil. For three years drought ensued, and half a million cattle starved throughout southeastern Arizona. By the time the summer monsoons returned in 1888, the *cienegas* had been stripped of vegetation and pounded into dust. Rather than percolate slowly into the groundwater, the rains slid down the hillsides, carving deep arroyos and taking the topsoil downstream with them. Many springs ceased to flow that year, and most of the vast *cienegas* have yet to come back, having reverted from life-giving wetlands to weedy and dry gullies. Throughout this period, when populations of all riparian-dependent species declined dramatically with the disappearance of the willows and cottonwoods and the waters themselves, the abundant cattle carcasses probably provided plentiful food for the diminutive Mexican gray wolves of the desert Southwest and northern Mexico.[19]

As a Forest Service surveyor between February and April 1917, Young may have taken on tasks similar to those performed by another Forest Service employee in the region eight years earlier. In 1909, the same year he shot a wolf, Aldo Leopold was engaged in the search for and tabulation of merchantable timber, and in so doing he started to note declining range conditions and severe erosion in the Apache National Forest a few dozen miles northeast of the Coronado National Forest. At the time of Young's induction into Forest Service employment, Leopold still regarded predators as "varmints," although he was also beginning to understand the role of cattle in destroying hydrological cycles. Perhaps the later split in attitude toward predators between the two scholarly naturalists stemmed in part from Leopold's ongoing employment with the Forest Service, from which he could explore in more depth the issue of "Pioneers and Gullies" (the title of one of his essays) in the southwestern landscape.[20] The Forest Service, although highly attentive to the interests of the livestock industry, was primarily interested in silviculture. Young, in contrast, went on to work for an agency whose basic clientele—the livestock industry—did not encourage such free-ranging investigations.

Unlike Leopold, Young appeared oblivious to the recent history of his adopted home. His later reflections in an essay entitled "Natural History as Learned in the Canelo Hills of Arizona" omitted any discussion of how the introducton of livestock had shaped the landscape. Once again John Muir, fifty-one years Young's senior, serves as an idiosyncratic benchmark to more conventional frontiersmen. Like Young, Muir had studied geology in college, and, also like Young, he was a keen observer of the natural world and a skilled woodsman. But whereas the nature-worshipping Muir had put his academic background to work explaining to the world the mystery of thousands of years of glacial influence on natural vegetation in the Sierra Nevadas,[21] Young entirely missed the short-term and ongoing biological events—of a geological magnitude—and centered on vulnerable water-courses such as Turkey Creek that were triggered by the introduction of livestock to the region.

On August 16, 1917, Mark E. Musgrave, the predatory animal inspector for the Biological Survey's Arizona–New Mexico district, visited the Forest Service office in Tucson to discuss his agency's need for a trapper in the Huachuca region, which encompassed the Canelo Hills. Heretofore, most of the predator-killing effort in the Southwest had been focused in New Mexico, to good effect. But Arizona had been relatively neglected.

Musgrave could only pay a trapper seventy-five dollars per month and, aside from traps, would not provide equipment. A new employee would have to bring his own horse to the job. But Musgrave had high standards nonetheless. He wanted to hire not only a skilled outdoorsman as a trapper but someone sufficiently educated to be able to fill out reports and paperwork properly. Beyond competence, Musgrave wanted employees who would be proud to work for the bureau and whose enthusiastic spirit would permeate each carefully placed trap as well as every interaction with the public. Young's former boss and current father-in-law, Coronado forest ranger Robert A. Rodgers, stationed in Tucson at the time, wrote to Young shortly after the meeting: "It seems that they do not want the old style trapper but young men wide awake and anxious to earn the money and ones that would be really interested in the work."[22]

Rodgers immediately suggested his son-in-law, Stanley P. Young—interested in "God's out-doors," college degreed, and just shy of his twenty-eighth birthday—for the position. Musgrave was intrigued. Could Young be persuaded to sign on with the Biological Survey? Although he was looking for a full-time trapper, he would be glad to hire Young part-time to allow him time to work on his brother's ranch. Musgrave prevailed upon Rodgers to ask Young to apply.[23]

The job attracted Young like "a worm to a hungry trout," and, with his brother's encouragement, he applied. Six months after the end of his Forest Service job, he was hired by the Bureau of Biological Survey as one of a handful of predatory animal hunters in Arizona.

Right after his employment began, Young set to work trying to kill a pair of wolves whose territory ranged from Mexico into the Canelo Hills. It appears that one of his first assignments as a survey hunter directly benefited both him and his brother.

The wolf pair had been killing newborn calves, and their tracks were distinguishable by the male's missing middle toe on his right front foot—almost certainly lost to a leghold trap. For that reason he was particularly wary of traps. The pair had avoided poison and attempts to track them down with hunting dogs.

For four weeks Young tracked the wolves on their regular circuit of about 70 miles, crossing the international border at two places. On most of their route the wolves' trail ranged too widely—from a few to dozens of yards in width—for Young to be able to set traps accurately. In addition, much of their trail was also used by free-ranging cattle and cowboys, and the traps would not likely stay unsprung long enough to catch the wolves. But Young finally discovered a spot on a 6,000-foot-high pass in the Canelo Hills where the animals detoured about 30 feet from their main route to a flat limestone rock, from which they could rest while observing the San Rafael Valley below. At the spot where the wolves stepped from the ground to the rock, Young placed two traps.

The wolf pair was always suspicious of new odors on the trail, particularly scent posts seemingly established by strange wolves. But nothing alerted the female wolf to the trap beneath the soil as she approached the rock. As she felt the steel teeth bite into her foot she lunged away, pulling the trap (attached to 8 feet of quarter-inch linked chain) with her and yanking a foot-and-a-half-long steel stake pin out of the ground. Pulling these objects behind her, she ran 200 yards into the thick cover of manzanita bushes and then stopped to bite at the trap, seeking freedom and respite.

When Young returned to the spot on October 12, 1917, he saw that the trap was sprung and missing. Although he could have tracked the wolf on his own, he went back to the valley and returned with two ranchers and their hounds. The dogs tracked the wolf into the nearby thicket. The wolf, trailing the chain and pin, scrambled nearly 500 feet up a ridge and then down into a creek bed, running down a rocky gully thick with vegetation. Each time the dogs got close she turned on them and snapped, leaving no doubt that even handicapped she could ably defend herself. After 5 miles she reached the open valley and kept running. Every time she leaped, the steel stake swung around and hit her in the flank. Still, she was alive, and escape seemed possible. But Young and the ranchers followed the hounds on horseback. After more than a mile of pursuit in the valley, they gained on the wolf and her seven-pound encumbrance. She could not keep ahead of the galloping horses, and as they came upon her Young ended the wolf's travail with a shot from a .38-caliber Colt revolver.[24]

Young was proud of his achievement, believing this was the first wolf killed by the Biological Survey in Arizona. (Other records indicate the survey had killed wolves in the state during its first year of organized predator killing, 1915, although at the time the survey administered Arizona and New Mexico as a single unit, potentially confusing any claims for an Arizona precedent.[25]) But he still wanted the male wolf, the trap-wary animal.

Seventeen days later the male wolf returned, and from following his distinctive track Young surmised he was searching for his lost mate. In anticipation, Young had collected the dead female's urine, ground up her gall bladder and anal glands, and combined these elements into an odiferous tonic. He sprinkled the tonic on a "scent post," a bush or other upraised feature where the dominant wolf in a pack habitually urinated to mark his territory; this one was at the point where the wolf trail detoured to the fatal rock outcropping. Three days later, on November 1, 1917, the male wolf, his caution overpowered by longing, stepped into another trap at that spot.[26]

Within a couple of months Young's arduous pursuit of wolves in southern Arizona landed him in a trap. A wolf in one of his traps had headed south, crossing the international border near the town of Santa Cruz with a chain and drag that left a prominent track. Young pursued and was captured by renegades associated with Pancho Villa, the Mexican revolutionary. Young was not fluent in Spanish, and he had no papers indicating his business. The

Biological Survey hunter Stanley P. Young with Mexican gray wolf trapped near the Arizona border with Mexico, November 1, 1917. Young claimed this animal's mate as the first wolf trapped by the government in Arizona—the initial one of his many successes as he rose to power. (Biological Survey Unit, USGS, Patuxent Wildlife Research Center, National Museum of Natural History, Washington, D.C.)

revolutionaries thought their gringo prisoner was a wise investment to retain. For ten days they held him while a vigilant American customs patrol officer, evidently aware of Young's last-known general whereabouts and cognizant of border tensions in the region, spread the word of his disappearance. One of Young's professors at the University of Michigan notified officials in Washington, D.C., and a formal protest was lodged with the Mexican government. This diplomatic intervention had the desired effect, and Young was released to a squad of the Twenty-Fifth Infantry stationed on the border at Nogales, who escorted him back to American soil. Upon his return he had the Tom Sawyer–like pleasure of reading his own obituary, drafted by the Michigan professor whose hopes for his safe recovery had apparently been exhausted. Young left no record of the fate of the wolf (whose survival must have been difficult with a trap and a drag hook permanently affixed and likely suffering from gangrene in a foot cut off from normal circulation).[27]

The same fall day Young dispatched that second wolf, speakers at a conference in Albuquerque proclaimed that wolves and other predators were costing New Mexico livestock producers $2.71 million annually, a highly speculative but unchallenged figure used to justify unlimited expenditures for predator killing.[28]

The diverse landscapes of the Southwest still embraced a wealth of natural carnivores. In addition to wolves, the survey killed coyotes, black and grizzly bears, mountain lions, and even, in December 1918, a jaguar on Mount Wrightson in southern Arizona's Santa Rita Mountains, within sight of the sleepy hamlet of Tucson.[29] Young quickly progressed in his work, gaining wide experience with traps and poisons in Arizona and New Mexico. In the fall of 1918 he persuaded Musgrave to hire a hunter, B. A. Wilson, who owned a half-ton Ford truck. Although the agency furnished traps, survey hunters had to supply their own horses. Wilson had the fastest mount around, and he and Young ran a 200-mile trap line together in probably the first extensive use of an automobile in such work, doing "a land office business on coyotes."[30]

The description was Young's from decades later, but the phrase recalled the well-known abuses by the Interior Department's General Land Office in rapidly divesting the frontier federal domain to large corporate interests hiding behind supposed individual homesteaders. Was the reference an unconscious irony or an unconscious affirmation?

In October 1919, after Arizona had earned its own status as a Biological Survey district, with Musgrave as predator animal inspector, Young took a civil service exam to qualify for the same job. He spent two months as a rodent control foreman in Santa Cruz County, supervising the placement of poisons for the small animals that competed with domestic stock for forage.

That was followed by two months spent poisoning coyotes in southeastern New Mexico's Sacramento Mountains.[31] Here Young was supervised by Inspector Stokley Ligon, whose working principle—prominently placed at the bottom of a sheet listing six rules and given to new hunters—spoke to his pride in government service: "Don't Complain of Difficulties; Overcome Them With Victory. They Are the Stimulators That Help Us to Success."[32] Young applied that philosophy more consistently than Ligon might have intended. One day in the field he purchased several oranges and itemized them on his government expense account. Amid a ledger that might have included old horses to slay for bait and perhaps feed for his horses, the fruit stood out. Ligon returned the form to him unpaid for lack of an explanation for the oranges. Young filled in "[g]ratification of the human palate," and Ligon approved the reimbursement.[33]

In March 1920, having passed the civil service exam, Young was promoted to Musgrave's assistant in the survey's main Arizona office in Phoenix. Musgrave took the same pride as Ligon in conquering challenges, and when funds from Arizona's state legislature had temporarily dried up in 1917, he managed to finagle money to hire hunters from the State Council of Defense.[34]

Young thrived on the can-do spirit. As Musgrave's assistant, his first assignment was supervising several coyote-poisoning campaigns throughout the state. North and west of Tucson he worked to protect poultry "in a region where coyote infestation is so thick as to make the raising of poultry impossible on the farms" and where farmers "are compelled to keep their poultry locked in pens and do not dare to let them run loose on the range."[35] He also spent five weeks in the valley of Arivaca (near the Mexican border) supervising trappers killing wolves. And just south of the Grand Canyon, to protect 200,000 sheep, he used "the standard strychnine alkaloid one-grain tablet" to kill 340 coyotes in ten days, putting Arizona "again to the front" of the nation in predator extermination, as a survey report from Washington noted. The "cooperating sheep men were so much delighted with the work," the report continued, "that they insisted that the baiting operations be pushed without regard to finding and counting the animals killed. Such campaigns as this clinch the position of the bureau and prove that it has worked out successful methods for predatory animal destruction."[36]

Sometime during this period Young divorced his wife, the daughter of his old Forest Service boss. A Biological Survey personnel form he filled out on March 15, 1920, notes that he was still married to Helen. But in mid to late August he attended the traditional Snake Dance of the Hopi of northeastern Arizona, a ceremonial event few tourists ever viewed. There he met Nydia Marie Acker, just shy of her twenty-sixth birthday, born in Salt Lake City but living in the northern Arizona high valley town of Prescott. (Her parents had moved there for her father's health.) Acker was with another man, but Young evidently impressed her. The next June they were wed.[37]

In December 1920 Young was transferred to Colorado and became Logan B. Crawford's assistant, an assignment probably taken to familiarize the younger man with the Colorado district in preparation for assuming the leadership there. Although subordinate to Crawford until July 1921, he seems to have taken effective charge of much of the fieldwork in Colorado from the moment he was on the Colorado district's payroll.

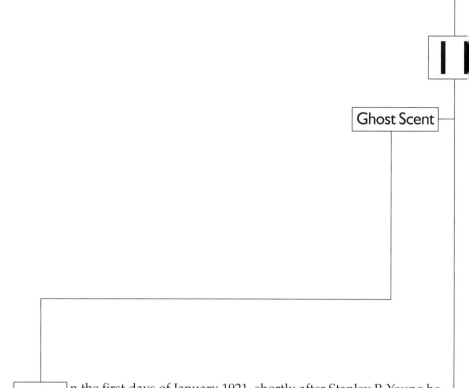

Ghost Scent

I n the first days of January 1921, shortly after Stanley P. Young became assistant predatory animal inspector for the Biological Survey's Colorado district, he dispatched a skilled wolf hunter to the public domain (now Bureau of Land Management) country between the Colorado River and the point at which the Eagle River joins it from the east. From this area a pack of wolves made regular forays into the lowland ranches where cattle were concentrated during the snow-packed winter months. Setting a high standard for wolf eradication, Young let the hunter, Hegewa A. Roberts, know his job depended on wiping out these wolves, which were led by "Lefty," a male who had lost his entire front left foot in a trap eight years before.

When Roberts arrived at the Burns Hole region, as it was known, local ranchers directed him to a one-room log cabin at the head of Bull Gulch, below the crenellated cliffs of Castle Peak. The rough-hewn shack—located in a meadow surrounded by aspen, lodgepole, and ponderosa pines—served as shelter for cowboys and ranch hands. A languid Texan was residing there when Roberts showed up to stow his bedroll and traps and get the lay of the land.[1]

Bull Gulch enters the Colorado River at around 6,400 feet above sea level, cutting a canyon through maroon-colored rock and mesas crowded with squat pinyons and junipers reminiscent of the Colorado Plateau. But its headwaters are more than 3,000 feet higher, above the intermediate sage flats in dark coniferous forests, and this elevational diversity furnishes year-round deer and elk habitat. Along with almost every other place in the Rocky Mountains, it was fully stocked with cattle pushed up from riverside ranches as soon as the retreating snow permitted. On the serrated volcanic slopes of 11,000-foot Castle Peak perched a fire lookout peering down over extensive beaver ponds and expanses of forest. Even today, much of the country remains wild. Although the Eagle River to the south now echoes with the littoral-like hum of Interstate 70, 31,000 acres (almost 50 square miles) of Burns Hole are without roads save for a single private ranch road on a ridge that separates Castle Peak from Bull Gulch.[2]

Roberts, an accomplished skier in his early thirties, spent his first two weeks on long excursions from the cabin looking for the wolf pack's trails. He eventually located the pack's runway and noted one of Lefty's scent posts. The hunter sprinkled a few drops of another male wolf's odor on the post and set his traps between the post and the trail.

When the pack discovered the strange wolf's odor, Lefty's suspicions were aroused, according to the later account by Young, who recorded the battle against Lefty and other wolves in an action-packed book entitled *The Last Stand of the Pack.* The danger of hidden metal beneath the ground had been incised into Lefty's memory, along with images of a young wolf in his pack writhing from strychnine poisoning after snatching a morsel of beef-flank fat. Instead of approaching to mark his own scent over that of the stranger, he signaled his packmates to back off and he led them off the trail. Despite his adjuration, however, as they were leaving one female wolf, enticed by the strange odor, rolled on the ground near it, setting off a trap. Fortunately for her, it only claimed tufts of her fur and did not nip the flesh.[3]

Meanwhile, Roberts's cabin companion reported that friendly wagers within the ranching community along the Colorado River put the odds at five to one against Lefty being captured within six months. But Roberts kept reconnoitering further on his skis, suffering a frostbitten finger after spending one blizzardy night under the shelter of a spruce tree. His next bunch of traps caught a coyote, which Lefty keenly observed struggling for freedom. Once again he led his pack out of the normal route through a thicket of young oaks. When Roberts returned to the cabin disappointed, carrying the luckless coyote's hide, he was almost ready to give up.

But not quite. His next traps anticipated the pack's detour around the scene of the coyote's demise. In tracking the wolves, Roberts had observed an unusual lurching step Lefty made to leap over fallen logs and other obstructions. The crippled wolf momentarily put down his avulsed leg to bring his good front foot into position for the jump. With that in mind, the trapper placed an obstructing stick in the pack's new route through the oak thicket to force Lefty's right front foot into a new trap.

It worked, and the cagey wolf found himself once again in a trap. Even worse, in his struggles another paw floundered into a second trap. The traps weren't staked down, each instead pulling a drag with twisted prongs at the end of a chain. His pack fled the scene of terror, and the wolf plunged through the snow and down a gully, painfully wrenching his legs to break down sage clumps and scrub oaks on which the prongs caught and bending the metal hooks when trees would not give way.

The next morning Roberts was ecstatic to discover the traps missing and a plain record in the snow of the wolf's travail. He returned to the cabin and summoned the ranch hand, who brought along his lariat. The two men followed the two-mile trail that marked a night of struggle and torment. At the end of it stood the wolf, facing them.

The Texan lassoed Lefty's unencumbered legs and pulled the rope taut, stringing the wolf out between the rope and the traps' drag hooks. Roberts axed down a four-inch-thick aspen tree and laid it on the struggling wolf's neck, walking out on the tree up to the strangling animal to where he could muzzle him with a noose. Once done, he hog-tied the wolf's four legs, "trussed up until he could barely move."

Finally, Roberts placed a collar and chain on Lefty and staked him out to entice his packmates toward further traps. Within three nights two more wolves were caught, and the remaining wolves fled the region.[4] In a last triumph, described by Stanley P. Young and his co-author, "Hegewa brought in a bottle of Lefty's scent and the green hide of the old leader, while magpies pecked at his freezing carcass."[5]

A short time later, in early February, with state funds having run out and his few other expert wolf hunters already in the field, Young drove to southeastern Colorado to personally engage another pack adept at survival. In all but a titular sense, Young was already in charge of the Colorado district. It was he who worked closely with the Colorado Stockgrowers Association to prepare a new funding request to the Colorado General Assembly, and as field supervisor he oversaw the men spread throughout the state setting poison and traps.[6] He may have claimed the title "Inspector" prematurely; a newspaper article covering the capture of Lefty, almost certainly written at Young's instigation, referred to him as such—although in fact he was still officially an assistant to Logan B. Crawford.[7]

The wolves of southeastern Colorado—the region inscribed by wagon ruts of the Santa Fe Trail and home to the Bent brothers' pioneering adobe trading post—had not only survived the nineteenth century but endured into the 1920s. With a few wolves still roaming the San Juan Mountains as well, it is likely that the entire southern tier of the state, along with northern New Mexico, retained a meta-population—allowing dispersing yearlings from any pack in the mountains, for instance, to replenish the population on the plains. For despite a wolf run down by hounds on the plains in 1919 and three trapped there by the survey in October 1920, the choppy grassland headwaters of the Apishipa, Huerfano, and Purgatoire rivers supported a pack of nine wolves. The pack was led by a once-trapped female known as "Three-Toes" and her equally wary mate, an exceptionally large animal the local ranchers dubbed "Whitey" for his age-bleached pelage.

Predatory animal inspector, or still just an assistant? Young with the first wolf of old Whitey's pack in southeastern Colorado. Ranchers would not only treat Young to dinner, but support him as he built a network of government and private entities to fund the extermination campaign. (Bureau of Biological Survey)

For a week Young scouted the terrain on horseback, searching out the pack's travel routes and returning each evening to the home of rancher Jim Shaw, whose enthusiasm for ridding his range of these last, canny wolves was reflected in his warm hospitality to Young. But like his cohorts on the Colorado River the previous month, Shaw was skeptical about the ability of anyone to trick a long-surviving wolf into a trap. Shaw told Young, "You're a better man than we've had here before if you can set a trap with a pan about two inches across and catch him, in all that range."

"I've got something else that will bring old Whitey around," responded Young, showing Shaw a bottle of Lefty's urine and ground-up scent glands—an odd amber mixture.[8]

The next morning Young, Shaw, and another local rancher rode out to set traps. Young, characteristically self-confident, bet the two scoffers a dinner at the best eatery in the nearby town of Rocky Ford that he could trap a wolf within twenty-four hours if they showed him one fresh paw print. Within a mile Shaw found a print, and Young followed it to a scent post—a small tuft of gama grass—where he carefully laid his trap, baited with Lefty's "ghost scent," as he called it. The next morning he found a female wolf struggling in vain for her freedom, and the ranchers were happy to buy him dinner.

Young eagerly anticipated capturing Whitey, who typically walked first in the pack's single-file line of travel. But within a few days his traps started disappearing.[9] Local dryland ranchers, who had settled the region too late to claim tracts of grazing land with access to water, often found themselves at odds with cattle kings such as Shaw.[10] With their few cattle and horses typically fenced in close to the safety of their homestead, they had no strong interest in exterminating the wolves. More important, the Biological Survey's success would eliminate the occasional bounty they might claim by killing wolves themselves. As Shaw put it, "Their kind just resent any Federal man coming into this section."[11]

More frustrating to Young than the loss of traps were the lost opportunities. The site of each trap carelessly dug up became tainted with the odor of humanity, warning Whitey away. A bobcat had stumbled into one of Young's traps but had been removed—most likely for its fur—before Young could retrieve it. Young and the ranchers were furious. In an attempt to ride the trap line before the "two-legged wolves" could get to the traps, Young and Shaw set out early one morning—and for the first time since his arrival Young forgot to bring his rifle.

Riding to the scene of Young's latest trap set, they discovered Whitey's characteristic large paw print in the lead of several wolves but none in the traps. Whitey would not be enticed to approach the strange wolf scent. Following the pack's trail, Young and Shaw came upon a recently killed steer. Following the trail ten minutes further they rode up on Whitey, napping a few hundred yards away under a pinyon tree. Young reached for his rifle and discovered his holster was empty.

Whitey suddenly looked up, thrust out his nose to pinpoint the danger, then leaped up and disappeared through the sagebrush into a thicket of pinyons. Young spewed out imprecations like bullets after the retreating wolf.

Young decided to abandon trying to catch Whitey with baited traps. Not only were traps still disappearing, but the wolf clearly knew he was being hunted and did not follow normal wolf behavior, eschewing the temptation to investigate unusual odors. So Young began laying so-called blind sets, unscented traps along the wolf's customary trails.[12]

Before he could check on the results, however, Young was summoned into a different battlefield—facing advocates of bounty payments who regarded the Biological Survey as competition. After receiving an urgent telegram in March from the Colorado Stockgrowers Association, Young hurried back to Denver to help coordinate a legislative battle to ensure the survey another two years of funding from the state. The bill was supported by the legislature's sizable ranching contingent and opposed by those fearful of the survey's efficient dispatch of predators. "There is a bunch in this state that have been making money from trapping predatory animals for bounty, and they are bringing all the pressure they can to defeat that bill," Young explained to Shaw. "If we clean out the animal killers, there'll not be any bounty left for them." Fresh from a field campaign hindered by the same type of people, Young relished the opportunity of "licking those bounty advocates." But he also rued having to leave Whitey uncaught and vowed to return as soon as he could.[13]

Meanwhile, Whitey's mate, Three-Toes, had borne a litter of pups. The six surviving pups from the previous year could now hunt on their own, and with the new danger Whitey sensed in his long-established territory, perhaps he felt the yearlings and the new pups would all be safer if the pack split up. He led the six surviving one-year-olds south out of the pack's range into the rolling juniper country of northern New Mexico and then headed back alone to his nursing mate, who waited for him to bring back food.

He never made it. After an all-night run of many miles, upon approaching his den along one of his old trails Whitey stepped into one of Young's blind traps. In his struggle he stepped into another trap. Mile after mile and hour after hour he struggled to free himself, to no avail. He was found—we do not know whether the next morning or many days later—by a dryland rancher named Nate Strang, the person Shaw had suspected of stealing Young's traps.[14]

To the Biological Survey and Colorado's established ranchers, Strang represented an enemy of progress, more interested in collecting a bounty than in solving the problem the bounty had been intended to address. But to Whitey, Strang was first and foremost a human—bearing the scent he recognized as having been fatal to so many of his kind. If anything, Strang may have represented a kinder death than Young would have, since the small-scale rancher would not have known to keep the old wolf chained up to lure his mate. Strang would not, as survey trappers were known to do, have tightened a wire around the wolf's penis to collect urine in the bladder for future scent baits before dealing the death blow.[15]

Strang collected a long-standing twenty-five dollar bounty on Whitey, paid out by local ranchers. For good measure, Strang wrote Young a letter detailing his luck at having caught the wolf in a small coyote trap set behind his house and offering to sell Young the pelt and skull.

But Young's disappointed pride kept him from accepting the offer. "As long as I didn't catch him myself, I don't know as I would want it," he later quoted himself in *The Last Stand of the Pack*. "It would always remind me of the fact that the Survey had one whale of a try catching this old fellow and then had a rank amateur come right in after our campaign and catch him in a dinky little trap." Returning to southeastern Colorado after having passed the funding bill, and preparing to pursue Three-Toes and any other wolves still in the vicinity, Young lamented his failure to catch the animal. "I sure would like to have nabbed him myself," he muttered wistfully. "Wish I had been the man to stop his raiding."[16]

Then, while inspecting his old trap line with Shaw and another rancher, Young found all the marks of a trapped wolf—the tiny furrow in the ground indicating a trailing drag hook, signs of struggle, a huge wolf print, and, lastly, tufts of white hair that only could have come from the singularly canescent wolf. "That hair is enough for me," exclaimed Young. "He dragged the trap and chain here, got hung up and thrashed around something awful."[17]

The three men remounted their horses and followed the trail. Young later described the story written into the earth:

> The hook had caught, released, caught again and gouged into the earth. At times the riders traveled at a slow trot, at others they walked their horses. Through thickets, down little cliffs, on through the brush Whitey had fought with two traps on his feet. The track led to a tangle of cedar and piñon where there had been a terrific struggle. Here it stopped.[18]

Young and the two ranchers, infuriated by Strang's deception, rode directly to his homestead, a squalid and haphazard assemblage of house, barn, and rickety corrals. After a tense confrontation in the dirt yard, Young asked Shaw, who also served as the local marshal, to arrest Strang. "I mean to see that you land in Leavenworth just to show other trap thieves that they can't get away with this rough stuff they've been pulling," declared Young.[19]

But before Shaw could act, Strang's wife called out to him, asking why he hadn't brought in the firewood. And one of Strang's three children, undernourished and unkempt, wandered into the yard. Young and his cohorts suddenly lost their zeal for justice. After a quick consultation they decided to let Strang off with a return of the bounty money, Whitey's pelt and skull, and a letter of confession to Edward W. Nelson, the head of the Biological Survey in Washington.[20]

And thus old Whitey, no more to roam the plains or nuzzle his blunt-nosed, blind-born pups, served to extend a bit the reach of human grace and mercy.

| Your Uncle |

A few days after Lefty's demise at the hands of Biological Survey hunter Hegewa A. Roberts but before Stanley P. Young headed southeast to engage Whitey, the assistant predatory animal inspector received a visitor in his Denver office. Joseph N. Neal, who during the twentieth-century's early teen years had been active in the Wolf Bounty Association, was visiting Denver from his home in Meeker. Having survived wolf depredations when they were common, Neal now made his living through cattle and also through ownership of a bank that made substantial loans on livestock.

Young pulled out a chair for his well-heeled guest. Neal sat down and pulled out two cigars, lighting his own before touching the match to that of his thirty-two-year-old host.[1]

Despite his poise and aplomb, Neal had plenty to worry about. From its recently balmy heyday, the nation's economy had quickly turned south. Agriculture had been particularly hard-hit. During the war, despite patriotic exhortations to the contrary, the public had heartily enjoyed its steaks and burgers. But with incomes dropping precipitously in late 1920, beef consumption seemed a luxury that might best be deferred. Although the genial banker could not have known it for a certainty, 1921 was destined to be the worst year for cattle producers since at least the turn of the century.[2] Neal and Young talked about the stock market, Neal's trip to Denver, and mutual friends. Then Neal signaled the end of the chitchat with a forceful exhalation of blue-gray smoke.

"When can Caywood get on the trail of that wolf Rags?"

Young had been expecting the question, but he could not give a satisfactory answer. The Colorado district's best wolf hunter had suffered a riding accident the past autumn and had broken his leg, ending up in the hospital for several months.[3] William Henry Caywood, who shared the nickname "Big Bill" with Colorado anarchist and labor leader William Haywood, had joined the survey as one of its first hunters in 1915. Caywood was the son of pioneers from Iowa who had arrived in Colorado in an ox-drawn prairie schooner in 1863 to work in the mines. The next year Caywood's parents returned to Iowa, but in 1877 they came back to Colorado by train with seven-year-old Bill and his six siblings in tow—this time for good.[4] Caywood had bought himself a ranch eight years back with the $7,000 he earned killing 140 wolves for Neal and his cohorts in the Piceance Creek Stock-Growers Association and its Wolf Bounty Association.

Caywood had deeply impressed Neal at the time. No other bounty hunter seemed to understand wolf behavior as well as he did. Neal still retained the white hide of a wolf Caywood had trapped within sight of Neal's ranch house, and he was convinced that no other survey hunter would solve his present problem.[5]

The wolf nicknamed "Rags" had roamed the Piceance Creek region of northwestern Colorado and deep into Utah for about seventeen years. Once part of a pack, since the successive loss of two of his mates he had shunned other wolves' company. His first mate had stepped into a trap set by a local rancher, Bob Coats, and the second had died, along with all their pups, when Coats discovered their den and dug them out.

Now Rags traveled a vast circuit of pinyon- and juniper-covered escarpments and desert canyons, occasionally joined by a pair of younger wolves. Profoundly unsocial, Rags eschewed wolf custom and permitted the smaller, subordinate male wolf to mate with the female. Another atypical behavior helped account for his advanced age: Rags seldom traveled on trails or dirt roads, loping a few feet to one side or the other of any pathway.[6]

In April 1921, when Caywood had recovered from his accident sufficiently to ride again, Young assigned him to his old hunting ground along Piceance Creek in pursuit of Rags. Caywood was a hefty fifty-year-old with broad shoulders that were stooped from peering down on tracks from his horse. He was delighted to be out of the hospital and back on the trail that wound through the apple green of budding oak leaves, the soft purplish gray of aspen catkins, and the stubby green needles of pinyon pines.

Toward evening, the packhorse in front of the big bay Caywood rode stopped to graze in a little gopher-scarred meadow tucked between a bend in the creek and the low limestone cliffs. There Caywood set up his campsite and base of operations for the coming weeks, erecting a pyramid-shaped canvas tent. He built a fire, cooked ham in a blackened skillet, and went to bed relishing the freedom of the wilderness, kept comfortably awake only by his suppertime coffee and a brief chorus of coyotes.[7] Two weeks later, having as yet picked up no sign of Rags, Caywood rode with rancher Bob Coats on yet another reconnoitering expedition. Coats was no novice at killing wolves, counting almost fifty to his credit. But Rags, marked by hind feet larger than his front feet—an anomaly among wolves—had evaded him year after year, taking a regular toll on Coats's cattle herds.[8] He deferred to Big Bill and his reputation for uncanny success at getting the most cautious wolf to step into a trap.

Caywood's genius for trapping wolves stemmed from an ability to think like his prey. He had grown up on a ranch along Grape Creek—a stream issuing northeast from the Sangre de Cristo range—at a time before much of the resident wildlife had learned to fear human presence. His outdoor childhood (he quit school after fourth grade) taught him well to observe the local animals.[9]

Caywood professed not only to respect wolves but even to love them. "He's a real fellow, the big gray is," he told Coats. "Lots of brains. I feel sorry for him. It's his way of livin'. He don't know better." His terse words came out with the textureless earnestness preceding the summary judgment of a log cabin courthouse.

"And I feel sorry every time I see one of those big fellows thrashin' around in a trap bellowin' bloody murder." The survey hunter's pale blue eyes seemed to recede into themselves as his thin lips recounted the intimately familiar last moments of countless wolves, now amalgamated into a single scene of pain and desperate fear.

But he didn't feel too sorry for them. "It's part the way that wolves go after poor defenseless steers, murder does and fawns and drag down bucks that helps me go out and bring them in," he concluded.[10]

Within a few years, recovering from a serious illness but back at work on the Olympic Peninsula in Washington state, Caywood would evince nostalgia for the species he had helped wipe out in Colorado. "There is a report that there is some Gray Wolvs in there I hope the report is true for I am getting home sick to see and hear some of them old boys again," he wrote Young, then stationed in Washington, D.C.[11]

If Caywood felt almost as kin to wolves, it is not surprising that ambivalence typified his familial relationships as well. He grew up witnessing his father, George Washington Caywood, viciously beat his mother. George had married Mary in Iowa when he was twenty-one and she just seventeen. When the couple made its second move to Colorado in 1877, George abandoned contact with his parents and four siblings. Mary bore nine children, of whom William was the fourth. But when Mary reached her mid-forties and after years of abuse, George kicked her out of the homestead. (After she got on her feet she homesteaded an abandoned cabin at an old sawmill site and eventually sold it and bought a house in Cañon City, Colorado.)[12]

Big Bill seems to have picked up at least some of his father's proclivities. In his early sixties, ten or so years after chasing Rags, a drinking habit began consuming most of his income, leaving little for paying bills or supporting his wife and the two youngest of their fifteen children. In 1935, about two years after this condition started, survey officials abruptly retired him on disability, citing the injury he had received in the 1920 riding accident. Although he had apparently developed serious back pains from that incident, on his last day of work he still managed to kill a bobcat and was surprised to receive notice of his termination.[13] It seems at least as likely that his good friend and old boss Young, by that time a senior official in the Washington office, had orchestrated a respectable exit for Caywood to spare the old trapper and the survey embarrassment over his dipsomania.

Caywood's spree didn't end there. Four months after his retirement, like his father before him, he abandoned his wife of thirty-eight years, Laura. In the midst of the Great Depression, she was in no shape to support the three youngest of their fifteen children on her own, especially since she had been injured in an auto accident after fleeing his wrath. He left her their house in New Castle (near Glenwood Springs) but continued to drink away each monthly disability payment, leading her to write Young a plaintive and desperate appeal for the survey's help in getting part of the money. Young wrote back with the bad news that the government had to send Bill Caywood's monthly checks to him but informing her of his last known postmark.[14] Big Bill was also not particularly close to his children. A great-nephew recalled him as a distant and harsh figure who assigned the smallest of his children to crawl into the narrow confines of wolf dens to pull out the pups.[15] His son Joe, who also became a trapper, recalled his father's absence for up to a year at a time when pursuing wolves.[16] Four years before his death at age eighty-three Caywood wrote Young that he thought his grown children must be doing all right or else he would have heard from them.[17]

Now, in 1921, searching for signs of Rags, Caywood found nothing. The wolf was probably in the western part of its range in Utah, he concluded. But come summer and the melting of the high-country snows, the season when Utah sheep were herded into Colorado, Rags would again appear.

Before too long, five of Coats's cattle were killed by a lone wolf in one night, and Caywood hurried to pick up the track. Rags, so the local ranchers speculated, killed out of bitterness or revenge. Indeed, the lone wolf killed more cattle than he needed to sate his hunger. Caywood, the master of his trade, began to set his traps.

But Rags seemed to comprehend Caywood as well as the survey hunter understood wolves. Around dusk shortly after the wolf's return to Colorado, awakened from a nap by Caywood's approach along the trail below, Rags—careful not to show himself—followed the man on the reddish-brown horse to his camp by Piceance Creek, departing only when the campfire kindled into flame.

Then there were the traps. Although he had never been caught in one himself, Rags remembered his mate's struggles and understood the traps' intent; he even had a notion of how they operated. Trotting along a ridge one evening, he caught whiff of Caywood's scent and sensed danger, mincing

Survey hunter William Caywood saw wolves as kin and could think like a wolf to trick one into a trap. Big Bill didn't treat his human kin much better; his wife ended up injured after fleeing his rage, and he drank up his monthly disability checks, leaving her alone and in poverty during the Great Depression. (Denver Public Library, Western History Collection, Call number F-45783)

around a few innocuous-looking oak leaves no different in appearance from any others.

He sidled up carefully to the suspect spot, extending the claws of one foreleg to the edge of the danger zone. He scratched and pulled a few leaves toward himself, then a few more, revealing loose dirt and the steel edge of a trap. He started digging at an angle an inch from the trap edge until it sagged. He approached it from the other side, scraping away first leaves and then the substrate of earth until the whole trap was exposed in its delicately wrought brutality. He sniffed at it, catching the merest taint of the man he had followed to the camp at the bend in the creek. Then, with a final flip of his paw from underneath the trap, the wolf popped it out of its hollow and onto the adjacent ground, right side up, the chain still extending from the earth like the umbilicus to a misformed birth.

That night Rags headed west again, back into Utah, where the scent of Bill Caywood adhered to no gust of wind.[18]

Caywood was astounded when he found his trap dug up, but the ranchers desperate for Rags's demise seemed to take the incident almost as vindication of their travails. "You've met your match," declared Neal. "Rags is your equal, Bill. He's the headiest wolf that ever roamed the White River country. He's outguessing you."

"Didn't I tell you, Bill, that that ain't no common wolf?" Coats exclaimed. "Rags has more sense than any wolf I ever took and that is quite a number to measure him up by. I've had him dig out three or four traps of mine in a night."

"Mad? Why, man, I just went hog wild tryin' to catch that old duffer after he dug up my first traps," Coats continued. "Seemed like he just dared me to set a trap in such a way that he could not throw it up on the ground surface unsprung. And now he's turned the trick on you. Well, that's good!"

But Caywood took the incident as a dare. "If he gets away the next time, then I'll be waitin' fer [sic] him. . . . Some day I'll roll his hide up and ship it to the Denver office, and inside of it will be his big old skull. I'm not sayin' when I'll get him, but I will."[19]

So he kept setting traps for the wolf. Almost every night another coyote would fall victim to a trap and a young, inexperienced wolf—recently dispersed from its natal pack—was caught. But not Rags.

Then, in late June, Rags returned to the region and was joined by the wolf pair, which in those perilous times seemed to take some solace from his company despite his lack of requital. The odd threesome (Rags, as was his custom, off to the side of the trail) soon came to a scent post, the urine of a male wolf deposited on a tuft of grama grass. Rags was suspicious and edged away. But the smaller male, after first following Rags, could not resist turning back to meet the territorial challenge of the unknown wolf. His surrender to normal wolf behavior landed him in one of Caywood's traps.[20]

The next night Rags followed a few feet to the side of a trail ascending to the striking, tree-lined Cathedral Bluffs, just south of Calamity Ridge. Cathedral Bluffs is a bow-shaped escarpment curving north to south and dropping off on either side into sharp declivities. From the top one can see to the east the cliffy edge of the White River Plateau (now largely protected as the Flat Tops Wilderness) and to the west more plateaus and canyons dropping into the Green and Colorado rivers. It was familiar territory to Rags but, like everywhere else, full of potential hazards. And here, once again, he caught scent of Caywood, along with a foreign wolf smell. He started scraping at the dirt, carefully uncovering the edge of another trap.

Wolves are creatures of habit, adding through accretion new behaviors to an old repertoire. Caywood had decided to use a carelessly set trap as bait. Behind the trap Rags had discovered were two others, placed with all the subterfuge of which Caywood was capable. "You're a smart boy," he had intoned in admiration on discovering his first dug-up trap weeks before. "You're a darned crafty old codger, Ragsy. But your uncle'll get you before the summer is over, and he'll get you just because you are so darned smart. You'll start to dig up one of my traps just once too often, old-timer, just once too often."[21]

Now, as Rags repositioned himself to scrape from the other side of the trap, a hind paw was snatched up and held tightly. Leaping away, he yanked the three-foot chain attached to a drag hook out of the earth behind him; attached to the hook was another chain and trap that bounced and clanked in pursuit.

The next day Caywood rode up toward Cathedral Bluffs, noting Rags's faint but distinct paw prints in the dirt alongside the trail. When he reached his trap set and noted the torn-up ground, he sprang off his horse in excitement, oblivious to the pain in the leg still weakened from the break. Jumping back on the bay, he eagerly followed the tine marks from the trap's drag hook.

Rags had followed the trail a short distance, then turned off, crossing a meadow and then a grove of pines. Caywood noted the familiar marks of a trapped wolf—the turmoil where Rags pulled past vegetation that snagged the two hooks, the bite marks, and the tiny bubbles of saliva where the wolf had battled brush impeding his escape.

At the edge of a cliff the trail disappeared. Caywood looked up and down the ridgetop but saw no mark. He got off his horse and ventured to the drop-off point. The trail went over the edge, but protrusions in the broken and exfoliating cliff face kept him from seeing the bottom, more than a hundred feet below.

Caywood remounted his horse and found a less direct route to the base of the cliff. There, instead of the twisted carcass of the wolf he had expected to find, the scrape marks from the drag hook and loose trap continued, wending through sage and oak thickets and up and down shallow draws flanked with yellow and red cliffs.

Finally, he saw the shaggy-coated wolf in the distance, ducking into a narrow canyon. The mounted hunter followed, his horse barely fitting between the sheer walls. The canyon split into two tributaries, and, following the distinct marks, Caywood turned left.

But his horse, with a snort of fear, stopped and would go no farther. Rags was clearly visible in the distance. Caywood urged the bay a few feet forward and loosened his .25-.35 rifle from the saddle scabbard. Rags looked back, assessing the horse and rider, then plodded on. Perhaps he was beyond panic; except for his fetters, he could have been returning to a den site and the familiar comforts of a pack life he had long since lost.

The arroyo was narrowing, and Caywood decided he would have to make the last few feet on foot. Leaving the horse bellowing nervously behind, he limped ahead with rifle in hand. The drag hook had caught on a small branch. Rags pulled but without force, his red tongue drooping from exhaustion. Perhaps in the spring runoff this arroyo trickled with water, but now in late June it radiated heat. The hook held.

For a long moment the wolf looked ahead into the canyon. From his years of wandering, he may have known exactly where it topped out on a ridge or where a spring moistened a shadowed cleft soft with moss. But he knew he would not get there.

Slowly, Rags turned to face Caywood, seventy-five yards distant. Their eyes met. Then the wolf advanced, a slow, tired walk toward the man who had tricked him into the trap. The drag hook, released from its obstruction, followed like a clanking coda to a life born into a fatal era.

We can never know precisely how an animal thinks; some maintain that even two human beings, toggled together with the magic of words, understand each other only through a leap of speculative faith. Nobody can be sure, and perhaps even the wolf himself did not know, why he turned back to approach Caywood. Did Rags expect salvation, release from the trap, at the hands of Big Bill?

Caywood didn't think so. The ranchers who had suffered Rags's depredations had painted a picture of a mythical beast, shaggy in appearance, wise beyond belief, large for his kind, and a potential killer of humans. Their physical descriptions, Caywood could see, were unimpeachable. He had experienced the wolf's cunning. Now, with Rags plodding toward him—and although encumbered by steel little more crippled than Caywood himself—the ranchers' warnings about the danger of this wolf came back to him.

"Whatever you do, Bill, don't let that old devil catch you on foot without a gun," Neal had warned from the comfortable safety of his office in the Meeker bank. "With your leg crippled he'd make mincemeat of you in forty seconds."[22]

And Bob Coats, on that languid spring day when they had searched for the wolf's tracks: "You've never been on the trail of a worse killer than this Rags. He's a murderer—straight out animal murderer. I believe he'd tackle a man if he got the chance, I really do."[23]

Caywood raised his rifle and aimed. He pulled back the hammer with his thumb. But it wouldn't catch. He tried again, to no avail. With his leg still healing, he found walking difficult. Climbing the canyon walls would not be an option. He stared at the approaching Rags as if the routine of trapping and killing wolves had twisted into a dream-like reversal he was destined to witness in amazed paralysis.

He tried the rifle again, working the trigger to try to hold the hammer. But now the trigger was jammed. His horse snorted again and started to back out of the canyon. He could see Rags's hair standing up on the back of his neck and could hear a deep rumbling in the wolf's throat. Whatever his purpose, surely Rags felt at least the same anxiety as Caywood did.

But Rags's intentions, whether bellicose or supplicatory, died in that narrow canyon. With only eight feet between them, Caywood yanked again at the hammer, and this time it held. He squeezed the trigger, and a bullet exited the barrel and careened through the heart of Rags, the trap-excavating wolf.[24]

That the Conquerors May Live

In a world not even wise old Rags could have imagined, change was afoot. Within a few days of the wolf's death, on July 1, 1921, Stanley P. Young, just returned from his wedding to Nydia M. Acker back in Prescott, Arizona, replaced his nominal supervisor, Logan B. Crawford, as predatory animal inspector. Young spent most of that summer reorganizing his district, instituting procedures for his cadre of hunters to follow, retraining them, and creating a better system of record-keeping in the Denver office.

He also renamed the Colorado district of the Biological Survey, expanding it to the "Colorado-Kansas district." This ambitious move proved premature, as indicated in his reports to Washington over the next two years—punctuated with the adverse phrase "No work was performed in Kansas."[1] (Young's failure to establish a strong survey presence in Kansas made the state an Achilles' heel for the agency. In 1973, fifty-two years after he claimed the state for the survey and four years after his death, Young's organizational handiwork was challenged and his legacy of wolf extermination undermined when Republican president Richard M. Nixon signed into law the Endangered Species Act. As will be seen, some of the first rumblings that led to this act originated in Kansas.)

In the summer of 1921, however, there was plenty for the energetic Young to accomplish in a state where the threat of wolves and mountain lions remained acute—Colorado. (Coyotes and bobcats still inhabited Kansas, but wolves were not known to have persisted there into the twentieth century.[2])

Much of the reorganizing involved building stronger ties with the survey's current and, Young hoped, future constituencies. He emphasized to his hunters the importance of "maintain[ing] the best possible relations with ranchmen, stockmen and sportsmen."[3] Having come of age in the Progressive era and been schooled by the demanding Mark E. Musgrave and Stokley Ligon (his Arizona and New Mexico supervisors, respectively), Young believed deeply in government employment as a public service.

Young also urged the local livestock groups cooperating with the survey to pool their predator extermination funds to give the survey more flexibility as to where and when it placed hunters. This required the ranchers to believe the survey's actions in their collective interest would yield greater results for all than would strictly localized work for those able to pay in any given season.

Prior to this innovation, a local livestock association would expect the survey to keep a hunter on its turf until its money ran out, even if every coyote had been poisoned within the first few weeks of the hunter's arrival. But now the survey could move on to an adjoining area rather than spend inordinate resources killing the few coyotes migrating into the newly vacant habitat. Attacking a robust population elsewhere while the funds were available would do more to prevent "re-infestation" than would staying put.

Young's reform, which resulted in the formation of the Western Slope Coyote Association and the North Fork Predatory Animal Association (the latter based on the North Fork of Gunnison River and comprising two local wool growers' associations), would enable the same amount of money to be distributed far more efficiently. "We intend to make one dollar produce as big results next year as two dollars did last year," he asserted confidently in a report to Washington, D.C. Nevertheless, he reported that the reorganization "necessarily consumed a considerable length of time, and it was not until early fall that real work on the extermination of predatory animals got under way."[4]

But even through the summer the killing of wolves continued apace. While William H. Caywood was still working to capture Rags in the Piceance Creek region, Young sent Hegewa A. Roberts almost a hundred miles south of there. In 1913 Roberts, then working for bounties, had trapped a female wolf by the toes. In the process of freeing herself she had broken a toe, which had then grown at an odd angle, crossed over another toe. Later, he trapped her again, but a stick fortuitously jammed in the trap had enabled her to escape. Now, like so many other wolves that survived into the 1920s, she could be identified by the track created from that first encounter with steel.

Dubbed "Unaweep" for the 4,000-foot canyon into which she descended for her camisadoes onto ranches, this wolf and her mate and pups made their summer home in the cool oak, pine, aspen, spruce, and fir forests of the massive Uncompahgre Plateau. The plateau rises in west-central Colorado between the desert canyons of the Dolores, Gunnison, and (its tributary) Uncompahgre rivers. In the winter the pack ranged southwest into the foothills of the La Sal Mountains, across the border in Utah.

At the start of the summer, Unaweep's foraging mate had been spotted by a ranch hand and shot on sight. Without knowing why he never returned to their den, she began hunting on her own to support their eight pups from the previous year and their four several-month-old whelps. In early July Roberts, even though he guessed that Unaweep would be too savvy for such tactics, managed to poison six of her eight unschooled yearling pups before turning his attention to the matriarch, who had narrowly escaped death at his hands twice before.

After losing half her progeny, Unaweep was determined to shelter the remaining two yearlings and the four newborns. When Roberts next began to set traps, she taught her surviving pack to avoid the customary scent posts and routes. As the summer passed she kept feeding them fresh beef—never again carrion—from the free-ranging cattle on the plateau. Roberts's poison baits only brought down coyotes and magpies.

Roberts became so frustrated that he wrote his boss, Stanley Young, asking for assistance. Young and his second in command, George Trickel, based nearby in Montrose, came out to see what they could do. Roberts's problem resulted not only from Unaweep's savvy but also, ironically, from the very livestock he was trying to protect. The wolves wouldn't come to scent posts, and blind sets left on roads and trails were routinely sprung by the ubiquitous cattle. After several days of riding the trails with Roberts and Trickel, Young advised asking the ranchers to remove their cattle from a small aspen-bordered park through which the pack traveled and setting traps there without scent.

Then, with a few words of encouragement, Young departed. Since taking over two months previously, he had sorted out the chaotic files in the Denver office, written the fiscal year 1921 annual report for the district, and completed his administrative improvements. But he had sixteen other hunters (not counting Trickel) to supervise throughout the state and was in the midst of a 1,200-mile automobile trip to visit them all. That September his agency had accounted for three more dead wolves trapped in Rags's old territory south of Meeker. As much as he may have been tempted, the new predatory animal inspector could no longer stay with a single trapping project until its conclusion.

On his own again (or perhaps still accompanied by Trickel), Roberts found the neighboring rancher happy to move his stock if it might help the government man catch Unaweep. With the meadow clear of cattle, Roberts set his traps and waited. It took about three weeks, but the pack returned to Unaweep Canyon, and on October 1, 1921, Roberts's traps claimed the canyon's namesake wolf. The pups escaped.[5]

Having returned to Denver assured that field operations were progressing smoothly, Young worked to broaden the constituency for his agency by getting the survey's exploits reported in the media. "Get Home, Lobo! Uncle Sam's Hunters Are on Your Trail" proclaimed the headline of a short article in the *Denver Express* that September. "Two thousand predatory beasts will perish in

Colorado this year. That is the goal of the U.S. biological survey branch in Denver," the piece began. But raw numbers, then as now, fail to engage people's emotions. So in a tribute to the difficulty Roberts (and perhaps also Trickel) was still experiencing with the wary Unaweep, Young emphasized to the reporter the drama of man against wolf: "Two of Young's men have tackled the task of capturing the worst wolf in Colorado. This old criminal, operating in Uncompahgre forest, is reputed to have destroyed $40,000 worth of livestock in eight years."

Since estimates of money lost to predators came from the ranchers, who were inclined to exaggerate even in their own minds the value of each cow or calf killed, the accuracy of the $40,000 figure might be challenged. Clearly, however, because Unaweep and any other long-surviving wolf would have to kill for each meal to avoid poison, the cumulative toll was significant.

The article closed on a positive note, one that would have warmed the hearts of every citizen awakened to William Temple Hornaday's warnings a few years back: "Young attributes the increase in wild game birds largely to destruction of predatory beasts."[6] In December the paper ran another blurb on the survey's exploits. Titled "Capture Wolf: Hunters Dispose of Colorado 'Killer,'" the piece recounted the previous month's body count: "One hundred and seevnty-eight coyotes, one grey wolf, two lynx, and nearly two hundred small fur-bearing animals were captured by federal hunters of the predatory animal section of the biological survey during November, says tSanley P. Young, head of the bureau." The article continued: "The wolf captured was one of the most destrutcive 'killers' known in recent years in Colorado. Together with her mate ,who was killed recently, the animal had done thousands of dollars of daamge to herds and flocks."[7]

Despite the article's histrionic tone, the wolf in question was never given a name or written up further for popular edification. Suffice it to say that almost every wolf from that point on would be known as a "killer," a "criminal," or some similarly dramatic epithet—reflecting the increasing rarity of wolves and the attendant interest in each remaining one. In 1921 the survey recorded killing twenty-five wolves in Colorado, seven fewer than the previous year but once again more than would die in any future year.[8]

The appellations also reflected growing popular concern over the violent crime beginning to plague the nation as bootleggers battled each other and police to profit from Prohibition. A longer article from January 1921 (twelve months after Prohibition had gone into effect but before the criminality it would engender had become apparent), noting the capture of Lefty, had described the wolf merely as "cunning" but not as a criminal or a killer. The introduction of these terms in the later articles indicated Young's adeptness (conscious or not) at molding the Biological Survey's image to the evolving zeitgeist.

Young's ability to garner press attention had first surfaced in Arizona, where he had used the media to encourage cooperative relationships between the Biological Survey and local ranchers who initially might have shied away from any entanglement with the federal government. For example, Young had publicly heralded a state senator-elect as "one of the most willing of the Apache county men who have stock interests in co-operating with the survey service in exterminating the coyote on Arizona ranges," probably thereby winning his subject's long-term support.[9]

Proselytizing came naturally to Young, whose middle name, Paul, honored the apostle who had gone forth to convert gentiles in a foreign land. The Biological Survey's gentiles were urban dwellers with no experience with predators' destructiveness to cattle and sheep. Even at this early stage in his career, Young recognized intuitively that the backing of the growing urban majority would go far in enabling the survey to carry on its extermination agenda, and he took pains not to alienate potential supporters. The January 1921 article on Lefty's capture had included a summary of conditions attending his sequestration: "With food and water within easy reach, and after receiving the best of medical attention to avert suffering, 'Big Lefty' has been tied near one of the principal runways of the pack and around him officers have set a score of steel traps as well as poisoned bait stations."[10] Although water and perhaps even food might have been left for Lefty, it is hard to believe Roberts gave the condemned wolf any medical attention. Clearly, the statement reflected Young's sensitivity to the feelings of a public that had neither been sold on nor deeply considered the extermination policy.

Young's shrewdness in portraying the survey's work to a largely urban audience stood in stark contrast to the recently retired Crawford's awkward scuffles with his agricultural constituency—whether over poisoning dogs or exterminating bears. The difference in styles in part reflected generations. The very concept of a public opinion to manipulate dated from Young's formative adolescent years, during which President Teddy Roosevelt had developed a "bully pulpit" to command the nation's attention. Public opinion's great boom, at least as measured by commercial advertising, was still several years away.[11]

Ideologically, Young was a man of his era, a believer in progress and never a deep questioner of the verities of the times. Yet he was sufficiently bright to use the central insight and technique of advertising—the association of a product with a topic that already commands subjects' emotions (as wolves with criminals)—before the methodology became standard procedure. In 1921 such strategic communication was still somewhat a novelty—not unknown, yet no more integrated into the daily considerations of most Biological Survey officials than were the automobiles that occasionally transported hunters from one end of a wolf's range to another. (Not just the survey but also its animal targets were taken in by the newness of cars. In the fall of that year Young's former Arizona supervisor, Mark E. Musgrave, riding shotgun in one of the newfangled contraptions, had spotted a wolf 150 yards away on a ridge. Musgrave stepped out of the slowly moving vehicle and, with the wolf's attention focused on the animate-seeming car, fatally shot it. The incident merited mention in a newspaper and stuck in Young's memory for decades.[12])

The automobile, representing modernity, became the perfect prop to hang the remains of creatures whose ongoing eradication marked the march of progress, including these coyotes and skunks. (J. Stokley Ligon Papers, CONS92, Conservation Collection, Denver Public Library)

Like the automobile, the concept of public opinion reflected a world that had expanded beyond the boundaries of the small-town general store. Public opinion was formed less by personal experiences or over-the-fence anecdotes between neighbors and more by mediated and mass-produced information and points of view.[13]

Young's canny association of wolves with criminals in the December 1921 news article took advantage of the demise of provincialism and the emergence in its stead of a new era of public opinion. Those individuals and institutions, such as Young and his Colorado outpost of the Biological Survey, capable of deliberately shaping and distilling information would henceforth enjoy a tremendous advantage in determining public policy.[14]

Young also pursued support the traditional way—in person. In January 1922 he gave a talk at the annual stockgrowers' association meeting. Such outreach allowed him to pitch the survey, get direct feedback from its primary constituents, and request their public backing. The ranchers were happy to give him their endorsements. In March 1922 the Colorado Stockgrowers Association formally requested that both its local affiliates and counties suspend bounty payments and rely entirely on the survey's efforts. Other resolutions from county-level ranching associations explicitly commended the survey's work and called for increased appropriations for the agency.[15] Young worked to ensure that every time his hunters completed a job—whether trapping a single wolf or poisoning all the coyotes in a valley—they solicited a thank-you letter as testimonial from the happy rancher. He well understood that both formal resolutions and individual expressions of support would prove useful in future appropriation requests—whether to the state legislature or the U.S. Congress. Nor, he realized, would such documentation hurt appraisals of his own performance at the survey office in Washington.

Young's comfortable relationship with ranchers helped make 1922 another successful year for the survey. The same month he attended the stockgrowers' meeting, another rancher-banker, referred to only by his surname Wilcoxson, dropped by the survey's Denver office. Like his colleague Joseph Neal, Wilcoxson—hailing from the town of Debeque near the area where Rags used to roam—requested a wolf hunter for the region. Young readily agreed, with one proviso: that Wilcoxson and his fellow ranchers withdraw a $500 bounty they had posted for the male of the runagate wolf pair, known as Bigfoot. Young explained, "[w]e can't have any amateurs messing up that den, smearing the trails, putting in clumsy trap sets and scaring these wolves."[16]

With the condition met, Young dispatched Hegewa Roberts to the job. It took Roberts a month, but in March he located Bigfoot and his mate's den, occupied by a new litter of pups. Local cowboys urged him to dig the den out for the pups, but he demurred. "I can poison them," he said. "If it comes to a final showdown, I can get poison into a yearling wolf. Even a two-year-old will take it. But it's trappin' that old he-leader that takes the pains. And as long as there is a chance to catch him on his runs from the den, I'm goin' to stick to that plan."[17]

On April 4 Roberts's plan came to fruition with the capture of savvy old Bigfoot within a mile of the den. Before riding back to the cow camp for assistance in taking the wolf from the trap alive, Roberts left his handkerchief hanging from a stick in front of the den, dug into the base of a shaley cliff. "I was afraid the old she-wolf would come to that den and get out those whelps," he explained. "No wolf will go back to a den with a cap or rag on a stick stuck up in front of it. You can't block them by filling in rocks or dirt in the mouth of the den. They'll dig right through that. But this mysterious rag with the man scent will keep 'em away for hours—and keep the whelps in, too."[18]

The trick worked, and after hours of digging with a pick and shovel Roberts snaked into the den with thick leather gloves. One by one he grabbed each of seven shivering pups from among its brothers and sisters, clustered against the back of the den, and stuffed it into a canvas bag to be killed later.

After killing the pups, he dissected their scent glands and concocted an olfactory lure for their mother, still at large. A three-legged wolf armed with the cautionary lesson of her missing limb, she would enter a trap only with the strongest enticement. But as Roberts expected, the scent of her missing pups dabbed near the den did the trick, and on April 26 the final member of that wolf family was trapped and killed.[19] Roberts wrote Young a summary note:

I had almost given up being able to trap her, as she was one with trap experience, having lost the left hind foot, when, on going to the traps yesterday morning, what should be in No. 14, but the old sister! Tickled is how I felt, and the job of taking her hide off was a pleasure I had looked forward to for months.[20]

That same blustery April the survey unearthed six other wolf pups from their den north of the town of Fruita along the Colorado River near Utah. In May Bill Caywood killed another wolf in northwestern Colorado, and in June he killed two more, all from the same pack. Another wolf that June was caught in one of the survey's coyote traps and escaped. Then in November the survey trapped a wolf near the town of Thatcher on the southeastern plains, for a total of nineteen wolves killed in the calendar year. Once again, although this number was lower than the tally for 1921, it was more than would be killed in subsequent years.[21]

To cap the year's successful captures, in the last two weeks of 1922 and the first two weeks of the new year Young landed a much bigger media catch than the previous year's short news clips: four Sunday spreads in the *Rocky Mountain News,* comprising one full-page photo essay and three lengthy narrative articles, that revealed, if nothing else, how remote from urban interests predator extermination had become.

Since 1915, when Congress had first authorized the survey to systematically kill predators and rodents, the nation had fought and won a world war. Even before that, in the period since the first state bounty had been offered, Denver had evolved from a frontier agricultural and mining post to a commercial center, and Pueblo had industrialized. Turn-of-the-century articles, predicated on a common base of knowledge and lore, had seldom needed to provide background information on wolves or on efforts to kill them. In contrast, the prolix title alone of the *Rocky Mountain News*'s December 31, 1922, full-page spread sought to recast the war against the species in a fresh societal context—one amalgamating crime-fighting and pioneering: "U.S. AGENTS STALK 'DESPERADOES' OF ANIMAL WORLD THRU DESERTS AND OVER MOUNTAIN RANGES OF WEST: Grim Sun-Bronzed Men Trail Predatory Creatures to Death in Government Campaign to Protect Civilization, Simple Diary Entries of Kills and Captures Conceal Record of Many Hardships and Thrilling Battles of Wits and Brute Force in Silences of Wood and Hill." The feature article opened by laboring to explain the moral significance of exterminating the last few remaining wolves:

NOT YET is the wilderness won. Grim, relentless, trammeled, yet untamed, the spirit of nature battles against encroaching civilization—battles and seems temporarily to win, although inevitably the struggle must be a losing one. Mighty in its untutored majesty is the out-of-doors, but mightier is man. The progress of nature is in unerring circles: She moves forward only to swing back again. Man's progress is ever onward, forward. He is impeded, never stopped.

"Animal criminals" along with "soldiers of the wilderness." Young is at the far right, and Albert K. Fisher, his boss in D.C., whom he would eventually replace, is pictured on the bottom. (Rocky Mountain News, *Denver, CO*)

The history of civilization is written in terms of its struggle against enemies. Thru immemorial aeons there have been forces to contend against—forces which have threatened at times to overcome even the ever-conquering deity which is the spirit of man.[22]

The piece went on to explain the economic rationale for exterminating predators and the failure of the bounty system, echoing the Biological Survey's orthodox policy line. But clearly its appeal for a public enjoying the fresh fruits of 1920s prosperity[23] lay in evoking the self-sacrificing heroism of war, crime-fighting, and pioneering:

> What are they like—these men of the out-of-doors—these soldiers of the wilderness who work day in, day out to protect civilization against the desperadoes of the desert and mountain.
>
> Grim, sun-bronzed, taciturn fellows, many of them are with a great love of the silences of wood and hill, and a devotion to duty under every circumstance which reminds one strongly of the men of the Northwest mounted police. When one thinks of the hunter doggedly pursuing the trail of some animal criminal across rocky wastes, over wind-swept crags, and thru dark forests, waiting, watching, and scheming relentlessly until at last he makes his capture, the strength of the comparison with the policeman of Canada who undergoes inconceivable hardship and danger to track down an outlaw is evident. . . .
>
> The hunter's descriptions of his work are brief. He is a matter-of-fact sort of person. When he writes in his daily diary, which constitutes the basis for his report to headquarters, "Thursday, July 20. Took two wolves up Higby gulch. Put out poison baits and riding my trap line," his duties for the day sound quite prosaic. In reality, however, the capture of the two wolves may be a thrilling climax to many long days of waiting and watching and working to bring a pair of villains with a long record of crime back of them to justice.[24]

In concluding such a heart-throbbing tale of good versus evil, the article abandoned verisimilitude entirely to better serve Young's propagandistic agenda. Blithely contradicting the decades-long observations of strychnine's often prolonged and always agonizing effects, the reporter addressed any compunctions readers might hold about the humaneness of the survey's work:

> "Unutterably hideous, inspeakably cruel" someone may murmur, shuddering. Not so. Poisoning has been found the cheapest, the surest, the quickest, the kindest and hence the most effiicent method of operation in eradicating animal pests. The creature does not know what is happening to him. It acts so quickly that death comes without preliminary suffering. When one remembers that nearly every creature of the wilds meets a tragic death, it seems almost that poisoning animals is a boon to them rather than a bane.[25]

The sensitivity to animal suffering reflected the continued strength in the early 1920s of the humane movement, one of the many initiatives for reform that had blossomed thanks to the energies of the broader women's movement. By 1925 this concern over treatment of animals led to the formation of the Anti–Steel Trap League, which paid little attention to poisoning, much less to whether extermination was appropriate at all.[26] But whereas Young sought to depict poisoning as humane, his supervisor in Washington, D.C., Albert K. Fisher, in charge of the Division of Economic Investigations for the survey,

Young poisoning part of a carcass. (Bureau of Biological Survey)

counterattacked on a more fundamental level and to a national audience. In a November 1922 article for *The Farm Journal* entitled "Steel Traps, Animals and Pain," Fisher outlined a hierarchy of sensitivity to pain. "To students of anthropology it is a well-known fact," he wrote to an audience accustomed to reading about the latest farming improvements, "that savages and illiterate men suffer less from pain than those with high-strung mental development." From that premise, in sections of the article subtitled "The Natives Suffer Little" and "Reflex Action Mistaken for Pain" he argued that the "lower forms of animal life" likewise feel little pain from injuries and that even mammals in traps do not suffer unduly.[27]

The *Rocky Mountain News* series also sought to build public support by emphasizing the survey's reliance on science. The paper's full-page photo essay on December 24, 1922, called the agency "a scientific and efficient machine," whereas the January 7, 1923, article appropriated language directly from the survey's annual report in referring to the agency's "[d]iligent field studies."[28]

Such rhetoric took advantage of the contemporary adulation of science. As the chief chronicler of the age, social historian Frederick Lewis Allen, wrote, "The prestige of science was colossal." He added, "The word science had become a shibboleth. To preface a statement with 'Science teaches us' was enough to silence argument. If a sales manager wanted to put over a promotion scheme or a clergyman to recommend a charity, they both hastened to say that it was scientific."[29]

The survey had been born to a scientific mission in 1885, and vestiges of that legacy remained. The survey's leadership remained vitally interested in properly classifying species and subspecies, including those they consigned to extinction.[30] Nevertheless, science was now largely subordinated to the survey's "economic" functions, chief among them predator and rodent extermination. Back at the turn of the century "approximately three times more was spent on scientific work than on economic work," according to the survey's semi-official biographer of the late 1920s, Jenks Cameron. But by 1921 pure science had shrunk to around 3 percent of the agency's budget,[31] and the field studies mentioned in the 1923 annual report and the *Rocky Mountain News* article consisted of reports of depredations passed on by ranchers. Young, who later matured into a genuine scholar, may have wanted to view his agency as still primarily scientific. But whatever it meant to his self-image, by attaching the patina of science to the survey in 1923 he also further inoculated the agency against potential public disapproval.

The *Rocky Mountain News* article from January 7, 1923—the next-to-last in the series—bore a title fully as dramatic as the one the week before: "LOBO, MASTER MARAUDER OF PREDATORY ANIMALS, MATCHES CUNNING AGAINST WITS OF U.S. HUNTERS: Wolves Are Most Crafty of Four-Footed Outlaws, Gifted With Almost Uncanny Faculty of Evading Traps and Snares of Men of Biological Survey, Who Live Rigorous Lives Tracking Down Destroyers of Herds of Cattle and Sheep Flocks of Ranchers in Valleys and on Plains." Surprisingly, however, this piece opened with a sympathetic glimpse of life at a wolf den:

> There are an even dozen of them, funny, fat furry, little fellows with short, wabbly legs, big ears and eyes as bright as buttons. The wolf mother, mate of old Lefty, famous three-footed animal outlaw, is inordinately proud of them as they roll and waddle about in the dusky shadows of the den, nosing about among the refuse of bones, hair and feathers which remain from yesterday's feast, or snapping at each others' tails with a playfulness so vehement that it is accompanied by frequent squeaky yelps. Not unlike little dogs they are, these wolf pups with their roly-poly bodies and their desire to romp. Perhaps the reason their mother watches them so solicitously and pricks her ears at every tiny sound outside is that last year her young ones mysteriously disappeared one night. The strange toeless tracks made by man animals had been about the opening of the cave.

But the semblance of balanced reporting represented in this portrayal of wolf domesticity quickly succumbed to the article's main points—the challenge the survey faced in exterminating such canny wolves and a reminder of why they must die:

> The pilgrimage for food is often made at night thru black forests and across deep-shadowed ravines. Every stick and stone is carefully

observed by the foragers. Hunters have long ago discovered that wolves will circle a trap that is carelessly concealed. They are suspicious if even a broken twig is on the trail which was not there when last they passed over. If the trapper has left loose earth upturned or has dropped a matchstick in the grass these most sagacious members of the animal kingdom will mark it. . . .

Presently the grim foragers emerge upon a grassy mesa where several hundred head of cattle are grazing. With the discrimination of experienced epicures they choose the victim for their kill. Tonight it is the tender, succulent flesh of a 2-year-old steer that is sought. A few sharp-fanged nips at the creature's flanks are enough to start the excitement of the attack. Mad with fright and pain the harrassed animal plunges and reels, pursued by a mysterious terror. The wolves follow, one at either side, tearing off great pieces of flesh and snapping at the vitals.

Sometimes thru human interference or other intervention the wolves do not complete their gruesome task. Often a steer has the tail torn off in some such combat. Occasionally the hunter or stockman finds a stricken creature suffering from wounds inflicted in his hind quarters thru which the entrails may be exuding. There is nothing to be done in such a case but to put an end to the animal's misery. It is another addition to the record of crime which civilization is writing against wolves.

Ebullient with a sense of history in the making, striving to evoke the frustrations evinced by actual frontiersmen, the piece went on to describe experiences remote from those of most readers:

Bob [the survey trapper], who had been detailed to the region after years of fruitless effort on the part of bounty seekers and suffering ranchers to annihilate the plunderer, worked with a patience equaled in almost no other profession. In determining Grit's [the wolf's] course, he had spent long days out under a blazing sun with little food to stay his hunger. He had slept out many a night when a chill, drizzling rain spattered thru the branches of his tree shelter, stiffening his joints and filling him with a sense of grim foreboding.

The conclusion was unambiguous in outcome, although almost regretful in tone:

The story of Lobo, the outlaw, master marauder, is a story of yesterday and today. His cruel, rapacious devastations give him no place in modern civilization. Were it not for the work of the United States government, he would continue to be the villain in tales of torture to innocent wild life, destruction of protected game, and ravages on the cattle ranges incurring millions of dollars' economic waste, for many years to come. As it is, tomorrow he will be gone. In the fastnesses of our mountains he is making his last stand agains humanity, and with his passing something of spirit of the wilderness must die, too, that the conquerors may live.[32]

On January 19, 1923, Young again appeared at the annual stockgrowers' convention, this time armed with a slide projector to better illustrate the survey's work. Unlike the readers of the recent *Rocky Mountain News* series, this far more partisan audience needed no philosophical maundering to convince them of the need to exterminate carnivores. Young was happy to cut to the chase at the outset:

> Gentlemen, since I talked to your meeting a year ago, I am going to try to give you something a little different. I am going to talk about predatory animals, of course, but I [am] going to tell you that we have about 3,000 less predatory animals in the state of Colorado than we had at that time. There have been some notorious wolf packs cleaned up entirely. . . . Well, doubtless you all say, or think, "we have them yet on our ranges and you haven't reached us yet." Well, we practically know the existence of every wolf pack in Colorado and it is just a question of time as to when we will be able to get around to your place and eradicate them.[33]

Unlike the more general audience, the stockgrowers' association also needed no reassurance that the survey's work was painless. One slide indicated a coyote hanging by a trapped leg over the bank of an irrigation ditch. "When he was caught he jumped and went over in the ditch," Young explained. "That is a part of the method of the government trapper in making the wolf and coyote set." Other slides graphically illustrated the techniques and results of poisoning campaigns. "Now here is [a] typical view of the one of many thousands poisoned by us in Colorado," Young expounded as the audience focused on the strangely contorted remains of a coyote. "If you ever find one of those in the range you will find everyone laying in that shape. It is from the final convulsions of strychnine poison. You see this fellow—the end of the tail is straight out. This was on Mr. Brown's sheep range at Montrose."[34]

Shortly after Young's appearance at the stockgrowers' convention, local sheep ranchers in the Tennessee Pass area near Leadville raised $500 to join the survey's network of private cooperators. Beyond continuing the high-quality service it had come to expect on the ground, Young reciprocated the ranching community's confidence in his agency through his enthusiasm for a bill giving ranchers more direct oversight over the survey's performance. The legislation appropriating a new batch of state money for the extermination campaign included a provision establishing the Colorado State Board of Stock Inspection Commissioners as the body representing the state's interests in ensuring the survey used its predator extermination funds properly. Previous to this, the state Game and Fish Commission had worked with the survey, but the Stock Inspection Commissioners, responsible for fighting rustlers and determining ownership of any livestock in dispute, more closely represented ranching interests, and the Colorado Stockgrowers Association had pressed for its new assignment. In mentioning passage of the bill in a report to his supervisors, Young heralded the Stock Inspection Commissioners' "enthusiasm and whole-hearted feeling of real cooperation with the Bureau," adding that many members of its board "have game matters and the protection of game much at heart."[35] He did not need to mention their equally fervid interest in protecting their own industry.

The new state appropriations bill also set up an account, called the predatory animal fund, to provide additional and more convenient moneys for the extermination campaign. Pelts taken from wolves, coyotes, bobcats, lynx, or mountain lions captured by hunters whose wages were paid by the state appropriation would be sold and the proceeds deposited in the fund, to be tapped later. Designed so remains of these animals would help finance the killing of more creatures, the fund provided a source of revenue available to the survey during the recurring periods after state funds had run out and before new appropriations could be approved. The first fur sale, in December 1923, yielded $2,561.55—a substantial sum for the time, roughly equivalent to one month's total expenditures for the survey in Colorado.

Although the Stock Inspection Commissioners would oversee the accounting, their job was not difficult. Survey reports already broke down which funds— federal, state, county, or local ranching association—paid for which hunters and when. Although every hunter answered directly to Young or his assistants, the breakdown of animals killed according to the various "co-operators" had long helped members of each cooperating body—from state legislators and county commissioners to members of a local wool growers' association— better visualize what they got for their money.[36]

The momentum of so many entities, under one competent person's supervision, putting their money and sometimes their volunteer effort toward exterminating predators yielded significant results. The survey planted 31,255 poison baits in Colorado during 1923, accounting for many of the 1,406 coyotes it recorded killed. That year rangers in the Pike National Forest began guiding the survey's hunters to areas they knew were frequented by mountain lions. "As the result of this team work, it is easily seen that any particular forest can be given a good combing by said policy and help considerably towards the eradication of any known lion existing therein," Young noted in anticipating expansion of the procedure. Although only 7 mountain lions were killed in the state that year, the survey accounted for 97 bobcats and 37 lynxes as well.[37]

But as usual, the wolves interested Young most, and the fiscal year 1923 annual report, written in July of that year, assessed progress in eradicating the species:

> Continued work toward complete eradication of known wolf packs in the district has been the policy adhered to in the twelve-months' period. From evidence gained of known wolves in Colorado, the number at present on the ranges approximate [sic] fifty. With the exception of this year's increase, each one of these wolves is noted for its shyness and its uncanny knowledge of avoiding any method toward capture. Complete eradication of wolves in Colorado is going to take time, and it is felt this can only be accomplished by concentrating on known ranges and staying with the job until each area is cleaned of wolf packs.[38]

As it turned out, fifty animals was a significant overestimation of the state's remaining wolf population. In 1923 the survey managed to kill seventeen wolves (one carrying an unborn litter of seven pups), two fewer than the year before. Just like the year before, most of these wolves had lived and died in the northwestern portion of the state—the area that had previously housed Rags, Lefty, and Bigfoot.[39] But consistent digging out of the pup-filled dens in northwestern Colorado had prevented any rebound in the region's wolf population, and 1923 turned out to be the last year for multiple wolf killings. Each subsequent year in the 1920s, 1930s, and 1940s would yield at most a single dead wolf, with increasingly long intervals between the killings.

Young's excellent relations with the livestock industry undoubtedly contributed to the accomplishments of this 1923 endgame in the Colorado front of the wolf extermination campaign. Young, the ranchers sensed instinctively, was one of them—a man who understood both the hardships of wresting a living from an untamed landscape and the proper relationship of the national government to those on the frontier. His hunters could always count on housing, spare horses, tools, and any other assistance they needed from local ranchers. His efforts to enlist more of the general public and a larger constituency of those concerned with game animals likely also helped ensure continuing financial support from the Colorado General Assembly. But a third reason for the agency's success was explained by the high spirits and the sense of mission Young instilled among his hunters. The pride he felt in government service carried over to his employees. His standards were tough, but whatever the difficulties his men experienced in the forests and deserts, they knew Young had probably endured the same in his rise from hired trapper to predatory animal inspector. One employee acknowledged this in a report submitted in verse and printed in the *Rocky Mountain News* series:

> Dear Mr. Young: You know how I feel perhaps
> When I ain't had no luck with my other traps,
> When Sat. the Bix line I run
> Find six sets dugout and another sprung
> Then tonight I say in my report
> Seven sets spoilt by a coyote sport.
> I can see you shake your head and hear you say
> You're not much of a trapper, hey?
> But I thinks me a few years back or so
> And I think maybe it happened to you, you know,
> And if for this day's work you turn me down in sad disgrace,
> Get a worser man to take my place.
> I will always think to my dieing day
> That I worked dam hard to earn my pay;
> But working hard don't amount to a dam
> If I don't deliver to Uncle Sam.
> I hope to say in my next report
> I brought in that darned old sport.

P.S.—And I did also an old male today. It was a female that got my goat and that is not unusual in life.[40]

It is easy to understand the sedulousness toward the work and the loyalty to Young beneath this doggerel. Young most enjoyed working in the field with his men, and they sensed it.[41] In the spring of 1923 Young roped together a local Farm Bureau chapter and the Kansas Agricultural College to pay for an inaugural coyote-trapping project in Kansas—which he heretofore had lacked the resources to cover. Three months later Young drove east from the Denver offices in the company of Bill Caywood to complete work on the campaign. It rained almost the entire time they spent on the prairie. But decades later both Caywood and Young remembered how much they enjoyed each other's company. "It was 25 years yesterday that you & I came back from Kansas to Denver & if I remeber ritely I was out to your house the next night & took Diner With you & famely," Big Bill wrote in 1948. "I mis those visits when I am in Denver."[42] Young wrote back: "Well do I remember our Kansas trip of a quarter century ago, and how you chewed so much tobacco, and in getting rid of each squirt plastered my rear fender with the aid of the wind until it looked more like a deloused chicken house than a fender. Them were the happy days!"[43]

The value of such esprit de corps came into cameo relief on the southeastern plains in the spring of 1923. Just a few years prior, this region had constituted one of the state's wolf population strongholds. But between 1915 and 1919 the survey had killed around eighteen wolves. Then the killing slowed somewhat. In 1919 a wolf had been run down by hounds owned by a private party. In October 1920 the survey trapped three more wolves in the region. Early the next year Young had trapped Whitey and a female wolf from the same pack. Subsequently, Whitey's newborn pups were dug out of their den. Finally, in November 1922 another wolf was killed—likely a pup from Whitey's previous litter.

Now Three-Toes, old Whitey's trap-scarred mate, wandered the grasslands of southeastern Colorado alone. Young's administrative and political responsibilities had kept him from staying on the job until Three-Toes was captured. Nevertheless, he hadn't forgotten the female wolf, and neither had local ranchers. Without a pack she represented much less of a threat than the wolves in northwestern Colorado, whose continued breeding threatened to undo years of survey work. But her procreative instincts were not stymied by the absence of male wolves in the region, and that brought the survey back.

In the fall of 1922 Three-Toes mated with a ranch dog, who subsequently abandoned his owners and accompanied the wolf on her peregrinations and occasional cattle-killing raids. Young sent Hegewa Roberts to the region, and the experienced wolf hunter quickly managed to poison the collie, but not Three-Toes.

The next spring the wolf bitch gave birth to a litter of wolf-dog hybrids, but before Roberts could continue setting traps and poison, he was fired for what

Roy Spangler pursued Three-Toes while his wife lay dying of smallpox in June 1923. Capturing this last reproducing wolf on the Great Plains meant he could keep his new Biological Survey job and support his four motherless children. (Willard R. Prator, grandson of Roy C. Spangler)

remains an undisclosed transgression of survey regulations. To replace him in the hunt for Three-Toes, one of Young's field assistants, John W. Crook, hired a local ranch hand named Roy C. Spangler, whose eagerness to work for the survey induced him to offer his labors for free if he failed to get the wolf—on the condition that his job would be permanent should he succeed.

Having just lost a man for violating survey rules, Crook took pains in emphasizing to Spangler the seriousness of the trust bestowed in him as a predatory animal hunter for the United States government, Department of Agriculture, Bureau of Biological Survey. He emphasized the need for self-sacrifice and regaled the applicant with tales of survey hunters' heroic perseverance in the face of blizzards and every other obstacle.

Spangler took the job imbued with the full sense of purpose and obligation his employment entailed. For weeks he set traps for Three-Toes and her hybrid offspring, taking to the trail early each morning and often returning after nightfall. When his wife took sick in early June, she urged him to stay on the job rather than care for her. On June 11, 1923, Three-Toes finally fell into one of his traps and fled for miles with the trap and drag hook attached to her. Despite his wife's worsening condition, Spangler trailed the wolf to ensure nobody else would find her and claim credit for the kill. Returning in triumph with the trussed-up wolf on his horse, still alive, he found his wife dead, a victim of smallpox.

Spangler was left alone with four young children, but his work had finally put an end to this determinedly prolific wolf. Such was the dedication to the job Young managed to inspire. Never again in the twentieth century, as far as is known, did a wild wolf give birth on the U.S. portion of the once-great plains.[44]

A Campaign Against Magpies

With all but a handful of wolves gone from the West, the Biological Survey turned with increased vigor to killing coyotes, now nominated as the number-one predatory threat. On June 29, 1922, one of Colorado's deputy state game wardens, J. D. Jennings, wrote the survey a note of appreciation for its poisoning operations in the Gunnison area, calling coyotes "the most destructive beast that roams the home of our game."[1] The survey echoed that theme nationally: "Clearing the ranges of coyotes is proving a boon to the cattlemen as well as to the sheepmen," the chief of the survey wrote in the agency's fiscal year 1923 annual report. "With the practical elimination of the gray or timber wolf over much of the range country of the Western States, cattlemen have discovered that heavy losses of calves heretofore attributed to wolves have evidently been due to coyotes."[2]

It is likely, in fact, that not only were some wolf depredations actually the work of coyotes (as well as of feral dogs) but that coyotes began to take over wolves' ecological niche—the cooperative hunting of ungulates. Wolves had evolved complex social behaviors precisely to kill large animals that would be difficult and dangerous to attack alone, leaving coyotes to rely mostly on smaller animals such as rodents. There had always been some crossover in prey selection; wolves will readily eat hares, rabbits, and mice, and coyotes would occasionally cooperate to bring down ungulates—particularly individuals more vulnerable because of old age, disease, starvation, or other such factors. From the early 1920s onward, with wolves absent from most of the

West, coyotes likely banded together more often to take advantage of such prey.

In addition, killing wolves removed the most significant natural control on the coyote population. Despite the differences in their niches, wolves regard coyotes as competitors and kill them regularly. Studies at Yellowstone National Park in the mid-1990s, after the reintroduction of wolves to the ecosystem, revealed a dramatic decline in coyote numbers within wolf pack territories.[3] Despite the Biological Survey's official stance that rigorous scientific investigations determined their actions on the ground, the agency's officials had no idea that wiping out wolves would increase the number of coyotes. But judging by the agency's commitment to continue its work at any cost, there is no reason to believe such information would have made an iota of difference in its policies. (In 1937 Aldo Leopold published an essay noting the absence of coyotes in Mexico's Sierra Madre range and positing that wolves "kept the coyotes out." But although he suggested allowing wolves and mountain lions to "come back in reasonable numbers" in the "rougher mountains" of the United States,[4] the survey's course did not change.)

Aside from whatever was happening on the ground, survey officials clearly needed to elevate the coyote's status for purely budgetary reasons. By fiscal year 1923 federal animal-killing appropriations amounted to $276,890, and the cooperators chipped in an additional $243,000—totaling more than half the agency's budget of $913,123.[5] If the threat of wolves had opened the purse strings of Congress, western states, counties, and private associations, then wolves' imminent disappearance left a serious void to be filled. Stanley P. Young wrote in the calendar year 1925 progress report for his Colorado-Kansas district that "[w]ith the wolf problem at this time requiring so little effort and expenditure of money, allows [sic] of more effort to be devoted to the coyote problem which is the range problem in Colorado."[6]

The most efficient weapon against coyotes remained strychnine. Each year in the early 1920s the survey's plant in Denver (it had been moved from Albuquerque in October 1921 at Young's urging and been named the Eradication Methods Laboratory) churned out more strychnine tablets for hunters throughout the West to insert in baits or to give ranchers for their use. The agency's fiscal year 1922 annual report boasted of setting "about 1,229,000 specially prepared and highly effective poisoned baits devised by bureau experts" and cited some of the results: "In a period of five weeks two Utah hunters put out a poison line approximately 300 miles long in a great loop and around their first two stations on their return found about 40 dead coyotes. A stockman wrote that these men did good work, for, as he put it, they left a string of dead coyotes wherever they went."[7]

In 1923 the survey upped the number of baits to 1,703,000, and in 1924 it more than doubled the number to 3,567,000, covering, by its own estimation, 284,400 square miles.[8]

We have seen that poison could inadvertently kill domestic dogs, a recurring problem for the survey throughout the West. That risk, combined with the growing use of poison, ironically led to vast areas in which hound hunting of mountain lions, bobcats, and lynxes was infeasible, thus eliminating the surest means to bring about the eradication of these felids. Trained and highly valuable hunting dogs were at least as likely to gulp down a bait as were coyotes or wolves, and lions could also be poisoned, although less reliably. As early as the teen years, with narrower time frames and locations in which to hunt with dogs, the survey's Colorado district could not afford to keep on staff a hunter dedicated to training and maintaining them. As a result, hunters with other duties kept survey-owned dogs but brought them on a hunt only when a mountain lion was reported.[9] In 1924 Young's old boss in New Mexico, Stokley Ligon, complained that poison put out by ranchers (but likely supplied by the survey) in the southwestern part of the state had kept out the survey's lion hunters for several years.[10] And in Arizona, Mark E. Musgrave lost a lion dog to the agency's poison and later told his fellow state predatory animal inspectors that "coyote poisoning work on mountain lion infested ranges will defeat mountain lion eradication."[11] The decision to rely so extensively on poison is the most significant reason wolves vanished from the West while cougars did not. (The survey continued to kill predatory cats whenever feasible, but the inadequacy of these efforts in Colorado may have contributed to the 1919 decision of *The Denver Post* and the Douglas County Stock Growers Association to institute and fund new mountain lion bounties.[12])

The new emphasis on poisoning coyotes brought about other problems as well. "It is impossible to conduct coyote poisoning work on account of magpies, because these birds will clean out all poison baits around coyote poison stations so that no baits are exposed at the time coyotes visit the same," Young reported in January 1926. The solution was "a campaign against magpies to be instituted over the major portion of the San Luis Valley." Although the survey's strychnine coyote baits killed the black-and-white scavenging birds as well, the agency developed a special "processed magpie poison" that was easier for the birds to gulp down and issued it to its cooperators in the region.[13]

Those cooperators reflected the survey's ability to develop a loose alliance of hunters and ranchers against a species that had never before been notorious for impinging on human interests. In addition to local agriculturalists, the eager cooperating poison contingent included the Three River Fish and Game Association, a hunting group that had been introducing to the area Hungarian partridges, Mongolian pheasants, and California valley quail— on whose eggs the magpies had apparently been dining. Having assembled the requisite cooperating interest group, the survey proceeded to attack the birds it resented for stealing poison baits from the intended victims, themselves newly ascendant to the top tier of animal enemies only since the demise of wolf populations. "Heretofore," Young concluded without a hint of the burlesque, "in many localities of the San Luis Valley it has been necessary to eradicate magpies first before any effective work with coyote poisoning could be done."[14]

"Coyote poisoning work on mountain lion infested ranges will defeat mountain lion eradication," according to the survey's Arizona district predatory animal inspector, Mark E. Musgrave (not pictured). Here, Musgrave's former employee Chas. Miller, standing, contemplates his six lion dogs, intended for his new career as an independent hunting outfitter, but accidentally poisoned by the survey shortly after his retirement from the agency in 1923. The squatting man is not identified. (Outdoor Life, *December 1932*)

Not only did wiping out wolves increase the number of coyotes and change their behavior, in turn requiring the killing of magpies, but killing the coyotes also released the principal lid on the rodent population. The last of the fawning four-part *Rocky Mountain News* feature series on the survey from 1922–1923, entitled "Rodents Are Everlasting Menace to Civilization," acknowledged that "man has also destroyed the natural enemies of the rodents by aimlessly killing off those birds and animals provided by nature as a check."[15] (The journalist did not make the connection to her previous three articles, perhaps because none of the killing described in them was aimless.) In 1927 the director of the Utah Agricultural College made the case to the delegates at the American National Livestock Association that, in the words of the survey's semi-official historian, "the coyote in earlier times had done much to keep the rodent within bounds," and therefore, "if the government removed coyote pressure upon the rodent it should be prepared to stop the rodent seethe-up which would inevitably follow."[16]

In the upper Arkansas River valley of Colorado, ground squirrels increased markedly in the mid- to late 1920s—an irruption the survey characterized as an "invasion." In the San Juans, porcupines—normally controlled by coyotes, wolves, bobcats, and mountain lions—ate the bark of so many trees that the survey contended they were more destructive than forest fires.[17] The same effect was noted elsewhere in the Southwest, and occasional Biological Survey

The Biological Survey provided poisoned grain for local people, often recruited by the Federal Extension Service and the Farm Bureau, to kill prairie dogs. This program would accelerate greatly after most of the prairie dogs' own predators had been killed off. (Yearbook of the U.S. Department of Agriculture, 1917)

hunter Ben V. Lilly of New Mexico—a life-long predator hunter and keen observer of the wilderness in which he lived—thought the porcupine increase was a result of the killing off of mountain lions.[18] The survey responded—characteristically—with a renewed emphasis on poisoning prairie dogs, ground squirrels, gophers, hares, porcupines, and other small creatures that consumed farmers' crops, ate grass that might sustain livestock, or damaged trees.[19]

The shift in emphasis from killing wolves to coyotes to rodents and even to magpies reveals the self-perpetuating aspect of the survey's work. Before it realized a budgetary incentive to do so, the survey had oscillated between regarding coyotes as a predatory foe and viewing them as beneficial. In 1908, for instance, Albert K. Fisher had written:

> In parts of the West where fruit growing and farming are dominant industries, it may be wise to encourage coyotes and bobcats within certain limits, provided poultry and sheep are properly protected at night. Numerous ranchmen and fruit growers have learned by experience that these animals if unmolested will free their premises from rabbits and other crop or tree destroyers. Where coyotes and bobcats have been allowed to do their work thoroughly they are fully appreciated, and many ranchers would almost as soon shoot their own dogs and cats as their wild benefactors. At times the coyote feeds entirely on large insects, as May beetles, crickets, and grasshoppers, and accomplishes much good.[20]

This sentiment conflicted with the intent of state bounty laws in the West, but the survey during that period regarded one of its most important functions as educating state legislatures on the most efficacious wildlife policies and was not unused to gainsaying accepted wisdom.[21] But since Congress had first appropriated money in 1915 for the survey to hire its own predator hunters, the agency had placed coyotes on its list of established enemies.

Nevertheless, the species had never elicited the same degree of vitriol and even respect as wolves had. Much of the survey's institutional identity, promulgated in newspaper articles such as the *Rocky Mountain News* series in 1922–1923, reflected the difficulty and hardship entailed in killing wolves and, to a lesser degree, mountain lions. It was only when wolves started to disappear from Colorado in the early to mid-1920s that Young began citing the wariness of individual coyotes and the consequent prestige attending their deaths, as he had long done with wolves. "Hunter W. J. Wilder, working in the Weston Pass country, succeeded in capturing what is believed to be the noted Rick Creek coyote that had been of considerable menace to sheepmen in the South Park country," he reported in 1923. "This coyote was trapped and was found to have the left front leg entirely missing at the elbow joint, which had evidently been shot off formerly in that country. This necessarily meant that the coyote limped considerably in his running the country, which was often noted by sheepmen."[22]

Notwithstanding the survey's increased attention to killing other animals, the few surviving wolves gained no respite. The fact that the killing infrastructure had a reason and a means to sustain itself meant it would still be prepared to act against the occasional wolf that might make an appearance. By the early to mid-1920s most wolves showing up in the West were migrants from Mexico or Canada, where the absence of anything approaching the survey's organized extermination program allowed wolf populations to persist. For example, the survey's fiscal year 1922 annual report boasted of "a total of 30 wolves destroyed along the international border [with Mexico] without allowing a wolf to drift more than 25 miles into the United States, and only one to escape back into Mexico."[23] And the few wolves remaining in the western United States would have faced, had the survey ceased its attentions toward them, daunting odds in re-establishing any population.

In Colorado, an old female wolf had long occupied an adjoining territory to that of Three-Toes, wandering from the foothills of the Wet Mountains (a small range west and southwest of Pueblo) down through the Huerfano River valley and into the plains, then south along the eastern flanks of the Sangre de Cristos to the Purgatoire River. It is almost certain that the two bitches had run across each other's scent markings, but with neither having found a male, the wolf tribe had no chance at perpetuation in the region.

Not only did Three-Toes likely know of this wolf, but so did local ranchers. In December 1923, six months after Three-Toes's demise, Young sent Bill Caywood to the region to finish off the other wolf, subsequently known as Greenhorn for the prominent peak in the Wet Mountains that dominated the heart of her range. This was not new country to the wolf hunter; he had spent his childhood wandering these forests and canyons.

Caywood was greeted at the Pueblo train station by the local U.S. Department of Agriculture County Extension agent, who told him the Greenhorn wolf didn't bite her prey so much as strangle it. From that, Caywood deduced that she was old and her teeth were worn down. He guessed she was having trouble killing prey and that, despite her advanced age (later estimated at eighteen years), she would be vulnerable to poison.

He was right. The Greenhorn wolf had tasted strychnine before and managed to disgorge the poison before it took effect. She had had both her front feet caught in traps and escaped. She had even survived a bullet and certainly understood that her old packmates' absences were caused by human hands. But in the chill of late December she was desperately hungry. A week before she had eaten an antelope, and a few days later she had devoured a rabbit. The day after Christmas 1923 she wandered on the plains east of her namesake mountain, searching for sustenance. She happened upon the scent of meat and, despite her forebodings, followed the trail it left to the head of a horse, dragged there by Caywood several days before and tied with metal wire to a scrubby oak. She circled warily, with slow, mincing steps alert for traps. She disdained to swallow the squares of flank fat scattered around and tore herself away from the temptations of the baits and trotted away.

But her ravenousness was too much for her, and the Greenhorn wolf returned to the enticing horse head and the deceitful beef and pork squares surrounding it. She sniffed at a square, mouthed it, and dropped it. She headed to the horse head and tried to rip some dried-up tissue from around the skull, already pecked at and stripped by magpies. The elusive taste of meat accentuated her hunger. She turned from the skull and found a loose mass of ground fat by a clump of oak. This was different from the solid squares she knew and feared. But it was just as deadly—magpie bait laced with the same strychnine as that in the squares. She sniffed at it suspiciously and walked away. But she couldn't stay away long. She turned back, sniffed again, and then yielded to her hunger and gulped down the shredded beef suet.

It only took a few minutes for the poison to strike, and when it did the agony in her bowels overcame the hunger of moments before. The Greenhorn wolf ran through brush to the top of a little ridge, fell down, got up again to struggle on, bit at her belly in desperation, and fell down again, quivering uncontrollably. She never rose.

Several days later, when Caywood returned from a Christmas vacation to check on his poison stations and a few trap sets, he discovered the Greenhorn wolf's tracks and traced her hesitation and acquiescence at the baits and her final travail. As he skinned the stiff carcass, removing the skull and hide for the Biological Survey's collection, he thought he had killed the last wolf that had been born in Colorado.[24]

Caywood might have been right, but wolves still occupied the state's borders, perhaps receiving some respite through the inefficiency of a system in which hunters were assigned on a state-by-state basis. Half a year later, in July 1924, the Biological Survey managed to kill one more wolf, believed to be a migrant from Wyoming, in northwestern Colorado's Burns Hole region where Lefty and his pack had been killed three and a half years previous.[25] In April 1925 the survey killed another wolf whose territory ranged from eastern Utah to western Colorado.[26] And in June of that year another wolf was spotted by a mammalogist, high in an alpine cirque in southern Wyoming. The wolf had just killed a marmot, reported the scientist, who—notwithstanding the growing interest of his professional society, the American Society of Mammalogists, in conserving predators—regretted his lack of a "firearm with which to disturb its somewhat exasperating nonchalance."[27]

The general collapse of wolf populations in the southern Rockies was summarized by Young in early February of that year:

> Relative to wolf work, gray wolves in Colorado are becoming a negligible quantity. We question whether there are more than ten existent in the district at this writing. These wolves in the main are what we have termed "border wolves", in that they cross back and forth from Colorado across the boundary lines to adjacent States and return at certain intervals of time. Plans have been laid and are being put into effect for eradicating these wolves, but this is going to take time as the known wolves of this

nature cover a vast scope of country in their travelways. The only wolf taken during the calendar year was of the kind that is particularly noted for heavy depredations. This wolf was one of the so-called "border wolves" that ranged from northern New Mexico into southern Colorado. It had been dubbed the name "Old Stubby" on account of the fact that its left front foot was missing which, evidently, was the work of a trap set by some private hunter in years past. The track of this wolf was first noticed across the Colorado side during a snow storm in April. The Survey hunters, in tracking this wolf at that time, came across the carcasses of two freshly killed calves. They succeeded in sighting the wolf on that day but could never get within rifle range.[28]

Young added, "The gray wolf problem in Colorado is practically under control, and funds formerly utilized in this work can now be utilized on increased coyote control."[29]

In re-orienting itself to newly significant challenges, the survey acted perhaps no differently than any other government bureaucracy whose officials believe their own work is important to the degree they themselves have invested their energies into it. But ranchers' unabated enthusiasm for the survey as wolves became a thing of the past also indicates a reliance on the agency that combined a financial motivation with more complicated psychological motives.

The pecuniary rationales for keeping the survey's hunters setting poison and traps for coyotes (and mountain lions, bobcats, lynx, and "stock-killing bears") are obvious. Beyond this convenience, however, lay deeper and no less powerful reasons for ranchers' dependence on the survey's work. Many ranchers had come to view a host of wild animals as affronts to their life mission of improving the untamed landscape. To such people, any animal whose flesh or pelt could not be sold symbolized a frontier as yet unredeemed by civilization. "I wish to congratulate the Department," rancher E. S. Edmundson wrote Young in February 1924 after Bill Caywood had spent two weeks setting poison in his vicinity on the prairie south of Pueblo, "for the diligence with which he has ridden the country of the magpies and stray dogs, and whatever coyotes there might have been."[30] It is almost as if the survey hunter served as a stress-reduction device in the presence of obstreperously noisy birds, dogs that might harass his stock, and anything else threatening to intrude on his ideal of bucolic pastoralism.

Intelligent Conservation

W hile the Biological Survey addressed ranchers' economic and psychological needs in the emerging post-wolf era, the first squeaks of opposition to predator extermination began to be voiced. In 1916 an article in *Science* magazine had suggested preserving carnivores in the national parks for the benefit of recreation and scientific research. "As a rule predaceous animals should be left unmolested and allowed to retain their primitive relation to the rest of the fauna," wrote the authors, Dr. Joseph Grinnell and Dr. Tracy Storer, "even though this may entail a considerable annual levy on the animals forming their prey."[1]

Grinnell was one of the most accomplished field naturalists in the country. Raised on Indian reservations served by his physician father, his "well-trained ear and quick eye" stemmed from his early association with Indian playmates, according to his wife.[2] But reservation life proved dangerous to the thirteen-year-old Joseph on the morning of December 29, 1890, at the Sioux encampment on Wounded Knee Creek in South Dakota. As U.S. troops demanded relinquishment of Indian weapons, his mother placed him for safekeeping with the wife of Chief Red Cloud, who brought him to their tepee. When the soldiers opened fire, Joseph couldn't help but peek out the flap at puffs of dust from bullets landing nearby but was jerked to greater safety inside by Red Cloud's wife. Unlike 150 or more Indians, Grinnell survived that day.[3]

Grinnell earned his bachelor's degree at age twenty while having found the time to travel to the rain forest of southeastern Alaska and to shoot animals

*Joseph Grinnell preparing specimens in the field. As early as 1916, Dr. Grinnell, the first director of the Museum of Vertebrate Zoology at the University of California at Berkeley, proposed preserving carnivores in national parks. The museum became a locus of scientific activism against the survey's poisoning campaign. (*The Condor, XLII, 1, January-February 1940, © Cooper Ornithological Society)

in the pursuit of science. Thirty-nine years old in 1916, he was a meticulous curator who eight years before had become director of the newly established Museum of Vertebrate Zoology on the University of California campus at Berkeley—a position he held until his death in 1939.[4]

Under Grinnell's strict oversight, the museum cataloged tens of thousands of animal specimens collected by his staff and by cooperating biologists. Grinnell's neat goatee and wire-rimmed glasses seemed to embody his compulsion for order. A martinet for proper procedure in the museum, he personally chose the tags and ink by which each animal's species identification, origin, and date of death were recorded. Correspondence with museum personnel, no matter how casual or personal in nature, was carefully filed and cross-referenced (an invaluable tool for historians). When subordinates fell short in following his system, Grinnell would deliver a written citation detailing the mistake. The note was to be returned to him when the condition was corrected, and after confirming that fact for himself he would initial the citation and place it in the employee's file.[5]

Storer was one of Grinnell's protégés at the Museum of Vertebrate Zoology, and he co-authored several guidebooks with the master. In 1916 the two, along with a third biologist, were working on *The Game Birds of California,* their first book together, eventually published in 1918.[6] Their article in *Science* magazine was in the nature of helpful advice proffered by scientists accustomed to weighing in on wildlife issues.

Two years later, in early December 1918, three survey scientists (including Albert K. Fisher and Vernon Bailey) met at Bailey's Washington, D.C., home and decided to create a professional society of mammalogists. Since the survey had been born of the American Ornithologists' Union in the 1880s, it seemed appropriate for the now-prominent government science bureau to help nurture its own scientific roots. Further, despite the increasing number of scientists specializing in the study of mammals, no mammal organization similar to the ornithological union existed. Eight days later a committee was appointed to assist with the birth of the new organization. It was only natural that the founders asked Joseph Grinnell to serve as one of the ten committee members. Thus was born the American Society of Mammalogists, led by the universally esteemed C. Hart Merriam—retired from the survey but hardly retired from mammalogy—as its first president.[7]

None of the founders could likely have imagined that Grinnell's idea for preserving predators in national parks would eventually turn their genteel creation into a stubborn institutional critic of the survey and even eventually turn Merriam himself against policies of the government bureau he had founded. Nor could Grinnell or his colleagues in museums and universities throughout the country conceive that their affection for the survey, and their personal comfort with killing, might lead them to make strategic misjudgments and to miss opportunities for reform. The learning of that lesson was destined to stretch out over many years.

In 1919 the American Society of Mammalogists began publishing the *Journal of Mammalogy,* in which its members detailed the results of their research (and which still comes out quarterly today). The society held an annual conference, and some discussion of the idea of conserving carnivores simmered in informal discussions. But it wasn't until five years after the group's founding and eight years after publication of Grinnell and Storer's article that the issue erupted in full force, by this time honed by the keen edge of ecological observation and made urgent by the accelerating poisoning campaign.

In April 1924 the annual meeting of the American Society of Mammalogists was held at Harvard University. In the sanctuary of the venerable buildings of America's oldest institution of higher learning, several academics gently took issue with the survey's extermination policy and, in turn, listened courteously as the agency's senior biologists responded. Lee R. Dice of the University of Michigan, previously a doctoral student of Grinnell's,[8] described the loss to science represented by extinctions:

Progress in all branches of zoology is dependent upon the study of living forms, and our knowledge of no species nor subspecies is sufficiently complete to assume that it is no longer needed for scientific observation. There is no substitute in scientific work for the living animal and the fresh specimen, and every species exterminated marks a decided loss for the scientific world.[9]

Milton P. Skinner, also an academic and a former ranger in Yellowstone National Park, gave a talk urging "[c]ontrol . . . for animals *proved* [original italics] detrimental to the general good, but not extermination."[10] His argument, directed only toward national parks, was based largely on predators' ecological function:

Wildlife is benefited by the predacious animals which serve us well by removing weak and sickly animals, thus keeping the breeding stock vigorous and free from epidemics. . . . The bison of the tame herd in Yellowstone National Park are subject to hemorrhagic septicemia which breaks out at intervals with tragic results. Since the wild animals do not have the disease, we are beginning to wonder if a few predators would not normally have stopped the disease with the first weakened animal before it could spread to others. I know of an instance back in 1917 where I found a single mule deer infected with actinomycosis, or lumpy jaw. This deer avoided all natural enemies by living near Mammoth where the crowds of people scared off the coyotes that would otherwise have killed him during the early stages of his trouble. But as it was, this deer lingered on for two years more. From that date to 1921, I saw five different mule deer that were infected with this disease although I had never noticed a case among them before. Unfortunately, I was not able to trace the disease back from the five mule deer to the one first seen in 1917, but the presumptive evidence is very strong that they contracted it from the first deer.[11]

Another scientist, Dr. Charles C. Adams of the New York State Museum, acknowledged the scientific and economic rationales for conserving predators, then addressed "the actual practice of conservation of the predatory mammals." He proposed a type of national zoning to ensure that predators survived in national parks and other lands ill-suited to agriculture. Acknowledging that in national forests "economic standards are generally considered paramount" and that "there will be a marked tendency to restrict predators in favor of game and domestic grazing animals," he still argued that

in the remote regions there will be less need of predatory control. At any time the production of fur may become a more important economic crop in forests, and then this will put new values on these animals. A certain number of minor fur-bearers should be preserved in these forests, even if the larger ones are sacrificed on account of grazing animals and game, because many of these smaller species will materially aid in rodent control, as well as produce a valuable crop of fur.

But for national parks Adams urged the strongest protections:

> Without question our National Parks should be one of our main sanctuaries for predacious mammals, and these parks should be of sufficient size to insure the safety and perpetuity of such mammals. At present they are not numerous enough, satisfactorily located, and properly isolated by natural boundaries to make the predacious fauna safe. The grazing of domestic animals should be prohibited in order to preserve the forage for wild species, some of which should be sacrificed for the maintenance of the predators.[12]

Then, and with utmost gentility, Adams broached a sensitive topic heretofore avoided—that government policies might not always follow scientific recommendations. He managed to get his point across without mentioning the Biological Survey:

> One should not conclude this discussion of policies without reference to the menace of "political" interference and to vicious propaganda which so frequently obscures conservation measures. The predators have come in for their full share. Without question this is one of the most serious menaces to American wild life. One can recognize these influences at work in almost every locality where inside information is available. In dealing with scientific studies, naturalists are seldom concerned with these influences, but as soon as they attempt to apply their science to human affairs in the form of public policies they come into direct contact with these influences.

Lest offense be inadvertently taken, Adams finished his remarks on a positive note:

> It should be clearly understood, however, that all officials, politicians or even propaganda, are not corrupt, but unfortunately the superior, large-minded men of high ideals who take an active interest in public affairs are lamentably few, so that it is a welcome event to see them battling for constructive public measures. These men deserve better support than they usually receive. As naturalists, and as citizens, we should not take a passive attitude and allow these abuses to continue without opposition, or allow ourselves to be used as tools by unscrupulous leaders, to promote selfish and personal interests at the expense of public welfare. Until our state fish, game, forest and conservation departments, and all others concerned with these problems, are relatively "out of politics", and placed on a real merit basis, a definite goal stands before us that invites our support.[13]

Over the next decade, Adams would find out how difficult such a goal would prove to be.

It fell to Major Edward A. Goldman, a World War I veteran and Biological Survey naturalist who later co-authored a landmark book on wolves with Stanley P. Young, to provide the principal defense of the agency's policies. "As nature lovers we are loath to contemplate the destruction of any species," he began, acknowledging the unstated yet powerful motivations of most of his opposition. "But as practical conservationists we are forced by the records to decide against such predatory animals as mountain lions, wolves, and coyotes."[14] Goldman continued:

> We can not consistently protect them and expect our game to be maintained in satisfactory numbers. Such a course would also alienate the livestock industry, the interests of which must be considered in connection with game administration, and would arouse opposition to such conservation projects as the establishment of game preserves, which might otherwise be favored.[15]

But rather than attack unequivocally the idea of preserving predators, Goldman stressed the animals' unsuitability in agricultural areas:

> Large predatory mammals, destructive to livestock and to game, no longer have a place in our advancing civilization. To advocate their protection in areas occupied by the homes of civilized man and his domestic animals is to invite being discredited as practical conservationists and to risk through prejudice the defeat of measures which may be vital to the future welfare of the country.[16]

Despite the differences between the two sides, it appeared possible to develop a consensus around policies delineating a safe haven for carnivores. The attending mammalogists passed a resolution authorizing a committee of their membership to "formulate policies for the preservation of predatory mammals" and to "recommend the location of certain wild life preserves suitable for the preservation of such animals."[17] The committee consisted of Goldman and Vernon Bailey of the survey, along with Adams, Edmund Heller of the Milwaukee Museum, and Joseph Dixon of Grinnell's Museum of Vertebrate Zoology.

No one was more of an insider at the Biological Survey than Bailey, the second of survey founder C. Hart Merriam's assistants back when the survey had been known as the Division of Economic Ornithology and Mammalogy. He was even married to Merriam's sister.

Bailey also represented the Biological Survey's scientific authority as one of the nation's most accomplished field naturalists, along with his wife, Florence. And Bailey had authored *Wolves in Relation to Stock, Game, and the National Forest Reserves*, the 1907 booklet that marked the agency's first shift from a scientific bureau to an agricultural service organization. If anyone epitomized the dual faces of the survey in seemingly perfect harmony, it was Vernon Bailey.

The three nonsurvey biologists were professional acquaintances on friendly terms with each other, but each had a full-time job involving extensive fieldwork.[18] The committee started off slowly. Perhaps the academics felt so relieved at having achieved the establishment of an investigative committee that some of their battleground urgency simply disappeared. After all, the survey had already softened its rhetoric slightly at the conference that authorized the committee.

The mammalogists shared with the survey the methodology of making lists and taking measurements of dead animals, so they had no reason to be shocked at the agency's mass killing of predators. "I have just finished the mouse harvest. We have put up about 1550 flat skins of Peromyscus from our colony," reported mammalogist Dice to his colleague E. Raymond Hall in 1930.[19] Merriam himself had conducted a study involving the examination of 27,000 mouse carcasses.[20] They exchanged avian specimens with a cavalierism that would discomfit contemporary bird lovers: "I have the song sparrow safely put away," wrote naturalist and predator proponent A. Brazier Howell to Grinnell, also in 1930. "Will send it as soon as I can get to Washington to see if I have not a couple of bird skins left to keep it company on the way west."[21] The survey's extermination campaign, rather than jarring the mammalogists' sensibilities, at first seemed a natural evolution from killing and tabulating animals for science to killing them for agriculture. The question to them revolved simply around a balance between the agricultural necessity for killing predators in some areas and their professional interest in conserving such species elsewhere.

The Biological Survey took advantage of the reservoir of good will afforded it to further reassure critics. Its 1924 nation-wide annual report was intended to help clarify the easily misunderstood impact of the agency's work:

> The fierce destructiveness of large wolves and of mountain lions, both to domestic animals and game, is so great that it becomes a necessity to eliminate them from certain areas. This, however, does not mean the actual destruction of these species, since they range over such a vast area in both North and South America that the possibility of their actual extermination undoubtedly lies many centuries in the future. . . . In northern Mexico, Canada, and Alaska these animals [wolves] still occur in considerable numbers and will long persist as picturesque elements of the fauna.[22]

The nonsurvey scientists had no reason to disbelieve this sentiment. In 1924 the survey still had a longer tenure as a scientific institution than as an extermination service. Despite a decade of increasing dedication to its agricultural constituency, biologists continued to regard the federal agency as a scientific partner and valued its employees as colleagues and friends. With the field of biology still largely focused on taxonomy and identification, survey biologists and those in academia were accustomed to cooperating in the acquisition of animals for identification and in exchanging specimens to round out museum collections for further research. They saw each other at conferences and turned to each other for specialized expertise. Bailey and Goldman were still first and foremost their esteemed colleagues. So Adams, not having attended to the predator committee during 1924, was delighted upon first hearing news of the survey's amended policy at the end of that year: "I am very glad to hear the the [*sic*] Survey is to soft pedal extermination," he wrote Joseph Dixon. "I have not heard of this change of heart."[23]

Indeed, the Biological Survey's nation-wide annual report for the 1925 fiscal year explicitly renounced extermination as a policy, assuring the reader that each animal targeted was surviving amply somewhere:

> Little objection can be raised to the continuance of a limited number of predatory animals in national parks and in wilderness areas remote from civilization, so long as they do not prove too destructive to the other wild life there. It must be taken into consideration, however, that with the growing numbers of hunters and the improved facilities for getting into the haunts of game, either the number of predatory animals permitted to roam the forest must be reduced, or the resulting drain on game will mean its extermination.

But in the case of wolves the annual report equivocated, arguing first for their "elimination in occupied country" and then implying that occupied country constituted all of American soil:

> Owing to their destructiveness of livestock and game, these animals [wolves] can be tolerated only in unsettled country. Aside from purely economic reasons, their elimination in occupied country is essential to an intelligent conservation of the useful and attractive forms of wild life. This does not mean complete extermination of the species, for wolves will doubtless continue to exist indefinitely in the wilder parts of Canada and Mexico, where they now occur in large numbers.
>
> Skilled hunters have been detailed to take destructive individuals wherever they appear and to patrol the borders, especially in Arizona and New Mexico, for those animals coming across the international boundary. . . . So far as known, scarcely a litter of young wolves was permitted to escape in these States during the year. . . . As the wolves become fewer, it becomes increasingly difficult to locate them, for they travel long distances and change their range frequently. In spite of this, however, the hunters assigned particularly to wolf work have become so skillful that it usually takes only a few days to capture any wolf reported doing damage.[24]

In fact, wolves would not persist indefinitely in Mexico because the previous year the survey had begun assisting American ranchers south of the border to kill wolves there, probably through shipments of strychnine.[25] As will be seen, the last known wolves from Mexico were destined to be captured alive between 1977 and 1980 for an emergency captive breeding program to save the Mexican subspecies from extinction and prepare for its reintroduction into the United States. Although reports of wolves south of the border persist, none of them has been confirmed, and, so far as is known today, no wild wolves are left in Mexico.

Notwithstanding the shift in the Biological Survey's rhetoric, nothing was changing on the ground. No instructions reached the survey's trappers and poisoners directing them to spare some animals in some regions. Young had to remind himself of his own agency's tempered ambitions in preparing to deliver a radio address in Denver explaining the survey's work in late July 1926.[26] His original script for the talk included the sentence "In Colorado the Biological Survey is cooperating with Colorado State Board of Livestock Inspection Commissioners and eight Wool Growers Associations and many individual stockmen in the destruction of the predatory animal." But before going on the air he changed the last phrase to read "the destruction of predatory animals," reflecting the new notion that perhaps "the predatory animal" as a catch-phrase for all predators was too broad a target.

Nor did the Biological Survey develop new measures to save the fur-bearing, and hence economically valuable, animals that died incidental to coyote-poisoning operations. Instead, the agency simply denied the magnitude of the problem, claiming that few skunks, wolverines, badgers, raccoons, bears, and other scavengers were poisoned. Since the issue had arisen in 1922, the agency claimed its poisoners returned at the end of each winter to destroy the toxic predator baits they had distributed the previous fall—even though the baits numbered in the millions and many were given to ranchers for distribution. Since survey employees' job performance rested solely on how many predators they killed, however, they had no incentive to search for uneaten baits (if they even knew they were supposed to do so).

The Biological Survey's initial attempts to reform its reputation helped lull the independent scientists on the predator committee into inactivity, and more than a year passed with no substantive action from the committee. But the illusions of change at the survey could not last forever. "Dr. Nelson [the survey's chief] has been somewhat concerned about the complaints that have come in from various people regarding the animals that have been killed by poisoned pellets put out for coyotes," Dixon wrote to Adams in the fall of 1925. "Of course, you know the Survey attitude is to minimize the number of fur-bearing animals which may thus be killed, while at the same time, they claim that not over one out of every three coyotes killed by poison is found."[27] Beginning that same year, the survey ceased publishing the number of baits it distributed, perhaps concerned that figures that had once indicated rapid progress toward a goal were now interpreted as evidence of misconduct.

Despite obfuscating its field procedures and their results and disavowing the goal of extermination to quell the revolt among scientists, the Biological Survey could not afford to alienate the members of the House and Senate funding committees. Members of Congress who paid attention to the obscure federal agency were most interested in the type of efficiency represented by its old argument against bounties. Ever since the first federal appropriation to kill predators and rodents was allocated, the survey had premised its definitive case for receiving public money for that purpose on the financial savings only extinction could guarantee. If the goal was merely control, then by its own well-worn pitch the old bounty system had been perfect for the job. In 1919 Albert Fisher, the head of the survey's Division of Economic Investigations, had made that very point in an article published by a Denver-based national ranching magazine. The survey, he wrote, "naturally placed little reliance upon the bounty system, but adopted a method which promised permanent relief—namely, actual extermination of the pests."[28] And the survey's fiscal year 1923 nationwide annual report made the same case:

> From the beginning of this work the survey has maintained that eventually it would be practicable completely to destroy some of the worst of these animal pests and thus forever eliminate the heavy losses they have been causing. Through the campaigns against them prairie dogs have been exterminated on considerable areas, and the large wolves, of which 4,900 have been killed, are being so reduced in numbers that over most if not all of the West their end is in sight.[29]

The Biological Survey had to keep two unreconcilable ideological factions happy. So undoubtedly with an eye to pleasing its traditional constituency and its political funders, its 1926 national annual report acknowledged that the agency's goal in New Mexico—and implicitly everywhere else as well—was "to get the last one [wolf] in the State." The report also celebrated the fact that "[f]or the first year in the history of the work not a single lobo wolf was taken in Colorado and less than half a dozen are known to range within the State."[30]

But the survey was still fighting to retain the loyalty of the scientific community. So the report also reflected the tension between competing interests in an ambiguously worded statement on killing bobcats and lynxes "wherever they prove seriously destructive to livestock interests."[31] Presumably the reader, depending on his or her prior assumptions and inclination, would be happy to assume that these animals were either killed or spared elsewhere.

The fact remained, however, that livestock still existed in huge numbers almost everywhere throughout the West, with the exception of the national parks. Rocky Mountain National Park, the biggest stretch of non-grazed, non-urban land in Colorado, contained almost no winter range; it almost certainly could not serve as a year-round home for even a single wolf pack, and there is no evidence it ever had. But just as with the claims of poison bait retrieval, the new, half-articulated policy from Washington of providing carnivores respite in national parks did not exist in the field offices. In Yellowstone National Park in northwestern Wyoming, several times as large as Rocky Mountain and containing considerably more winter range, the last two wolves were trapped and killed that same year—1926.[32]

As members of the American Society of Mammalogists grew to question the Biological Survey's sincerity and debated at their annual meetings whether it intended to exterminate species, the remnant of the wolf population of the southern Rocky Mountains continued to diminish. In fiscal year 1924 (ending

Wolves Killed by the Biological Survey in Colorado Under Stanley P. Young's Supervision, 1921–1927

Fiscal Year	Wolves Killed
1921	6
1922	26
1923	11
1924	8
1925	1
1926	0
1927	1

Source: Colorado-Kansas district reports, Bureau of Biological Survey, NA.

June 30 of that year) the survey had killed ten wolves in the San Juans in New Mexico near the Colorado border. The next fiscal year the agency killed six wolves in the same region, and in 1926 it killed two more. In calendar year 1928 the survey trapped a pack of seven wolves in northern New Mexico, reported to have migrated from Colorado the previous year. These were the last known wolves in New Mexico's portion of the San Juans. And assuming—as is likely from the quick time line and the discrete area in which they were trapped—that these seven wolves constituted a pack, they were the last pack of wolves to roam the southern Rocky Mountains at all.[33] From this point on, each remaining wolf was a loner.

One of those last loners was a Great Plains wolf. On a January day in 1927, Roy C. Spangler, the survey trapper who had lost his wife to smallpox while chasing Three-Toes three and a half years earlier, was skinning poisoned coyotes on Colorado's southeastern plains—in the Purgatoire River area where Whitey used to live—when he came upon a wolf that had succumbed to his baits. The survey, in its report on the wolf, did not mention its sex, speculating instead that it had come from either northern New Mexico or the Oklahoma panhandle.[34] But where that wolf had wandered was a secret that died with the animal. The spaces between wolves were widening in the western United States, widening almost beyond the ability of members of that wide-ranging species to find each other. It no longer mattered what sex they were.

True Value

In early 1927 the non–Biological Survey members of the predator committee appointed at the American Society of Mammalogists conference almost three years previously had reached some definite conclusions about the effects of the Biological Survey's policies. They had perused survey data, interviewed survey employees, and conferred with scientists throughout the West. Most exciting, in January 1927 a promising young mammalogy student at Joseph Grinnell's Museum of Vertebrate Zoology, E. Raymond Hall, had caught wind of an outbreak of mice in south-central California and had rushed to the region to investigate. Millions of mice had swarmed out of a dry lake bed, devouring crops and dying by the hundreds of thousands on local roads.

Two years earlier, at Grinnell's urging, the twenty-three-year-old Hall had accompanied Edward A. Goldman of the survey on a trip to the Kaibab Plateau in northern Arizona to investigate a dramatic increase in deer numbers.[1] Just as elsewhere, predators had been largely eliminated from that forested region; unlike elsewhere, the Grand Canyon served as a barrier that may have deterred wolves from recolonizing from the Mogollon Rim to the south (and wolf populations in the arid Colorado Plateau to the north had always been as sparse as the desert itself). By the early 1920s the burgeoning number of deer had stripped the Kaibab Plateau bare of browse, and then, during the winters, they starved by the thousands.

Now it seemed to Hall that a similar dynamic was at work. He linked the mouse irruption in California's Central Valley to the survey's killing of predators

Grinnell protégé E. Raymond Hall investigating the deer irruption on the Kaibab Plateau, 1924, a result of the extermination of wolves and mountain lions. During this summer, his horse bucked, launching his rifle into the Grand Canyon. Hall climbed down to retrieve it from a ledge, but the stock was broken and, even after being replaced, the gun never sighted quite true. Hall's own aim, however, was dead on: his experience on the Kaibab propelled him into half a century of highly effective scientific advocacy against eradicating predators. (Mrs. E. R. Hall [Mary F. Hall])

such as coyotes. (Although agency officials at first vigorously disputed this interpretation, the next year recently retired survey chief Edward W. Nelson admitted as much by acknowledging that predator poisoning in the region had been overdone.)[2]

The mouse report was Hall's first weighing in on a debate he would pursue vigorously throughout his long life. Born in 1902 on a Kansas farm, Eugene Raymond Hall dreamed of becoming a trapper in the uncharted forests of Canada. In preparation, he took up trapping on the farm, selling the pelts of skunks, possums, and other small animals to a commercial buyer in a nearby town.

Although Hall eventually gave up on the idea of a career as a north woods trapper, he replaced that dream with the reality of trapping for science. Eventually, he became one of the twentieth century's most accomplished mammalogists, identifying and naming 9 new genera, 23 new species, and 138 subspecies—as well as authoring the discipline's definitive overview, *The Mammals of North America* (first published in 1959).

Although a childhood friend described him as a "mamma's boy"—obedient and well-behaved—Hall's indefatigable energy and resolve made him a thorn in the survey's side for decades. Many of his cohorts in mammalogy eventually gave up or compromised unnecessarily, whereas others never succeeded in translating their academic perspective into a politically effective voice.[3]

Hall, in contrast, persevered, eventually succeeding in kicking the survey out of his home state of Kansas, kicking up enough dust to precipitate a series of investigations and bills that helped lead to passage of the Endangered Species Act, and along the way fighting off not just the rhetorical jabs of Stanley P. Young and supporters but also two street thugs who accosted him in Washington, D.C., as he prepared to testify in Congress against the survey.[4]

But those events were years and decades into the future. In 1927, with Hall's mouse study as ammunition, the independent scientists on the predator committee were finally ready to write a report. Then word came that the Biological Survey was shortly to have a new chief, Paul G. Redington, a Forest Service official. Once again the outsiders hoped the survey might reform itself. Someone who had not been involved in the controversy, they thought, might be open to the kind of reasoned suggestions they had long been proffering. In anticipation of releasing their findings in time for the American Society of Mammalogists' April meeting, which would take place a mere week and a half before Redington was to take charge on May 9, Charles C. Adams drafted the long-awaited report. He sent it first to Joseph Dixon and Edmund Heller for review, intending to then send it to the two survey representatives on the committee, Edward A. Goldman and Vernon Bailey.[5]

But Dixon had another idea. He intended to conduct a detailed field study of the Biological Survey's poisoning campaign in Nevada to ascertain precisely how many fur-bearing animals were being inadvertently killed. Several furriers had promised to front his research expenses, and survey officials had promised their full cooperation. He worried that signing a report damning the survey before embarking on his investigation would open him to charges of prejudice:

> I do not feel that it would be advisable for me to say much at this particular time in view of the fact that I must be able and willing to take up the poison investigation and to carry it on with a free, unbiased, open mind. It would not be fair or just for me to express a decided partiality toward either the fur industry or the Survey at this time.

He offered to withdraw from the committee if Adams thought issuing the report immediately was paramount. Otherwise, he suggested, "it would be much better to leave the final statement until I can conclude the poison investigation."[6]

Adams agreed to delay the report. Undoubtedly, he thought losing Dixon's imprimatur would weaken its credibility. But he also thought it might not hurt to give Redington time to get his bearings. Goldman and Bailey, although suspicious of Adams's motives, were happy for any delay to further animadversion of their agency.[7]

Redington arrived in Washington in early May to take over the Biological Survey. The same day Redington assumed power, Stanley P. Young became the number-two man for predator and rodent control operations for the nation, having been promoted out of his position in Colorado.[8] It is likely that Albert K. Fisher—the head of the Division of Economic Investigations and a survey employee since its founding in 1885—in preparing for his upcoming transfer to a research job within the survey, wanted to groom a reliable successor to ensure that Redington would not succumb to the mammalogists' pleas. In any event, as the assistant director of the survey's largest and most active division, Young was admirably poised to help shape an agency whose future direction was very much up for grabs.

Joseph Dixon, in the meantime, preparing for his investigation in Nevada and ever concerned about objectivity, resigned from a position he held with the survey as an inspector of animals imported through the port in San Francisco Bay. But inexplicably, the money promised by the fur industry failed to arrive. For over a year Dixon awaited the promised funds, but they never came.[9] Years later he found out that Fisher had prevailed on the fur dealers to hang on to their money by telling them that the results of Dixon's investigation would make little difference to their fur supply.[10] (The survey's ability to influence the fur industry likely stemmed in part from its longtime research into and promotion of captive breeding of wild mammals.)

Although Dixon suspected that survey influence was behind his inability to secure funds for a field investigation of the poisoning campaign, he did not despair of Redington's ability to mold the agency. The key, he thought, was to avoid rash criticism that Redington might dismiss out of hand and to cultivate a more productive relationship than the one that had developed between the mammalogists and the recently retired chief, Edward W. Nelson, who was still on the survey's payroll as a biologist. Attacking the credibility of Dixon's colleague from New York, Charles C. Adams, for example, Nelson wrote Adams: "You will remember within the last two years coyotes suddenly appeared in one or two counties of western New York State and committed there the same kind of damage on the live-stock of the farmers as they are doing to the settlers in the west." No doubt reveling in the oratorical freedom his shift in duties allowed, Nelson continued:

> If these animals are such desirable citizens, why was it that the naturalists of New York State did not arise in their might and demand that these interesting beasts be permitted to go on and enjoy their interesting lives without man's brutal interference? Can it be that the naturalists of New York disapprove of predatory animals roaming in their own State but have a tremendous desire for their perpetuation in other communities?[11]

Both Adams and Dixon were amused by the attack, but the incident further impressed upon Dixon the importance of not opposing the entirety of the survey's killing program. "Of course, no one would think of making a coyote reservation in a poultry yard," he wrote Adams. "The whole attitude of that sort of talk is too foolish to be considered seriously."[12]

Despite Dixon's insistence on mere reform of the Biological Survey's practices, from the first Redington seemed to side with his agency's long-standing methods. When Dixon, still anticipating fur industry funding for his study, asked the survey for such information as the number of baits it both distributed and recovered, Redington sent back a stiff letter questioning his need for the data. Still maintaining studied neutrality, Dixon responded by noting his participation on the American Society of Mammalogists' predator committee and disavowing any hostile intent: "There have been attempts to discredit certain worthy work of the Survey. I have tried to prevent any *unfair* or *unjust* [emphasis in original] criticism of the Survey's good work. At the same time, I have not hestitated [sic] to condemn certain things which I believe to be ill-advised or harmful."[13]

Eventually, Dixon dropped his investigation,[14] and in April 1928 the predator committee issued its report on policy toward predators at the annual meeting of the American Society of Mammalogists in Washington, D.C. The report, delivered four years after it was first authorized, represented the split on the committee between the three academics and the two survey representatives.

Adams had initially intended that the committee issue a report that would move the survey toward allowing respite in certain areas for both predators and the miscellaneous animals valued for their fur. Goldman's and Bailey's signatures on such a document would leave Redington practically no choice but to begin at least some rudimentary reforms. In addition, he intended to submit a supplementary report, one he knew neither survey representative could sign, that would not mince words in describing the true extent of the mammalogists' disapprobation of the agency's practices.

The intended consensus report began by stating that predators "should be preserved under suitable conditions" because of their "scientific, educational and economic value." Bailey and Goldman had no objections to that. And all agreed that "the main practical problem is *how* and *where* [emphasis in original] to do so" and that "[t]he safest general policy with respect to species usually injurious to human interests is intelligent control, rather than wholesale extermination."

But when the report advised on specific policies, Adams's bid for unanimity came apart—the consensus document evidently proving too pointed for the survey representatives. Although no records indicate who insisted on changes to Adams's draft, both Goldman and Bailey undoubtedly recognized the danger to the survey's interests in pinning the agency down to an unequivocal set of policy principles. The draft's first recommendation read: "Careful scientific studies of predators regarded as injurious, their ecology and *role* in our general economic and social life should be made in *advance* of drastic control measures [emphasis in original]." But when published, the report also included the phrase "when practicable" at the end of that sentence—thus creating a loop-hole that could always justify continued killing.

Adams's second policy prescription read: "At the present state of our knowledge we are not justified in advocating an extermination policy for any of our predatory mammals." But the published report substituted "most" for "any." With the survey so tantalizingly close to exterminating wolves from the United States (excluding Alaska, which was not yet a state), certainly Bailey and Goldman did not want to help provide a surefire basis for an argument to cease killing the few remaining wolves.

Similarly, in discussing conserving predators in the national forests, the draft pointed out that "[w]ith grazing and game interests paramount in many regions, the larger predators are controlled severely." The final report changed the last phrase to read "the larger predators must be fully controlled." The draft followed this by recommending setting aside the Kaibab Plateau and the Gila region of southwestern New Mexico (which was also experiencing a deer irruption) as refugia for a limited number of large predators. But the final report deleted mention of these heavily grazed areas, conceding only that "a few predatory animals" could be preserved in national parks or in national forests in Alaska and Washington state—areas with no livestock.[15]

Adams, Dixon, and Heller accepted these changes, having already intended to include a scathing critique of the survey's practices in their supplementary report. The latter document excoriated the survey for pursuing a de facto extermination campaign without regard for scientific principles. The mammalogists criticized the lack of investigation into the relation between predators and prey animals (such as rodents) and the dubious figures for livestock losses used to justify the killing, and they questioned the degree to which public funds should be used to protect the livestock industry.[16]

Redington responded by arguing that predator killing could not wait for research results. "No farmer," he wrote in an open letter to Adams published over a year later in the *Journal of Mammalogy*, "would consent to permit a predatory animal to make constant raids on his livestock while research reports were being awaited to show whether the same predator might be saving him the trouble of combating injurious rodents." And he denied that the outbreak of mice in central California had had anything to do with the survey's activities.[17]

Stanley Young, however, knew the Biological Survey had to get beyond fighting scientists on scientific grounds. He recognized the need to articulate a broad policy that would effectively insulate the survey from the mammalogists' fustigations. Shortly after he arrived in Washington, Young had helped staunch the criticism of the survey's policies. In September 1927, for instance, he convinced a concerned Smith Riley (who following a stint as the Forest Service's regional chief for Colorado had worked as the survey's principal official in charge of wildlife refuges) that the survey no longer practiced extermination and was allowing some wolves and mountain lions to continue living in national parks.[18] (Indeed, the previous year Rocky Mountain National Park had terminated an intensive carnivore-killing campaign initiated by Young in 1922, but other parks still allowed the survey free rein.[19])

On February 7, 1928, Young backed up Redington at the yearly House hearing on the survey's budget. The survey's annual federal appropriation had almost quadrupled, from $281,290 in fiscal year 1915 to $1,035,020 for fiscal year 1928, of which $437,310 went to its Division of Economic Investigations (and much of the rest to management of game refuges). In addition, by 1928 cooperating states, counties, and stockmen's associations contributed a hefty $946,800 to kill predators and rodents. Now survey officials were back before Congress to request another increase. Before a sympathetic committee, clearly impressed at the level of support demonstrated by non-federal contributions, Redington boasted that "the gray wolf of the western range country is practically reaching the point of extermination," and Young explained that insufficient funds had kept the survey from fully controlling the coyote. "We have a dirty back yard on some of the national forests," Young told the committee. Young continued:

> Take the State of Colorado, for instance, where we have 15 national
> forests surrounding a lot of stock ranges, where the livestock come down
> from summer grazing. Our land areas there are infestating [sic] the lower
> privately owned lands in the matter of predatory animals. For that reason
> we figure we should clean up our own back yard.[20]

Redington's and Young's remarks prompted Representative James P. Buchanan of Texas to ponder the possibility of increasing funds to the survey for five years to "wipe out" coyotes and after that "appropriate only a small amount from year to year."[21] At Buchanan's request, the committee instructed the secretary of agriculture to report on the feasibility and cost of such a campaign.[22]

Nine days later, on February 16, 1928, Young replaced Albert Fisher as head of the survey's Division of Economic Investigations—the department that ran the killing campaign and assisted fur farmers. Fisher stayed with the survey in a research capacity.[23]

Young's latest career rise followed the same pattern as had his replacement of Logan B. Crawford in July 1921 after half a year as Crawford's nominal assistant. In 1928, just as in 1921, he was taking title to a position he had effectively taken to a new level of competence while still an underling. And just as when he turned the Colorado district of the survey into the Colorado-Kansas district, so too, after assuming the position of biologist in charge of the Division of Economic Investigations, he prepared to change its name to the "Division of Predatory Animal and Rodent Control."[24] Young liked to denominate his posts.

One facet of Young's competence can be read in the pleasure and pride his friends in Colorado and Arizona felt at his promotion. The secretary of the

Colorado Game and Fish Protective Association wrote a letter of congratulations—with the proper salutation "Dear Mr. Young"—and concluded: "Your membership card in this Association is dated, I believe, sometime late in 1927. Our 1928 card is of a little different design—we think, an improvement. May I take the liberty of enclosing one, showing dues paid till the end of the current year." He added, "Please accept kindest personal regards and best wishes."[25]

Arthur H. Carhart, a Colorado writer who pioneered with Aldo Leopold and Robert Marshall the push to protect wilderness areas, was more informal. "Dear Stan," typed Carhart affectionately, "Think you're smart, eh? Gettin' a new job." Carhart, who was collaborating with Young on a book recounting the killing of Rags, Three-Toes, and the other "renegade" wolves in Colorado, congratulated him and gave him the latest on publishing prospects. He ended, "Missed out on my lion hunt but I've got one coming when I can get time, down on the Mexico border, haven't I?"[26]

In Arizona, the Prescott *Journal-Miner* ran a story entitled "Trapper of First Wolf in the State for Biological Survey Now Heads Economic Division." The newspaper regarded Young as its native son of a sort, identifying him in the first line as the "son-in-law of Mr. and Mrs. J. S. Acker of this city."[27] (Young's ties to the town were genuine and sustained. His son, Acker Young, recalled that his sister and mother typically escaped the capital's summer humidity by estivating in the high-elevation Arizona town but that his father only managed to get back for around a week at the end of each summer.[28])

Young's new post as head of the Division of Economic Investigations (the name did not officially change until July 1, 1929, although the new name was in use shortly after he got the job in February 1928) proved powerful. The enduring affection of professional colleagues and acquaintances in the places he left behind gives one hint as to why he was effective in wielding that power.

Young started as division head by convening a conference. In April 1928, less than two weeks after the release of the dueling reports at the mammalogists' annual convention, the survey convened a five-day meeting of the state leaders and Washington brass of its Division of Economic Investigations. They met in Ogden, Utah, a small town north of Salt Lake City in the shadow of the snowcapped peaks of the Wasatch Front.

The conference was intended to standardize the division's operational procedures in every conceivable activity, ranging from filling out forms to setting up displays at outdoor fairs to cooperating with the Indian Service (later known as the Bureau of Indian Affairs). But not surprisingly, the most urgent topic for discussion was the agency's stance on extermination. Redington opened the conference by noting the opposition the agency faced:

> Sharply aligned against us in connection with our predatory animal work are several elements whose voices at times are loud in condemnation of our efforts to reduce the numbers of stock-killing animals. There are those who still feel that nature's balance operates and that it must be main-

tained. There are those whose interests are deleteriously affected by our taking of the bobcat and the coyote because of the value of the furs at the present time. There are those who condemn us mercilessly because of our use of poison. On the other hand, we have, I feel sure, the general and sincere support of the livestock men of the Western States and of those who appreciate the harm which is being done to various forms of wild life by predatory animals. It is indeed necessary in handling this work that we first fully agree upon consistent policies, and then talk the same language in our exposition of the policies; and it is for this purpose primarily that this conference has been arranged.[29]

Beyond the relatively simple matter of developing a set of policies and standardizing a position statement, the conference was designed as a type of strategic planning process to position the Biological Survey to meet the political exigencies of a changing era. The survey had been born in 1885 as a frontier-era scientific institution that (nominally) assisted farmers. Largely swimming against the agricultural and utilitarian tides of its first twenty-five years until around 1910, when C. Hart Merriam retired, the survey charted its own course as the nation's premier scientific body. In 1915 Congress ordered the agency to enter the predator-killing business on a systematic basis, and the body counts started racking up all over the West. By the early 1920s, when science was highly esteemed, the agency was fully immersed in 1880s-type agricultural service.

An acute observer might have surmised that the survey's institutional culture worked best in opposition to society's dominant trends. Now, in the spring of 1928, the survey had managed to antagonize a good portion of the scientists who had worked with the agency. It remained to be seen how an attempt to re-invent itself would comport with a worldly and often cynical public enjoying the height of the Jazz Age. Unlike 1915, the year Congress had set in motion new funding that decisively changed the agency's purpose, this time its activities would stay the course, but it would project a new image. And to do that, everyone whose job it was to supervise trappers and poisoners and to coordinate activities with ranchers and county commissions would have to learn to be a publicist also.

The conference was elaborately planned, with state predatory animal and rodent control leaders required to think about and answer questions in writing before the event even began.[30] This preparation facilitated extensive discussion within each policy committee. Fifty-two people attended, including Redington, Young, each state's predator and rodent control leader, and a state assistant or two, as well as the four biologists who staffed the Eradication Methods Laboratory—the survey's national poison development facility in Denver, which Young had helped get off the ground in 1921. But no one traditionally associated with the scientific branch of the survey appeared—not even Edward Goldman or Vernon Bailey, although they had justified the extermination activities to a skeptical scientific community. The absence of scientists at a gathering representing a crucial institutional juncture for the survey clearly bespoke the agency's future—particularly since the survey's scientific credentials were central to fending off criticism.

Young made no formal presentations at the conference, nor was he quoted in the records of its proceedings. He didn't have to speak. As the conference's coordinator he structured the proceedings so as to make others grapple with the problems the survey faced and feel ownership of the solutions they reached.[31] And agreement on policies proved easy. Although the conference was structured to foster open and friendly debate among state leaders (and, indeed, in such matters as which poison formulas worked the best they strongly disagreed), it was obvious to all that advocating extermination would only get them into further trouble. Accordingly, in the most formal process yet enacted, *control* replaced *extermination* as the operative term for the survey's killing activities, and the Eradication Methods Laboratory became the Control Methods Laboratory—although previously "control," "eradication," and "extermination" had often been used interchangeably. To ensure that everyone understood the new company line, Redington elaborated on the change:

> There are some predatory animals and rodents that, because of their great harm to agriculture and livestock, must be eradicated from large areas of the country. For example, the gray wolf and the prairie dog in their operations so deleteriously affect agricultural interests that their presence in large numbers can not be tolerated. Other species, such as the coyote and the ground squirrel, are so prolific and occur over such wide areas that although their reputation for destructiveness is well known, no one in the Biological Survey would have the temerity to assert that these animals could be exterminated. The idea of extermination of any species is abhorrent to thousands of people throughout the United States, and the use of the word "exterminate" should, I think, be eliminated from our vocabulary. We know full well that there will continue to be left many wild areas where the mountain lion, the coyote, the bobcat, and many species of rodents will perhaps always be present, and I feel sure that the members of the Biological Survey will be just as happy in the assurance that these animals are on such areas as will the nature lovers of the country. The fact remains that we must work for the eradication of certain species from areas where their destructiveness is so impressive in an economic way that no other policy of handling them there could be followed, and we should frankly admit this fact to our critics, pointing out, on the other hand, that we are not embarked upon a general extermination program, and that our main objective is so to control the predatory animals and the rodent pests as to reduce to a minimum the economic losses for which they are responsible.[32]

The conference also resulted in the development of policies for field procedures that addressed the most egregious abuses cited by fur trappers and the mammalogists. State leaders were supposed to cease issuing predator poisons to people not working under their supervision. (This did not mean that only employees could receive poison; ranchers who agreed to follow survey directions could continue their own poisoning campaigns.) The agency also vowed to stop poisoning operations in "high timbered country" and areas along streams "where careful investigation shows that valuable fur bearers, other than species to be controlled, would be endangered." And it became policy to "[l]iberate all furbearing animals from traps . . . except those that are destructive to livestock, game, and poultry."[33] (A survey biologist not present at the conference innocently asked several months later, "Are there any fur-bearers not occasionally destructive to livestock, game, and poultry?" He added, "As written this recommendation does not seem to mean very much."[34])

Despite this one person's confusion after the fact, nobody at the conference suffered from the misapprehension that basic goals had changed. In several cases participants resorted to a standard phrase that covered their past—and future—activities in the field: "clean up." A. E. Gray, the survey's leader for New Mexico, used the term to explain that the present use of strychnine on rodents was inefficient:

> If extensive work is contemplated with no idea of a clean up our present
> methods in most instances might be considered efficient, but I find that
> this type of work is not desired as the people are demanding a clean up.
> Under these conditions the work becomes intensive rather than extensive,
> and the methods now in use are wholly inadequate.[35]

He added, "The use of strychnine when studied from every angle is not practical for the control of the prairie dog and ground squirrel group of rodents; by control I mean reducing their numbers to a point so low that increase is impossible."[36] Such a point would be tantamount to extermination for such prolific animals, since any remaining pair of prairie dogs or ground squirrels would begin to increase the population again. The moderator of this discussion, D. A. Gilchrist of Arizona, made clear that his colleagues should hold themselves to the same high standard:

> A county completely cleared of a rodent pest is a beautiful and convincing
> sight. Taxpayers, legislatures and congressmen are willing to pay real
> money to the personnel and will readily raise adequate funds for depart-
> ments who will get upon their toes and secure definite results.
> Will the poisons now used in your state give you permanent and far
> reaching results as described or does each season's effort only add to the
> number of "strychnine proof" rodents which you have to contend with, and
> if so, how long do you think the public will stand for such a procedure?[37]

Gilchrist adhered to his own rigorous criterion and in listing his successes in Arizona disdained to employ the standard euphemisms of "clean up" or "control":

1. The black tail prairie dog, "cynomys ludovicianus Arizonesis," has been completely exterminated from the state. This rodent infested 650,000

acres in Cochise and Graham counties. It took three years time, 83,826 quarts of poisoned grain, 1920 quarts of CS_2 gas and $75,381.00 or .11½ per acre to finish the job. The last dog was killed on June 25, 1922 and is on display at this conference.

2. By following the prebait system the last prairie dog in Gila county, the white tail "Cyonomys gunnisoni zuniensis" was exterminated upon September 16, 1923.

3. Again following the prebait system the last prairie dog in Greenlee county was exterminated during August 1926. Mohave county will be next if adequate funds are forthcoming.

4. Again following the prebait system and this time using the modified standard formula, Ben E. Foster has succeeded in clearing 82,468 acres of "Zuniensis" white tailed prairie dogs, from the Tusayan forest.

5. The original prairie dog infestation in Arizona national forests was 1,122,620 acres. Todate [sic] through the use of the prebait strychnine system and, more recently, thallium we have completely cleared 601,805 acres leaving a balance of 510,815 acres remaining to be exterminated.[38]

Other speakers were equally frank. The rodent control leader from Montana, O. E. Stephl, admitted that "[p]rairie dogs are being eradicated for all time" in his state. Stephl complained, however, that with other rodents "there is nothing to indicate that we are making progress toward complete eradication" and, in particular concerning ground squirrels, "control only and no permanent relief can be expected."[39] Stephl's colleague from Montana, R. E. Bateman, in charge of the predator campaign, likewise directly referred to the goal as "the extermination of predatory animals."[40]

Admittedly, some of these candid remarks regarding the survey's real goals had been prepared before the conference and reflected prior operating assumptions. But during the conference Redington added numerous clarifying statements to the various policy recommendations developed in committees, and aside from his general introductory remarks disavowing extermination he made no effort to disabuse his employees of the notion that the survey practiced extermination.

More tellingly, of the over 100 detailed policy changes emanating from the conference, not one spelled out any steps to delineate the "many wild areas" Redington had magnanimously proclaimed would always be available even to the most reprobate of predators. Not even national parks were to receive definitive exemption from the survey's attentions, as the policy adopted on the subject makes clear:

That inasmuch as the National Park Service desires to maintain the parks in a natural condition as far as practicable, the Biological Survey officers should not, as a rule, take the initiative in cleaning up these areas, but that they should feel free to cooperate with the park officers upon request. . . .

Situations will be found, however, on national park areas and on national monuments under the supervision of the National Park Service, where the presence of predatory animals and rodents threatens the success of large regional control projects of the Biological Survey in adjacent territory. Where in the opinion of the district leader this condition exists it is felt that the Biological Survey should take the initiative in discussing the matter with the National Park Service officials and suggest plans for control. Definite cooperative agreements in such instances should be entered into.[41]

Addressing the question of whether predators should be killed "where there is an over abundance of deer or other game animals," the conference resolved that "[t]he Bureau stands for protection of game, not for allowing predators to exist and subsist upon game" and that "[a]reas having a game surplus are just as vital in furnishing predatory animal breeding grounds as areas where no game animals are present. We cannot favor sanctuaries for the breeding of mountain lions, wolves, bobcats, and coyotes."[42] Clearly, the much ballyhooed policy shift from extermination to "control" was never intended to influence procedures in the field.

The development of a set of new safeguards (however porous) for non-depredating fur-bearers, and of a sanitized vocabulary to describe the survey's activities, constituted defensive measures in the face of political attacks. But the conference also set up the basis for future expanded capabilities. First, it addressed the lexical and bureaucratic quandary posed by the fact that its soon-to-be-called Division of Predatory Animal and Rodent Control technically would not be authorized to kill many types of birds, since officials astutely recognized that not all birds were predators and none of them were rodents. In fact, another division of the survey was responsible for balancing various bird-hunting seasons against an attempt to recover those same species, and yet another survey division was managing game refuges intended to ensure habitat for migratory birds. (These bird protection divisions soon merged.) Just as Young had formally inaugurated magpie killing in Colorado in 1925, however, so throughout the West the survey found reasons to kill similar scavengers, such as crows, ravens, Clark's nutcrackers, and eagles. Stephl, chairing the committee to address the issue, noted that "because of the sentiment involved," killing birds was "a delicate subject." Indeed, activism for bird protection hearkened back decades and included among its early leaders Florence Merriam Bailey, the sister of the survey's founder and the wife of its most renowned biologist still on the payroll in 1928.[43]

Stephl also admitted that "investigations by the Bureau indicate that crows, ravens and magpies are not as undesirable as most people believe." Nevertheless, "[s]entiment of sportsmen, farmers, and stockmen is so strong against these species that it may be best not to attempt to defend these birds too strongly." He noted that the species to be targeted by the survey had survived hunting and would probably survive campaigns by the survey. These ruminations led him and his committee to make three recommendations adopted by the conference: first, that before the survey undertake a program of killing birds, it "ascertain the facts with a view of avoiding, if possible, any such controversy as has been experienced in the past"; second, that it avoid "the use of poisons . . . in bird control whenever possible and practical"; and third, that "the Division of Predatory Animal and Rodent Control not be required to first obtain the approval of any other Division of the Bureau" before killing birds.[44] Whereas the first two policies reflected a prudent entry into a potential political minefield, the last one cemented a niche for future specialists in bird control to operate with no outside restrictions. (The bird control program's scope of victims and the reasons advanced for their killing expanded dramatically in decades to come.)

The conference also prepared the survey to expand its operations geographically and fiscally. Central to the survey's success to date had been its extensive network of cooperating ranchers, county officials, and state legislators who helped secure matching funds. Young took that idea to the next level of organization by getting the conferees to commit the survey to develop similar funding arrangements with other government agencies. The Forest Service and the Office of Indian Affairs, for instance, could be expected to "furnish all available labor and such equipment as trucks, tools, tents, etc." to kill rodents on lands under their supervision (although one conferee commented on Indians' reluctance to participate in the killing campaigns, noting that they "look upon all animals as a source of food"[45]). And in addition, "inasmuch as this is a definite range improvement program, directly benefiting the national forests and the Indian reservations by enhancing the grazing values, a portion of the grazing revenues [should] be allotted to the Survey for control operations."[46]

Similarly, the public domain lands (largely the low-elevation deserts eventually managed by the Bureau of Land Management) should be targeted despite their low productivity for grazing because "where the rodents are removing the ground cover . . . millions of tons of earth are washed from these low-productive areas and are eventually deposited as detrimental silt in valuable reservoirs or upon valuable irrigation projects in the lower valleys."[47] (Of course, as Aldo Leopold had noted four years previously and as irrigation interests throughout the 1890s had complained as well, the cause of such disastrous erosion was not native rodents but unregulated livestock.[48])

The conference also urged close cooperation with state fish and game commissions and with the Federal Extension Service.[49] The Extension Service's county agents, whose job—ostensibly—was to disseminate information from federally-funded state agricultural colleges, had long provided the survey with manpower for its rodent-poisoning campaigns, as well as with a connection to the American Farm Bureau Federation. The Extension Service's county agents often worked directly for the Farm Bureau, and local Farm Bureau offices were usually the same as those of the federal agency—which paid the rent.

The American Farm Bureau Federation served, in the words of its first president, as "a rock against radicalism," a counterweight to the agrarian populist resentment toward railroads and other faceless corporations. In the 1920s the Farm Bureau built up a series of insurance companies and other corporate holdings that sold farm equipment and services to agribusiness, whereas the local bureaus (and often the extension agents under them) acted as brokers to sell crops and livestock. To ensure continued markets for its equipment, the Farm Bureau fought against government policies that benefited poor subsistence farmers, those who raised food largely for their own consumption. (The Farm Bureau's work was effective; throughout the 1920s the percentage of absentee farm owners rose throughout Colorado and the West. With the onset of the Great Depression a few years later, many farmers who had gone into debt to buy Farm Bureau equipment lost their farms, and the corporate agriculture that took their land provided far more lucrative customers for such products.)[50]

With the Extension Service and the agricultural colleges both promoting a strictly mercantile type of agriculture at the behest of the Farm Bureau, the Biological Survey had found the perfect agency partners—fellow travelers in enhancing agricultural efficiency and partners that came with their own political base. Through these sister Department of Agriculture agencies, the survey had allied itself with the powerful Farm Bureau and its county-by-county network.

In one final aspect, the conference also prepared the survey to step into the future. Ira N. Gabrielson, the rodent control leader for Oregon (and a future survey chief who will be encountered in later chapters), noted that despite assiduous efforts at public outreach, heretofore only a handful of people recognized the survey:

> Newspaper publicity, articles in farm papers, talks before farmers' organizations, chambers of commerce, luncheon clubs, sportsmens' [sic] organizations, and others are all valuable and necessary. In fact, as a group we probably do too little rather than too much of this sort of thing. But no matter how much publicity of this kind has been carried on in a district, there are doubtless thousands of people who have no knowledge whatever of the work; thousands more who have in a vague way heard of the Biological Survey but don't remember whether it is a new face paint or some new fangled skin disease; a much smaller number who have a partial understanding; and a comparatively few who really understand the work and its purpose.

And even some of the agency's diehard supporters were not always the best representatives of the survey's position, as Gabrielson could testify from personal experience. "A farmer above the average in intelligence," he recalled, "succeeded in getting elected to the legislature."

> The time came for a hearing on an appropriation bill for rodent-control work. He having worked more or less with us and being familiar with the

field end of it, volunteered to appear in our behalf. He was asked if he needed any additional information and replied in the negative, saying that he understood the work thoroughly. He appeared and became hopelessly tangled up. He knew how we mixed poison, how we put it out, what it did, and that he was for the work. But he had vague ideas as to the needs of this particular appropriation. When questioned by the committee he didn't know whether the work was financed by the Federal, State, or county authorities or by charity. He did know that "these boys" did the work and he was for it. Needless to say, we profited by the experience so that future spokesmen were posted whether they wanted to be or not.

Gabrielson didn't have to mention that such thin reeds of public understanding and support made the agency inherently vulnerable to the type of negative publicity recently waged by one of the few groups that actually knew the agency well—scientists. The solution he proposed was a public relations program based on personal outreach to powerful individuals and to officials in state and local governments.

It is obviously impossible to contact every man of importance in a State, but a little study will usually reveal certain men to be leaders in their counties. There are certain farmers or stockmen whom the rest follow to a greater or less degree, and if these men are accurately informed as to the work it gives a tremendous impetus to the whole program in that community. Sometimes they are difficult to win, but that is part of the job.

One other thing in regard to personal contact—it doesn't hurt the case any for the members of the county court, the legislative committee, or other officials with whom we are working, to be able and willing to call us by our front [first] names. And if the county contacts are properly made and properly kept up it is gratifying to see how many of these same men later turn up at opportune monents [sic] as State officials, when their accurate information regarding the work can help over a tough place.[51]

Between allying itself with the Extension Service and land-grant colleges, and thus implicitly with the American Farm Bureau Federation, and cultivating individuals within political leadership, the Biological Survey embraced its rightful and lasting constituency: a rural elite that regarded ranching less as a semi-subsistence lifestyle than as a business. Since the agency's inception in 1885, survey officials had periodically gestured, with varying degrees of enthusiasm, toward their devotion to serving the small farmer. But they had ignored the growing populist agrarian rebellion of the last fifteen years of the nineteenth century while concentrating on scientific endeavors that primarily interested an academic elite ensconced in universities and museums.

In remaking itself into an agricultural service agency during the late teen years and early 1920s, the survey evinced no more real concern for small farmers than it had at its inception. The process had entailed defeating the bounty system, which primarily favored the type of rural proletariat to whom a few dollars in bounties and pelts was worth considerable time and effort. Although such people also owned domestic animals, they were often sufficiently close to the homestead to be relatively safe from predators. Thus in 1925 seventy stock-raising homesteaders in Elko County, Nevada, petitioned the survey to refrain from poisoning coyotes in their neighborhood: "The depression of the last few years has made trappers out of many of us who depend upon the sale of coyote furs for a part of our livelihood, and we feel that at this time it would be as unjust to destroy this part of our income with poison as it would be to destroy our timber with fire." Similarly, in Susanville, California, a delegation of set-tlers had appealed to the local stockmen's association not to raise money for a cooperative poisoning campaign with the survey because "any time you elimi-nate the coyote from that section you take our winter groceries."[52]

Winning the bounty war state by state had honed the agency's political skills and helped shape its identity. Young and his colleagues had taken pro-fessional pride in defeating bounty advocates in state legislatures, in turning former bounty hunters (such as Bill Caywood, Hegewa A. Roberts, and Rattle-snake Jack Junior) into salaried professionals, and in catching the occasional bounty-seeking trap thief such as the impecunious Nate Strang.

The beneficiaries of the salaried hunter program that replaced the bounty system were those who owned large and dispersed herds of cattle or flocks of sheep, not easily protected. Without articulating it as such, the survey had long thrown its lot in with these wealthier interests at the expense of those whose rural existence tended to be more marginal. With its official encouragement to work with the Farm Bureau–dominated extension agents, the survey implic-itly acknowledged its firm alliance with the rural elite of the western states.

Five days is a long time to confer with colleagues and hammer out policies and procedures, but the conference in Ogden likely energized the participants with a commonality of purpose. One working committee recommended bring-ing together the survey's Washington staff and its field supervisors at least once every five years to enhance communication. Enthusiasm builds on itself. "As representatives of the greatest conservationists' body on earth," exclaimed the state predator control supervisor for Oregon, "we as individuals must do all we can to protect the more valuable fur bearers and control those species that do not best serve man's purpose." Others saw through the day-to-day routine of supervising those inserting strychnine into cubes of horse flesh to recognize the transcendent worth of their work. "If every man here will culti-vate a critical appreciation of the other's point of view," said D. A. Gilchrist, "ours will be a real conference and the real dimensions and true value of our gathering will live long after most of us are gone and forgotten."[53]

The Biological Survey's official policy shift from extermination to control in April 1928 bought it two more years of respite from additional campaigning by scientists for reform. The new policy provided the substance contained in the 1929 letter sent by survey chief Paul Redington to Charles Adams repudi-ating the mammalogists' condemnatory report and Adams's cover letter. That report, along with the joint mammalogist-survey report, had stopped short of specifying areas where carnivores should be safe from persecution—a fatal weakness. Without such areas identified, the survey could continue to obfuscate the magnitude and ubiquitous impact of its work. "Our operations for the control of predatory animals and other injurious species merely hasten the inevitable elimination of various animals from areas occupied by man," Redington explained in his public letter to Adams, "a process that is defensible because of the great economic benefits that accrue."[54]

In April 1929 Redington gave a well-received talk at the annual American Society of Mammalogists meeting, once again convincing at least some in his audience (including the ever-optimistic Joseph Dixon) that he was open to their suggestions for reform.[55] Believing they had won a concession on basic policy goals, the independent scientists at first relaxed the intensity of their campaign. Dixon, largely satisfied at the change, wrote Redington with several suggestions intended to protect the fur industry. Licensed trappers, he recommended, "should be given a chance to trap coyotes before any intensive poison campaign be undertaken." Poison should not be left out all winter "in timbered country where there is a possibility of marten, fisher, and red foxes, or other valuable fur-bearers" getting at it. Eager to demonstrate his practical frame of mind, Dixon advised not poisoning "certain areas where the hunting of mountain lions with dogs is a necessity." Only one of Dixon's suggestions addressed non-utilitarian uses of wildlife—"That the use of steel traps and poison on lands *inside* [emphasis in original] National parks might be more carefully supervised." But lest he be misunderstood on that point, he stressed that "it is perfectly right and proper that the Survey should handle control of predatory animals in National parks."[56]

The Difference Between an Englishman and a Chinaman

Paul G. Redington, Stanley P. Young, and the rest of the Biological Survey's top brass had begun nursing ambitions grander than the mere improvement of relations with trappers and the mammalogists. As far as they were concerned, their change in policy should have ended the controversy, and Joseph Dixon's mild letter of December 7, 1928, did not destroy their sanguinity. In the meantime, the House Appropriations Committee's instruction to report on a possible five-year boost in the agency's budget to allow for the virtual extermination of coyotes offered a tantalizing opportunity. The survey took the idea one step further: a ten-year campaign at more than double its fiscal year 1929 budget that would effectively end the threat of both predators and rodents once and for all. On January 3, 1929, less than a year after the mammalogists' report had been presented and the survey's official policy amended, the secretary of agriculture sent Congress the survey's pitch for increased expenditures.

The survey's case was premised on efficiency. Relying on calculations of losses as a result of predators and rodents that the dissident mammalogists had long criticized as biased and unreliable, the report confidently asserted that increasing the annual predator and rodent control budget from fiscal year 1929's $566,634 to $1,378,700 would eventually save the government money:

> The estimated savings effected even from the inadequate work thus far made possible by Federal appropriations have been demonstrated to be

more than $10 for every dollar spent. It is believed that the funds esti-
mated to be necessary for a 10-year intensive program of control,
through preventing constant reinfestation of cleared areas, will make this
saving permanent.[1]

This new threat aroused the mammalogists again, inspiring Charles C.
Adams to address a pointed letter to Redington:

> I was pleased to see in your latest Annual Report of the Bureau that you
> stated positively that the Bureau policy was not one of *general extermina-*
> *tion.* The next practical step is to see how this practice will be *interpreted in*
> *the field,* and furthermore what *research program* will precede practice. So
> far so good, but when I secured a copy of House Doc. No. 496 (70th Cong.
> 2nd Session) on "Control of Predatory Animals," with its request for over
> 10 million dollars for a ten year program, in which I see *no provision for*
> *research to guide practice,* I again wondered where are we drifting! I think
> that before any such program is started you should consider this with the
> American Society of Mammalogists, no less than with the cattle and sheep
> interests, stating your case, and profiting by their suggestions, unless you
> consider them negligible [all original italics].[2]

Redington's explanation—in the same public letter in which he had repudiated the mammalogists' predatory animal committee report—was that the
absence of a research component to the ten-year budget request merely reflected the fact that research fell into a different line item. His answer revealed
more, perhaps, than he intended, reflecting the well-established dominance of
the Division of Predatory Animal and Rodent Control over the agency's scientific divisions.[3]

That same year, 1929, two books were published about the survey's activities that seemed strikingly at odds with the agency's newly-struck positions.
The Bureau of Biological Survey: Its History, Activities, and Organization, a semi-
official history produced by the non-profit Institute of Government Research
(later renamed the Brookings Institution), panegyrized the survey's glorious
past but frequently employed such defunct terms as *extermination* to refer to its
goals. "The best gauge of the success of the work is its measure of accomplishment," author Jenks Cameron wrote, continuing:

> Predatory animals in the great stock-raising areas of the West have not
> been exterminated. They still exact a not inconsiderable yearly toll from
> the herds. But that toll is no longer the twenty to thirty million dollars that
> it used to be, and it is constantly being reduced with the passage of time
> and with the tightening-up of the cooperative control system, which year
> by year strengthens its grip on the situation, through riper experience and
> progressive improvement in method. It is now pretty generally agreed
> that the end of the wolf is in sight. His known casualties, accounted for by
> hides and heads, had reached a total of about six thousand by 1926, and
> practically all of the most notorious stock-killers had been accounted for.
> In a general way, similar comment may be said to apply to the cougar (or

mountain lion), the lynx, and the bobcat. Their depredations have been controlled, and their ultimate elimination, though not so apparently imminent as that of the wolf, is only a matter of time.[4]

That fall another survey history appeared, *The Last Stand of the Pack,* co-authored by none other than Stanley Young. Written by Colorado outdoor writer and wilderness enthusiast Arthur H. Carhart, with factual details provided by Young, *Last Stand* described in breathless prose the battle between the survey's Colorado hunters and such "renegades" as Whitey, Three-Toes, Lefty, Bigfoot, and Rags. Like Cameron's eponymous tome, *Last Stand* seemed curiously dated in its ideology. "There is no place in to-day's civilization for the gray wolf," Carhart and Young proclaimed, "except in fur shops, museums, and zoos."[5]

Contrasting the book's over-heated rhetoric with Redington's cool and professional letter to Adams would perhaps reveal nothing in itself. After all, Carhart had penned the words to *The Last Stand of the Pack,* certainly informed in every detail by Young, whereas Redington's signature backed up the survey's official statements, whether to the mammalogists or to Congress. Yet here, also, Young's hand may perhaps be traced through the palimpsest of time. For later events consistently revealed that Redington—although boasting a background in public relations from his tenure with the Forest Service—was unable to muster facts and explanations for his agency's actions when he most needed to think on his feet. And Young, in enumerating his professional accomplishments when he retired three decades hence, indicated his own not-too-subtle role in formulating "a set of policies to follow in mammal control work, where none had existed previously."[6] It seems likely that many, if not most, of Redington's writings and public statements in this period were handed him by Young.

The real difference between *The Last Stand of the Pack* and official survey pronouncements was one of timing. The first was conceived in the mid-1920s, when Young must have spent considerable time briefing Carhart, who then apparently wrote the book in 1927 and 1928 during the period Young left Colorado for Washington.[7] Up to that period, Young's life and career had largely revolved around a series of escapades. That romantic spirit of engagement against the wolves and the wild (and, on another level, against bounty hunters) animates *Last Stand.* The book is structured around, and in essence comprises, nine hunting adventure stories about the "outlaw" wolves Young and his dedicated nimrods pursued. (One publisher, in turning down a bid to reprint the book in 1949, helpfully suggested the authors submit it to presses specializing in works for juveniles.[8])

But after moving to the capitol and taking on greater responsibility, Young's challenge was to expand his agency's de facto extermination campaign in the face of a growing bloc of opposition that might eventually shut it down entirely. The policies that emanated out of the five-day conference in Ogden, and

Redington's subsequent articulation of those policies, also represented Young's transition from deadly adventurer to deadly bureaucrat. Now, instead of wandering off a pier as in childhood or traipsing across an international border by mistake or tricking a wolf to step just where he intended, Young would battle mammalogists to build support for a ten-year campaign of increased predator and rodent killing.

The key to building that support would be the business-like network strengthened by long-standing personal bonds that tied the survey's private and government cooperators to the survey itself. Young was the perfect man to link the survey's Washington brass and congressional supporters to those working on the ground in the West. "Bluff and hearty" (in the words of a feature article on him),[9] with a wide plexus of personal acquaintances in Colorado, Arizona, and New Mexico and increasing familiarity elsewhere, he was trusted by the grassroots network of western ranchers and state and local officials. With Young at the fore, the survey's state leaders throughout the West contacted their local cooperators, who in turn urged their elected representatives to support the funding increase.

In first raising the possibility of dramatically increasing the survey's appropriations, Representative James P. Buchanan had wanted a guarantee that matching funds would continue to be available in the same roughly two-to-one ratio that existed previously. Since the survey's cooperators in stock associations, counties, and state agencies typically financed the control campaign on a year-to-year basis, such a commitment would not come easily. But Colorado, still a bastion of political support for the livestock industry, rose to the occasion. Young's replacement as predatory animal inspector, Leo Laythe, met with thirteen local and regional stock associations, as well as with a rotary club and the women's bureau of the state chamber of commerce, garnering almost all of their endorsements for a new system of state financing to accompany the federal expenditures.[10]

In April 1929 the Colorado General Assembly approved a resolution urging Congress to adopt the ten-year campaign, and the next month the assembly passed a statewide funding mechanism specifically intended to help finance it—a three-mills-per-dollar tax on non-feedlot sheep and goats and a half-mill-per-dollar tax on range cattle. Now, for the first time, the state's contribution to the work would depend not on the vagaries of the legislature but simply on the number of livestock potentially vulnerable to predation in the state. As an interim measure until the taxes could be collected, however, the legislature appropriated another dollop of money for 1929—$10,000.[11]

The Biological Survey and its clientele in the livestock industry were not alone in preparing for congressional review of the agency's ten-year budget request. The dissident mammalogists had been reaching out to the growing number of trappers angry over the survey's waste of animals through poisoning and the effects of its practices on their livelihoods. In March 1929 an article appeared in *Hunter Trapper Trader* magazine decrying the survey's poisoning campaign. In "The Truth About the Poisoners," author W. N. Miller recounted his personal experiences competing with the Biological Survey for animals to kill. "I have seen two Biological poisoners (one here in Wyo., and one in Arizona) driving along in their cars and about every fifty feet they would throw out several poison baits," he wrote. The survey man in Wyoming, poisoning as close as his automobile would allow to a creek Miller wanted to trap along, particularly angered him, but to no avail:

> His defense was that this was the age of progress and that the Bilogical [sic] stopped at nothing and that the Biological slogan was "Get the Animal." Mind you this was in June, the middle of the summer. No doubt all the young of the skunk, mink and coon were killed as he put out over 2000 baits along forty miles of that creek.

But that technique didn't even catch most of the coyotes, who, according to Miller, knew better than to take baits. In trapping from the Black Hills of South Dakota to the Gila River of southwestern New Mexico, he saw the same picture unfold. "It has been proven here in the West that the government poisoners are actually destroying every fur bearer but coyotes, and I believe that they are just as plentiful as ever," he wrote. "Is it necessary to kill every other fur bearer just to destroy the coyote?"[12]

Young then appealed to the same audience of hunters and trappers in his article in *Southwest Wilds and Waters,* romantically entitled "Conquering Wolfdom and Catdom." Appearing in January 1930, the article explained the cooperative program led by the survey and (despite its broader title) its success against wolves. The piece did not attempt to answer the survey's critics but merely to present the agency's program in a positive light.[13] Another article, consisting entirely of quotes from Paul Redington explaining the importance of the survey's work, appeared in February in the press briefing paper of the American Game Protective Association, a hook and bullet group financed by firearms manufacturers.[14]

Despite mounting such counterattacks, in the face of the opposition the survey and its supporters in Congress put off bringing to a vote the legislation enacting the ten-year budget increase. But the resistance continued to grow. A handful of mammalogists had been volunteering their energies for over five years in an attempt to reform the agency. Many others—constituting an overwhelming majority of the professionals in the field—had passively supported their colleagues' efforts. But the survey's proposed ten-year program proved the final straw to those scientists who thought change within the survey was always just around the bend. Although the dissident scientists still clung to the language of reform, they seemed revolutionized, suddenly and shockingly cognizant of the intractability of the agency with which they had once been proud to associate.

In January 1930 one of those mammalogists, formerly employed by the survey as a "dollar-a-year man," A. Brazier Howell of Johns Hopkins Medical

School, formalized the rift with the survey. Howell was a complex man. Respected by his colleagues for his wide-ranging intellect,[15] he was accustomed to the supremacy engendered by a convincing argument. But the traits that made him a force in academia sometimes hindered his effectiveness in the world of politics. Bold in his ideas and eager to reform the survey, in the years to come he would occasionally veer between hopelessly naive idealism and equally illusory stabs at reaching a pragmatic compromise.

As the new decade began, however, Howell read the political situation more astutely than many of his colleagues. Realizing that the mammalogists' differences with the survey could no longer be considered a family feud best settled quietly, he decided instead to take them to the level of a public campaign. He drafted a petition intended for public release and sent it to his colleagues throughout the country. Squeezing his litany of complaints into two run-on sentences that he sternly termed a "Protest," his text read as follows:

> We, the undersigned, having taken cognizance of the fact that conditions operating for the destruction of American wild life are becoming increasingly intolerable, view with the gravest concern the present wholesale and largely indiscriminate use of poison at the hands of paid, and frequently irresponsible hunters, whereby it appears that the very existence of all carnivorous mammals, including those valuable species which constitute the chief check upon injurious rodents and are a vital element of our fauna, is imminently threatened over large areas. We therefore earnestly petition that this extensive program of poisoning operations be immediately abandoned, and that no extensive and general destruction of any form of wild life, by trapping or other means, be permitted in the name of expediency, without this course having first been abundantly proved as justifiable from an economic viewpoint by having made available a thorough investigation of the food habits of the species concerned, prosecuted by disinterested and properly qualified parties.[16]

The response from Howell's colleagues was electric. "Here is your petition, signed freely and joyously by everyone within reach," responded Joseph Grinnell, widely regarded as the dean of nonsurvey mammalogists. "Use it in the best possible way toward saving our North American mammalfauna [*sic*] from complete extermination!" Even Dixon signed the petition, following it with a letter to Redington assuring the chief "that I am not against the control of predatory animals" but criticizing the survey's bias in calculating the damage wrought by predators.[17] In the end, 148 scientists from most major biological research institutions in the country attached their names. With signatures attached, Howell sent the protest to every United States senator and member of Congress, Secretary of Agriculture Arthur M. Hyde, Biological Survey chief Paul G. Redington, around 500 daily newspapers, and every major outdoor, hunting, agricultural, and nature magazine.

Although Howell and his colleagues regarded any public break with the survey as an extreme sign of their frustration, Howell's actual position, in fact,

A force in academia, sometimes a naif in politics, A. Brazier Howell was the first to publicize the American Society of Mammalogists' rift with the survey. (Courtesy, Elmer C. Birney and Jerry R. Choate, editors, Seventy-five Years of Mammalogy (1919–1994), *Special Publication No. 11, The American Society of Mammalogists)*

was more moderate than that of Dixon in 1927 and even than that of the joint survey-mammalogists' predator committee report published in April 1928. That report had urged "preservation of a few predatory animals, and particularly the larger types in the national parks . . . as well as in certain carefully selected wilderness areas if this should prove practicable in the national forests." And in February 1927 Dixon had recounted his own participation, as a mammalogist seeking specimens, in a survey-sponsored killing of three or four mountain lions in Sequoia National Park, followed by his argument that those killings should suffice and a few lions be allowed to remain. "We cannot hope to maintain a large population of predatory animals in the immediate vicinity of flocks and herds of man, but we can, and I think justly should, keep them in our National Parks."[18]

In an April letter to Redington explaining his petition, Howell reiterated the long-standing dissident position that "control of predatory mammals is advisable in certain instances and in certain places" but that "it is greatly and dangerously overdone." But he also gave ground in stating that "we make no mention of wolves and mountain lions which, whatever their value from an aesthetic viewpoint, are truly killers and are destructive." To avoid the dreaded charge of sentimentality he added, "Our claims are based on the economic viewpoint alone."[19]

Despite Howell's trimmed objectives for reform, the survey's top brass took the scientists' new fighting spirit as an attack on the agency's fundamentals. Dr. E. Raymond Hall, the mammalogist who three years earlier had concluded that the California mouse outbreak resulted from the survey's killing of predators, reported—in a confidential letter to Grinnell—on an April 1930 working visit to the capital's National Museum, during which he also dropped by the survey's offices:

> I saw Mr. Young (chief coyote destroyer) and am to see Redington tomorrow a.m. They are really much alarmed over A.B. Howell's recently sent out material. The [sic] assume a hurt expression and say "well if this wrecks the Survey it will be worse with the inevitable return to the local bounty system." Young is belligerent and says "That gang are at least going to know they have had a h— of a fight before they are through." Howell is regarded as a 3-tailed devil. Dixon is not much more popular.[20]

A few days after Hall's visit, while he remained in the capital, the authorizing bill for the survey's ten-year budget request was unexpectedly brought to a hearing after remaining dormant for five and a half months. The bill's principal sponsor was Representative Scott Leavitt of Montana, whose interest in what he frankly termed "extermination" stemmed from his early days with the Forest Service, supervising the killing of wolves and coyotes. In introducing the bill in December 1929, Leavitt had brought the pelt of a Mexican gray wolf, trapped by the survey in Arizona, onto the floor of the House—prompting his colleague from Minnesota, Representative Harold Knutson, to exclaim, "[d]oes the gentleman mean to state that the Federal Government was a party to the dastardly murder of that animal?" Other members chortled at the remark.[21]

Unfortunately for the survey, however, Leavitt would not get to vote on his own bill until, and unless, it reached the House floor. In fact, although the subcommittee on agriculture within the House Appropriations Committee—the survey's regular funding conduit—was decidedly sympathetic, it could only consider funding requests one year at a time. It would make no sense for the survey to hire the staff and build up the infrastructure for a ten-year campaign without a reasonable assurance of adequate funding for all ten years. Authorizing legislation of this sort would have to go first through the House Agriculture Committee—which, thanks in part to the intransigence of the autocratic former speaker of the House, Joe Cannon of Illinois, boasted not a single member from the eleven western public-lands states.[22] With economic conditions plummeting from the stock market crash six months before, its members would not automatically augment a budget largely intended to benefit states not represented on the committee.

Of course, the Agriculture Committee members were not immune to the concerns of their colleagues off the committee. To ensure full appreciation of the bill's regional importance, eleven members of Congress from the West and Midwest—many of them ranchers—appeared before the committee to testify to the urgency of more than doubling the survey's budget for predator and rodent control.

Representative Edward T. Taylor of Colorado, a rancher and lawyer from Glenwood Springs and one of the livestock industry's most accomplished allies throughout a distinguished career as a state and federal legislator, was one of the eleven who testified. Taylor credited his early understanding of the issue to his experience trapping, poisoning, and shooting wolves and coyotes on his father's ranch in western Kansas. He argued that "Congress should go at this thing in a wholesale and businesslike way and clean out this scourge," referring to predators. "If we could ever get them cleaned out once, we would be relieved very largely of that scourge and the Government relieved of this expense."[23]

To back up Taylor and the other western congressmen appearing as witnesses in the hearing, dozens of the survey's cooperators who contributed matching funds for predator and rodent control had mailed and telegrammed endorsements, testimonials, and resolutions favoring the legislation. Chambers of commerce, farm bureaus, state departments of agriculture, stockmen's associations, county commissions, and state legislatures throughout the West weighed in—comprising people who owned thousands of head of cattle and sheep and who turned the wheels in the western states' political machinery.In the words of Representative Albert G. Simms of New Mexico, another cameo witness at the hearing, these people constituted "the most substantial individuals and the most substantial taxpayers in our section."[24]

According to many of the endorsements, the best part of the proposed legislation lay in the agricultural efficiency it would engender. Letter after letter and telegram after telegram delivered to the committee addressed the increases in agricultural production resulting from the survey's elimination of predators and rodents from various areas. Every grain of wheat consumed by a ground squirrel, every tuft of hay nibbled by a jackrabbit, and every ewe eaten by a coyote retarded the proper development of the country and cut intolerably into private businesses' profit margins. And the promise of even greater efficiency lay just around the corner. Touting the fact that non-federal sources already outnumbered congressional appropriations two to one, the survey's supporters generously promised to maintain that ratio should the increase be granted, despite the fact that the federal public domain represented more than half of many western states' territories.[25]

But the survey's traditional and proposed emphasis on the western states hardly impressed a committee whose westernmost representative was from the Territory of Hawaii and whose only other western representatives hailed from North Dakota, Kansas, and Texas. The chairman was Gilbert N. Haugen of Iowa, a state for which no survey attention was intended. Not only was no money to be spent in his district, but Haugen was concerned that predator control elsewhere might lead to further rodent outbreaks, to the detriment of wheat farmers everywhere whom he had long championed.[26]

Under Haugen's sharp questioning on a variety of such issues, Redington proved the wrong man to finesse the geopolitical weakness of his agency's budget request. Although the official transcript of the hearing reveals the chief's circumlocutory responses to difficult questions, Hall's firsthand account of the "rather nervous" Redington conveys a fuller picture:

> He could get nowhere. He was asked several times by congressmen to state his policy. Each time he went off on a tangent. Finally one congressman swore, others got up and began talking to Redington. He broke down and turned the thing over to Stanley Young who is as hard boiled as the next one and who made a pretty good showing of it.[27]

The hearing adjourned at noon, and that afternoon Hall buttonholed Representative Charles Adkins—a bluff, tobacco-chewing congressman from Illinois whose skeptical questions for the bill's supporters had indicated to the young scientist an openness to opposing the bill.

When the hearing resumed the next morning Redington was absent, reportedly (although not convincingly) required at the last moment to attend to business at the White House. In his stead, the survey's assistant chief, W. C. Henderson (an attorney by training), along with Young, defended the bill in the face of Adkins's pointed questioning about the survey's poisoning of songbirds and badgers, the federal agency's systematic violation of a state of California anti-poisoning law, and the waste of tax-payers' money.

Toward the end of the day, E. Raymond Hall was allowed to testify, along with two of his fellow mammalogists—A. Brazier Howell, author of the dissidents' formal protest petition to the survey, and Tracy Storer, co-author of the seminal 1916 *Science* magazine article suggesting the preservation of predators in national parks. Unfortunately for the bill's opponents, Howell evidently mistook the proceedings for a scientific contest of ideas. He read from some of his considerable data on the number of animals killed and the cost per animal, boring the congressmen until Hall, gaining permission from the committee's acting chair, approached his colleague and practically yelled into his ear, "[t]he committee is sitting late. May it not be best to insert the remainder of your evidence in the record?" Storer did even worse—getting cold feet, as he later admitted, at the prospect of becoming an apostate to the fraternity of scientists within the survey and stating that he would not oppose the bill if it were amended to provide adequate monies for scientific investigation of the economic impact of predators.[28]

But Hall saved the day, giving skeptical committee members solid reasons to oppose the legislation. Ten days short of his twenty-eighth birthday but fast becoming a veteran in the mammalogists' struggle with the survey, Hall cited his experience conducting fieldwork alongside a survey hunter in Nevada, who in a two-month period had inadvertently killed sixty badgers, five or six gray foxes, two golden eagles, and "a few" turkey vultures—but failed to report most of his victims except coyotes and bobcats, the survey's prescribed targets. "It's too much bother and they don't count much in a fellow's record," Hall quoted the hunter. He added: "We have here in the desert regions a tremendous destruction of a valuable fur-bearing animal, namely, the badger. . . . This is entirely aside from the great value which the badger has as a destroyer of rodents, and even insects injurious to crops and to forage on range lands."[29]

In the end, perhaps bolstered by the mammalogists' objections, the chairman held up the bill until the survey could come up with a definite policy addressing the mammalogists' concerns and the uneven geographic distribution of its work. Hall and Howell were ecstatic at winning the first round in the battle, but, as Howell speculated, the final vote may have already been decided.[30] Indeed, Representative Leavitt had already indicated his acceptance that fiscal year 1932 (beginning in summer 1931) would inaugurate the first year of increased funding, reflecting an agreement worked out previously with the Hoover administration's director of the budget.[31] Given such a generous timeline, the bill's delay in April 1930 would not likely prove decisive.

The hearing initially scheduled for May 6 in the Senate was postponed, and Hall got word that inquiries were being made as to how long he intended to stay in the capitol. The day after his departure on May 9, the Senate Agriculture and Forestry Committee convened to examine the bill. This hearing was much shorter, consisting only of testimony by a representative of the California Wool Growers' Association and by Senator Carl Hayden of Arizona, standing in for the bill's sponsor, Senator Peter Norbeck of South Dakota. Once again the committee took no action. But following the hearing the committee appointed a Special Committee on Conservation of Wild-life Resources to investigate an array of issues—including the survey and its control program—to be chaired by Senator Frederic C. Walcott of Connecticut. Walcott, in turn, requested that the survey conduct an investigation of its own practices in the field, accompanied, if possible, by a representative of the American Society of Mammalogists.[32] Despite this openness to new information, however, Walcott also indicated he intended to find a solution to the controversy that would "satisfy the stockmen without offending the mammalogists,"[33] indicating perhaps the greater importance in his view of the former group.

On May 21, 1930, less than two weeks after the Senate Agriculture and Forestry Committee met, the American Society of Mammalogists held a symposium on predatory animal control as part of its annual meeting, this time in New York City. Once again Edward Goldman and Vernon Bailey, joined by the survey's number-two man, W. C. Henderson, and by Albert K. Fisher (the first head of the Division of Economic Investigations), gamely defended the agency's policies. "Wolves will continue indefinitely in sparsely inhabited regions," Goldman claimed, "and there seems to be no definite evidence of any marked decrease in small fur bearers due to poison used under the direction of the Biological Survey." But like his agency as a whole, he focused his attention on the coyote:

> How can we treat as of little importance the inroads of an animal that in many places threatens the success of the livestock industry, in which many millions of dollars are invested, and which furnishes a livelihood for a large section of our people? How can we ignore its destruction of useful wild life, and its menace to public health as a carrier of rabies? If the present program of control is to be abandoned or greatly modified, what clear-cut, practical alternative will serve the purpose? It seems a reasonable forecast that additional studies will confirm the conclusion that the coyote is the archpredator of our time.[34]

But the independent scientists were not impressed, and unlike their understated criticisms voiced at the 1924 meeting, this time they did not hesitate to express the full force of their disagreement with the survey. Charles Adams, who six years previously—without naming the survey—had obliquely criticized the agency's "vicious propaganda," now pulled out a copy of Jenks Cameron's history of the survey, published the previous year, and began quoting its liberal use of the word *extermination.* "I wanted to bring out these statements to show again," he concluded, "that it is not an accident that the word 'extermination' is used; this is the term emphasized, as it seems necessary to describe the actual work."[35]

This challenge prompted the iconoclastic Fisher to broach another line of argument, along a similar train of thought to that in his 1922 article rating the capacity to experience pain among civilized people, "savages," and animals. "What is the difference between an Englishman and a Chinaman except meat?" the adipose survey veteran asked as the audience broke out laughing. Undaunted, he answered his own question:

The Englishman went over the world and made it better for civilized people because he is a meat eater, a beef eater. Now we are running short of beef and it is our duty to save all the beef and mutton that we can. Is there anyone who wants to pay seventy-five cents or a dollar a pound for steak? If we kill off those things which are destroying our meat, we will have more meat for our increasing population. We should have more meat and the only way that I know of getting it is to save it, and if necessary in certain places exterminate the destroyers of it.[36]

These remarks prompted humorous wisecracks among the assemblage and may have even broken up the uneasy tension between the two factions. But the gulf, once opened, would not disappear. Howell, whose recent talk before the House Agriculture Committee had set the congressmen to bored fidgeting, now commanded his colleagues' attention in the symposium's final speech, titled "At the Cross-roads." He summarized the moderation of the mammalogists' position:

We have no objection to reasonable control. Whatever in our own minds we would like to see obtaining in wild life conditions we admit that concessions must be made by pure conservation to the economic exigencies of present day civilization. As the most practical viewpoint I therefore base my arguments on economic considerations, and leave the aesthetic side, of equal or even greater interest to me, to others.

Accordingly I pass over the plight of the mountain lion and the wolf. You already know it. But I may mention that among the tens of thousands of carnivores killed in 1928 by federal hunters there were only 11 gray wolves. The rest have gone from the far west.

The root of the problem lay, according to Howell, in the relationship between the survey and its present constituency:

Coyote damage has been much overestimated in many instances. Sheep men have told me that when a sheep was killed all that was necessary to get a hunter to clean out the coyotes in a region was to yell loud enough that they were being ruined. Not only are the sheep men powerful enough politically to get such service, but they can get almost anything else they want, and they want a lot. Great stretches of western country have been practically ruined by overgrazing, and several years ago the sheep men even tried to have all deer and elk in Utah killed so there would be more grass for live stock. I was assured by a senator not three weeks ago that the grazing interests could count on sufficient votes to pass almost any bill they wished.

Each coyote may do $50 worth of damage a year as claimed by the Survey. I cannot prove the contrary, but many of us doubt it. . . . I want to see this evidence of destruction put down in black and white. Perhaps Mr. Bailey or Major Goldman has it in convincing form, but neither one of them has shown it to us. It seems to us decidedly odd that if this evidence be so readily available the Biological Survey has been unable during the past 14 years to spend $1000 for placing it in print, while spending 10 millions for destruction.

He saw no more reason to trust the agency's claimed goals and methods than he did its damage estimates:

> The statement is constantly made by the Biological Survey that its policy is not one of extermination but only one of moderate control. Now I strongly object to be assured that the Biological Survey policy is one thing when the policy of the field force is quite different. . . .
>
> I cannot agree with the exalted opinion voiced by Mr. Young, in the book which he wrote with Mr. Carhart, that federal hunters are *"friends of all animals, the compassionate, regretful executioners of animal renegades when such outlaws must die that other wildlings may live* [original italics]." They are hired to kill and their jobs depend upon killing. What is a skunk or badger to them but vermin which gets into their traps and prevents them from taking so many more coyotes! Rather than turn the beasts loose they knock them in the head, that they may be bothered no more!

Finally, Howell invited his fellow scientists to take responsibility for reforming the survey before it could inflict even more damage:

> For a number of years now wild life matters have been going from bad to worse. . . . We are told that the procupine [sic] damages the forests and must be killed, the nests of the wood rat constitute a fire hazard and must be eliminated, and badger holes are dangerous to horses and the animals should be destroyed (as were actually 1450 of them in Wyoming by federal hunters in 11 years, and we know not how many more unreported). At any moment there is danger that some one will arise to label some additional species as destructive and successfully demand its elimination.

Immediately following Howell's remarks, a colleague corroborated his last point:

> Mr. Chairman, I should like to call the attention of the gentlemen here to the fact that the coyote extermination involves still another kind of poisoning which we have just learned about. The ramifications of it seem to be endless. According to the Bulletin Number 24 of the Department of Agriculture, October, 1927, they in a single year poisoned 5000 magpies. It was felt that this had to be done as the magpies interfered with the traps set for the coyotes. As a result the Department says, "Campaigns of magpie extermination (they use the term 'extermination') often must be carried out before successful work in coyote control can be conducted."
>
> I wonder how many other species of birds were poisoned besides the 5000 magpies in one year?[37]

The survey men had nothing to say.

Squawking Stockmen

W ith the Biological Survey's ten-year control bill still not reported out of committee, on June 20, 1930, a month after the American Society of Mammalogists' symposium on predator control, Secretary of Agriculture Arthur M. Hyde wrote A. Brazier Howell to invite the American Society of Mammalogists to participate in a survey tour of poison and trap lines in the West—the joint survey-mammalogists tour requested by Senator Frederic C. Walcott's special committee.[1] Such a field inspection to determine the truth of the mammalogists' claims, to take place in the fall, would play a key role, Howell and his fellow activists believed, in Congress's vote on the bill.

In the meantime, however, the activist scientists would not rely on the investigation alone to push their case. Howell published his closing speech to the mammalogists in the hunting and fishing magazine *Outdoor Life*'s August issue, and the magazine itself editorialized against the poisoning campaign. Furthermore, the scientists' growing alliance with trappers and furriers contributed to a unanimously approved resolution by the Western Association of State Game and Fish Commissioners, a remarkable ally to pick up given the survey's long association with precisely such bodies on a state-by-state basis. The resolution, adopted September 16 at the association's meeting in Santa Fe, New Mexico, cited "meager and conflicting" scientific data on the effects of the poisoning campaign. It urged the appointment of a commission of scientists to investigate "with open minds" such issues as the coyote's diet at different times of the year and in different areas (and hence, whether coyotes should be killed in all agricultural areas) and the numbers and kinds of non-target species poisoned. Most significant for the survey's ten-year budget request, the game commissioners opposed any expansion of poisoning operations until such a commission could report on its results.[2]

Equally dramatic, Nevada's electorate narrowly approved a referendum repealing the state's appropriation to cooperate with the survey. The vote, pushed by a state assemblyman and trapper who supported a return to the bounty system, played on the image survey officials held of all opponents as bounty advocates. But the mammalogists, happy to pick up support wherever it lay, trumpeted the results as the setback it genuinely was for the survey. (Ultimately, however, the vote was nullified by the state's attorney general, thus obviating both the mammalogists' triumph and the survey's fears.)[3]

The rift grew wider than the survey's brass had imagined it would. Arthur H. Carhart, who had authored *The Last Stand of the Pack* with Stanley P. Young and seen it published only the year before, now questioned the homilies he had so cavalierly written about the killing of Colorado's last known wolves. Echoing the mammalogists' many arguments, Carhart wrote Young a tartly worded letter questioning the livestock loss figures used to justify the killing, the secondary impacts on fur-bearers and birds, and other implications of the survey's work.[4] In *The Last Stand of the Pack* he had penned these words about survey hunter Bill Caywood and his Christmas 1923 pursuit of the Greenhorn wolf, thought at the time to be the last resident wolf in Colorado:

> Caywood was selected to write finis to the history of the renegades of the rangeland; would close the book against the gray raiders. In the pages of that book were written acts of bloody slaughter. The wolf account of stock killed could be written in the form of thousands of dollars. On the other pages there were months and years of silent trailing by dogged hunters.
>
> It was fitting that big Bill Caywood, the craftiest, the most learned of all wolfers in the Rockies, should ring down the curtain on this tragedy of the gray wolf killers. No other man of modern days has ever equalled his knowledge of the big gray—knowledge wrung from days on snowy trails, nights in wet, chill camps, hours under baking suns, and weeks of stark, frosty winter.
>
> Caywood's sympathies were against the wolf without the slightest hesitation.
>
> For he knew wolves. . . .
>
> The West was passing. It was falling before the march of the new West of finest auto roads, hydroelectric plants, industry and commerce. Even here in the big pasture there dwelt side by side the fading wild life, represented by the antelope, and that lonely old wolf, and the new order which demanded grade whitefaces in the place of the buffalo and the old longhorns.[5]

But now Carhart viewed the survey's activities quite differently. Was the extermination of wolves "to please squawking stockmen" justifiable, he asked

Young. "Isn't it a just consideration," he wrote, "that the cats and wolves and coyotes have a damn sight better basic right to live in the hills and have the use of that part of the world as their own than the domestic stock of the stockmen?"[6]

"Dear Art," began the head of the Division of Predatory Animal and Rodent Control for the U.S. Bureau of Biological Survey, writing back to his longtime friend in Denver, before repeating the survey's now common lines of defense in a formal eleven -page letter accompanied by dozens of pages of attachments. "The grey wolf has no place in modern civilization," he wrote, turning to Carhart's criticism of the subject the two had hashed over so many times in their work on *The Last Stand of the Pack*. Young continued:

> In my opinion this animal is one hundred percent criminal, killing for sheer blood lust, more often killing to satisfy his lust than to satisfy a natural and reasonable hunger. However, even with the inroads made against the wolf since the beginning of the settlement of the western country, it is questionable in my mind whether the species will ever be blotted out. Strange as it may seem to you, we had them in Colorado in the Telluride country at the time I left the State. We were making no attempt to control them at that time or the present time as little complaint is being received relative to their depredations so far as the stock industry is concerned for the reason that in the main they presumably are preying on the wildlife that you and I like to see roaming the hillsides. The same is true in the Jackson Hole where there are probably 18 to 25 wolves and we are taking no steps toward their control, although we are constantly being harassed to go in and eliminate them because of their inroads on wild game.
>
> I think you will agree with me that the depredations of the wolf make the desire for his obliteration in many areas inevitable in the face of advancing civilization. I have talked with you so much on this particular subject that it seems to me further discussion of the matter would be unnecessary. Nevertheless, in spite of all that is bad about the wolf I personally consider this animal our greatest American quadruped and have often wished that it would change its ways just a little so that the hand of man would not be raised so constantly against this predator. In my opinion he is the "king of predators."[7]

In fact, in Yellowstone National Park near Jackson Hole, Wyoming, the last wolves had been killed four years earlier, in 1926. In 1928 two wolves had roamed Jackson Hole. But one would have to have been male and the other female, they would have to have mated and had two large litters over a two-year period, and they all would indeed have to have remained unmolested for the extravagant figure of eighteen to twenty-five wolves to be credible. Given that the last Wyoming wolf was killed in 1940 and that none had been seen for several years prior,[8] either Young was purposefully playing dense in the letter to his friend or soon after writing to Carhart he sent his men to wipe out that budding wolf population. And in the southwestern San Juan's Telluride region, no other extant records indicate the survey knew of a wolf in 1927, when Young left the state. (In spring 1933, however, the survey would report a wolf in the canyon and mountain country of San Miguel and Dolores counties. The agency did not report on any livestock losses to the wolf but set out traps for it nonetheless. The animal was not captured—although it could have succumbed to poison without anyone's knowledge.[9])

Young also strongly contested Carhart's claim that the survey's use of poison was responsible for the decline of non-target animals, and he took issue with Carhart's attack on livestock grazing in national forests as a destroyer of wildlife habitat. But more striking than the arguments Young marshaled is the incongruity between the easy tone of his salutation and the unyielding defense he proffered. In an era in which most men's professional correspondence, even among good friends, began with a last-name salutation, Young's use of Carhart's first name contrasts sharply with his adamant position. And his almost pained admonition near the end of the letter makes clear his shock that Carhart, of all people, now opposed the survey:

> In the main I have answered the many questions you ask. Possibly there are some that I have overlooked. Matters of this kind are better discussed personally rather than to attempt to answer in the form of a letter. I returned here the latter part of October with many things to attend to and many interruptions, even during the dictation of this letter. Consequently I may have done a poor job of it.
>
> I will be quite frank, however, in stating that after reading your questions and turning them over in my mind I have wondered whether or not you are as ignorant in this entire matter as you would have me believe. On second thought, I believe you are; but at the same time I can hardly understand why you ask some of the questions in view of the outdoor experience you have had. Has not someone been talking to you and filled you full of opinions. At the present time, opinions are what have raised the present rumpus over our control work. The rumpus is based on what the opposition *thinks* of our work and not on what they *know* in actual facts which will stand up under investigation.[10]

The non-survey scientists certainly thought their objections were based on actual facts, and when in Washington they did not hesitate to push their case with Senator Walcott and his co-committee member Senator Charles McNary of Oregon, both of whom they thought were amenable to their objections.[11] But it was not always easy to obtain facts from the survey, hence the mammalogists also used the clout of a congressional office to ferret out information. F. E. Garlough, a Young protégé and director of the Control Methods Laboratory in Denver, had let slip to Joseph Grinnell that the survey kept a count of the number of poisoned baits produced at the laboratory for use nationwide. Grinnell—notwithstanding his 1916 article with Tracy Storer in *Science* magazine supporting predator preservation in the national parks and another mildly worded essay in 1925 criticizing "the absolute extermination of any native vertebrate species" as "unwise"—had not been at the forefront of the battle with the survey. But in "joyously" signing Howell's January 1930 protest, Grinnell had lent his considerable academic authority to the reformers, and he had written directly to Paul G. Redington criticizing the control campaign and the ten-year funding bill. His own protégé, E. Raymond Hall, who worked under Grinnell at the University of California at Berkeley's Museum of Vertebrate Zoology, was given freedom to pursue the issue on staff time. Garlough should have known better, as Redington and W. C. Henderson let him know later, than to let slip the possible availability of data that just a few years before the survey had boastfully released in its annual reports.[12]

The mammalogists had not sought this information, but the sensitivity it seemed to engender among the top survey brass made them all the more eager to obtain it. "Doubtless it is puerile and indicative of a deplorable tendency to treat a government inst. with levity, but I am getting some kick out of my effort to get the poison bait figures," Howell wrote to Hall. With their queries rebuffed, they enlisted the aid of Senator Charles W. Waterman of Colorado to query the survey. "If it is anything the BS [Biological Survey] hates it is to risk offending a senator or congressman, and farnkly [sic] I am surprised that it is running this for the sake of a few figures that cannot be of great importance to it," continued Howell.[13] Redington finally gave Waterman the number—more than 2 million poisoned predator baits put out nationwide. "To one unacquainted with the methods used in exposing these poison baits this total no doubt seems enormous," Redington explained to the senator. "When it is considered, however, that these 2,174,886 poison baits were used over the vast territory of the Western States, it is really by no means an excessive number."[14]

The survey officials didn't just defend, they counterattacked as well. Young, who in 1918 had persuaded Arizona's predatory animal inspector Mark E. Musgrave to hire a hunter who possessed an automobile and who in 1926 had used another newfangled technology—the radio—to reach an audience in Denver, now worked to produce the Department of Agriculture's first television broadcast. He orchestrated the production of a short silent film, *The Cougar Hunt*, picturing the depredations of mountain lions and coyotes in Utah, urgent telephone calls and telegrams informing the survey's Salt Lake City office of attacks by the animals, and the setting of traps for the coyotes and pursuit of the lion by dogs. Conspicuously absent from the film was any mention of poison. After the lion was treed, the film showed it being shot, adding in ornate text on the screen that it was "[a] 'good' lion at last" and explaining: "No more will these sharp claws and fangs tear the throat of calf, or lamb, or fawn." But lest such summary rangeland justice provoke undue sympathy, the film concluded with "a less tragical ending" for another lion pulled down with lariats from the boulder on which it sought refuge. The caption read: "Here the fugitive is taken alive—to spend the remainder of his days in the 'Zoo.'" Released in January 1931, the film received widespread national coverage on the big screen and, via a radio station, was broadcast on television as well.[15]

The survey also used targeted outreach. Back in 1912 the agency had begun to research fur farming. Now it used that background, never a large part of its work, to try to mitigate furriers' opposition by stressing the gains to the industry of using furs from captive foxes and other fur-bearers.[16] Finally, the survey's chief and assistant chief toured the West, meeting with state game officials and others to bolster their cause among doubters and to rally supporters. "I had two unlooked-for visitors yesterday, namely, no less of a personage than Paul G. Redington, accompanied by W.C. Henderson," Hall impishly informed Howell. "I had great fun talking with the former, and would have had more fun had not the last-named gentleman chimed in at strategic points to guide the faltering footsteps of his superior officer from gaping pitfalls."[17]

Despite skirmishes and pleas for support at the periphery of the issue, everyone knew the joint survey-mammalogists tour of the West could prove instrumental for the fate of the ten-year funding bill. But none of the principals in the fight against the survey's practices could spare six weeks from his academic research to accompany the survey investigators.[18] Nor did they trust the survey to stumble onto its employees' misdeeds, even with an outsider present. "As a way of showing their good faith in an impartial investigation of possible damage to fur-bearers by poison, the B.S. have selected [Edward A.] Goldman and [Vernon] Bailey to make an investigation of a number of such workers," wrote Remmington Kellogg, one of the many mammalogists who supported their more vocal colleagues from behind the scenes. Kellogg, working for the Smithsonian Institution in Washington, D.C., probably conferred frequently with survey officials but didn't trust them, as his note to Grinnell in Berkeley indicates:

> Some of us have facetiously inquired whether or not the reports by Goldman and Bailey have not as yet already been written. They will leave here some time this fall, and Goldman states he is confident that nothing will turn up to disprove the opinion they now hold. The field men will be notified when they are to arrive, and everything will be got in ship-shape for their visit. You fellows out there have much to learn about the ways business can be conducted. Well heres to you, but dont get discouraged and dont pick on BOUNTY HUNTERS for supporting evidence.[19]

Despite the limitations of time, Hall prepared to take off a few days to traverse his former study area in Nevada and seek evidence. And a naturalist associated with the California Fish and Game Commission, at Hall's and Howell's urging, similarly planned to take off a day or two per week to seek evidence in the field. But the activists knew such excursions would not suffice to obtain the information they needed.[20]

So the mammalogists convinced the fur industry to donate almost $800 to pay the expenses of two independent field investigators who would spend six weeks in the field and report directly to the mammalogists' Special Committee on Problems of Predatory Mammal Control.[21] The focus of the investigation was to be the survey's use of poison. "If we can stop poisoning then we can attack the program on some other specific count," explained H. E. Anthony, the committee chair. "But if we do not check the poisoning in the meantime there will shortly be no problem because there will be no mammals left to worry about."[22] The two furrier-paid investigators worked with Anthony at the American Museum of Natural History in New York,[23] but neither had been active in the fight against the survey. The first, George P. Goodwin, traveled with survey officials and, predictably, found nothing untoward—to the disappointment of the activist scientists.[24] The other man, T. Donald Carter, traveled to Colorado to start his investigation through the network of supporting fur houses rather than through the survey. He found a very different set of circumstances.

In 1930 Denver was a metropolis of 287,861 residents (more than a quarter of the state's population) whose multistoried buildings seemed emblematic of its dominant stature in the economy of Colorado and much of the Rocky Mountain region as a whole. It was an important, if not the principal, Rocky Mountain outpost of a fur network that stretched through St. Louis and eastward. The city had not yet been hit by the full force of the previous fall's economic collapse; nevertheless, its 7.2 percent unemployment rate was two points higher than that of the nation as a whole.[25]

Carter arrived in the Mile High City on October 30, 1930 (coincidentally, the forty-first birthday of Stanley Young, who was coordinating the survey's investigators on the ground.[26]) After conferring with local fur dealers, Carter set out the next day for North Park to begin his field investigation. Despite 69,000 miles of road throughout the state,[27] the North Park region was still somewhat remote. And although thousands of tourists were pouring into northern Colorado to see the lower stretches of Trail Ridge Road as it was constructed from Estes Park through Rocky Mountain National Park and over the Continental Divide,[28] North Park took longer to access.

Perhaps this remoteness and any consequently lower cattle-stocking rates accounted in part for an unusual attribute the area sported: wolves. In 1992 elderly physician Wayne Pettee recalled growing up on a North Park ranch. At age six, in 1929, while riding with his grandfather through a meadow, they came across a half-eaten elk carcass surrounded by wolf tracks. His grandfather pointed out the long tooth-scrapes on the bones where the wolves had stripped off the flesh. From the tracks they could see where the wolves came into the meadow and where they left. They followed the tracks for a short distance, discovering pieces of the carcass scattered about. The next day almost all the flesh had disappeared. Pettee saw the animals in subsequent years, too, claiming that "[a]lmost every day we were out on the range we saw or heard them."[29]

Although it seems likely that one or two recollections of such sightings at so young an age have been magnified by memory, other records, as we will see, indicate that wolves survived in northwest Colorado. But there are no extant reports of losses of livestock to wolves or of other signs of the animal in survey records for the period, and the agency's principal target remained coyotes.

Carter's investigative technique recalled that of the Biological Survey's original naturalists, who sought out local informants before traipsing into the wilderness. Carter asked ranchers, farmers, private trappers, and former survey hunters about the survey's poisoning campaign. "I would be riding along and perhaps meet a man on the road and pass the time of day with him," he described his polling method. "When I came to a town I would inquire as to the names of the leading cattle and sheep men."[30]

The mammalogists soon found that their suspicion about going through survey channels in the investigation seemed justified, as Carter reported "I found out that trappers have received a letter from the Biological Survey stating that inspectors were coming around and that everything was to be in good shape."[31] Although the survey was attempting to ensure that its own hunters did not provide grist for a negative report, it could not control statements from those outside federal employment. Surprisingly, Carter repeatedly heard that the agency did not command the support of many ranchers: "My whole trip goes to show that the sheepmen alone are for the poison," he concluded after returning to Denver from an almost 1,200-mile excursion to North Park and through southern Wyoming. "None of the cattle men are for it."[32] The reason was two-fold. First, most of the ranchers Carter talked with had lost dogs to survey poison, including small-scale sheep owners whose valuable sheep dogs had gulped down the survey's enticing strychnine baits. In addition, despite the survey's increasing reports of coyote predation on calves, almost all the cattle producers Carter talked with had lost more hay to rodents than calves to coyotes, and they faulted the survey for drastically reducing the principal control on rodents. A dry farmer in North Park told him:

> I do not approve of poison. Would not allow Biological Survey men to put out poison on my place. The coyote is a benefit to me as he kills the animals that eat my truck. If he must be caught I would not mind the trappers, but no poison. In North Park you will find that the big sheep men are in favor of poison, but everyone else is against it.[33]

Carter's next excursion, begun December 12, was to southern Colorado, in the company of a Denver furrier.

> Our route took us from Pueblo west to Canon City and then south to Silver Cliff and Westcliffe and Westcliffe Valley. Here in the San Isabel National Forest, on the eastern side of the slope, Johnson [the furrier] said to me, "Although we are a little late we will go up and see a trapper about five miles above here and I will guarantee he will have four or five foxes. The place never has had any poison placed in it. Every year approximately the same number of foxes are taken out of there." . . . We rode up and the man had caught seven, besides three wildcats, one martin [sic], a number of skunks, and nine coyotes. Some of them were taken on the very crest of the mountain range.
> We spent the night at Salida. In the morning we continued north to Buea Vista [sic]. Then south through the San Luis Valley to Monte Vista.

here we spent the night and here we heard another story. Although separated only by a mountain range from the Westcliffe Valley, the government poisoners (five of them) were at work there. In that whole valley, which used to be very productive, we bought only five coyotes and a few muskrats. According to Johnson, this used to be one of the most fertile fields.[34]

Carter also talked with several trappers distraught at the effects of the survey's poison campaign. This was not an insignificant issue—even with declining fur prices—because of the increasing importance of whatever extra cash could be generated as the year-long economic downturn started to snowball into the Great Depression. "I generally trap through the winter and can guarantee to catch fur if there is any to catch," said one San Luis Valley man Carter interviewed—who, in fact, had previously worked for the survey. "But it is useless to try in this valley. Everything is wiped out. I am looking for another section in which to try my luck." Another trapper, A. L. Pearsall of Monte Vista, recalled the survey's arrival at one of his old trapping sites in the southern San Juans. "I was down in La Jara meadow in 1928 when a government trapper went in there. At that time badgers were thick. I was there in 1929 and found but one, although there were plenty of old holes, diggings, and dens."[35]

Southern Colorado was not the only region saturated with poison, but it still supported wolves. The first wolf to be killed in the state since January 1927 was poisoned by the survey in Saguache County sometime in fiscal year 1930—between July 1, 1929, and June 30, 1930. (Saguache County stretches from the northeastern San Juans through the northern half of the San Luis Valley to the western side of the Sangre de Cristos.) The animal had gulped one of the 181,887 poisoned coyote baits planted in the state that year.[36]

Young had done his utmost to structure a field investigation whose strict appearance of propriety was matched only by the inevitability of its reaching positive conclusions. But he had made a mistake in judgment. In addition to assigning Goldman and Bailey to the investigative trail, he also selected Olaus J. Murie, one of the survey's remaining biologists not involved in the control campaign. Murie had spent years in the backcountry of Alaska engaged in various biological studies of the sort the survey had first made its mark pursuing. Since 1927 he had been assigned to Wyoming's Jackson Hole region at the edge of Yellowstone National Park to conduct in-depth studies of elk and then coyotes. Murie was a close friend of Bailey's (who had inspired him to join the survey a decade before), and he must have seemed an ideal choice as an investigator to Young, who was seeking credibility for the survey's own look at its control program.

But Young got more credibility than he bargained for. Murie's probity was central to his conception of himself. "All a scientist has is his integrity," he had explained to his future wife many years before. Through his years in Alaska he had developed an independence of judgment about biological phenomena and a refusal to accept others' judgments over his own observations.[37]

Like the mammalogists' Carter, Murie traveled throughout Colorado and Wyoming in his inspection, visiting hunters as they put out poison stations before abandoning the high elevations for the winter. Starting in Denver, where he conferred with state leader (the new term for predatory animal inspector) Leo L. Laythe and other survey officials on November 21, he conducted a train and automobile circuit of Colorado through December 3—passing through the San Luis Valley, South Park, and Montrose before heading off for more meetings in Denver and a similar circuit in western Wyoming.

During Murie's travels, which began just after Carter's trip through the same region ended, the survey hunters were just setting up their seasonal poisoning operations while finishing up the trapping that occupied warmer weather. In one visit Murie reported that a hunter "had established several stations but only a few were baited with poison. He was watching them carefully, anxious to have the coyotes begin work on them and become confident before placing any poison." At others, the baits were already out. These bait stations consisted of non-poisoned butchered horses intended to draw in and habituate coyotes, each surrounded by 100 to 150 small poisoned baits. Murie also inspected the less extensively used "studded stations," where the horse carcasses were impregnated with strychnine.[38]

The previous year, he learned, 477 poison stations of both types had been set up in the higher elevations of the San Juan National Forest alone—probably including the station that drew in the wolf poisoned in Saguache County. But in 1930, for some reason, only 250 had been set up in the same area, apparently reflecting a general reduction of poisoning in Colorado to about 80 percent of the 1929 level and not any cut in the agency's budget. Although the reason is not apparent, it may be that the presence of inspectors themselves had led to fewer stations in order to ensure that haste wouldn't mar adherence to proper procedures.

Nevertheless, the hunters still had a big workload, and the quickest way to kill coyotes was not to ensure that every bait was sniffed out by a coyote yet concealed from birds but rather to kill off the birds first:

> Hunters are bothered a great deal by mice and birds when the station is first put out and find it necessary to eliminate these before success with coyotes can be assured. Even after this "clean-up" magpies, hawks, and eagles, may still visit the station. In many cases I found that the hunter placed his poison baits on the ground in plain sight.[39]

Given the earliness of the season and perhaps also because of the warnings passed down the administrative line, Murie saw few poisoned animals—only two coyotes, a dog, and some magpies and rodents. Survey hunters told him that they had poisoned badgers and skunks before his arrival and killed jackrabbits and raccoons in traps. "Those reported to me," he explained in his own report, "were entered in the itinerary of the hunter and I made no effort to obtain a complete list of such animals."[40]

Even though he could confirm only a relatively small number of unintended animal victims in the recent past, Murie was disturbed by his observations. Having spent seven years traveling thousands of miles by foot, dogsled, and hand-poled boat in the wilds of Alaska and three years in and around the relatively pristine Yellowstone National Park, he knew how to read animal signs and he knew the kinds of habitats different creatures occupied. But his inspection tour revealed few signs of furbearers anywhere: "I saw hardly any badger holes in the areas I visited and no tracks in snow areas except an occasional weasel track." The reasons were not hard to ascertain. "Time after time, we found baits missing with no animals to show for it," evidently because the animals that picked them up flew or crawled away before succumbing. In the case of one poison station he inspected, tracks revealed that a coyote had picked up two baits, then dropped them a considerable distance away—where they lay exposed for any other animal to pick up.[41]

Murie offered some modest suggestions on how to minimize the killing of non-target animals. "It seems to me that baits could be hidden under a light litter of leaves, in a tussock of grass or other light available cover" was one of his recommendations. "Surely the coyote would find it with his keen scent and the birds would miss it."[42] But he also acknowledged that at the scale on which the survey operated, an unknown level of random mortality would always be a factor:

My own opinion is that one cannot expect the hunter to account for every poisoned bait. If he is to operate on a large enough scale to do effective work it cannot be done. The hunter finds a bait gone—no dead animal. What can he do about it? He may have a pretty fair idea what happened, and some of these men are pretty shrewd in sizing up such situations. But after all, there is considerable doubt. No one, it appears to me, can be certain what animals might be killed or how many.[43]

Next, Murie addressed the "economic status of the coyote" itself. And, much as Carter had, he found that not all ranchers were eager for its extermination. He quoted a survey hunter's straightforward question: "Who, besides the sheep man, is benefited by predatory animal control?" He added that "[s]ome cattlemen report that they have never had losses from coyotes, or that losses are insignificant, or that coyotes take only very weak or injured calves."[44]

Just as the survey had reported in 1923 that losses attributable to wolves were turning out to be the work of coyotes, Murie found that a fair number of the sheep supposedly killed by coyotes in fact were disappearing for other reasons:

[A] number of sheepmen and many assistant leaders and hunters stated that more sheep are killed by dogs than by coyotes. One sheep man, who highly prized the poisoning of coyotes, remarked, "One good thing it does is to kill off the dogs." One assistant leader, who is also a sheep owner, lost a sheep by a dog during my visit. He declared that he lost more by dogs than by coyotes. Such statements were repeated everywhere I went. . . .

I was told by some of the hunters as well as others that the coyote is often blamed for the work of dogs. . . .

The dog menace apparently has become more noticeable in many sections since the coyotes have been brought under control[.] Several sheep men stated it this way, "In the last two or three years, since the coyotes have been brought under control I have lost a lot more sheep by dogs."

A forest supervisor, who was heartily in favor of coyote control, remarked, "Since the coyotes have been killed off the 'unknown' loss has increased, and the sheepmen are beginning to realize the fact." He was referring to the dishonest sheep herders. I was told by many that not only are the herders careless with their sheep, allowing them to stray, going off visiting relatives or other sheep herders, but that they give sheep to their relatives and even sell them.

I was visiting a fur trader. He remarked that on that one day alone about 25 sheep hides had been brought in by Mexicans, most of the hides with the head cut off, some with the marks partly destroyed. I was informed repeatedly that many such sheep are reported "killed by coyotes."

A sheep man complained he was losing lambs every night and had lost 16. A government hunter went to destroy coyotes. He asked the herder if any [lambs] had been lost the previous night. "Yes", the herder said, "by pinyon," pointing up the hill.

"Where is the carcass?" the hunter asked.

"No, coyote vamoose!" replied the herder.

No carcasses were found and the killings stopped, although no coyotes were killed. The hunter was convinced the Mexican had done the killing.[45]

Murie also examined the conflicting evidence of coyotes' harm or benefit to game animals, but he was reluctant to draw any conclusions before completing his comprehensive study of coyotes in Jackson Hole.

Toward the end of his report, Murie went beyond analyzing information from the ground to address the larger societal questions represented by the survey's practices. He listed the "factions interested in [the] coyote question," weighing what he saw as the legitimate views of sheep ranchers, trappers, and hunters.[46] But it was a fourth faction, one he counted himself as part of, that seemed most incongruous with his agency's dominant tendency:

4. The Nature Lover. It is difficult to find a satisfactory term, for we must not appear "sentimental." Sometimes we speak of "recreational value," which sounds less effeminate, and of late even "inspirational values" of wild life. At any rate under some such head I would list those who may or may not be hunters but who enjoy animals without shooting; and those who are naturalists or scientists and look upon wild life as valuable, per se.

"All a scientist has is his integrity," according to Olaus J. Murie, pictured on right with Aldo Leopold. In 1930, sixteen years before this picture was taken, survey employee Murie was appointed by Young to investigate predator control (the term that in 1928 had officially replaced "eradication" and "extermination"). But his damning report was kept under wraps until after passage of the Animal Damage Control Act the following year. By the 1930s, Leopold was entertaining his own doubts about wiping out predators, but he turned down the 1934 offer to become chief of the Biological Survey, thus wielding more influence in the long run through his writings. (Courtesy, The Murie Center Archives)

It must be admitted that this class is the most altruistic in motives. Perhaps it is largely instinctive. I have given much thought to this question, and it appears to me, in tracing man's growth from the savage state, that the urge to protect animal life for its own sake is a natural development in man's intellectual growth. It is perfectly proper, in my opinion, to look far ahead and try to anticipate what proportions this tendency will reach at some future time.[47]

Building on that ethical foundation, Murie criticized the routine propaganda pervading almost all the survey's operations: "Assistant leaders in the field are continually called upon to advertise the harmful side of predatory animals, in order to arouse enough interest to obtain the necessary cooperative funds. They sometimes go to special pains to convince a farmer that certain species are harming him." As a result of such one-sided information, "the public gains the impression that a predatory animal is distinct from others, just as one would speak of sparrows being different from warblers. Placing an animal in the predatory class becomes a matter similar to the shifting of a species from one genus to another." That attitude was becoming insinuated into the society at large: "One day I picked up a Wyoming school book in which I found the following statement: 'The magpie, although he destroys insects and small rodents, is a thief and a murderer.'" And the cascade of victims, as the mammalogists had charged at their conference the previous spring, never seemed to stop—with foxes, badgers, skunks, and mourning doves all falling into disfavor with either the survey or the constituency it served. Even eagles "are generally hated by the hunters," Murie reported, "largely for the reason that they tear up coyotes which have been poisoned and spoil the hides for sale. Cyanide baits are sometimes issued to get rid of them. If this were the only mark against the eagle, one could reason that after all the hunter is out to destroy coyotes and that fur sale is of only secondary importance."[48]

Murie concluded his report by advising a change in attitude:

> It appears to me that there is an incipient landslide in the direction of denouncing everything with fur or feathers that has the slightest adverse effect on any human interest and it makes one wonder where it will end. . . . We profess to believe that interest in wild life is a most desirable influence in our lives. Should not young people on the farm be encouraged in the *enjoyment* [original italics] of wild life, in any form it may take? Should we not welcome and encourage any tolerance toward wild life on the part of rural people? What better environment could there be for young people than a farm where appreciation of Nature is a rule rather than bitterness toward animals? Many farms are rather barren of healthful interests, and even the casual visitor cannot help but be aware of sordid elements in the environment. If the coyote, for instance, must go, let us by all means send him on his way. But in doing so, I firmly believe that it is working against the best interests of humanity to discourage sentiment in his favor, and to ridicule those who see beauty in a coyote's howl, merely to further temporary ends.
>
> After all, the wild life question is a human one. Man is affected directly by his attitude toward Nature. When man decides to protect song birds because of their beauty and their music, man is improved more than the birds that are saved. . . .
>
> It appears to me, that if we keep in mind the factors making toward any form of cultural improvement we shall make the least mistakes. I feel that we should not discourage interest and enjoyment of any form of wild life, even if we are killing off such animals for economic reasons. Furthermore, we should consider sympathetically any plan which might be proposed, if any plan is proposed, which shows leniency toward species that are in conflict with certain interests, provided of course that such a plan is at all workable.[49]

Murie's report, issued at the end of December 1930 or in early January 1931, must have stunned the Biological Survey's brass, and some survey officials evidently execrated him.[50] Murie's close friend Vernon Bailey, who had helped the younger amateur naturalist gain survey employment, forcefully expressed his disagreement with Murie.[51] Three years later, during an even greater battle over the survey's future, Young mentioned cryptically that he had difficulty maintaining cordial relations with some survey employees, although he did not mention Murie or others by name: "Sometimes I really wonder how it is possible for me to speak civilly to my associates here in the office." But Young kept his lid on: "Maybe, it is because I blow off some steam at home, probably to the discomfiture of my family."[52] Bailey kept the tenor of his direct criticism eminently respectful. Perhaps it was hard to take issue with a man like Murie whose ingenuous bearing could not be reproached. "Somehow it never occurred to me that my position or standing would be endangered in any way," Murie recalled seven months later, in July 1931, in a letter to H. E. Anthony. Murie continued:

> To be real honest about it, I have received no hint of displeasure from Mr. Redington or any one else and they have all treated me very well. When I sent in this report (or any other report) I simply took it for granted that it could be used in any way anyone saw fit, that it could be picked to pieces and attacked at will. I said nothing that had not been carefully considered and I was and am prepared to defend it on every count.[53]

Murie backed up his report with a private letter to Assistant Chief Henderson that went further than his official notations, mentioning that survey officials in the field had tried to influence his report by offering him (illegal) licenseless hunting and complaining that the agency's hunters displayed not "the slightest interest in the broader phases of conservation of wild life":

> They do share the popular idea that conservation consists of preserving anything that may be shot. They do speak of the great saving of game effected by the predatory animal control. But I failed to note the slightest interest in non-game species, with one possible exception. Some of them hold in contempt such people who enjoy wild life without shooting. In fact sometimes it was very evident that the hunter took great delight in excrutiating [sic] suffering of an animal, particularly a predatory one.[54]

The independent mammalogists had long trusted Murie's judgment as a biologist not associated with the control campaign. But not having accompanied him in the field, after his inspection tour they neglected to contact him, perhaps simply because of the distraction of the holiday season. For whatever reason, they thus failed to request a copy of his report either from him or from the survey.[55] During the same period, Senator Walcott's special committee finished its report and issued it on January 21, 1931. But the report was no longer about predator control. Rather, the committee had been steered into producing a nineteen-page generalized homiletic description of the challenges to wildlife in a new era and the importance of conservation.[56]

Young realized the danger the recreant survey employee's report represented to the passage of his ten-year funding bill and sat on it for as long as he could. But no doubt realizing that he could not squelch it forever, he had to try to get the bill passed as soon as possible.

Much Less Necessary in the Future

T he earliest the Biological Survey's supporters in the Senate could schedule a hearing for the ten-year funding bill was in late January 1931, which was when the Senate Agriculture and Forestry Committee reconvened. The night before the hearing, the bill's opponents within the fur industry threw a big party for the senators' aides, replete with illegal alcohol. But in facing senators Charles McNary's and Frederic C. Walcott's sharp questions the next day, the agency had come well prepared. "[Paul G.] Redington had been called south (ahem) and [W. C.] Henderson presided for the BS [Biological Survey], supported by [Stanley P.] Young,"[1] wrote mammalogist A. Brazier Howell to his colleague E. Raymond Hall in a letter describing the hearing. Most important, the survey had support from several westerners on the committee. Senators Peter Norbeck of South Dakota, John Thomas of Idaho, and John P. Kendrick of Wyoming gave mammalogist H. E. Anthony as sharp a grilling as the survey's officials had undergone in the House Agriculture Committee, when Anthony tried to introduce the evidence gathered by his colleague T. Donald Carter during his furrier-sponsored western tour:

> Mr. ANTHONY. I should like to introduce into the record of the committee several of these reports made, one of them jointly and another independently of the Biological Survey, this fall, because they will give you a valuable cross section of opinion, methods, and results.

One of our investigators was sent out there to investigate wherever a promising clue developed. He was Mr. Carter, and he covered 4,000 miles in Utah, New Mexico, Wyoming, and Colorado, and only returned when the snow became so deep he could not continue his studies.

Senator Thomas. I think the committee might be interested in knowing who Mr. Carter is, and what experience he has had with the ranch, and what he knows about conditions, what his knowledge would be before he traveled those 4,000 miles.

Mr. Anthony. Mr. Carter's intention was to interview—

Senator Thomas (interposing). I can understand what his intention was, but what was his groundwork? How does he qualify on this particular line?

Mr. Anthony. I want to point out that his particular part was the taking of statements made on the ground. He does not need to express an opinion. He also has an opinion, but I attach the greatest weight to the testimony taken, in the presence of the witness, written out and read back to the witness, and the witness agreed to the use of his name.

Senator Thomas. He was not traveling as an expert himself?

Mr. Anthony. He qualifies as an expert. But he does not qualify from personal acquaintance with the field on many of these controversial points.

Senator Thomas. That is what I want to know, whether he is an expert witness along this line, or just some fellow who went out to look.

Mr. Anthony. Many of these people he quotes are possibly known to you. Some are influential citizens and some are the average citizen. When he went into a post office or a gas-filling station or wherever people gathered, he asked questions and often he interviewed influential people by special appointment. He interviewed men wherever he found them, and he wrote down statements of 56; some are very brief. I want to offer these just as they come. I am willing to let the points that work against us appear right along with the points that favor us, as an evidence of good faith.

Senator Norbeck. What is the general trend of them?

Mr. Anthony. Let me read one of them.

Senator Norbeck. I am asking you for the general trend so that we may have it as we go along.

Mr. Anthony. They are 10 to 1 against poisoning. And they represent trappers, sheepmen, stockmen, agriculturists, nature lovers, and just as they came. There is nothing hand picked about them.

Senator Thomas. Are they in the nature of the affidavits of these people?

Mr. ANTHONY They are not sworn to, but the men have agreed to the use of their names. But they can be verified because we have their addresses. I will read a short one:

M. H. Willadsen, Granite Canyon, Wyo., 7,000 acres: "I do not believe in the use of poison. As far as I know, no calf or sheep belonging to our company has been killed by coyotes, although I have raised sheep for 25 years. The stray dog is our greatest menace."

You might say that because he has lost no sheep by coyotes he doesn't know anything about it. I read the first one, and there are 56 statements in which the sentiment is generally against poisoning, the ground taken being that—

Senator NORBECK (interposing). May I ask you, do stockmen generally say that they have not lost anything through the coyote?

Anthony admitted that some suffered small losses and distinguished between the sheep men who favored the poisoning and the cattlemen who opposed it. This prompted a discussion of the cattlemen's old bane—wolves—and Senator Kendrick of Wyoming, who owned ranches in his own state and in Montana, reminisced on utilizing "guns, traps, dogs, and poison, any way in the world we could exterminate them. They were given no quarter whatsoever," he said. "It was a fight to the finish."[2]

The committee adjourned that day, but, not surprisingly, it approved the bill in early February. In the meantime, the House Agriculture Committee amended the bill by limiting annual appropriations for the ten-year period to $1 million—$378,700 less than originally proposed. The committee then passed the bill unanimously.

A few days later on the floor of the House of Representatives, Congressman Scott Leavitt of Montana faced questions about the need for the bill. His response was a throwback to older days before the survey disavowed extermination:

In the past, the appropriation has been just about enough; for instance, in the case of coyotes, to keep up with the natural increase of that predatory animal. But the problem is always one calling for solution. Often the wolves in an area are largely exterminated, but, because of a shortage of funds or lack of appropriation, the area becomes reinfested. . . .

The adoption of this 10-year program will establish a campaign that will not only take care of the natural increase, as we have done with some of these predatory animals in the past, but which will enable us to get control of them and make it much less necessary in the future to appropriate large sums of money annually.[3]

Leavitt was backed up by several of his colleagues, and he made sure to emphasize the hefty contributions the survey received from state and private sources. But he did not convince everybody. Representative John J. Cochran of St. Louis, Missouri, denounced the bill:

> Mr. Speaker, we have passed legislation to-day of almost every character, but at this late hour it seems to me the House is called upon to pass a measure which could well remain on the calendar. At a glance it is doubtful what fitting title should be given to the bill, but it certainly can be classed as a destructive measure. Its purpose is to destroy—destroy everything in the way of wild animals from a mountain lion to a field mouse.
>
> It is another obnoxious Federal-aid measure, increasing the fund for the destruction of wild animals to $1,000,000 a year over a period of ten years.[4]

Cochran read a telegram expressing opposition to the bill from the Raw Fur and Wool Association of St. Louis, noting that his city "is the largest fur market in the world" and that it "originated as a fur market or fur-trading post." In response to Leavitt pointing out that Missouri would receive Biological Survey attention under the proposed ten-year funding authorization, Cochran switched his criticism to fiscal principles: "You are simply handing out more money to bait the States. It is done in the nature of Federal aid. I am opposed to the principle of Federal aid, be it for a good or a bad purpose. I hope the time is not far distant when the Congress will discontinue all Federal-aid programs."[5]

Survey work had begun relatively late in Missouri and was increasing rapidly as the agency began to eliminate a population of wolves surviving in the Ozark Mountains. Cochran's principled opposition to the legislation, despite the enticement of service for his state, points to a political freedom largely absent among elected officials from states with more developed Biological Survey–created political networks. But Cochran also understood the power of the survey's constituency: "I know it is futile to argue against the passage of this measure, but I rise to enter my protest. . . . I know the people in distress throughout the country will not understand appropriations of this character, especially at a time when money is needed to feed and clothe people in distress." In a voice vote taken a few minutes later, Cochran was in a minority of around one-third of his colleagues.[6]

When the bill reached the Senate floor two weeks later, Utah senator William H. King at first objected, citing his lack of familiarity with the legislation but noting "several communications from my State in opposition to it."[7] At King's objection, a vote on the bill was deferred. Nine days later when the bill reappeared, he was the first senator to signal whole-hearted support. Evidently, King had either been convinced of its merits or had received sufficient correspondence from the well-developed network the survey had established back home—or both.

But some senators from the Midwest and the Pacific Northwest were still not ready to pass the bill. Senator Clarence C. Dill of Washington objected, as had Cochran in the House, to the federal government's assumption of responsibilities that should be the concern of individual states. His colleague

Arthur H. Vandenberg of Michigan mentioned protests by the American Society of Mammalogists and the University of Michigan. Senator John Blaine from Wisconsin extolled the virtues of the gopher as a destroyer of cutworms and grubworms that prey on corn. "Mr. President, does the Senator from South Dakota [Peter Norbeck] seriously propose that the Department of Agriculture shall find out the best way of destroying gophers in the corn-growing regions of the United States?" he asked. "I know of no reason why they should be exterminated. The fact is, many believe they should be protected."[8] Blaine's comment prompted Senator Thomas J. Walsh of Montana to defend the survey on grounds even more anomalous—if considerably less accurate—than those that conceded extermination was the agency's objective. "Mr. President, as I understand it the bill makes no provision for the extermination of rodents," he averred. "It applies to animals like the wolf and the coyote, which prey on others. The argument is that they ought to be killed, because they kill the rodents."[9]

Blaine ran out of time to make his argument, and with no one inclined to prolong the debate, the Senate approved the measure.[10] A few days later, on March 2, 1931, forty-six years (minus one day) after President Chester A. Arthur had signed the spending bill creating the Office of Economic Ornithology and Mammalogy, President Herbert Hoover signed what later became known as the Animal Damage Control Act. The language of the new law echoed the phraseology of earlier appropriations bills for the survey and sounded almost innocuous, authorizing and directing the secretary of agriculture

> to conduct such investigations, experiments, and tests as he may deem necessary in order to determine, demonstrate and promulgate the best methods of eradication, suppression, or bringing under control on national forests and other areas of the public domain as well as on State, Territory, or privately owned lands of mountain lions, wolves, coyotes, bobcats, prairie dogs, gophers, ground squirrels, jack rabbits, and other animals injurious to agriculture, horticulture, forestry, animal husbandry, wild game animals, fur-bearing animals, and birds, and for the protection of stock and other domestic animals through the suppression of rabies and tularemia in predatory or other wild animals; and to conduct campaigns for the destruction or control of such animals.

The new law also provided for the secretary of agriculture to "cooperate with individuals and public and private agencies, organizations, and institutions" and authorized the appropriation of $1 million per year through fiscal year 1941, in accordance with the proposed ten-year program submitted by the Biological Survey back in 1928.

"To me this ten year bill is more important in principle than in fact," wrote an undaunted Howell to ally Clinton W. Rowley, secretary of the Western Association of State Game and Fish Commissioners. Howell looked forward to trying to cut the survey's budget in the yearly appropriations process or by pressuring the president's director of the budget, in charge of putting together the administration's funding requests to Congress. Howell continued, "If we fail in our efforts against this the Survey can continue to flout the advice and wishes of those concerned with wild life, while if we win I am sure the result will be that the Survey must adopt rather drastic changes."[11]

Howell was right that the bill represented more principle than fact. But the principle represented the outcome of the first instance in which Congress as a whole had actually debated the survey's control campaign on the floor and then taken a vote rather than simply approving funding measures buried within the annual appropriations bills. Passage of the measure vindicated the survey and handed it a green light to proceed as before, with greater financial assets.

The mammalogists had put up a tremendous fight, given their resources and the emotional and cultural distance they had traveled collectively merely to break publicly with the survey. Their opposition had helped delay approval of the funding bill for over two years, even if the House Agriculture Committee members' primary motivation in initially shelving the bill stemmed from reluctance to vote for money for other districts in tight times.

The mammalogists' loss can be attributed primarily to the survey's powerful political machine (a manifestation of the livestock industry's vast political network). But one cannot help but wonder whether the outcome would have been different had the mammalogists been less moderate, quicker to realize the depth of their differences with the survey.

Joseph Dixon's official neutrality back in 1927 had helped delay the American Society of Mammalogists' special predator committee report. Even as an advocate, he failed to use all the tools at hand. His cousin had served first as a U.S. senator and then as assistant secretary of the interior, yet there is no indication that Dixon ever asked his cousin to use his influence to reform the survey.[12] Dixon's colleagues recognized his shortcomings. As Charles C. Adams put it in December 1932, "Dixon is in the machine now and none who are in are free."[13]

Tracy Storer had retracted his opposition to the bill during his 1930 congressional testimony, signaling his acceptance of "the present eradication program" so long as it was tempered with a research component.[14] Howell, who maintained his fortitude after the loss, privately described Storer as "a good fellow gone wrong, a fence straddler with poor circulation in the nether extremities, and who fancies himself as an astute, and rather devious politiciean [sic]," adding, "I would rather have a strong, outspoken enemy, and am well pleased that you chaps in the west have him rather than we in the east."[15]

Howell's political potency varied widely. In early 1932 he confidentially proposed removing all livestock from all national forests, not only to eliminate the rationale for the survey's extermination activities on those lands but also in recognition of the extreme overgrazing to which they were subject. The idea was bold, profoundly idealistic, and politically utopian. But Howell, whose 1930 address to the House Agriculture Committee had fallen short of his usual ability to communicate with and inspire his colleagues, similarly did not seem to grasp the powerful opposition his idea would have engendered. "High officials of two federal bureaus will back it," he wrote Hall naively, adding, "[a]ll I want to do is to get a number of topnotchers enthusiastic and then fade from the picture, but the prospects seem bright."[16]

Contrast that stance with his assiduously moderate position on the survey's control campaign, as expressed in a letter filled with minor quibbles he wrote to colleague Aldo Leopold in April 1932:

> I have insisted, in print and out, that I believe in control of predators, that the harmful hawks should be killed, that the wolf should be exterminated in the United States, that the mountain lion can be tolerated only in the smallest numbers and in few places, that coyotes should be rigorously dealt with by trapping and hunting where they are definitely harmful, that destructive rodents should be kept at a minimum where it is shown that such is needed; and I know of no competent vertebrate zoologist who does not feel much the same, with minor variations. Also we are anxious to reach a common ground of compromise, while yet there is time. Yet the opposition, including one class of sportsmen, graziers, the Biological Survey et al, are constantly reiterating that we are a bunch of sentimentalists who would prohibit the killing of everything and would allow wild life to fatten on the farmer and his crops, prohibit hunting, and such fantastic things.[17]

Moderate in their stances though they were, the activists among the mammalogists felt embattled and often found themselves postponing research—and thus professional advancement—for days that stretched into weeks and sometimes months of testimony, impassioned writings, and organizing among colleagues. They made real sacrifices in careers they might have reasonably expected to be free of strife. In 1984, having outlived Stanley Young and most of the other principals in the battle, Hall recalled that he had been physically attacked as a means of shutting him up. "I went to Washington to testify against these predator control people, and I knew for a fact that their jobs were on the line and that they were out to get me," he told a writer for *Audubon Magazine*. "I was walking back to my hotel after dinner when a couple of thugs jumped me and tried to rough me up."

Hall threw one man over his shoulder and scrambled up a nearby rock pile, grabbing two rocks for self-protection. Thus armed, he frightened off his attackers. "I know who put them up to it," he told the magazine, "but I never said anything."

It cannot be known whether indeed this was a political attack rather than a common mugging, nor is the timing of the event clear. Hall recalled the incident as occurring in the summer of 1931, but his crucial testimony had been given the previous year, and he did not mention the attack in his correspondence of the time. More than half a century later, it is not surprising that he would get the year wrong (and 1931 would have stuck in his mind as the year the bill had passed). In any event, Hall continued to fight the survey for many years to come, undaunted.[18]

Howell's letter to Rowley of the Western Association of State Game and Fish Commissioners indicated a similar tenacity:

During my visit to Washington last week I ascertained that one group in the Survey is celebrating the fact that they have licked the scientists. This is evidently headed by Young and his killers. Another opinion, emanating from at least one B.S. man, was to the effect that they should have dropped the bill, instead of pushing it through and having a bitter ten year fight on its hands. A shrewder Survey element is trying hard to find out if we mean to continue the fight. They are apprehensive that we may be so dumb that we dont [sic] know when we are licked, and may even endeavor to cause them future discomfiture. I let it be speedily known that we are hardly warmed up yet and are having a bully time.

More important still, I was told by someone whom I consider entirely reliable, but whose name I can not mention, that the second highest source in the Survey, meaning Henderson, had breathed a sigh of relief when he heard the bill was passed and said he never had been afraid of the naturalists, or of the sportsman contingent, because they controlled most of the latter of influence [sportsmen], but he had been most apprehensive all along that we would secure the aid of the Federated Womens [sic] Clubs, and of the Humane Society. What the latter can do I dont [sic] know, but the former can do anything they start out to accomplish and we are dubs not to have enlisted their aid before. Anyway, I am going after them hotfoot and may want some help before long. This is a second detail of the plan.

Trot out any suggestions you have to offer. The more the merrier, but at any rate, no matter what we do in addition, we must hammer away at [Secretary of Agriculture Arthur M.] Hyde and the director of the budget, not so much ourselves, as to get others to do it, so that there may be an imposing number. Send the latter copies of your resolutions, and better let me have a few more, for the ladies.[19]

D espite A. Brazier Howell's optimism a week after the March enactment of the Animal Damage Control Act of 1931, the General Federation of Women's Clubs was not nearly the force it had been in the
teen years. Contrary to the expectations of many early supporters,
the 1920 passage of the Nineteenth Amendment granting women suffrage
failed to bring about the feminization of the nation or to reform the national
culture. Instead, society's increasing complexity had made such comprehensive reform seem ever less likely. Although Howell exchanged a few ineffectual
letters with federation officials, there is no indication the clubs mounted any
sort of campaign.[1]

Although the organized women's movement was in decline, one of its
earlier activists was inspired by the mammalogists' pleas for assistance in
fighting the survey. Rosalie Barrow Edge, unlike the mammalogists, was not
handicapped by nostalgia for the survey's lost scientific soul or by the easy
familiarity with killing numerous animals that had at first anesthetized the
mammalogists to the significance of the survey's killing machine. Rather, she
had become radicalized by the realization that social change would always be
resisted, and she was enthralled by the beauty of nature. Most promising,
through one of her associates she gained the ear of the next president of the
United States.

Edge's first awakening to the world of activism occurred in 1913 while
traveling on a steamship to the United States after living overseas for four

years. At age thirty-five and pregnant with her second child (a previous son had died), Edge was returning home with her husband, a British consulting engineer, to ensure her child would be born a U.S. citizen and thus eligible to run for president.[2] Onboard she met radical suffragist Lady Linda Rhondda, and despite her husband's resolute lack of interest in women's participation in the electoral process, Lady Rhondda deeply impressed Edge.[3]

Edge's love of the wild and disregard for adversity were evident when she was in her early thirties, newly married, and living in the Far East. According to a later feature article on Edge in the *New Yorker Magazine,* "Hurricanes, pirates, floods, man-eating tigers, uprisings, and epidemics failed to deter their progress once she had set her mind on a port of call."[4] Rosalie Edge had grit and determination.

Edge had been drawn into the fight against the Biological Survey almost as a by-product of another battle against another intransigent and deceptive institution—the National Association of Audubon Societies. During the teen years she barnstormed New York as vice president of the Women's Suffrage Party, developing organizational skills and a working familiarity with the media and transforming her formidable verbal acuity (her father was Charles Dickens's cousin, and she seems to have shared the writer's wry wit) into a blistering presence on the stump. In 1917 New York became the first eastern state to allow women to vote, testimony in part to Edge's effectiveness. But behind her public persona she developed a fascination with birds and once arrived to a suffrage meeting late because she had stopped to watch a heron. When her husband, Charles, who appreciated avifauna as much as he did women's rights, would ask about her day, Rosalie would recite her bird sightings—testimony that each wren, robin, or blue jay stood as chief currency in the daily budget of her emotions.[5]

In late August 1929, at age fifty-two and separated from Charles, Edge was visiting Europe with her two teenage children when she received a sixteen-page pamphlet from a fellow bird enthusiast in New York. Dr. Willard Van Name, the sender and principal author, was curator of marine invertebrates at the American Museum of Natural History. A monastic lover of wilderness and animals, he never quite fit in to the chic society of many of his fellow academic zoologists. His pamphlet, "A Crisis in Conservation," without ever naming the Audubon Society, criticized the bird group for its inaction on efforts to set bag limits for bird hunting and on passing legislation to establish bird refuges in which hunting was banned. Van Name connected the society's silence on these issues to money it received from firearms manufacturers and to the society's close ties to the Biological Survey, which opposed any limits on bird shooting despite the sharp decline in water fowl populations and the foreseeable extinction of some species.

Edge, who hadn't yet met Van Name, was appalled when she read the pamphlet. "For what to me were dinner and the boulevards of Paris," she recalled of her reaction in her hotel room as her family waited to go to dinner, "when my mind was filled with the tragedy of beautiful birds, disappearing through the neglect and indifference of those who had at their disposal wealth beyond avarice with which these creatures might be saved?"[6]

Less than two months later (and a few days after the stock market's collapse), back in New York, Edge attended the Audubon Society's annual meeting, seating herself in the front row of a sparse audience. At a presentation clearly intended only for insiders, the speaker mentioned that "[t]he Society has dignifiedly stepped aside from criticism in a pamphlet that is not worth further reference." Edge, a lifetime member of the organization, interrupted to request a response to the pamphlet's charges. Audubon officials' answers did not satisfy her, and she kept asking questions—eventually to be informed by the society's president that she had spoiled the meeting, that she had left no time for the scheduled film, and that lunch was getting cold. She left and "returned to the birds in Central Park."[7]

Around the same time, Van Name was censured by the American Museum's administration, part of a small wildlife clique that included Audubon Society and Biological Survey officials. They forbade him to write any more pamphlets. Edge had already contacted him to help distribute additional copies of "A Crisis in Conservation," and now she offered to publish any additional pamphlets he wrote anonymously. Van Name liked the arrangement. "They can prevent my signing them," he said. "But they cannot prevent my writing them."[8]

Edge and Van Name were soon joined by another instigator, Irving Brant, a journalist (and later editor) for the St. Louis *Star-Times* and a nature lover. Brant had tried to break the story of the Audubon Society's close collusion with gun manufacturers but had found publication blocked by the Biological Survey's influence over his publishers.[9] The three established a group they called the Emergency Conservation Committee. Brant or Van Name would write an exhortatory pamphlet and Van Name would pay to have them produced, then Edge would print and mail the pamphlets.

Her experience as a high-level suffragist campaigner, along with an inherited nest egg that gave her the luxury of independence, served Edge well as a wildlife activist. She launched into a flurry of actions, including filing in June 1931 what may have been the first private citizen environmental lawsuit—four decades before environmental litigation became established—in a successful bid to obtain the Audubon Society's mailing list.[10] "She is always mettlesome," wrote a journalist for the *New Yorker Magazine* in its 1948 feature on her, "and she sleeps, eats, and thinks best when the fray is hottest."[11] Her passion to save the birds, and her righteous anger at Audubon's half-hearted and duplicitous advocacy, began to attract more people—including William T. Hornaday, who was seventy-six years old when Edge filed her suit.

Hornaday's initiative to turn the national forests into game sanctuaries had stalled in the 1920s, and although he kept pushing to "stop the shooting," many now regarded his voice as a one-note alarm, easy to ignore. When he heard about Edge's confrontation with the Audubon Society he contacted her,

Bird lover, suffragist, truth-teller, and inveterate foe of the Biological Survey: Rosalie Edge with red-tailed hawk. (Courtesy of Hawk Mountain Sanctuary)

commending her "courage of a lion" and inviting a meeting. He was happy to fill her in on conservation battles from long before, and she was eager to learn from the man she called a "fierce, militant, old Saint Francis." Hornaday gave her his mailing list and began strategizing with Edge and Brant. This involvement led the Audubon Society to suspect that behind the shockingly outspoken but always impeccably proper New York lady and the accomplished newspaper man lurked a more substantial enemy: the curmudgeonly Hornaday.[12]

But in truth, although the Emergency Conservation Committee seemed to echo the Hornaday of two decades past as the shrill voice of conscience for wildlife, Edge's very different persona still suffused the small group. The pamphlets the committee produced were as acerbic as anything Hornaday had written, but Edge was far more graceful in social settings than the gruff Hornaday and far more capable of building alliances and soliciting others' active involvement. And guided by Brant's political acumen, the committee operated more strategically than Hornaday had. Further, as we will see, Edge, Brant, and Van Name were not blind to the value of predators in the landscape.

The Emergency Conservation Committee started out purely as a group of wildlife advocates dedicated to protecting birds. But within a few years its purview expanded dramatically to include activism for wilderness and habitat preservation, placing the group's policy triumvirate among a tiny group of people successfully advocating for these issues. The committee's support for the wilderness was based overwhelmingly on ecological considerations rather than on the cultural benefits Aldo Leopold tended to emphasize. Tellingly, a pamphlet written by Brant in 1935 included a Muir-like criticism of those who would exterminate ducks: "The idea that the world exists in part for its non-human inhabitants is beyond their ken."[13]

The group's ecological emphasis also led it to espouse, in a Van Name–authored pamphlet published in September 1934, removal of all livestock from national forests—an idea no one else publicly endorsed but that the three members may have picked up from Howell.[14] Unlike the naive mammalogist, however, Edge understood the insurmountable obstacles to such a dramatic change in land use; and although several Emergency Conservation Committee pamphlets mentioned the idea, there is no indication she actively pushed it—never, for instance, devoting an entire pamphlet to the notion. She and Van Name did pursue ending the Biological Survey's control program.

The Emergency Conservation Committee was pure muscle, bogged down with no bureaucracy beyond Edge's meticulous daily maintenance of a growing mailing list of pamphlet recipients. Within a few years the group had issued dozens of pamphlets, each one hand-addressed by Edge, her sister, and her son. By early 1932 the mailing list contained about a thousand names. The pamphlets never equivocated, and the recipients seemed animated by the same sentiment that boldly adorned the group's letterhead: "The time to protect a species is while it is still common. The way to prevent the extinction of a species is never to let it become rare."[15] Edge and Brant (although not likely the professional biologist Van Name) were the most successful conservationists since John Muir, who had died in 1914, and Enos Mills, who died in 1922, without extensive personal experience in killing animals. C. Hart Merriam, Teddy Roosevelt, William Hornaday, Aldo Leopold, Joseph Grinnell, E. Raymond Hall, Olaus J. Murie, and almost every other man who pushed for protection for some form of wildlife had been a hunter—whether for science or sport. Edge followed in the largely female tradition of bird protectors as a non-hunter. She was also the first person to introduce the issue of cruelty into the debate about the Biological Survey's control program.

After each Emergency Conservation Committee pamphlet was mailed out to an audience that included newspaper editors and other people of influence, editorials and articles would appear in prominent papers throughout the country, including the *New York Times*. Public officials would feel the heat of angry letters, and contributions of usually no more than a few dollars each would wing their way to Edge's mailbox—always answered with a thank you letter written in longhand. In 1933 the committee spent $3,370, and the annual budget never reached $10,000. (In 1936, while testifying at a congressional hearing on the proposed Olympic National Park and answering the questions of a suspicious and hostile congressman as to who gave her big contributions, she held out her cupped hand and asked him to donate—enraging him further but winning the amused sympathies of other representatives.[16])

While the fight against the Audubon Society lasted two decades—and eventually resulted in the bird group's abandonment of trapping at its refuges, reversal of its hostility toward raptors, and reformation into a true advocate for wildlife—the Emergency Conservation Committee quickly branched out to take on other enemies of wildlife. Although Van Name was a colleague of H. E. Anthony's, the former's abrasive style had alienated many people, and before joining with Edge he had long operated alone. But he was sufficiently connected to the broader scientific community to have become familiar with the survey's ten-year funding bill. Strikingly, the Audubon Society had failed to join in the near-universal conservationist condemnation of the legislation.[17]

In May 1930 the Emergency Conservation Committee issued a Van Name–authored pamphlet condemning the survey and urging opposition to the legislation. Although it echoed the mammalogists' criticisms of the same period, the twenty-three-page committee pamphlet was considerably more trenchant than the typically measured and sometimes dry utterances of Howell, Hall, and their associates. The pamphlet indicted the Biological Survey's "wholesale poisoning and trapping operations" as "one of the biggest factors in the extermination of the animals and birds of the Western United States." To devastating effect, the tract juxtaposed the survey's boastful statements in reports from the early 1920s of poison distributed and animals destroyed with the agency's careful reiteration of official policy current in 1930. The pamphlet emphasized the animal suffering attendant to the survey's use of poison and traps. Up until then, the only mention of such issues had emanated from survey representatives in declaring their sensitivity to animals, while the mammalogists had stressed their independence from such concerns. Finally, the pamphlet went further than any of the mammalogists in calling not just for rejection of the funding bill but for an end to the survey's entire predator-killing program.[18]

In the Emergency Conservation Committee's first year of existence it took on a host of new campaigns for birds and against Audubon misconduct, but it seemed that little traction could be gained in the fight against the Biological Survey's control program. In April 1931, however—two months after passage of the Animal Damage Control Act—Stanley P. Young authored his own pamphlet for the survey, intended to mitigate some of the public relations damage from the recent legislative brouhaha. Young's publication was a routine iteration of the survey's official line, but it provoked the Emergency Conservation Committee to renewed engagement on the issue. "Poison for Our Wildlife: An Answer to the Biological Survey," a four-page broadsheet issued the following month again blasted the agency. "The Biological Survey is not being and has not been for years conducted according to scientific methods," Van Name wrote. He continued:

> Appropriations are all that it is interested in, and it seems to be quite willing to wipe out of existence the wild life, which it was established to protect, if it can get appropriations for doing so. The Bureau has the support of the powerful lobby of the sheep-raisers who are quite willing to have the public expend millions and destroy all our wild creatures if it will save them some insignificant losses or some trifling expense in caring for their flocks.[19]

But much of "Poison for Our Wildlife" consisted of the same material from the Emergency Conservation Committee's previous missive on the subject, and Edge knew she needed more information. She tried, unsuccessfully, to have one of Hall's contacts in Nevada film coyotes in traps to arouse animal lovers against the cruelty for which their tax money paid.[20] But without new grist to generate public outrage (Murie's report had not yet reached her or the mammalogists), the committee could not build additional opposition to the survey's control program.

In the meantime, Howell, Hall, and a few of their colleagues continued their battle as well, and sometimes the battle came to them. In the autumn of 1931 California sheep ranchers complained to the president of the University of California at Berkeley about the advocacy stemming from that institution's Museum of Vertebrate Zoology. The president resisted the pressure and refused to censure the two principal malefactors, Grinnell and Hall. The mammalogists had better fortune attacking the survey on its own turf, successfully recruiting the agency's founder, C. Hart Merriam, seventy-six years old, to come out against the poisoning program.[21] To the chagrin of survey officials, Merriam published a letter in the *Journal of Mammalogy* that read in part:

Most of us believe that in certain places and at certain times it is highly desirable to destroy harmful animals, but when it comes to employing upward *of three hundred men* to distribute poisons broadcast over vast areas, I must confess that my sympathy is with the animals. . . .

As I look at the matter, the fight is between the stock men, who have *enormous* influence in Congress, and the rest of us, who have *no influence at all.*

Just why the Government should force all the States to pay the cost of poisoning alleged injurious animals in *one third of the States,* is beyond my comprehension.

I have long felt that this is a *State* affair, and that such trapping and poisoning as may be necessary should be paid for by the *States concerned, not* by the United States as a whole [original italics].[22]

As the economic downturn turned into the Great Depression in late 1931 and early 1932, the dissident scientists and the Emergency Conservation Committee were aided by a force that carried more weight than either pamphlets or Merriam's endorsement: a tightening federal budget. President Hoover's budget director, J. Clausen Roop, who had been receiving letters urging cuts or outright elimination of the survey's Division of Predatory Animal and Rodent Control, recommended a 30 percent cut in the survey's authorized $1 million animal killing appropriation for fiscal year 1933.[23]

To keep up the pressure, in April 1932 the Emergency Conservation Committee put out a third pamphlet about the survey, acerbically entitled "It's Alive! Kill It!" The pamphlet exposed the survey's increasing emphasis on killing birds and the development of a relatively new poison—thallium sulfate—that facilitated the killing. Edge had received a report from an ornithologist in Berkeley about the survey's poisoning of 1,700 tri-colored blackbirds, and she re-printed his account of the "almost solid floor of floating bodies" of the birds in a shallow wetland and of the few surviving fledglings "feebly alive in some stage of starvation or grilling and parching by sunburn." The ornithologist estimated, based on his banding of birds throughout the region and the number found dead, that at least 30,000 had been poisoned. Recounting the predator control campaign as well (and the Audubon Society's close ties with and failure to fight the survey), the pamphlet urged readers to write their senators, representatives, and the director of the budget to "*stop its appropriations for killing*" or simply to "*abolish it as a bureau*" [original italics].[24]

Although the Emergency Conservation Committee's pamphlets were based on the best information available to those outside the survey and they demonstrated perspicacious analysis and a keen sense of irony, they also seemed to contribute to the opposition through their stridency. An October 1931 opinion piece in *The New York Sun* reiterated the mammalogists' long-standing complaints about the survey's poisoning program, quoting H. E. Anthony that "surely a young, faunally rich country does not wish the great open spaces swept clear of all wild life in order to make the West a sheepman's paradise."

The paper praised Anthony's position as possessing "a merit often conspicuously lacking from the arguments of conservationists—it is calm and non-abusive."[25] In fact, every public statement on the subject by the mammalogists over the past seven years had been imbued with the same moderate tone, but the issue seldom reached the public beyond those exposed to the academic or hunting media; the only difference was the Emergency Conservation Committee's new voice in the debate. Thus, although it implicitly criticized the committee, the paper tacitly acknowledged the group's success in keeping alive the controversy over the poisoning campaign.

But the survey ploughed ahead, notwithstanding the new tone of some of its critics. Despite the cuts in its budget and the now vague threat of greater cuts, the survey moved into larger quarters in the capital. In June 1932, when Paul G. Redington was not available, Stanley Young—the man who more than any other had guided the survey into its modern stance and august stature—was signing official letters defending the survey against the Emergency Conservation Committee's attack over the title acting chief."[26]

Young never became chief of the agency, testament likely to his political prudence. New administrations, wanting a break with the past, typically replace agency heads, whereas lower-level bureaucrats (thanks to civil service rules) generally remain. Young kept his profile low.

Full Blast of the Machine

P assage of the Animal Damage Control Act stalled the momentum for reform of the Biological Survey. "I think things conservational are unpromising," A. Brazier Howell wrote to Joseph Grinnell in December 1932. "The waiting game of the B.S. [Biological Survey] is bearing fruit, for people become uninterested in scrapping, and the belligerents have dropped off one by one."[1] Economic worries during the Depression, as well as political uncertainty, also kept the scientists from vigorous action. By the time of Howell's writing, the nation's entire populace seemed to be simply waiting. With the November elections past but no inauguration of the new president until almost spring of the following year, there was little else for the nation to do.

When New York governor Franklin D. Roosevelt finally assumed the presidency on March 4, 1933, the Depression was near its nadir. By virtue of the country's desperation, the new president had greater power than perhaps any of his predecessors had enjoyed; some observers expected him to trespass far beyond the U.S. Constitution's limits, and not a few welcomed the prospect. "This nation asks for action, and action now," the president said at his inauguration. "We must act, and act quickly." Although nobody knew exactly what to expect, Washington, D.C., was electric with anticipation at the new president's arrival, and across the country desperate people huddled by their radios to listen to his message of hope.[2]

One of the first measures proposed by Roosevelt, and approved by Congress on the last day of his first month in office, was the Emergency Conservation Work, popularly known as the Civilian Conservation Corps (CCC). Intended to put unemployed young men to work on conservation measures, the CCC reflected the president's personal commitment to rebuild a devastated society from the dirt up. Roosevelt, despite his confinement to a wheelchair, felt a deep-rooted emotional connection to trees—nurtured by his years of loving oversight of the planting of tens of thousands of pines, poplars, and hemlocks on his Hyde Park estate. New Deal historian Arthur M. Schlesinger Jr. described this arbophilia as the president's "desire to renew the land" that had been impoverished through deforestation and poor farming. The CCC was as much intended to combat cynicism among the nation's youth as it was to build up the countryside—and Roosevelt knew of no better way to do so than by putting young men to work making things grow and protecting the soil.

The challenge of mobilizing millions of men into hundreds of outdoor camps across the nation was to be met in record time. The CCC, a program that only came into existence on March 31, was to put 300,000 young men into the forests by July. Run by the U.S. Army and the Labor Department, the CCC had to recruit and screen enlistees, establish camps in remote locations, and arrange for food and supplies to arrive on time in each camp. Such an undertaking would leave it unable to make informed decisions on the projects on which its enrollees were to work, so the CCC was to rely on other federal agencies for leadership on such issues as where to build roads and trails, where to plant trees, which trees to plant, and similar questions. The Forest Service provided much of the direction for the CCC. But in wildlife matters the CCC turned to the federal wildlife agency.[3]

The Bureau of Biological Survey took charge of implementing the CCC's wildlife management programs. The agency put the CCC's men to work on its rodent-poisoning campaigns, with the general purposes of controlling erosion, saving forage for livestock, and protecting the public from animal-borne diseases. Later, the survey also garnered resources from several other New Deal programs: the Public Works Administration (PWA), Works Progress Administration, Agricultural Adjustment Administration, Farm Security Administration, Federal Emergency Relief Administration, Civil Works Administration, and Soil Conservation Service. By February 1934, the CCC and PWA alone had purchased 153,000 ounces of strychnine.

So even though the budget approved in the Animal Damage Control Act had been cut because of the deteriorating economy, resources from the "alphabet agencies" more than made up the difference, extending poisoning operations into ever more remote areas. Now not only was the survey tapping federal, state, and local coffers and garnering direct support from livestock associations, but it also gained tens of thousands of full-time and, usually, highly motivated young men to carry out its programs on the ground, as well as gaining the supplies and poisons they were to use. Thus the survey took advantage of the incredible growth of new government programs designed to meet a national emergency to appropriate additional resources for its own program.[4]

While activities on the ground were worsening for wildlife, it seemed reasonable to expect reforms in policy before too long. For despite the sudden infusion of new resources for the survey, the Emergency Conservation Committee was quickly developing unparalleled access in the new administration through newspaper editor Irving Brant.

Throughout his multiple terms in office, even while battling the Depression or the Axis powers, Roosevelt maintained his interest in the minute details of conservation. In his closing speech during the 1940 election, for example, the president extolled a vision of an America "whose rivers and valleys and lakes—hills and streams and plains—the mountains over our land and nature's wealth deep under the earth—are protected as the rightful heritage of all the people."[5] And the year before, in a memo to his budget director as the administration worked to simplify administrative responsibilities in the wake of a government reorganization plan, Roosevelt wrote, "[p]lease have it carried out so that fur-bearing animals remain in the Department of the Interior." The president continued:

> You might find out if any Alaska bears are still supervised by (a) War Department (b) Department of Agriculture (c) Department of Commerce. They have all had jurisdiction over Alaska bears in the past and many embarrassing situations have been created by the mating of a bear belonging to one Department with another bear belonging to another Department.
>
> P.S. I don't think the Navy is involved but it may be. Check also on the Coast Guard. You never can tell![6]

With this level of interest in wildlife and other conservation affairs, it is not surprising that Roosevelt wanted to hear what the Emergency Conservation Committee had to say. Just four days after Roosevelt's 1932 election victory, Brant wrote the president-elect a congratulatory letter that also suggested the nomination of Henry A. Wallace for secretary of agriculture. Although conservationists were not the only ones recommending Wallace, after Roosevelt ended up appointing Wallace to the position his secretary wrote Brant a note stating, "I know Mr. Roosevelt would very much like to receive your ideas on re-organization in the various bureaus you mention, and may I ask that you send them along?"[7]

So on March 31, the same day Congress approved the creation of the Civilian Conservation Corps, Brant wrote Roosevelt to describe the problems within the Biological Survey. He described Chief Paul Redington as "an honest, well intentioned man . . . bewildered by his environment" and assistant chief W. C. Henderson as "the real head of the bureau"—a man who "affiliates easily and naturally with reactionary agents, and not at all with others."[8]

The Emergency Conservation Committee was not the only group with access within the new administration. The American Farm Bureau Federation had backed Roosevelt in his bid for the presidency. When it came time to choose a secretary of agriculture, Farm Bureau officials informed Roosevelt that his long time friend Henry Morganthau wouldn't do. Instead, they offered a short list of alternatives, including Henry Wallace.[9]

Agriculture Secretary (and later Vice President) Wallace was a brilliant but troubled man who seemed driven by a need to bridge a gap in his personality between his interest in helping farmers and a series of metaphysical quests. As it turned out, Wallace (like his predecessors) seemed largely indifferent to the policies of his Bureau of Biological Survey, evidently concerning himself more with the intricacies of farm prices and a successful campaign to place the pyramidical and cyclopian Great Seal of the United States (which he admired for its occult properties) on the dollar bill.[10]

Brant and Rosalie B. Edge's main agenda regarding the survey was to enact hunting regulations protecting waterfowl from their trajectory toward extinction—and on this measure the survey had long proved as immovable as it had toward suggestions it curtail its poisoning program. Eventually, Brant and Edge took on a multitude of battles, including the creation of Olympic National Park in Washington state and expansion of Sequoia National Park in California. Brant conferred personally with the president on these and other issues and had ready access to Interior Secretary Harold L. Ickes—thereby allowing the Emergency Conservation Committee to prevail in numerous policy objectives. But he had to pick his fights. Although ending the survey's control program was one of Edge's priorities, for some reason she never asked Brant to take up the issue with the administration; it wasn't until 1939 that Brant did so at the instigation of fellow committee member Willard Van Name.[11]

The cumulative pressure generated through the Emergency Conservation Committee's three anti-poisoning pamphlets and continued pressure from the mammalogists, along with a sympathetic administration, had the desired result, however. The new administration's first budget request in essence reversed the mandate of the Animal Damage Control Act of just three years before by slashing the budget for the Biological Survey. On January 4, 1934, the president's director of the Bureau of the Budget, former Arizona congressman Lewis W. Douglas, released a budget that cut the survey's federal allotment almost in half, from $1,017,261 for fiscal year 1934 to $582,741 for the coming fiscal year. The agency's remaining research would be cut practically to the point of elimination, including the mammalogist-supported investigations into the food habits of predators and the research at the Control Methods Laboratory into new poisons. But almost as dramatic, and much larger from a dollar point of view, was the effect on the animal-killing budget, which would drop from $382,981 to just $91,343.[12]

Although the actual appropriations still had to be developed and approved by Congress, during Roosevelt's first nine months in office Congress had approved most administration requests with little change. The fact that the most powerful president yet to occupy the White House proposed the virtual elimination of the Biological Survey's control campaign represented the biggest

257

Newspaper editor Irving Brant, Rosalie Edge's fellow activist at the Emergency Conservation Committee, worked closely with Interior Secretary Harold L. Ickes, and met with President Franklin D. Roosevelt, but was bested in the bureaucratic battlefield by Young. (Courtesy, Ruth Brant Davis and Robin Brant Lodewick)

reversal to the agency since Congress had first authorized its systematic killing activities in 1915. Later that January, at a game conference attended by Aldo Leopold and by Redington's soon-to-be-appointed successor, J. "Ding" Darling, rumors swirled that the survey might be closed down.[13]

Stanley P. Young was not about to acquiesce to the end of federal predator control or even to its drastic curtailment. The day after the Roosevelt administration released its proposed budget, Young sent a memo to each of his state field leaders outlining the cuts. His memo warned that if the cuts were implemented the survey would have to shut down the Control Methods Laboratory in Denver, eliminate all federal hunters and rodent control men, end all work on public lands, and leave only a skeleton force consisting of a leader and possibly a clerk in some of the states presently covered. Their jobs would presumably consist of supervising whatever hunters could be retained based on state, local, and private funds. Young concluded his missive by explaining congressional procedure and listing the members of the House Appropriations Committee's subcommittee on agriculture and the states they represented. Only one hailed from the West, although Young noted that the committee was chaired by the survey's old friend (and instigator of the survey's 1929 report that had led to the passage of the Animal Damage Control Act) James P. Buchanan of Texas.[14]

Young went further than just giving information. Working through the survey's offices in the West, he mobilized the agency's cooperators into action. The decades spent building a political network of farm bureau organizers, county commissioners, state legislators, state game and fish departments, not to mention state predator control agencies came to fruition. On January 9, Ira N. Gabrielson—the former Oregon rodent control leader who had delivered the public relations talk at the 1928 Ogden conference and who now acted as a Pacific regional supervisor for the control division—reported back on the early results of his outreach:

> Word is getting around rapidly as to the predicament of the Survey under the set-up proposed by the present budget. Chambers of Commerce, Granges, Farm Bureaus, County Agricultural Commissioners, State Department of Agriculture, Wool Growers and all of our other numerous cooperators in California are very much stirred up over the proposed cuts. Things are also getting very warm here in Oregon. I was just up to Washington for a day and intend to return there as soon as I can get certain work out of the way here in Portland. Word is spreading around in that state and reaction is beginning to come in. We cannot of course tell out here, what the reaction on Congress will be but we are hopeful that some increase will be made in our allotment, at least enough to permit retention of the Civil Service employees now on the payroll. Most of our cooperators out here are asking that the Division be given a minimum of $600,000 for rodent and predatory animal control and some of them have already received pledges from some of the Congressional delegation that they will go down theline [sic] for such an appropriation.[15]

At the same time, Young worked with supporters in Congress, providing them with talking points toward reversing the cuts and marshaling them to pressure the administration. He served as both strategist and cheerleader. In a January 11 letter to Gabrielson labeled "STRICTLY CONFIDENTIAL," Young inveighed against giving up. "Some of you regional men are beginning to worry," he said with considerable understatement, "as to a new set-up for the Division if the final figures are as recommended by the Budget." Young continued:

> My advice to you for the time being is to forget any such worry as this. Our job is to see to it that cooperators get a perfect picture of the situation in the hope that through their efforts there may be a full restoration of our funds. Our efforts therefore should be bent in that direction and not in taking time at the present to worry along as to the proper set-up for the Division with this drastic cut. There will be plenty of time left for that worry. We realize what a nasty job that is going to be if it becomes necessary for us to fit the present Division into the sum of $91,343.[16]

Three weeks later Young was able to send Gabrielson good news. "Boys, we are on our way!" he wrote:

> Three days after my letter to you of January 11, I had a conference with twenty representatives of the Far West, gotten together by Representative Lea, which included Mrs. Greenway of Arizona, Mr. Pierce, Mr. Buck and others from the range states. Also I might add that Congressman Taylor of Colorado, next in authority to Mr. Buchanan on the Appropriations Committee, was also very active. An executive session was held with a group of these people, and it was decided that Congressmen Lea and Taylor should be designated by interested Congressmen as a committee of two to work out ways and means of restoring our appropriation. . . .
>
> Mr. Lea has been in constant communication with me with reference to facts on the work and he has worked exceedingly hard in our behalf. A week ago today in conjunction with twenty congressmen from the West he called upon the Secretary of Agriculture to plead our cause. The Secretary, I am informed, stated that the delegation had made a very fine case and that as far as he was concerned he would like to see all of the money restored.
>
> Following the meeting with the Secretary, this group descended on the Budget Bureau last Saturday morning in a two-hour session. This session was being held while the Chief, Mr. Henderson and a few other members of the Bureau, including yours truly, were before the Subcommittee in the hearing on the Bureau's part of the Agricultural Supply Bill. When Henderson and I returned to the Bureau we found awaiting us a hurry up call from the Budget Bureau.

After spending two hours on the next Saturday afternoon with officials from the Budget Bureau who were very ready to please, Young, Henderson and an associate were assured things looked much better for the survey. Young closed his summation of recent events by sending his congratulations and best wishes to his staff and the state, local and private cooperators. "If there are any future developments that appear disastrous to the fine way in which things are developing," he added, "we will communicate with you immediately. In the mean time, call off the dogs!"[17]

"Word has gone out calling off the dogs," wrote back Gabrielson. "I am mighty glad that it is over, but on the other hand sorry that we did not get the full blast of the machine in operation. We were in position to increase the barrage and had some interesting things planned for the next two weeks. However, we can save this for the next time, if it should come."[18]

Who backed up this impressive display of political might? Several of the twenty-odd western members of Congress who descended on the Budget office were ranchers—including (as we have seen) Colorado's Edward T. Taylor, Oregon's Walter M. Pierce, and Arizona's congresswoman Isabella Greenway, who occupied the budget director's old congressional seat in Arizona. In addition, Representative Frank T. Buck of California had grown up on a ranch. This substantial bloc of legislators, in the words of a sympathetic columnist, "sat on his [the budget director's] official neck with their whole weight and with the whole weight of their constituents."[19] This political avoirdupois extended beyond rancher-representatives; politicians of all backgrounds from the West were accustomed to heeding the livestock industry. In 1939, Irving Brant was working closely with Senator Alva Adams of Colorado—who chaired the Senate Committee on Public Lands—on legislation to establish Kings Canyon National Park in California. Adams, although willing to take on the timber industry, had a far different relationship with the livestock industry—as Brant's account of a meeting with Adams's administrative assistant, Raoul Camalier, indicates:

> One day as I sat talking with Camalier, the doorway darkened and the 350-pound congressional lobbyist of the American stockmen's organization entered the room. Without a preliminary word he said, "I want a meeting of the committee next Thursday." "Yes, sir," said Camalier. The cattle-and-sheep agent then said a few words about the purpose of the meeting and rolled out of the room.[20]

Although the livestock industry's political clout ensured reversal of the survey's funding cut, the key role played by Young also reflects the different orientation to political challenges displayed by the departments of Agriculture and Interior. Departmental cultures still reflected the dynamics that had led Gifford Pinchot to insist in 1904 that his Forest Service reside within the Department of Agriculture to insulate it from the dissoluteness of the Interior Department, stained by its nineteenth-century record.[21] Interior had supervised—or, rather, failed to supervise—the giveaway of much of the public domain to timber companies, railroads, and speculators, thereby frustrating the idealistic mid-nineteenth-century assumption that yeoman farmers would settle the West. Interior officials had taken over from the War Department custody of the West's conquered Indian population and, in a similar betrayal of responsibilities, had facilitated the systematic dispossession of tribal lands and resources. In large part, these breaches resulted from Interior's traditional status as a repository for presidential benefactors; once ensconced within the department, many extracted extra emolument from their offices. As late as 1922, Interior Secretary Albert B. Fall, a New Mexico rancher, was granting oil leases on government land to an old friend who had handed the secretary a $100,000 "loan"—delivered in cash with no records maintained—in the scandal that became known as Teapot Dome (named for the landmark on one of the leased parcels).[22]

The Forest Service was the paragon for the general Department of Agriculture professionalism—intended as a bulwark against improper political pressure but also serving to resist more prosaic pressures. Thus, for example, in 1937, when President Roosevelt visited Olympic National Forest in Washington state to express his support for turning much of the forest into a national park, the Forest Service's regional forester ordered that the national forest boundary sign along the presidential motorcade route be moved two miles inward, thus deceiving the president into believing that the agency's desolate clearcuts were in fact on private land and that the Forest Service was protecting the primeval forest.

When Roosevelt found out about the deceit and ordered the regional forester transferred, Agriculture Secretary Wallace defied the order until ordered a second time by the president.[23] No mere president would dictate the agenda of the Forest Service—an agency that Roosevelt's interior secretary, Harold Ickes, and Senator Charles McNary of Oregon both believed was the strongest lobby in Washington, D.C., and that Wallace admitted he could not control.[24]

Young's 1934 outreach to Congress for help in thwarting Roosevelt's budget director's original decision on the survey's funding stemmed not just from his own propensity toward decisive action. His inclinations and abilities were well fitted to the Agriculture Department's long-established institutional culture of aggressively asserting its own agenda.

The survey's opponents seemed asleep at the switch as the administration quickly changed course on the budget. But just a month after the reversal was accomplished, it seemed they still had reason for optimism. Paul G. Redington—in poor health and likely demoralized by the constant controversy and the continued sense of impending change—resigned as chief of the survey. On March 1, 1934, three days short of his first anniversary in office, Roosevelt asked J. "Ding" Darling—a nationally syndicated editorial cartoonist who had repeatedly put his pen to work in urging the Biological Survey to adopt stricter duck-hunting regulations—to serve as the new chief of the survey. Darling, determined to save the ducks, accepted on a temporary basis at the government salary of $8,000 per annum, planning to return to his $100,000-a-year career as an editorial caricaturist within six months.[25] Conservationists were delighted at Darling's appointment. Darling had lent his name to the Emergency Conservation Committee as an advisory board member, was a personal friend of both Edge and Brant, and had long expressed concern over the survey's laxness in protecting migratory waterfowl; he entered determined to clean house in the troubled agency.[26]

Young recognized the threat to the survey's operations that Darling's arrival represented. Just three and a half weeks after Darling's appointment, feature articles began appearing in newspapers across the country—including the *Washington Post Sunday Magazine* and the *St. Louis Post-Dispatch Sunday Magazine*—explaining the survey's work. The articles conveyed a theme first seen in Colorado in the 1920s—a theme of predators and rodents as "gangsters," reflecting the repeal of Prohibition less than four months previous and the still vivid memories of the violence of the bootlegging era. The *Post-Dispatch* feature, entitled "Declaring War on the Gangsters of the Animal Kingdom: Coyotes, Bobcats, Wolves and Porcupines Are Among Those Cited by the United States Bureau of Biological Survey in Its List of Four-Footed Public Enemies"— although assuming a martial metaphor, assured readers of the survey's limited objectives:

> On the wall in Young's office there is a large map showing each county in the United States. The map is liberally sprinkled with pins, each pin representing a Biological Survey hunter engaged in predator or rodent control work. As conditions change, these pins are shifted about.
> Young emphasized that campaigns are carried on only where they are economically justifiable.
> "We are not concerned," he explained, "with wiping out these species."
> "We would not go to an isolated mountain top, where the animals can do no harm to man or his property or menace his health, for the purpose of wholesale slaughter.
> Thus, our hunters are always on the move, endeavoring to bring about effective control where such control is urgently needed."

Despite such disavowals, the article closed on the same exhortatory tone seen in the *Rocky Mountain News* series over a decade before:

> That map on Young's office wall is a graphic picture of the battle front. In one section the fight is against an uprising among the wolves. In another, mountain lions are killing sheep and cattle and deer. Elsewhere swarms of pocket gophers are doing the work of sappers.
> As the tide of battle changes, Young moves his daily colored pins.
> And so the never-ending campaign goes on, increasing in scope and intensity as the Federal Government seeks to give adequate protection to society, to man and beast, against the animal underworld![27]

Another recycled theme in the articles, reflecting the national interest in forest conservation inspired by the commander-in-chief, was the damage porcupines inflicted on trees by gnawing their bark. Although the survey had long warred against porcupines for that reason, never before were these proclivities so heavily touted. (The survey had first emphasized the damage porcupines caused during the presidency of another Roosevelt, also known for his silvicultural inclinations.)

In the meantime, despite the restoration of the survey's appropriations, Howell took heart at Darling's appointment. In a May 1934 letter to Grinnell, Howell intimated at the changes to come:

> I have, confidentially as far as the source is concerned, seen a private communication from Darling in much the same vein, indicating that the sheepmen have had their inning and the old order changeth, but stating that it could not be done overnight, for appropriations already made must be spent and it will take much work to keep more money from being appropriated for the purpose. . . .
>
> All in all things look much rosier than I thought they ever would again, and I have much confidence in the future, and more in Darling. It looked for a while like all our efforts had been in vain, but I am now confident that we dissenters did good work. Our labors have borne a bit of fruit, undoubtedly, which, although still green, may be expected to ripen in due course of time, providing the cutworms and scale insects do not ruin it. So I am patting the MVZ [Grinnell's Museum of Vertebrate Zoology] spirit on the back, with a pat for myself and a couple for Rosalie.[28]

But Darling was quickly becoming frustrated with the politics of his new job, and a week after Howell's optimistic assessment he resigned. He advised that his replacement be Aldo Leopold, who the previous year had published a landmark textbook entitled *Game Management*. Secretary of Agriculture Henry Wallace, after consulting with Roosevelt and officials in his own department, offered Leopold the job.[29]

It was the second job offer Leopold had received from the survey. Almost fifteen years earlier, in December 1919 (when Leopold still campaigned for predator extermination), then–survey chief Edward W. Nelson had asked the young Forest Service employee to administer the seventy-four bird and game refuges. Leopold stayed with the Forest Service.[30]

In 1934, at the University of Wisconsin as professor of game management (a niche created largely because Leopold had virtually invented the field of "game management"), Leopold sought to understand the ecological dynamics of predation and how factors such as habitat played into the interaction between predator and prey. "We are not trying to render a judgment" about predators or predator control, he wrote in *Game Management*, "but rather to qualify our minds to comprehend the meaning of evidence."[31]

Although Leopold had closely followed the arguments on both sides and repudiated the thoughtlessness of the extermination campaign he had once championed, he had refrained from criticizing the survey's actual practices. One possible reason, aside from his scientific agnosticism, may have been a sense of loyalty to Redington, who in 1919 had recruited Leopold back to the Forest Service from an unsatisfactory stint with the Albuquerque Chamber of Commerce.

Whatever the reason for his inaction, Leopold did not smell like a reformer. He hadn't yet reached his mature conclusion that predators were essential to the functioning of natural ecosystems. In *Game Management* the closest he came to a judgment was in advocating "determining and practicing such kind and degree of control as comes nearest serving the interests" of "(1) agriculturists, (2) game managers and sportsmen, (3) students of natural history, (4) the fur industry." That position sounded little different from the survey's rhetoric.[32]

Furthermore, Leopold had received gun and ammunition manufacturers' money as a researcher during the late 1920s. Those manufacturers had long contributed to a variety of organizations, including the Audubon Society, to stymie momentum for waterfowl-hunting limits. Although Leopold never succumbed to the Audubon Society's crass venality in tailoring his positions to those of his funders, he was tainted by a general association with those who had long pressured the survey to oppose meaningful hunting limits.[33]

Not surprisingly, as the rumors reached them of Leopold's possible ascent, the mammalogists familiar with his work expressed concern. "I think Darling is just hanging on for the purpose of keeping a worse man out," wrote Howell to Hall, evidently unaware that Darling himself had recommended Leopold. "Rumor to that effect persists; that it has been offered Leopold and he declined."[34]

Indeed Leopold, after agonizing over it for a week, did decline the offer, writing Darling that "[i]t boils down, in my mind, to a choice between policy-making and research" and opting for the latter.[35] And Darling decided to stay on after all.

Sometime during Darling's tenure another heavy hitter ventured into the fray over the survey's control program: Eleanor Roosevelt, the president's wife. Stanley Young's manuscript on the history of predator control, a work completed in the 1960s toward the end of his life (but never published), provides the only known record of her brief intervention. "For the historical record," wrote Young (while neglecting to note the all-important date or the name of the First Lady's informant):

> the late Mrs. Eleanor Roosevelt became concerned with the injurious mammal activities. . . . Her interest was aroused by an unfriendly biologist formerly employed by the Biological Survey who had several years previously left the Bureau in a huff because of disagreement with the Chief of the Bureau, through his wife, who had obtained Mrs. Roosevelt's ear on this controversial question.[36]

It was likely ornithologist and bird lover Florence Merriam Bailey who contacted Mrs. Roosevelt. In July 1933, Redington had unexpectedly retired

Field scientists Vernon and Florence Merriam Bailey (sister of the Biological Survey's founder) in the Grand Canyon, 1929. After Vernon's retirement in 1933, was it Florence who tipped off Eleanor Roosevelt about the Biological Survey's control program? (Barbara H. McKee collection, courtesy of Edwin H. McKee)

her husband, Vernon Bailey—who at age sixty-nine still held the position of chief field naturalist, a position that had allowed both Baileys to continue wandering the West together in pursuit of science. Although there is no reason to believe he had left in a huff, his departure was abrupt, and his views on the survey's control program had changed.

Perhaps the couple's near continuous immersion in wilderness and a newly cast appreciation for wildlife as they witnessed its tremendous decline had slowly reshaped their view of the survey's activities. As early as 1919, Henry W. Henshaw, the former survey chief, wrote that Florence preferred "study of the living bird over the stuffed specimen and she was ever alert to urge the advantages of this method of study as against the less humane use of the shot-gun."[37]

Vernon may have felt the same. Very early in his career he had sent some specimens to C. Hart Merriam's capitol office unimpaired—inspiring panic at the post office when a package broke open, releasing its cargo of live snakes. Merriam had admonished him for the mishap, and from then on Bailey dutifully killed and preserved animals before mailing them. In addition to whatever suasion his wife may have exerted, it is possible he also took seriously the frank criticisms rendered by his friend and colleague Olaus J. Murie at the conclusion of his 1930 investigation of the poisoning campaign.

Even before Bailey's forced retirement he reverted to his childhood activity of building live traps intended for non-lethal relocation of animals that were inconveniencing humanity, and he began marketing them.[38] The man whose 1906 investigations led him to write the groundbreaking monograph *Wolves in Relation to Stock, Game, and the National Forest Reserves* and who vigorously defended the killing program throughout the 1920s came to doubt the results of his labors. His personal records include a photo of a trapped wolf with his annotation "Feet Frozen but no less Painful. Yes, he killed Cattle to Eat. But, Did he Deserve This?"[39]

Whatever influence her informant had with Eleanor Roosevelt was blunted by the fact that, as Young put it, the "majority of the reports" made by the investigators from the joint survey-mammalogists inquiry had exonerated the survey. Young's manuscript recounts that "Mrs. Roosevelt wrote to the Secretary of Agriculture calling for a full investigation" and that Henry Wallace passed the letter on to Darling. "Much pro and con took place," Young wrote obliquely, "but finally when Mrs. Roosevelt was apprized [*sic*] of the field investigations that had taken place with the American Society of Mammalogists . . . the matter was dropped."[40]

Young's abilities as a bureaucrat also frustrated Howell's high expectations of Darling. Beyond propagandizing the survey's work in newspapers, Young worked on the administrative front to ensure survival of the control campaign. He knew that to be effective in the short period the new chief intended to serve, Darling would have to rely on somebody's administrative skills and knowledge of the agency. Young was anything but reticent, and he knew how to get things done. If a re-organization was in the works, he would help make it successful.

Darling, following one of the mammalogists' long-standing recommendations, bolstered the survey's reliance on science, requiring "that no predator work or field work . . . should be carried out or undertaken without first having a scientific prescription written by the research division."[41] Although Darling planned to oust several stalwarts of the control campaign, including W. C. Henderson and Dr. W. B. Bell, Young convinced the new chief not to get rid of them and in fact to put Bell (who had been Albert K. Fisher's assistant at the Division of Economic Investigations until Young took that job) in charge of the newly created Division of Wildlife Research (which combined the functions of several previous administrative designations, including Bailey's old Division of Biological Investigations). Also on Young's advice, Darling promoted Ira Gabrielson to the capital to be Bell's chief assistant. Now the research program the mammalogists had intended as a check on the control program was headed by two of the control program's advocates.

Darling also combined the Division of Predatory Animal and Rodent Control, headed by Young, and the Division of Game and Bird Conservation (in charge of Lacey Act enforcement and preserve management). The new Division of Game Management controlled 41 percent of the agency's budget, and Young was placed in charge of it.[42] When a stunned Howell protested this expanded authority, Darling explained that "Mr. Stanley Young is by all odds the best administrator who has so far appeared." Darling continued:

> He already had a skeletonized organization out over the country. I had them all in here to Washington and I want to say that I never saw a better bunch of conservationists, even in the Society of Mammalogists, than gathered in here for that meeting. A lot of prejudices exist which are not deserved, and while they have made many errors in the predator control field in the past, we shall hope to avoid as many mistakes as possible in the future.[43]

Howell responded frankly. "I do not question the administrative or other abilities of Mr. Young," he wrote. "I have always assumed he is a very capable man." He continued, however:

> But the fact remains that we have seen him in action for many years, and during that time he has built up a reputation as the foremost exponent of a wild life policy that is considered by professional biologists as the most undesirable and harmful yet advanced. He may modify his actions in the face of necessity but he has demonstrated his basic beliefs, and biologists will never be reconciled to leave wild life at the mercy of these beliefs.
>   I feel thoroughly conversant with the opinions of biologists at large anont [sic] wild life policies and have heard from a sufficient number on the question of your reorganization so that I have no hesitation in stating that vertebrate zoologists interested in the handling of wild life look upon this now being in the hands of Mr. Young as nothing short of a catastrophe. That is a fact that will increasingly manifest itself, and it must be faced that he not only lacks the confidence, but has the distrust, of the above group. I state it for your own information.[44]

Privately, Howell was even more dejected. "I'm glad I got out of mammalogy before everything was exterminated," he wrote to Hall at the end of 1934.[45]

The year 1934, particularly the rollercoaster first six months that opened with the administration's proposed budget cuts released in early January, may have been the busiest period of Young's life. He paid a steep personal price for being overworked—similar to, if slightly less dramatic than, Roy C. Spangler's loss of his wife to smallpox while he pursued Three-Toes on the Colorado plains in 1923. Young lost the chance to visit his brother Arthur in southern Arizona shortly before Arthur's death on June 29, 1934, at age forty-nine, and he was too busy to attend Arthur's funeral on July 2. Young's wife, Nydia, attended in his stead.[46]

Arthur's death, and Young's absence from his side, represented caustic ironies. For while his brother was busy saving the federal animal-killing program, Arthur, a federal employee engaged in another branch of taming nature, was killed by a wild animal. His fate may have been sealed by his own inattention to bureaucratic procedure even as his younger brother mastered the bureaucracy in Washington.

Arthur B. Young, who served as the Forest Service's senior road engineer in Arizona, building access into the isolated mountain ranges of southern Arizona (now known as Sky Islands) and through the pine-shrouded Mogollon Rim, was stung on the leg by a scorpion on March 10, 1933, while building a road into Bloody Basin in the Tonto National Forest. He failed to report the injury within forty-eight hours, as required by federal regulations. After over a year, during which period necrosis spread from the bite wound, he filed the report on April 19, 1934, right before taking unpaid leave to recuperate and after having exhausted his sick leave. By May his condition was worsening rapidly, and his finances had declined as well—precluding the possibility of receiving serious medical attention.

That month the Forest Service filed additional forms on his behalf with the United States Employees' Compensation Commission, corroborating the previous year's injury. But the commission did not rule on whether Young's illness was work-related and thus, presumably, on whether he would have been eligible for paid leave or paid medical treatment until after his death. (It ruled he was ineligible, a moot point by then.) In May, Stanley Young first received word of his brother's condition and penurious straits from Arthur's Forest Service supervisor, Ed G. Miller. Stanley wrote to Arthur on May 18, offering financial help, but it was too late.[47]

Young remembered his brother fondly but believed his death "was in the cards and that there was nothing any of us could do about it to hinder or forestall it," according to an August 1934 letter he wrote to Miller thanking him for his support of Arthur.[48] But the loss would have tempered Young's elation over his significant professional accomplishments in early 1934.

With the survey's control program intact and still aided by untold resources from the CCC and other public relief agencies, western ecosystems continued to unravel. Wolves were not the only carnivores rapidly disappearing. The survey had killed hundreds of lynxes throughout the Rocky Mountains, and the population was greatly diminished by 1934. Likewise, the wolverine—the famed scavenger whose Latin name means "gluttonous glutton" and which explorer George Frederick Ruxton had described as "a cross between the devil and a bear"[49]—was a rarity and well on its way to extinction in the southern Rocky Mountains, the proliferation of strychnine baits a factor in its doom.

Blackfooted ferrets, which live in large prairie dog towns and subsist on the residents, were likewise declining rapidly. Olaus Murie had received a report of a place where the ferrets "are fairly common" in Colorado during his 1930 field investigation,[50] and millions of acres containing the prairie dogs ferrets require as prey still survived into the early 1930s. But times were changing. The survey had poisoned ferrets without intending to, and those that survived had to contend with the survey's unrelenting warfare against prairie dogs.

In fiscal year 1931, before Roosevelt's election and the start of the New Deal, the survey distributed over 220,000 pounds of poisoned grains over 609,000 acres of prairie dog towns in Colorado.[51] But it was the advent of manpower and funds from Depression-era relief organizations that sealed the fate of prairie dog ecosystems. By June 30, 1936, the CCC alone had poisoned prairie dogs and other rodents on 21,507,889 acres throughout the West.[52] During 1938 an estimated 3 million prairie dogs were killed over 200,000 acres in northeastern Colorado's Weld County alone.[53] Following World War II, the last significant prairie dog colonies were eliminated with the help of a new poison, Compound 1080; by 1962, considerably less than 500,000 acres occupied by the species remained in Colorado.[54]

As a result, the blackfooted ferret was destined to be extirpated from the entire West except for one population in Wyoming. But as will be seen, in the mid- to late 1980s, with the plague killing ferrets from this remnant population, the last remaining eighteen would be taken into captivity for an emergency breeding program and subsequent reintroductions.

The survey's work also helped eliminate grizzly bears over most of their range by the early 1930s. Again, many black and grizzly bears were probably poisoned inadvertently, and whenever a bear killed livestock it was targeted for elimination—an exception to the survey's long-held policy that bears were to be preserved. In spring 1925 a survey hunter in the Gila National Forest of New Mexico explained how he knew a certain bear his hounds had treed was guilty of killing livestock: "There was an old bear that was fat and I know she had to be eating beef to be in that shape this time of year so I killed her," he reported for the survey's records. After cutting open her stomach, he indeed found cattle remains.[55] The soundness of his judgment reflected the high stocking rates in the Gila, which so limited other bear food sources that any non-starving grizzly was almost certain to be eating cattle. In 1931 New Mexico's last confirmed grizzly was killed (by a rancher, not the survey) around 40 miles farther south; and four years after that, in 1935, Arizona's last grizzly was killed in the same ecosystem around fifty miles to the southwest.[56]

In the mid-1930s a small grizzly bear population survived in the San Juan Mountains of Colorado, the southernmost remaining U.S. population. The other populations were centered around Yellowstone and Glacier national parks; the Cabinet-Yaak area of northern Idaho; along the Washington, Idaho, and Montana borders with Canada; and in the Sierra Madre in Mexico. (As will be seen, the survey's successor agency eventually helped poison out this Mexican population.) The grizzly's survival at least until 1979 in the San Juans was facilitated by minimal livestock presence on the 58,000-acre Tierra Amarilla ranch south of today's South San Juan Wilderness. But that private land was not sufficient to provide sanctuary from the survey for more than a handful of bears.[57]

By the 1930s, with very low numbers of wolves, mountain lions, and grizzly bears to control them, deer and elk populations were oscillating wildly throughout much of the West. In 1928, as seen, the American Society of Mammalogists' predator committee had proposed—in the draft report ultimately changed by Vernon Bailey and Edward A. Goldman—exempting from predator control the Kaibab Plateau north of the Grand Canyon and the Gila National Forest in southwestern New Mexico, which had both experienced severe deer irruptions. Deer numbers also exploded on the Uncompahgre Plateau in Colorado and in the nearby La Sal Mountains of eastern Utah, prompting both states to open up hunts on does.

But the solution in the Gila permanently affected the landscape. In 1924, at the urging of Aldo Leopold, 755,000 acres of the Gila had been designated the nation's (and the world's) first primitive area (later renamed wilderness area), intended to be kept free of roads and automobiles forever. Five years later, however, as the number of deer increased alarmingly, the Forest Service decided to breach the designation and the wilderness to provide easier access for deer hunters. In 1931 the agency completed construction of a winding dirt road across a plateau and down into canyons. The road bisected the Gila Primitive Area, splitting off the eastern third (later named the Aldo Leopold Wilderness).[58]

Leopold eventually came to understand how his support for predator extermination undermined his support for wilderness. "I was hoist of my own petard," he wrote.[59]

In the Jackson Hole area south of Yellowstone National Park, elk were the most prominent animal to boom in the absence of predators. As early as the winter of 1908–1909, thousands of elk starved when heavy snows covered the closely cropped winter ranges that had been turned into private ranches. In 1911 Congress had appropriated money for supplemental feeding of the elk, and two years later a National Elk Refuge was established to provide them with winter range. But the problem continued. In the winter of 1916–1917 starvation struck once more, and it hit the elk again in the winter of 1919–1920—the latter catastrophe reducing Yellowstone's northern herd from around 25,000 to 11,000. At the end of the winter the southern herd numbered around

9,000 animals. By spring 1927, however, it had more than doubled to 19,000, leading Goldman to warn that catastrophic mass starvation was inevitable during the next severe winter. In 1934 the National Park Service began capturing elk to ship them for re-stocking elsewhere (including, apparently, on private game ranches).[60]

In Colorado, the Department of Game and Fish also fed thousands of elk and deer that faced starvation in the harsh winters of 1921 and 1922. In 1929 elk in North Park had become sufficiently numerous—and damaging to ranchers' hay fields—to support the first hunting season since 1903.[61] In Rocky Mountain National Park's limited winter ranges, where hunting was banned, the elk over-population impacted vegetation much the way cattle grazing affected other areas. The park's willows and aspens were severely defoliated, eventually resulting in declines in beaver populations and even in bighorn sheep whose forage was taken over by elk. By the 1940s park rangers and the Department of Game and Fish were shooting hundreds of elk to control the population. In 1943, Senator Patrick A. McCarran of Nevada introduced a bill (but withdrew it before it reached the floor) to authorize the Forest Service to slaughter game animals wherever they were deemed in excess.[62]

The chain of unintended consequences went even further. In the San Isabel National Forest and "other timbered sections" of Colorado, the widespread killing of birds incidental to poisoning of gophers led to an irruption of ticks in the early 1930s, which in turn took "a heavy toll of wild animals and live stock," according to an article in the *New York Sun* that specifically named the survey as the culprit in the incidental bird poisoning. Deer, cattle, and sheep were found dying while covered with hundreds of the blood-sucking parasites, and Colorado governor Edwin C. Johnson pledged the state's help in addressing the crisis.[63] Thus the federal agency that worked so hard to save cattle and sheep from predators was inadvertently injuring the livestock industry through its efforts to also kill off the predators' prey.

On the plains in the early 1930s, an enormous irruption of grasshoppers devoured farmers' crops, a result Howell attributed to the poisoning campaign as well. "This is a case of sowing the wind and reaping the whirlwind," he wrote to Senator Charles McNary in what constituted an "I-told-you-so" letter decrying the inevitable results of having poisoned off the grasshoppers' natural enemies:

> Almost all rodents are to a considerable extent insectivorous. I have many times watched ground squirrels pursue, catch, and eat grasshoppers and they are especially given to this practice when the latter are particularly numerous. Furthermore, some sorts of rodents have the habit of searching out the egg cases of the grasshoppers, buried just beneath the surface of the ground. In the treeless sections of the west there are very few insectivorous birds, and mammals, both rodents and carnivores, constitute the chief check (other than by disease and parasites, perhaps) to the undue increase of such insects.[64]

Before long, the chain of unintended consequences extended to the soil, exposed to the wind by too much grazing and then, in many places on the plains, ripped up to grow wheat. In 1931 the rains largely stopped in the West. The next year, with the rains failing again, a few localized dust storms began cropping up. In November 1933 a much more severe dust storm carried dirt all the way to New York. But it was the events of 1934 and 1935 that gave the region the appellation "Dust Bowl." With the drought showing no signs of relenting, in May 1934 winds swept up an estimated 350 million tons of earth and sent them east. Similar storms continued throughout the remainder of the decade, blanketing entire communities on the plains in black, choking clouds that blotted out the sun for days. The dust suffocated dozens of people and untold numbers of livestock and wild animals throughout the plains states and dropped like an evil snow on the eastern seaboard—even falling on ships hundreds of miles out on the Atlantic Ocean.[65] Although not a direct result of the predator extermination campaign, the dust storms of the 1930s reflected the same rush to exploit the land that had precipitated the killing off of wolves. Leopold came to recognize this link, articulating it as a failure to develop what he called a "land ethic." In 1944, toward the end of his life, Leopold claimed that when he shot an Arizona wolf pack back in 1909 and saw a "fierce green fire dying" in the mother wolf's eyes, he had awakened to "something new . . . in those eyes—something known only to her and to the mountain." In his posthumously published magnum opus *A Sand County Almanac with Essays on Conservation from Round River,* he elaborated on the playing out of that vision:

> Since then I have lived to see state after state extirpate its wolves. I have watched the face of many a newly wolfless mountain, and seen the south-facing slopes wrinkle with a maze of new deer trails. I have seen every edible bush and seedling browsed, first to anaemic desuetude, and then to death. I have seen every edible tree defoliated to the height of a saddlehorn. Such a mountain looks as if someone had given God a new pruning shears, and forbidden Him all other exercise. In the end the starved bones of the hoped-for deer herd, dead of its own too-much, bleach with the bones of the dead sage, or molder under the high-lined junipers.
>
> I now suspect that just as a deer herd lives in mortal fear of its wolves, so does a mountain live in mortal fear of its deer. And perhaps with better cause, for while a buck pulled down by wolves can be replaced in two or three years, a range pulled down by too many deer may fail of replacement in as many decades.
>
> So also with cows. The cowman who cleans his range of wolves does not realize that he is taking over the wolf's job of trimming the herd to fit the range. He has not learned to think like a mountain. Hence we have dustbowls, and rivers washing the future into the sea.[66]

Settlement of the West, as we have seen, was never a matter of creating an economy to fit regional ecosystems. Any natural obstacle was seen as a challenge or an enemy or both. In the 1870s the railroad had opened up the West to a profitable livestock industry, leading to the perceived need to rid the region of the wolves that threatened to limit that industry. Similarly, in the 1920s the profitability of wheat, and the financial exigencies brought about by the purchase of tractors and other expensive equipment, led to the churning up of soil for crops—regardless of the plains' irregular rainfall. Just as plagues of ticks and grasshoppers were the end product of a process of seemingly common sense decisions that started with the building of the railroad, so, too, the dust storms were the inevitable result of the commercial and technological system that encouraged ubiquitous overgrazing and widespread sod-busting. In fact, the same "techno-fix" mentality that had targeted species after species once wolves were largely gone arose on the plains, leading several would-be plains saviors to suggest paving over the enormous region to prevent the dust from flying while others advocated the development of dams for irrigation. The Roosevelt administration largely adopted the latter idea and also increased plantings of non-native plants to stabilize the soil. Both attempts at mitigation were destined to wreak additional ecological havoc in the decades to follow.[67]

Dust was not the only problem faced by farmers. Too many years of expanded agricultural production, fueled largely by the need to pay for modern farm equipment, combined with the nation's loss of purchasing power brought on by the Depression resulted in the collapse of agricultural prices. In an emergency effort to boost farmers' buying power, the Roosevelt administration—which regarded the salvation of agriculturalists as fundamental to the nation's recovery—responded by buying farm products and in many cases simply destroying them. By fall 1934, 7 million cattle had been purchased by the government and either slaughtered (some of which, but not all, to be canned) or moved to pastures in the better-watered East.[68]

The collapse of agriculture and the crisis of failed settlement throughout so much of the West inspired some within Roosevelt's Department of Agriculture to search deeper for the lessons to be learned. They might have considered the fact that the war on predators and rodents had not, after all, resulted in greater agricultural efficiency. Instead, it had helped encourage the same frenzy of overstocking that had devastated the cattle industry back in the 1880s.

Ultimately, in the hurly-burly of the New Deal, the search for answers got pushed behind the implementation of solutions. Some solutions worked spectacularly, some made things worse, and many had the character of muddle-throughs. One New Deal program that fit within the last category was conceived to account for the western landscape's limited ability to grow livestock and, using Forest Service management as a model, to regulate grazing for the good of all. But like the Forest Service, the new agency created to implement the program failed to subordinate economic interests to the land's limits. Instead, the Division of Grazing gave effective control of its grazing management to the ranchers using the public domain.

There could be no more reliable tool to ensure that the dream of unlimited productivity would prevail over any thought to restrict grazing than to systematize the funneling of money from the Division of Grazing—money the ranchers paid as grazing fees—into rodent and predator control. The Biological Survey was ready for the task.

With Little Molestation

On November 15, 1935, Ding Darling finally escaped from directing the Biological Survey and returned to his career in public art. The Department of Agriculture press release announcing his resignation included the departing chief's frank remarks on the state of conservation:

> I have come to realize that most of our wildlife conservation troubles are due to lack of organization among those who are interested but ineffective in the conservation of wildlife. There is no mass strength to enforce adequate legislation and executive attention to wildlife interests. Every other element of American life has a national organization to get effective results. Wildlife interests remind me of an unorganized army, beaten in every battle, zealous and brave but unable to combat the trained legions who are organized to get what they want.[1]

At Darling's suggestion, he was replaced by Ira N. Gabrielson, the public relations instructor at the survey's 1928 conference and Stanley P. Young's primary lieutenant and operative in the 1934 battle over the survey's budget cut—in other words, a leader among those very trained legions.

"A very large pachyderm type of man," as Darling described him, the jocular 260-pound "Gabe" was the master of persuasion. When Darling was beginning his tenure as chief in early 1934, Gabrielson had impressed him with "a very well-stated analysis" of the prospects for wildlife restoration in

Retiring Biological Survey chief Ding Darling, left, receives a shotgun from his chosen successor, Ira N. Gabrielson, November 15, 1935. Gabrielson, Young's lieutenant in the previous year's fight over the predator and rodent control budget, maintained the survey's core mission of agricultural service, which Darling thought he had downgraded. Five years later, Gabrielson became the first chief of the survey's successor organization, the U.S. Fish and Wildlife Service. (Courtesy, the J. N. "Ding" Darling Foundation)

the Pacific Northwest—thus securing his initial promotion to Washington that Young had been instigating.[2]

The appointment of Gabrielson as chief represented the culmination of Young's influence. In 1915 Gabrielson, a high school teacher and avid ornithologist in his native Iowa, had wanted to join the survey as a bird warden enforcing the Lacey Act, and he even offered to work without a salary just for the chance to serve. But the survey job he was given on October 1 of that year, four days after his twenty-sixth birthday, was to kill birds so their stomach contents could be inspected. Three years later he was transferred to the rodent eradication campaign in the Dakotas and Minnesota. He rose within the ranks of the control program for sixteen years before being elevated to the capital, taking to his work with the same sense of mission characteristic of other successful Department of Agriculture employees.[3]

Ultimately, Gabrielson's communication skills, like Young's, turned out to be far more valuable than his ability to kill animals. Young had been observing Gabe in action for many years and had played a key role, in what he later recalled as a "conflab with Darling," in persuading the latter to promote Gabrielson out of Oregon and into his position as the number-two man in the Division of Wildlife Research.[4]

Despite his early and sustained interest in protecting birds, Gabrielson's ascent to the chieftainship maintained the survey's core mission of agricultural service, as the mammalogists glumly understood. "And what do you think of the new B.S. [Biological Survey] Chief," wrote A. Brazier Howell to E. Raymond Hall in December 1935. "I haven't heard anything about what policy will be followed, but I hardly need to be told. Anyway, when the little wild life now left is finally gone you and I will have the satisfaction of knowing that we got in a couple of good licks on the opposition."[5]

Gabrielson used his oratorical skills to further dig the survey out of the public relations morass into which it had fallen. Darling had started the survey's public rehabilitation through his reputation as incorruptible. As chief, he had enacted meaningful hunting regulations to save waterfowl, pushed an aggressive program of land acquisitions for game reserves, and fenced cattle and sheep out of the Sheldon Antelope Refuge in Wyoming—thereby saving its starving pronghorn herd.[6]

The survey's image could not have been hurt by the self-evident fact that Darling—a Republican in a Democratic administration and a man who had taken a substantial pay cut to work for the government—genuinely cared for the wildlife for which he was responsible and had no ulterior motive for his service. His actions spoke for themselves, as when he secured a $6 million federal appropriation for waterfowl refuges through a connivance with Senator Peter Norbeck.

In early summer of 1934, with funds tight, that was a large amount of money to be soliciting on behalf of ducks, and many of Norbeck's colleagues were bound to object. The senator spoke with a thick Scandinavian accent, and to enhance his unintelligibility when requesting unanimous consent to pass the appropriation he removed his false teeth—thus speaking "in words totally devoid of understandable articulation," according to the admiring Darling.[7] No senators objected to what they did not understand, and Darling persuaded President Roosevelt to sign the bill immediately, apparently unread.

The president, with fond exasperation, called Darling "the only man in history who got an appropriation through Congress, past the Budget and signed by the President without anybody realizing that the Treasury had been raided."[8] The only pressing reform Darling failed to enact (although he thought he had) was reining in the control program.

Gabrielson enthusiastically continued many of Darling's policy innovations and thus inherited the mantle of reform. Darling had induced the survey to take protection of game animals more seriously. Gabrielson, whose early and sustained avocation had been bird conservation, had no inclination to reverse such popular initiatives.

Gabrielson was electrifying on the stump. The "voice of Mr. Gabrielson has a deep issuance, withal melodious, and the pleasing eye of the chief of the United States biological survey is none the less sharply commanding," reported the *Morning Oregonian* after Gabrielson gave a talk in Portland in late 1936 or early 1937. "[A]nd besides," continued the account, "he knows ducks, from the tundra to the Gulf coast, and anywhere else you may mention. The way that jaded assemblage, full of good cheer and vague if noble ambition, snapped out of it was a positive caution." The *Oregonian* writer said Gabrielson "turned a very tame party, bromidic and possibly dyspeptic, into an occasion of veritable inspiration and high informative value."[9]

But however ducky Gabrielson waxed in front of a crowd, he did not waver in keeping the survey's established emphasis on control of predators, rodents, and birds; never did the dog of game conservation threaten to wag the tail of control. In a 1941 book—whose title, *Wildlife Conservation,* can be viewed as a euphonious update of Aldo Leopold's well-received 1933 work, *Game Management*—Gabrielson managed to platitudinize about predator control without ever grappling with Leopold's serious probing at the relationship between predators and prey.

Leopold's work was hard-headed and crisply worded, although he often refrained from offering prescriptions in favor of developing ways of thinking about conditions in the field. To read *Game Management* is to be subject to a Socratic interrogator, repeatedly asking us to consider a new and occasionally dissonant wildlife observation. To read *Wildlife Conservation,* in contrast, is to be assured that although scientific questions remain to be answered, the proper authorities are judiciously striving for a balanced solution. "Some contend that the predators have as much right to the game as do the human hunters," Gabrielson summed up one line of thought in *Wildlife Conservation,* continuing:

Others assert that human interests are paramount. There is much controversy over these conflicting viewpoints, though in actual practice the direct human interest in increased food or game supplies usually wins out and control is undertaken to reduce the predator population and the pressure on the game species. Under such conditions, to determine whether predators shall be allowed to harvest a part of the game crop or whether efforts shall be made to reserve as much of that part as possible for human use becomes a question of public policy.[10]

Gabrielson did not mention the 1934 machinations of which he was a part that maintained that public policy.

Under Gabrielson's chieftainship, in early 1938 Young's bailiwick was renamed again, this time to the Division of Predator and Rodent Control.[11] In his newly redesignated post, with his former underling comfortably established as his supervisor, Young did not need to be shy. As new government programs appeared to reconcile the wounded landscape to conquering humanity, Young quickly tapped their budgets for his own.

The Taylor Grazing Act, yet another New Deal reform, created one such opportunity. Named for Colorado rancher and senior congressman Edward T. Taylor, the 1934 law gave the Interior Department the authority and responsibility to regulate grazing on the public domain—the same power the Forest Service had been exercising since its inception in 1905. The Taylor Grazing Act represented federal recognition of the closing of the frontier proclaimed by historian Frederick Jackson Turner in 1893, for it authorized the president to close the public domain to homestead entry and divide the land into grazing districts.

Closing the West to new pioneering hardly dampened western settlement during a period in which westerners were fleeing drought and dust storms by the thousands. Many of the lands already privatized were not even habitable (and some of those were bought up by yet another New Deal program for conservation purposes). Several key people in Roosevelt's administration viewed the Dust Bowl as a consequence of capitalism's worst excesses and wanted to replace capitalistic land stewardship with federal scientific management.[12]

Taylor, whose early career was built on developing water laws to aid irrigation and whose later career branched out in myriad acts of legislation that funneled federal lands and appropriations to the livestock industry,[13] had different intentions. He wanted to protect established ranchers from competition for grass from their itinerant competition. He also recognized that the catastrophic loss of soil resulted in part from cutthroat competition. Districts in which only one person was authorized to graze would keep interlopers out and ensure a long-term basis for the industry.

But Taylor and his ally, Senator Patrick A. McCarran of Nevada (who had grown up on a sheep ranch), also wanted to protect permitted ranchers from the heavy hand of the federal government. Their bill subordinated federal authority to regulate grazing to state laws and forbade the cancellation of grazing permits that had been staked as collateral in obtaining any loan. Roosevelt signaled he would veto these provisions, however, and they were dropped.[14]

Thus the compromise that was signed into law on June 28, 1934, along with subsequent amendments, retained federal authority (and in the year 2000 proved the basis for the Supreme Court to reaffirm its 1911 decision and rule unanimously that there is no "right" to graze livestock on public lands). But in other respects the law gave the livestock industry complete practical control of the public domain. Local grazing boards composed almost entirely of ranchers became the primary decision-making bodies. These boards and their projects were funded by the grazing fees authorized under the Taylor Grazing Act, and it was those funds that the survey tapped for rodent-killing projects under the general rubric of range improvement.

For the first few years after passage of the Taylor Grazing Act, 25 percent of the grazing fees were spent directly by the newly created Division of Grazing close to where they were collected (and an additional 50 percent of the fees were shunted to livestock industry improvements through state governments). The grazing boards became one more conduit for the ranchers to exercise political power—as intended by the Division of Grazing's first director, Farrington R. Carpenter, who wrote, "we hope to build up an hierarchy of local advisers which will be able to act as a policy advising council and determine all-important matters of fees, cuts, needed legislation, etc., for grazing districts."[15]

Carpenter—a northwestern Colorado rancher, Ivy League lawyer, and cattle industry lobbyist—was Taylor's protégé and had been appointed in part at the latter's urging.[16] Under Carpenter's loose supervision, grazing fees were heavily tapped for control programs, principally targeted at rodents. Members of the grazing boards planned such programs with survey staff and the directors of CCC camps, all working together.

Carpenter's boss, however, felt it was important that the federal government retain functional control of its lands, and he appreciated the importance of those lands for wildlife. The Division of Grazing had been placed within the Department of the Interior, and Secretary of the Interior Harold L. Ickes was a different type of public official—selected by the president in part because of his imperviousness to corruption. A Chicago lawyer, long-time civic reformer, and political activist, Ickes had backed the first President Roosevelt and was a power broker in the Progressive movement Roosevelt had spearheaded. But as that movement sank from view and influence in the post–Theodore Roosevelt 1920s, Ickes's power waned. When he decided to leave the Republican Party and throw his lot in with the second Roosevelt to run for the presidency, his losing streak ended. But the ascent to the president's inner circle was accomplished almost accidentally.

Anna Wilmarth Ickes, running for re-election to the Illinois state legislature as a Republican in 1932, initially protested her husband's decision to lead a new group of midwestern Republicans who were backing Roosevelt. Ickes won her support by promising to seek for himself, should Roosevelt win, the appointment that touched Anna the most deeply—commissioner of Indian affairs—since she had long taken an interest in the plight of American Indians.

After Roosevelt's victory, John Collier, an erstwhile Ickes ally, urged Ickes to seek a higher (and presumably more competitive) post instead to ensure that Collier himself would get the commissioner position. Ickes upped his request to become secretary of the interior—the department overseeing the Bureau of Indian Affairs—in consideration that "[i]t would be no more painful or fatal to be hung for a secretary than for a commissioner," according to his book of memoirs, *Autobiography of a Curmudgeon.* He asked friends from his long career in the Progressive movement to reach out to the president-elect's camp.[17]

After two U.S. senators turned down the position and just three weeks before Roosevelt's inauguration, Ickes garnered an interview with the president-elect. The next day, in what a Roosevelt aide called "one of the most casual appointments to a cabinet position in American history," Ickes learned of his appointment when Roosevelt introduced him to his soon-to-be-colleague Francis Perkins: "It is nice to have the Secretary of Labor meet the Secretary of the Interior here tonight."[18]

Like the president (who identified his occupation for a *Who's Who in America* listing as "tree-grower"[19]), Ickes had a visceral love of nature. Shortly after his appointment, speaking to the superintendents of the national parks, Ickes declared:

> I do not want any Coney Island. I want as much wilderness, as much nature preserved and maintained as possible. . . . I recognize that a great many people, an increasing number every year, take their nature from the automobile. I am more or less in that class now on account of age and obesity. But I think the parks ought to be for people who love to camp and love to hike and who like to ride horseback and wander about and have . . . a renewed communion with Nature.[20]

Pugnacious and determined, Ickes ended up protecting more wildlife habitat than any other interior secretary before or since.

Yet Ickes increasingly found himself unable to exercise his full authority because of the resistance of his underling, Farrington Carpenter. The Division of Grazing director failed to hire sufficient staff to enable oversight of the grazing boards' decisions. But in the face of Carpenter's support by the vast western network of ranchers, including congressmen Taylor and McCarran, Ickes felt constrained from firing his vexatious employee until late 1939.[21]

In 1938, in an attempt to assert federal control over management of the grazing lands under his jurisdiction, Ickes began requiring that the grazing fees go first to the United States Treasury, from whence Congress could then appropriate the 25 percent allocated for range improvements. Although the political climate at the time made the prospect doubtful, the possibility of such congressional oversight opened up potential vulnerabilities in this spigot of the survey's funding stream—for instance, the possibility of Congress consolidating control funds in one appropriation and thereby capping the amount.

The administrative change prompted Young to develop a memorandum of understanding with the Division of Grazing formalizing the allocation of resources to survey-directed control projects. With an unerring compass for navigating the bureaucracy, he intended as much as possible to keep the survey's funding subterranean, below the level of scrutiny customarily exercised by a president's budget director.

In March Young sent his staff throughout the West a memorandum entitled "Cooperative control projects with the Division of Grazing, Department of the Interior," warning that "[f]unds that are available at the present time, if not expended by June 30, 1938, will revert to the United States Treasury." Since many control programs would extend beyond that date, he advised that it would be appropriate to purchase "reasonable quantities of supplies and materials" in advance. With the prudence of someone who had witnessed his share of public discord, he added that "no large surplus should be purchased purely from the standpoint of obligating available funds." And for emphasis he added:

> We wish to caution you that definite plans should be worked out only for
> *such projects that can be economically and justifiably carried on* [original italics].
> We do not want any such projects undertaken purely from the standpoint
> of expending money, and they should only be approved where they are
> actually needed and where the control of injurious mammals will be a
> definite benefit to the range areas concerned.[22]

Of course, for all the policy development conducted for over ten years under Young's direction, there had been no attempt to define economic or any other objective criteria for inception of control operations. The lines seem intended to be read with a knowing wink and nod.

Young's talent for prose as unmelodious as it was exculpatory was nicely balanced by Gabrielson's ability to wax flowery on the stump. In October 1938, Gabrielson gave a well-received talk on predator control to the Audubon Society. Rosalie Edge described the chief's rhetorical power in a letter to E. Raymond Hall:

> Yesterday I listened to Gabrielson expound the beauties of Biological
> Survey poisoning at the Convention of the Audubon Association. I never
> heard anyone so persuasive; it was as though I was smoking opium. The
> fumes went to my head, and I began to think how beautiful it was that the
> Biological Survey was destroying all these little mammals, so painlessly
> and skillfully. I got up and left—I was so utterly disgusted.
>
> The big hall of the American Museum was crowded with teachers,
> various officials of organizations, garden clubs, etc., and there was
> Gabrielson making wholesale poisoning sound perfectly beautiful, almost
> lyric. And none of us are doing anything about it. It makes me sick.[23]

She added, "You are the only one who gives me any help, I do thank you very much." But she would not have been aware that Young was at the same time formalizing procedures to ensure that funds from the Division of Grazing would continue to flow smoothly into the survey's troughs.

With the survey back in the hands of control advocates, the best chance to end the poisoning appeared to lie with Interior Secretary Ickes, in charge not just of the Division of Grazing but also of the Civilian Conservation Corps and the Public Works Administration—among his many agencies. On May 9, 1939, as part of an executive reorganization, the Bureau of Biological Survey was transferred from the Department of Agriculture to Interior and a year later renamed the Fish and Wildlife Service.

Opponents of the control program took heart, although their campaign had long since lost momentum. The American Society of Mammalogists continued on occasion to pass resolutions opposing poisoning, but the three-member Emergency Conservation Committee was the only entity still actively pushing to end the killing. Irving Brant wrote Ickes in June of that year informing him of the mammalogists' long-standing opposition and urging a "careful study" of the control program, and Rosalie Edge secured a meeting with the secretary in January 1940 to push for reform. "The Secretary was sympathetic and receptive," Edge reported to Hall. "He appeared to know that an inquiry should be made into the Biological Survey."[24]

Whether the inquiry occurred or not, Gabrielson had positioned himself well to block significant changes. He had earned Ickes's trust by his prior support for transferring the survey to Interior—a key move in Ickes's long-sought (although ultimately unsuccessful) ambition to transform his Department of the Interior into a broader Department of Conservation with jurisdiction over a host of Department of Agriculture agencies, most notably the Forest Service.[25] (In contrast, Ding Darling, retired and heading up a private wildlife advocacy organization, had reversed his initial support and by 1937 was lobbying against putting the survey into Interior, thus earning Ickes's enmity.[26])

Young later attributed Ickes's eventual support for the control program to an incident that touched him personally: "One night a pack of roving wild dogs proceeded to attack and kill some of his prize turkeys," prompting the secretary to turn to his predator-killing agency for relief.[27] Whatever the reason, Ickes failed to follow Brant and Edge's wishes.

The last wolves died hard but hardly noticed, their truncated lives inspiring little of the drama of those of their predecessors. Along the nation's borders with Canada and Mexico, wolves continued to show up, albeit less and less frequently, for decades to come. A small population was even allowed to persist in the Boundary Waters region of northern Minnesota, where the extensive lakes limited most human transport to canoes and had long precluded livestock grazing. In neighboring Wisconsin and Michigan the cessation of the survey's activities in 1932 and 1935, respectively—the former in response to hostility by local bounty hunters who regarded the newly arrived survey as competition—also enabled a few wolves to persist.[28]

In the interior regions of the West, a handful of lone wolves survived through the Roosevelt years, their occasional deaths popping up in the survey's reports and other records like incongruous reminders of a bygone era. In the Bighorn Mountains east of Yellowstone National Park, a Wyoming state game warden shot the last regional wolf in 1940—two years after having shot and wounded the same animal.[29] In Arizona's arid grasslands north of the Mogollon Rim, the last wolf was said to have been killed in 1942.[30] It may have dispersed from the southern Rocky Mountains.

For despite the epitaph written in the late 1920s by Arthur H. Carhart and Stanley Young in *The Last Stand of the Pack*, wolves had persisted in Colorado. The species appeared "far from extinct" to a mammalogist from the Colorado Museum of Natural History, writing in 1932.[31] But that assessment, likely based on the fact that wolves kept re-appearing time upon time despite their supposedly final demise, proved untrue.

The sheer 2,000-foot chalk-colored Book Cliffs rise from the lowlands of Grand Junction and the Colorado River in western Colorado to a forest of pinyon pines and twisted junipers. In 1932, according to a report the survey judged authentic, private hunters in the Book Cliffs killed two wolves.[32] The following year the survey received reports of wolf depredations in the Book Cliffs. It seemed likely the job of "control" had not been completed in the region, and Bill Caywood was sent to the scene. But the West's best wolf hunter concluded that large coyotes and a dog were the culprits. He could find no trace of wolves.[33]

Along the state line between Colorado and New Mexico, wolves survived over a decade longer. As seen, the last pack in this region, consisting of seven wolves, was trapped in northern New Mexico in 1927. Then, one early morning in 1933 or 1934 in northern New Mexico's Jemez Mountains—a spur of the San Juans—between the towns of Ojo Caliente and Tres Piedras, sheep rancher John Davenport spotted a wolf at close range through the sagebrush and shot it. And in 1934 the survey killed another in Colfax County to the east, where high mountains slope down to the plains.[34]

On the Colorado side, in fiscal year 1933 a wolf was reported in the western San Juan Mountains of Dolores and San Miguel counties, although there were no reports of depredations. The survey sent a hunter to set traps, but the animal was not caught. It was not until 1938 that a survey hunter could take credit for another wolf killed in the state. In November of that year, a wolf was shot at the head of the Navajo River in Archuleta County's south San Juan region. (The putative last grizzly in the southern Rocky Mountains was killed along the same river forty-one years later.) Finally, in 1945, after ten sheep were reported killed by a wolf, the Fish and Wildlife Service trapped Colorado's last known wild wolf in Conejos County, in the southeast San Juans.[35]

In Oregon, five wolves were killed in the 1940s, and it is not clear whether these animals were the last of a resident population or, more likely, migrants from Canada. Wolves' survival in the Cascade Mountains had been enhanced

Wolves Killed by the Biological Survey Fish and Wildlife Service in Colorado Following Stanley P. Young's Departure from the State

Fiscal Year	Wolves Killed
1930	1
1939	1
1945	1

Sources: "Number and Species of Animals Taken and Cost Per Month, FY 1916–1917," USDA-APHIS Wildlife Services; "History of Predator and Rodent Control Colorado District," 2, National Archives, Washington, D.C.

by the wet, Pacific-facing mountains' jumble of downed trees, rendering the national forest lands largely inaccessible to cattle and sheep. Dropping off either side of the mountains, however, a wolf would readily run into stock.

Ironically, in the state in which Stanley Young was born and Ira Gabrielson spent much of his early career, the last wolves were killed not by the survey but by bounty hunters. The last wolf in the state was turned in from Lane County, which extends from the coast to the Cascade Mountains, on February 7, 1947, for a thirty dollar payment by the state.[36]

Although wolves continued to show up and be killed along the nation's borders, either the Oregon animal or the Colorado one in 1945 was likely the last native wolf that had been born in the western United States in the first half of the twentieth century. Three years before the Oregon wolf's death, in 1944, Young had published this excerpt in his book *The Wolves of North America*:

> Except in local areas where wolves have continued to present a pressing economic problem the Fish and Wildlife Service has felt that little wolf control work is now justified. There still remain, even in the United States, some areas of considerable size in which we feel that both the red and gray species, in their respective habitats, may be allowed to continue their existence with little molestation.[37]

Young could hardly have imagined, at the height of his prestige, how alarmingly close to accurate his prevaricating words would prove to be half a century later.

Honorable Chief Cur

T he transfer of the survey to the Department of the Interior in 1939 and its re-organization the following year as the Fish and Wildlife Service marked the permanence of Stanley P. Young's influence on wildlife policy. He had not only helped name that policy, branding it "control," but he had built its statutory authority by shepherding the 1931 Animal Damage Control Act into law and ensured its persistence and growth through changes in the executive branch. Now, with control assumed by the same agency under a new name and with Ira N. Gabrielson securely ensconced, he could leave the nuts and bolts of running the program to others.

On January 1, 1939, Young, forty-nine years old, transferred out of his administrative capacity and into a research role as a senior biologist in the survey, following in the footsteps of many of the survey's former leaders. His position was filled by yet another of his protégés, Dorr D. Green.

For someone as meticulously attentive to bureaucratic lexicon as Young, his new title was distinctly nebulous, outlining no job description. In subsequent autobiographical sketches he described his duties and accomplishments but not where he resided in the bureaucracy from 1939 until his retirement twenty years later. The press release issued to announce the new assignment noted only that he was "on the staff of the Bureau to conduct special work under the direction of the chief, Dr. Ira N. Gabrielson."[1] (The doctorate was an honorary Ph.D. in science from Oregon State College—testimony to Gabrielson's remarkable ability and agility in public relations.[2])

Perhaps Young did not need a descriptive title because he was practically an institution. Three years before his transfer of responsibilities, in 1936, he had acquired a more colorful title that presaged, if only on a psychological level, his shift of duties. This private and decidedly informal name, Honorable Chief Cur, reflected his central participation in the Biological Survey Kennel of the Ancient and Honorable, Independent and Effervescent Order of Yellow Dogs.

A ribald society of Agriculture Department employees, the order was modeled after more traditional men's social clubs and their august and secret rituals. The Yellow Dogs' prospective members were initiated by urinating on posts and baying at the moon—plus repeating a solemn oath while sitting naked in a faux-outhouse.[3]

Young's role in this association appears to have included authorship of two vulgar poems apparently read aloud at Yellow Dogs convocations and sent by Young to the director of the Control Methods Laboratory in Denver, F. E. Garlough (known by his Yellow Dogs appellation Custodian of the Bone). One poem, "The Grooving of Dan McGrew," is a take-off on Robert Service's ballad "The Shooting of Dan McGrew" and substitutes a syphilitic barroom rape for Service's shooting. The other poem, "The Piddling Pup," spared such gruesome descriptions but indecorously depicted a farmer's dog whose powers of urination awed his urban brethren.[4] The bawdy verses are so unlike any of Young's dry memoranda and other attributable writings that it is tempting to dismiss his membership in the Yellow Dogs as an irrelevant sideshow to his serious endeavors. A Yellow Dogs initiation instruction paper, also apparently written by Young, confirms that the order "is founded on Friendship, Frivolity and Fun," with an emphasis on fun.[5]

But the order also reflected a distinct political view. The initiation instructions jeered at the New Deal and, in a sign of Young's adherence to modern values, prescribed as toilet paper for the "outhouse" a 1929 book entitled *The Specialist*, which satirized the ascent of specialists and the accompanying eclipse of common sense.[6] Clearly, the leader of the nation's predator and rodent control specialists, although skeptical of the administration, had sharp opinions on a work that mocked the milieu in which he thrived.

On a more personal level, the canine motif to some Yellow Dogs' rituals and one of its poems might indicate the Chief Cur's occasional chafing at his bureaucratic responsibilities, so remote from the escapades of his early career that had inspired his life-long fascination with wolves. Young's 1939 transfer from directing the control program to becoming a researcher freed him from those administrative responsibilities.

The transfer also may have fulfilled his intellectual ambitions. Beginning in the mid-1930s, he styled himself as a sort of frontier scientist along the lines of the survey's early field naturalists (but with an up-to-date conservationist tinge, as he pursued the protection of game animals). He joined the American Society of Mammalogists, the Biological Society of Washington, and the Explorers' Club of New York—as well as the gun manufacturers–funded American Game Protective Association.

He also began implying that he had a Master of Science degree in biology from the University of Michigan—a misstatement that repeatedly made it into print in the increasing number of biographical articles that focused on Young.[7] Perhaps behind this small and unnecessary measure of dishonesty was a man who, although supremely accomplished, felt chastened by the narrowness of his own outook—or perhaps simply a man disgruntled at the increasing esteem accorded the author of *Game Management*.

In November 1939, Aldo Leopold, then professor of wildlife management at the University of Wisconsin, wrote Young a warm letter of praise for an article he had written that appeared in the journal *American Forests*. Addressing Young as "Stanley," Leopold included the comment, "You and I often differ in our views on predator control, but good information is the backlog of any policy, and this is certainly good information authored on coyote biology." Young passed the note to Gabrielson with his own handwritten annotation: "Thought you would be interested in reading what 'Aldo the Great' had to say, As I recall,—I didn't think any member of the Bureau could ever write any thing he didn't already know! However, I seem to have done so in one particular at least."[8]

It had been a challenge for Young to become a scientist. Previous challenges in earlier stages of his life had defined Young to himself and to the world at large. As a young man he had tested his mettle against the frontier and against the wits of wary wolves. He had graduated to supervising fellow trappers and building a system of cooperating institutions sufficient to outlast and out-compete a population of wolves in Colorado, as well as a human population of bounty hunters.

Each challenge had added a facet to his life, a shimmering set of experiences by which he would be known. A 1925 publicity release authored by Young and apparently intended for biographical articles described some of his employment details. "[C]onferences with the Governor of the State and other high officials" comprised one day, according to his blithe account, "thence twenty-four hours later a sleep [*sic*] under a cedar tree on the open range near the camp ground of some illiterate Mexican sheep herder."[9]

Clearly, Young had thrived on his early work, and his competence and love of responsibility were rewarded by his transfer to Washington in 1927, followed quickly by promotion to head of the Division of Economic Investigations. Without doubt, he must have felt immense pride in captaining an army of hunters from among whose ranks he had risen.

The challenge immediately following that promotion, however, started a countdown to the time when he could no longer fully revel in his post. In 1928 he had proscribed the survey's use of "extermination" and replaced it with "control." By 1934 that lexical change had helped vanquish the political threat that precipitated it. But in beating the scientists on the political battleground,

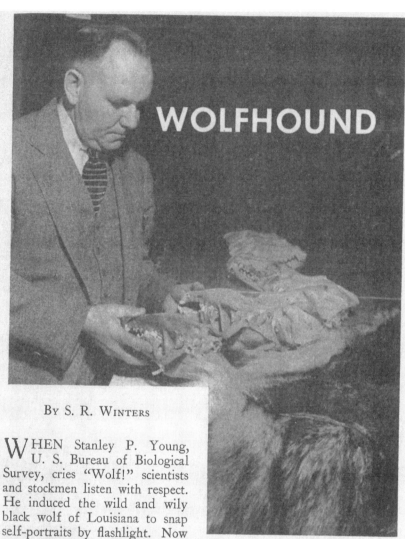

WOLFHOUND

By S. R. Winters

WHEN Stanley P. Young, U. S. Bureau of Biological Survey, cries "Wolf!" scientists and stockmen listen with respect. He induced the wild and wily black wolf of Louisiana to snap self-portraits by flashlight. Now leaves his post as Chief of the Survey's Division of Predator and Rodent Control for a different kind of wolf hunt, tracking down the last secrets of Ranchers' Enemy Number One via scientific skull - measuring and fossilized bones.

Started his wolf-hunting career as one of the Survey's hunters of predatory animals in the wolf-country of Arizona in 1917 two years after receiving his M. S. degree from the University of Michigan. Twelve years later, still with the

Stanley P. Young, already an institution in Washington in 1940, touting his fictional graduate degree in biology in the magazine American Wildlife. *(American Wildlife magazine, courtesy of the Wildlife Management Institute)*

Young had undermined the honor of heading an extermination campaign; he could not take credit where it was due him.

In the mid-1930s, having won every battle he had taken on, Young was ready for new challenges. Developing credentials as a biologist promised the respect he could no longer claim as an exterminator.

Playing the role of exterminator while disavowing extermination would also have jarred with Young's life-long faith in the integrity of public service. After years of stating that no species would be wiped out and that wolves not causing problems would not be killed, it is likely he believed his own rhetoric, at least in part. In the fall of 1935 he began, albeit in a small way, acting in accordance with his own pronouncements.

In an act he would recall fondly for the rest of his life, that year Young set a very different type of trap for a wolf—a trap that burnished not only his scientific standing but also his sense of allegiance to his own official line. In the first use of a trip-operated camera to photograph wildlife, Young worked with two non-governmental scientists to take pictures of wild black wolves (of the red wolf species, different from the gray wolves in the West) in the Singer Wildlife Refuge of Louisiana, apparently with no intent or attempt to kill them.[10] (The survey's long-term disposition toward these wolves was less charitable, as the refuge no longer exists and the agency and its cooperators eventually wiped out this photogenic population of distinctly colored canids.)

As a researcher, Young's first major project was to write a book about wolves—a project destined to take five years and, when published in 1944, to become the definitive natural history overview of both the red and gray species, never surpassed in thoroughness and comprehensive scope. It is evident in *The Wolves of North America,* co-authored with survey colleague Edward A. Goldman (who wrote the relatively short and technical taxonomic section only), that Young applied the same care and dedication to research as he had to setting a trap for the most savvy wolf. His bibliography alone comprised eighty pages. Over the years he wrote books on the mountain lion, bobcat, and coyote, but none was as encyclopedic and filled with lore as *The Wolves of North America.*

At its appearance in 1944, the 636-page opus confirmed Young's legitimacy as a biologist of substance. Leopold, in a review for the *Journal of Forestry,* praised the volume as "the outstanding contemporary treatise on an outstanding animal." But he also used the review as a vehicle to level harsh criticism against Young's legacy. In response to the book's cavalier assertion that "some areas of considerable size" might serve as refuge for wolves, the professor of game management asked, "[w]hy, in the necessary process of extirpating wolves from the livestock ranges of Wyoming and Montana, were not some of the uninjured animals used to restock the Yellowstone?" "How can it be done now," he chided, "when the only available stocks are the desert wolf of Arizona, and the subarctic form of the Canadian Rockies?"[11]

The split between Leopold and Young, although slow in developing, embodied the schism in policy that had plagued the U.S. Fish and Wildlife Service since its inception in 1885 and the sowing of doubt as to its purpose with placement of the errant comma in its congressional appropriation act that year. Leopold died in 1948, at age sixty-one, before publication of his own masterpiece, *A Sand County Almanac*. Although that book's influence grew throughout the remainder of the twentieth century, in the short term—three decades— Young's agency and the Department of the Interior that housed it were destined to continue on their reckless course unimpeded.

On April 12, 1945, shortly after beginning to serve his fourth term as president, Franklin D. Roosevelt died of a sudden cerebral hemorrhage at age sixty-three. The wildly popular Roosevelt had so long seemed synonymous with the presidency that the nation seemed to mourn not just the passing of the man but the passing of an era as well. Roosevelt had brought the country out of depression and through the most harrowing years of a global war. The world, so it seemed in retrospect with his passing, had been held together by his moral force.

Roosevelt's personal fortitude had been rooted in the earth. He may have been the last president, at least until Jimmy Carter, who cherished the rasp of the wind in tree limbs, the feel of soil in his hand, and the warbling of birds— and whose secretary of the interior shared those feelings.

Ten months after Vice President Harry Truman assumed the presidency, on February 15, 1946, he jettisoned Secretary of Interior Harold L. Ickes in consequence of a dispute over the administration's nomination of a wealthy California oilman, Edwin Pauley, to be under-secretary of the Navy. Ickes asserted that in 1944 Pauley, who served as treasurer of the Democratic National Committee, had baldly attempted to bribe him with $300,000 in campaign contributions in return for access to offshore oil deposits. Ickes had scorned the offer and left this comment in his diary: "I don't intend to smear my record with oil at this stage of the game even to help win the reelection of the President" (Roosevelt). Almost two years later Truman, open to any rationale for removing a secretary of the interior whose scruples made him a pain in the administration's hindquarters, eagerly accepted Ickes's resignation.[12]

Truman offered the Interior position to Supreme Court Justice William O. Douglas, a mountaineer and ardent lover of the wild (who much later wrote in opposition to the government's poisoning program and against the public-lands sheep grazing it supported). But Douglas had been privy to Ickes's deep reservations about Pauley and, in Truman's words as recorded in his diary, "hummed and hawed about the offer." (Douglas would dither again in 1948, with the same results, when Truman offered to make him vice-president.) Truman instead appointed Julius A. Krug, who ensconced Colorado cattleman and longtime Interior official Oscar Chapman as his number two at the department. Krug was phobic about paperwork and liked to tour Interior lands, at times incommunicado even to the president. Chapman ran the department and in 1949 was promoted to secretary in his own right.[13]

Ickes's removal and Chapman's ascent as the powerhouse in the Department of the Interior seemed to embolden the livestock industry. Since ousting

Farrington R. Carpenter in 1939, the interior secretary had recast the Division of Grazing as the "Grazing Service" in emulation of the Forest Service's professionalism. In part to demonstrate that he would better protect forests if the latter agency were added to his portfolio, Ickes labored to turn his Grazing Service into a meaningful protector of the public lands, an agency that would guard against stocking too many animals lest they result in further damage to the soil.

The threat was clear: If the federal government could limit livestock use to protect soil, what would prevent it from adopting the same measures for more far-reaching aims—for instance, protecting game animals? Ding Darling, with Ickes's approval, had already shut out grazing from the Sheldon Antelope Refuge in Wyoming. The only sure protection from such extremism lay in private ownership of the federal domain.

Six months after Ickes's departure, on August 17, 1946, the National Livestock and National Woolgrowers associations appointed a joint committee to work toward transferring the Taylor Grazing Act lands and, later, other "grazing lands" (never defined) managed by the Forest Service and the National Park Service to private ownership. The proposal, unveiled in February 1947, would allow only those currently holding permits to graze those lands to buy them. The price tag would range between $.09 per acre and an estimated $2.80 per acre, based solely on the tracts' value for livestock.[14]

Nevada senator Patrick A. McCarran, the erstwhile ally of the late Representative Edward T. Taylor, had been holding a series of investigations and hostile hearings on the Grazing Service since shortly after Carpenter's firing. By 1946, McCarran had succeeded in cutting the Grazing Service budget to the bone in an attempt to make sure it had sufficient personnel to keep trespass graziers off the allotments held by permittees but no additional resources to monitor the range or make informed decisions about management. In July 1946, as a result of his budget cut, the Grazing Service was replaced by a new, toothless agency named the Bureau of Land Management (BLM).[15]

Over the next decade, as McCarran repeatedly introduced legislation to privatize the public domain, the BLM responded by abandoning any attempt to manage its lands. The grazing boards run by ranchers decided stocking rates and all aspects of management. BLM officials, under the gun in Congress, did not dare—and in most cases probably did not care to—challenge the livestock industry's complete control over the lands owned by the American public.

The Forest Service was also cowed by the cow (and sheep) men. In 1951 Congress extended grazing boards' advisory jurisdiction to cover national forest lands as well—thus providing the same institutional leverage for ranchers as those they used to control the BLM. In the 1952 election campaign, the Republican Party platform endorsed "opportunity for ownership" of public lands along with vague suggestions of establishing "rights" to graze. Heretofore, the courts had sided with the federal government in holding that grazing leases only extended privileges that could be revoked to serve other uses.

That November, General Dwight David Eisenhower, the Republican nominee, won the presidency, and the Republican Party captured both houses of Congress. Legislation to privatize the public domain outright was stymied as the result of a vigorous publicity campaign led by Arthur H. Carhart—supported by Rosalie Edge, among others, and joined by the retired Ira Gabrielson, whose New Deal sympathies for government evidently prevailed over any loyalty to the prosperous ranchers who were its principal intended beneficiaries.[16] But with presidential support, in 1954 a legislative rider was tacked onto a farm bill to create a private property right for public-land range "improvements" (such as fences and water tanks) and to prohibit the government from reducing stocking rates for any rancher who had pledged his federal grazing lease as security for a loan. (The latter provision mirrored the measure Roosevelt's administration had kept out of the 1934 Taylor Grazing Act.)

Although the 1954 rider was nixed at the last moment in a conference committee between the Senate and the House, the Forest Service no longer needed to be told who ruled the range. With the professionalism indigenous to their agency and the Department of Agriculture of which it was a part, some Forest Service employees had tried to adhere to their mandate not to degrade the long-term capacity of the land. But Forest Service supervisors, district rangers, and range specialists lived with the knowledge that the ranchers whose stock grazed the forest could reach a U.S. senator by phone more quickly than they could—and sometimes the rancher and senator were one and the same. In many cases, reductions in stocking levels resulted in aborted careers.

Decisions on how many animals to permit were not the only things ranchers cared about. In a 1951 demonstration of the clout of local woolgrowers in Wyoming, Big Horn National Forest supervisor Roy Williams was transferred to a dead-end administrative job without responsibilities as retaliation for proposing a reduction in the number of poison baits placed by the Fish and Wildlife Service.[17]

Just as the Bureau of Land Management and the Forest Service abandoned any pretense of meaningful regulation of grazing on the public domain, the Fish and Wildlife Service reverted to its old relaxed posture after over a decade and a half of adamant insistence that the control program was under control. While the BLM, born of a Grazing Service shaped by Harold Ickes's conservation ethic, performed less and less, the Fish and Wildlife Service—rooted much more deeply in the soil of the western livestock industry—bloomed in an efflorescence of new and expanded programs.

On December 5, 1946, Ira Gabrielson retired as chief of the Fish and Wildlife Service. His successor was Albert M. Day, yet another Young protégé promoted from within the ranks of the control program.[18] In December 1946, within weeks of becoming chief, Day approved two new predacides for Fish and Wildlife Service use—thallium sulfate and sodium fluoroacetate.

Since 1928 the Biological Survey had used thallium sulphate, a by-product of an industrial smelting process, to kill rodents.[19] Interest grew in its predator-killing properties because coyote populations were surviving strychnine—not to mention traps, den excavating operations, and auditory lures to bring them within rifle range. Remarkably, not only was the little "song dog" seemingly holding its own, but the species—originally limited to the temperate regions of western North America—was actually expanding its range to include Alaska and the East Coast.

The coyote fared so well, even as the wolf was extirpated from the West, for three reasons. First, coyotes are more fecund animals, reaching reproductive maturity at age one—a year earlier than wolves. This accelerated fertility helped compensate for extraordinarily high rates of mortality.

Second, coyotes maintain a higher population density over any given area than wolves do because coyotes' primary food sources—rodents—are naturally more numerous than wolves' prey—ungulates. Higher population density helped ensure that discrete areas in which persecution lapsed might harbor a coyote or two, even if the region was too small to encompass the home range of a wolf.

Lastly, rodents had not disappeared from vast landscapes as completely or as abruptly as wild ungulates had over the last three decades of the nineteenth century. As a result, coyotes had relied less completely on domestic livestock than wolves had and consequently were not subject to the universal persecution that had befallen wolves.

But coyotes' tenacity would not necessarily last. By the late 1930s, with the eradication of prairie dogs and other rodents accomplished over vast distances and the forage they would have consumed allocated to domestic livestock, more coyotes were likely forced to prey on such vulnerable animals as sheep. They were also forced to travel farther in seeking food and thus became more exposed to the dangers of poison. Perhaps "control," gray wolf style, might be possible for the coyote after all.

Strychnine killed many coyotes, but it had drawbacks. First, its bitter flavor would impel any animal to spit it out. The government's one-inch meat and fat baits had overcome this limitation because canids' natural tendency is to gulp down such morsels without biting into them. But baits that small could only be relied upon during the warm months, or they would be covered with snow.

Strychnine's other drawback was that animals started to succumb within minutes after ingesting the poison. Any animal that arrived to feed late might learn from its fellows' suffering to be wary of what it swallowed.

Thallium sulphate solved both these problems. It was tasteless and undetectable, so it need not be confined to small, gulp-sized baits. Applied in powder form, it could be dusted into slits of a carcass big enough to stay exposed through the winter.

Thallium sulphate also acted slowly. Poisoned animals took anywhere from a few days to weeks to die (depending on the dose they received), first losing the pads on their feet, then going bald, and then becoming blind before expiring. This slow demise masked the link between a poisoned carcass and the result of consuming it. In fact, poisoned animals sometimes returned over and over to feed on the carcass that was killing them.[20]

In 1937 the survey had begun experiments, supervised by the Control Methods Laboratory in Denver, in which field personnel in Wyoming set up thallium poison stations and then attempted to monitor the results through reports from sheep growers and a running census of carcasses reported found. The experiments continued for years, expanding to Colorado, but the poison was not approved for general agency use until December 1946 when Gabrielson retired—a hint that perhaps Gabe in his later years was inclined to join Young in heeding his own statements against exterminating any creature.

Sodium fluoroacetate, the second poison approved by Day, was just as insidious as thallium sulphate. It was invented in 1944 by Polish scientists for use in public health campaigns against rodents. Fish and Wildlife Service scientists at the Wildlife Research Laboratory (the new name, since 1940, for the Control Methods Laboratory), in their 1,080th attempt at finding the perfect killer of coyotes, formulated it into the substance they called Compound 1080. Odorless and tasteless, it was designed for injection into a dying animal whose capillary action would spread the toxin into every bit of flesh. A horse shot for use as bait required only one syringe of Compound 1080 to render each small chunk of meat, no larger than the old strychnine one-inch baits, deadly. But Compound 1080 was far cheaper and, more important, easier to handle than thallium (since it could be dissolved in water for injection into an entire carcass) and much easier than the old, laborious process of planting strychnine tabs in small chunks of meat and fat.[21] As with thallium sulphate seven years earlier, Compound 1080 was tested in the field in Wyoming, Colorado, Idaho, and Nevada but not yet approved for general use. Both new poisons yielded dynamic effects. "[T]he control of coyotes sometimes approached local extirpation," a Fish and Wildlife Service researcher reported.[22] Compound 1080 appeared even more painful than thallium, although the dying process was considerably shorter. Around thirty minutes after ingestion, the victim would lapse into violent convulsions ending in death within several hours. Like thallium, Compound 1080 would leave its victims, and the vomit they inevitably disgorged in their dying spasms, as toxic as the original baits—thus leading to additional deaths of scavengers.[23]

In addition to thallium and Compound 1080, Fish and Wildlife began using a new coyote-killing technique, the Orwellian named "humane coyote getter," which used powdered sodium cyanide to kill. As early as 1924, Stanley Young had reported in a memo to the head of the Eradication Methods Laboratory on the results of his discovery that a glass bottle of cyanide flakes, tossed into a coyote den too rocky to be excavated, had killed the occupants.[24] But the "getter" had the advantage of bringing the coyote to the cyanide. Consisting of a several-inch-long metal tube like a pistol barrel that was hammered partway into the ground and capped with a soft fabric soaked in alluring scent, the device would fire a load of the poison when the odiferous top was disturbed. Typically, coyotes (and other creatures) would mouth the device, and the cyanide expelled into their mouths would absorb into the bloodstream and cause a violent but relatively quick death—that is, in the span of a few minutes.

In 1945 the Fish and Wildlife Service also began aerial gunning for coyotes in the winter, when they could be spotted against a sparkling white landscape and hindered from rapid escape by deep snow.[25]

With all these new weapons in play, it finally seemed possible to achieve what survey officials from long ago had not dared imagine—broadscale extirpation of the coyote. Although officials could no longer openly boast of the prospect, complete "control" seemed in sight. John W. Crook, a survey hunter in Colorado since November 1914 (and a field deputy for both Logan B. Crawford and Stanley Young), who retired at age sixty-two at the end of 1944, recalled the trajectory of coyote population declines during his entire career and predicted that "[i]n southern Colorado at least, the animal is doomed to go the same way that the lobo went."[26]

The Fish and Wildlife Service expanded its operations not only technologically but geographically as well. In the late 1940s and early 1950s the agency began shopping around its methodology and its custom-concocted poisons to thirty-six separate nations and colonies of foreign nations. This resulted in twelve countries ordering strychnine, almost all in the Western Hemisphere. Five nations ordered Compound 1080. Seven engaged in unspecified "miscellaneous cooperation" with the service, and personnel in five countries received specialized training.

The upshot was that every inhabited continent on earth (and many islands) began receiving the same poisons, training in the same techniques and institutional approaches, and, along the way, inculcated key people in the same agricultural utilitarianism that had transformed the American West. From Korea to Venezuela, strychnine baits were being set. From Greece to Columbia, Compound 1080 flourished. From Indonesia to the Congo, local operatives received training in the survey's methods. Whether the problem was depredations by baboons and black-backed jackals in South Africa, to be handled by that country's Department of Nature Conservation, or the old stand-by rationale—rabies—in Mexico, addressed by the Pan American Sanitary Bureau, the service's response was Compound 1080.[27]

In Canada the shift from a bounty system to cooperative control mirrored the state-by-state and county-by-county shift in the United States decades earlier. In early February 1947, Stanley Young visited British Columbia as part of a Canadian research tour for his upcoming book on coyotes and appeared on a radio program named *Sportsman's Guide* and in the pages of the *Northwest Sportsman* to blast bounties and tout cooperative wolf control. (The apparently pre-scripted radio interview, preserved in Young's records in the form of a typewritten transcript with extensive passages revised by hand, misidentifies Young as having received a Ph.D. and includes this dialogue: "So Doctor, if you'll just pull up a chair we will fire some questions at you," followed by "Thank you, Hal. Let's be very informal on this programme. I prefer that you call me Stan and I'll call you Hal." Even as he conferred on himself yet another fictional degree, Young had not forgotten that the common touch counted for much more.)[28]

Later that year, British Columbia created a predator control agency and within a few years was importing hundreds of thousands of strychnine tabs designed for insertion into baits, followed, beginning in 1952, with 1080 for both small baits and whole-carcass poison stations. Many of the small baits were dropped by airplanes over vast roadless forests and tundras inhabited not just by wolves and coyotes (the prescribed targets) but also by bears, foxes, wolverines, and other scavengers. Other provinces soon followed suit.[29] In 1948 the Fish and Wildlife Service, also at Young's prompting and with a special trap he developed for conditions in the far north, inaugurated cooperative wolf control in the Territory of Alaska as well.[30]

Beginning in 1950 the Fish and Wildlife Service sent Compound 1080 (along with two of its employees) to Mexico to kill Mexican gray wolves, known by their Spanish name *lobos*, the smallest and southernmost subspecies of gray wolf.[31] In an article published in *American Forests* following a 1936 hunting trip to the Sierra Madre, Aldo Leopold had described those mountains as refugia from the effects of livestock grazing as a result, first, of Apache resistance to European settlement and later because of the presence of bandits:

> It is this chain of historical accidents which enables the American conservationist to go to Chihuahua today and feast his eyes on what his own mountains were like before the Juggernaut. To my mind, these live oak-dotted hills fat with side oats grama, these pine-clad mesas spangled with flowers, these lazy trout streams burbling along under great sycamores and cottonwoods, come near to being the cream of creation. But on our side of the line the grama is mostly gone, the mesas are spangled with snakeweed, the trout streams are now cobble-bars.[32]

"Mountain lions and wolves are still common," wrote Leopold then. And whitetailed deer were "abundant . . . but not excessive." But in New Mexico and Arizona, sharing similar landforms and climates, "there are in general two kinds of deer range, the overstocked and the nearly empty," he reported. "Most of the herds are very thin, but every few years some new spot flares up with a sudden overpopulation of deer."[33]

Notwithstanding Leopold's plea in this 1937 article for protection of the Sierra Madre and his question as to "whether the presence of a normal complement of predators is not, at least in part, accountable for the absence of irruption,"[34] little more than a decade later Fish and Wildlife Service–provided Compound 1080 upset that balance, playing a significant role not just in reducing wolf populations drastically but also in wiping out the southernmost population of grizzly bears remaining in North America. These last thirty or so grizzlies, living on an isolated and jagged twenty-mile-long mountain range in central Chihuahua province, were deliberately poisoned off during the early 1960s (and the extirpation documented in 1967 by Leopold's son, Dr. A. Starker Leopold, who had followed in his father's footsteps in exploring Mexico and seeking to understand its biota).[35]

Aldo Leopold died in 1948. Soon after his death the landscape that prompted his epiphany about the value of predators was rapidly being rendered safe for an invasion of livestock.

During the post-war period the United States greatly increased its foreign development projects, premised explicitly on an altruistic urge to rebuild after the ravages of war but also motivated by economic self-interest. In Mexico, American ranchers were among the most prominent beneficiaries of the rabies suppression/wolf control program, although a service employee opined that the campaign "generated good will for our country from the Mexican stockmen" as well.[36] This combination of motives typified post-war foreign aid. In dispensing the benefits of American technological prowess and economic might, the United States sought to inoculate the world against the seductions of communism. Economic efficiency was the lingua franca of America's offer to the rest of the world, the ink in the contracts for numerous foreign aid programs. The Fish and Wildlife control program, premised on eliminating the waste represented by wild predators and rodents, embodied that zeitgeist. Technological wonders such as Compound 1080 not only continued the expansion of the frontiers of agriculture such efficiency demanded but also helped introduce to foreign societies an inevitable corollary to that efficiency: the American agribusiness-government relationship to natural landscapes.

Could the specific benefits of foreign goodwill and aid to expatriate ranchers have been only minor factors in the Fish and Wildlife Service's mission overseas? Judging from its past, the service may have needed little external prompting to embark on an international extension of its yeomanly work in the western United States. Perhaps neither technological nor geographic expansion was optional for an agency whose internal culture had been molded by its long role as conqueror of the frontier. It somehow seems only natural that when the frontiers of America's growth-oriented economy significantly breached the nation's borders, the Fish and Wildlife Service was on the front lines.

Although Canada, Mexico, and lands further afield represented fertile new territory for cooperative predator control, coyotes failed to disappear from the western United States. It is unclear over what vast distances coyotes were actually extirpated throughout the poison-heavy two decades that followed World War II. In 1952, Olaus J. Murie—retired from federal service and active in an organization called the Wilderness Society—in reviewing Stanley Young's book *The Clever Coyote,* warned that the species was heading "over the Great Divide." He concluded with this poignant remark: "In extensive areas, many who had formerly taken for granted the presence of Señor Coyote and his song, without much thought, now miss him, now that he is gone."[37]

We will never know precisely how close coyotes came to extinction. Most likely, the vagaries of budget allocations allowed a few to survive in various scattered locales and replenish adjacent areas whenever persecution lapsed. "Compound 1080 baits will drastically thin out a coyote population, but I have never seen it do more than that," avowed the Fish and Wildlife agent in charge of Nebraska and the Dakotas in the winter of 1955–1956. He continued, "You frequently hear that 'coyotes are all gone' or 'there isn't a coyote left' but such statements are in error."[38]

One of the most significant factors in allowing coyotes to survive was the presence of national parks, which had finally been put off-limits to the Biological Survey in 1931. The parks, although only a small and widely scattered portion of the public domain, provided vital sanctuaries from which coyotes could re-occupy surrounding landscapes whenever poisoning was relaxed for budgetary or other reasons.

By the early 1950s, however, the Fish and Wildlife Service was encircling the western national parks with rings of Compound 1080 stations, intended to catch coyotes crossing the line. In one incident, brought to light in 1952, the agency finagled the introduction of 1080 into the interior of Zion National Monument in Utah by making arrangements to poison private land contained within the park—and by cavalierly assuring Zion's superintendent that strychnine had been used there in the past, so no additional harm could be done.

Coyotes were "all but exterminated" as a result, according to a letter National Park Service director Conrad L. Wirth wrote to his counterpart, Albert Day, at Fish and Wildlife. "The Monument and adjacent Park are a section of a severe deer-problem area," Wirth reported, "where predation is sorely needed."

Day responded by agreeing to keep poisons out of the exterior boundaries of the parks but hedged when requested to limit poisoning to exceptional circumstances within three miles of a park's borders, as the two agencies had agreed the previous year.[39] Clearly, coyotes were to be controlled as closely as possible around such refugia as the parks represented.

Although the eleven western public-land states were saturated with new poisons in the post-war period, the Midwest was less so. The paucity of public lands necessitated greater coordination with private land owners. East of the 100th meridian (approximately the easternmost line delineating the Texas panhandle) a wetter climate, and hence more productive land, had allowed smaller farms to prosper. Altogether, this meant there were a lot more land owners to consult and that stock need not be as dispersed as in the West nor, for that very reason, would they be as vulnerable to predators.

Both factors militated against a smoothly functioning cooperative control program such as Fish and Wildlife had long operated. It is striking that while a national border would prove porous to the federal government's poisons, the 100th meridian—a delineator of rainfall—would prove a substantial (although not consistent) obstacle to Fish and Wildlife Service expansion.

As seen, Wisconsin and Michigan had rejected the old Biological Survey in 1932 and 1935, respectively, in favor of bounties. The following decade two other midwestern states, Missouri and Kansas, also began to slip from the agency's fold. In the case of Kansas, the western-most of the four states and bisected by the 100th meridian, the Fish and Wildlife Service would not leave without a fight.

Stanley Young had targeted Kansas for expansion of his and the survey's responsibilities when he took over the Colorado district in 1921. His optimism had bubbled forth in his fiscal year 1923 report to Washington, written less than three weeks after he and Bill Caywood returned from the latter's four-month stint trapping coyotes in northwestern Kansas—the first and last time Young had been able to institute cooperation within the state. Young wrote, "We are of the opinion that cooperation will be forthcoming on a larger scale from this state in the near future, and it is felt the program as outlined by the Biological Survey will in due course of time be inaugurated in Kansas and financed in the main by the aid of state and county funds."[40]

Instead, the state's officials had persisted in championing bounties for coyotes, even as those payments ballooned into thousands of dollars annually and strained the state's budget. The Biological Survey and later the Fish and Wildlife Service offered their services within Kansas at various times after 1923; and in 1941, 1948, 1950, and 1961 the agency entered into temporary cooperative arrangements with state officials. But the agreements were never made permanent, to the frustration of Fish and Wildlife Service officials.

In 1949 the Kansas State Legislature followed Missouri's lead from three years before and began requiring counties that wanted to offer bounties (half of which were reimbursed by the state) to first contact the state agricultural college and work with extension agents on a county-wide control program. Unlike such programs elsewhere, the Fish and Wildlife Service would not be at the helm in directing the extension agents.

From that point on, Kansas's control program evolved in opposite ways to the federal agency's program. Rather than merging larger and larger units for comprehensive control and trying to suppress the entire coyote population, as pioneered by the survey, extension agents in Kansas targeted individual depredating coyotes. For that purpose, traps and not poison were the weapons of choice.[41] That allowed many non-depredating coyotes to maintain their territories and keep out young, dispersing coyotes seeking new territories—in other words, to keep out competitors that would not be familiar with the patterns of local prey populations and would thus be more likely to turn to sheep.

The success of the Kansas program in reducing livestock losses led many of the state's counties to opt out of offering bounties. As the program evolved, the extension agents spent more of their time teaching individual farmers how to trap for themselves or otherwise better protect their stock. The system encouraged personal responsibility in preventing losses.

By killing fewer coyotes and specifically targeting the ones responsible for attacks on livestock, Kansas and Missouri had stumbled onto a means of keeping such losses to a minimum. These states had, in effect, pioneered a viable alternative (at least in the Midwest) to the two established systems for dealing with predators: the bounty and the cooperative federal control program.

But it was more than stumbling that made the Kansas system work. Five years before the system was inaugurated, in 1944, forty-two-year-old E. Raymond Hall had moved back to his home state to chair the zoology department at the University of Kansas in Lawrence and direct its natural history museum. Hall's move reflected his frustration at having served for six years, since Joseph Grinnell's death in 1939, as acting director of the University of California at Berkeley's Museum of Vertebrate Zoology without being named its director—in consequence of his outspokenness over the federal control program. Within a few years of his return, he would direct the state's own academically-oriented Biological Survey, modeled on the federal agency of that name in its early days before the era of control.[42]

Hall built both of the institutions he took over in Kansas into world-class centers of scholarship, reflecting his prodigious output of 350 scientific publications throughout his career. But he also made time to meet and get to know people in power in Kansas. He played a key role in conceiving the Kansas extension trapper program and prompting its formative legislation and in establishing its operating principles, such as eschewing poison. Eventually, in 1969, his former student and protégé, F. Robert Henderson, was appointed director of the Kansas program and ran the system until 1995, eleven years after Hall's death.[43]

But in 1944, at his arrival, Hall probably could not have guessed that establishing himself beyond, but temptingly close to, the Fish and Wildlife Service's western empire would finally give him the opportunity to best the agency on the political battlefield. It only took another three decades for him to do so.

Since the 1961 temporary agreement had been reached between Kansas and the bureau, Hall had complained to officials in President John F. Kennedy's administration about the impacts of poisoning.[44] The new president's secretary of the interior, former Arizona congressman Stewart L. Udall, had just been appointed and was ambitious to enact conservation reforms. With broad policy latitude—first from Kennedy and, after the president's assassination on November 22, 1963, extended by President Lyndon B. Johnson[45]—Udall pursued the establishment of a new series of public seashores to be preserved by the National Park Service, enactment of legislation establishing a system of wilderness areas forever protected from motorized incursions, a permanent funding mechanism to protect land from development, and a host of other initiatives inspired largely by Aldo Leopold's "land ethic" as articulated in *A Sand County Almanac*.[46]

But in an era of increasing public appreciation for natural beauty, predator control was still a sensitive subject. Udall had been raised on a ranch in the eastern Arizona town of St. Johns astride the Little Colorado River. With this background and three terms as a western congressman under his belt, he understood well the political danger in taking on the Bureau of Sport Fisheries and Wildlife—the new operational name, since 1956, for the Fish and Wildlife Service (which continued to exist as the shell entity supervising the bureau but consisted only of an extra layer of bureaucracy and not as a functioning agency).

A growing number of members of Congress answered to constituents who felt menaced by technological progress and who sought salvation in nature. The advent of nuclear warfare against Japanese cities in August 1945 had demonstrated the fearful lethality of science in the service of the sword. Science tethered to ploughshares, it turned out, might prove just as deadly. In 1962 a bombshell of a book appeared, authored by federally employed marine biologist Rachel Carson. *Silent Spring* warned that new agricultural insecticides and herbicides were poised to wipe out bird populations and threatened human health as well. "On the mornings that had once throbbed with the dawn chorus of robins, catbirds, doves, jays, wrens, and scores of other bird voices there was now no sound," Carson prophesied darkly in her first chapter. "Only silence lay over the fields and woods and marsh."[47]

In this intellectual atmosphere, government poisoning of predators and rodents was bound to be viewed quite differently than it had been in the past. Unlike the early 1930s, the last time significant opposition to the Biological Survey had garnered the attention of Congress, by the early 1960s an entire generation had been raised during a period of robust expansion of economic opportunities and without having to worry about poverty in their old age. Franklin D. Roosevelt's Social Security program enabled many people to consider matters of public policy through a prism not of fear for economic survival but rather of concern for how the world might be ideally constituted. Massive poisoning of wildlife seemed to epitomize the lack of foresight and sensitivity that generation was turning against.

Events in the nation's capital over the next decade—the issuance of reports, holding of congressional hearings, enactment of laws, and decisive action by the executive branch—may have appeared like a film of the brouhaha in the early 1930s, spooled in reverse or proceeding in proper order but animated by an inversion of values. Few people alive in the 1960s, however, had been close enough to events in the earlier era to gain a sense of déjà vu. E. Raymond Hall was one of those people. Another was Stanley Young.

Young had retired from federal service when required by law on his seventieth birthday, October 30, 1959. He had one last unpaid contract, however, to write a book on the history of predator control[48]—in essence, to tease out and synthesize the strands of practice and policy that were the heart of much of his previous writing.

Clearly, Young paid enough attention to public affairs to understand where his legacy was headed. The sense of legacy, personal adventure written onto the land, is how he had made sense of his life. The boy who grew up by the river that had carried Lewis and Clark; the young man who wandered, prospected, raised stock, and always hunted—these loose ends of manhood had found their coherence and meaning in the successful federal career to follow. This last book, titled "Management of Injurious Mammals in the United States: Its History and Philosophy," was his chance to have, as it were, the last word.[49]

But Young's writing in this final work is curiously flat. He could not help but realize that wiping out the last wolves decades previously would be increasingly regarded not as heroic but as tragically shortsighted. Absent the heroic element, his prose reads as a bland recitation of events, with nothing to enliven them. The work was never published.

Instead, the heart of Aldo Leopold's land ethic, disseminated more and more widely through A Sand County Almanac, was partially written into federal law. It was pushed and prodded into something called the Endangered Species Act by, among others, that indefatigable agitator from the Kansas prairie, E. Raymond Hall.

Not His to Take Away

t is not clear precisely what prompted congressional stirrings of revolt against the Bureau of Sport Fisheries and Wildlife's cooperative control program in the early 1960s, but the issue of poisoning had never ceased to invite controversy. In November 1959, Arthur H. Carhart (Stanley P. Young's old friend and co-author of *The Last Stand of the Pack*) published an article in the magazine *Sports Afield* entitled "Poisons—The Creeping Killer." Carhart attacked the bureau and its use of Compound 1080 and, presaging Rachel Carson's more detailed arguments in *Silent Spring*, also warned of new insecticides such as DDT. Nervous bureau officials, carefully monitoring Carhart's writing, had "tried to sway him into a broader article on insecticides, herbicides, etc.," according to the director of the agency's Wildlife Research Laboratory in Denver, so as to lessen the indictment of their agency by comparison. Nonetheless, Carhart's article focused on the poisoning of vertebrate animals and explained both the cumulative nature of some poisons and their stability over time—their capacity to render each victim a toxic bait for the next scavenger to arrive.[1]

When *Silent Spring* appeared in 1962, the issue of poisons took on a life of its own, garnering attention largely because of the compelling argument that whatever befell birds, fish, and mammals would not exempt humanity. The general backlash against toxins naturally encompassed skepticism about their use by the Bureau of Sport Fisheries and Wildlife—the only arm of the U.S.

government with its own counter-constituency of scientists and conservationists who had long loathed poisoning.

On April 19, 1962, Representative Silvio O. Conte, a forty-year-old Republican from Massachusetts only in his second term but already seated on the powerful House Appropriations Committee, fired the first shot across Interior's bow by introducing a resolution calling for the secretary of the interior to establish a Special Committee on Predatory Mammal Control. Interior Secretary Stewart L. Udall had already appointed a five-person Advisory Board on Wildlife and Game Management to address management of the national parks, in particular the conundrum posed by exploding elk numbers in Yellowstone. In 1963 he instructed the board to report on predator and rodent control as well.[2]

Like the American Society of Mammalogists' special predator committee appointed in 1924 and the investigators who scrutinized the field activities of the Biological Survey in 1930, the panel was divided between agency insiders and outsiders. The five included two biologists previously connected to the Fish and Wildlife Service: the seventy-three-year-old former chief, Ira N. Gabrielson, and a former assistant chief and aggressive stalwart of control, Dr. Clarence M. Cottam.[3] The board also included a former director of both the Arizona and Colorado state game departments, Thomas L. Kimball, with a background in range ecology and agronomy and recently installed as the head of the hunting-oriented conservation group, the National Wildlife Federation. The final two members were well-respected scientists from academia: Dr. Stanley A. Cain, a botanist at the University of Michigan, plus the committee's chairman from the University of California at Berkeley's Museum of Vertebrate Zoology, A. Starker Leopold, who had been investigating the status of grizzly bears in Mexico and was losing his subjects to Fish and Wildlife Service poison.

A perspective not represented on the committee was that of the recently deceased Rosalie Edge, who had never accepted the necessity of a federal agency to kill animals. On November 12, 1962, the eighty-five-year-old Edge had attended the National Audubon Society's annual meeting in Corpus Christi, Texas. Age had slowed her down but had not halted the steadfast commitment to wildlife protection that had first publicly surfaced at another Audubon meeting thirty-three years earlier.

The conference included a talk by Clifford C. Pressnall, who occupied Young's old position as head of the Branch of Predator and Rodent Control (it had changed from a "Division" in 1948). Pressnall spoke glowingly about the cooperative control program, which he called "an outstanding example of teamwork between industry and government." He emphasized his employees' dedication to conservation, their care in sparing species that were becoming rare, the general reduction in reliance on toxins, and the initiation of research to develop birth control for coyotes as an alternative to killing them.[4] That night at the formal dinner Edge was accorded a seat of honor at the speaker's table and was formally introduced by Audubon president Carl W. Buchheister. The organization she had once battled had, in the later words of Emergency Conservation Committee cofounder Irving Brant, "recovered its virginity."[5] It fought vigorously for birds and, despite inviting Pressnall to speak, had established significant independence from the Bureau of Sport Fisheries and Wildlife.

Rosalie Edge deserved a large part of the credit for this revolution, having pummeled the Audubon Society with adverse publicity and forced out its old corrupt leadership. Now, on November 12, 1962, the Audubon members gave her a standing ovation. She phoned her son that night, redolent with pride.

Edge had spent most of her life as a force for change, but she had not built up the Emergency Conservation Committee as an institution to last beyond her lifetime. The recognition she received represented more than a personal triumph; it also symbolized a passing of the torch to an old institutional nemesis, one that would henceforth help advance her agenda and her values. That phone call was the last time Edge's son spoke with her; ten days later, she died.[6]

In early March 1964 the Advisory Board on Wildlife and Game Management turned in to Interior Secretary Udall its report on "predator and rodent control in the United States," commonly known as the Leopold Report. Like previous reports, its recommendations reflected the committee's split. On the one hand, it criticized vigorously almost every aspect of the control program, from use of Compound 1080 in densities that violated Interior's regulations, to the inadequate factual basis for deciding when to initiate predator and rodent control, to absence of scientific proof that killing animals to control rabies actually helped. The report's summary pulled no punches:

> Federal responsibility for minimizing animal damage is properly assigned to the Fish and Wildlife Service. But the program of animal control, under the Branch of Predator and Rodent Control, has become an end in itself and no longer is a balanced component of an overall scheme of wildlife husbandry and management. In the opinion of this Board, far more animals are being killed than would be required for effective protection of livestock, agricultural crops, wildland resources, and human health. . . .
> [T]he Branch of Predator and Rodent Control has developed into a semi-autonomous bureaucracy whose function in many localities bears scant relationship to real need and less still to scientific management.[7]

Despite this conclusion, the Leopold Report included no recommendations that would force the agency to change. The balance on the committee—two retired federal control adherents, two academics, and one person with a background with state agencies and new responsibilities to a game protection constituency—may account for its dissonance in identifying a structural problem while recommending only cosmetic changes. The committee recommended the appointment of a permanent advisory board on predator and rodent control, a search for a new name that "clearly connotes a broad management function" to replace the "Branch of Predator and Rodent Control," an internal reassessment of the branch's goals, "explicit criteria to guide control decisions," a greater emphasis on research, and the strengthening of federal law to control non-federal access to Compound 1080 and other long-lasting poisons—but nothing to constrain federal use of poison.[8]

Perhaps it was obvious that the committee was not prepared to endorse drastic change. Four months before the report was issued, on November 6, 1963, thirty-seven-year old Democratic congressman from Michigan John D. Dingell, who chaired a subcommittee on wildlife and fisheries, introduced a bill to force the Bureau of Sport Fisheries and Wildlife to use only the Kansas and Missouri model for control.

Dingell was part of what he later called "the old red-shirted hunting fraternity and fishing fraternity."[9] But his early life was also informed by the preservation ethic of the national parks; he worked as a ranger at Rocky Mountain National Park for five summers during his early twenties and one summer at Rainier National Park in Washington state. During his period at Rocky Mountain (although not in the summers), rangers were shooting overpopulated elk by the hundreds, a stark and controversial lesson in an ecosystem out of balance.

The congressman had been elected in 1955 to succeed his father, who had died that fall. Congressman John D. Dingell Senior, also a hunter and a leader in conservation efforts, had introduced his son to his friend Ira Gabrielson.[10] Inspired by his father, Gabrielson, and others, the junior Dingell entered public life deeply imbued with a sense of public service. In 2005 he was the longest-serving member in the House of Representatives, and during his extended tenure, especially in the 1960s and 1970s, Dingell had helped pass every significant conservation measure that became law. Dingell was the most effective conservationist in the House of Representatives since John F. Lacey, the Iowa congressman who had served from 1889 to 1907 (except for one term)—twelve years of that as chairman of the Public Lands Committee—and had played a similarly decisive role in the spate of laws enacted during that period to protect wildlife and wild habitats.

John Dingell did not oppose predator control, but he did oppose extermination. His bill opened with a declaration "that the wolf, the coyote, the mountain lion, the lynx, the bobcat, the several species of bear, and other large, wild carnivores native to North America and commonly known as predatory mammals, are among the wildlife resources of interest and value to the people of the United States." The bill would limit federal "extension mammal control agents" to teaching state personnel, who would then show members of the public how to protect their properties. No state could be assigned more than six such federal agents.[11] In the same congressional session, another Democratic member of Congress from Michigan, Martha Griffiths, introduced a bill that was identical to Dingell's except for one provision: her bill banned the extension mammal control agents from using poison.[12] (Dingell, in a February 2003 interview, stressed that "to achieve the good is often better than to strive for the perfect."[13])

Secretary of the Interior Udall opposed both bills, contending that internal reform was under way and restrictive legislation unnecessary.[14] On July 1, 1965, the bureau moved to begin implementing the wildlife board's recommendations. The Branch of Predator and Rodent Control became the Division of Wildlife Services, and the mammal control agents were renamed "district field assistants."[15] Shortly afterward, Udall appointed botanist Stanley Cain of the wildlife board to be assistant secretary of the interior for fish and wildlife and parks, overseeing several agencies including the Bureau of Sport Fisheries and Wildlife. He also replaced the bureau's chief.

Clearly, change was the scent on the wind and the talk of the bureau. But no other tangible reform seemed forthcoming. In the field, most control work continued unimpeded.

Notwithstanding that the red wolf of the southeastern United States was known to be imperiled, the bureau continued to kill one of the last populations in Arkansas, shifting to state hunters employed and supervised by the federal government only when orders to cease direct federal control efforts were issued. The population was thought to be completely eliminated as a result.[16] In Arizona and New Mexico the agency continued to kill the few remaining Mexican gray wolves that crossed the border from Mexico every few years, notwithstanding that it had already deprived this subspecies of any substantial sanctuary south of the border as well.[17]

In South Dakota in the summer of 1965, the bureau poisoned one of the largest remaining populations of prairie dogs remaining on the plains, despite protests from biologists who had reason to believe the region was the last stronghold of the blackfooted ferret and who appealed to Cain to cancel the poisoning.[18] In southern California throughout the 1960s, some of the last California condors—black-and-white scavengers with wing spans in excess of nine feet—were poisoned by the bureau's Compound 1080. The Museum of Vertebrate Zoology acquired one condor carcass to preserve its skeleton but could not use the museum's standard absterging procedure of allowing beetle larvae to consume the feathers and flesh off the bones—the condor's remains killed off the entire colony of larvae.[19]

In the case of each predator—the red wolf, Mexican gray wolf, and blackfooted ferret—the Fish and Wildlife Service did its job so well in the 1960s that the next decade, when its marching orders were finally changed by Congress, the last remaining members of each species had to be captured alive for an emergency captive breeding program to ward off extinction and provide a seed stock for reintroduction. Condors lasted a decade longer, but with one killed in November 1983 by a sodium cyanide gun and others dying from ingesting lead shot in carcasses, the giant birds also had to be taken in for their own good. The last condor was captured on Easter Sunday 1987 for a similar captive breeding program.[20]

In February 1966, Cain testified about his reform efforts before the House Subcommittee on Fisheries and Wildlife Conservation chaired by Dingell. It became apparent that the reformer brought in to steer the federal wildlife bureaucracy in a new direction was being steered by his agency. Dingell sympathized with Cain's intent and the difficulty of changing an entrenched bureaucracy. "But actually," the congressman asked, his incredulity growing at a series of nebulous answers by Cain, "you really as of this time have nothing to show this committee in terms of concrete changes, with the exception of revision of the internal structure of your agency. . . . Am I correct?"

"You are not completely correct," Cain answered.

"But I am sort of correct?" Dingell pressed.

"You are essentially correct," the scientist-cum-bureaucrat conceded.[21]

E. Raymond Hall told the subcommittee that "[h]istory repeats itself" and that, as in the shake-up three decades before, "the 700 to 900 employees in the field are not about to change. They know," he said presciently, "that the average tenure is short for the makers of policy; many of the 700 have served under more than one Director, Assistant Secretary, and Secretary and aim to serve under several more." Unless the system is changed, he warned, "we have every reason to expect the deplorable practices to be back again, and in a few years the juggernaut itself bigger than ever."[22]

Another poisoning opponent, Paul Maxwell of Grand Junction, Colorado, representing the National Trappers Association, compared sheep ranchers and the federal employees who did their bidding to "dope fiends," adding, "[t]hey just can't do without it. There are no extremes they won't go to in order to get poison and will break every law of God and man to use it for their selfish, inhuman purposes."[23]

The National Wool Growers Association, the Farm Bureau, and four western congressmen spoke up for increased control. George K. Hislop from Utah, president of the Wool Growers Association, tried to refute the perception that the control program was wiping out predators, prompting Dingell to offer the mountain lion, grizzly bear, and wolf as counter examples. "Is this necessarily bad?" responded Hislop, referring to extinction of the wolf. "I am not discussing goodness or badness," said Dingell. "I am not fencing with you. It is true that the wolf and grizzly bear are extinct in many large areas of the United States?" Hislop conceded that they were.[24]

The momentum had turned against the control program, but the question remained as to how far Congress would take reforms. Democrats controlled both chambers and were naturally inclined to work cooperatively with the Democratic president, Lyndon B. Johnson. Despite the growing movement to rein in the bureau, the administration's opposition prevailed, and neither Dingell's nor Griffiths's reform bills received consideration by the full House.[25]

The opposition to federally coordinated predator and rodent control did not go away. Instead, it became one of the streams in a broader torrent of concern—one that echoed the earlier sentiments and language of William T. Hornaday and Rosalie Edge—over extinction.

On June 5, 1965, Udall sent draft legislation to Congress intended to "conserve, protect, restore, and where necessary to establish wild populations [and] propagate selected species of native fish and wildlife . . . that are found to be threatened with extinction." The secretary, as early as August 1964, had issued a list of sixty-three "rare or endangered species," and by 1966 the list included eighty-three species.[26]

The administration bill, entitled the Endangered Species Preservation Act, prohibited the killing of endangered species on national wildlife refuges and authorized (subject to the annual appropriations cycles) the purchase of additional refuges for the purpose of protecting rare animals. It also encouraged, although vaguely, broader cooperation and habitat conservation within the Interior Department in the service of endangered species protection—but only to the "extent practicable."[27]

Dingell introduced the bill, and with little controversy it passed on October 15, 1966. But it had no practical effect on slowing down the Bureau of Sport Fisheries and Wildlife, since wildlife refuges constituted a small minority of the western landscape and the endangered wildlife they held—such as whooping cranes—was already protected by administrative policy.

Passage of the Endangered Species Preservation Act ultimately created a lasting imprint not by directly changing human activities in the homes of wild creatures but through providing statutory backing to a specific template for future attempts to reform wildlife policy. The law took a different approach than reform attempts based on banning or limiting specific activities destructive to wildlife, such as poisoning or, in the case of the 1964 Wilderness Act, motorized travel and industrial activity. Instead, the 1966 act focused on identifying and classifying which species were imperiled, designating them as "endangered," and changing policies on a species-specific basis. When refined in two future endangered species laws to be passed over the course of seven years, this model proved to have the winning combination of political support and conservation effectiveness sufficient not just to check predator control but also to sharply curtail the work of a host of other public institutions responsible for tearing apart the natural world.

But that winning combination was hardly apparent at first. In the short term, growing adverse publicity and opposition on the ground challenged the Bureau of Sport Fisheries and Wildlife. In particular, the agency faced increasing opposition east of the 100th meridian—that delineator of rainfall that now seemed to delineate bureaucratic turf as well.

On September 26, 1966, the bureau finally secured its coveted long-term cooperative control agreement in Kansas. The agreement was signed by the state's Republican governor, William H. Avery, at the behest of the Kansas Livestock Association, less than a month and a half before the November elections without any announcement to the public. Although the promised federal aid may have swayed some ranchers to vote for him, Avery lost to Democratic challenger Robert Docking.

By then, the sixty-four-year-old E. Raymond Hall was highly influential. Officials knew he was one of the giant figures in the field of biology, drawing some of the best and brightest young people from throughout the nation to study in Kansas. His students occupied positions of responsibility, and his long-term active courtship of other influential people made him a force to be reckoned with. In contrast, the Bureau of Sport Fisheries and Wildlife was a stranger.

When news about the agreement broke in April 1967, it was roundly condemned, even by some ranchers. The *Kansas City Star* editorialized against "a Frankenstein army of Federal exterminators" and urged the new governor, a member of the Kansas Livestock Association, to abrogate the agreement.[28]

The state's functional system of limiting depredations—rendered even more practical by the smaller, more manageable size of many eastern Kansas farms—militated against any ostensible predator crisis and the proffered federal solution. But the final shove was Hall's. He visited Governor Docking, a longtime acquaintance, and delivered an ultimatum "that it was either me or them [the federal agency]. And I was earnest about it," he recalled sternly to the writer of an *Audubon Magazine* article published in 1984, shortly before his death. The governor terminated the agreement and asked Hall to write the letter informing the federal agency of the change in policy. Hall stayed on as Kansas's star scientist and the overseer of a small but powerful academic empire.[29]

Resistance against federal control in Kansas was matched by growing momentum in Washington, D.C., to protect endangered species. In February 1967, less than four months after the Endangered Species Preservation Act was signed into law, Representative Dingell introduced an amendment drafted by the Interior Department that would prohibit trade in endangered species, including foreign creatures. This bill, unlike the last one, aroused the opposition of the fur industry, which succeeded in weakening it and delayed its passage for over two years.[30]

The bureau, characteristically, was not passive in the face of the building momentum for protection of rare animals and the integrity of the natural world. In April 1969 it issued its hunters a handbook to ensure that they put forth the best possible image. "Much of the terminology that has been used over the years is for various reasons now distasteful to some segments of the public and there is need for a careful review of verbal and written expressions," the manual advised. It continued: "We think the word 'poison' should be replaced by 'toxicant' or 'toxic chemical compounds' or other appropriate phraseology. 'Kill' should be replaced by 'reduction' or 'removal.'"[31]

This time, however, the old lexical tricks did not suffice to screen cooperative federal control from unfriendly eyes. Perhaps the bureau's spirit had been weakened by over twenty years within the lackluster Department of the Interior, and its staff in the Division of Wildlife Services may not fully have been up to the immense challenge. The most direct threat to the bureau, a law banning it from killing animals, was defeated. But a new law passed that ultimately rolled back the agency's signature accomplishment, the elimination of wolves, and limited how and where the agency exercised control. Could that old master of office intrigue, Stanley Young, possibly have staved off such an unthinkable train of events? We do not know what outline of the future Young foresaw from his cancer deathbed. Bureaucrat emeritus, general of the corps of federal trappers and poisoners, and chronicler of their exploits, Stanley Paul Young died on May 15, 1969, at age seventy-nine. He was survived by his wife, Nydia, and son, Acker.

Young had spent his last years active and engaged. He cultivated rose bushes, socialized at the exclusive Cosmos Club of Washington, continued writing and publishing articles, and kept up a correspondence with friends and admiring strangers.[32] "Shall look forward to reading the article in the 'Post' about your pet wolf, Kunu. I, too, hope the wolf will never disappear as part of our fauna," he wrote to a Seattle man who had contacted him in 1963, adding:

Have thought about the problem of stirring up enough interest among some of the "wildlifers" to establish some sort of a sanctuary for it, but the trouble would be to get him (the wolf) to stay put in such a set up, and there are many other problems that arise too. So much so that I fear it is not a practical idea.[33]

In the foreword to his final unpublished manuscript chronicling and defending the cooperative federal control program, Young opened with the phrase "[e]very book is a deed—bad or good." In introducing his would-be book, he seemed to veer into an unexpected retrospective of the deeds on which it was based:

An author, writing even with the best of faith may have moments of doubt, whether instead of bread he did not give poison, whether his work is not a great mistake or misdeed, whether it has brought profit to humanity, or whether, were it not better for the people and himself, had he not written anything, nothing accomplished.

But that was the most he would concede to the drumbeats of reform. "The control, or management if you please, of injurious mammals," he continued, "has always been a controversial issue." He added, "Much of this criticism originates from sincere but musguided [sic] individuals who are unacquainted with many of the facts of the case. Mammal control has served, and still serves, a vital purpose, of great value to public health, the stockmen, nurserymen, agriculturists, sportsmen, and others."[34]

On December 5, 1969, President Richard M. Nixon signed the strengthening measure, newly renamed the "Endangered Species Conservation Act, initiated

A triumph of persistence and savvy aided by reliable rainfall. In 1967, Dr. E. Raymond Hall convinced the governor of Kansas to evict the Bureau of Sport Fisheries and Wildlife and its poisons. (University Archives, Spencer Research Library, University of Kansas Libraries)

by the previous administration. Nixon's attitude toward this and a minor blizzard of other environmental legislation he was about to sign stemmed entirely from political considerations. In private, he despised environmental activists as "hopeless softheads," but at the beginning of his first term he hoped to build an image as an aggressive environmentalist and gain the support of the disaffected, ecology-minded young voters (whose ranks swelled in the next presidential election because of passage in 1971 of a constitutional amendment guaranteeing the right to vote to those age eighteen or older).[35]

Nixon's quest for the environmentalist vote eventually faltered in the face of adept Democratic opponents in Congress, including 1972 presidential challenger Edmund Muskie, a senator from Maine who offered greater credibility in his long-standing advocacy for environmental measures. Despite this advantage, Muskie ended his bid during the primary, and the eventual Democratic nominee, Senator George McGovern of South Dakota, was overwhelmingly defeated in November 1972 in spite of his support from environmentally conscious youth.

Nixon began spending less political capital on environmental initiatives in 1971, and eventually, in March 1974, he admonished his cabinet to "get off the environmental kick."[36] Ironically, however, the policy development already under way, and the authority he had vested in a handful of senior aides who cared about the natural world, resulted in the biggest turnaround for the animal control establishment since its inception—as well as similarly seismic shifts in wildlife policy in other arenas.

That reversal was galvanized by resistance in the West. In Colorado, a bastion of Young's empire, state regulations issued in 1969 banned the use of poisons. But neither state nor its own regulations were about to stop the bureau, which spread poisons throughout the state at will.[37]

Notwithstanding its new manual instructing its poisoners to call the contents of their baits "toxic chemical compounds," the agency's improprieties were gaining visibility. In fall 1969 the Defenders of Wildlife, a small but rapidly growing membership organization for which E. Raymond Hall served as vice-president, ran an article in its newsletter on the poisoning program in central Colorado's Pitkin County. In this single county the Defenders of Wildlife's ecologist, Dr. Alfred G. Etter (who had lost a dog to government poison), wrote that the bureau had violated ten of its own regulations, several repeatedly. Compound 1080 was applied at much higher densities than allowed, was used in places that were supposed to be off-limits, and in multiple other ways was used by the government hunter entirely as expedient—with no regard for the latest iteration of official policy.[38]

Then, in early 1970 the Defenders of Wildlife ran an article and photos that revealed surreptitious government poisoning on a southern Arizona ranch belonging to an absentee American diplomat, whose adult daughter managed it and forbade poisoning on the premises. She had discovered on the property the partial carcasses of a horse and a cow, with poison warning signs erected, and five coyotes and a raven already dead nearby. She buried the entire bait station and contacted the Defenders of Wildlife. Two weeks later the disgruntled poisoner (whose salary was paid by the bureau's cooperator, the Farm Bureau–dominated Federal Extension Service), returned to the ranch. In his rage over the halting of his project he seized a shovel and, in the presence of a ranch employee, beat a pig to death—behavior not explicitly covered in the bureau's employee policy manual and one the Defenders of Wildlife noted without editorial comment in their article.[39]

In May of that year, Boy Scouts near Casper, Wyoming, stumbled upon several dead eagles. Members of the local Audubon chapter searched the region and uncovered the carcasses of two dozen bald and golden eagles, which turned out to have been poisoned by thallium sulfate. In June the Senate held hearings to investigate the matter.

That June, *New Yorker Magazine* ran a lengthy cover article, written with understated eloquence by journalist Faith McNulty, about rodent control on the South Dakota prairie and the impending extinction of the blackfooted ferret.[40] Despite elaborate regulations imposed in the mid-1960s by Stanley Cain under Interior Secretary Udall's general shake-up of the agency, prairie dog control was wiping out the last stronghold of the blackfooted ferret. McNulty documented the ins and outs of prairie dog ecology and the bizarre bureaucratic ecology of a conflicted Department of the Interior. Her article was republished in 1971 as the book *Must They Die? The Strange Case of the Prairie Dog and the Black-Footed Ferret*, a title that presaged equally direct prose. "The sky was beautifully clear, the sun benevolent and warm," she wrote in the book's final passage, continuing:

> The wind pressed the grass into silver waves ahead of the work crew, who were now walking from crater to crater on a methodical course, dropping poisoned oats from long-handled spoons as though they were leaving a tiny gift on each doorstep. The prairie dogs had disappeared.
>
> "They don't come out and eat right away," McDaniel [the bureau's worker] said. "But if you come back later and watch, you'll see 'em feeding. Then, all of a sudden, you'll hear that little ol' dog scream, and see him head for his hole."[41]

The spotlight of negative publicity, once trained on the Bureau of Sport Fisheries and Wildlife, proved unrelenting. In 1971 another exposé of the agency appeared in print. True crime writer Jack Olsen, churning out investigative non-fiction while living in idyllic splendor in Colorado's mountains, had stumbled on the poisoning story and wrote *Slaughter the Animals, Poison the Earth,* first excerpted in successive issues of the magazine *Sports Illustrated.* The book chronicled federal poisoners out of control and the destruction they wrought along with cooperating sheep ranchers. The narrative jumped around the American West, naming names and citing episode after episode in a grisly succession of poisoned dogs, eagles, bears, and even human beings. Olsen documented the gunning down of antelope from the air simply to poison the carcasses, as well as the systematic aerial poisoning of wildlife sanctuaries that were officially protected. *Slaughter the Animals* indicted the bureau as the central cog in a sheep ranchers' culture of poisoning that knew no limits and a blatant violator of all the gentle homilies on responsible control that had so often been written into official policy.[42]

In March 1971 the Defenders of Wildlife and the Sierra Club filed suit against the bureau, followed the next month by the Humane Society of the United States—all demanding more detailed analysis of the effects of its killing program, as required by the 1970 National Environmental Policy Act. With public outrage at the poisoning at a fine boil, members of Congress demanding action, and marching orders from the president to get out in front of environmental policies so as not to cede the high ground to his Democratic challengers, in April three senior Nixon administration officials met to plan the dismantlement of the cooperative federal animal control program.[43]

Russell E. Train, born in 1920, had served as a congressional aide, Treasury Department lawyer, and a tax judge. In 1956 he had gone to Africa on a hunting safari and was stunned and moved by what he saw. "We were enthralled by the strangeness and beauty around us," he recalled in his 2003 memoirs after over twenty more trips to the continent—only one of which was to hunt. He reminisced about the "Masai warriors leaning on their spears, the early morning chill, the quiet breeze that flowed through the camp at first light, the sibilant calling of the doves in the dawn, the heat of midday spent in the shade of an acacia, the hot, dry smell of the African earth, the spoor of the passing game." The game itself, as he called his prey, was part of that beauty:

> elephants bathing in a stream below, the gentle grace of giraffes browsing
> through the thorn trees, the tension and concentration of the hunt, the
> beauty and incredible variety of the birds, the sundowner beside the fire
> and the tales told at such a time, the soft sound of African voices, the
> nights full of stars, the occasional roar of a distant lion, the call of a hyena.[44]

In 1959 Train founded the African Wildlife Leadership Foundation to set up infrastructure and policies to preserve wildlife in African nations. Six years later he left government service to take the helm of another international conservation organization.[45] His sojourn in the non-profit world did not last long. Nixon recruited the loyal Republican to help create and oversee the administration's environmental policy. It was in this capacity that Train, along with presidential scientific adviser Dr. Lee Talbot and Secretary of the Interior C. B. Morton, decided to do something about the federal poisoning corps. The first step was to conduct another formal examination of the issue.

On July 9, 1971, Morton convened a new panel to scrutinize predator control. "I personally pledge," Morton said, "that performance will follow program so that our imperiled predators will not perish in a sea of platitudes."[46]

The new investigative committee, chaired by Stanley Cain, who in 1968 had returned to academia after his three-year stint as assistant secretary of the interior, was composed entirely of non-bureau scientists—again including A. Starker Leopold. Their 207-page report, named for the chairman and completed on October 30, 1971, echoed the strong language of the Leopold Report of seven years before, including criticism of the bureau's institutional culture. "It is clear that the basic machinery of the federal cooperative-supervised program contains a high degree of built-in resistance to change," the Cain Report charged. It continued, "The substantial monetary contribution by the livestock industry serves as a gyroscope to keep the bureaucratic machinery pointed towards the familiar goal of general reduction of predator popula- tions, with little attention to the effects of this on the native wildlife fauna."

But the Cain Report went one crucial step farther than its predecessors in committee review. "Guidelines and good intentions will no longer suffice," it urged and advised, among fifteen recommendations, banning the bureau's arsenal of poisons.[47]

The Nixon administration waited over three months to make the report public, and when it did so, on February 8, 1972, it was in the context of a broad- ranging environmental policy speech by the president, addressed to Congress. In seventeen pages of remarks, Nixon unveiled new administrative programs, suggested legislation, and announced executive orders. He asked Congress to designate an additional 1.3 million acres of areas protected from motorized incursions (although not from grazing or predator control) by authority of the 1964 Wilderness Act; announced programs to regulate off-road vehicle use of public lands, limit air and water pollution, and protect children from lead- based paint; and resurrected former secretary of the interior Harold L. Ickes's old idea of merging the Departments of Interior and Agriculture, this time into a single "Department of Natural Resources."

Nixon's words harmonized his diverse platform around Aldo Leopold's "land ethic"—a phrase the president used but did not cite (and almost cer- tainly could not have attributed) but one his speech's likely author, Russell Train, would have well understood.

"The time has come for man to make his peace with nature," Nixon pro- claimed in the introduction to his remarks. "[T]o a significant extent man com- mands . . . the very destiny of this planet where he lives, and the destiny of all life upon it. We have even begun to see that these destinies are not many and separate at all—that in fact they are indivisibly one. This is the environmental awakening," he proclaimed, explaining:

> It marks a new sensitivity of the American spirit and a new maturity of American public life. It is working a revolution in values, as commitment to responsible partnership with nature replaces cavalier assumptions that we can play God with our surroundings and survive. It is leading to broad reforms in action, as individuals, corporations, government, and civic groups mobilize to conserve resources, to control pollution, to anticipate and prevent emerging environmental problems, to manage the land more wisely, and to preserve wildness.

When it came to predators and other imperiled species, Nixon's remarks did justice to this clarion call:

> Wild places and wild things constitute a treasure to be cherished and protected for all time. The pleasure and refreshment which they give man

Environmental aide Russell E. Train was the moving force behind President Richard M. Nixon's banning of poisons in February 1972 and the president's concurrent proposal to pass a new endangered species law. Here Train meets with Nixon in July 1973, five months before the president signs the Endangered Species Act into law. (Nixon Presidential Materials Staff, National Archives and Records Administration, College Park, MD)

confirm their value to society. More importantly perhaps, the wonder, beauty, and elemental force in which the least of them share suggest a higher right to exist—not granted to them by man and not his to take away.

Summarizing the Cain Committee's findings in his speech, Nixon announced that "persistent poisons have been applied to range and forest lands without adequate knowledge of their effects on the ecology or their utility in preventing losses to livestock. The large-scale use of poisons for control of predators and field rodents has resulted in unintended losses of other animals."[48] Nixon announced an executive order banning use of poisons for federal predator and bird control (but not for rodent control) and banning federal use of any toxicant that causes secondary poisoning. He allowed for exceptions in cases of emergency but defined such situations narrowly. Another executive order barred anyone from poisoning federal lands and called for canceling the grazing lease of any violator. Yet another measure stopped interstate shipment of the same poisons evicted from federal lands and barred from federal use. And just to be sure, Nixon called on Congress to pass a bill drafted by his administration, titled the Animal Damage Control Act of 1972.

This legislation went beyond the Cain Committee's recommendations in that it would repeal the 1931 law of the same name and carry forward Representative Dingell's previous efforts to confine the federal role in control operations to advising the states. But most of the bill's provisions took their lead from the Cain Report and its insistence that the "bureaucratic machinery" of cooperative control be dismantled. To ensure the states would follow the Kansas and Missouri models and not maintain the cooperative control program, during a three-year transitional period the federal government would help fund state control operations—but only if matching state monies were entirely appropriated by their legislatures. No more would stock associations, counties, and game departments be permitted to chip in funds from coffers over which the state legislature had little, if any, direct control. And the bill would codify into law the administrative order banning poisons so no future president could unilaterally re-initiate widespread poisoning.[49]

After mentioning these executive orders and the Animal Damage Control Act of 1972, Nixon moved to the next cure in his environmental pharmacopoeia. Following a Cain Report recommendation that Congress pass legislation to protect endangered predators, the president presented another administration bill, the Endangered Species Conservation Act of 1972, which he said would "make the taking of endangered species a Federal offense for the first time, and would permit protective measures to be undertaken before a species is so depleted that regeneration is difficult or impossible." In effect, he proposed a comprehensive program to rescue animals from extinction, largely to be implemented by the Department of the Interior.[50]

That same day, Representative Dingell and twenty-four co-sponsors introduced both pieces of legislation (jointly drafted by the administration and Dingell's subcommittee staff). Hearings on the bills and on over two dozen similar measures (including some to ban trapping and other "inhumane" methods of killing animals), introduced with broad bipartisan support, commenced the following month, March 1972.[51]

Once again, the livestock industry and its institutional allies in animal control stoked the well-oiled political machinery that had so effectively served the cause in the past. This time, most likely (documentation has not come to light) the American Farm Bureau Federation provided leadership that the Bureau of Sport Fisheries and Wildlife could no longer muster. (The ranchers' lack of confidence in the bureau's political effectiveness was reflected in one of their counterrequests to Congress—that the agency be transferred out of Interior and back to the Agriculture Department.[52])

Local elected officials throughout the West passed resolutions condemning the executive orders. Representatives of western states' woolgrowers associations brought coyote-killed lambs into a congressional hearing room to provide corporal evidence of the need for poisons. The grassroots ranching backlash against the anti-poisoning initiatives was strong enough to turn one of the original sponsors of the 1972 Animal Damage Control bill, Representative

Robert L. Leggett, a Democrat from California who sat on Dingell's subcommittee that considered the bill, into an active opponent of his own legislation. Western members of Congress lined up to testify against the legislation.[53] "I think," admonished Representative George Mahon of Texas in his committee testimony in March 1973, "bad animals ought to be put in their place." He continued: "We hear talk about the cruelty to the coyote. Well, I am not concerned about cruelty to the coyote because he is a bad animal, a destructive animal. I am concerned about the cruelty to the lamb, to the sheep, to the young calf, the victims of the coyote."[54]

But the coyotes and even their larger and more dreaded canine cousins commanded lawmakers' attention and demanded their sympathies as well. Republican representative George A. Goodling of Pennsylvania, who also sat on Dingell's subcommittee, responded to the remarks of Mahon and other members of the Texas delegation by noting that a wolf on a leash had been active in his district: "Right now I am busy answering letters coming from the high school students with this plea, 'Please save our wolves.'"[55]

The Animal Damage Control Act of 1972 passed in the House of Representatives on July 17, 1972, but did not come to a vote in the Senate before adjournment for the November elections[56]—reflecting the fact that each senator had far greater power to halt legislation than individual representatives customarily exercised. Despite its introduction in both the House and the Senate again the next year, the ban on poisons and dismantlement of the federal control apparatus were never enacted into law.

In committing all its political capital to the successful fight against the anti-poison, anti–federal control legislation, the ranching establishment had nothing left to spend to oppose the broader endangered species bill, which presented a vaguer threat and in the spring of 1972 was being considered in the same four hearings in which testimony on the Animal Damage Control Act had been proceeding in the wake of Nixon's February announcement. Representatives for neither the Farm Bureau nor woolgrowers organizations testified against the bill—perhaps because opposition to the goal of protecting wildlife would impeach their credibility in standing up for the use of poisons.

One of the few people to testify against the endangered species legislation was the president of the Wildlife Management Institute, previously known as the American Game Protective Association—which had counted among its luminaries Aldo Leopold during the teen years of the twentieth century, when he had supported predator extermination, and Ira N. Gabrielson, who had headed the group from the time he left federal service in 1946 until 1970. Gabrielson's successor, Daniel A. Poole, also a veteran of the old Fish and Wildlife Service, suggested amending the bill to pre-empt federal responsibility to protect endangered species by granting individual states primary authority for enforcement. But when it came to the Animal Damage Control Act of 1972, under consideration in the same hearing, Poole testified against it for the converse reason—opposing delegation of this established federal responsibility to the states.[57] (Since 1972 the profession of wildlife management has continued to adhere to this particular view of federal and state responsibilities.)

By this time advocates for animals were at the peak of their power. The Society for Animal Protective Legislation, Defenders of Wildlife, Sierra Club, Fund for Animals, National Audubon Society, Friends of the Earth, and the Humane Society of the United States testified for abolishing federal predator control and for protecting endangered species.[58] The latter measure steadily gained ground in hearing after hearing. It passed the Senate in September 1972, but with no time left for reconciliation with the House bill it did not pass that year. The measure was resurrected in 1973, and the version developed in late 1972 started through another series of committee hearings and further emendations.

Committee members, in effect, solicited a series of seminars by scientific and lay witnesses on the plight of wildlife, the connections between species and their habitats, and what one ardent supporter of the legislation—Senator Alan Cranston, a Democrat from California—called "the unfortunate marriage of man's technological know-how to his ecological myopia."[59]

"Could you enlighten me on this balance of nature?" asked Representative Ralph Metcalfe on April 10, 1972, referring to a phrase from the Cain Report. The newly seated member of Dingell's subcommittee, a Democrat from Illinois, added with genuine curiosity, "Is it necessary to have these predators, and especially do they have their own value?" In response, presidential aide Russell Train, at the witness table, summarized the ecology of predators and their prey and how the absence of predators might disrupt vegetation and the entire ecosystem.[60] Longer-term members of the subcommittee, as well as many of their colleagues with less authority over passage of the bill, had heard their constituents recite the same themes—deeply felt and expressed with urgency—over a period of months and in some cases even years.

Cranston, whose opposition to predator control broke with the position of his western colleagues, told the committee the following day, "In our scramble after 'infinite progress,' we have scarred and mutilated the face of the earth." He believed endangered species protection should not be subject to the give-and-take of the political tides: "[M]an has an ethical and moral responsibility to protect other life forms."[61]

On July 24, 1973, the Endangered Species Act passed the Senate 92 to 0 (with eight senators not voting). On September 18 the House approved it by a vote of 390 to 12 (with 31 abstentions). It then went to a conference committee between the two houses and when it emerged was again approved unanimously by the Senate, on December 19, and the next day approved 345 to 4 by the House.[62]

As the endangered species measure advanced through committees, it became stronger than the original proposed by Nixon's aides. The administration's first version of the bill provided for designating species as either threatened or endangered (the latter closer to extinction) at the government's "discretion." It instructed federal bureaus, agencies, and services to utilize their authorities to protect such species, "insofar as is practicable and consistent" with their primary purposes.[63]

But legislators had witnessed how a federal agency might chart its own course in defiance of congressional intent, and they did not trust the Interior Department. At one hearing Dingell grew frustrated trying to find out how many coyotes the government had killed. "We have been engaging in body counts in Vietnam. Body counts are not very well received by me," he said. "[W]e may just very well decide to call Interior back here and have a day of playing the numbers game with them."[64]

The plight of the grizzly bear at the outskirts of one of its last refuges, Yellowstone National Park, and the prospect of continued federal persecution of the bears and destruction of their habitats led Dingell to require federal agencies to utilize their authorities to protect species regardless of whether it was practical and consistent. The sense that the federal government might stray from conservation unless compelled otherwise was reflected in the precise prescriptive language amended into the bill as it worked its way through committees. The legislation President Nixon ended up signing on December 28, 1973, bristled with the compulsory word *shall*. Species were to be placed on the threatened and endangered species list based on their degree of imperilment as a result of any or all of five factors: habitat loss, hunting, disease or predation, the inadequacy of existing regulations, or "other natural or manmade factors affecting [their] continued existence." The Department of the Interior—and in the case of marine and anadromous species the Commerce Department—was to issue regulations, enter into cooperative agreements with states, and buy land in order to save species and bring them to the point where they could be taken off the list. Neither private entities nor the government were permitted to take any action that would doom a listed species, including destroying its habitat. And citizens were given the right to sue the government—and to recoup their fees if they won—to compel enforcement.[65]

Most of the discussion of endangered species had focused on charismatic mammals and birds such as wolves, blackfooted ferrets, eagles, and whooping cranes (as well as foreign and marine mammals such as elephants, kangaroos, spotted cats, and whales), and the original impetus for Nixon's bill was the recommendation by the Cain Report that endangered predators be protected. In the version of the Endangered Species Act that ended up passing, however—thanks to Dingell's and other committee members' broad understanding of their role in ecosystems—plants and invertebrate animals were also eligible for listing (although plants did not enjoy the same level of protection as animals).[66]

Remarkably, amid the storm of environmental laws enacted from the mid-1960s through the early 1970s—a list that included (among many others) the Wilderness Act (1964), National Environmental Policy Act (1970), Federal Insecticide, Fungicide, and Rodenticide Act (1972; passed to regulate poisons),

Marine Mammal Protection Act (1972), and the two previous endangered species bills—a jaded media failed to note the significance of the 1973 Endangered Species Act. The *New York Times* mentioned the bill's signing in passing, within an article about another act that transferred job-training funds to the states: "In addition to the manpower act today, the President signed bills that do the following: . . . Grant the Government, through the Endangered Species Act of 1973, authority to make early identification of endangered species and to act quickly to save the designated species from extinction."[67] The *Washington Post*, which had repeatedly editorialized in favor of stronger endangered species legislation (in one editorial focusing on the need to rescue wolves), similarly buried the Endangered Species Act's passage in text about another issue.[68]

Perhaps the statement of intent of the Endangered Species Act best bespoke the magnitude of influence it was destined to wield. "The purposes of this Act are to provide a means whereby the ecosystems upon which endangered species and threatened species depend may be conserved," Congress had proclaimed, as well as "to provide a program for the conservation of such endangered species and threatened species."[69]

Wildlife Services

I n 1973 a district supervisor for the Bureau of Sport Fisheries and Wildlife in Wyoming underwent a radical change of heart followed by a revolutionary change of career. Forty-nine-year-old World War II veteran Dick Randall had worked for the agency for ten years in two shifts, with extensive experience in poisoning, aerial gunning, and trapping. He was also an avid photographer and had taken hundreds of pictures of animals dead and waiting to die in his traps.

One day in southern Wyoming's Red Desert, Randall and his eleven-year-old son, Andy, approached a male bobcat that had been struggling for days in one of Randall's traps. The animal had probably dislocated a leg and had bitten through much of the ligament, cartilage, and muscle; but perhaps because of dehydration and shock, he had not succeeded in separating himself from the trap.

As the two walked up on a scene that was routine for the adult Randall, the bobcat mustered the energy for a last, desperate maneuver. "As we walked up, the cat took one furious leap at us," Randall recalled seventeen years later in an interview for *U.S. News and World Report.* "He hit the end of the chain, dropped down and died staring right at us." His son whispered, "Look, Dad. The light just went out in its eyes" and then asked "[w]hy are you doing this, Dad?"

Andy's straightforward question caused Randall to ask himself the same thing. "After being in the Air Force, I believed in our government," he later told

"The light just went out in its eyes," Dick Randall's son, Andy, pointed out to his father as a bobcat died in a trap in front of them in 1973. "Why are you doing this, Dad?" The question inspired Randall to quit his government job and reveal the killings of animals that were officially protected, and other violations of regulations. (J. Stokley Ligon Papers, CONS92, Conservation Collection, Denver Public Library)

reporters. "I never questioned that I was doing humanity a real favor," he said. "I was convinced that the killing was worthwhile."[1]

Seeing his own actions through his son's eyes began kindling in Randall a sense of empathy with the animals he killed. Six months after his epiphany with the dying bobcat, Randall quit the agency, made public his gruesome photos, and began a career representing the Defenders of Wildlife and later the Humane Society of the United States in their campaigns against the control program. He wrote and spoke about the black and grizzly bears, pine martens, badgers, wolverines, and eagles he had poisoned inadvertently; of trapping black bears ("They would look at you and bawl like a baby"); and of thallium-poisoned hairless coyotes huddling in barns for warmth and dispatched with pitchforks.[2]

He also alleged that bureau employees often violated regulations and that hunters were encouraged to turn a blind eye to deaths of protected animals. And he recounted the driving force behind the agency's actions: the never-ending complaints of sheep ranchers.[3]

In the heavy snowfall winter of 1971–1972, Randall wrote in a 1992 article, he and his men had shot hundreds of coyotes from airplanes: "With no place to hide, coyotes were visible from a mile away. One day that winter, I killed 42 coyotes in six hours . . . a state record. In one month I killed 230. Another record." Following up in the spring by digging out coyote dens, he

Dick Randall, denning coyotes before his defection from government predator control: "Smoke den to move pups out of side tunnels where hooks won't reach. If any still breathing, whack 'em!" (Photo by Dick Randall, courtesy of The Humane Society of the United States)

found "it was nearly impossible to find a coyote track, let alone a den of pups: the winter's work had been a job well done." But that year "sheep ranchers reported that predation by coyotes was up slightly on the year before. It appeared that either those sheep-killing coyotes had burrowed into the snow and we missed 'em, or else it was a case of the fairy tales again."[4]

Opponents of the control program welcomed Randall's defection because in the face of ranchers' determination and perseverance, President Richard M. Nixon's executive order banning poisons proved ephemeral. The strategic wisdom in the livestock industry's efforts to prevent enactment of the statutory poison ban became evident after Nixon's impeachment and his resignation on August 8, 1974, followed by the ascent of Vice President Gerald R. Ford to the executive office. On July 18, 1975, Ford amended Nixon's February 8, 1972, executive order. Ford authorized the U.S. Fish and Wildlife Service (the old agency name, restored in 1974) and its "Office of Animal Damage Control" to again set sodium cyanide guns (first known as the "Humane Coyote Getter" but now called simply the M-44), but only for "experimental" use. Less than a year later he issued another order allowing general (non-experimental) use of the device. He also led a successful push to provide Animal Damage Control with an additional $1.2 million in fiscal year 1977.[5]

Appropriations were like desert rainfall to Animal Damage Control, and, not surprisingly, the agency remained true to its roots. Neither law nor regulation was destined to stop an efflorescence of killing wild animals. Between 1975 and 1977 a federal trapper in Texas participated in an organized campaign of gunning down at least 100 golden and bald eagles by helicopter, in defiance of the Bald Eagle Protection Act (which covered both eagle species). After a thorough investigation, in December 1977 he was convicted, fined, and suspended from his job, along with his supervisor. But after the brouhaha died down, both men were quietly rehired.[6]

President Ford's pro-control measures may have played a role in his sweep of the West in the 1976 election; he won every western public-land state. But Georgia governor Jimmy Carter won almost the entire eastern portion of the country and the election as a whole. On January 19, 1977, his last full day in office, President Ford transmitted to Congress proposed legislation to transfer Animal Damage Control from the Department of the Interior to the Department of Agriculture.[7]

The legislation, as Ford surely knew, went nowhere. The president-elect and his Democratic majorities in the House and Senate had no motivation to push through the losing candidate's agenda. The bill was a signal—one not contradicted since—of the Republicans' repudiation of Nixon's conservation record, an affirmation of the party's allegiance to the traditional rulers of the West. (The thank you was remembered: in November 1978, Ford's former chief of staff Richard B. Cheney, the son of a Bureau of Land Management employee, was elected to the House of Representatives from his home in Wyoming.)

Although the Republican Party committed an about-face on wildlife policy between the first Nixon term and the end of Ford's short tenure, the Democrats continued the policies of faux-reform. President Carter's new secretary of the interior, Cecil Andrus (previously the governor of Idaho), followed a venerable tradition whose lineage he probably knew only incompletely by appointing a committee to examine predator control.

Following the committee's recommendations, a new statement of Animal Damage Control policy flourished—one that, like many such policies before it, was billed as a reform but amounted to little real change on the ground. Its most important component was a ban on killing coyote pups in their dens—a ban that left the agency free to inform ranchers about den locations. Even if pups remained unmolested, discovery of a den inevitably entailed killing the adults, thus dooming their offspring to starvation.

Not all aspects of the new policy could be acted upon immediately. The implementation plan for Andrus's policy included as a future objective the development of "criteria for defining unacceptable livestock losses," as well as development of "guidelines for documentation of losses." A mere fifteen years after the 1964 Leopold Report had urged doing so, the Fish and Wildlife Service was almost ready to identify the criteria that would guide site-specific control decisions.[8] Ultimately, however, the November 1980 election of former

California governor Ronald Reagan to the presidency spared the agency the indignity of basing its control decisions on a formula that included calculation of livestock losses.

Reagan had campaigned in the West in favor of the "Sagebrush Rebellion," the revitalized movement to give public lands to individual western states or, if that could not be achieved, to keep site-specific decision making in ranchers' hands. In July 1979 the Nevada State Legislature passed legislation demanding ownership of the public lands in the state and appropriated $250,000 for a campaign to wrest them from federal control. Other western states followed Nevada's lead, and western members of Congress introduced legislation to achieve this end—hardly the first such bill and destined not to be the last. Utah Republican senator Orrin Hatch, a sponsor, asserted that the bill would "return control of our destiny to the people of Utah by transferring title to the unappropriated public lands to state control, and from there to the county authorities, and ultimately to private citizens."[9]

Although the broader movement to quash environmental protections on public land was destined to prosper under Reagan and in subsequent administrations, legislation to divest the federal estate repeatedly failed to pass. Had Hatch's legislation passed, many western states would likely have apportioned the lands to the ranchers whose political machinery had pushed it along—perhaps simply by drawing property lines along the former grazing allotment boundary lines. (State legislatures also may have chosen to give some lands to oil, gas, and mining companies—the other long-time powerhouse of western politics and a force that compensated for its less developed grassroots network with deeper pockets available for political engagement.)

The administration was eager to reward the western ranching establishment that had contributed to Reagan's victory. The president's administrator of the Environmental Protection Agency, in charge of regulating poisons, Anne Gorsuch of Wyoming, wrote to the National Wool Growers and the National Cattlemen's associations before even being sworn in on May 20, 1981, to invite them to petition for re-authorization of Compound 1080. The new interior secretary, James G. Watt, began the process of unshackling the Fish and Wildlife Service's Division of Animal Damage Control as one of his first tasks upon assuming office.[10]

The process for re-authorizing widespread poison use was lengthy, and members of Congress from the West rode herd on the administration every step of the way. On January 4, 1982, seven western senators from both political parties wrote presidential counselor Edwin Meese III to urge reversal of Nixon's poison ban (which Ford had only partially undone). On January 27, 1982, Reagan issued an executive order reversing the ban (as well as rescinding Carter's ban on killing coyote pups in their dens).[11]

But that was only the first step, since under the laws Nixon had signed—specifically the Endangered Species Act, the National Environmental Policy Act, and the Federal Insecticide, Fungicide, and Rodenticide Act—a dispositive record had to be established that poisoning would not jeopardize the survival of threatened or endangered species. Defenders of Wildlife and other groups watchdogged and countered the administration's moves as the Environmental Protection Agency and the Interior Department convened technical hearings on the matter.

In 1985, after the Republicans captured control of the Senate, a rider on a funding bill transferred the Animal Damage Control program back to the Department of Agriculture. Interior retained responsibility for the Endangered Species Act's enforcement, implemented under the old agency name, Fish and Wildlife Service.

Finally, the agency schizophrenia that hearkened back to the Office of Economic Ornithology and Mammalogy—the split that could be boiled down to the interpretation of a comma in the agency's original enabling legislation of March 3, 1885—was resolved by separating the conservation scientists from the exterminators. The split had lasted 100 years, 9 months, and 9 days.

The Fish and Wildlife Service—in character with its position within the Department of the Interior and without the support of grassroots cooperating institutions—evolved into a timid agency whose actions to protect endangered species today are almost all a result of litigation by private conservation groups. Animal Damage Control, in contrast, took full advantage of residing back within the bosom of the Agriculture Department.

With the liberation of Animal Damage Control from any remaining political constraints within the Department of the Interior, the Endangered Species Act served as the last line of defense against poisoning. In August 1986, as the Environmental Protection Agency was nearing its decision to re-authorize registration of strychnine for rodent control under the regulatory authority it exercised by dint of the 1972 Federal Insecticide, Fungicide, and Rodenticide Act, Defenders of Wildlife and the Sierra Club sued under that law as well as under the Endangered Species Act. The groups claimed that strychnine would inevitably kill members of eighteen threatened and endangered species. These included meat eaters such as the gray and red wolf, grizzly bear, blackfooted ferret, San Joaquin kit fox, and California condor, as well as rodents such as the Utah prairie dog.

A federal court agreed with the environmentalists and in April 1988 enjoined the Environmental Protection Agency from allowing the products without complying with the Endangered Species Act's stringent requirements. (The constraints have not been shaken, and strychnine's above-ground, non-arboreal field use is still illegal, although Animal Damage Control developed a system of poisoning rodents in their underground burrows as well as a method to poison tree-climbing porcupines.)

The same legal argument forced a series of restrictions on the use of Compound 1080 as well. No longer could carcass segments or small poisoned baits be scattered about; rather, the poison was to be contained as a liquid within a collar on potential prey animals, such as sheep, so that only the

Golden eagle in leghold trap, released alive with a broken leg. Passage of the Endangered Species Act led to requirements that meat baits be placed away from traps to protect bald eagles. (Photo by Dick Randall, courtesy of The Humane Society of the United States)

individual coyote attacking that sheep's neck would be poisoned. The Endangered Species Act also eventually led to limitations on how close to meat baits leghold traps could be placed, in order to protect bald eagles, and to restrictions on neck snares and M-44s in the habitats of endangered wolves, foxes, and jaguars.[12]

The animal control establishment of the West, as might be expected, did not universally adhere to the law and regulations. Throughout the late 1980s dead eagles and sometimes dead bears and other scavenging animals kept showing up in New Mexico, Colorado, Utah, and—most of all—Wyoming. Individual ranchers were occasionally caught and convicted of using banned poisons, but the unnatural deaths continued unabated.

In 1989 a former government trapper from Texas, Rex Shaddox, who was taking predator control classes at the University of Wyoming in Laramie, contacted the Fish and Wildlife Service's law enforcement division. Shaddox maintained that after class one day his instructor, Randy Graham, the head of the Wyoming Department of Agriculture's predator control office, repeated advice he said he had earlier given one of his employees that was intended to be passed on to ranchers: dead eagles must be gotten rid of with the utmost discretion. Graham had told Shaddox that the state Department of Agriculture had

Dick Randall and a golden eagle that didn't survive government poison. (Photo by Dick Randall, courtesy of The Humane Society of the United States)

hoarded banned poisons after Nixon's February 1972 executive order while falsifying records to make it appear they had been destroyed.

The tip corroborated information already available to investigators. In the mid-1970s the Environmental Protection Agency had investigated poisoning in Wyoming and asked to see the state's records on disposal of Compound 1080 but was refused and thwarted by Wyoming Department of Agriculture officials who asserted that federal law did not apply to the state's actions. (The assertion of the primacy of states' rights conflicted with the seemingly interstate nature of the poisoning—reflected in the spread of Compound 1080 to various locations in the West and Midwest.) In response to Wyoming's opposition, the Environmental Protection Agency never followed up with warrants or indictments.

Then, in the early 1980s Graham's predecessor at the Wyoming Department of Agriculture, Lyle Crosby, had testified before an administrative judge for the Environmental Protection Agency deciding whether to re-grant authority for widespread above-ground use of Compound 1080. Crosby testified that the Wyoming Department of Agriculture had continued to use Compound 1080 between 1975 and 1977, despite the ban. In 1989, Crosby was employed by the federal Animal Damage Control and worked closely with Graham.

The Fish and Wildlife Service recruited Shaddox to become a paid informant, and he began purchasing Compound 1080 and strychnine tabs from Graham. The Wyoming official's office and warehouse contained several safes full of cans of strychnine and Compound 1080—over 100 of the latter, enough, according to a later statement by a Fish and Wildlife Service official, to kill "every predator, man, woman, and child west of the Mississippi."[13] At every sale, Graham, a small thirty-four-year-old man who liked to wear black and whose desk sported a plaque of a blackfooted ferret adorned with a circle and slash, would look up the safe's combination in his daybook, pull out the requisite cans, and scratch off their serial numbers with his pocket knife before handing over the tins.

In the fall of 1990 the Fish and Wildlife Service brought in officer Doug McKenna, who had recently obtained the conviction of a Utah rancher for poisoning eagles. McKenna became "Nick Koutralakos," supposedly Shaddox's unemployed brother-in-law, and the two opened a business in Laramie as "Wyoming Predator Control Consultants." Their business card sported a helicopter and the suggestive slogan "The Private Approach."

Graham was happy to work with them. The two men seemed to share his delight with poisons. Graham treated poison with the sacramental respect befitting its efficacy at transubstantiating predators into flocks and herds. He collected DDT and other commercial pesticides, legal and illegal. He scraped unknown poisons from nineteenth-century doctors bags. He even melted the used and empty plastic collars of Compound 1080 that had been turned in to his office by ranchers following federal regulations—the toxic residue went into creating illegal small baits of meat and fat. He liked to share whiffs of his various and sundry toxic concoctions with his new partners and even prevailed on McKenna to taste a pinch of strychnine; the agent suffered a three-day headache afterward.

Wyoming Predator Control Consultants turned in the toxic baits to a law enforcement lab for analysis and substituted placebo baits, laced with a harmless emetic, in their work with Wyoming ranchers. Most of the ranchers, who had long been saturating the landscape with poison, did not notice the difference.

The investigation seemed to lead everywhere, to dozens if not hundreds of ranchers and to the federal Animal Damage Control agency and Graham's close associate Lyle Crosby, who was taped recounting recent killings of eagles and who was evidently involved in the distribution of poisons. But the perennially underfunded Fish and Wildlife Service had few resources for law enforcement and could not adequately follow up on all the leads. In addition, law enforcement personnel felt an urgency to make arrests as soon as possible to limit the ongoing killing, which they estimated at 2,000 to 3,000 eagles per year across the West.

On September 5, 1991, the Fish and Wildlife Service and the Environmental Protection Agency raided the Wyoming Department of Agriculture and other poisoners but did not deliver any indictments against Animal Damage Control personnel—a reflection of the late date on which evidence against the agency came to the fore and the consequently weaker case they would have had. Ultimately, several ranchers, as well as Randy Graham, were convicted and fined. Graham was also sentenced to six months' house arrest, monitored by a telemetry ankle bracelet.[14]

As a renaissance of opposition to federal predator control mounted in the 1990s, the agency's staff sought to squelch criticism. In 1989 Sierra Club volunteer Patricia Wolff of Santa Fe began researching and opposing the animal-killing program in New Mexico. In response, Animal Damage Control employees showed up at public meetings at which she spoke and once at her place of employment, where a federal trapper told her "I just wanted to see what you looked like" before driving off in his government vehicle.[15]

After one incident in the summer of 1992 in which a group of Animal Damage Control (ADC) personnel surrounded and harangued Wolff at a meeting of a citizen council advising the state game commission—a council to which the commission had appointed her—she received an anonymous death threat referring to statements she had made at that meeting and calling her a "witch who worshipped animals." The indomitable Wolff redoubled her activism against the agency, gaining headlines throughout the country about its activities. "I may not have changed ADC, but ADC changed me," she later recounted. "In 1989 I was a run-of-the-mill environmentalist and meat eater. After the radicalizing experience of fighting ADC, I evolved to become a staunch supporter of animal rights and veganism."[16]

Other revelations suggested, but could not prove, the likelihood of widespread illegalities conducted or facilitated by the agency. On the Gila National

Forest of New Mexico, in March 1996 a non-profit organization, Sangre de Cristo Animal Protection, discovered M-44 cyanide guns set by Animal Damage Control in violation of regulations. The guns were too close to a stream and to a hiking trail and were missing mandated warning signs, as well as having been placed in an area with no recent documented coyote depredations—a prerequisite for authorizing the devices. Sangre de Cristo's executive director, Elisabeth A. Jennings, videotaped the field violations and demanded that federal and state authorities take action.

After an investigation by the New Mexico Department of Agriculture (like its Wyoming counterpart, the federal agency's long-time state control partner), conducted under Jennings's watchful eye, the state agency referred the case to the Environmental Protection Agency for prosecution. The evidence pointed to violations of the Federal Insecticide, Fungicide, and Rodenticide Act by an Animal Damage Control "specialist" (the latest name for the one-time "mammal control agents") and his supervisor. In August 1996 Animal Damage Control admitted to several violations and shielded its employees from prosecution by another arm of the federal government by agreeing to pay a $1,000 fine. The fine, as if to flaunt the control establishment's impunity, was payable to the state Department of Agriculture.[17]

Even with violations, legal limits on Animal Damage Control activity greatly reduced the numbers of poisoned baits, traps, and snares in the habitats of wild creatures and the level of lethality exercised by the federal killers. In 1973 two converging shadows had been cast over Animal Damage Control's future: the Endangered Species Act and the prospect of another Dick Randall popping up from within the agency to air its bloody laundry. Violating regulations might carry a price, and that fact alone continues to significantly inhibit the scale of lawbreaking.

Legal or not, Animal Damage Control still relies on its old but proven tricks to duck public scrutiny, never more brazenly than in the present. In August 1997 the agency changed its name to "Wildlife Services." The new appellation, through its similarity to "Fish and Wildlife Service," may have been intended to blur the distinction between the agency that controls animals and the one that enforces the Endangered Species Act—just a dozen years after these functions had been split between departments.

Despite the name change, in 1998 a critic of federal predator control, Representative Peter A. DeFazio, a Democrat from Oregon, joined by New Hampshire Republican representative Charles Bass, introduced an amendment to the Department of Agriculture appropriation bill to strip Wildlife Services of all funds for lethal control, totaling $10 million. In a June 23 vote on the House floor, the amendment passed by a vote of 229 to 193—a stunning setback for the agency, even though it had yet to be reconciled with the Senate appropriation bill.

The vote did not stand. Representative Joseph R. Skeen—a southern New Mexico sheep rancher, recipient of federal predator control services, and Republican chairman of the House agricultural appropriations subcommittee—

organized his colleagues. Democratic president Bill Clinton's secretary of agriculture, Dan Glickman, backed up Skeen with a letter urging a re-vote, and the Farm Bureau worked congressional offices and organized its far-flung constituency to contact their representatives. The following day the House voted again, and with over 30 representatives having changed their minds, the amendment was defeated 232 to 192—a performance that might have qualified for Ira N. Gabrielson's praise as a "full blast of the machine."[18]

On November 1, 1999, a federal judge in Waco, Texas, responding to a Farm Bureau lawsuit that was not vigorously opposed by the federal government, enjoined Wildlife Services from revealing to the public the names of, or any other identifying information about, its various cooperators. The ruling was so broad as to allow the agency subsequently to withhold information revealing in which counties it conducted various activities and even to stop issuing copies of its programmatic environmental impact statement, previously published in compliance with the public participation provisions of the National Environmental Policy Act.[19]

With that ruling, the agency achieved a perfect opaqueness that belied the need for further mendacity. But just to be sure, the following year, at Wildlife Services' request, Congress amended the 1931 Animal Damage Control Act—Stanley P. Young's masterpiece—to remove the language referring to "eradication" of wildlife. Instead, the agency was authorized to "take any action the Secretary [of Agriculture] considers necessary . . . consistent with all the wildlife services authorities in effect" the day before the amendment took effect.[20]

Now or in the Future

T he Endangered Species Act not only blocked—or, more frequently, redirected or mitigated—federally funded actions that harmed listed animals and plants; the 1973 law also promised to initiate actions to recover species, actions laid out in official recovery plans developed by the Fish and Wildlife Service. Those recovery plans ultimately effected a much more dramatic reversal of the legacy left by the institution of cooperative federal predator control through the reintroduction of gray wolves to the West in the mid- and late 1990s.

Before a type of animal or plant could have the benefit of a recovery plan, it had to be formally placed on the list of threatened and endangered species. The list could include species, subspecies, and populations. Wolves had been identified and named through cranial and body measurements, along with details of pelage, during the 1920s and 1930s. In 1944 Biological Survey scientist (and extermination advocate at the 1924 and 1930 meetings of the American Society of Mammalogists) Edward A. Goldman published a systematized taxonomy and map of the various subspecies as his contribution to *The Wolves of North America,* co-authored with Stanley P. Young. He identified twenty-three subspecies of the gray wolf, along with three subspecies of the red wolf.[1] These subspecies, and the ranges they had once occupied, guided wolf-listing decisions.

As already seen, the endangered species list had originated in 1964 under the direction of Stewart L. Udall and received statutory authority with passage of the 1966 Endangered Species Preservation Act. In 1967 the eastern gray wolf (also known as the timber wolf), which survived in the upper Great Lakes region (primarily in the Boundary Waters of northern Minnesota), was listed as endangered.

Just days after President Richard M. Nixon signed the Endangered Species Act into law on December 28, 1973, on January 4 of the new year the Fish and Wildlife Service listed two subspecies whose ranges encompassed borderlands. The northern Rocky Mountain gray wolf, had formerly ranged through most of Idaho, Wyoming, and western Montana, as well as eastern Alberta, Canada. The Texas gray wolf had roamed western Texas and deep into Mexico, primarily the province of Chihuahua. (Reflecting the toothlessness of the Endangered Species Act's predecessors, in 1970 two wolves had been legally killed in Texas—the first of their kind recorded in the state for over two decades and evidently also the last.) Two years later, in May 1976, the Mexican gray wolf, ranging from central Mexico to the borderlands of southeastern Arizona and southwestern New Mexico, was also listed as endangered.

Areas of the United States within and close to the original ranges of these subspecies became the focus of conservation planners, even as the Fish and Wildlife Service in 1978 consolidated the disparate subspecific listings into two simple designations: a "threatened" status for wolves in Minnesota and a more imperiled "endangered" status for wolves everywhere else in the contiguous forty-eight states. This move acknowledged the modern reality that any wild wolf outside of the population in northern Minnesota had significant conservation value and that the subtle gradations in phenotype that originally demarcated wolf races should not form the basis of policy or law enforcement in an era in which a wolf might travel many miles outside its natural range in an effort to find a mate. (In January 1975 a wild wolf had been killed in Washington state, but it was identified as a subspecies from Canada not listed under the Endangered Species Act.)[2]

In 1975 the Northern Rocky Mountain Wolf Recovery Team was formed, consisting of biologists from the Fish and Wildlife Service and the Forest Service, academic Robert Ream, and a representative from the National Audubon Society. Six years later the team identified Glacier National Park in northwestern Montana, Yellowstone National Park, and the wilderness of central Idaho as likely recovery areas.[3]

Both Glacier and Yellowstone were favored for possible reintroduction in part by institutional tradition. The National Park Service was the only agency to have broken out of the Biological Survey's clutches, first in 1931 and then with more finality in 1936. In an era in which every other federal, state, and local government agency adhered to the creed of cooperative federal control, the National Park Service stood alone, an apostate.[4] Just as the survey had molded ambitious individuals to direct their dreams toward grander and more efficient control operations, so the Park Service had shaped some of its staff to dream about ecological restoration. Each agency had its own value system, and to a significant degree that of the Park Service had come to embody the points of view long championed by the American Society of Mammalogists.

Glacier National Park, adjoining the international border and Canada's Waterton National Park, was recognized as a natural place for wolves to recolonize. In 1950 and 1970 Canadian wolves migrated to Glacier and its immediate environs, only to be killed. In 1973, Dr. Robert Ream of the University of Montana established a program to study any wolves that might return. Notwithstanding the occasional lone wolf wandering through southeastern British Columbia and southwestern Alberta, the nearest known population was 200 miles north in Jasper National Park, Alberta.

In 1978 a wolf was spotted immediately north of Glacier, but it could not be captured for study. The next year another appeared, an adult female, which Ream and his associates captured in Canada and outfitted with a radio telemetry collar. They named her Kishinena, for a creek near where she was caught. Two years later, in 1981, a male appeared and paired up with the female. Although he was killed in 1983 in a wire slipknot snare intended for bears, the pups he and his mate raised began recolonizing Glacier and other regions in northwestern Montana.

The wolves were closely monitored by Ream's graduate student, Diane Boyd, who spent the next two decades trapping, radio collaring, and following the animals—recording the life histories of generations of wolves through their day-to-day movements as they reoccupied their former habitats. During the same years, Ream, in addition to his university teaching and supervision of the wolf project, took an unusual step for a wildlife scientist: serving in the Montana State Legislature and eventually chairing the state Democratic Party. But in the early 1980s, before Ream's rise to prominence, the wolves recolonizing Glacier and the presence of biologists tracking their fate made northwestern Montana a natural area for the recovery team to identify.

Beginning in December 1980, on the plains to the east of Glacier National Park, another recolonizer nicknamed the Bearpaw Wolf killed livestock and evaded traps with all the élan and savvy of the best of his kind decades before. The Fish and Wildlife Service first asked Animal Damage Control to capture the wolf alive, apparently intending to relocate it to Glacier. But with the wolf uncannily alert to traps and continuing to bring down stock, senior Fish and Wildlife Service officials then asked Animal Damage Control to kill the wolf and claim the death was an accident incidental to a capture operation, according to a memo written by an indignant Animal Damage Control official who refused to allow his agency to take the fall for another agency's illegal decision. At that point Fish and Wildlife Service proclaimed the depredator not a wolf but a wolf-dog hybrid and formally ordered Animal Damage Control to kill it. The next day, December 30, 1981, Animal Damage Control launched a plane, located the animal's tracks in the snow, pursued them for fifteen miles, and shot the enigmatic canid. A subsequent laboratory investigation revealed the animal was a male wolf with no evidence of hybridization.[5]

Yellowstone National Park, at 2,221,766 acres and all of it free of livestock, had been mentioned for many decades as sufficiently large to support some wolves. Indeed, reports had surfaced for decades of wolves in and around Yellowstone, particularly in the 1960s, only to drop off again in the 1970s. Some maintained that these wolves represented a residual population that had survived extermination. Others thought they might be migrants from Canada. And surrounding these mystery canids was speculation that they might have stemmed from surreptitious reintroductions—perhaps, some whispered, brought in by the National Park Service. But regardless of what people saw or heard, no carcasses of a wolf had been confirmed from the Yellowstone region since 1940. No pack activity could be confirmed either. (If there were wolves, their numbers didn't seem to be growing the way an unmolested population would. If wolves had been reintroduced on the sly, perhaps they had been killed that way also, by aerial poisoning; what one government agency or individual might do under cover of darkness, another could undo with the same anonymity.)

Central Idaho made the short list for wolf recovery, in part for the sheer scale of its wildness; the state included the largest roadless area in the United States outside of Alaska. Northern Idaho, near the Canadian border, also had an unbroken history of wolf sightings, even reports of pack activity; and in the 1950s wolves were reliably reported to have been killed by private individuals. After Nixon's 1972 poison ban, it appeared wolves were making their way further south and recolonizing old territory in the state.[6]

The recurring rumors of wolves throughout the northern Rocky Mountains from the 1950s through the 1970s contrast with a near cessation of wolf reports in the southern Rockies. During the same period, only two wolf reports can be found in Wildlife Services records for Colorado (released in response to a Freedom of Information Act request). Those two reports, from May 1955 and November 1961, related to captive wolves that escaped their owners and were killed by a group of ranchers and by the Fish and Wildlife Service, respectively.[7] But the reports from the north largely reflected wolves dispersing from Canada to the United States. The fact that no reproduction was documented and that evidently a population did not become established until the 1970s may vouch for the efficacy of Nixon's poison ban, combined with passage of the Endangered Species Act and the vigilance of a university department.

In the southern Rocky Mountains, the animal killed in 1945 in southern Colorado's San Juan range was the last southern Rocky Mountain gray wolf. With none still available to save, there was no urgency to designate the southern Rocky Mountains as a recovery area.

Daunting political problems also limited the possibility of recovering wolves within Colorado. Rangers at Rocky Mountain National Park were interested in the prospect, and in 1974 the Colorado Division of Wildlife had made wolf recovery an official objective of its nongame division. But it was obvious that the high-elevation park, at only 265,769 acres (roughly a square with twenty-mile sides), would primarily provide a summer range for wolves and was not nearly big enough to support a viable population. In 1976 division officials sought backing for a feasibility study for wolf and grizzly bear reintroduction in Colorado, but the study was never conducted.

Three years later, on September 23, 1979, a grizzly bear—supposedly extirpated in Colorado—materialized out of the high coniferous forest of the South San Juan Wilderness and ended up mauling bear-hunter and outfitter Ed Wiseman. (The last Colorado grizzlies confirmed before that date had been trapped and poisoned by the Fish and Wildlife Service and ranchers in the early 1950s.) The man survived, although barely, but the grizzly bear—a sixteen-year-old female—did not, perforated by arrow wounds in her side. Wiseman claimed he had stabbed the bear with a steel-tipped hunting arrow as she bit at him. Others suspected that Wiseman and his client had shot the sleeping bear with a bow and then were charged by the dying animal. A subsequent search for additional grizzlies was inconclusive.

To squelch further discussion of either species, in January 1982 the Colorado Wildlife Commission, dominated by ranchers, passed a resolution declaring its "opposition to every person or entity which may now or in the future suggest or plan" reintroduction of either species to the state. With the environmental activist community in Colorado not paying close attention, that sufficed to kill the issue for the next six years.[8]

The national momentum toward wolf reintroduction in Yellowstone National Park, the region deemed least likely for wolves to recolonize on their own, was buoyed by efforts to meet ranchers' objections head-on. In 1987, following a recommendation made by National Park Service director William Penn Mott Jr., who had become personally enamored of reintroduction, Defenders of Wildlife promised to reimburse ranchers for the cost of livestock killed or injured by wolves. The organization also supported the notion, in the best tradition of the mammalogists, that wolves that preyed on livestock could be killed. And conservationists as well as the Fish and Wildlife Service disclaimed any intention of protecting habitat for wolves—a hot-button item in the wake of a 1978 Supreme Court decision (and a congressional rider overturning it) that blocked construction of the Tellico Dam in Tennessee because of its impact on an endangered fish, the snail darter.[9]

In 1982, as part of one of a succession of amendments to the 1973 Endangered Species Act, Congress added a clause permitting an exception to many of the protections afforded threatened and endangered wildlife in the case of a reintroduced population. The new amendment was largely written to facilitate reintroduction of wolves in the face of ranchers' opposition. A reintroduced population might be designated "experimental" or "non-essential" or both as long as it was wholly separate geographically from other populations of the species, was in fact not essential to the survival of the species, and if reduced protection would reduce incidents of illegal killings and thus ultimately benefit recovery. Members of a population so designated could be killed or otherwise harmed under circumstances spelled out in regulations promulgated for the reintroduction, and they were not eligible for designation and protection of critical habitat.[10]

In 1980 and 1985 the interagency Northern Rocky Mountain Wolf Recovery Team completed successively more detailed iterations of a *Northern Rocky Mountain Wolf Recovery Plan,* the second version of which called for recovery through continued natural migration in northwest Montana, reintroduction into Yellowstone, and—unless natural recovery built a population in Idaho—reintroduction to that state as well. The recovery plan called for designation of the reintroduced wolves as experimental and for controlling wolves that preyed on livestock.

In the winter of 1986, a pack of wolves emanating from Glacier National Park began killing cattle east of the park. The Fish and Wildlife Service had by now developed the legal mechanisms to allow the Animal Danger Control to kill depredating wolves, and with that authority the federal killing corps first trapped and relocated several of the wolves. When that failed to stop the depredations, they wiped out the pack. The livestock killings only reinforced ranchers' determination to block reintroduction, concessions from pro-wolf forces notwithstanding. Representative (and future vice-president) Richard B. Cheney, a Republican from Wyoming, warned President Ronald Reagan's secretary of the interior, Donald Hodel, who had replaced James Watt, that he was "as committed to preventing government introduction of wolves to Yellowstone as Bill Mott is determined to put them there." Montana Senator Conrad Burns, also a Republican, predicted that if reintroduction did occur, a child would be killed by wolves within a year. They were aided by the director of the Fish and Wildlife Service, Frank Dunkle, who blocked release of the revised recovery plan for almost two years—until August 1987—and relented only after conservationists threatened to sue to compel its issuance.[11]

Republican lawmakers from the northern Rocky Mountains vigorously opposed the prospect of reintroduction, but no Democratic lawmakers from the area supported it either. Senator Max Baucus of Montana, a Democrat from a sheep-raising family, walked out of a meeting with Defenders of Wildlife representative Hank Fischer when the latter broached the topic of wolves.[12]

But opponents were badly outnumbered and out-organized nationwide, and reintroduction of wolves to Yellowstone was fast becoming a cause célèbre for an army of volunteer activists throughout the country. In September 1987 a Democratic member of Congress representing Salt Lake City, Utah, Wayne Owens (the son of a sheep herder), introduced legislation to require wolf reintroduction (first outright and, in subsequent versions of his bill, by initiating an environmental impact statement—the more detailed of the two categories of public notice and planning documents required for major federal actions under authority of the 1970 National Environmental Policy Act). Although Owens had no hope that his bill would pass, the fact of a westerner repeatedly sponsoring such legislation provided moral support and a rallying cry for proponents.[13]

Ranchers and their supporters could not hope to get Congress to simply terminate the planning. Instead, they obtained moratoriums on planning for the releases through riders on appropriations bills. Some of these blocked reintroduction outright, others required voluminous studies of wolves' projected impacts far beyond analysis already required under the National Environmental Policy Act, and still another rider convened a committee of ranchers, environmentalists, and government representatives who were to agree to some kind of compromise on reintroduction. (Compromise was not achieved.) But opponents of reintroduction could not secure complete regional unity because of the ongoing recolonization of Idaho by wolves. Whereas Wyoming legislators stood firm against the prospect, Senator James McClure, a Republican from Idaho, realized that reintroduction with an experimental designation offered the opportunity to avoid land-use restrictions that would protect critical habitat. In 1990, McClure introduced a bill to reintroduce wolves to Yellowstone and Idaho, but with provisions capping the number of wolves in his state to three packs and requiring the control of wolves that strayed outside a limited recovery area. His bill failed and was replaced with a measure providing funds to study the impact of wolves in Yellowstone.[14]

Ultimately, anti-wolf members of Congress managed only to delay reintroduction, and eventually they ran out of reasons and political capital to block what was mandated by the Endangered Species Act and actively supported by many of their colleagues. In January 1995, with much fanfare and with the enthusiastic participation of Secretary of the Interior Bruce Babbitt (from an Arizona ranching family), twenty-nine wolves that had been captured in Canada were released into Yellowstone National Park and central Idaho's wilderness—but not without a near setback. The wolves almost died in their small metal transport containers at the edges of their new homes when an American Farm Bureau Federation lawsuit resulted in a last-minute restraining order against their release, thereby confining the wolves to containers that Babbitt warned could become their coffins. The restraining order was lifted just in time, although full briefings were yet to be reviewed in federal court. The next year, absent the same drama, an additional thirty-seven animals were brought in.[15]

The Farm Bureau was not the only entity suing over wolf reintroduction. A coalition of conservation groups (one of which I led) sued to ensure that naturally occurring wolves in Idaho, and the progeny of these wolves with reintroduced wolves, would not lose their protection under the Endangered Species Act when the Canadian wolves arrived with their control-friendly regulations as experimental, non-essential animals.[16] Throughout the 1980s and early 1990s sightings of wolves increased in Idaho, as well as in Yellowstone and its environs. In Idaho, pairs of wolves had been recorded, indicating the likelihood that reproduction was occurring or was likely to occur soon, according to an analysis by the Fish and Wildlife Service. In Yellowstone, in August 1992 a black wolf was videotaped feeding on a bison carcass along with grizzly bears, coyotes, and ravens. The next month a gray-colored wolf was shot and killed by a hunting outfitter immediately south of the park's boundary (near the spot furthest from a road anywhere in the lower forty-eight states). But even though these encounters proved that some individual wolves were utilizing the park, unlike in Idaho, wolves in Yellowstone in the 1980s and 1990s were seldom observed in groups. So the wolf-friendly lawsuit pertained only to Idaho, where, we argued, a naturally occurring wolf population existed that could not be stripped of protection because it would not be "wholly separate geographically" from the experimental, non-essential population.[17] The same logic did not apply to Yellowstone because the Endangered Species Act spoke to the separation of populations, not individual animals.

The conservationists' suit touched on some of the same issues as the Farm Bureau suit, and so, to the pro-wolf groups' chagrin and against our objections, the two cases seeking opposing remedies were heard as one case before a federal judge in Wyoming. The judge ruled in December 1997 and at the same time (in a highly unusual move) stayed his own order—that is, he put its enforcement in abeyance until a higher court could rule—that the wolves in both Idaho and Yellowstone could not be designated experimental and non-essential and thus must be removed from the wild.

The adverse ruling put the conservationists on the defensive and permanently derailed our effort to provide full protection for the Idaho wolves. The National Audubon Society, shocked that in a case in which it was listed as a plaintiff a judge could agree with the premises and yet decide to reverse what Audubon had fought for, dropped out of the coalition and filed a brief in opposition to the plaintiffs' previous arguments. On appeal, the entire environmental effort switched to the ultimately successful argument to reverse the nightmarish prospect of the recently established wolf populations being annihilated by another control program. Authorities in Canada had declared they would not take the wolves back. The wolves, and the humans who had stood up for them, had nowhere else to go.[18]

In January 2000 the Tenth Circuit Court of Appeals reversed the district court's ruling and allowed the wolves to stay. The court interpreted the phrase "wholly separate geographically from nonexperimental populations" to emphasize the final word at the expense of the first; that is, it emphasized that a few wolves, even seen together, do not a population make and downgraded the meaning of "wholly separate." In so doing, the appeals court veered between the choices of removing the wolves, as ranchers sought, and granting them significant protection from control (as well as the prospect of eventual designation of critical habitat that could have closed down grazing allotments) as conservationists had sought.[19]

Instead, the court affirmed and put the seal of legality on the course designed by the Fish and Wildlife Service—a management schemata that looks not unlike a plan the American Society of Mammalogists at its most idealistic might have prescribed had that group ruled the West during the 1920s and

1930s. It was a course supported by environmental groups such as Defenders of Wildlife and the National Wildlife Federation, which dreaded their colleagues' litigation and were informed by a sense that they had struck the right balance in wolf reintroduction. The leaders of these groups believed that by asking too much, their more radical brethren risked destroying the progress so precariously gained.

The wolf population took off quickly in the protected confines of the national park. But outside Yellowstone and throughout western Montana, most of Idaho, and northwestern Wyoming—a region soon home to an amalgamated metapopulation of several hundred wolves—most wolf packs whose ranges overlapped with livestock were heavily controlled, in the first few years through trapping and relocation but soon through aerial gunning and traps that offered no second chances.

Capturing and killing wolves was both more difficult and easier than in the past. Single lethal dose baits—the old one-inch cubes of meat or fat imbedded with strychnine—could no longer be used. Nor could whole carcasses laced with Compound 1080 or thallium. Instead, that old standby, the leghold trap, stood duty. And an innovation, the radio collar, was put to expanded use.

Twin scientists Frank and John Craighead had begun experimenting with radio collars in 1961 to study the movement of grizzly bears in Yellowstone. Mapping out the bears' home ranges through the use of telemetry taught the brothers that the national park alone would not suffice for a viable grizzly population; the animals relied on areas outside the park for many of their life needs. The realization served as an ecological epiphany for the brothers and later for environmental activists and land managers—crystallized in the term *greater Yellowstone ecosystem,* a multi-jurisdictional region largely defined by the bears' peregrinations.[20]

Now radio collars would be used to pinpoint wolves' locations. But rather than promote a view of the wolves' wanderings as a template for defining ecosystems, the radio collars would aid in the animals' apprehension. The Fish and Wildlife Service maintained an active program to catch at least one wolf in each pack to outfit with a radio collar. If the pack was suspected of or known to be preying on livestock, collared animals known as "Judas wolves" would disclose the pack's location to shotgun-armed Wildlife Services hunters in planes and helicopters.

But Yellowstone offered salvation and seemed to deliver. America's landscapes and their frontier influence that, according to historian Frederick Jackson Turner, had sculpted our national character and helped build our democratic institutions, had crown jewels that glittered like those housed in London's Buckingham Palace. The national parks were those jewels. And the first of those was the most brilliant gem in America's tiara: Yellowstone.

Yellowstone National Park now had wolves, unmolested wolves whose lineages could be tracked, whose packs received names, and whose exploits in hunting and in lupine romance could be observed from park roads and tracked on a new medium—the Internet. The millions of park visitors, many of whom had written letters to support the reintroduction, fed a popular craze for wolves. By 2005—despite the control program outside the national parks—over 900 wolves roamed Wyoming, Idaho, and Montana. During the first five years of the twenty-first century, dispersers found their way to Washington, Oregon, Utah, and Colorado; more would surely follow.

The word *Yellowstone*, and the more plebeian or at least lesser-known landscapes outside the park, seemed to vindicate the U.S. Fish and Wildlife Service, seemed proof that it could change. In 2005, 120 years after its founding and 133 years after its founder had collected birds and their nests and eggs in Yellowstone as the official ornithologist with the Hayden expedition, it seemed the agency had finally struck the right balance in C. Hart Merriam's old stomping grounds.

It remained for the shadows of the West—the dry lands of southeastern Arizona and southwestern New Mexico at the headwaters of the Gila River, the ponderosa parks and oak and juniper savannas that had seduced Aldo Leopold into organizing against wolves and for primitive area designation and then taught him that his wilderness needed wolves—to give the Fish and Wildlife Service a chance to lose its balance yet again.

27

Detectable Ambivalence

lthough Yellowstone was the locus of national attention on wolves throughout the 1980s and 1990s, the plight of the Mexican gray wolf (*Canis lupus baileyi*) was much more dire than that of wolves in the northern Rocky Mountains. *Canis lupus baileyi* was first identified as a unique subspecies from a diminutive male wolf killed at around 6,700-feet elevation in the mountains of Chihuahua, Mexico. Edward W. Nelson, later chief of the Bureau of Biological Survey, and Edward A. Goldman, the Biological Survey man who later co-authored—with Stanley P. Young—*The Wolves of North America,* had "collected" the animal during an 1899 expedition. Three decades later and with sixty-four more specimens having become available for their examination (including the two killed by Young in the Canelo Hills in 1917), they published a description of the creature in a May 1929 *Journal of Mammalogy* article, classified it as a subspecies, and named it "for Vernon Bailey in recognition of his extensive studies of the life habits of wolves."[1]

What seemed striking to the two scientists in 1929, and to Goldman in his 1944 taxonomic contribution to *The Wolves of North America,* was the Mexican wolf's smaller size and distinct dentition in comparison to the subspecies to its north and east. "In southeastern Arizona and southwestern New Mexico, *baileyi* intergraded with *mogollonesis,*" Goldman wrote. "Although wolves are known to wander over considerable distances, the transition from *baileyi* to *mogollonesis* is remarkably abrupt."[2]

That abrupt morphological transition reflected a dramatic change in the landscapes occupied by wolves and in their prey inhabiting those landscapes. The Mexican gray wolf—the animal Aldo Leopold had called the "desert wolf" in his chiding review of *The Wolves of North America*—before widespread persecution had extended only a few dozen miles into the United States, ranging in an area with few elk and preying on the Coues whitetailed deer, itself a diminutive subspecies, and on the piglike javelina, or collared peccary, that roamed the Chihuahuan and Sonoran deserts and the Sky Islands. Although mammals' sizes generally decrease with distance from the poles, the precipitous changes in body type noted by Nelson and Goldman and by subsequent taxonomists may have had specific adaptive value. Perhaps a little wolf found it easier to travel through the dense and prickly Sonoran Desert and relying on smaller prey may have found no advantage in larger mass.

By the time the Endangered Species Act became law at the end of 1973, Fish and Wildlife Service biologists knew the "lobo" had long been extirpated from the United States and was rapidly declining in Mexico. In November 1976, six months after it was listed as endangered, the agency issued a contract with a former federal trapper—who was working as a bounty hunter in Mexico (and who in 1990 was implicated but not charged in the Wyoming poisoning case and in 1993 pleaded guilty to a charge of illegally selling a commercial pesticide, Furdan, for the purpose of killing livestock predators)—to determine the status of the Mexican wolf south of the border.[3]

Roy T. McBride was the last of generations of American citizens who had killed Mexico's wolves, usually to protect American-owned cattle south of the border. As early as 1933, according to the New Mexico supervisor of the Biological Survey at the time, a majority of wolf hunters in the Republic of Mexico were United States citizens.[4] McBride was one of the most talented: patient and willing to study the tracks and behavioral patterns of individual animals as long as it took to trick them into a trap or to poison them.

To fulfill his new contract, McBride conducted an extensive investigation of the old haunts of wolves in Mexico, asking cattlemen and bankers who loaned money to ranchers to advise him as to where the last few animals remained. He followed up with trapping; his efforts, along with ranchers he was in contact with, resulted in the trapping of four wolves, poisoning of one, and shooting of an additional six—confirmation that indeed the Sierra Madre still held wolves.

The Fish and Wildlife Service then contracted with McBride to bring in wolves alive as a hedge against the loss of the last remaining, widely scattered animals. Between 1978 and 1980 he managed to trap six lobos, but one died before it could be retrieved. (He also documented the poisoning of an additional three.) The last wolf he captured, in March 1980, was a male. Unable to find a female of his kind, he had mated with a ranch dog and sired hybrid pups. McBride caught him on a visit to his would-be pack. The veteran trapper, based on his several years' of recent efforts for the Fish and Wildlife Service and his decades of wolf-hunting experience in Mexico, concluded that fewer than fifty wolves still inhabited the country and that the subspecies "faces imminent extinction."[5]

At the May 1981 meeting of the Mexican Wolf Recovery Team, a biologist from Mexico's national wildlife agency told his five counterparts from the Fish and Wildlife Service, the Forest Service, the New Mexico Department of Game and Fish, and two zoological parks (which were taking care of the captured wolves) that probably only around thirty wolves still survived in his country. Lobos had already disappeared from some of the areas in which McBride had found their sign a year or two previously. The recovery team concluded that capturing the remaining animals was imperative to bolster the very limited genetic diversity among those they already had, and formally requested funds from the Fish and Wildlife Service to survey and capture these last free wolves. But Ronald Reagan had ascended to the White House in January of that year and was already cutting the budget for listing species as threatened or endangered. Funds for wolf captures were not allocated.[6]

In January 1982 the Fish and Wildlife Service released the Mexican wolf recovery plan written by the recovery team, and it again contained a plea for resources: "The team therefore recommends that money be made available for additional intensive survey work and attempts to capture wolves located during the survey. The feeling is that this final attempt is a now-or-never effort."[7] But this plea, too, was ignored.

The recovery team's sense of the Mexican wolf's extreme vulnerability led it to disregard a key and required element in writing recovery plans: providing criteria for downlisting the species to threatened status and criteria to eventually delist it entirely, whereupon Endangered Species Act protections would no longer apply. They could not, they wrote, visualize complete recovery of the Mexican wolf and outlined instead as an interim step a plan for breeding animals in captivity and then establishing a population of at least 100 wild wolves—followed by a second population.[8]

Breeding the animals almost ended before it began. Only one of the five wild-caught wolves was female, named "Nina" by the recovery team. Her first litter, conceived in the wild (possibly by one of the other wolves caught near her), had contained only one female pup, which had died shortly after birth. Nina was estimated to be six years old at capture, and by 1981 she was nine years old and had not bred in captivity. A haunting question hung over the team's deliberations: Might she be too old to reproduce again, leaving the entire captive population consisting only of males? The team prepared to collect and preserve sperm from the males so that if the entire generation in captivity were to die off without contributing offspring, some future wild-caught female could still be impregnated. As events turned out, despite subsequent unconfirmed reports in Mexico and in the United States, no more live wolves—female or male—have since been documented from Mexico. But that spring Nina became pregnant and gave birth, and that litter included the precious female pups.

The Fish and Wildlife Service seemed less than enthusiastic about the prospect of eventual reintroduction to either Mexico or the United States. It remained for three private captive breeding facilities and the recovery team, led by Norma Ames, a biologist with the New Mexico Department of Game and Fish, to keep that goal alive.

Ames was admirably suited to push the Fish and Wildlife Service into enforcing its responsibilities. In her early sixties and living on an old ranch in the Sangre de Cristo range, she raised Mexican wolf pups born to a pair of lobos caught and kept alive as curiosities before Roy McBride was hired by the Fish and Wildlife Service. (This lineage was eventually certified as purebred Mexican wolves and added to the captive breeding program.) Ames was independent, an adept writer (and published novelist), and, most of all, deeply committed to saving the species. She was also accustomed to overcoming institutional barriers. Three decades earlier she had broken through the glass ceiling of gender and become one of the few women to assume substantial responsibilities in a wildlife management agency.[9]

Members of the recovery team believed that the more pups that were born to earlier generations of the captive population, the better the chance of retaining the maximum proportion of the original breeding stock's genetic inheritance. And the sooner the population was built up, the sooner some animals could be released into the wild. But the Fish and Wildlife Service gave that goal little support. In November 1981, Ames wrote a Fish and Wildlife official in Albuquerque to complain about "your office's present detectable ambivalence about pushing the breeding program to produce many wolves as soon as possible." She deplored "the premature setting of a trend toward the holding of a small, token population of captive Mexican wolves, held in check by drugs."[10] Under Ames's leadership the recovery team and three private captive breeding facilities blocked the use of potentially risky contraceptive drugs on the wolves.

With Mexican wolf breeding under way, the Wild Canid Survival and Research Center in Missouri, the first of the breeding facilities, applied for federal funds to build enclosures to house the expanding population. In 1983 the Fish and Wildlife Service turned down the request, explaining that "we have not as yet firmly determined the direction and needs of the Mexican Wolf Recovery Program" and that thus it "was not of a high enough regional priority." (The Wild Canid center went into debt to create the needed infrastructure.) The federal agency would not even reimburse Ames's basic expenses after she retired from her state job and continued to lead the far-flung recovery team as a volunteer.[11]

That year an Arizona Department of Game and Fish biologist, David E. Brown, published *The Wolf in the Southwest: The Making of an Endangered Species,* a compendium of different accounts of Mexican wolves that documented the extermination campaign. In an afterword titled "A Dire Prognosis," Brown cited the lack of "administrative commitment" as one reason for doubting the possibility that there would ever be a reintroduction.[12]

Norma Ames continued to battle the inertia of an uninterested federal government. In March 1984 she wrote her own agency director and the Fish and Wildlife Service's chief of endangered species recovery for the southwestern region about credible reports that wild Mexican wolves were recolonizing the southwestern corner of New Mexico. She accused the Fish and Wildlife Service (FWS) regional office of verbally advising Animal Damage Control in that area "to bring in a specimen for identification, dead or alive, if they happen to catch one." As in Montana three years earlier, Animal Damage Control would not accept such an ambiguous and politically dangerous mandate. "I am informed that the ADC people are dissatisfied with that situation and would appreciate having written guidance," Ames reported, along with reiterating the genetic importance of any additional wolves and requesting "that FWS take stronger, more positive action in this matter."[13] (The rumors of the wolves remained unconfirmed, as did continuing rumors of a surreptitious program to control them.)

Under constant prodding by the recovery team, six years after the last wild wolf had been caught in Mexico the Fish and Wildlife Service was finally induced to broach the issue of reintroduction.[14] Because (1) there is always a degree of arbitrariness in demarcations of original ranges for subspecies, (2) there was genetic mixing at the edges of wolf subspecies' ranges (as Nelson and Goldman had noted), and (3) the range established for *Canis lupus baileyi* barely entered the United States in extreme southwestern New Mexico and southeastern Arizona, the recovery team adopted a revised taxonomic classification that combined *baileyi* with the other listed but apparently extinct southwestern and Mexican type, *Canis lupus monstrabilis,* and with the long-extinct *Canis lupus mogollonesis* of the Mogollon Rim in Arizona and the Mogollon Mountains in New Mexico—the headwaters of the Gila River. Through this taxonomic revision the official range of the Mexican wolf was extended 200 miles northward to allow for greater flexibility in choosing places for reintroduction in the United States.[15]

In March 1986, Michael J. Spear, the Southwest regional director of the Fish and Wildlife Service, formally requested that the states of Arizona, New Mexico, and Texas identify permissible areas for wolf reintroduction, and he attached a short list of areas the recovery team had identified as possibilities over two years earlier. Spear translated the "states' rights" rhetoric of the Reagan administration into a new policy—that "[a]ffected States and land managers shall have the right to refuse authorization of the reintroduction effort within their jurisdiction"[16]—although the Endangered Species Act held no such provision. Texas officials pointed to a state law banning the private release of wolves as indicating their opposition to a federal release (although later analysts read the law as not in conflict with reintroduction). The question then turned to the two states farther west.

The director of the New Mexico Game and Fish Department, Harold F. Olson, responded to Spear, saying wolves could be reintroduced onto the White

Sands Missile Range, which did not carry domestic livestock. "On the other hand," Olson insisted—referring to the area first designated as a "primitive area" at the behest of Aldo Leopold and where the mammalogists had urged a predator refuge be created—"the Gila National Forest would not be acceptable."[17]

At 2,087,624 acres, the missile range, along with an adjoining U.S. Air Force base, was almost as big as Yellowstone National Park. (Contiguous areas potentially usable for wolves subsequently identified by Fish and Wildlife Service planners brought a potential recovery area up to over 2.5 million acres—larger than Yellowstone.) The missile range included within its boundaries two little-explored mountain ranges, the San Andres and Oscura mountains, the latter so obscure it had heretofore escaped virtually any notice or investigation by biologists. Even aside from their status within a military reservation closed to most public entry, the two ranges exuded an austere and foreboding aspect: two giant sedimentary fault blocks tilting steeply into dry valleys.[18]

Military operations impacted a very small portion of the area and disrupted the ecology far less than cattle would have done. (The cattle were removed in 1942 after the military seized the private land through eminent domain.)[19] But unlike the snow- and rain-soaked Yellowstone, the missile range consisted of Chihuahuan desert and arid woodlands. Much of it was composed of shifting gypsum dunes and alkali flats. Other parts comprised habitats, such as grasslands and pinyon pine mixed with juniper, considered the Mexican wolf's preferred terrain; but those areas were small and water was scarce. As a result, the wolves' presumed primary prey, mule deer, existed at low densities. Wolf packs would have to roam vast distances to find enough to eat and drink, and thus the region could not support very many wolves.[20]

In Arizona the question posed by federal officials about possible reintroduction sites garnered a positive response from biologist Terry B. Johnson, in charge of endangered species for the state's Department of Game and Fish. Johnson, a compact man with a wry and ironic sense of humor, seemed an instinctive master of the bureaucracy—patient, attentive to detail, and destined to be embroiled in controversy over Mexican wolves for the next two decades. He was also committed to recovering the species.

Two weeks after Spear's query to the states was mailed on July 14, 1986, the Arizona Department of Game and Fish's director, Bud Bristow, wrote back with a list and map of seventeen possible reintroduction sites. By October of that year, Johnson had developed an action plan to refine that list down, to solicit and evaluate public input, and, by September of the following year, to select one or more sites for reintroduction.[21]

As in New Mexico's game department, however, movement toward reintroduction by agency biologists was thwarted by higher-level officials. In June 1987 a new director of the Arizona game department formally requested of the Fish and Wildlife Service that reintroduction of wolves (and grizzly bears, which had even less support) "be put on the back burner for several years." The agency proposed in the interim implementation of a public education program about the species. To underlie that program, it would first conduct a public attitudes study. (The attitudes survey, which eventually indicated 77 percent support for wolf reintroduction, took three years to complete.)[22]

In mid-April 1987 the U.S. Army agreed to study the possibility of wolf releases on the missile range, and the Fish and Wildlife Service initiated an evaluation of the habitat there. But the thought not just of wolves but of their being placed on lands that had been seized from ranchers incensed the ranching community. On September 29 the commander of White Sands Missile Range wrote Michael Spear informing him that the army would not agree to host wolves. Less than two weeks later, Spear announced that for lack of reintroduction sites, "the wolf reintroduction program, as of now, is terminated."[23]

Wolf advocates believed Spear had deliberately orchestrated a failure. A New Mexico Game and Fish biologist wrote a memo accusing the Fish and Wildlife Service of a plan "to erect a series of obstacles to hinder and eventually thwart" its legal obligation to conserve wolves. A representative of the Arizona Sonoran Desert Museum, which bred the wolves, contended that the previous August Spear had asked her and an Audubon Society official to put off public education about wolf reintroduction until that October. That delay allowed the livestock industry to quietly organize against wolves.[24]

The habitat evaluation of White Sands was completed in February 1988, despite the previous year's announcement, but Fish and Wildlife delayed its release until that June. The study found the area could support a maximum of thirty-two wolves. The report, while acknowledging that the prey base on the missile range was scanty, urged an "experimental" release of the animals there to see how they would fare, with strict management parameters requiring that any wolf that strayed outside the recovery area be removed from the wild.[25]

That was enough to spur hope. In February 1990 a coalition of environmental groups—including the Sierra Club, the Audubon Society, and the Wolf Action Group, based in New Mexico—formally notified the Departments of Defense and Interior that they would be sued for failing to adhere to the recovery mandates of the Endangered Species Act. The threat induced the army to reverse course and commit itself to cooperate with planning for a reintroduction program, contingent on Fish and Wildlife Service evaluating alternate locales as well.[26]

The army still bore only part of the responsibility for enforcing the law; the Fish and Wildlife Service was supposed to spearhead recovery. The environmentalists filed suit, and with litigation under way, the agency reinitiated the planning process. In October 1991 it assigned biologist David R. Parsons to the new position of Mexican wolf recovery coordinator.

Parsons, soft-spoken, raised on a farm on the Iowa prairie, had begun his career with the Fish and Wildlife Service after passage of the Endangered Species Act, and he enthusiastically embraced the act's goals. In addition to beginning the process to choose and evaluate reintroduction sites, one of his first tasks as recovery coordinator was to negotiate with the environmentalists an end to the litigation before a court could rule. In a 1993 settlement agreement, the Fish and Wildlife Service pledged to continue planning work that would lead to a reintroduction program, and the lawsuit was dropped.

Meanwhile, White Sands's caveat to its offer to participate had to be followed. The army had requested that alternate reintroduction sites be evaluated, and Arizona's Game and Fish Department, having completed its public opinion survey, in December 1990 began the process of evaluating habitats. The results were released in October 1992. The state identified three overlapping study areas within the Mexican wolf's originally conceived historical range, each drawn to include over 2 million acres centered around one or two Sky Islands: the Chiricahua Mountains, the Galiuro-Pinaleno Mountains, and the Atascosa-Patagonia Mountains.[27]

A fourth study area, the Blue range on the Apache National Forest in the southeastern part of the state, was within the Mexican wolf's range only as reinterpreted to include that of the neighboring subspecies. The region in which Aldo Leopold had shot a wolf in 1909, it was the southeastern terminus in Arizona of a broad forested plateau—the Mogollon Rim—that runs diagonally from the Grand Canyon to the New Mexico border. Unlike the other three analysis areas, the Blue range had elk, not just deer. The Blue range was only 1 million acres, but it adjoined the 3.3 million-acre Gila National Forest in New Mexico.

The Arizona game department analysis found all four regions capable of supporting wolves. But the greatest extent of roadless land and wilderness within the Mexican wolf's revised range in the United States was not on the department's list to evaluate. The Gila National Forest is a land of streams enveloped in towering canyons—with grasslands; pinyon pine, oak, and juniper woodlands; and ponderosa pine and mixed conifer forests above. Just over three quarters of a million acres of the headwaters of the Gila River had first been protected from motorized incursion in 1924 at Aldo Leopold's urging, until split apart by the unpaved North Star Road constructed between 1929 and 1931 to provide hunting access to the overpopulated deer. Now the Aldo Leopold Wilderness lay to the east of the road and the Gila Wilderness to its west, and a portion of the latter had been retired from grazing in the 1950s— with the permittee's assent—to prevent competition with elk that were being reintroduced.

Parsons wanted to get wolves into the Gila, but New Mexico officials had made clear that the only place they might conceivably acquiesce to allowing wolves was White Sands—and only if the animals could be confined to the missile range. The draft environmental impact statement for the reintroduction, released in 1996, evaluated releases in both White Sands and the Blue range and left the decision on which to choose to the final environmental impact statement to follow. Arizona's game commission, despite having okayed its department's study that identified the Blue range, now opposed releasing animals within the state—testimony to the livestock industry having regained control of the game commission through new appointments and of the sense among some state officials that in evaluating possible recovery areas they were merely humoring the authorities at White Sands. The notion that wolves might actually be released in the state came as a shock.

The draft impact statement Parsons wrote managed to offend both states' wildlife commissions, although it abided by New Mexico's insistence that wolves not be released anywhere but White Sands and Arizona's original adherence to a scientific-based decision-making process that had identified the Blue range. Parsons drew the Blue Range Wolf Recovery Area to include not just the Apache National Forest in Arizona but also all of the much bigger Gila National Forest, because the two areas are ecologically inseparable. The two jurisdictions comprised just under 4.4 million acres.

If the Blue range was chosen over White Sands, the wolves could only be released from the captive breeding program into Arizona but would be allowed to wander into and set up territories in New Mexico. As a further concession, one that had been averted in the Idaho and Yellowstone reintroductions, any wolves that established home ranges outside of whichever recovery area was chosen in the Southwest would be removed from the wild, even if they were on other national forests or Bureau of Land Management (BLM) public lands. And like the Yellowstone and Idaho program, wolves would be designated as experimental and non-essential, their freedom and lives contingent on their not preying on cattle.

These conciliatory policies failed to temper ranchers' strident opposition to the release. On May 12, 1994, during the planning process for the reintroduction environmental impact statement, Parsons and others met with Dr. Alex Thal and Howard Hutchinson, the former an instructor at Western New Mexico University in Silver City and a rancher on the Gila National Forest and the latter an anti-environmental activist in Catron County, New Mexico, which overlaps much of the Gila National Forest. The meeting was intended to properly document the county commissioners' insistence that social pathology—unemployment, alcohol and drug abuse, and family violence—would result from the effects on ranchers of releasing wolves. Thal introduced a new issue for Parsons and his colleagues to consider. "Someone is going to get shot over this," he repeatedly warned the government biologists and bureaucrats.[28]

With that tenor to the opposition, senior Fish and Wildlife Service officials and the Clinton administration seemed to get cold feet. They delayed release of the final environmental impact statement for over six months. Environmentalists threatened to sue again to require action.

Michael Spear, the Southwest regional director, and his successor, John Rogers, worked to steer the reintroduction to White Sands, where the wolves would be few and wide-ranging. But with management parameters that would require removal of wolves that left the missile range and adjoining areas and, according to the habitat evaluation, a maximum of thirty-two wolves that might subsist there, the region was clearly inferior to the Blue Range Wolf Recovery

Area—which encompassed twice as much land and much more water and prey. (Unbeknownst to anyone in 1997, a multi-year drought soon to begin would lead to a sharp drop in White Sands's already low deer population, reducing even further the area's capacity to support wolves.) Despite Spear's and Rogers's efforts, Parsons outmaneuvered the bureaucracy above him and managed to formally propose to Interior Secretary Bruce Babbitt that wolves be released in the Blue Range Wolf Recovery Area. Babbitt, apparently ignorant of the turmoil over geography within his Fish and Wildlife Service, readily assented and signed the final authorization.[29]

In the successful struggle to secure the only biologically viable recovery area under discussion, Parsons gave little thought to the provisions requiring the removal of wolves outside the recovery area, assuming that at some point when the wolf population grew sufficiently the provision could be rescinded and the wolves allowed to occupy other regions—as indeed they would have to in order to comply with his anticipated but as yet unwritten recovery criteria. He gave somewhat more thought to the provision limiting his authority to release the animals to Arizona, although most of the recovery area was in New Mexico. In the final decision document, Parsons had added an exception to that provision, allowing translocations of wolves captured from the wild into New Mexico. Little did he imagine that the geographic limitations on wolves and on his agency's authority would retard recovery, or the personal cost he would incur in trying to fix those limitations later.

The spring of 1998 turned out to be exceedingly wet in the Southwest, the last year with a substantial snowpack for the next seven years. On March 29, 1998, in the middle of a storm that coated the Blue range with several more inches of snow, eleven wolves in three packs were released in the Apache National Forest. Born in captivity, they had never hunted for their food and never roamed beyond a few hundred feet of fence line. But three females were pregnant, and the hope for recovery lay in wild-born pups.

Roadkill was initially provided for the animals, but soon they were successfully hunting elk; and each of the three packs was staying together, establishing territories, and avoiding livestock. But in that summer and fall, wolf after wolf was found shot to death. By November 1998 five had been killed and two were missing, including the first wild-born Mexican wolf pup in the United States in over half a century, which could not be found after its mother was killed. The remaining animals were captured, some for having left the recovery area and the others because their mates had been killed and they were at risk.[30]

Ultimately, the surviving five wolves were re-released into the forest, and over the next six years dozens of others followed them from captivity into the wild. As time went by, illegal killings of these wolves continued at a level far exceeding that in the northern Rockies, a sporadic but continuing toll on a population that struggled to maintain itself. But private killings, as so often in the past, failed to make the same inroads as that old and efficient standby—federal cooperative control.

So much effort had gone into meeting the objections of ranchers, so much stock was placed on wolves' ability to reproduce themselves out of harm's way, and the experience in the northern Rockies had made biologists too cavalier in their judgments. But several things were different between the Southwest and the northern Rockies. First, there was no Yellowstone National Park down south, no 2-million-acre well-watered stretch without livestock and with a prey base buoyed by the exclusion of human hunting. Rather, most of the Gila and Apache national forests' area was grazed, and all of it was open to hunting. In addition, unlike the snow-covered north, the areas that were grazed often had cattle all year, at least in their lowlands; grazing pressure, and attendant competition with native ungulates, was high.

Moreover, the arid Southwest is less productive and holds a naturally lower density of prey. The authors of the 1982 Mexican Wolf Recovery Plan had speculated that wolves in the Southwest maintained larger home ranges to compensate for the lower wildlife density.[31] This density was lowered even further by habitat degradation through years of livestock grazing and fire suppression, which together reduced grasslands favored by deer, elk, bighorn sheep, and pronghorn and replaced them with brush or dense forest.

The further Mexican wolves roamed, the more susceptible they were to the hazard of encountering and scavenging on livestock carcasses. Cattle frequently die of starvation, accidents, and disease; and their remains litter the forests and private inholdings. The problem first surfaced in the summer of 1999, after the seven-member Pipestem Pack in Arizona frequented an area with such carcasses and turned to preying on cattle. The pack was trapped and removed from the wild, and in the course of the trapping three wild-born pups died of parvovirus. A veterinarian who necropsied them observed that they had earlier been exposed to the disease and beaten it, and he attributed parvo's fatal recrudescence to the stress from their capture.[32]

Parsons wanted to re-release the survivors into the Gila Wilderness in New Mexico, where they would enjoy the security of around 700,000 acres with no cattle and almost no roads to give access to poachers. But with ranchers up in arms, the Fish and Wildlife Service's Southwest regional director, Nancy Kaufman, backed by a skittish Clinton administration, would not permit the re-release of the wolves into New Mexico. In September, with aid of a campaign led by the non-profit Center for Biological Diversity and pressure from two members of Congress from New Mexico and Colorado, respectively, cousins Tom and Mark Udall (the former the son and the latter the nephew of the former interior secretary), Parsons received approval from Babbitt's undersecretary to proceed with planning for the release. But shortly afterward, as Parsons began the planning, through an administrative sleight of hand Kaufman rid herself of the troublesome recovery coordinator, refusing to retain him as a rehired annuitant (a common practice in the agency) after he took advantage of a routine early retirement opportunity and reapplied—the only applicant—for his old position on an annual basis.[33]

Without a recovery coordinator, remaining Fish and Wildlife Service staff were handicapped in conducting the legally required planning. So as fall turned to a dry winter in the Blue Range Wolf Recovery Area, the survivors of the Pipestem Pack, including wild-born pups, paced the fenced perimeter of their enclosure an hour south of Albuquerque.

As the year 2000 began, two more packs rapidly fell into captivity. The eight-member Gavilan Pack had been released in late 1999 in a portion of the Apache National Forest that was supposed to be rested from livestock, but the area was so heavily grazed by trespassing cattle that wild prey was exceedingly scarce. The wolves were soon killing cattle. Government biologists, unable to force a wavering Forest Service to enforce its own regulations against trespass, lured the pack with road-kill and zoo "carnivore logs" out of the conflict zone and a few miles to the northeast. But livestock roamed everywhere. In the first few days of the new millennium, the Gavilan Pack scavenged on a dead cow in New Mexico's Gila National Forest and was soon killing cattle again. The pack was trapped and removed from the wild, save for a single pup and a yearling that were never captured—the pup was assumed dead, and the radio-collared yearling was reported in various locales but never retrieved.[34]

Meanwhile, that January the Mule Pack in Arizona scavenged on both a dead cow and a dead horse. The wolves, as well as the Fish and Wildlife Service, were under intense attack in the media by an enraged ranching community. Agency biologists worried that the Mule Pack would turn from carrion to live animals as well. They trapped the wolves to move them to an area seasonally vacant of livestock. But the trapping went awry, and the Mule Pack's alpha female was left overnight in wintry weather. When retrieved the next day she was suffering from frostbite, and her leg had to be amputated to save her life. Given this trauma, the pack was not immediately re-released.[35]

By the end of January 2000 only eight wolves were left in the wild, and three packs languished behind bars. The livestock industry ramped up a campaign against the wolves. At a rally in Catron County, the owner of the cattle on which the Gavilan Pack had scavenged and then begun to kill, who two years previously had left her job with Bank of America in Colorado to buy a New Mexico ranch and become a rancher, waxed eloquent on the rural lifestyle threatened by the wolves. (She may have been the first such urban émigré since Theodore Roosevelt to utter those complaints, but within two years the Mexican wolves would inspire the same response from another urban business couple–turned–cowboy and cowgirl.)[36]

Fish and Wildlife Service biologists issued an environmental assessment to solidify the agency's legal position on re-releasing these and future wolves in New Mexico. The document's completion—following a public comment period and two public hearings—had to be timed to occur before the female wolves eligible for re-release gave birth, since their pups—never having been in the wild—could only be released in Arizona. The hearings were held on

The alpha female of the Mule Pack of Mexican gray wolves, descendant of the last seven "lobos" not wiped out by predator control, was released into Arizona as part of a reintroduction project. But after scavenging on a cow and horse carcass left on the Apache National Forest, she was trapped to prevent her from beginning to prey on cattle. Here her leg has just been amputated to save her life after developing frostbite while caught in January 2000 in a government trap. When re-released, she wandered alone for months, surviving like the three-legged wolves of another century, and may still be out there. (U.S. Fish and Wildlife Service)

March 1, 2000, in Reserve, New Mexico, a redoubt of the ranching oligarchy, and on March 2 in the more cosmopolitan copper mining, tourist, and college town of Silver City. The hearings drew around a thousand people, seemingly evenly split on the issue. Having tried but failed to activate a mob with threatening rhetoric in Reserve, the next night in Silver City J. Zane Walley, a ranching activist, took a swing at Tucson reporter John Dougherty. (Walley was taken outside by campus police, apologized to the flabbergasted Dougherty, and was allowed back in.)[37]

After all the controversy the Fish and Wildlife Service re-released two of the packs, Pipestem and Mule, in the Gila Wilderness. Both packs disintegrated, however, despite their members having stuck together before their capture. The three-legged female, left on her own by her mate and yearlings and unable to keep her pups alive despite initial supplemental feeding by government biologists, wandered for the rest of the year back and forth between Arizona and New Mexico—apparently bringing down native prey despite her injury or successfully scavenging until she disappeared from telemetry and her fate became hidden from official eyes in early 2001. Like Lefty and many other amputee wolves of the century past, she had kept herself alive as long as she could despite long odds.

Traumatized wolves that wandered from their kin and mates became the hallmark of those and subsequent animals re-released in the Gila. In Arizona, where wolves could be released directly from the captive breeding population, packs became established over the first five years of repeated releases and adhered to the ancient wolf regimen of establishing a territory and raising pups. But over the next two years the state line, and the provisions only allowing wolves to be re-released there, kept New Mexico's wolf population perennially marginal.

In addition to the peril of encountering livestock carcasses, another danger wandering wolves risked was the possibility of crossing the odorless boundary of the recovery area, which comprised the Gila and Apache national forests as well as the Fort Apache Indian Reservation in Arizona, west and northwest of the Apache National Forest area and home to an Apache tribal government that had formally welcomed the wolves' presence. Wolves that established territories outside those two forests and that reservation—whether they were on BLM lands, other national forests, or privately owned or tribal lands where they were not welcome—were to be removed.

Captures of Mexican wolves were effected through leghold traps and aerial pursuit to either dart wolves with a tranquilizer or drop a net over them. Not only traps were liable to lead to unexpected troubles. On November 9, 2001, a non-depredating wolf living off of the recovery areas was accidentally run to death during an aerial effort to capture him.[38]

Six months after ousting Parsons, Fish and Wildlife Service regional director Kaufman hired in his stead Brian T. Kelly, a biologist who had formerly worked for a dog food company, in the similarly troubled red wolf reintroduction program in South Carolina, and in Ogden, Utah, conducting experiments on coyotes with the University of Utah under the auspices of Animal Damage Control. The federal agency will not fully disclose the nature of his work there, citing the Farm Bureau court order.[39]

As Kelly began his tenure in April 2000, it became evident that the exponential population growth following wolf reintroduction in the northern Rocky Mountains in 1995 was not being replicated in the Southwest. Rather, the population was repeatedly set back through control actions. But Kelly, a consummate bureaucrat, unleashed a multi-year planning process rather than initiate the changes that would allow Fish and Wildlife to release wolves directly from the captive breeding program into the Gila National Forest.

Amid a profusion of administrative shuffling, a scientific study of the Mexican wolf reintroduction program was conducted for Fish and Wildlife Service by four non-governmental scientists, led by renowned carnivore expert Dr. Paul C. Paquet of the University of Calgary. The eighty-six-page Paquet Report, released in June 2001, warned that the control program was disrupting pack structures, estimated a 39 percent chance that without changes the population would go down rather than up, and advised three crucial reforms: first, that the government gain the authority to release wolves directly into the Gila National Forest; second, that wolves be allowed to roam and set up territories outside the recovery area boundary as long as they weren't creating any problems; and third, that ranchers be required to dispose of the carcasses of their livestock before wolves scavenged on them and became habituated to domestic animals.[40]

In the two years after the report was released and despite wild oscillations in the wolf population, Kelly and the Fish and Wildlife Service did not heed the scientists' warnings and did not begin the process of changing the Mexican wolf reintroduction rules. Kelly applied for a transfer to a Fish and Wildlife Service position in Wyoming and resigned as Mexican wolf recovery coordinator in June 2003, acutely aware of the political difficulties in reforming the program and unwilling to press the matter with his new boss, Southwest regional director H. Dale Hall, who had replaced Nancy Kaufman in June 2002.

The lax federal regulations governing Mexican wolf reintroduction were taken advantage of by savvy ranchers intent on the removal of what they considered a pestilence imposed on them by a hostile government and conservation groups. In reintroducing wolves to the northern Rocky Mountains, the Fish and Wildlife Service rules proscribed control actions where "attractants," including livestock carcasses, had drawn wolves into conflict with ranchers.[41] No such regulation protected Mexican wolves.

In the summer of 2000, a pair of wolves emigrated outside the Apache National Forest. The wolves were dubbed the Campbell Blue Pack, named for the Campbell Blue River, a slender mountain tributary of the Blue River. According to Aldo Leopold, the waterway was named for a Campbell piano laboriously packed into the wilderness by mule for the new bride of an early cowman. "But the piano failed to bring contentment," Leopold wrote. "[T]he lady decamped; and when the story was told me, the ranch cabin was already a ruin of sagging logs."[42] Likely with somewhat different sensibilities than those of that long-ago couple, the two wolves also left their home range and wandered to the southwest.

The male, named "Rio" by those who raised him in the private Wild Canid Survival and Research Center in Missouri but numbered "166" as a Fish and Wildlife Service–managed animal, and the female, numbered 592, were trapped and taken into captivity. She broke her leg, evidently trying to climb out of a chain-link fence. After she received veterinary care and recovered, they were both released into the Gila National Forest in January 2001. The pair split apart.

What happened afterward is perhaps most remarkable not for its occurrence but for the documentation that came to light. Both wolves, separated by dozens of miles, found cattle carcasses and settled down to eat. Rumor in the local community had it, although this could not be documented, that the owners of both kine coordinated their responses. When the Fish and Wildlife Service, tracking the wolves by their radio collars, discovered the carcasses, they were examined and determined not to have been killed by wolves. The animal fed upon by wolf 166 had "slipped and fallen on a steep, icey [sic] hillside and broken a leg," according to a Fish and Wildlife Service biologist's e-mail report, "probably lying there for up to a week before dying. There was no evidence that the wolf had chased or attacked the bull," the biologist reported.[43]

Government staff wanted to pack the dead animal out but were blocked by the rancher, who demanded payment for release of his half-eaten carcass at the bottom of a canyon far from a road. (It turned out that his livestock were trespassing on this portion of the national forest in contravention of his grazing permit, but that did not bear on the Fish and Wildlife Service's decision to back down and allow the wolf to continue eating.) Mexican wolf 166 fed on the carcass for over a week, and from that point on the male animal, which previous to first being trapped had once killed an elk a few hundred yards from a corral full of cows and calves, focused on livestock carcasses—and managed to find plenty to feed on in and around the Gila National Forest.[44]

Meanwhile, his mate found a dead cow on private land belonging to rancher Laura Schneberger, the president of the Gila Forest Permittee's Association. Schneberger also insisted that the wolf be allowed to continue feeding on a carcass located just a few hundred yards from her house. Shortly afterward the two wolves reunited in a region of mixed private and public lands and began killing livestock together—the first time for either of them. Too savvy for traps and frequenting an open area with long vistas and only a few scattered juniper and pinyon trees, in June 2001 the pair was recaptured by a net shot out of a pursuing helicopter.[45]

The male animal, 166, one of the initial eleven wolves released in 1998— and one of the few not to have been shot that year—was sentenced to life in captivity. He now lives behind wire mesh in the foothills of southern California.

His mate, 592, was paired with another wolf and re-released in a different part of the Gila National Forest in spring of 2003. She left her new companion and traveled dozens of miles back to Schneberger's cattle, now grazing in the national forest. There 592 began hunting them, and in response, on May 27, 2003, Fish and Wildlife Service wolf biologist Daniel W. Stark, under instructions from recovery coordinator Brian Kelly, shot the female dead—the first (but not destined to be the last) Mexican gray wolf killed in the wild by the federal government since the reintroduction began.

When a draft of the next scheduled assessment of the Mexican wolf reintroduction program was released in December 2004, this one written by federal and state biologists who cooperated in the reintroduction program, the previously identified problems had not been solved. Nor had the number of radio-collared and radio-monitored wolves increased; despite continuing releases from captivity, twenty-seven lobos could be tracked across the canyons, mesas, and forests of the Apache and Gila national forests both in June 2001 and three and a half years later—although there was anecdotal evidence that the number of uncollared wolves, born in the wild or released while too young to support collars, had increased somewhat in the interim. The review explicitly identified the obstacle to change as regional director Hall and his insistence that any action must follow unanimous support of various "stakeholders," including ranchers who had been fighting for the termination of the reintroduction program and the removal of the wolves.[46]

As a result, the 2004 review seemed to expose a similar institutional schizophrenia to that attending the birth of the Office of Economic Ornithology and Mammalogy almost 120 years earlier. The new review recommended, like the previous one, allowing the release of wolves from captivity into New Mexico and permitting wolves to roam outside the boundaries of their recovery area. But it all but acknowledged that the requisite rule change in the Federal Register would not happen under Hall's criteria for action. In a sign that even the agency biologists would not or perhaps could not conceive of limitations on ranchers' use of the public lands, the report documented that 91 percent of the wolves known to have scavenged on livestock had also attacked livestock—but it rejected the Paquet Report's suggestion that ranchers be required to take responsibility for removing such carcasses or rendering them impalatable (as by lime).[47]

On April 1, 2003, United States troops entered the outskirts of Baghdad, the climax, as it then appeared, of the invasion of Iraq launched less than two weeks earlier. On the same day, the U.S. Fish and Wildlife Service issued sweeping new regulations to guide the removal of gray wolves throughout the United States from the protections of the Endangered Species Act. Not surprisingly, the television images that night and the headlines the next day were not of wolves, but of war. The new regulations divided the range of the gray wolf in the lower forty-eight states and Mexico into three "distinct population segments," based on the Endangered Species Act's flexibility in allowing the listing of threatened and endangered creatures on the species level, the subspecies level, and (for vertebrate animals only) the population level. Most of the eastern United States, including the thriving population of wolves in Minnesota, Wisconsin, and Michigan and extending to the Atlantic Ocean, became part of the Eastern Gray Wolf Distinct Population Segment. In the West, Interstate 70 in north-central Colorado and Highway 50 in Utah divided the Western Gray Wolf Distinct Population Segment to the north from the Southwestern Gray Wolf Distinct Population Segment to the south—including the entire Republic of Mexico.

All gray wolves regardless of subspecies found within each of these boundaries constituted an official listed taxon, and each distinct population segment was intended to be delisted individually. The western and eastern populations were simultaneously down-listed to threatened, and the few limits on control actions in these areas were largely lifted. The southwestern population, consisting only of the demographically oscillating population of the Blue Range Wolf Recovery Area, was maintained as endangered.[48]

The genesis of this rule change was a June 1994 Fish and Wildlife Service meeting (half a year before reintroduction to Yellowstone and central Idaho began) that resulted in two successive draft planning documents at the end of that year and in 1995. "The recovery goals (numbers of wolves) for each plan would remain the same as already approved," the 1995 version explained. "However, when those goals are met for any given plan, the wolf would be delisted for the entire population area." The intent was to address the "problem" of wolves recolonizing the Pacific Northwest and the Great Plains and eventually other areas "where recovery is not practical or planned at this time. Under present recovery goals and criteria the species would continue to be listed as endangered in such areas, and the opportunities for wolf management would be limited by that classification." Another problem, according to the 1995 memo, was the growing support for restoring wolves to Colorado (a campaign I led) and the successful effort in 1993 of Representative David E. Skaggs, a Democrat from Boulder with a seat on the House Appropriations Committee, to appropriate $50,000 to study the feasibility of reintroduction to his state—"independent of any stated objective by the Service to recover the wolf there."[49]

When given official sanction with publication eight years later in the Federal Register on April Fool's Day 2003, the southwestern distinct population segment, which encompassed the native range of the Mexican gray wolf and much more, was the only segment without previously established mileposts for delisting—in consequence of the seeming hopelessness of that goal when the Mexican wolf recovery plan was finalized in 1982. To create such criteria, Hall appointed a recovery team, heavily stacked with ranchers and outfitters but also including a smaller minority of conservationist representatives (including myself, representing the Center for Biological Diversity).

This team, also well stocked with agency biologists, by the end of 2004 was well on its way to identifying three recovery areas within its geographic bailiwick: the existing Blue range recovery area, the Grand Canyon region (including the Kaibab Plateau), and the San Juan Mountains of southern Colorado.[50] Only one of these tentatively identified recovery areas, the Blue range, is within the expanded definition of the Mexican gray wolf's original range. (The others were roamed by the much larger southern Rocky Mountain gray wolf, *Canis lupus youngi,* named for Stanley P. Young.) But the Blue range wasn't even part of *baileyi's* originally delineated range. The Apache and Gila national forests, perched above the desert floor frequented by *baileyi,* had been the ancestral home of the Mogollon Mountain wolf, *Canis lupus mogollensis.*

The original range of the Mexican wolf, in its purest conception, consisted of vast swaths of the Republic of Mexico as well as the Sky Islands region of southeastern Arizona and southwestern New Mexico. The latter ecosystem consists of mountains rising out of saguaro- and ocotillo-covered lowlands.

The highlands are covered in oak savannas, ponderosa parks, and, at the top, thick boreal forests that issue forth snow-fed streams to join the Santa Cruz and San Pedro rivers, tributaries of the Gila River.

But most of the rivers in the region had been drained for agriculture and residential development. Even before the waters had been whisked away, the isolated mountains were too small and too dry to support large numbers of ungulates. The Mexican wolf had to cross from one mountain to another and occupy vast home ranges to survive in this region. With wolves traveling farther than elsewhere, the inevitable conflicts with livestock were magnified.

Just as state game officials in Colorado had declared in 1982 that wolf reintroduction was a taboo subject and New Mexico Game and Fish director Harold Olson had proscribed consideration of the Gila National Forest for reintroduction in 1986, so also in the upcoming 2006 southwestern wolf recovery plan were the Sky Islands to be written off because of sensitivities over land use. Wolves in the Southwest, if the U.S. Fish and Wildlife Service were to have its way, would be officially recovered even with no *Canis lupus baileyi,* no desert wolves, at large in their evolutionary home.

O n December 16, 2003, a male Mexican gray wolf, number 796, was located by aerial telemetry in the San Mateo Mountains of New Mexico, northeast of the Gila National Forest. Born in the wild, 796 was first trapped in September 2002 while still a pup in the Cienega Pack in the Apache National Forest in Arizona, so he and his brother could be outfitted with radio collars. In the spring of 2003 he had been occasionally located away from the pack, apparently undertaking reconnoitering expeditions on his own. In the summer he dispersed, eventually finding his way across several mountain ranges of the Apache and Gila national forests—some of them claimed by established wolf packs—and across heavily stocked grasslands that lay between his natal Blue range and the San Mateo Mountains. "I counted numerous dead cows throughout the Slash and Adobe ranches," wrote Fish and Wildlife Service wolf biologist Melissa Woolf in May 2001 about an expanse of grasslands in which private, state, Bureau of Land Management, and national forest lands intermingled—a region that was drawing wolves to scavenge before 796 was born. "They just received a huge shipment of cattle from Mexico, and many of them are dying due to traveling stress, etc.," Woolf had written.[1] But wolf 796 had gotten through, or around, this perennial trouble spot that lay immediately west of the San Mateos.

He also found a mate, an uncollared wild-born female—spotted with him at the end of April 2004, visibly pregnant. In June of that year a cow was killed by one or both of them on nearby private lands. The Fish and Wildlife Service, sensitive to complaints that its control program was dangerously depressing the Mexican wolf population—and noticing small canine tracks alongside those of the adult wolves, as well as receiving reports of puppy-like vocalizations—instead of initiating trapping, closely monitored the male animal's movements and successfully hazed him and his mate away from cattle, thereby preventing any further depredations.

But although the San Mateo Pack's new range skirted to within a dozen miles of the northeastern corner of the Gila National Forest, it was wholly outside that forest in the Cibola National Forest instead. And although the 1996 environmental impact statement on reintroduction had predicted that the San Mateos would be colonized by dispersing wolves, the Fish and Wildlife Service had bound itself not to permit that. "The Service and cooperating agencies will not allow the wolves to establish territories on public lands wholly outside these wolf recovery area boundaries," the agency's 1998 experimental, non-essential rule governing Mexican wolves had proclaimed, pledging that "the Service will capture and return to a recovery area or to captivity" any wolves that so transgressed.[2] So in August 2004 the pair was trapped—first the female and eleven days later her trap-experienced mate—and taken into captivity. No sign of pups could be found; the litter was assumed lost.

Five weeks after 796's capture the pair—with the female now collared—was released in the Gila Wilderness, but the two wolves immediately split apart. First the female and then the male made their way back to the San Mateo Mountains, where they re-united.

This mountain range had been the last refuge for the last Apache warrior still fighting the invasion of his homeland through raids on ranches throughout southwestern New Mexico and southeastern Arizona. In September 1906 the so-called Apache Kid was gunned down by a posse following a trail of stolen horses up a hidden valley high in the San Mateos. His widow, who escaped the bullets, was caught a few days later rummaging through garbage in the nearby town of San Marcial.

The Cibola National Forest was named for the mythical Seven Cities of Cibola sought by conquistador Don Francisco Vasquez de Coronado in 1540. Like the Coronado National Forest to the southwest in Arizona, home to the Sky Islands, the Cibola National Forest consists of separate mountain ranges scattered throughout New Mexico and consolidated under one administration—a forest united not by geography but under the rubric of mythical golden metropolises.

Although the San Mateos in the Cibola National Forest might seem an ironic promised land to one steeped in history, the rocky soil retains no scent of calamity or of epic quests unfulfilled. From the 10,048-foot Apache Kid Peak, the line of cars on Interstate 25 almost twenty miles to the east emits not even a whisper. To a wolf the range might seem blessed. A sky island–type landscape, although well to the north and east of the Sky Islands ecosystem, the San Mateos form an escarpment rising west of the northernmost portion of the

Chihuahuan Desert along the Rio Grande. Dropping off on their western edge into grasslands, to their southwest, across an isthmus of scrub and desert, lies the Gila National Forest. Although countless motorists traversing the highway between Albuquerque and Las Cruces have seen the blunt ridges of the San Mateos, almost nobody visits the range. With vegetation changing dramatically from their desert and grassland roots to their spruce- and fir-covered ridgetops, the San Mateos are home to deer, elk, and pronghorn antelope.

The return of wolves to the San Mateos is a forerunner of what many western landscapes will experience soon. Cooperative federal control and, to a lesser extent, non-governmental hunting will define the limits of wolves' distribution and abundance. Where that control takes place will largely be determined by how the Endangered Species Act is interpreted and applied.

On January 31, 2005, federal district judge Robert E. Jones in Portland, Oregon, citing that law's definition of an endangered species as one likely to become extinct in "all or a significant portion of its range," overturned the Battle of Baghdad wolf regulation.[3] The plaintiffs in the case were nineteen non-profit organizations that included Defenders of Wildlife, the Humane Society of the United States, the Sierra Club, and the Center for Biological Diversity—all opposed to de-listing wolves with only tiny portions of their original ranges occupied (and with the Mexican wolf entirely deracinated).

The ruling repudiated the Fish and Wildlife Service's biological gerrymandering and put the brakes on rapid de-listing. Unless the ruling is reversed on appeal, the agency will have to come up with new recovery areas in more of the vast haunts of wolves that are still vacant.

Beyond the question of where wolves will be allowed to live, the broader issue of whether the government has an affirmative duty to protect animals and plants from extermination will again be addressed by Congress. Western Republicans, as well as at least one Democrat, have introduced legislation that would substantially weaken the Endangered Species Act. Not surprisingly, the livestock industry and the Farm Bureau in particular are at the heart of this effort—personified by Representative Richard W. Pombo, a rancher from California who chairs the House Committee on Resources.

If the Endangered Species Act is eviscerated, wildlife persecution will intensify and the pace of habitat destruction will accelerate as the institutions of government revert to their old policies. At best, wolves and other creatures whose existences conflict with some human enterprise will largely be relegated to national parks, and there is no reason to believe that even those sanctuaries will remain unbreached in the long run.

Alternatively, if the Endangered Species Act survives the current Republican control of Congress and the presidency—if its ethic continues to take root in the American conscience and its protocols remain the habits of public institutions—then scientific and ecological considerations will be heard and will continue to balance out, mitigate, and occasionally block short-sighted and rapacious land-use decisions.

San Mateos, Cibola, Apache Kid Peak: the names resonate with the stories of timeless human passions—desperation, revenge, and avarice, to name but three—played out on a stage grander than our own. Landscapes evoke strong responses in our species, those with large predators all the more so.

In southeastern Arizona not far from Mexican wolf 796's place of birth lies another mountain whose name has entered a murky zone between history and myth. Escudilla Mountain, along whose southeastern slopes the yearling wolf had been located on early excursions away from his parents, had represented to a young Aldo Leopold a broader perspective on his world. "Life in Arizona was bounded under foot by grama grass, overhead by sky, and on the horizon by Escudilla," he recalled in *A Sand County Almanac*. Leopold continued:

> To the north of the mountain you rode on honey-colored plains. Look up anywhere, any time, and you saw Escudilla.
>
> To the east you rode over a confusion of wooded mesas. Each hollow seemed its own small world, soaked in sun, fragrant with juniper, and cozy with the chatter of pinon jays. But top out on a ridge and you at once became a speck in an immensity. On its edge hung Escudilla.
>
> "There was only one place from which you did not see Escudilla on the skyline: that was the top of Escudilla itself. Up there you could not see the mountain, but you could feel it. The reason was the big bear."
>
> "Old Bigfoot was a robber-barron, and Escudilla was his castle. Each spring, when the warm winds had softened the shadows on the snow, the old grizzly crawled out of his hibernation den in the rock slides and, descending the mountain, bashed in the head of a cow. Eating his fill, he climbed back to his crags, and there summered peaceably on marmots, conies, berries, and roots."[4]

Here Leopold's desire to tell a good story, or his faulty memory (he wrote the account in 1940), implausibly assigns a federal trapper to the task of killing the bear, although he was killed in 1911,[5] four years before the Bureau of Biological Survey had salaried hunters:

> Those were the days when progress first came to the cow country. Progress had various emissaries.
>
> One was the first transcontinental automobilist. The cowboys understood this breaker of roads; he talked the same breezy bravado as any breaker of bronchos.
>
> They did not understand, but they listened to and looked at, the pretty lady in black velvet who came to enlighten them, in a Boston accent, about woman suffrage.
>
> They marveled, too, at the telephone engineer who strung wires on the junipers and brought instantaneous messages from town. An old man asked whether the wire could bring him a side of bacon.
>
> One spring, progress sent still another emissary, a government trapper, a sort of St. George in overalls, seeking dragons to slay at government expense. Were there, he asked, any destructive animals in need of slaying? Yes, there was the big bear.

The grizzly was duly killed, and it had not occurred to Leopold to object:

> We forest officers, who acquiesced in the extinguishment of the bear, knew a local rancher who had plowed up a dagger engraved with the name of one of Coronado's captains. We spoke harshly of the Spaniards who, in their zeal for gold and converts, had needlessly extinguished the native Indians. It did not occur to us that we, too, were the captains of an invasion too sure of its own righteousness.
>
> Escudilla still hangs on the horizon, but when you see it you no longer think of bear. It's only a mountain now.[6]

But when you see the San Mateos today, they are not just another mountain range—they're home for two wild-born lobos. The Fish and Wildlife Service and the Department of Agriculture's Wildlife Services will trap them again, then perhaps give them another shot at freedom and hope they don't go back. But their kind will not be kept away.

They're out there still, outlaw wolves.

A Methodological Note on Demographic Data in Appendixes

E stimating the number of wolves killed in Colorado based on an examination of remaining bounty receipts is not an exact science. Three significant factors cloud the data. First, the amount of information varies widely because of several breaks in statewide bounty payments and disparities between counties in record collection at the time and record maintenance subsequently. Second, even when records were carefully maintained, a significant number of wolves might have traveled far from the baits after ingesting poison and, although killed, would not have been found and counted. The final confusing factor is qualitative: most county clerks accepting scalps from the local open-range poisoner did not distinguish wolves from coyotes and commonly lumped the two together. Also, few of the standardized forms drawn up by each county required identification of the specific canid whose remains were brought in.

In 1883 and 1884, however, one diligent courthouse employee in northeastern Colorado's Weld County took the trouble to note the species for which he disbursed funds. Likewise, officials in Elbert County (also on the plains) distinguished wolves from coyotes on their forms between 1893 and 1898, and those records indicate almost the identical proportion of wolves to coyotes as that found in Weld County. Using these records as a rough template, I applied the proportion of wolves to coyotes—approximately 5.5 wolves out of each 100 animals turned in for bounty—as a general guide to estimate the number of wolves killed by strychnine on the plains of Colorado.

To estimate the number of wolves killed in the western mountainous counties, I used Routt County's ratio of wolves to coyotes—7.7 wolves out of each 100 animals killed, slightly higher than on the plains—between 1882 and 1885, a period in which that county almost invariably distinguished the species in its bounty receipts. This higher incidence of wolves to coyotes than was found on the plains does not indicate a higher original population of wolves in the mountains (the contrary is almost certainly true). Rather, it indicates that the plains probably supported an overwhelmingly greater number of coyotes, preying on prairie dogs and other rodents.

The mountain formula is more problematic than the plains formula for two additional reasons. First, the sample size for these years in Routt County is smaller than the one on the plains, increasing the likelihood of one fluke (for instance, one large pack of wolves poisoned together) invalidating the data. Additionally, habitats within the western counties, because of their great elevational range, varied considerably more than habitats on the more uniform plains—and some of the western counties encompassed plains, foothills, and mountains. So even accurate figures obtained from Routt County may not reflect other western counties.

In addition, the proportion of wolves to coyotes may underestimate the killing of wolves during the late 1870s. Within the first few years after so much of their prey, the bison, disappeared and other prey species such as antelope and elk were greatly reduced, wolves might have been more susceptible to poison than the coyotes, whose much smaller prey—such as prairie dogs, mice, and hares—had not vanished abruptly. Altogether, my estimates of the number of wolves killed in any region can best convey a sense of magnitude and scale.

Keeping these several epistemological constraints in mind, one can draw rough demographic conclusions. For the first few years of the bounty law there are no remaining receipts for scalps turned in, but there is a record of annual statewide expenditures. I have assumed that these animals were largely killed on the plains, where stocking was heaviest, and applied the plains ratio of 5.5 percent wolves for those years—even though coyotes had not yet formally been added as targets but assuming that both bounty hunters and state officials regarded them as a type of "wolf." In 1869, when Colorado's territorial legislature first approved the bounty, $247 was spent for that purpose. The next year the allocation was $1,000, but only $567 was spent. In 1871 another $1,000 was allocated, and $599 was spent.[1] Since each scalp was worth fifty cents, an estimated twenty-seven wolves were killed in 1869, fifty-seven in 1870, and sixty-six in 1871.

What this means for other periods is difficult to discern. Between 1858, when significant white settlement began in Colorado, and 1869, when the bounty was first instituted, large numbers of wolves were killed solely for the market value of their pelts. Between 1872 and 1875 and again between 1886 and 1888, the bounty was not operative, although ranchers and hide hunters still killed an unknown number of wolves (some of which could have been bountied through private livestock associations). For example, in the southeastern corner of Colorado, as the last bison were being hunted down around 1874, a Mr. Rush made around $1,000 on hides from poisoned wolves—which perhaps included coyotes[2]—representing between 500 and 1,000 skinless carcasses strewn across the plains.

Virtually no records remain of bounty payments in 1876 and 1877, although there is no reason to doubt that large numbers of wolves were killed then also. After the bounty was reinstated in 1889, the data become patchy because the receipts stayed at the county courthouses where the bounty was paid, not at the Colorado State Archives where those from previous years ended up. Some counties retained the receipts over the decades, but many did not.[3]

Appendix I: Wolves and Coyotes Bountied in 1878

Northern Plains	Wolves	Coyotes	Unspecified
Arapahoe	14	254	93
Douglas	—	—	14
Elbert	11	6	60
Jefferson	—	—	2
Weld	12	104	52
Total	37	364	221

Southern Plains	Wolves	Coyotes	Unspecified
Bent*	62	0	212
El Paso	—	—	42
Las Animas	—	27	6
Pueblo	—	29	26
Total	62	56	286

*Bent County originally encompassed most of the southern plains before other counties were carved out of its territory.

San Luis Valley	Wolves	Coyotes	Unspecified
Conejos	—	1	—
Costilla	—	—	7
Total	—	1	7

Mountains, Parks, and Foothills	Wolves	Coyotes	Unspecified
Fremont	—	—	3
Grand	—	—	1
Larimer	—	—	26
Park	—	—	2
Routt	2	37	—
Total	2	37	32

Appendix II: Revised (Estimated) Wolves and Coyotes Bountied in 1878

Northern Plains	Wolves	Coyotes
Arapahoe	19	342
Douglas	1	13
Elbert	14	63
Jefferson	—	2
Weld	15	153
Total	49	573

Southern Plains	Wolves	Coyotes
Bent	74	200
El Paso	2	40
Las Animas	—	33
Pueblo	1	54
Total	77	327

San Luis Valley	Wolves	Coyotes
Conejos	—	1
Costilla	—	7
Total	—	8

Mountains, Parks, and Foothills	Wolves	Coyotes
Fremont	—	3
Grand	—	1
Larimer	2	24
Park	—	2
Routt	2	37
Total	4	67

Appendix III: Wolves and Coyotes Bountied in 1879

Northern Plains	Wolves	Coyotes	Unspecified
Arapahoe	18	459	31
Boulder	—	11	1
Douglas	9	23	39
Elbert	—	5	99
Jefferson	—	24	14
Weld	39	642	15
Total	66	1,164	199

Southern Plains	Wolves	Coyotes	Unspecified
Bent*	22	10	609
Custer	—	8	1
El Paso	—	—	151
Huerfano	—	30	5
Las Animas	—	0	123
Pueblo	—	151	27
Total	22	199	916

*Bent County originally encompassed most of the southern plains before other counties were carved out of its territory.

San Luis Valley	Wolves	Coyotes	Unspecified
Conejos	—	9	—
Costilla	—	—	36
Rio Grande	—	—	7
Total	—	9	43

Mountains, Parks, and Foothills	Wolves	Coyotes	Unspecified
Fremont	—	9	13
Grand	1	—	5
La Plata	21	7	24
Larimer	—	5	28
Park	—	9	—
Routt	5	—	—
Total	27	30	70

Appendix IV: Revised (Estimated) Wolves and Coyotes Bountied in 1879

Northern Plains	Wolves	Coyotes
Arapahoe	20	488
Boulder	0	12
Douglas	11	60
Elbert	5	99
Jefferson	1	37
Weld	40	656
Total	77	1,352

Southern Plains	Wolves	Coyotes
Bent	55	586
Custer	—	9
El Paso	8	143
Huerfano	—	35
Las Animas	7	116
Pueblo	1	177
Total	71	1,066

San Luis Valley	Wolves	Coyotes
Conejos	—	9
Costilla	3	33
Rio Grande	—	7
Total	3	49

Mountains, Parks, and Foothills	Wolves	Coyotes
Fremont	1	21
Grand	1	5
La Plata	23	29
Larimer	2	31
Park	—	9
Routt	5	—
Total	32	95

Appendix V: 1880 Livestock Production[4]/Wolf and Coyote Bounty Figures

Northern Plains	Wolves	Coyotes	Unspecified	Cows*	Sheep
Arapahoe	14	433	98	55,840	84,854
Boulder	0	0	17	6,016	0
Douglas	0	57	11	18,776	1,468
Elbert	4	0	103	12,275	66,893
Jefferson	0	0	19	9,088	2,025
Weld	11	367	271	25,135	54,015
Total	29	857	519	127,130	209,255

*Excluding dairy cows and working oxen, both of which are likely to have been better protected from possible depredations than range cattle were.

Southern Plains	Wolves	Coyotes	Unspecified	Cows	Sheep
Bent	7	141	673	15,216	61,800
Custer	0	13	7	6,778	148
El Paso	0	0	198	16,322	122,416
Huerfano	2	53	2	8,264	36,762
Las Animas	0	3	139	38,119	113,055
Pueblo	4	119	84	16,666	68,860
Total	13	329	1,103	101,365	403,041

Appendix V—continued

San Luis Valley	Wolves	Coyotes	Unspecified	Cows	Sheep
Conejos	0	14	25	2,773	25,325
Costilla	0	2	63	5,146	22,676
Rio Grande	0	15	0	8,883	3,243
Saguache	4	37	28	16,530	22,247
Total	4	68	116	33,332	73,491

Southern Mountains	Wolves	Coyotes	Unspecified	Cows	Sheep
Hinsdale	0	0	0	0	0
La Plata	10	83	99	16,287	16,100
Ouray	0	0	0	450	0
Total	10	83	99	16,737	16,100

Central Mountains and Foothills	Wolves	Coyotes	Unspecified	Cows	Sheep
Chaffee	0	1	0	1,567	0
Fremont	0	6	14	4,551	906
Gunnison	0	0	0	1,329	0
Park	1	5	13	20,000	2,205
Total	1	12	27	27,447	3,111

Northern Mountains and Foothills	Wolves	Coyotes	Unspecified	Cows	Sheep
Gilpin	0	0	0	324	0
Grand	0	33	0	1,877	1,046
Larimer	11	50	63	14,220	45,410
Routt	3	7	4	3,625	0
Summit	0	0	0	0	0
Total	14	90	67	20,046	46,456

Appendix VI: 1880 Livestock Production/ Revised (Estimated) Wolves and Coyotes Killed

Northern Plains	Wolves	Coyotes	Cows	Sheep
Arapahoe	19	526	55,840	84,854
Boulder	1	16	6,016	0
Douglas	1	67	18,776	1,468
Elbert	10	97	12,275	66,893
Jefferson	1	18	9,088	2,025
Weld	26	623	25,135	54,015
Total	58	1,347	127,130	209,255

Appendix VI—*continued*

Southern Plains	Wolves	Coyotes	Cows	Sheep
Bent	44	777	15,216	61,800
Custer	0	20	6,778	148
El Paso	11	187	16,322	122,416
Huerfano	2	55	8,264	36,762
Las Animas	8	134	38,119	113,055
Pueblo	9	198	16,666	68,860
Total	74	1,371	101,365	403,041

San Luis Valley	Wolves	Coyotes	Cows	Sheep
Conejos	2	37	2,773	25,325
Costilla	5	60	5,146	22,676
Rio Grande	0	15	8,883	3,243
Saguache	6	63	16,530	22,247
Total	13	175	33,332	73,491

Southern Mountains	Wolves	Coyotes	Cows	Sheep
Hinsdale	0	0	0	0
La Plata	18	174	16,287	16,100
Ouray	0	0	450	0
Total	18	174	16,737	16,100

Central Mountains and Foothills	Wolves	Coyotes	Cows	Sheep
Chaffee	0	1	1,567	0
Fremont	1	19	4,551	906
Gunnison	0	0	1,329	0
Park	2	17	20,000	2,205
Total	3	37	27,447	3,111

Northern Mountains and Foothills	Wolves	Coyotes	Cows	Sheep
Gilpin	0	0	324	0
Grand	0	33	1,877	1,046
Larimer	16	108	14,220	45,410
Routt	3	11	3,625	0
Summit	0	0	0	0
Total	19	152	20,046	46,456

Appendix VII: Wolves and Coyotes Bountied in 1881

Northern Plains	Wolves	Coyotes	Unspecified	Southern Plains	Wolves	Coyotes	Unspecified
Arapahoe	23	350	129	Bent	2	111	104
Boulder	1	3	1	Custer	0	5	5
Douglas	2	31	15	El Paso	0	0	80
Elbert	5	58	188	Huerfano	0	58	0
Jefferson	3	9	8	Las Animas	12	128	9
Weld	12	331	162	Pueblo	8	133	43
Total	46	782	503	Total	22	435	241

San Luis Valley	Wolves	Coyotes	Unspecified	Southern Mountains	Wolves	Coyotes	Unspecified
Conejos	0	49	9	La Plata	0	21	16
Costilla	0	11	91	Total	0	21	16
Rio Grande	0	10	0				
Saguache	3	22	14				
Total	3	92	114				

Central Mountains and Foothills	Wolves	Coyotes	Unspecified	Northern Mountains and Foothills	Wolves	Coyotes	Unspecified
Chaffee	0	4	0	Gilpin	3	0	0
Fremont	4	11	19	Grand	7	17	0
Gunnison	0	1	0	Larimer	1	86	8
Park	0	8	0	Routt	4	133	55
Total	4	24	19	Summit	20	3	14
				Total	35	239	77

Appendix VIII: Revised (Estimated) Wolves and Coyotes Bountied in 1881

Northern Plains	Wolves	Coyotes	Southern Plains	Wolves	Coyotes
Arapahoe	30	472	Bent	8	209
Boulder	1	4	Custer	0	10
Douglas	3	45	El Paso	4	76
Elbert	15	236	Huerfano	0	58
Jefferson	3	17	Las Animas	12	137
Weld	21	484	Pueblo	10	174
Total	73	1,258	Total	34	664

San Luis Valley	Wolves	Coyotes	Southern Mountains	Wolves	Coyotes
Conejos	1	57	La Plata	1	36
Costilla	7	95	Total	1	36
Rio Grande	0	10			
Saguache	4	35			
Total	12	197			

Central Mountains and Foothills	Wolves	Coyotes	Northern Mountains and Foothills	Wolves	Coyotes
Chaffee	0	4	Gilpin	3	0
Fremont	5	29	Grand	7	17
Gunnison	0	1	Larimer	2	93
Park	0	8	Routt	8	184
Total	5	42	Summit	21	16
			Total	41	310

Appendix IX: Wolves and Coyotes Bountied in 1882

Northern Plains	Wolves	Coyotes	Unspecified	Southern Plains	Wolves	Coyotes	Unspecified
Arapahoe	63	501	102	Bent	147	601	21
Boulder	5	6	8	Custer	0	9	10
Douglas	1	98	3	El Paso	37	8	158
Elbert	9	203	165	Huerfano	1	57	0
Jefferson	1	20	1	Las Animas	1	226	5
Weld	29	521	117	Pueblo	20	157	5
Total	108	1,349	396	Total	206	1,058	199

San Luis Valley	Wolves	Coyotes	Unspecified	Southern Mountains	Wolves	Coyotes	Unspecified
Conejos	2	11	22	Dolores	4	0	0
Costilla	15	1	105	La Plata	30	97	84
Rio Grande	0	3	28	Total	34	97	84
Saguache	18	94	1				
Total	35	109	156				

Central Mountains and Foothills	Wolves	Coyotes	Unspecified	Northern Mountains and Foothills	Wolves	Coyotes	Unspecified
Chaffee	2	13	1	Gilpin	1	0	1
Fremont	1	2	61	Grand	1	6	0
Gunnison	5	36	91	Larimer	2	116	39
Park	24	30	46	Routt	0	28	0
Pitkin	2	2	0	Total	4	150	40
Total	34	83	199				

Appendix X: Revised (Estimated) Wolves and Coyotes Bountied in 1882

Northern Plains	Wolves	Coyotes	Southern Plains	Wolves	Coyotes
Arapahoe	69	597	Bent	148	621
Boulder	5	14	Custer	1	18
Douglas	1	101	El Paso	46	157
Elbert	18	359	Huerfano	1	57
Jefferson	1	21	Las Animas	1	231
Weld	35	632	Pueblo	20	162
Total	129	1,724	Total	217	1,246

San Luis Valley	Wolves	Coyotes	Southern Mountains	Wolves	Coyotes
Conejos	4	31	Dolores	4	0
Costilla	24	97	La Plata	36	175
Rio Grande	2	29	Total	40	175
Saguache	18	95			
Total	48	252			

Central Mountains and Foothills	Wolves	Coyotes	Northern Mountains and Foothills	Wolves	Coyotes
Chaffee	2	14	Gilpin	1	1
Fremont	6	58	Grand	1	6
Gunnison	12	120	Larimer	5	152
Park	28	72	Routt	0	28
Pitkin	2	2	Total	7	187
Total	50	266			

Appendix XI: Wolves and Coyotes Bountied in 1883

Northern Plains	Wolves	Coyotes	Unspecified
Arapahoe	81	335	399
Boulder	18	32	38
Douglas	0	105	0
Elbert	12	323	49
Jefferson	7	24	0
Weld	59	662	17
Total	177	1,481	503

Southern Plains	Wolves	Coyotes	Unspecified
Bent	122	408	81
Custer	3	9	23
El Paso	26	199	47
Huerfano	2	63	6
Las Animas	9	242	0
Pueblo	23	231	22
Total	185	1,152	179

San Luis Valley	Wolves	Coyotes	Unspecified
Conejos	1	72	38
Costilla	11	1	93
Rio Grande	10	15	5
Saguache	55	40	15
Total	77	128	151

Southern Mountains	Wolves	Coyotes	Unspecified
Hinsdale	—	8	—
La Plata	32	119	17
Ouray	2	6	10
Total	34	133	27

Central Mountains and Foothills	Wolves	Coyotes	Unspecified
Chaffee	4	6	0
Delta	2	26	0
Fremont	0	2	30
Gunnison	6	397	356
Mesa	8	50	0
Montrose	12	3	7
Park	7	15	65
Pitkin	9	30	0
Total	48	529	458

Northern Mountains and Foothills	Wolves	Coyotes	Unspecified
Eagle	1	6	0
Gilpin	2	0	0
Grand	9	16	9
Larimer	11	120	118
Routt	5	3	0
Summit	20	3	12
Total	48	148	139

Appendix XII: Revised (Estimated) Wolves and Coyotes Bountied in 1883

Northern Plains	Wolves	Coyotes	Southern Plains	Wolves	Coyotes
Arapahoe	103	712	Bent	126	485
Boulder	20	68	Custer	4	31
Douglas	0	105	El Paso	29	243
Elbert	15	369	Huerfano	2	69
Jefferson	7	24	Las Animas	9	242
Weld	60	678	Pueblo	24	252
Total	205	1,956	Total	194	1,322

San Luis Valley	Wolves	Coyotes	Southern Mountains	Wolves	Coyotes
Conejos	4	107	Hinsdale	—	8
Costilla	18	87	La Plata	33	135
Rio Grande	10	20	Ouray	3	15
Saguache	56	54	Total	36	158
Total	88	268			

Central Mountains and Foothills	Wolves	Coyotes	Northern Mountains and Foothills	Wolves	Coyotes
Chaffee	4	6	Eagle	1	6
Delta	2	26	Gilpin	2	0
Fremont	2	30	Grand	10	24
Gunnison	33	726	Larimer	20	229
Mesa	8	50	Routt	5	3
Montrose	13	9	Summit	21	14
Park	12	75	Total	59	276
Pitkin	9	30			
Total	83	952			

Appendix XIII: Wolves and Coyotes Bountied in 1884

Northern Plains	Wolves	Coyotes	Unspecified	Southern Plains	Wolves	Coyotes	Unspecified
Arapahoe	203	1,109	50	Bent	20	1,062	112
Boulder	7	33	2	Custer	2	12	29
Douglas	2	89	0	El Paso	0	251	6
Elbert	7	371	33	Huerfano	0	129	2
Jefferson	2	50	0	Las Animas	24	180	0
Weld	42	1,055	114	Pueblo	28	419	25
Total	263	2,707	199	Total	74	2,053	174

San Luis Valley	Wolves	Coyotes	Unspecified	Southern Mountains	Wolves	Coyotes	Unspecified
Conejos	1	219	4	Dolores	0	5	0
Costilla	29	16	76	La Plata	65	195	2
Rio Grande	2	40	2	Ouray	5	16	0
Saguache	19	151	13	San Miguel	0	1	18
Total	51	426	95	Total	70	217	20

Central Mountains and Foothills	Wolves	Coyotes	Unspecified	Northern Mountains and Foothills	Wolves	Coyotes	Unspecified
Chaffee	3	13	2	Eagle	7	0	2
Delta	6	39	8	Garfield	9	53	1
Fremont	3	10	32	Grand	8	42	6
Gunnison	39	362	131	Larimer	72	143	141
Mesa	19	24	45	Routt	14	113	8
Montrose	14	176	1	Summit	0	0	2
Park	3	69	40	Total	110	351	160
Pitkin	3	8	0				
Total	90	701	259				

Appendix XIV: Revised (Estimated) Wolves and Coyotes Bountied in 1884

Northern Plains	Wolves	Coyotes
Arapahoe	206	1,156
Boulder	7	35
Douglas	2	89
Elbert	9	402
Jefferson	2	50
Weld	48	1,163
Total	274	2,895

Southern Plains	Wolves	Coyotes
Bent	26	1,168
Custer	4	39
El Paso	0	257
Huerfano	0	131
Las Animas	24	180
Pueblo	29	443
Total	83	2,218

San Luis Valley	Wolves	Coyotes
Conejos	1	223
Costilla	35	86
Rio Grande	2	42
Saguache	20	173
Total	58	514

Southern Mountains	Wolves	Coyotes
Dolores	0	5
La Plata	65	197
Ouray	5	16
San Miguel	1	18
Total	71	236

Central Mountains and Foothills	Wolves	Coyotes
Chaffee	3	15
Delta	7	46
Fremont	5	40
Gunnison	49	483
Mesa	22	66
Montrose	14	177
Park	6	106
Pitkin	3	8
Total	109	941

Northern Mountains and Foothills	Wolves	Coyotes
Eagle	7	2
Garfield	9	54
Grand	8	48
Larimer	83	273
Routt	15	120
Summit	0	2
Total	122	499

Appendix XV: Wolves and Coyotes Bountied in 1885

Northern Plains	Wolves	Coyotes	Unspecified
Arapahoe	8	560	4
Boulder	4	8	0
Douglas	0	47	0
Elbert	0	138	1
Jefferson	0	19	0
Weld	16	558	23
Total	28	1,330	28

Southern Plains	Wolves	Coyotes	Unspecified
Bent	12	124	34
Custer	0	0	11
El Paso	0	110	0
Huerfano	0	17	1
Las Animas	4	46	0
Pueblo	25	234	0
Total	41	531	46

San Luis Valley	Wolves	Coyotes	Unspecified
Conejos	0	124	3
Costilla	2	9	20
Rio Grande	2	9	0
Saguache	0	74	0
Total	4	216	23

Southern Mountains	Wolves	Coyotes	Unspecified
La Plata	0	35	0
Ouray	0	3	0
San Miguel	0	0	1
Total	0	38	1

Central Mountains and Foothills	Wolves	Coyotes	Unspecified
Chaffee	0	8	0
Delta	2	0	0
Fremont	5	6	11
Gunnison	2	7	62
Mesa	2	0	47
Montrose	0	61	0
Park	0	6	5
Pitkin	1	0	0
Total	12	88	125

Northern Mountains and Foothills	Wolves	Coyotes	Unspecified
Eagle	0	1	0
Garfield	1	11	0
Grand	0	20	1
Larimer	2	44	2
Routt	0	136	0
Total	3	212	3

Appendix XVI: Revised (Estimated) Wolves and Coyotes Bountied in 1885

Northern Plains	Wolves	Coyotes
Arapahoe	8	564
Boulder	4	8
Douglas	0	47
Elbert	0	139
Jefferson	0	19
Weld	17	580
Total	29	1,357

Southern Plains	Wolves	Coyotes
Bent	14	156
Custer	1	10
El Paso	0	110
Huerfano	0	18
Las Animas	4	46
Pueblo	25	234
Total	44	574

San Luis Valley	Wolves	Coyotes
Conejos	0	127
Costilla	4	27
Rio Grande	2	9
Saguache	0	74
Total	6	237

Southern Mountains	Wolves	Coyotes
La Plata	0	35
Ouray	0	3
San Miguel	0	1
Total	0	39

Central Mountains and Foothills	Wolves	Coyotes
Chaffee	0	8
Delta	2	0
Fremont	6	16
Gunnison	7	64
Mesa	6	43
Montrose	0	61
Park	0	11
Pitkin	1	0
Total	22	203

Northern Mountains and Foothills	Wolves	Coyotes
Eagle	0	1
Garfield	1	11
Grand	0	21
Larimer	2	46
Routt	0	136
Total	3	215

Appendix XVII: Wolves and Coyotes Bountied From 1889 Onward

Northern Plains	Wolves	Coyotes	Unspecified	Southern Plains	Wolves	Coyotes	Unspecified
Arapahoe	11	321	0	Prowers	197	1,264	71
Boulder	5	136	0	Total	197	1,264	71
Elbert	90	1,684	1				
Weld*	416	1	0				
Total	522	2,142	1				

*Archived in county courthouse.

Southern Mountains	Wolves	Coyotes	Unspecified	Central Mountains and Foothills	Wolves	Coyotes	Unspecified
La Plata*	6	—	—	Park	—	222	—
Total	6	—	—	Total	—	222	—

*Archived in county courthouse.

Appendix XVIII:
Revised (Estimated) Wolves and Coyotes Bountied From 1889 Onward

Northern Plains	Wolves	Coyotes	Southern Plains	Wolves	Coyotes
Arapahoe	11	321	Prowers	201	1,331
Boulder	5	136	Total	201	1,331
Elbert	90	1,685			
Weld	416	1			
Total	522	2,143			

Southern Mountains	Wolves	Coyotes	Central Mountains and Foothills	Wolves	Coyotes
La Plata	6	—	Park	—	222
Total	6	—	Total	—	222

APHIS	Animal and Plant Health Inspection Service
AZGF	Arizona Department of Game and Fish Wolf Files
CBD	Center for Biological Diversity
CHS	Colorado Historical Society
CSA	Colorado State Archives
DPL	Denver Public Library
DPL-OJM	DPL, Olaus J. Murie Files
DPL-RBE	DPL, Rosalie B. Edge Files
DPL-SPY	DPL, Stanley P. Young Papers
DPL-wolf	DPL, Wolf Files
EIS	environmental impact statement
EMCC	Enos Mills Cabin Collection
FOIA	Freedom of Information Act
JM	*Journal of Mammalogy*
MVZ	Museum of Vertebrate Zoology, University of California, Berkeley
NA	National Archives
NA-Ogden	National Archives, Ogden Conference Records
NMGF	New Mexico Game and Fish Mexican Gray Wolf Files
OPM	Office of Personnel Management
OPM-ABY	OPM, Arthur B. Young Files
OPM-AM	OPM, Albert McIntyre Files
OPM-CHM	OPM, C. Hart Merriam Files
OPM-ING	OPM, Ira N. Gabrielson Files
OPM-LBC	OPM, Logan B. Crawford Files

OPM-SPY	OPM, Stanley P. Young Files
OPM-VB	OPM, Vernon Bailey Files
OPM-WHC	OPM, William H. Caywood Files
SIA	Smithsonian Institution Archives
SIA-SPY	SIA, Stanley P. Young Papers
SIN	Sinapu (Boulder, Colorado)
USDA	U.S. Department of Agriculture
WS	Wildlife Services

CHAPTER I

1. Ruxton (1951), 226–234. Ruxton's favorite haunt throughout his travels was South Park, a South Platte tributary, known at the time as Bayou Salado.

2. Ruxton (1973), 281.

3. Ruxton (1973), 279.

4. Ibid.

5. Ibid., 280.

6. Ibid., 265.

7. Ibid., 279.

8. Ruxton (1951), 67. Although this book recounts his companions' and not his own adventures, there is every reason to believe the sentiment is Ruxton's.

9. Ruxton (1973), 215.

10. J. Audubon, 600.

11. Quoted in Matthiessen, 135.

12. J. Audubon, 609–610.

13. Ibid.

14. M. R. Audubon, in Preface to J. Audubon.

15. J. Audubon, 625–627.

16. Casteñeda et al., 75; Morris, 205.

17. Chrisman, 28; Gregg, 252.

18. Custer, 9.

19. Chrisman, 16–17.

20. Cronon, 214–215; Chrisman, 205.

21. Gard, 100.

22. Casteñeda et al., 110.

23. Ibid., 45.

24. Ibid., 60.

25. Ibid., 25–43, 45, 60, 110.

26. Quoted in DeVoto, 27–28; original spelling, italicization, and punctuation.

27. Ruxton (1973), 297–298; original spelling.

28. Ibid., 297–299.

29. Parkman, 67.

30. Ibid., 67–68.

31. Ibid., 67.

32. Quoted in DeVoto, 29; original spelling.

33. Dodge, 201–203.

34. Ruxton (1973), 211–212.

35. Gregg, 216.

36. Parkman, 265–266.

37. Conner, 52–53.

38. Ibid., 56.

39. Lavender (1954), 190.

40. Parkman, 49.

41. J. Audubon, 637.

42. Ruxton (1973), 304.

43. Lavender (1954), 85–86.

44. Ibid., 219.

45. Ibid., 234.

46. Parkman, 246.

47. Ibid., 266.

48. Matthiessen, 79.

49. Lavender (1954), 56–62.

50. Ibid., 69–71.

51. Ibid., 207, 399. Although technically a ranch, domestic animals were not the primary products of Bent's Fort, unlike later ranches that demanded the extirpation of wolves.

52. Ibid., 126–139, 180; Lavender (1964), 411–412; Wishart, 107, 161–162; Haeger, 228, 236.

53. Lavender (1954), 184; Chittenden, 32.

54. Wishart, 107.

55. Quoted in Lavender (1954), 229.

56. J. Audubon, 585, 712.

57. Cronon, 438.

58. Nash, 101.

59. Ruxton (1973), 266, original spelling.

60. Ibid., 279; original italicization.

61. J. Audubon, 592.

62. Dodge, Introduction, original spelling.

63. Lopez, 115–117.

64. Hoebel, 30–33.

65. Quoted in Athearn (1971), 144.

66. Young (1930), 20–22, 62–63; (1967), 32, 52–53. During the height of the commercial wolf-poisoning campaign decades later, each wolf pelt was worth between $1 and $2; in 1862 in the same region, each pelt fetched $1.25. Prices were lower in the mid-1850s.

67. Belknap, 168.

68. Ibid; Parkman, 15.

69. Quoted in Young and Goldman, 325, 327–329.

70. Ibid., 327; Stanley Young, "Management of Injurious Mammals in the United States: Its History and Philosophy," unpublished manuscript in Western History Department, Stanley Young Papers, Box 223, Denver Public Library (DPL-SPY); O. J. Murie, Report on Investigations of Predatory Animal Poisoning Wyoming and Colorado, Nov. 19–Dec. 19, 1930, in Record Unit 7176, Box 45, 9, Smithsonian Institution Archives (SIA), Washington, D.C.

71. Young and Goldman, 331.

72. See Frederick Turner (1980), for a full explication of that fervid imagination.

73. Quoted in Lavender (1954), 379–380.
74. Parkman, 99, 265, 272–273.
75. Gregg, 46.
76. DeVoto, 102, 111, 177.
77. Conner, 59–60.
78. Parkman, 59.

CHAPTER 2

1. Lavender (1954), 252, 294.
2. For example, according to Curnow (34), in 1846 Jesuit missionaries first brought cattle into Montana.
3. Lavender (1954), 257.
4. Ibid., 285, 287.
5. Ibid., 412.
6. Ibid., 298, 326, 329–330.
7. Ubbelohde, Benson, and Smith, 60–66, 75, 100–102, 156.
8. Peake, 22.
9. Martin, 173.
10. "The Bent-Prowers Cattle and Horse Growers Association," Manuscript MSS699 C2:37, Colorado Historical Society (CHS), Denver.
11. Peake, 209.
12. The population of Denver only grew by ten individuals between 1860 and 1870. Ubbelohde, Benson, and Smith, 156.
13. Steinel, 112.
14. Ibid.
15. Ibid., 130.
16. Peake, 270; Sprague, 69.
17. Ubbelohde, Benson, and Smith, 124–125.
18. Steinel, 122.
19. Chrisman, 38.
20. See, for example, Morris, 190–191, recounting the killing of 5,000 bison by Sioux in 1883.
21. Cronon, 216–217.
22. McHugh, 253.
23. Chrisman, 19–20.
24. Roy Welch, recalling his father's stories and his own youthful experiences in Baca County, on Colorado's southeastern plains. Interview with Morris Snider, 1977. Audiotape made available by Snider.
25. Cronon, 216–217; Steinel, 113–115; Athearn (1971), 157, 184.
26. Gard, 206–210; *Rocky Mountain News* editorial quoted in Gard, 210.
27. Steinel, 115–116; Hornaday (1889), 514–519.
28. Gard, 210–212.
29. Townshend (1968), 259–260.
30. Ibid., 260.
31. Ibid., 263
32. Ibid., 260–263, 263 (quotation).
33. Ibid., 178.
34. Peake, 240 (quotation); Athearn (1971), 228.

35. Cronon, 233–237, discusses the perceptual and psychological distance between nature and consumers, largely created by the railroads.

36. Ubbelohde, Benson, and Smith, 129; Cronon, 82–83; Athearn (1971), 30–32.

37. Cronon, 83–86.

38. Everett, 159.

39. Steinel, 127, 143.

40. Kimball, 78.

41. Cook, 128–129.

42. Matthiessen, 136.

43. Allen (1952), 38.

44. Thompson, 349.

45. Hornaday (1914), 33.

46. Barrows and Holmes, 9–10, 15, 17, 19.

47. Cary, 58; USDA Annual Report, fiscal year 1912, 83.

48. Matthiessen, 143–144.

49. Vernon Bailey's notes of September 5, 1909, Record Unit 7176, Box 42, U.S. Fish and Wildlife Service, 1860–1961, Field Reports, SIA.

50. Hornaday (1913), 71, 161, 272.

51. Barrows and Holmes, 39.

52. F. M. Fryxell, "The Former Range of the Bison in the Rocky Mountains," *Journal of Mammology* (JM) 9, 2, May 9, 1928.

53. Barrows and Holmes, 10; Hornaday (1913), 69.

54. Stegner, 38–39, 62, 217.

55. Quoted at an El Paso County Pioneers Society meeting by an unidentified 1927 newspaper. Denver Public Library, Western History Department, wolf file (DPL-wolf). Stark was from Elbert County.

56. Peake, 126. Its first recorded meeting was held in 1872 (Steinel, 120), and its earliest affiliate, the Bent (later Bent-Prowers) Cattlemen's Association, first met in 1870 (Peake, 103).

57. Richthofen, 60; Peake, 104, 106–110, 114, 140–141.

58. Young and Goldman, 361–362; Peake, 103.

59. Peake, 140.

60. Quoted in Osgood, 94.

61. George, 8.

62. Cronon, 438; Steinel, 115.

63. Richthofen, 48; Steinel, 137–140; Osgood, 216–217. Abundant incorporation papers for new cattle companies of the era can be found in Box 70, Manuscript 699, CHS.

64. Richthofen, 59.

65. Welch.

66. Young and Goldman, 362.

67. Ibid., 359, 361; Brown, 43.

68. Young and Goldman, 381.

69. McIntyre, 118; ibid., 340–352, 360; Curnow, 33; Fleharty, 195.

70. Peake, 231–232.

71. The subsequent figures on wolves and coyotes "bountied" in Colorado from 1878–1885 come from tabulations of each of 38,451 bounty receipts stored at the Colorado State Archives (CSA) and in a few individual county courthouses. Figures from 1869–1871 are from Peake, 231–232.

72. Ubbelohde, Benson, and Smith, 171–172; Peake, 123–124, 272.

73. Thomas, 6–8.

74. Townshend (1968), 34, 41, 54 (quotation).

75. Quoted in Jackson, 376.

76. Wentworth, 331.

77. Ibid., 113, 430–445; Richthofen, 76–77.

78. Sprague, 100.

79. From bounty receipts stored at CSA and at county courthouses.

80. Gregg, 133–134.

81. Wentworth (334) quotes an 1868 newspaper report that the southern half of the San Luis Valley and the adjacent mountains supported as many as 195,000 sheep—two and a half times as many as recorded in 1880. Either the census figures from 1880 reflected significant underreporting (perhaps for the purpose of tax evasion) or the newspaper was engaged in boosterism, for during the interval sheep production expanded dramatically in the state overall.

82. Quoted in Peake, 233.

83. Ibid.

CHAPTER 3

1. Osgood, 217–222; Curnow, 46–51, 56; Stegner, 294–296; R. M. Allen to T. S. Palmer, April 3, 1896, in Record Unit 7174, Box 9, SIA, Smithsonian Institution Manuscript Collections, Stanley Young Papers, 1921–1965 (SIA-SPY).

2. Theodore Roosevelt, "A Wolf Hunt in Oklahoma," *Scribner's Magazine,* November 1905, 530.

3. Stegner, 298–300; Athearn (1971), 173–174, 219.

4. Peake, 234.

5. Ibid., 234–235.

6. *Colorado Revised Statutes,* 1893, 68–70.

7. Young and Goldman, 367.

8. Peake, 334–335.

9. Ibid., 232.

10. Young and Goldman, 362–363.

11. Curnow, 44.

12. "The Gray Wolf," *Forest and Stream* 5, 58, February 1, 1902, 84.

13. Belknap, 168.

14. Mills (1922), 141–142.

15. Ibid., 141.

16. Ibid., 147–148.

17. Ibid., 142.

18. Peake, 234.

19. Reprinted in Don and Jean Griswold, "Man-Chasing Wolves, Fact or Fiction?" *Carbonate Chronicle* [Leadville, Colorado], March 6, 1967.

20. Ise (1936), 32–37.

21. Chrisman, 266–268.

22. "When the Wolf Prowled as Shark of the Plain: Most Dreaded Carnivore Enemy of Pioneers, Described as Ravenous, Crafty, Merciless," undated newspaper article in DPL-wolf.

23. Chrisman, 204.

24. Gard, 208–209.

25. Chrisman, 96–99, 99 (quotation).

26. R. M. Allen to T. S. Palmer, April 3, 1896, Record Unit 7174, Box 9, SIA-SPY.

27. Young and Goldman, 363–364; notes from interview between Stanley Young and J. N. Neal at Meeker, Colorado, February 13, 1940, Record Unit 7174, Box 9, SIA-SPY. Young's handwritten notes from this interview refer to the group "known as wolf bounty assoc." It appears Young immediately crossed out that name and replaced it with the group's proper name, the Piceance Creek Stock-Growers Protective Association. The concept of a "wolf bounty association" separate from the more general stockmen's associations did not originate in Rio Blanco County; in 1901 ranchers in Montana's Sun River area formed the Augusta Wolf Bounty Asssociation specifically to raise bounty payments in their region (Curnow, 71), and in North Park, Colorado, a Wolf Bounty Fund was in existence in early 1902 (see "Wolves in Wyoming and Colorado," *Forest and Stream* 9, 58, March 1, 1902).

28. U.S. Department of Commerce, *Census Reports, Volume V: Twelfth Census of the United States Taken in the Year 1900, Agriculture*, 422–423; see also the slightly different figures from U.S. Department of Commerce, *United States Census of Agriculture: 1945*, 377, which includes a tabulation of cattle and calves in each state for every decade between 1840 and 1940. The figures remained within the same scale of magnitude between 1900 and 1910.

29. Cary, 53.

30. Cameron, 15; Gard, 129. A compelling case has also been made that such irruptions are part of the natural population cycle for these grasshoppers; see Jeffrey Lockwood, "The Death of the Super Hopper: How Early Settlers Unwittingly Drove Their Nemesis Extinct, and What It Means for Us Today," *High Country News* 35, 2, February 3, 2003.

31. C. S. Crandall, "Reproduction of Trees and Range Cattle," *The Forester,* July 1901, 170.

32. Drummond, 63–64.

33. Crandall, 172.

34. Phillips, 232.

35. Drummond, 155–154.

36. These floods are well-known locally, and the detail presented here came from World Wide Web pages for the respective towns.

37. Leopold (1990), 164–167, 167 (quotation).

38. Quoted in Pickering, 102.

39. Roosevelt (1927), 305.

40. Horace Greeley, quoted in Fleharty, 24.

41. Steinel, 152–153.

CHAPTER 4

1. Martin, 65, 127, 307–322.

2. Ibid., 69–70.

3. Quoted in ibid., 128–133.

4. Ibid., 437–438; Steinel, 151.

5. Martin, 132–133, 134.

6. Martin, 128–133, 134 (quotation).
7. Ibid., 21–24.
8. Young and Goldman, 380–381.
9. Quoted in Young and Goldman, 379.
10. Peake, 164–166.
11. Martin, 145.
12. Bird, 179.
13. Cronon, 200–202.
14. Ise (1920), 63–118, 81 (quotation).
15. Quoted in McCarthy, 92–93.
16. The census defined the frontier as an area with fewer than two people per square mile. See Matthews, 33–34.
17. See Turner (1985); Drummond.
18. Nash, 141–160.
19. Hays (1959), 22–25; McCarthy, 18–21, 278; Ise (1920), 45.
20. Ise (1920), 114–118; McCarthy, 16.
21. Pinchot, 85.
22. McCarthy, 25, 29–74; Hays (1959), 55; Ise (1920), 121.
23. Pinchot, 22, 31 (quotation), 182.
24. Quoted in McCarthy, 125.
25. Nash, 111–113.
26. Drummond, 226–227.
27. Quoted in Ise (1920), 271.
28. Crandall.
29. Pinchot, 177.
30. Ibid., 181.
31. McCarthy, 56–57.
32. Martin, 202–219.
33. Muir (1987), 97; Ise (1920), 169. See also Fox, 109–114.
34. Ise (1920), 190–191.
35. McCarthy, 116–118; ibid., 156, 172; Hays, 253.
36. Drummond, 173, 175; Muir (1987), 95.
37. Quoted in Pinchot, 198.
38. Drummond, 172.
39. Ise (1920), 157, 172, 175; Pinchot, 271–272.
40. Miller (2001), 159–161; *Light v. U.S.*, 220 U.S. 523, 31 S. Ct. 485.
41. *Light v. U.S.*.
42. Young and Goldman, 382.
43. Ibid.

CHAPTER 5

1. Sterling, 54–56.
2. Ibid., 56–64.
3. Ibid., 8–10.
4. Dunlap, 35–38; Kofalk, 14; Nash, 108–113.
5. Sterling, 3, 16, 34, 56–59.
6. Stegner, 44–45, 113, 188, 202–204, 240.

7. Sterling, 59–64; Cameron, 2 (quotation).

8. Cameron, 2, note.

9. Ibid., 20–23.

10. Ibid., 25.

11. Ibid., 229; Merriam (1899).

12. See Sterling, 76, 198–199, for Merriam's naturalist philosophy that guided the agency.

13. Ibid., 28–29, 45, 47, 64–65.

14. Throughout his years of government service, on some required personnel forms Bailey gave his birthday as June 21, 1863, and in others as June 21, 1864. In 1923, with the advent of a government retirement system based on age, Department of Agriculture officials insisted he take an oath as to one year or another. He chose 1864 but subsequently used 1863 again, prompting the punctilious administrators to demand he dredge up proof. A family Bible finally settled his birth date as 1864.

15. Vernon Bailey, "My Early Days in the Biological Survey," *The Survey* (periodic publication of the U.S. Biological Survey) 16, 7–9, July–September 1935, USG Patuxent Wildlife Research Center, http://www.prwc.usgs.gov/history/survey7–9.pdf (accessed January 3, 2005); Sterling, 66.

16. C. H. Merriam to C. W. Dabney, June 17, 1896, C. Hart Merriam Files, Office of Personnel Management (OPM-CHM, St. Louis, Missouri).

17. "Agricultural Report 1886," *Farmers Home Journal* [Louisville, Kentucky], August 20, 1887, Box 330, DPL-SPY.

18. *Prairie Farmer* [Chicago], October 22, 1887, Box 330, DPL-SPY.

19. "Is a Boon to Farmers: Work and Methods of United States Biological Survey: Dr. Merriam, Chief of the Survey, Tells What Is Being Done in Oregon and Elsewhere," *Morning Oregonian* [Portland], September 10, 1896.

20. "A Monumental Sham," *The Sun*, March 9, 1896, incompletely identified newspaper article in Box 330, DPL-SPY.

21. For an example of a prototypical state bird protection law distinguishing "game" birds from songbirds, see Doughty, 105–106.

22. Dunlap, 35–38.

23. Cameron, 1.

24. "Two Veteran Scientists to Retire From Biological Survey: Vernon Bailey and Dr. T. S. Palmer End Notable Services in the Federal Government," press release, July 20, 1933, in Vernon Bailey Files, Office of Personnel Management (OPM-VB).

25. *Morning Oregonian* [Portland], September 10, 1896.

26. Various documents in OPM-VB.

27. Cameron, 37–38; Sterling, 242–272.

28. Title page of the U.S. Department of Agriculture (USDA) Annual Report, fiscal year 1910.

29. Memo from Gifford Pinchot to Secretary of Agriculture, March 14, 1906, OPM-VB.

30. Bailey (1907), 5.

31. Ibid., 19.

32. Ibid., 16.

33. Ibid., 17.

34. Ibid., 18.

35. Ibid., 19.

36. Ibid., 20.

37. Bailey (1908), 3, 5.

38. Vernon Bailey (1908).

39. USDA Annual Report, fiscal year 1907, 486–487.

40. Vernon Bailey had arrived at the figure in his 1907 *Wolves in Relation to Stock, Game, and the National Forest Reserves,* citing his own and ranchers' observations that each wolf in the Gila National Forest of New Mexico killed "approximately a hundred head of cattle a year," each valued "as calves, at the very low rate of $10 a head," 12.

41. Brown (1992), 48; Dunlap, 38. See also Fox, 114–115.

42. USDA Annual Report, fiscal year 1907, 487.

43. Lopez, 189.

44. Cameron, 58.

45. USDA Annual Report, fiscal year 1908, 112.

46. USDA Annual Report, fiscal year 1911, 537–538.

47. Sterling, 262–264, 280–281.

48. Cameron, 58–59; USDA Annual Report, fiscal year 1911, 536–537.

49. Sterling, 28–29, 45, 47, 64–65, 109.

50. Memo from H. W. Henshaw to Secretary of Agriculture, May 21, 1913, OPM-VB.

51. E. W. Nelson Death Valley Journal, 1890–1891, Record Unit 7364, Box 13, folder 1, Edward William Nelson and Edward Alphonso Goldman Collection, ca. 1873–1946, SIA.

52. Birney and Choate, 67; Sterling, 92–93, 102, 105.

CHAPTER 6

1. Peake, 114, 235.

2. Stanley Young's notes from an interview with Neal, February 13, 1940, Record Unit 7174, Box 9, SIA-SPY.

3. Ibid.

4. Ibid.

5. *The Golden Interlude 1900–1910* (Alexandria, Virginia: Time-Life Books, 1969), (no author), 6–9.

6. Quoted in Lukas, 570.

7. Peake, 243–249.

8. Ubbelohde, Benson, and Smith, 250–260; Lukas, 218–231.

9. Lukas, 61–63.

10. *Times,* June 5, 1902, unidentified newspaper in DPL-wolf.

11. "Timber Wolves Make Havoc With Herds, and Kill Even Ranch Dogs," March 9, 1902, unidentified newspaper in DPL-wolf.

12. Roosevelt (1905), 529–530.

13. Payne (1965), 13, 20, 39, 125–130, 283, 309–320, 357.

14. T. John Payne to Enos Mills, March 3, 1910, in Enos Mills Cabin Collection, Estes Park, Colorado, courtesty of Beth Mills (EMCC).

15. According to McIntrye's son, the incident occurred when the Burlington Northern Railroad was being built through Gillette, Wyoming. That was August 1891, according to Nelson (1966), 19. Nelson's depiction of the town at this time makes the senior McIntyre's barroom experience seem not at all out of place.

16. Barth, 62; Payne, 312.

17. Payne, 312.

18. Albert McIntyre to Enos Mills, April 1, 1916.

19. Payne, 314.

20. Barth, 62–63; Payne, 312.

21. T. John Payne to Enos Mills, March 3, 1910, EMCC. According to this account, up to this point McIntyre had trapped five wolves, and an additional two were shot. In contrast, according to Stephen Payne's memoirs (1965), the McIntyres trapped only two wolves (of which one was stolen) until they dug up the den in April. I have assumed that the contemporaneous account is correct.

22. Barth, 64–65.

23. Albert McIntyre to Enos Mills, April 1, 1916, EMCC, original spelling, punctuation, and grammar.

24. Ibid.

CHAPTER 7

1. Harding, 49.

2. Young and Goldman, 383.

3. Bailey (1907), 25.

4. Sterling, 263–264.

5. Henry Wetherbee Henshaw, "The Policemen of the Air: An Account of the Biological Survey of the Department of Agriculture," *National Geographic* 19, 2, February 1908, 79.

6. Young and Goldman, 383–384.

7. Quoted in McIntyre, 129, 131–132.

8. Quoted in Ibid., 166–167.

9. Ibid., 160–172.

10. Quoted in ibid., 168.

11. Quoted in ibid., 165.

12. Quoted in ibid., 170–171.

13. Ibid., 172.

14. Young and Goldman, 383; Cameron, 275; map of BBS districts and hunters, in Box 345, DPL-SPY.

15. Stone, 751–753; Pritchett.

16. "Very early day answer received by Biological Survey when choosing predatory animal personal [*sic*]," Box 359, DPL-SPY.

17. Albert McIntyre to Enos Mills, April 1, 1916, EMCC.

18. Arthur Hawthorne Carhart, "Buckskin Pay-Off," *Rocky Mountain Sportsman*, February 1939. Today Colorado supports several hundred thousand mule deer.

19. Albert McIntyre to Enos Mills, April 1, 1916, and undated questionnaire filled out by McIntyre, both in EMCC, original spelling, punctuation, and grammar.

20. Ibid. (Letter of 4/1/16.)

21. Albert McIntyre to BBS, September 25, 1915, in Albert McIntyre Files, Office of Personnel Management (OPM-AM).

22. Ibid.

23. A. K. Fisher to Logan B. Crawford, September 27, 1915, OPM-AM.

24. Correspondence in OPM-AM.

25. Albert McIntyre to A. K. Fisher, October 31, 1915, OPM-AM.

26. Albert McIntyre to H. N. Wheeler, March 15, 1916, OPM-AM.

27. Albert McIntyre to Enos Mills, April 1, 1916, and undated questionnaire filled out by McIntyre, both in EMCC; original spelling, punctuation, and grammar; correspondence in OPM-AM.

28. Albert McIntyre to Enos Mills, May 13, 1916, EMCC.

CHAPTER 8

1. Hagedorn, 4–45, 43 (quotation).

2. Quoted in Hays (1959), 125.

3. Brands, 221–226, 273–285.

4. Although Marshall's phrase is part of the literary currency of today's conservation movement, no reference seems to be available as to when he uttered it (Dave Foreman, personal communication, December 2000).

5. See Allen (1952), 8; Hays (1957), 24–47, 189–190.

6. Kazin, 79–106; Smith, 253–254, 267; Beard; Hymowitz and Weissman, 218–222; Riegel, 291–292; Lukas, 170–172; Allen (1952), 99 (quotation), 99–105, 131, 136–137.

7. Quoted in Drummond, 186–187.

8. Ibid., 183–188.

9. Quoted in ibid., 130.

10. Ibid., 183–188; Sprague, 126–127; Nash, 176; *Colorado Federation of Women's Clubs Official Year Book 1911–'12*, 39–42.

11. Ubbelohde, Benson, and Smith, 233; P. Smith, 173. Utah in fact preceded Colorado in suffrage leadership, but Utah's suffrage law was enacted while it was still a territory and was invalidated by the U.S. Congress (Flexner, 162–163).

12. Webb, 504.

13. Sullivan and Rather, 310.

14. The link is embodied in the wife of Edward Costigan, a Roosevelt-allied, Progressive candidate for Colorado governor and later conservationist senator. Mrs. Costigan was active in the Colorado Federation of Women's Clubs. *Colorado Federation of Women's Clubs Official Year Book 1911–'12*, 7.

15. See Brands, 27, 36; Nash, 145–153; Sullivan and Rather, 171, 298.

16. Hornaday, *Campfires* (1909), advertisement at back of book.

17. McHugh, 291–292, 291 (quotation).

18. Hornaday (1889), 533.

19. Ibid., 533–545.

20. Quoted in ibid., 546.

21. Ibid., 520.

22. Hornaday (1913), cover page.

23. Hornaday (1889), 542.

24. Hornaday, *Campfires on Desert and Lava* (1909), 355–6.

25. Hornaday (1913), x.

26. Ibid., 8.

27. Hornaday (1914), 179.

28. Ibid., 35–36, 41–42, 193 (quotation).

29. Brown and Carmony, 24; Meine, 149; Cameron, 88.

30. Hornaday (1914), 140–142.

31. Hornaday (1913), 9, 78–79.

32. Hornday (1914), 103–104.

33. Hornaday (1913), 335, 348.

34. Ibid., 38–39.

35. Fox, 164; Cameron, 319, note. (The limitations on hunting did not apply to "predatory and noxious animals"—Cameron, 64.)

36. Hornaday (1913), 46, 159, 172, 248–250, 250 (quotation), 340–341, 387–388, 388 (quotations).

37. Grinnell (1913), 500–501 (quotations); Nash, 152.

38. Grinnell (1913), 423, 430, 509. Biological Survey leaders included C. Hart Merriam and E. W. Nelson. The club also included prominent men from other federal agencies, including Gifford Pinchot of the Forest Service. Members of Congress were represented as well, some synonomous with conservation policy, such as Representative John F. Lacey and Senator Francis G. Newlands (author of the Newlands Act creating the Bureau of Reclamation). Francis Parkman, who died in 1893, had been an "honorary member" exempt from paying dues, and Aldo Leopold joined in 1923.

39. Quoted in Trefethern, 165; Cameron, 241.

40. Quoted in Athearn (1976), 224.

41. Limerick, 131.

42. Barrows and Holmes, 35–36, 39–40, 257; John Ellenberger, Colorado Division of Wildlife, personal communication, May 16, 2000.

43. Riley, January 10, 1917.

44. Wiebe, 286.

45. Barrows and Holmes, 40–41.

46. These figures, as well as the previous ones for deer, from four pages of charts in Record Unit 7176, Box 42, SIA.

47. Meine, 128.

48. Quoted in Brown and Carmony, 56.

49. Ibid., 57.

50. Ibid., 56–60, 59 (quotation).

51. Meine, 149–150.

52. Quoted in ibid., 146.

53. Quoted in Brown and Carmony, 57.

54. Flader and Callicott, 47.

55. Ibid., 47–48.

56. Flader, 60.

57. Leopold (1966), 138.

58. Ibid., 138.

59. Ibid., 137; Meine, 93–94.

60. Muir (1987), 122.

61. Quoted in Drummond, 116; originally appearing in E. A. Mills (1990), 134.

62. Drummond, 257.

63. Cohen, 180. In an ambivalently worded testament to the tractability of "ferocious animals," Muir (1974, 149) noted that even "the faithful dog . . . is a descendent of the blood-thirsty wolf or jackal."

64. Drummond, 221–247.

65. Nash, 174–181.

66. Drummond, 217, 337, 376.

CHAPTER 9

1. Pritchett, 35–45; Stone, 751–753; Office of Personnel Management, Logan B. Crawford File (OPM-LBC).

2. Athearn (1982), 6; Athearn (1976), 252–253.

3. Letter from Geo E. Holman to Dr. A. K. Fisher, December 15, 1916, made available by USDA–Animal and Plant Health Inspection Service (APHIS) Wildlife Services (WS) through the Freedom of Information Act (FOIA) (all subsequent WS references also acquired via FOIA). Because WS only released the portions of records directly germane to the request, in some subsequent citations the document cannot be fully referenced.

4. "History of Predator and Rodent Control Colorado District" (1953), 1, unpublished manuscript, National Archives (NA).

5. "Predatory Animals Destroyed by Govt. Hunters During Fiscal Year 1916," WS.

6. Smith Riley to "His Excellency, the Governor of Colorado," January 10, 1917, Record Unit 7176, Box 42, SIA.

7. Schlebecker, 57–58; Rowley, 111–116.

8. U.S. Department of Commerce, *Census Reports, Volume V Fourteenth Census of the United States Taken in the Year 1920, Agriculture General Report and Analytical Tables,* 566, 631. The proportionately slight increase over the 1910 figures may reflect changes in enumeration (550–553) or the recent increase in livestock production to meet war demands, despite an almost certain reduction in the Colorado landscapes' ability to support livestock.

9. Sheep numbers from ibid., 632; again, the sheep numbers were for the following year, 1920. 1910 figures from U.S. Department of Commerce, *Census Reports, Thirteenth Census of the United States Taken in the Year 1910, Agriculture,* 193. Elk and deer numbers from Riley, January 10, 1917.

10. USDA, Bureau of Biological Survey, "Narrative Report. Predatory Animal Inspector. State of Colorado. July 1, 1916 to September 30, 1916," NA.

11. Sterling, 264.

12. Henry Wetherbee Henshaw, "Autographical Notes," *The Condor* 22, March 1920, 58.

13. "History of Predator and Rodent Control Colorado District" (1953), 2, NA; "Number and Species of Animals Taken and Cost Per Month" (fiscal year 1918), table, WS; March 1918 report, Biological Survey, Colorado District, NA.

14. "Bureau of Biological Survey District of Colorado, Monthly Summary Report," September 1919, NA.

15. See Peake for the most thorough look at the industry's activities and for the years 1910–1920, particularly 139–145.

16. Untitled transcript, Manuscript 153, 127, January 1922, CHS.

17. Peake, 152.

18. Ibid.

19. Ibid., 115–116, 151–154, 310.

20. September 1919 report, Biological Survey, Colorado District, NA.

21. "Resolution No. 5 Asking for Appropriations for Destruction of Predatory Animals," Manuscript 153, Box 146, CHS; CHS legislative records.

22. Colorado Legislative Council, *Presidents and Speakers of the Colorado General Assembly, a Biographical Portrait From 1876* (Denver: Eastwood Printing, 1980), 45–46.

23. House Bill no. 259, Chapter 52, Session Laws, 1919, NA. Although no available records prove that Rockwell attended the conference, a transcript from the following year's meeting of the Colorado Stockgrowers Association indicated his presence then, so it is likely he had attended the 1919 convention as well. See Manuscript 153, no. 123, 12, 14, CHS.

24. Sowers and Connor, 36; *Portrait and Biographical Record of the State of Colorado* (1899), 746–747.

25. CSA and CHS legislative records.

26. "Bureau of Biological Survey District of Colorado, Monthly Summary Report," September and November 1919, NA (quotation); "Semi-annual Report Colorado District, Bureau of Biological Survey United States Department of Agriculture July 1–December 31, 1919," NA.

27. "Narrative Report Colorado District, December 1919," Bureau of Biological Survey, NA, original spelling.

28. "Some Celebrated Government Hunters," portion of an unpublished manuscript by Young entitled "Saga of Predatory Animal Control," 84–85, Box 331, DPL-SPY.

29. Bureau of Biological Survey, "Annual Report 1920, Colorado District," NA; Victor H. Cahalane, "The Evolution of Predator Control Policy in the National Parks," *Journal of Wildlife Management* 3, 3, July 1939, 232, 234; Lloyd K. Musselman, *Rocky Mountain National Park Administrative History 1915–1965,* published by the National Park Service, July 1971, 128–130.

30. Victor H. Cahalane, "The Evolution of Predator Control Policy in the National Parks," *Journal of Wildlife Management* 3, 3, July 1939, 232, 234; Lloyd K. Musselman, *Rocky Mountain National Park Administrative History 1915–1965,* published by the National Park Service, July 1971, 128–130; "Annual Report 1920, Colorado District," NA.

31. Smith Riley of the Forest Service forwarded a letter from an official of the San Juan National Forest in southwestern Colorado requesting help in exterminating wolves, which were said to be increasing. Hundreds of miles north of there, in the second week of the new year, fifteen wolves were reported "doing considerable damage in the Piceance country," long-standing deer winter range west of today's Flat Tops Wilderness and the locale of exorbitant bounty payments a few years earlier. Five days later Monroe Bros. and Henerson, a ranch outfit near Thatcher on Colorado's southeastern plains, complained about the loss of nearly $4,000 worth of stock to wolves. Noting the failure of three men (either bounty hunters or ranch employees) to capture the chief culprit after several weeks of effort, the ranch asked Crawford for "assistance in ridding the country of them." The man Crawford sent out caught the offending wolf just three nights after setting out traps. Other wolf depredations that January included the loss of a yearling calf to a rancher near Jelm, Wyoming, and of a horse in the lower reaches of the southern San Juan Mountains at the edge of the San Luis Valley (close to the border of Conejos and Rio Grande counties). In March a survey hunter detailed to southwestern Colorado reported "the finding of a freshly killed cow by wolves. The cow had given birth to a calf and the wolves had eaten most of the calf, but the cow was untouched." In June, on the central border with Wyoming, rancher John Hohnholz again found himself feeding wolves, this time contributing a yearling colt to an animal likely descended from his old nemesis, Two Toes. Other ranchers in the region evidently shared the burden, which they estimated at more than $1,000 in losses within the previous seven months. A week later, in the southwestern desert country around the Dolores River, a survey

hunter "reported that he had found 3 calves that had been killed by wolves in the neighborhood of Mesa Creek." Other reports in June had wolves active in central Colorado's Middle Park, around Kremmling and Sulphur (now Hot Sulphur Springs), and around the Purgatoire River canyons of the southeastern plains—where a single dead sheep hinted that even after the animal bothering the Monroe Bros. and Henerson ranch six months previously had been killed, the old habitat of bison and antelope still harbored at least one wolf. (WS records released under provisions of the Freedom of Information Act. WS deleted all names of ranchers involved before releasing the information. Monroe Bros. and Henerson is identified in Carhart and Young. The unidentified rancher in documents released by WS wrote a thank-you letter to Stanley Young, which was reprinted with full attribution in *Last Stand*.)

32. "Predatory Animal Control District of Colorado 1918," Biological Survey, NA, original wording.

33. "Summary of Work Done, F.Y. 1920, Colorado District," "FY 1921 (Table A)," and untitled narrative report, fiscal year 1921, WS; "Semi-annual Report, State of Colorado, Predatory Animal Control, July 1st to December 31st 1920," Biological Survey, NA.

34. "Semi-annual Report, State of Colorado, Predatory Animal Control, July 1st to December 31st 1920," and "Annual Report of the Predatory Animal Division, Colorado-Kansas District, Fiscal Year 1921," Biological Survey, NA.

35. A. K. Fisher to E. A. Goldman, September 19, 1921, Record Unit 7176, Box 44, SIA.

36. The last known Colorado wolverine was recorded killed in 1979 in Utah, across the state line from northwestern Colorado's Dinosaur National Monument. Knowledgeable sources report that the shooter of the animal first asked about Colorado's game laws. Hearing that it is illegal to kill a wolverine in Colorado, he announced that he had shot one in Utah, where it is legal. Despite its imperiled status, in 2005 the wolverine was still not protected under the federal Endangered Species Act.

37. "Predatory Animal Control, District of Colorado, Fiscal Year 1919," Biological Survey, NA.

38. "Semi-annual Report Colorado District, July 1–December 31, 1919," NA.

39. "Predatory Animal Control, District of Colorado, Fiscal Year 1919," NA.

40. Transcript of annual meeting of the Colorado Stockgrowers Association, January 16–17, 1920, Manuscript 153, no. 123, 12, CHS; "Semi-annual Report Colorado District, Bureau of Biological Survey United States Department of Agriculture July 1–December 31, 1919," NA.

41. Cameron, 60; various documents from WS; McIntyire, 194.

42. Link, 56–59, 225–226.

43. Schlesinger, 60; Wiebe, 127, 298; Hays (1957), 111–112; Berger, 89–112.

44. Dodge, 97–99.

45. Peake, 219.

46. WS documents.

47. Cameron, 276–277.

48. Ibid., 314. The survey's responsibilities were expanding across the board, and although the predator expenditures represented the most dramatic increase, other survey departments were getting more money as well.

49. "Monthly Narrative Report, April 1918, for the Colorado District," Bureau of Biological Survey, NA.

50. "Predatory Animal Control District of Colorado, Fiscal Year 1919," Bureau of Biological Survey, NA; Crosby, 66, 213.

51. Ira N. Gabrielson to W. B. Bell, November 11, 1918, Ira N. Gabrielson Files, Office of Personnel Management (OPM-ING).

52. S. Young to E. M. Mercer, February 11, 1953, Record Unit 7174, Box 2, SIA-SPY.

53. Allen (1931), 8–9.

54. "Annual Report 1920, Colorado District," Biological Survey, NA.

55. "Narrative Report Colorado District, December 1919," Biological Survey, NA, original spelling and grammar.

56. "Predatory Animal Control District of Colorado 1918," Biological Survey, NA.

57. "Monthly Narrative Report April 1918," Biological Survey, NA.

58. Bailey (1907), 21.

59. "Narrative Report Colorado District, December 1919," Biological Survey, NA.

60. Transcript of annual meeting of the Colorado Stockgrowers Association, January 16–17, 1920, Manuscript 153, no. 123, 12, 14, CHS.

61. Ibid.

62. Smith Riley, District Forester, to the Governor of Colorado, January 10, 1917, Record Unit 7176, Box 42, SIA.

63. Wright (1977), iv; Dobie (1950), 167.

64. Annual Report, fiscal year 1922, Biological Survey, SIA.

65. "A Brief Synopsis of the Life History of Stanley Young," August 18, 1925, Box 351, DPL-SP; "History of Predator and Rodent Control Colorado District" (1953), 5, NA.

66. Personnel records in OPM-LBC.

67. "Annual Report 1920, Colorado District," Biological Survey, NA.

68. Brown (1992), 46; the phrase was actually used in reference to Stokely Ligon, not Young.

CHAPTER 10

1. Stanley Young, "Wolf!" *The American Rifleman,* June 1944, 10; parts of this account are copied verbatim from the article.

2. Carolyn Young Ogilvie, "The Benjamin Young House," CUMTUX, *Clatsop County Historical Society Quarterly* 6, 3, Summer 1986.

3. John White, "Did You Happen to See Stanley Young," *Times-Herald* [Washington, D.C.], January 5, 1949, Box 359, SPY-DPL.

4. Ogilvie, "The Benjamin Young House.

5. Turner (1985).

6. Ogilvie, "The Benjamin Young House," and "Artifacts, People and History," both in CUMTUX, *Clatsop County Historical Society Quarterly* 6, 3, Summer 1986; Vera Gault, "A Brief History of Astoria, Oregon 1811–1900," brochure for Benjamin Young Inn, 1393 Franklin Ave., Astoria, Oregon 97103, 1982.

7. White, 15.

8. Ibid.

9. Throughout his life Young mentioned Lewis and Clark in reference to his birthplace. See, for example, Young, "Natural History as Learned in the Canelo Hills of Arizona," 8, Box 331, DPL-SPY.

10. "Statement by the Candidate," March 7, 1927, Office of Personnel Management, Stanley P. Young Files (OPM-SPY).

11. For a thorough discussion of this model, see Cronon, 23–54.

12. Ogilvie, "Artifacts, People and History," 21.

13. See, for example, Young, "Natural History," 8; Dorothy G. Palmer, "Naturalist Comes Back to Cochise," *The Bisbee Daily Review* [Arizona] July 1, 1958, Box 358b, DPL-SPY; "Trapper of First Wolf in This State for Biological Survey Now Heads Economic Division," *Prescott Journal-Miner,* February 1928 (no specific date recorded), Box 325, DPL-SPY.

14. Information on the Panama-Pacific Exposition comes from The Virtual Museum of the City of San Francisco, www.sfmuseum.org (accessed May 25, 2005).

15. A. S. Potter, February 3, 1917, OPM-SPY.

16. Unsigned memo by "Chief of Bureau," December 15, 1920, OPM-SPY. It seems unlikely that the hunting Young was said to be employed in from "the fall of 1916" until his hiring by the survey in fall 1917 (presumably excepting the two months he worked for the Forest Service) was bounty hunting for the simple reason that he likely would have written subsequently about his pre-survey employment exploits killing predators. That leaves the distinct possibility that this consisted of market hunting.

17. Young, "Natural History; Palmer; various documents in OPM-SPY.

18. P. P. Pitchlynn to "District Forester" (Albuquerque), September 30, 1918, in Office of Personnel Management, Arthur B. Young Files (OPM-ABY).

19. Young, "Natural History," 5, 6; Young and Goldman, 85–86; Gehlbach, 208–229; Bowden, 71–74.

20. See Brown and Carmony for a view of Leopold's evolving conservation ethics and Meine, 134–136, for the development of his understanding of grazing at the time.

21. Turner (1985), 199–200.

22. R. S. Rodgers to Stanley Young, August 16, 1917, SIA-SPY.

23. Ibid.

24. Young, "Natural History; Young and Goldman, 14; Pam Uihlein, telephone interview with Acker Young (Stanley Young's son), January 8, 2000; letter from Young to Everett M. Mercer, February 11, 1953, Record Unit 7174, SIA.

25. Brown (1992), 53.

26. There is a discrepency in dates between Young's unpublished recollections in "Natural History," which states that the first wolf was trapped and shot on November 1, 1917, and the caption in Young and Goldman's *The Wolves of North America* for a photo of a wolf that is very much alive, trussed up on Young's horse, and attributed to the same day. It seems likely that the photo, clearly of the second wolf, was correctly captioned and the first one was, as Young described in his manuscript, killed twenty days earlier—on October 12.

27. Young, "Natural History; Young to Everett M. Mercer, February 11, 1953, Record Unit 7174, SIA-SPY.

28. Brown (1992), 57.

29. Young to Everett M. Mercer, February 11, 1953, Record Unit 7174, SIA-SPY. Young refers to "Mt. Baldy," another name for Mount Wrightson.

30. Ibid.

31. "Record of Government Service," May 23, 1947, OPM-SPY; ibid.

32. "Rules Governing Hunters and Trappers," August 30, 1917, Record Unit 7174, SIA-SPY.

33. Pam Uihlein, telephone interview with Acker Young, January 8, 2000. Acker Young did not specify Ligon in the story, but I have assumed he was the supervisor in question because the exchange took place in New Mexico.

34. Young to E. M. Mercer, February 11, 1953, Record Unit 7174, SIA-SPY.

35. "Senator Stars as Coyote Poisoner," undated newspaper article in Box 345, DPL-SPY; Young, "A Brief Synopsis of the Life History of Stanley Young," unpublished essay, Box 351, DPL-SPY.

36. USDA report, September 1920, Box 345, DPL-SPY.

37. "Nydia A. Young, Husband Was a U.S. Biologist," obituary in *The Evening Star and Daily News* [Washington, D.C.], May 21, 1973, Box 344, DPL-SPY; Pam Uihlein, interview with Acker Young, April 1998. Acker Young, Stanley and Nydia's son, was clearly uncomfortable discussing his father's first marriage; thus I assume it ended in divorce and not widowhood. Acker said his parents met at the Snake Dance, that she was with another man, and that they were married in Prescott in 1921. Various Web sites indicate the dance always takes place in mid- to late August. According to a form Young filled out when he retired in 1959, their marriage took place on June 4, 1921 (OPM-SPY).

CHAPTER II

1. Carhart and Young, 1–14. Hegewa Roberts's identity is problematic. Young called him simply Hegewa in *The Last Stand of the Pack,* but that may have been an alias to preserve his anonymity after he was fired from the survey.

2. Ibid., 12; Pearson, 165–172.

3. Carhart and Young, 7–15.

4. Ibid., 14–33; " 'Big Lefty,' Noted Wolf, Is Captured After Eight Years: Three-Legged Leader of Pack Tied Where He Will Serve as Decoy to Others," undated newspaper article, Box 345, DPL-SPY; "Progress Report, State of Colorado, Predatory Animal Control, January 1 to June 30, 1921" and "Progress Report, State of Colorado, July 1st to December 31st 1920," both in NA. The account in *The Last Stand of the Pack* recounts three wolves enticed toward the chained Lefty and killed, but the other records indicate a total of three wolves killed—including Lefty. Because *Last Stand* was written several years after the fact, I assume the contemporary survey records unearthed from the National Archives contain the correct figures. Direct quotes from this and subsequent wolf-pursuing accounts are from *The Last Stand of the Pack,* in which, according to a publicity release, "exact conversations are reproduced."

5. Carhart and Young, 32.

6. "Annual Report of the Predatory Animal Division, Colorado-Kansas District, Fiscal Year 1921," NA.

7. " 'Big Lefty,' Noted Wolf, Is Captured After Eight Years," DPL-SPY.

8. Carhart and Young, 38–40.

9. Ibid., 41–45.

10. Schlebecker, 50–51.

11. Carhart and Young, 39.

12. Ibid., 45–48.

13. Ibid., 36–37, 49–51, 55.

14. Ibid., 51–55, 57–60.

15. McIntyre, 140.

16. Carhart and Young, 55–56.

17. Ibid., 58.
18. Ibid., 57–60, 60 (quotation).
19. Ibid., 64.
20. Ibid., 61–67.

CHAPTER 12

1. Carhart and Young, 69.
2. Allen (1931), 159, 161; Schlebecker, 72–73.
3. Carhart and Young, 69.
4. "The Story of a Pioneer Family," unpublished history of the Caywood clan written by Phyllis and Bill Duncan, November 1971; Personal Statement, July 23, 1932, of William H. Caywood,William H. Caywood Files, OPM (OPM-WHC); "In Memory of WILLIAM HENRY CAYWOOD October 6, 1869–January 4, 1953," funeral announcement, Delta Mortuary, Delta, Colorado, DPL-SPY. (Throughout his life Caywood cited his birthday as October 6, 1870, not 1869; the apparent mistake in the funeral announcement may indicate his surviving family's remoteness in his last years.)
5. Carhart and Young, 70.
6. Ibid., 75, 77, 82, 84.
7. Ibid., 69–74.
8. Ibid., 75–76.
9. Duncan.
10. Carhart and Young, 76, 78 (quotations).
11. Caywood to S. P. Young, April 7, 1928, Box 358b, DPL-SPY; original spelling and punctuation.
12. Duncan.
13. J. N. Darling to William H. Caywood, April 12, 1935, William H. Caywood to Darling, April 25, 1935, and Personal Statement, July 23, 1932, of William H. Caywood, all in OPM-WHC.
14. Laura Caywood to Stanley Young, January 20, 1936, and Stanley Young to Laura Caywood, February 7, 1936, both in OPM-WHC; "Hunter Who Slew Famed Killer Wolves Retires," *Rocky Mountain News,* April 1935, Box 345, DPL-SPY.
15. Interview between Douglas Caywood and Pam Uihlein, summer 1996. This technique of Caywood's was also mentioned by Stanley Young in "Some Celebrated Government Hunters," in "Saga of Predatory Animal Control," Box 331, DPL-SPY.
16. Pat O'Neill, "Trapper Joe: The Last of a Breed?" *The Weekly Newspaper* [northwestern Colorado], January 30, 1980.
17. Caywood to Stanley Young, June 7, 1949, Box 325, DPL-SPY.
18. Carhart and Young, 83–86.
19. Ibid., 87–89.
20. Ibid., 88–89; Bureau of Biological Survey, fiscal year 1921, table A, WS. Again, a disparity exists between the account in *The Last Stand of the Pack,* which mentions two wolves trapped in addition to Rags, and the records kept by the Biological Survey, which notes a total of two wolves killed in Colorado during that period, one in April and the other in June. In this case I have sided with the *Last Stand* account because of the specificity with which Carhart and Young describe the successive trapping of Rags's companion and then of Rags himself within two days in June. It is possible, however, that Caywood erred in remembering the random capture of a two-year-old wolf while Rags was in Utah in the spring and that in fact Rags's male

companion was caught in April when the survey records note one wolf killed. Because the focus of the *Last Stand* story is on Rags himself, it seems less plausible that his June demise was in error.

21. Carhart and Young, 87 (quotation), 90.

22. Ibid., 80.

23. Ibid., 78.

24. Ibid., 78, 80, 90–104.

CHAPTER 13

1. "Narrative Report, Colorado-Kansas District, October 1921," Biological Survey, NA; "Some Highlights on the Official Career of Stanley Young," Record Unit 7174, Box 2, SIA-SPY.

2. Jay Antle, "Against Kansas's Top Dog: Coyotes, Politics, and Ecology, 1877–1970," *Kansas History: A Journal of the Central Plains* 20, 3, Autumn 1997, 163.

3. Progress Report, Colorado-Kansas District, U.S. Biological Survey Cooperating With the Game and Fish Department of the State of Colorado in Predatory Animal Control, July 1 to December 31, 1921," NA.

4. Ibid., and "Progress Report, State of Colorado, Predatory Animal Control, January 1 to June 30, 1921," NA.

5. Carhart and Young, 105–136; "Get Home, Lobo! Uncle Sam's Hunters Are on Your Trail," *Denver Express,* September 7, 1921, Box 345, SPY-DPL; "FY 1922, Table C," Biological Survey, NA; "Narrative Report for the Month of September, 1921, Colorado-Kansas District," Biological Survey, NA. Once again *Last Stand* recounts wolf deaths not recorded in the Biological Survey's tally sheets. In this case I have accepted the 1929 account as definitive because it states that Roberts found the decomposed body of one yearling but also mentions five other poisoning deaths Roberts might have inferred from close reading of the pack's tracks, even without finding the carcasses. In another contradiction, the newspaper article "Get Home, Lobo!" mentions only twelve hunters under Young's supervision while the Biological Survey's records mention eighteen hunters altogether, of which two would have been Young and Trickel. In this case, keeping in mind my experiences with newspaper stories, I have accepted the survey's records as the more plausible.

6. "Get Home, Lobo!," DPL-SPY.

7. "Capture Wolf: Hunters Dispose of Colorado 'Killer,'" *Denver Express,* December 1921, Box 345, DPL-SPY, original spelling and punctuation.

8. "FY 1922, Table C," Biological Survey; "Narrative Report for the Month of September, 1921," Colorado-Kansas District, Biological Survey, NA.

9. "Senator Stars as Coyote Poisoner," undated and unidentified newspaper article in Box 345, DPL-SPY.

10. "'Big Lefty,' Noted Wolf, Is Captured After Eight Years: Three-Legged Leader of Pack Tied Where He Will Serve as Decoy to Others," undated newspaper article in Box 345, DPL-SPY (January 1921 date assumed from context).

11. Lukas, 635; Allen (1931) 168–173; Tye, 23–44, 51–56, 63–80, 96, 248.

12. Stanley Young, "Some Celebrated Government Hunters," in "Saga of Predatory Animal Control," Box 331, DPL-SPY; "Lobo, Noted Cattle Killer, Succumbs to Hunter's Rifle," *Weekly News Letter* (unidentified newspaper), October 19, 1921, Box 345, DPL-SPY.

13. Allen (1952), 22–23.

14. Young's success at using mass media did not reflect universal comfort with the expanded intellectual horizons of the age. The appeal of presidential candidate Warren G. Harding's much ballyhooed call for "normalcy" in 1920 involved not only relief at the recent end of a world war but also an optimistic (and ultimately frustrated) nostalgic reflex toward local communities and away from an often exhausting national dialogue. See Allen (1931), 41.

15. Annual Report, Colorado-Kansas District, 1922, Biological Survey; Annual Report, Colorado-Kansas District, 1923, Biological Survey; "Resolutions Favoring Predatory Animal Control Work as Conducted by the U.S. Biological Survey"; and "Narrative Report, Colorado-Kansas District" June 1922, Biological Survey, all in NA.

16. Carhart and Young, 142.

17. Quoted in ibid., 162.

18. Quoted in ibid., 164.

19. *Rocky Mountain News*, January 7, 1923.

20. Biological Survey, fiscal years 1921, 1922, 1923, and 1924 Annual Reports, calendar year 1923 Progress Report, all in WS. Once again a discrepancy exists between the number of pups recorded dug out of Bigfoot's den by Roberts in *The Last Stand of the Pack*—six—and the number recorded in contemporaneous survey reports: seven. In the absence of evidence to the contrary, I have assumed here that the survey reports are more accurate.

21. Annual Report, Colorado-Kansas District, 1922, Biological Survey; Annual Report, Colorado-Kansas District, 1923, Biological Survey, all in NA.

22. Doris Wilder, "U.S. Agents Stalk 'Desperados' of Animal World Thru Deserts and Over Mountain Ranges of West," *Rocky Mountain News* [Denver], December 31, 1922.

23. Allen (1931), 159.

24. Wilder, "U.S. Agents," original punctuation.

25. Ibid.

26. Mighetto, 50–51, 57–58.

27. A. K. Fisher, "Steel Traps, Animals and Pain," *The Farm Journal* 46, 11, November 1922, 76.

28. Wilder, "U.S. Agents"; "War on Predatory Animals," *Rocky Mountain News*, December 24, 1922; Doris Wilder, "Lobo, Master Marauder of Predatory Animals, Matches Cunning Against Wits of U.S. Hunters," *Rocky Mountain News* [Denver], January 7, 1923.

29. Allen (1931), 197, 199.

30. See, for example, C. Hart Merriam's article in *Outdoor Life*, December 1922, titled "Distribution of Grizzly Bears in U.S.: The Founder of the Biological Survey—Also the Collector of America's Greatest Repository on Bear Geneology—Tells Us Some Interesting Things About a Fast-Disappearing Animal," which contained this quote: "[W]e hear every now and then of a 'dwarf grizzly' in the lava beds of Eastern Oregon—of which as yet no specimens have come to hand. . . . Here is an opportunity for some enterprising hunter to enjoy a fine outing and at the same time make a much needed contribution to the knowledge of American game animals," 406.

31. Cameron, 140.

32. Wilder, "Lobo, Master Marauder," original spelling and punctuation.

33. Untitled transcript, Manuscript 153, no. 146, CHS.

34. Ibid. Spelling in Young's draft has been corrected in the text, as the value of this never-published document lies in its oral presentation.

35. "Progress Report, Colorado-Kansas District," January 1–December 31, 1923; "Annual Report, Colorado-Kansas District, fiscal year 1923," both in Biological Survey, NA.

36. Ibid.; "Annual Report, Colorado-Kansas District, fiscal year 1924," Biological Survey, NA; "Progress Report, Colorado-Kansas District, calendar year 1923," Biological Survey, NA; ", Colorado-Kansas District, December 1923," Biological Survey, NA; "GET HOME, LOBO! Uncle Sam's Hunters Are on Your Trail," *Denver Express*, September 7, 1921; "CAPTURE WOLF: Hunters Dispose of Colorado 'Killer,'" *Denver Express*, December 1921; "Narrative Report, Colorado-Kansas District," June 1922, Biological Survey, NA.

37. "Annual Report, Colorado-Kansas District, fiscal year 1923," Biological Survey, NA; "Annual Report, Colorado-Kansas District, fiscal year 1924," Biological Survey, NA; "Progress Report, Colorado-Kansas District, calendar year 1923," Biological Survey, NA; and "Narrative Report, Colorado-Kansas District, December 1923," Biological Survey, NA.

38. "Annual Report, Colorado-Kansas District, fiscal year 1923," Biological Survey, NA.

39. "Annual Report, Colorado-Kansas District, fiscal year 1923," Biological Survey, NA; "Annual Report, Colorado-Kansas District, fiscal year 1924," Biological Survey, NA; "Progress Report, Colorado-Kansas District, calendar year 1923," Biological Survey, NA; and "Narrative Report, Colorado-Kansas District, December 1923," Biological Survey, NA.

40. Wilder, "U.S. Agents," original spelling.

41. Pam Uihlein, telephone interview with Acker Young (Stanley Young's son), April 1998.

42. Caywood to Young, July 2, 1948, Box 325, DPL-SPY, original spelling.

43. Young to Caywood, July 7, 1948, Box 325, DPL-SPY.

44. "Annual Report, Colorado-Kansas District, fiscal year 1921," Biological Survey, NA; "Annual Report, Colorado-Kansas District, fiscal year 1922," Biological Survey, NA; "Annual Report, Colorado-Kansas District, fiscal year 1923," Biological Survey, NA; "Annual Report, Colorado-Kansas District, fiscal year 1924," Biological Survey, NA; "Progress Report, Colorado-Kansas District, calendar year 1923," Biological Survey, NA; and "Narrative Report, Colorado-Kansas District, December 1923," Biological Survey, NA; Carhart and Young, 171–203.

CHAPTER 14

1. "Narrative Report, Colorado-Kansas District, June 1922," Biological Survey, NA.

2. "Report of Chief of Bureau of Biological Survey," fiscal year 1923, Record Unit 7171, Box 24, SIA.

3. Douglas W. Smith, Michael K. Phillips, and Bob Crabtree, "Interactions of Wolves and Other Wildlife in Yellowstone National Park," in Fascione and Cecil, eds., 141–145.

4. Leopold (1990), 205.

5. Cameron, 314; Emergency Conservation Committee pamphlet, "The United States Bureau of Destruction and Extermination: The Misnamed and Perverted 'Biological Survey,'" 11, September 1934, Denver Public Library, Rosalie B. Edge files (DPL-RBE).

6. Biological Survey, "Progress Report, Calendar Year 1925," NA.

7. Biological Survey, Annual Report, fiscal year 1922, Record Unit 7171, Box 24, SIA.

8. Biological Survey, Annual Reports, fiscal years 1923 and 1924, Record Unit 7171, Box 24, SIA.

9. "Predatory Animal Control, District of Colorado, Fiscal Year 1919," Biological Survey, NA.

10. Cited in Brown (1985), 145.

11. M. E. Musgrave, "Does Coyote Poisoning Work on the High Ranges Defeat Our Purpose in Mountain Lion Eradication," in 1928 Ogden Conference Records, NA (NA-Ogden).

12. Semi-annual Report, Colorado District Bureau of Biological Survey United States Department of Agriculture July 1–December 31, 1919, NA.

13. "Progress Report, Colorado-Kansas District, calendar year 1925," Biological Survey, NA.

14. Ibid.

15. Doris Wilder, "Rodents Are Everlasting Menace to Civilization," *Rocky Mountain News* [Denver], January 21, 1923.

16. Cameron, 183.

17. "Control of Predatory Animals: Letter From the Secretary of Agriculture, Report on Investigations Made by the Department of Agriculture as to the Feasibility of a Ten-Year Cooperative Program for the Control of Predatory Animals Within the United States," January 3, 1929, 70th Congress, 2nd Session, House Document no. 496, 17.

18. Cited in Dobie (1950), 163.

19. W. B. Bell, "Death to the Rodents," in USDA, *Yearbook 1920*, 432; Biological Survey Annual Reports for years 1921 and 1923, Record Unit 7171, Box 24, SIA; "Control of Predatory Animals," 15. Up through fiscal year 1921, the survey had poisoned an average of around 15 million acres of prairie dog towns and other rodent habitats every year nationwide. But in 1921 that figure shot up to 22 million acres, and just two years later it rose to 26 million acres. Although the statistics do not indicate a definitive trend (by 1926 the number of acres had dropped to 15 million), it appears that at least briefly the agency increased its rodent-killing operations dramatically. Perhaps more telling, in 1921, 18 million acres were poisoned for the first time, and 4 million acres were undergoing a second round designed to wipe out survivors from previous years' poisonings. By 1923, however, almost half of the 26 million acres had been gone over before and were being re-poisoned, suggesting that rodents were re-populating cleared lands at a faster rate.

20. A. K. Fisher, "The Economic Value of Predaceous Birds and Mammals," in *Yearbook of the United States Department of Agriculture*, 1908.

21. See, for example, "Statement of Dr. C. Hart Merriam, Chief of the Bureau of Biological Survey," in Hearings Before the Committee on Expenditures in Department of Agriculture, House of Representatives, March 4, 1910, 61st Congress, 2nd Session, 177.

22. "Narrative Report of Work Accomplished for August, 1923, Colorado-Kansas District," Biological Survey, NA.

23. Annual Report, fiscal year 1922, Biological Survey, SIA.

24. Carhart and Young, 263–289.

25. Biological Survey, fiscal year 1924, Colorado District Annual Report, NA. Accounting for the wolf killed in 1924 is problematic. Although this document places

the wolf's death on July 27, 1924 (outside the time period it covers), an untitled document provided by WS through a FOIA request and marked (by current WS employees) "FY 1924" indicates a wolf killed in June 1924. I have chosen to trust the annual report and to regard the June 1924 wolf as referring to the animal killed a month later. The annual report shows that Young wanted to at least mention the wolf killed a few days after the 1924 fiscal year ended, so it is not surprising that in another document he credited his organization with a wolf in fiscal year 1924 (which ended on June 30 of that year) by counting the July wolf as one killed in June. Adding to the confusion, the July 1948 correspondence between Young and Caywood (see July 2 and July 7, 1948, letters in Box 325, DPL-SPY) mentions that exactly twenty-five years previous (1923) Caywood had returned from a survey trip to Kansas; according to *The Last Stand of the Pack*, Caywood went directly from Kansas to Eagle County, where he killed this wolf. *Last Stand* also mentions that this same wolf occupied the region vacated two years previous (in 1921) by Lefty. Descriptions of the wolf and his capture in both *Last Stand* and the fiscal year 1924 annual report leave no doubt that it is the same animal. In this case, although I trust Caywood's memory of the year of his Kansas trip, I assume that Carhart and Young moved the 1924 event to 1923 in *Last Stand*. A possible reason to do so would be to allow the more dramatic storey of the Greenhorn wolf, which was actually killed in December 1923 before the Burns Hole wolf, to close the book.

26. Biological Survey, "Colorado District Progress Report, Calendar Year 1925," NA; Biological Survey, "Annual Report, Fiscal Year 1925," WS.

27. F. M. Fryxell, "An Observation on the Hunting Methods of the Timber Wolf," *Journal of Mammalogy* 7, 3, August 1926, 226–227.

28. Biological Survey, "Progress Report Calendar Year 1924," NA.

29. Ibid.

30. Biological Survey, "Annual Report, Fiscal Year 1924," Colorado District, NA.

CHAPTER 15

1. Joseph Grinnell and Tracy Storer, "Animal Life as an Asset of National Parks," *Science*, September 15, 1916, 378.

2. Hilda Wood Grinnell, "Joseph Grinnell: 1877–1939," *The Condor* 42, 1, January–February 1940, 3.

3. E. Raymond Hall, "Obituary, Joseph Grinnell," *The Murrelet* 20, August 10, 1939, 46.

4. Birney and Choate, 37–38.

5. Dunlap, 49.

6. Cited in Birney and Choate, 43–44.

7. Ibid., 11–19.

8. Ibid., 84.

9. Lee R. Dice, "The Scientific Value of Predatory Mammals," *Journal of Mammalogy* 6, 1, February 9, 1925, 25.

10. Quoted in McIntyre, 292, 295.

11. Quoted in ibid., 294.

12. Charles C. Adams, "The Conservation of Predatory Mammals," *Journal of Mammalogy* 6, 1, February 9, 1925, 90, 91.

13. Ibid., 93, original punctuation.

14. E. A. Goldman, "The Predatory Mammal Problem and the Balance of Nature," *Journal of Mammalogy* 6, 1, February 9, 1925, 33.

15. Ibid.

16. Ibid.

17. Vernon Bailey, Joseph Dixon, E. A. Goldman, Edmund Heller, and Chas. C. Adams. "Report of the Committee on Wild Life Sanctuaries, Including Provision for Predatory Mammals," *Journal of Mammalogy* 9, 4, November 1928, 354.

18. Dunlap, 51.

19. L. R. Dice to E. R. Hall, June 17, 1930, Archives of the Museum of Vertebrate Zoology, University of California, Berkeley (MVZ).

20. Sterling, ix.

21. A. B. Howell to J. Grinnell, October 28, 1930, MVZ.

22. Biological Survey, "Report of Chief of Bureau of Biological Survey," fiscal year 1924, Record Unit 7171, Box 24, SIA.

23. C. Adams to J. Dixon, January 9, 1925, MVZ.

24. Biological Survey, "Report of Chief of Bureau of Biological Survey," fiscal year 1925, Record Unit 7171, Box 24, SIA.

25. "Foreign Countries—Orders for Strychnine," undated document in Box 325, DPL-SPY (this document mentions Compound 1080, the poison that was not developed until 1946, so it must have postdated that year); Biological Survey, "Report of Chief of Biological Survey," fiscal year 1924, 4, Record Unit 7171, Box 24, SIA.

26. "A Brief Synopsis of the Work of the Bureau of Biological Survey of the United States Department of Agriculture," July 26, 1926, Box 331, DPL-SPY.

27. J. Dixon to C. Adams, September 28, 1925, Adams Files, MVZ.

28. A. K. Fisher, "Predatory Animals and Injurious Rodents," *The Producer, the National Live Stock Monthly* [Denver] 1, 3, August 1919, 10.

29. Biological Survey, "Report of Chief of Bureau of Biological Survey," fiscal year 1923, Record Unit 7171, Box 24, SIA.

30. Biological Survey, "Report of Chief of Bureau of Biological Survey," fiscal year 1926, Record Unit 7171, Box 24, SIA.

31. Ibid.

32. McIntyre, 329.

33. WS; Brown (1992), 79; Pickens (1980), 10–11.

34. Biological Survey, "Narrative Report of Work Accomplished for January, 1927, Colorado District," NA.

CHAPTER 16

1. Telephone interview with Hub Hall (E. Raymond Hall's son), December 2004.

2. Dunlap, 52–53; Adams to Dixon, July 30, 1928, MVZ.

3. Frank Graham Jr., "Hall's Mark of Excellence: The Many Battles of Mammalogist Raymond Hall," *Audubon Magazine* 86, 4, 1984, 91, 90.

4. Ibid.

5. Charles C. Adams to Joseph Grinnell, March 7, 1927, Joseph Dixon to Adams, April 18, 1927, and Adams to Dixon, April 12, 1927, and May 14, 1927, all in MVZ.

6. J. Dixon to C. Adams, April 18, 1927, MVZ.

7. C. Adams to J. Dixon, May 14, 1927, MVZ.

8. Dixon to Adams, April 18, 1927, MVZ; "Young Succeeds Fisher, National Head Predatory Animal Control," *Sheep and Goat Raisers' Magazine,* March 1928.

9. J. Dixon to Reddington, May 26, 1927, J. Dixon to C. Adams, June 11, 1927, and July 21, 1927, J. Dixon to O. J. Murie, June 12, 1928, and O. J. Murie to J. Dixon, October 31, 1928, all in MVZ.

10. E. R. Hall to A. Brazier Howell, August 26, 1930, MVZ; "Symposium on Predatory Animal Control," *Journal of Mammalogy* 11, 3, August 1930, 351.

11. E. W. Nelson to Charles C. Adams, May 27, 1927, MVZ.

12. J. Dixon to C. C. Adams, June 11, 1927, MVZ.

13. Redington to J. Dixon, June 30, 1927, and J. Dixon to Redington, July 5, 1927, both in MVZ.

14. O. J. Murie to J. Dixon, October 31, 1928, MVZ.

15. C. C. Adams to J. Dixon, April 12, 1927; Bailey, Dixon, Goldman, Heller, and Adams, 354–357 (quotations); original italics.

16. Chas. C. Adams, Joseph Dixon, and Edmund Heller, "Supplementary Report of the Committee on Wild Life Sanctuaries, Including Provision for Predatory Mammals," *Journal of Mammalogy* 9, 4, November 1928, 357–358.

17. Paul G. Redington, "Policy of the U.S. Biological Survey in Regard to Predatory Mammal Control," *Journal of Mammalogy* 10, 3, August 1929, 277.

18. Smith Riley to C. C. Adams, September 4, 1927, MVZ; Biological Survey, "Report of Chief of Bureau of Biological Survey," fiscal year 1925, Record Unit 7171, Box 24, SIA.

19. Musselman, 128–130; Cahalane, 232–233.

20. Hearings Before the House Committee on Appropriations, Department of Agriculture, 70th Congress, 1st Session, February 7, 1928, 622, 638.

21. Cameron, 314; Hearings Before the House Committee on Appropriations, Department of Agriculture, 70th Congress, 1st Session, February 7, 1928, 612–639, 631 (quotation).

22. Cameron, 54.

23. P. G Redington, "Memorandum to Field Leaders, Division of Economic Investigations," February 16, 1928, Box 325, DPL-SPY.

24. Biological Survey, "Report of the Chief of the Bureau of Biological Survey," fiscal year 1929, Record Unit 7171, Box 24, SIA. As in 1921, there is no direct proof that Young was behind the division's name change, except that it occurred after his arrival.

25. J. M. Scoville to S. P. Young, March 15, 1928, Box 345, DPL-SPY.

26. Arthur Carhart to S. P. Young, February 22, 1928, Box 325, DPL-SPY.

27. "Trapper of First Wolf in the State for Biological Survey Now Heads Economic Division," *Prescott Journal-Miner* [Arizona], February 1928 (not dated further), Box 325, DPL-SPY.

28. Pam Uihlein, telephone interview with Acker Young, January 8, 2000.

29. "Opening Statement by the Chief of Bureau at the Ogden Conference April 23," Records Concerning Conferences, Conference—Predators and Rodents, Ogden, Utah, April 23–28, 1928, NA-Ogden.

30. Memo from Paul G. Redington to state Predatory Animal and Rodent Control Leaders, November 9, 1927, NA-Ogden.

31. "Some Highlights on the Official Career of Stanley Young," Record Unit 7174, Box 2, SIA-SPY.

32. "Reports of Committees, With Comments by the Chief," April 23–28, 1928, NA-Ogden.

33. Ibid.

34. Memo from Walter Taylor to Paul G. Redington and Dr. Bell, August 2, 1928, in NA-Ogden.

35. "The Situation in Regard to Rodent Poisons Including Use of Thallium and Their Efficiency at the Present Time," April 23–28, 1928, NA-Ogden.

36. Ibid.

37. Ibid.

38. Ibid.; original grammar.

39. O. E. Stephl, "What Should Be Our Policies in Rodent Control on Federal Areas?" April 23–28, 1928, NA-Ogden.

40. R. E. Bateman, "What Should Be Our Policy on Local Cooperation With Counties, Associations and Clubs?" April 23–28, 1928, NA-Ogden.

41. "What Is the Nature of the Cooperation That We Should Establish and Maintain in Handling Rodent-Control Work on National Forests, the Public Domain, Indian Reservations, and National Parks?" April 23–28, 1928, NA-Ogden.

42. Ibid.

43. O. E. Stephl, "Report of Committee on Bird Control," NA-Ogden.

44. Ibid.; Biological Survey Annual Report, fiscal year 1928, Record Unit 7171, Box 24, SIA.

45. "What Part Should the Bureau Play in Interlocking Cooperation With Such as the Extension Service, State Departments of Agriculture, Horticultural Commissions, County Commissioners and Other Governmental Agencies?" April 23–28, 1928, NA-Ogden.

46. "What Is the Nature of the Cooperation That We Should Establish and Maintain in Handling Rodent-Control Work on National Forests, the Public Domain, Indian Reservations, and National Parks?" April 23–28, 1928, NA-Ogden.

47. Ibid.

48. Aldo Leopold, "Pioneers and Gullies," in Flader and Callicott; Hays (1959), 24–25.

49. "What Is the Nature of the Cooperation That We Should Establish and Maintain in Handling Rodent-Control Work on National Forests, the Public Domain, Indian Reservations, and National Parks?" and "Cooperative Use of Processed Poison. What Safeguards Should Be Put About Its Distribution to Extension Services, Farmer-Hunters, Stockmen's Associations, and to Individuals?" both April 23–28, 1928, in NA-Ogden.

50. Ubbelohde, Benson, and Smith, 310; Kramer, 18–19; Kile, 260–272; Berger, 89–112, 93 (quotation).

51. Ira N. Gabrielson, "Public Relations—The Value of Personal Contacts," April 23–28, 1928, NA-Ogden.

52. Cameron, 175–176.

53. Stanley G. Jewett, "Our Policy With Resepct to Fur Bearers in Predatory Animal Control" (quotation), "Report of Personnel Committee," and D. A. Gilchrist, "The Situation in Regard to Rodent Poisons Including Use of Thallium and Their Efficiency at the Present Time," all April 23–28, 1928, in NA-Ogden.

54. Redington.

55. Lee R. Dice to J. Dixon, April 16, 1929, and J. Dixon to Lee R. Dice, April 26, 1929, both in MVZ.

56. J. Dixon to G. Redington, December 7, 1928, MVZ; original italics. See also Dixon to Lee R. Dice, April 26, 1929, MVZ, for Dixon's eagerness to assume the best of the survey: "Redington appears to be open to education and . . . gives promise of being very amenable to reason."

CHAPTER 17

1. "Control of Predatory Animals: Letter From the Secretary of Agriculture, Report on Investigations Made by the Department of Agriculture as to the Feasibility of a Ten-Year Cooperative Program for the Control of Predatory Animals Within the United States," January 3, 1929, 70th Congress, 2nd Session, House Document no. 496.

2. Charles C. Adams to Paul G. Redington, February 19, 1929, reprinted in *Journal of Mammalogy* 10, 3, August 1929, 275.

3. Redington.

4. Cameron, 50–51.

5. Carhart and Young, 166.

6. "Some Highlights on the Official Career of Stanley Young," Record Unit 7174, Box 2, SIA-SPY.

7. The evidence of when *Last Stand* was conceived and written stems from the time frame of the events it covers, the likelihood that Young briefed Carhart on these events while both were living in Colorado (i.e., before Young's move to Washington, D.C., in May 1927)), and the fact that its individual stories first appeared in syndicated magazine form in 1928 and 1929 ("Bibliography of Stanley Young," Box 344, DPL-SPY).

8. C. R. Heck, Stackpole and Heck, Inc., to S. P. Young and A. H. Carhart, April 1, 1949, Box 351, DPL-SPY.

9. S. R. Winters, "Wolfhound," *American Wildlife* 29, 1, January-February 1940, Box 359, DPL-SPY.

10. "Predatory Animal Control," Colorado District, Fiscal year 1929, Biological Survey, NA.

11. An act, dated May 7, 1929, "For the control of predatory animals to provide for the control of coyotes, wolves, mountain lions, bobcats, lynx, and other predatory animals that are injurious to the livestock industry and public health," and "Cooperative Work in Destroying Predatory Animals by the Bureau of Biological Survey, United States Department of Agriculture, and the State Board of Stock Inspection Commissioners of Colorado" (memorandum of agreement), May 1, 1929, both in NA.

12. W. N. Miller, "The Truth About the Poisoners," *Hunter Trapper Trader*, March 1929, 17, 16.

13. Stanley Young, "Conquering Wolfdom and Catdom, *Southwest Wilds and Waters*, January 1930.

14. "Loss Account of Wild-Life: Chief of Biological Survey Lists Depredations of Predatory Animals on Debit Side—Heavy Liability on Game, Live Stock and Farms," *Clip Sheet of the American Game Protective Association*, February 1, 1930, Box 345, DPL-SPY.

15. Birney and Choate, 40.

16. "A Protest," petition, typewritten note, and associated letter of A. B. Howell to J. Grinnell, January 24, 1930, MVZ.

17. J. Grinnel to A. B. Howell, January 31, 1930, MVZ; J. Dixon to P. G. Redington, February 25, 1930, MVZ.

18. Bailey, Dixon, Goldman, Heller, and Adams, 355; J. Dixon to C. C. Adams, February 25, 1927, MVZ.

19. A. B. Howell to P. G. Redington, April 14, 1930, MVZ.

20. E. R. Hall to J. Grinnell, April 24, 1930, MVZ.

21. Hearing before the Committee on Agriculture, House of Representatives, 71st Congress, 2nd Session, on H.R. 9599, April 29, 30, and May 2, 1930, 5–7; Congressional Record—House, December 14, 1929, 679.

22. Hearing on H.R. 9599, April 29, 30, and May 2, 1930, 13.

23. Ibid., 11.

24. Ibid., 22 (quotation), 22–25, 28–32.

25. Ibid., 26.

26. Ibid., 34, 37, 44, 78.

27. E. R. Hall to J. Grinnell, April 30, 1930, MVZ.

28. Ibid.; E. R. Hall to J. Grinnell, May 16, 1930, and E. R. Hall to H. E. Anthony, July 21, 1930, both in MVZ.

29. Hearing on H.R. 9599, April 29, 30, and May 2, 1930, 61–63.

30. A. B. Howell to J. Grinnell, May 2, 1930, MVZ.

31. Hearing on H.R. 9599, April 29, 30, and May 2, 1930, 3.

32. Memoranda by E. R. Hall, September 13, 1930, and A. B. Howell to Annie M. Alexander, October 18, 1930, both in MVZ; Special Committee on Conservation of Wild-life Resources, "Wild-life Conservation," Report no. 1329, 71st Congress, 3rd Session, January 21, 1931.

33. Quoted in A. B. Howell to E. R. Hall, September 29, 1930, MVZ.

34. E. A. Goldman, "The Coyote—Archpredator," in "Symposium on Predatory Animal Control," *Journal of Mammalogy* 11, 3, August 1930, 332–334.

35. Charles C. Adams, "Rational Predatory Animal Control," in "Symposium on Predatory Animal Control," *Journal of Mammalogy* 11, 3, August 1930, 355–356.

36. "Symposium on Predatory Animal Control," *Journal of Mammalogy* 11, 3, August 1930, 358.

37. Ibid., 377–389.

CHAPTER 18

1. Arthur M. Hyde to A. Brazier Howell, June 20, 1930, MVZ.

2. A. Brazier Howell, "The Borgias of 1930," *Outdoor Life,* September 1930; "Poison," *Outdoor Life,* August 1930; A. B. Howell to F. C. Walcott, November 10, 1930, and A. B. Howell to A. M. Hyde, November 14, 1930, both in MVZ; Hearing before the Committee on Agriculture and Forestry, United States Senate, 71st Congress, 2nd Session, on S. 3483, January 28, 1931, 42.

3. H. E. Anthony to E. R. Hall, December 3, 1930, E. R. Hall to R. Edge, July 8, 1931, and E. R. Hall to A. B. Howell, August 26, 1930, all in MVZ; "Predatory Mammals," Hearings before the Subcommittee on Fisheries and Wildlife Conservation of the Committee on Merchant Marine and Fisheries, House of Representatives, 89th Congress, 2nd Session, February 2, 3, and March 22, 23, 1966, 95. Nevada's contribution to the survey was premised on fighting rabies. A second referendum in 1934 decisively ended the appropriation, and enacted a bounty.

4. S. P. Young to A. H. Carhart, November 24, 1930, Box 325, DPL-SPY. I was not able to locate Carhart's letter to Young that inspired this eleven-page defense, but Young quoted Carhart directly on a number of issues, and I could surmise other questions by the specificity of Young's responses.

5. Carhart and Young, 278–279.

6. S. P. Young to A. H. Carhart, November 24, 1930, Box 325, DPL-SPY.

7. Ibid.

8. King, 79–80, 141–143.

9. WS reports.

10. S. P. Young to A. H. Carhart, November 24, 1930, Box 325, DPL-SPY, emphasis in original.

11. A. B. Howell to H. E. Anthony, December 13, 1930, and A. B. Howell to E. R. Hall, December 19, 1930, both in MVZ.

12. Joseph Grinnell and Tracy Storer, "Animal Life as an Asset of National Parks," *Science*, September 15, 1916; J. Grinnell, *Philosophy of Nature* (1943), 165; J. Grinnell to P. G. Redington, August 21, 1930, and E. R. Hall to A. B. Howell, December 31, 1930, both in MVZ; "Some Highlights on the Official Career of Stanley Young," Record Unit 7174, Box 2, SIA-SPY.

13. A. B. Howell to E. R. Hall, January 11, 1931, MVZ.

14. G. Redington to Charles W. Waterman, February 10, 1931, MVZ.

15. Stanley Young, "The Cougar Hunt," A Biological Survey Picture, January 1931, from Dr. Steve Lacy, Footprints from the Past Museum; "Annual Report, 1931," Biological Survey.

16. Cameron, 127–128; A. B. Howell to H. E. Anthony, December 13, 1930, MVZ.

17. E. R. Hall to A. B. Howell, October 9, 1930, MVZ.

18. H. E. Anthony to P. G. Redington, August 14, 1930, and E. R. Hall to J. Grinnell et al., September 13, 1930, both in MVZ.

19. R. Kellogg to J. Grinnell, July 23, 1930, MVZ, original spelling.

20. H. E. Anthony to E. R. Hall, September 5, 1930, E. R. Hall to H. E. Anthony, September 17, 1930, and J. Grinnell to A. B. Howell, November 8, 1930, all in MVZ.

21. H. E. Anthony to E. R. Hall, October 25, 1930, and December 3, 1930, H. E. Anthony to P. G. Redington, August 14, 1930, and E. R. Hall to J. Grinnell et al., September 13, 1930, all in MVZ.

22. H. E. Anthony to E. R. Hall, December 3, 1930, MVZ.

23. Hearing before the Committee on Agriculture and Forestry, U.S. Senate, 71st Congress, 2nd Session, on S. 3483, January 29, 1931, 94.

24. H. E. Anthony to G. G. Goodwin, December 1, 1930, and H. E. Anthony to L. R. Dice, December 2, 1930, both in MVZ.

25. Wickens, 6–10, 19.

26. L. R. Dice to H. E. Anthony, December 2, 1930, MVZ.

27. Wickens, 5.

28. Sprague, 156.

29. Wayne Pettee, M.D., personal recollections, interview with M. Robinson, Lakewood, Colorado, April 29, 1992.

30. T. D. Carter to H. E. Anthony, November 11, 1930, MVZ.

31. Ibid.; H. E. Anthony to L. R. Dice, December 2, 1930, MVZ.

32. T. D. Carter to H. E. Anthony, November 11, 1930, MVZ.

33. T. D. Carter to H. E. Anthony, November 17, 1930, MVZ.

34. Ibid.

35. Ibid.

36. WS; P. G. Redington to U.S. senator Charles W. Waterman, February 10, 1931, MVZ.

37. Gregory D. Kendrick, "An Environmental Spokesman: Olaus J. Murie and a Democratic Defense of Wilderness," *Annals of Wyoming* 50, 2, Fall 1978, 213–302.

38. O. J. Murie, "Report on Investigations of Predatory Animal Poisoning, Wyoming and Colorado," U.S. Fish and Wildlife Service, 1860–1961, Field Reports, Record Unit 7176, Box 45, SIA, 20, 6.

39. Ibid., 10.

40. Ibid., 3.

41. Ibid., 7, 8.

42. Ibid., 10.

43. Ibid., 8–9.

44. Ibid., 14, 15.

45. Ibid., 14–15.

46. Ibid., 18.

47. Ibid., 19.

48. Ibid., 20, 22.

49. Ibid., 23–25.

50. Kendrick, 258, note.

51. Ibid., 230; Bailey cited in O. J. Murie to A. B. Howell, June 2, 1931, in Denver Public Library, Olaus J. Murie Files (DPL-OJM).

52. S. P. Young to E. R. Sans, February 13, 1934, Record Unit 7174, Box 7, SIA-SPY.

53. O. J. Murie to H. E. Anthony, July 13, 1931, DPL-OJM.

54. O. J. Murie to W. C. Henderson, January 9, 1931, DPL-OJM.

55. O. J. Murie to A. B. Howell, May 7, 1931, DPL-OJM.

56. F. C. Walcott to J. Grinnell, January 29, 1931, and J. Grinnell to F. C. Walcott, February 11, 1931, both in MVZ; Special Committee on Conservation of Wild-life Resources, "Wild-life Conservation," Report no. 1329, U.S. Senate, 71st Congress, 3rd Session, January 21, 1931.

CHAPTER 19

1. A. B. Howell to E. R. Hall, January 31, 1931, MVZ.

2. Hearing before the Committee on Agriculture and Forestry, U.S. Senate, 71st Congress, 2nd Session, on S. 3483, January 28, 1931, 96–97. The transcript refers to Thomas each time as "Senator THOMAS of Idaho," but I edited out this awkward formulation in the quotation.

3. Congressional Record—House of Representatives, February 1, 1931, 3817.

4. Ibid., 3818.

5. Ibid.

6. "Predatory-Animal and Rodent Control," Report no. 1565, Senate, 71st Congress, 3rd Session, January 26, 1931; "Predatory and Other Wild Animal Control," Report no. 2396, House of Representatives, 71st Congress, 3rd Session, January 27, 1931; Congressional Record—House of Representatives, February 1, 1931, 3817–3819, 3818 (quotation).

7. Congressional Record—Senate, February 17, 1931, 5190.

8. Ibid., February 26, 1931, 6109.

9. Ibid.

10. Ibid.

11. A. B. Howell to C. W. Rowley, March 9, 1931, MVZ.

12. J. Dixon to Lee R. Dice, April 26, 1929, MVZ.

13. C. A. Adams to J. Grinnell, December 5, 1932, MVZ.

14. Hearing before the Committee on Agriculture, House of Representatives, 71st Congress, Second Session, on H.R. 9599, April 29, 30, and May 2, 1930, 85.

15. A. B. Howell to J. Grinnell, February 26, 1932, MVZ.

16. A. B. Howell to E. R. Hall, January 2, 1932, and A. B. Howell to J. Grinnell, February 8, 1932, both in MVZ.

17. A. B. Howell to A. Leopold, April 17, 1932, MVZ.

18. Graham, 96.

19. A. B. Howell to C. W. Rowley, March 9, 1931, in MVZ.

CHAPTER 20

1. Evans, 187–195; E. R. Hall to A. B. Howell, October 6, 1931, MVZ.

2. Peter Edge, personal communication, June 18, 2000.

3. R. L. Taylor.

4. Ibid., 34. Edge's son, Peter Edge, believed the reference to man-eating tigers has no basis in her actual experiences; personal communication, June 18, 2000.

5. R. L. Taylor, 31–45; Fox, 176; Webb, 504.

6. Quoted in Fox, 174.

7. Peter Edge, "A Determined Lady," unpublished manuscript delivered as a talk before the Chicago Literary Club, April 10, 1989, made available by author.

8. Quoted in Fox, 173–174.

9. Ibid.

10. P. Edge, "A Determined Lady," and personal communication.

11. R. T. Taylor, 33.

12. Brant, 17–18, 30; Fox, 178; Edge, "A Determined Lady," 10 (quotation).

13. Brant, 52.

14. Emergency Conservation Committee pamphlet, "The United States Bureau of Destruction and Extermination: The Misnamed and Perverted 'Biological Survey,' " 11, September 1934; Lien, 421.

15. R. Edge to E. R. Hall, February 22, 1932, MVZ; P. Edge, "A Determined Lady."

16. P. Edge, "A Determined Lady."

17. Emergency Conservation Committee to Audubon members, October 6, 1932, MVZ; Fox, 174.

18. Emergency Conservation Committee, "The United States Biological Survey: Destruction, Not Scientific Investigation and Conservation, Now Its Chief Activity," May 1930, Emergency Conservation Committee Collection, DPL.

19. Van Name, "Poison for Our Wildlife: An Answer to the Biological Survey," May 1931, Emergency Conservation Committee Collection, DPL.

20. E. R. Hall to Rosalie B. Edge, July 8, 1931, MVZ.

21. E. R. Hall to A. B. Howell, October 6, 1931, A. B. Howell to E. R. Hall, January 2, 1932, A. B. Howell to J. Grinnell, February 8, 1932, A. B. Howell to E. R. Hall, February 14, 1932, A. B. Howell to J. Grinnell, February 20, 1932, and A. B. Howell to J. Grinnell, February 26, 1932, all in MVZ.

22. "Comment and News," *Journal of Mammalogy* 13, 1, May 1932, 97–98.

23. A. B. Howell to E. R. Hall, January 2, 1931, and R. Edge to J. C. Roop, August 11, 1931, both in MVZ.

24. "It's Alive!—Kill It," DPL-RBE.

25. "Extinction or Conservation?" *The New York Sun,* October 1, 1931, MVZ.

26. S. P. Young to W. E. Sanderson, June 21, 1932, MVZ.

CHAPTER 21

1. A. B. Howell to J. Grinnell, December 9, 1932, MVZ.

2. Schlesinger, 1 (quotation), 1–3; Watkins, 326–327.

3. Schlesinger, 336.

4. Schlesinger, 20, 335–340; USDA Annual Report, fiscal year 1938, Record Unit 7171, Box 24, SIA; Kendrick, 263; H. E. Anthony to Waldo L. McAtee, January 15, 1934, H. E. Anthony to E. A. Stephens, December 20, 1934, and E. R. Hall to H. E. Anthony, December 26, 1934, all in MVZ; "Annual Report, Colorado District, fiscal year 1934," Biological Survey, NA; "Annual Report, Colorado District, fiscal year 1936," Biological Survey, NA.

5. Quoted in Watkins, 697.

6. Quoted in Nixon, vol. 2, 361

7. Brant, 34.

8. Ibid.

9. Kile, 187–190, 194.

10. Schlesinger, 31; Ickes, vol. 3, 264.

11. Brant, 17, 210.

12. H. E. Anthony to R. G. Tugwell, January 22, 1934, MVZ; S. P. Young to "Field Leaders," January 5, 1934, and S. P. Young to I. N. Gabrielson, January 11, 1934, both in Record Unit 7174, Box 7, SIA-SPY; Nixon, vol. 1, 253–254.

13. Meine, 316–317.

14. S. P. Young to "Field Leaders," January 5, 1934, Record Unit 7174, Box 7, SIA-SPY.

15. I. N. Gabrielson to S. P. Young, January 9, 1934, Record Unit 7174, Box 7, SIA-SPY.

16. S. P. Young to I. N. Gabrielson, January 11, 1934, Record Unit 7174, Box 7, SIA-SPY.

17. "Some Highlights on the Official Career of Stanley Young," Record Unit 7174, Box 2, SIA-SPY; S. P. Young to I. N. Gabrielson, February 1, 1934, Record Unit 7174, Box 7, SIA-SPY.

18. I. N. Gabrielson to S. P. Young, February 8, 1934, Record Unit 7174, Box 7, SIA-SPY.

19. William Hard, "Bureaucracy in Need of Demarcation Line: Hard to Tell Good From Bad When Welfare of Wild Duck Collides With That of Duck Hunters," undated and unnamed Washington, D.C., newspaper, 1934, Box 345, DPL-SPY.

20. Brant, 213.

21. Pinchot, 116–117.

22. Schlesinger, 343–344; Watkins, 206–208, 308–320.

23. Lien, 177–178.

24. Ickes, vol. 2, 156; Brant, 161.

25. H. E. Anthony to E. R. Hall, April 11, 1934, and H. E. Anthony to Madison Grant, January 25, 1934, both in MVZ; Meine, 318–319; " 'Ding' Darling, 85, Prize Cartoonist," undated obituary in unknown newspaper, Box 344, DPL-SPY; Lendt, 68–69.

26. Peter Edge, personal communication, June 18, 2000; "Board of Consulting Biologists and Conservationists," October 25, 1933, MVZ; Brant, 36–39, 43; H. E. Anthony to E. R. Hall, April 11, 1934, MVZ; Lendt, 69–70.

27. "Declaring War on the Gangsters of the Animal Kingdom: Coyotes, Bobcats, Wolves and Porcupines Are Among Those Cited by the United States Bureau of

Biological Survey in Its List of Four-Footed Public Enemies," *St. Louis Post-Dispatch Sunday Magazine,* March 25, 1934, found with similar articles in Box 345, DPL-SPY.

28. A. B. Howell to J. Grinnell, May 3, 1934, MVZ.

29. Meine, 326.

30. Ibid., 179, 181.

31. Leopold (1986), 231.

32. Meine, 173, 175, 241–242, 255–256, 264, 270–271, 299; A. Leopold to E. R. Hall, June 20, 1930, and J. Grinnell to A. Leopold, July 31, 1930, both in MVZ; ibid., 230 (quotation).

33. Brant, 38.

34. A. B. Howell to E. R. Hall, December 27, 1934, MVZ.

35. Quoted in Meine, 327.

36. Young, "Management of Injurious Mammals," 509a, DPL-SPY.

37. Henshaw (1920), 58. I assume the article was written in 1919.

38. "Two Veteran Scientists to Retire From Biological Survey," USDA press release, July 20, 1933, OPM-VB; Kofalk, 19, 32–38, 78, 87, 155, 181, 190; Sterling, 112.

39. Quoted in Hampton, 132–133.

40. Young, "Management of Injurious Mammals," 509–509a, DPL-SPY.

41. J. N. Darling to A. B. Howell, September 25, 1934, MVZ.

42. Ibid.; W. B. Bell to I. N. Gabrielson, September 26, 1934, OPM-ING; "Some Highlights on the Official Career of Stanley Young," Record Unit 7174, Box 2, SIA-SPY; various documents in OPM-SPY. For Bell's background supporting the killing campaign, see W. B. Bell, "Hunting Down Stock Killers," Separate no. 845, from *Yearbok of the U.S. Department of Agriculture,* 1920. Bell's job as Fisher's assistant comes from a memo dated March 18, 1927, in OPM-SPY.

43. J. N. Darling to A. B. Howell, September 25, 1934, MVZ.

44. A. B. Howell to J. N. Darling, September 28, 1934, MVZ.

45. A. B. Howell to E. R. Hall, December 27, 1934, MVZ.

46. Memo of E. G. Miller, July 17, 1934, OPM-ABY.

47. S. P. Young to E. G. Miller, May 18, 1934, S. R. Young (Arthur's son) to E. G. Miller, June 26, 1934, E. G. Miller to T. E. McCullough, July 17, 1934, F.C.W. Pooler to "U.S. Employees Compensation Commission," Washington, D.C., May 23, 1934, W. R. Carpenter to "Forest Supervisor" (of an unspecified Flagstaff-based national forest), July 7, 1934, and miscellaneous other documents, all in OPM-ABY.

48. Pam Uihlein, telephone interview with Acker Young, May 1998; S. P. Young to E. G. Miller, August 8, 1934, OPM-ABY.

49. Ruxton (1973), 278.

50. O. J. Murie to Adolph Murie, December 18, 1930, Margaret E. Murie Personal Papers, Moose, Wyoming.

51. Peake, 94.

52. Nixon, vol. 1, 593.

53. "Three Million Killed," undated AP story included as attachment to letter of R. Edge to E. R. Hall, October 21, 1938, MVZ.

54. L. C. Bacus to S. P. Young, August 27, 1962, Box 344, DPL-SPY.

55. New Mexico District Annual Report, fiscal year 1925, Biological Survey, WS.

56. Brown (1985), 156–157.

57. Petersen (1995), 114–115.

58. Dunlap, 65–70; Range Net, www.rangebiome.org/genesis/colohist.html (accessed May 30, 2005); Meine, 224, 226, 254–256, 271; Murray (1988), xiv.

59. Quoted in J. Baird Callicott, ed., *Companion to a Sand County Almanac: Interpretive and Critical Essays*, 284.

60. E. A. Goldman, "What to Do With the Yellowstone Elk?" *American Forests and Forest Life*, May 1927; Chase, 19–20, 27–28; Kendrick, 248–249.

61. Barrows and Holmes, 45, 257.

62. Musselman, 134–143; Hess, 42–48; Voigt, 78, 86.

63. "Ticks Ravaging Colorado Game Gopher: Bait Kills Birds That Feed on Parasites," *The New York Sun*, August 28, 1933, MVZ.

64. A. B. Howell to C. N. McNary, August 11, 1931, Box 358b, DPL-SPY.

65. Worster, 10–23.

66. Leopold (1966), 131–132 (quotation); Meine, 458–459.

67. Worster, 38–39, 58–97, 195–197, 213; USDA (1948), 71–72, 670. Although wheat farming was the main factor in the dust storms, Worster makes clear that overgrazing was a significant factor also and argues forcefully that the zeitgeist of American expansionism was at the root of the disaster.

68. Lowitt, 34.

CHAPTER 22

1. "'Ding' Darling to Leave Federal Post and Return to Cartooning," USDA press release, November 11, 1935, OPM-ING.

2. Lendt, 72 (quotation), 85–86; "Like a Duck to Water," undated article from early 1937 in *The Morning Oregonian* [Portland], OPM-ING.

3. Memo of E. A. Cleasby, March 23, 1915, and various other documents in OPM-ING.

4. "Some Highlights on the Official Career of Stanley Young," Record Unit 7174, Box 2, SIA-SPY.

5. A. B. Howell to E. R. Hall, December 12, 1935, MVZ.

6. Lendt, 78–82.

7. Ibid., 76.

8. Ibid., 75–77.

9. "Like a Duck to Water," OPM-ING.

10. Gabrielson, 200.

11. "Nash Motors Conservation Award," 1953, Box 325, DPL-SPY; W. B. Morris to M. Gatlin, January 28, 1941, John W. Cook Files, OPM.

12. Worster, 188–197.

13. Byers, vol. 1, 264; "Rep. Edward T. Taylor, 83, Dies, Heart Attack in Denver Fatal to Congressman," front page *Rocky Mountain News* [Denver], September 4, 1941.

14. Watkins, 477–483; Clawson, 35–36.

15. Quoted in Voigt, 259.

16. "Colorado Leaders Laud Taylor for His Devotion to West's Cause," *Rocky Mountain News* [Denver], September 4, 1941, 1, 6. Carpenter was quoted in this article on Taylor's death: "He was a dear, dear friend. If I had been his own son he couldn't have done more for me." Carpenter called Taylor "partially responsible" for his appointment, in a 1981 interview. Range Net, www.rangebiome.org/genesis/interviewfrc.html (accessed May 18, 2005)

17. Quoted in Watkins, 275.

18. Ibid., 270, 274–280, 280 (quotations).

19. Lowitt, 78.

20. Quoted in Watkins, 550.

21. Ibid., 477–483; Brant, 48; Voigt, 253–261. The Farrington R. Carpenter file of the Office of Personnel Management is filled with livestock industry pleas—and occassionally demands—that Ickes retain Carpenter.

22. S. Young to Division Personnel and Regional Directors, "Cooperative Control Projects With the Division of Grazing, Department of the Interior," March 14, 1938, Box 344, DPL-SPY.

23. R. E. Edge to E. R. Hall, October 28, 1938, MVZ.

24. Brant, 210; R. E. Edge to E. R. Hall, February 1, 1940, MVZ.

25. Ickes, vol. 3, 71; Ickes, vol. 2, 629; Watkins, 489.

26. Ickes, vol. 2, 156; Watkins, 585.

27. Young, "Management of Injurious Mammals," 12, DPL-SPY. T. H. Watkins, Ickes's biographer, in a 1996 phone interview, confirmed that this incident sounded familiar but could not remember where Ickes had recorded the event.

28. Thiel, 79, 85–86, for dates of survey activity and hostility of bounty hunters. Thiel does not conclude that the survey's absence allowed the wolves to survive; that is my conclusion.

29. King, 141–143.

30. Hoffmeister, 468.

31. Frederic W. Miller, "Colorado's Mammals," *Nature Magazine* 19, 5, May 1932, 298.

32. "Third quarter 1932 report, Colorado District," Biological Survey, NA.

33. "Third quarter 1933 report, Colorado District," Biological Survey, NA.

34. Pickens, 11; Brown, 85.

35. "United States Department of the Interior Fish and Wildlife Service, Colorado District Annual Report, Fiscal Year 1945," WS.

36. Oregon Department of Fish and Game, Annual Reports 1941–1947, and state bounty ledger books for the same period; USDA (1948), 587: "As a result of the low value of forest lands for grazing, less than one-fifth of the total land area in the northern Pacific coast region is grazed by livestock." Records of wolves killed and sightings reported in Washington state suggest that the Cascade Mountains funneled wolves south for decades after the 1940s, although logging road construction rendered the range progressively more dangerous for wolves to traverse. See Jack R. Laufer and Peter T. Jenkins, "Historical and Present Status of the Grey Wolf in the Cascade Mountains of Washinton," *The Northwest Environmental Journal* 5, 1989, 313–327; University of Washington, Seattle, and Washington State Department of Game, 1974–1975 Big Game Status Report, Wolf Section, May 1975, 236–246.

37. Young and Goldman, 384.

CHAPTER 23

1. "Young Assigned to Wolf Studies," press release, December 30, 1938, and "Some Highlights on the Official Career of Stanley Young," both in Record Unit 7174, Box 2, SIA-SPY.

2. Telegram from Bell (first name not noted) to I. N. Gabrielson, May 2, 1936, OPM-ING.

3. S. P. Young ("Chief Cur") to F. E. Garlough ("Custodian of the Bone"), May 26, 1936, and F. E. Garlough to S. P. Young, July 13, 1936, both in Box 351, SPY; "Order of Square Holers," Box 331, DPL-SPY.

4. "The Grooving of Dan McGrew" and "The Piddling Pup," Box 331, DPL-SPY. Young's authorship is assumed because he sent the poems to Garlough and retained them in his personal records.

5. "A.H.I.E.O.Y.D.," Box 331, DPL-SPY.

6. "Order of Square Holers," Box 331, DPL-SPY; Sale.

7. Winters.

8. A. Leopold to S. P. Young, November 6, 1939, and Young's note to Gabrielson, November 9, 1939, both in Box 345, DPL-SPY, original wording.

9. Young, "A Brief Synopsis of the Life History of Stanley Young," August 18, 1925, Box 351, DPL-SPY.

10. "Black Wolf of Louisiana Takes His Own Photograph," *Science Newsletter,* November 23, 1935; Pam Uihlein, telephone interview with Acker Young, May 1998.

11. Aldo Leopold, review of *The Wolves of North America, Journal of Forestry* 42, 12, December 1944, 928–929.

12. Watkins, 829.

13. Ferrell, 233; Watkins, 820–833; oral history interview with Oscar Chapman, Truman Presidential Museum and Library, http://www.trumanlibrary.org/oralhist/Chapman6.htm (accessed January 3, 2003).

14. Arthur H. Carhart, "Don't Fence Us In!" undated article in *The Pacific Spectator* (Stanford, CA), Box 292, DPL, Rosalie B. Edge Files (DPL-RBE).

15. Clawson, 36–37; Foss, 84–85.

16. Raymond R. Camp, "Wood, Field and Stream: Wildlife Institute Head Fights Invasion of Public Lands by Stockmen," unidentified newspaper article, March 10, 1951; Carhart, "Don't Fence Us In!" DPL-RBE.

17. Voigt, 151–239.

18. "Some Highlights on the Official Career of Stanley Young," SIA-SPY.

19. "History of Predator and Rodent Control Colorado District" (1953), NA.

20. Weldon B. Robinson, "Thallium and Compound 1080 Impregnated Stations in Coyote Control," *Journal of Wildlife Management* 12, 3, July 1948; Dick Randall, "Wanted Dead or Alive?" *BBC Wildlife,* February 1992, 18–23; Olsen, 114.

21. Dobie (1949), 49; McNulty, 17–18.

22. Robinson, "Thallium and Compound 1080," 283.

23. McNulty, 18.

24. S. P. Young to S. E. Piper, July 1, 1924, NA.

25. "History of Predator and Rodent Control Colorado District" (1953), 24, NA.

26. Quoted in Dobie (1949), 45.

27. "Foreign Countries—Orders for Strychnine" and five similar lists, Box 325, DPL-SPY; McNulty, 20; Gary L. Nunley, *The Mexican Gray Wolf in New Mexico,* unpublished manuscript, the Division of Animal Damage Control, Albuquerque, New Mexico, 1977, 56–57.

28. "Sportsman's Guide" (radio transcript), February 1, 1947 (quotation), and "The Case Against the Bounty System," *Northwest Sportsman,* February 1947, both in Box 325, DPL-SPY.

29. Lopez, 194–195; McNulty, 19–20; Mowat, 176; Douglas H. Pimlott, "Wolf Control in Canada," *Canadian Audubon Magazine,* November-December 1961, Box 359, DPL-SPY.

30. Clarence Cottam, "Memorandum for the Files," July 12, 1950, Box 325, DPL-SPY; "Some Highlights on the Official Career of Stanley Young," SIA-SPY; National Research Council (1997), 29.

31. Nunley, 56.

32. Leopold (1990), 203.

33. Ibid., 205, 204.

34. Ibid., 204–205.

35. Brown (1985), 163; McNulty, 20; A. Starker Leopold, "Grizzlies of the Sierra Del Nido," *Pacific Discovery* 20, 1967, 30–32.

36. Nunley, 57.

37. Olaus J. Murie, "The Coyote in the Mind of Man," *The Living Wilderness* 41, 1952, 22. Others echoed Murie's sentiment. A central California cattle rancher and wheat farmer lamented in congressional testimony that coyotes "are very rare . . . practically exterminated" in his region. See "Predatory Mammals," Hearings before the Subcommittee on Fisheries and Wildlife Conservation of the Committee on Merchant Marine and Fisheries, House of Representatives, 89th Congress, 2nd Session, February 2, 3, and March 22–23, 1966, 152.

38. Memo of Clifford C. Presnall, May 10, 1956, Box 344, DPL-SPY.

39. C. L. Wirth to A. M. Day, April 9, 1952, Day to Wirth, May 9, 1952, and memo by D. D. Green, July 19, 1951, all in Box 344, DPL-SPY.

40. "Annual Report, Colorado-Kansas District, fiscal year 1923," Biological Survey, NA.

41. Antle, 169–171; McNulty, 32–33.

42. Birney and Choate, 41; Graham; telephone interview with Hub Hall, December 2004.

43. Graham; McNulty, 51; Hub Hall, personal communication.

44. Antle, 172.

45. Transcript, Stewart L. Udall oral history interview II, May 16, 1969, by Joe B. Frantz, Internet copy, Lyndon Baines Johnson Library and Museum, Independence, Missouri.

46. Udall, 196; Lyndon Baines Johnson Library and Museum, www.lbjlib.utex.edu/johnson/archives.hom/oralhistory.hom/UDALL/udall02.pdf (accessed May 30, 2005).

47. Carson, 14.

48. Marvin Tims, "UO Grad of 1911 Visits Campus," undated 1961 article in the *Eugene Register-Guard*, Box 344, DPL-SPY.

49. Stanley Young, "Management of Injurious Mammals," DPL-SPY.

CHAPTER 24

1. Arthur H. Carhart, "Poisons—The Creeping Killer," *Sports Afield*, November 1959, Box 325, DPL-SPY; memo by Cecil Williams, September 9, 1958, Record Unit 7174, Box 1, SIA-SPY.

2. "Predatory Mammals," Hearings before the Subcommittee on Fisheries and Wildlife Conservation of the Committee on Merchant Marine and Fisheries, House of Representatives, 89th Congress, 2nd Session, February 2–3 and March 22–23, 1966, 104.

3. Memorandum by Clarence Cottam, July 12, 1950, Box 325, DPL-SPY.

4. Circular memo and attached text, "Talk by Chief, Branch of Predator and Rodent Control," from H. A. Merrill, November 14, 1962, Box 325, DPL-SPY.

5. Brant, 22.

6. P. Edge, "A Determined Lady."

7. "Predatory Mammals," 15.

8. Ibid., 14–15.

9. Telephone interview with Representative John D. Dingell, February 17, 2003.

10. Ibid.; Musselman, 140–143.

11. "Predatory Mammals," 245–246.

12. Ibid., 246, 251.

13. Dingell interview, February 17, 2003.

14. "Predatory Mammals," 247–249.

15. Ibid., 17.

16. Ibid., 49–50, 128.

17. Nunley, 58–59.

18. McNulty, 57–77.

19. "ADC vs. the California Condor," *Congressional Record* 138, 9, 102nd Congress, 2nd Session, January 30, 1992, quoting from an article by Joe Bernhard in *Wild Earth*.

20. U.S. Department of Agriculture (1994) vol. 3, Appendix P, 269.

21. "Predatory Mammals," 42.

22. Ibid., 105.

23. Ibid., 181.

24. Ibid., 175.

25. McNulty, 40.

26. Yaffee, 35, 41; ibid., 7; Tobin, 84.

27. Yaffee, 39–41.

28. Quoted in Antle, 162.

29. Graham, 98.

30. Yaffee, 42–47.

31. "Predatory Mammals and Endangered Species," Hearings before the Subcommittee on Fisheries and Wildlife Conservation of the Committee on Merchant Marine and Fisheries, House of Representatives, 92nd Congress, 2nd Session, March 21, 1972, 162.

32. Stanley Young, "The Strychnine Caper," *American Forests*, June 1967; Stanley Young, "The Strychnine Onslaught," *American Forests*, July 1967.

33. S. P. Young to Jerome Hellmuth, June 3, 1963, Record Unit 7174, Box 2, SIA-SPY.

34. Stanley Young, "Management of Injurious Mammals in the United States: Its History and Philosophy," unpublished manuscript, Box 223, DPL-SPY, ii, iii.

35. Flippen, 166.

36. Ibid., 48–49, 132–136, 157, 166, 170, 214 (quotation).

37. Olsen, 40, 64–69.

38. Alfred G. Etter, "Wild Predatory Mammal Control," *Defenders of Wildlife News*, Fall 1969, 397–403; Alfred G. Etter, "Inside the Control Empire," *Defenders of Wildlife News*, April-June 1968, 169–174.

39. Harold L. Perry, "Arizona Ranch Poisoned Without Owner's Permission," *Defenders of Wildlife News*, January-March 1970, 40–41.

40. Cited in Dunlap, 135.

41. McNulty, 86.

42. Dunlap, 135; Olsen, 42, 47–49, 60–121, 135–141, 174–175, 182, 194–199, 209, 228–235.

43. "Predatory Mammals and Endangered Species," March 21 and April 10, 1972, 107, 241, 243; Stanley A. Cain et al., Advisory Committee on Predator Control, *Predator Control—1971: Report to the Council on Environmental Quality and the Department of the Interior*, Preface.

44. Train, 34.

45. Medal of Freedom, www.medaloffreedom.com/RussellTrain.htm (accessed on December 22, 2002).

46. "Predatory Mammals and Endangered Species," 92nd Congress, 2nd Session, March 20–21 and April 10–11, 1972, 6, 49; "Predatory Animals," Hearings before the Subcommittee on Fisheries and Wildlife Conservation and the Environment of the Committee on Merchant Marine and Fisheries, House of Representatives, March 19–20, 1973, 74.

47. Cain et al., 2, 5–6.

48. Richard Nixon Library and Birthplace, www.nixonfoundation.org/Research_Center/1972_pdf_files\1972_0051.pdf (accessed May 25, 2005).

49. "Predatory Mammals and Endangered Species," 1–2, 8–11, 49, 58–63, 91–94, 269, 279.

50. www.nixonfoundation.org/Research_Center/1972_pdf_files\1972_0051.pdf; ibid., 22–27, 36; Cain et al., 13.

51. Yaffee, 49; "Predatory Mammals and Endangered Species," 16.

52. "Predatory Mammals and Endangered Species," 349.

53. "Predatory Animals," 18–43; "Predatory Mammals and Endangered Species," 72–75, 96–97, 265–272, 300, 329–331, 337, 344.

54. "Predatory Animals," 21.

55. Ibid., 24.

56. Ibid., 1, 50.

57. "Predatory Mammals and Endangered Species," 292–300; Shannon Petersen, "Congress and Charismatic Megafauna: A Legislative History of the Endangered Species Act," *Environmental Law* 29, 2, Summer 1999, 474.

58. "Predatory Mammals and Endangered Species," 225–240, 306–310, 408–414, 573–576; Yaffee, 52.

59. "Predatory Mammals and Endangered Species," 480.

60. Ibid., 274.

61. Ibid., 480, 484.

62. Petersen (1999), 475–476.

63. "Predatory Mammals and Endangered Species," 22.

64. Ibid., 383.

65. "Endangered Species Act of 1973," Conference Report to accompany S. 1983, 93rd Congress, 1st Session, Report no. 93-740, December 19, 1973.

66. "Predatory Mammals and Endangered Species," 327; Yaffee, 47–56; Petersen (1999), 479–480; Dingell interview; Tobin, 93. According to Petersen (466), "Congress did not intend to pass a law that would protect seemingly insignificant species irrespective of economic considerations." But this statement relies more on the sentiments of members of Congress who did not participate in the hearings leading up to the act's passage than on those who did, and it is also contradicted by Dingell's recollections.

67. "President Signs Manpower Bill: States and Communities Get Larger Role in Job and Training Programs," *New York Times*, December 29, 1973.

68. Cited in Petersen (1999), 483.

69. "The Endangered Species Act of 1973," http://endangered.fws.gov/esa.html#Lnk07 (accessed May 8, 2005).

CHAPTER 25

1. Michael Satchell, "One Hunter's Epiphany," *U.S. News and World Report*, October 15, 1990, 46 (quotations); Susan Reed and Bill Shaw, "Dances With Coyotes," *People*, June 15, 1992, 67–70; Douglas Kreutz, "Ex-Coyote Killer Now Among Severest Slaughter Foes," *Arizona Daily Star* [Tucson], undated, provided by the Humane Society of the United States.

2. Reed and Shaw, "Dances With Coyotes," 70.

3. Dick Randall, "Wanted Dead or Alive?" *BBC Wildlife*, February 1992, 18–23; Jim Sibbison, "EPA and the Politics of Poison: The 1080 Story," *Defenders Magazine*, January-February 1984, 5–15; Reed and Shaw, "Dances With Coyotes," 67–70; Defenders of Wildlife booklet, "1080: The Case Against Poisoning Our Wildlife."

4. Randall, "Wanted Dead or Alive?" 18–23, 23 (quotation).

5. Executive Order 11870, "Environmental Safeguards on Activities for Animal Damage Control on Federal Lands," July 18, 1975, Federal Register 40 FR 30611; "Amending Executive Order 11643 of February 8, 1972, relating to environmental safeguards on activities for animal damage control on federal lands," Executive Order 11917, 41 FR 22239; Schueler, 148.

6. Schueler, 5–6, 10–13, 32, 37, 71, 140–152.

7. "Transfer of Predator Control Activities From the Department of the Interior to the Department of Agriculture," Communication from the President of the United States, House Document no. 95-60, 95th Congress, 1st Session, January 20, 1977.

8. Memo from Cecil D. Andrus, "Animal Damage Control Program," November 8, 1979, and memo from assistant secretaries to Andrus, April 16, 1980, both made available by the Humane Society of the United States; Schueler, 203.

9. Short, 9, 13, 32 (quotation).

10. Robert A. Jantzen, "Predator Control," undated policy overview by director of U.S. Fish and Wildlife Service, provided by the Humane Society of the United States; Sibbison, "EPA and the Politics of Poison," 5–15.

11. Letter from Senators Alan K. Simpson, Max Baucus, Paul Laxalt, James Abdnor, Malcolm Wallop, Dennis DeConcini, and John Melcher to Edwin Meese III, January 4, 1982, made available through the Humane Society of the United States; Executive Order 12342, "Environmental Safeguards for Animal Damage Control on Federal Lands," January 27, 1982, Federal Register 47, 20.

12. EPA Pesticide Fact Sheet, sodium fluoroacetate (1080) Chemical Profile August 90, Pesticide Active Ingredient Profiles, http://pmep.cce.cornell.edu/profiles/rodent/sodium-flouro/rod-prof-sod-fluoroacetate.html (accessed March 15, 2003); U.S. Department of Agriculture (1994), vol. 2, 12, 25, 22–27, Appendix G, 22–24; U.S. Department of Agriculture (1994), vol. 3, Appendix P, 38, Appendix Q, 10–11; U.S. Fish and Wildlife Service (FWS), Biological Opinion on Jaguar (David L. Harlow, FWS, to Michael V. Worthen, APHIS), June 22, 1999, 15; U.S. Department of Agriculture (1993), vol. 1, Appendix J, 8.

13. Beans, 215.

14. Ibid., 200–224; Sibbison, "EPA and the Politics of Poison," 5–15; interview with Doug McKenna, October 21, 2001.

15. Affidavit of Patricia Wolff to USDA's Office of Inspector General, September 12, 1993.

16. Personal communication, Patricia Wolff, February 4, 2003 (quotations); affidavit of Patricia Wolff to USDA's Office of Inspector General, September 12, 1993;

"Activist Receives Death Threat," *Albuquerque Tribune,* October 12, 1992; "Sierra Club Activist Threatened," *Rio Grande Sierran,* newsletter of the Rio Grande Chapter of the Sierra Club, September 1992, all supplied by Patricia Wolff and New West Research.

17. New Mexico Department of Agriculture, Investigative Report, Consent Agreement and Final Order for Case No. 96-24, and associated correspondence, obtained from Animal Protection of New Mexico (formerly Sangre de Cristo Animal Protection); *Albuquerque Journal,* "Feds Accused in Coyote Deaths," June 18, 1996; personal communication, Elisabeth A. Jennings, January 2000.

18. Al Kamen, "The France Chance," *The Washington Post,* March 17, 1997; Juliet Eilperin, "Chairman Skeen Not Shy to Go for the Kill—U.S. Helps Hill Rancher Thin Coyotes," *The Washington Post,* May 27, 1999; Defenders of Wildlife press release, May 26, 1999, http://www.defenders.org/releases/pr1999/pr052699.html (accessed May 8, 2003); Vicki Monks, "Farm Bureau vs. Nature," *Defenders Magazine,* Fall 1998. Representative Skeen's papers, housed at the Joseph R. Skeen Library of the New Mexico Institute of Mining and Technology, Socorro, New Mexico, include no records of the remarkable 1998 re-vote on funding for Wildlife Services. I was the first to peruse the archives after the congressman's 2002 retirement and was told by library staff that the University of New Mexico archivist who arranged the papers had commented that Skeen's records appeared to have been "sanitized" before being donated for public viewing—presumably by Skeen's long-time natural resources staff member James Hughes, who went on to serve as under-secretary of the interior under President George W. Bush.

19. Expanded and Modified Preliminary Injunction Order in *American Farm Bureau Federation v. USDA,* civil action no. W99CA335, U.S. District Court for the Western District of Texas, Waco Division, February 9, 2000. In February 2003 the New Mexico office of Wildlife Services cited this ruling in refusing to send me a copy of the environmental impact statement (EIS).

20. GAO, Appendix II, 52.

CHAPTER 26

1. Young and Goldman, 397–489.

2. Federal Register, 43, 47, March 9, 1978, 9608–9609; U.S. Fish and Wildlife Service (1987), 1; U.S. Fish and Wildlife Service (1982), 3, 6; Washington State Department of Game, 1974–1975 Big Game Status Report, Wolf Section, 241–242 (May 1975).

3. Fischer, 47–52.

4. Cahalane, 236.

5. Fischer, 44–46.

6. Diane Boyd, "The Return of the Wolf to Montana," in McIntyre, 360–361; George Gruell, "The Invisible Yellowstone Wolves," *High Country News* 25, 5, March 22, 1993; King, 141–143; U.S. Fish and Wildlife Service (1987), 1–6; Chase, 127–141; Hansen, 19–27; Verne Huser, "The Wolf Returns to Yellowstone," *Defenders of Wildlife News,* January–March 1969, 47–50; Ferris Weddle, "The Ghostly Wolves—Did Any Survive?" *Defenders of Wildlife News,* May 1973, 297–298; Weaver, 15–16.

7. Records from fiscal years 1955 and 1962, WS; Spence Conley, "Wolf Caught—1st in State in 40 Years," *Rocky Mountain News* [Denver], November 12, 1961.

8. Murray (1987), 183–192; *Colorado Wolf Tracks,* newsletter of Sinapu (SIN) [Boulder, Colorado] 2, 4, Winter 1993, 4 (quotation), SIN; Petersen (1995), 43, 68–69, 73–78.

9. Fischer, 53–164; Petersen (1999), 484–485.

10. "Endangered Species Act Amendments," *Report Together With Additional Views to Accompany H.R. 6133*, Report no. 97-567, House of Representatives, 97th Congress, 2nd Session, May 17, 1982, 33–34.

11. Fischer, 104, 163, 95–96.

12. Ibid., 90.

13. Ibid., 106, 123, 125–126.

14. McNamee, 36, 37; Fischer, 90–93, 121–122, 125–127.

15. Fischer, 161–162; McNamee, 84–86.

16. *National Audubon Society, et al. vs. Bruce Babbitt, et al.*, Case no. 95-0005-N-HLR.

17. *Wyoming Farm Bureau Fed'n v. Babbitt*, 987 F. Supp. 1349 (D. Wyo. 1997), Case no. 94-CV-286-D.

18. Brian B. O'Neill, Richard A. Duncan, and Jonathan W. Dettman, "Brief for Intervenor-Defendants-Appellants National Wildlife Federation, Defenders of Wildlife, et al.," June 22, 1998, U.S. Court of Appeals, Tenth Circuit, Case nos. 97-8127, 98-8000, 98-8007, 98-8008, 98-8009, 98-8011, SIN.

19. *Wyoming Farm Bureau Fed'n v. Babbitt*, 987 F. Supp. 1349 (D. Wyo. 1997), Case no. 94-CV-286-D; Brian B. O'Neill, Richard A. Duncan, and Jonathan W. Dettman, "Brief for Intervenor-Defendants-Appellants National Wildlife Federation, Defenders of Wildlife, et al.," June 22, 1998; *Wyoming Farm Bureau Fed'n v. Babbitt*, U.S. Court of Appeals, Tenth Circuit (January 13, 2000), Case nos. 97-8127, 98-8000, 98-8007, 98-8008, 98-8009, 98-8011, all in SIN.

20. Frank C. Craighead Jr. and John J. Craighead, *Grizzly Bear Prehibernation and Denning Activities as Determined by Radiotracking*, Wildlife Monographs of the Wildlife Society, 32, November 1972, 6.

CHAPTER 27

1. E. W. Nelson and E. A. Goldman, "A New Wolf From Mexico," *Journal of Mammalogy* 10, 2, May 1929, 165–166.

2. Young and Goldman, 460, 471.

3. Judgment in *USA v. Rancher's Supply, Inc.*, U.S. District Court, Wyoming (August 30, 1993), Case no. 92-CR-106-MAG; cited in Texas Center for Policy Studies monograph, *TDA's Failed Enforcement for Predator Poisons: Texas Ranchers Betrayed*, P.O. Box 2618, Austin, Texas 78768, April 1995, 5; interview with Douglas McKenna, October 21, 2001; "Contract for Investigation of the Gray Wolf (*Canis lupus baileyi* and *c.l. monstrabilis*) in Mexico," November 2, 1976, in New Mexico Game and Fish Mexican Gray Wolf Files (NMGF).

4. Nunley, 47–48.

5. McBride, 3, 8, 12, 33 (quotation); Brown (1992), 168.

6. Mexican Wolf Recovery Plan (1982), 9–10; Tobin, 126.

7. Mexican Wolf Recovery Plan (1982), 10.

8. Ibid., 23, 32.

9. Pythia Peay, "Call of the Mild," *Santa Fe Reporter*, May 16, 1982.

10. N. Ames to Jack B. Woody, FWS, November 13, 1981, NMGF.

11. FWS assistant regional director (name obscured in photocopy) to Bill Malloy of Wild Canid Survival and Research Center, September 2, 1983, N. Ames to FWS regional director, July 19, 1983, N. Ames letter to recovery team, September 22, 1983, Minutes of meeting of Mexican wolf recovery team, October 18–20, 1983, and N. Ames to James E. Johnson, FWS, December 30, 1983, all in NMGF.

12. Brown (1992 [1983]), 171.

13. N. Ames to James E. Johnson, FWS, and Harold F. Olson, New Mexico Department of Game and Fish, March 21, 1984, both in NMGF.

14. Burbank, 152–155.

15. Mexican Wolf Recovery Plan (1982), 3, 22–23, 63; McBride, 38; Ronald M. Nowak to J. Johnson, July 15, 1986, and other recovery team correspondence in NMGF.

16. M. Spear to H. Olson, March 12, 1986, and Spear to Senator Pete V. Domenici, September 21, 1987, both in NMGF.

17. Olson to Spear, July 17, 1986, NMGF.

18. Bednarz, 10, 23, 34.

19. Ibid., 61–66.

20. Ibid., 18–23, 34–40, 52.

21. Bud Bristow, AZGF, to Spear, July 28, 1986, and T. B. Johnson to Jim Johnson, FWS, October 9, 1986, both in Arizona Department of Game and Fish Wolf Files (AZGF).

22. Temple A. Reynolds, AZGF, to Frank H. Dunkle, FWS, June 9, 1987, AZGF; Johnson, Noel, and Ward, 5.

23. Joe S. Owens, U.S. Army, to Spear, September 29, 1987, NMGF; Mark Taylor, "Mexican Gray Wolf Condemned to Captivity," *Albuquerque Tribune,* October 9, 1987.

24. John Hubbard to W. H. Baltosser, both of NMGF, October 15, 1987, in NMGF; Taylor, "Mexican Gray Wolf."

25. Bednarz, ii, 95.

26. David Parsons, personal communication, November 2003.

27. Johnson, Noel, and Ward, 30.

28. Mexican wolf draft EIS ID team meeting minutes, May 12–13, 1994, 6, FWS. A decade later Parsons vividly recalled Thal's minatory statements: "He told us if wolves were released there somebody was likely to get killed." Personal communication, November 2003.

29. Author's interview with Parsons.

30. Mike Taugher, "5th Wolf Found Shot to Death: Reintroduction Effort Won't Stop, Scientist Says," *Albuquerque Journal,* November 25, 1998.

31. Mexican Wolf Recovery Plan (1982), 15.

32. FWS, "Mexican Wolf Reintroduction Update," April 7, 1999, and July 14, 1999 (e-mail and Web announcements); e-mail from Colleen Buchanan to David Parsons, both FWS, September 9, 1999 (forwarding an e-mail from veterinarian Bret Snyder), obtained via FOIA.

33. David Parsons, interviews, November 2003; personal involvement in representing Center for Biological Diversity (CBD) in these discussions.

34. Frank Hayes, Forest Service, to Carl and Martha Cathcart, ranchers, May 14, 1999, and June 2, 1999, Robert Whitten to Frank Hayes, both Forest Service, September 3, 1999, and Allotment Inspection, June 28, 1999, all in Apache National Forest Wildlbunch Allotment Files; "Mexican Wolf Complaint Investigation Forms," June 22, 1999, July 2, 1999, and August 29, 1999, FWS; discussions with various government employees; author's personal observation.

35. E-mail memos from Wendy Brown, FWS, January 7, 2000, January 13, 2000, and January 24, 2000, obtained via FOIA.

36. "Mexican Wolf Notes From the Field," U.S Fish and Wildlife Service Web site, http://mexicanwolf.fws.gov/notes (accessed May 25, 2005); author's personal observation.

37. John Dougherty, "Pack Mentality: The Fur Flies as Ranchers and Wolf-Huggers Argue Over a Plan to Put Lobos in the Wilderness," *New Times* [Tucson], March 9–14, 2000; author's personal observation.

38. FWS, "Mexican Wolf Reintroduction Update," November 2001, www.mexicanwolf.fws.gov/Notes.

39. Kimberly Pacheco to M. Robinson, APHIS response to FOIA request, September 28, 2000; "New Wolf Recovery Coordinator Named," *Silver City Daily Press,* March 13, 2000.

40. Paquet et al., 23, 27, 33, 41, 66–69.

41. Federal Register, November 22, 1994.

42. Leopold (1966), 136.

43. Wendy Brown, "Update on 166 and Dead Livestock," e-mail memo, February 9, 2001, FWS.

44. Ibid; Wendy Brown, "Wolf Update," e-mail memo, March 12, 2001, Dan Stark, "Journal Entries for 4/12–4/15," e-mail memo, April 15, 2001, Melany Benoit and Jason Hawley, untitled memo, March 8, 2001, and Mexican wolf coordination meeting, August 3, 1998, all in FWS.

45. Laura Schneberger to Onnie Byer, e-mail forwarded to Brian T. Kelly, March 27, 2001, and Alan R. Armistead, "Monthly Activity Report, June 1–30, 2001," July 3, 2001, both in FWS.

46. John K. Oakleaf, Dan Stark, Paul Overy, and Nick Smith, *Mexican Wolf Recovery: Technical Component of the Five-Year Program Review and Assessment,* December 2004, 41, 103, and Dave Bergman, Colleen Buchanan, Cynthia Dale, Chuck Hayes, Terry Johnson, and Wally Murphy, *Mexican Wolf Recovery: Five-Year Review, Section B, Administrative Component,* December 2004, 10, 23–24, both in FWS.

47. Ibid.

48. Federal Register 68, 62, April 1, 2003.

49. L. David Mech, "A Comprehensive Recovery Strategy for the Gray Wolf in the 48 Contiguous States, Draft," August 1, 1995, FWS. See also Michael Robinson, "Bruce Babbitt's Secret Plan to Prevent Wolf Recovery," *Wild Forest Review,* January-February 1996, 39–41.

50. Electa Draper, "Gray Wolves Lope toward Colorado Release, " *Denver Post,* December 13, 2004.

EPILOGUE

1. Melissa Woolf, "Journal Entries Tuesday, May 1st Through Saturday, May 5th" (2001), FWS, obtained via FOIA.

2. U.S. Fish and Wildlife Service, *Reintroduction of the Mexican Wolf Within Its Historic Range in the Southwestern United States, Final Environmental Impact Statement,* November 6, 1996, 3–25; Federal Register, 63, 7, January 12, 1998, 1754, 1771.

3. Judge Robert E. Jones, Civil Case no. 03-1348-JO, in U.S. District Court for the District of Oregon, Opinion and Order, January 31, 2005.

4. Leopold, 141, 142–143.

5. Meine, 88, 104, 408; Brown (1985), 78. Could the federal trapper have been a Forest Service employee? Possibly, although Leopold describes the "bureau chief who sent the trapper" as "a biologist versed in the architecture of evolution"—clearly the chief of the Bureau of Biological Survey and not of the Forest Service. He also says the grizzly was killed in June, although Brown reports grizzlies killed on Escudilla

only on September 7, 1908, and September 3, 1911 (both were males). Leopold arrived in the Apache National Forest in July 1909 and left in April 1911. Most likely he received the news of the last grizzly's demise after he left and folded his own experiences into the account as a rhetorical device. Leopold (1966), 144.

6. Leopold (1966), 141–145, 143 (quotation), 145 (quotation).

APPENDIXES

1. Peake, 231.

2. Chrisman, 32.

3. When researcher Pam Uihlein visited the Saguache County Courthouse in the fall of 1995, the courthouse staff told her that only the week before they had thrown out many of their old records, including all the wolf and coyote bounty receipts that had been stored there since the 1890s. In Rio Grande County a courthouse fire several years before had destroyed the bounty receipts. Because the records in this chart only include a few counties, the number and locale of wolves killed in the last decade of the nineteenth century were not estimated.

4. Census Bureau, *Statistics of Agriculture,* 1880, 178–179.

MANUSCRIPT COLLECTIONS

Animal Protection of New Mexico, Inc., Santa Fe (APNM)

Arizona Game and Fish Department Mexican Wolf Files, Phoenix (AZGF)

Colorado Historical Society, Denver (CHS)

Colorado State Archives, Denver (CSA)

Denver Public Library, Western History Department (DPL)

Enos Mills Cabin Collection, Estes Park, Colorado (EMCC)

Humane Society of the United States, Washington, D.C. (HSUS)

Margaret E. Murie Personal Papers, Moose, Wyoming (MM)

Museum of Vertebrate Zoology Archives, University of California, Berkeley (MVZ)

National Archives, Washington, D.C. (NA)

New Mexico Game and Fish Department, Mexican Wolf Files, Santa Fe (NMGF)

Sinapu, Boulder, Colorado (SIN)

Smithsonian Institution Archives, Washington, D.C. (SIA)

U.S. Department of Agriculture, Animal and Plant Health Inspection Service, Wildlife Services, Washington, D.C. (WS)

U.S. Fish and Wildlife Service, Albuquerque, New Mexico, and Washington, D.C. (FWS)

U.S. Office of Personnel Management, St. Louis, Missouri (OPM)

BOOKS

Allen, Frederick Lewis. *Only Yesterday: An Informal History of the Nineteen-Twenties.* New York: Harper and Brothers, 1931.

———. *The Big Change: America Transforms Itself 1900–1950.* New York: Harper and Row, 1952.

Athearn, Frederic J. *An Isolated Empire: A History of Northwestern Colorado.* Denver: Bureau of Land Management, 1982.

Athearn, Robert G. *Union Pacific Country.* Lincoln: University of Nebraska Press, 1971.

———. *The Coloradans.* Albuquerque: University of New Mexico Press, 1976.

Audubon, John James. *Writings and Drawings.* New York: Literary Classics of the United States, 1999.

Audubon, Maria R. *Audubon and His Journals, Volume I.* New York: Dover, 1986.

Barrows, Pete, and Judith Holmes. *Colorado's Wildlife Story.* Denver: Colorado Division of Wildlife, 1990.

Barth, Richard C. *Pioneers of the Colorado Parks.* Caldwell, Idaho: Caxton, 1997.

Beans, Bruce E. *Eagle's Plume: The Struggle to Preserve the Life and Haunts of America's Bald Eagle.* New York: Scribner, Simon and Schuster, 1996.

Beard, Mary Ritter. *Woman's Work in Municipalities.* New York: Appleton, 1915.

Bednarz, James C. *An Evaluation of the Ecological Potential of White Sands Missile Range to Support a Reintroduced Population of Mexican Wolves.* Albuquerque: U.S. Fish and Wildlife Service, Endangered Species Report 19, June 22, 1989.

Berger, Samuel R. *Dollar Harvest: The Story of the Farm Bureau.* Lexington, Mass.: D. C. Heath, 1971.

Bird, Isabella. *A Lady's Life in the Rocky Mountains.* New York: Ballantine, 1973.

Birney, Elmer C., and Jerry R. Choate, eds. *Seventy-Five Years of Mammalogy (1919–1994).* Provo, Utah: American Society of Mammalogists, 1994.

Bowden, Charles. *Killing the Hidden Waters: The Slow Destruction of Water Resources in the American Southwest.* Austin: University of Texas Press, 1977.

Brands, H. W. *T.R.: The Last Romantic.* New York: Basic, 1997.

Brant, Irving. *Adventures in Conservation With Franklin D. Roosevelt.* Flagstaff, Ariz.: Northland, 1988.

Brown, David E. *The Grizzly in the Southwest: Documentary of an Extinction.* Norman: University of Oklahoma Press, 1985.

———. *The Wolf in the Southwest: The Making of an Endangered Species.* Tucson: University of Arizona Press, 1992 [1983].

Burbank, James C. *Vanishing Lobo: The Mexican Wolf and the Southwest.* Boulder: Johnson, 1990.

Byers, William N. *Encyclopedia of Biography of Colorado: History of Colorado.* Chicago: Century Publishing and Engraving, 1901.

Callicott, J. Baird, ed. *Companion to a Sand County Almanac: Interpretive and Critical Essays.* Madison: University of Wisconsin Press, 1987.

Cameron, Jenks. *The Bureau of Biological Survey: Its History, Activities and Organization.* Baltimore: Johns Hopkins University Press, 1929.

Carhart, Arthur H., with Stanley P. Young. *The Last Stand of the Pack.* New York: J. H. Sears, 1929.

Carson, Rachel. *Silent Spring.* New York: Fawcett World Library, 1962.

Cary, Merritt. *A Biological Survey of Colorado.* Washington, D.C.: Government Printing Office, no. 33 in the series "North American Fauna," 1911.

Casteñeda, Pedro de, et al. *The Journey of Coronado.* New York: Dover, 1990.

Chase, Alston. *Playing God in Yellowstone: The Destruction of America's First National Park.* San Diego: Harcourt, Brace, Jovanovich, 1987.

Chittenden, Hiram Martin. *The American Fur Trade of the Far West: A History of the Pioneer Trading Posts and Early Fur Companies of the Missouri Valley and the Rocky Mountains and of the Overland Commerce With Santa Fe, Volume I.* Stanford, Calif.: Academic Reprints, 1954.

Chrisman, Harry E. *Lost Trails of the Cimmaron.* Denver: Sage, 1961.

Clawson, Marion. *The Bureau of Land Management.* New York: Praeger, 1971.

Cohen, Michael P. *The Pathless Way: John Muir and the Amercian Wilderness.* Madison: University of Wisconsin Press, 1984.

Colorado Federation of Women's Clubs. *Colorado Federation of Women's Clubs Official Year Book 1911–'12.* Denver: Colorado Federation of Women's Clubs, 1912.

Congressional Quarterly. *Presidential Elections 1789–1992.* Washington, D.C.: Congressional Quarterly, 1995.

Conner, Daniel Ellis. *A Confederate in the Colorado Gold Fields.* Norman: University of Oklahoma Press, 1970.

Cook, James H. *Fifty Years on the Old Frontier as Cowboy, Hunter, Guide, Scout, and Ranchman.* New Haven: Yale University Press, 1923.

Cremony, John C. *Life Among the Apaches.* Glorieta, N.M.: Rio Grande, 1969.

Cronon, William. *Nature's Metropolis: Chicago and the Great West.* New York: W. W. Norton, 1991.

Crosby, Alfred W. *America's Forgotten Pandemic: The Influenza of 1918.* Cambridge: Cambridge University Press, 1989.

Custer, George Armstrong. *My Life on the Plains: Or, Personal Experiences With Indians.* Norman: University of Oklahoma Press, 1962.

DeVoto, Bernard, ed. *The Journals of Lewis and Clark.* Boston: Houghton Mifflin, 1953.

Dobie, J. Frank. *The Voice of the Coyote.* Boston: Little Brown, 1949.

———. *The Ben Lilly Legend.* Boston: Little Brown, 1950.

Dodge, Richard Irving. *The Plains of the Great West and Their Inhabitants: Being a Description of the Plains, Game, Indians, &c. of the Great North American Desert.* New York: Archer House, 1959 [1877].

Doughty, Robin W. *Feather Fashions and Bird Preservation: A Study in Nature Protection.* Berkeley: University of California Press, 1975.

Drummond, Alexander. *Enos Mills: Citizen of Nature.* Niwot: University Press of Colorado, 1995.

Dunlap, Thomas R. *Saving America's Wildlife: Ecology and the Amercian Mind, 1850–1990.* Princeton, N.J.: Princeton University Press, 1988.

Evans, Sara M. *Born for Liberty: A History of Women in America.* New York: Free Press, 1989.

Everett, George G. *Cattle Cavalcade in Central Colorado.* Denver: Golden Bell, 1966.

Fascione, Nina, and Maria Cecil, eds. *Proceedings: Defenders of Wildlife's Wolves of America Conference, 14–16 November 1996.* Albany, N.Y.: Defenders of Wildlife, 1996.

Ferrell, Robert H., ed. *Off the Record: The Private Papers of Harry S. Truman.* New York: Harper and Row, 1980.

Fischer, Hank. *Wolf Wars: The Remarkable Inside Story of the Restoration of Wolves to Yellowstone.* Helena, Mont.: Falcon, 1995.

Flader, Susan L. *Thinking Like a Mountain: Aldo Leopold and the Evolution of an Ecological Attitude Toward Deer, Wolves, and Forests.* Columbia: University of Missouri Press, 1974.

Flader, Susan L., and J. Baird Callicott, eds. *The River of the Mother of God and Other Essays by Aldo Leopold.* Madison: University of Wisconsin Press, 1991.

Fleharty, Eugene. *Wild Animals and Settlers on the Great Plains*. Norman: University of Oklahoma Press, 1995.

Flexner, Eleanor. *Century of Struggle: The Woman's Rights Movement in the United States*. Cambridge, Mass.: Harvard University Press, 1970.

Flippen, J. Brooks. *Nixon and the Environment*. Albuquerque: University of New Mexico Press, 2000.

Foss, Phillip O. *Politics and Grass: The Administration of Grazing on the Public Domain*. Seattle: University of Washington Press, 1960.

Fox, Stephen. *The American Conservation Movement: John Muir and His Legacy*. Madison: University of Wisconsin Press, 1985.

Gabrielson, Ira N. *Wildlife Conservation*. New York: Macmillan, 1943 [1941].

Gard, Wayne. *The Great Buffalo Hunt*. Lincoln: University of Nebraska Press, 1959.

Gehlbach, Frederick R. *Mountain Islands and Desert Seas: A Natural History of the U.S.-Mexican Borderlands*. College Station: Texas A&M University Press, 1981.

George, Henry. *Our Land and Land Policy*. New York: Doubleday, Page, 1904.

The Golden Interlude 1900–1910. Alexandria, Virginia: Time-Life, 1992.

Gregg, Josiah. *Commerce of the Prairies, or, The Journal of a Santa Fe Trader During Eight Expeditions Across the Great Western Prairies, and a Residence of Nearly Nine Years in Northern Mexico*. New York: H. G. Langley, 1844.

Grinnell, George Bird, ed. *Hunting at High Altitudes: The Book of the Boone and Crockett Club*. New York: Harper and Brothers, 1913.

Grinnell, Joseph. *Joseph Grinnell's Philosophy of Nature: Selected Writings of a Western Naturalist*. Berkeley: University of California Press, 1943.

Haeger, John Denis. *John Jacob Astor: Business and Finance in the Early Republic*. Detroit: Wayne State University Press, 1991.

Hagedorn, Hermann. *Roosevelt in the Bad Lands*. Boston: Houghton Mifflin, 1930.

Hampton, Bruce. *The Great American Wolf*. New York: Henry Holt, 1997.

Hansen, H. Jerome. *Wolves of Northern Idaho and Northeastern Washington*. Missoula: U.S. Fish and Wildlife Service, 1986.

Harding, A. R. *Wolf and Coyote Trapping*. Columbus, Ohio: A. R. Harding, 1909.

Hays, Samuel P. *The Response to Industrialism 1885–1914*. Chicago: University of Chicago Press, 1957.

———. *Conservation and the Gospel of Efficiency: The Progressive Conservaton Movement, 1890–1920*. Cambridge, Mass.: Harvard University Press, 1959.

Hess, Karl. *Rocky Times in Rocky Mountain National Park: An Unnatural History*. Niwot: University Press of Colorado, 1993.

Hoebel, E. Adamson. *The Cheyennes: Indians of the Great Plains*, 2nd ed. New York: Holt, Rinehart and Winston, 1978.

Hoffmeister, Donald F. *Mammals of Arizona*. Tucson: University of Arizona Press and Arizona Game and Fish Department, 1986.

Hornaday, William T. "The Extermination of the American Bison, With a Sketch of Its Discovery and Life History." *Report of the U.S. National Museum, 1887*. Washington, D.C.: Government Printing Office, 1889.

———. *Campfires on Desert and Lava*. New York: Charles Scribner's Sons, 1909.

———. *Our Vanishing Wildlife: Its Extermination and Preservation*. New York: New York Zoological Society, 1913.

———. *Wild Life Conservation in Theory and Practice: Lectures Delivered Before the Forest School of Yale University, 1914*. New Haven: Yale University Press, 1914.

Hymowitz, Carol, and Michaele Weissman. *A History of Women in America.* New York: Bantam, 1978.

Ickes, Harold L. *The Secret Diary of Harold L. Ickes: Volume III—The Lowering Clouds: 1939–1941.* New York: Simon and Schuster, 1955.

Ise, John. *The United States Forest Policy.* New Haven: Yale University Press, 1920.

———. *Sod and Stubble.* Lincoln: University of Nebraska Press, 1936.

Jackson, Donald, ed. *The Journals of Pike, Zebulon Montgomery, With Letters and Related Documents, vol. I.* Norman: University of Oklahoma Press, 1966.

Johnson, Terry B., Debra C. Noel, and Laurie Z. Ward. *Summary of Information on Four Potential Mexican Wolf Reintroduction Areas in Arizona.* Phoenix: Arizona Game and Fish Department, Technical Report 23, 1992.

Kazin, Michael. *The Populist Persuasion: An American History.* Ithaca: Cornell University Press, 1998.

Kile, Orville Merton. *The Farm Bureau Through Three Decades.* Baltimore: Waverly, 1948.

Kimball, David, and Jim Kimball. *The Market Hunter.* Minneapolis: Dillon, 1969.

King, Calvin L. *Reasons for the Decline of Game in the Bighorn Basin of Wyoming.* New York: Vantage, 1965.

Kofalk, Harriet. *No Woman Tenderfoot: Florence Merriam Bailey, Pioneer Naturalist.* College Station: Texas A&M University Press, 1989.

Kramer, Dale. *The Truth About the Farm Bureau.* Denver: Golden Bell, 1964.

Lavender, David. *Bent's Fort.* New York: Doubleday, 1954.

———. *The Fist in the Wilderness.* Albuquerque: University of New Mexico Press, 1964.

Lendt, David L. *Ding: The Life of Jay Norwood Darling.* Des Moines, Iowa: Jay N. "Ding" Darling Conservation Foundation, 1984.

Leopold, Aldo. *A Sand County Almanac With Essays on Conservation From Round River.* New York: Oxford University Press, 1966.

———. *Game Management.* Madison: University of Wisconsin Press, 1986.

———. *Aldo Leopold's Wilderness: Selected Early Writings by the Author of A Sand County Almanac,* ed. David E. Brown and Neil B. Carmony. Harrisburg, Penn.: Stackpole, 1990.

Lien, Carsten. *Olympic Battleground: The Power Politics of Timber Preservation.* San Francisco: Sierra Club, 1991.

Limerick, Patricia Nelson. *The Legacy of Conquest: The Unbroken Past of the American West.* New York: W. W. Norton, 1987.

Link, Arthur S. *Woodrow Wilson and the Progressive Era: 1910–1917.* New York: Harper and Brothers, 1954.

Lopez, Barry Holstun. *Of Wolves and Men.* New York: Charles Scribner's Sons, 1978.

Lowitt, Richard. *The New Deal and the West.* Norman: University of Oklahoma Press, 1993.

Lukas, J. Anthony. *Big Trouble: A Murder in a Small Western Town Sets Off a Struggle for the Soul of America.* New York: Simon and Schuster, 1997.

Martin, Charles F., Secretary. *Proceedings of the Second Annual Convention of the National Live Stock Association.* Denver: Denver Chamber of Commerce, 1899.

Matthews, Anne. *Where the Buffalo Roam.* New York: Grove Weidenfeld, Grove, 1992.

Matthiessen, Peter. *Wildlife in America.* New York: Viking, 1987.

McCarthy, G. Michael. *Hour of Trial: The Conservation Conflict in Colorado and the West, 1891–1907.* Norman: University of Oklahoma Press, 1977.

McHugh, Tom. *The Time of the Buffalo.* New York: Alfred A. Knopf, 1972.

McIntyre, Rick, ed. *War Against the Wolf: America's Campaign to Exterminate the Wolf.* Stillwater, Minn.: Voyageur, 1995.

McNamee, Thomas. *The Return of the Wolf to Yellowstone.* New York: Henry Holt, 1997.

McNulty, Faith. *Must They Die? The Strange Case of the Prairie Dog and the Black-Footed Ferret.* New York: Doubleday, 1971.

Meine, Curt. *Aldo Leopold: His Life and Work.* Madison: University of Wisconsin Press, 1988.

Merriam, C. Hart. *Results of a Biological Survey of Mt. Shasta.* Washington, D.C.: Government Printing Office, 1899.

Mighetto, Lisa. *Wild Animals and American Environmental Ethics.* Tucson: University of Arizona Press, 1991.

Miller, Char. *Gifford Pinchot and the Making of Modern Environmentalism.* Washington, D.C.: Island, 2001.

Mills, Enos A. *Watched by Wild Animals.* Garden City, N.Y.: Doubleday, Page, 1922.

———. *The Grizzly.* Sausalito, Calif.: Comstock, 1976.

———. *Adventures of a Nature Guide and Essays in Interpretation,* ed. Enda Mills Kiley. Friendship, Wisc.: New Past, 1990.

Morris, Edmund. *The Rise of Theodore Roosevelt.* New York: Modern Library, 2001.

Mowat, Farley. *Never Cry Wolf.* New York: Dell, 1963.

Muir, John. *The Story of My Boyhood and Youth.* Madison: University of Wisconsin Press, 1974.

———. *My First Summer in the Sierra.* New York: Penguin, 1987.

Murray, John A. *Wildlife in Peril: The Endangered Mammals of Colorado.* Boulder: Roberts Rinehart, 1987.

———. *The Gila Wilderness Area.* Albuquerque: University of New Mexico Press, 1988.

Musselman, Lloyd K. *Rocky Mountain National Park Administrative History 1915–1965.* Washington, D.C.: National Park Service, 1971.

Nash, Roderick. *Wilderness and the American Mind.* New Haven: Yale University Press, 1982.

National Research Council. *Wolves, Bears, and Their Prey in Alaska: Biological and Social Challenges in Wildlife Management.* Washington, D.C.: National Academy, 1997.

Nelson, Dick. *Chicago, Burlington & Quincy: A "B & M" Excursion 1893 and Northern Wyoming.* Nairobi, Kenya: William Kirkpatrick Purdy, 1966.

Nixon, Edgar B., ed. *Franklin D. Roosevelt and Conservation 1911–1945.* Hyde Park, N.Y.: General Services Administration, Franklin D. Roosevelt Library, 1957.

Olsen, Jack. *Slaughter the Animals, Poison the Earth.* New York: Simon and Schuster, 1971.

Osgood, Ernest Staples. *The Day of the Cattleman.* Chicago: University of Chicago Press, 1966.

Paquet, P. C., J. Vucetich, M. L. Philips, and L. Vucetich. *Mexican Wolf Recovery: Three Year Review and Assessment.* Apple Valley, Minn.: Conservation Breeding Specialst Group for the U.S. Fish and Wildlife Service, 2001.

Parkman, Francis. *The Oregon Trail.* New York: New American Library, 1978.

Payne, Stephen. *Where the Rockies Ride Herd.* Denver: Sage, 1965.

Peake, Ora B. *The Colorado Range Cattle Industry.* Glendale, Calif.: Arthur H. Clark, 1937.

Pearson, Mark. *Colorado BLM Wildlands: A Guide to Hiking and Floating Colorado's Canyon Country.* Westcliffe, Colo.: Westcliffe Publishers, 1992.

Petersen, David. *Ghost Grizzlies.* New York: Henry Holt, 1995.

Phillips, Paul Chrisler. *The Fur Trade, Vol. II.* Norman: University of Oklahoma Press, 1967.

Pickens, H. D. *Tracks Across New Mexico.* Portales, N.M.: Bishop, 1980.

Pickering, Frederick H., and James H. Pickering, eds. *Frederick Chapin's Colorado: The Peaks About Estes Park and Other Writings.* Niwot: University Press of Colorado, 1995.

Pinchot, Gifford. *Breaking New Ground.* New York: Harcourt, Brace, 1947.

Portrait and Biographical Record of the State of Colorado. Chicago: Chapman, 1899.

Presidents and Speakers of the Colorado General Assembly, a Biographical Portrait From 1876. Denver: Colorado Legislative Council, Eastwood Printing, 1980.

Pritchett, Lulita Crawford. *Remember the Old Yampa Valley and the Boy That Loved It So True: Logan Bourn Crawford.* Steamboat Springs, Colo.: Tread of Pioneers Historical Commission, undated.

Richthofen, Walter Baron von. *Cattle-Raising on the Plains of North America.* New York: D. Appleton, 1885.

Riegel, Robert E. *American Women: A Story of Social Change.* Rutherford, N.J.: Fairleigh Dickinson University Press, 1970.

Rohlf, Daniel J. *The Endangered Species Act: A Guide to Its Protections and Implementation.* Stanford, Calif.: Stanford Environmental Law Society, 1989.

Roosevelt, Theodore. *Hunting Trips of a Ranchman.* Upper Saddle River, N.J.: Literature House, 1970.

———. *The Works of Theodore Roosevelt, Vol. 2,* ed. Herman Hagedorn. New York: Charles Scribner's Sons, 1927.

Rowley, W. Morgan. *U.S. Forest Service Grazing and Rangelands.* College Station: Texas A&M University Press, 1985.

Ruxton, George A.F. *Life in the Far West.* Norman: University of Oklahoma Press, 1951.

———. *Adventures in Mexico and the Rocky Mountains 1846–1847.* Glorieta, N.M.: Rio Grande, 1973.

Sale, Charles (Chic). *The Specialist.* St. Louis: Specialist Publishing, 1929.

Schlebecker, John T. *Cattle Raising on the Plains, 1900–1961.* Lincoln: University of Nebraska Press, 1963.

Schlesinger, Arthur M., Jr. *The Age of Roosevelt: The Coming of the New Deal.* Boston: Houghton Mifflin, 1953.

Schueler, Donald G. *Incident at Eagle Ranch: Man and Predator in the American West.* San Francisco: Sierra Club, 1980.

Sellars, Richard West. *Preserving Nature in the National Parks: A History.* New Haven: Yale University Press, 1997.

Short, C. Brant. *Ronald Reagan and the Public Lands: America's Conservation Debate, 1979–1984.* College Station: Texas A&M University Press, 1989.

Smith, Page. *Daughters of the Promised Land: Women in American History.* Boston: Little, Brown, 1970.

Sowers, A. W., and Cecil R. Connor. eds. *Pictorial Roster Eighteenth General Assembly of Colorado: State House, Denver, 1911.* Denver: A. W. Sowers and C. R. Conner, 1911.

Sprague, Marshall. *Colorado: A History.* New York: W. W. Norton, 1984.

Stegner, Wallace. *Beyond the Hundredth Meridian: John Wesley Powell and the Second Opening of the West.* Lincoln: University of Nebraska Press, 1982.

Steinel, Alvin T. *History of Agriculture in Colorado 1858 to 1926*. Fort Collins: State Agricultural College, 1926.

Sterling, Keir B. *Last of the Naturalists: The Career of C. Hart Merriam*. New York: Arno, 1977.

Stone, Wilbur F. *History of Colorado, Vol. 4*. Chicago: S. J. Clarke, 1919.

Sullivan, Mark, and Dan Rather. *Our Times: America at the Birth of the 20th Century*. New York: Scribner, 1996.

Thiel, Richard P. *The Timber Wolf in Wisconsin: The Death and Life of a Majestic Predator*. Madison: University of Wisconsin Press, 1993.

Thomas, Cyrus. *The Agricultural and Pastoral Resources of Southern Colorado and Northern New Mexico*. London: John King, 1872.

Thompson, Slason, ed. *The Railway Library 1910: A Collection of Noteworthy Addresses and Papers Mostly Delivered or Published During the Year Named*. Chicago: Gunthorp-Warren, 1911.

Tobin, Richard J. *Expendable Future: U.S. Politics and the Protection of Biological Diversity*. Durham: Duke University Press, 1990.

Townshend, R. B. *A Tenderfoot in Colorado*. Norman: University of Oklahoma Press, 1968.

Townshend, S. Nucent, JP. *Colorado: Its Agriculture, Stock-Feeding, Scenery and Shooting*. London: Field Office, 1879.

Train, Russell E. *Politics, Pollution, and Pandas: An Environmental Memoir*. Washington, D.C.: Island, 2003.

Trefethern, James B. *An American Crusade for Wildlife*. New York: Winchester, 1975.

Turner, Frederick. *Beyond Geography: The Western Spirit Against the Wilderness*. New York: Viking, 1980.

——. *Rediscovering America: John Muir in His Time and Ours*. New York: Viking, 1985.

Tye, Larry. *The Father of Spin: Edward L. Bernays and the Birth of Public Relations*. New York: Crown, 1998.

Ubbelohde, Carl, Maxine Benson, and Duane A. Smith. *A Colorado History*, 6th ed. Boulder: Pruett, 1988.

Udall, Stewart L. *The Quiet Crisis*. New York: Holt, Rinehart, and Winston, 1963.

U.S. Department of Agriculture. Annual Reports, various, fiscal years 1907–1912.

——. *Grass: The Yearbook of Agriculture 1948*. Washington, D.C.: Government Printing Office, 1948.

——. *Animal Damage Control Program, Supplement to the Draft Environmental Impact Statement*. January 1993. Two volumes. Hyattsville, Md.: Animal and Plant Health Inspection Service, USDA.

——. *Animal Damage Control Program, Final Environmental Impact Statement*. April 1994. Hyattsville, Md.: Animal and Plant Health Inspection Service, USDA.

U.S. Department of Commerce. *Census Reports, Volume V: Twelfth Census of the United States Taken in the Year 1900, Agriculture*. Washington, D.C.: Government Printing Office, 1922.

——. *United States Census of Agriculture: 1945, Vol. II*. Washington, D.C.: Government Printing Office, 1947.

U.S. Fish and Wildlife Service. *Mexican Wolf Recovery Plan*. Albuquerque: U.S. Fish and Wildlife Service, 1982.

——. *Northern Rocky Mountain Wolf Recovery Plan*. Denver: U.S. Fish and Wildlife Service, 1987.

———. *Reintroduction of the Mexican Wolf Within Its Historic Range in the Southwestern United States, Final Environmental Impact Statement.* Albuquerque: U.S. Fish and Wildlife Service, November 1996.

Voigt, William, Jr. *Public Grazing Lands: Use and Misuse by Industry and Government.* New Brunswick, N.J.: Rutgers University Press, 1976.

Watkins, T. H. *Righteous Pilgrim: The Life and Times of Harold L. Ickes 1874–1952.* New York: Henry Holt, 1990.

Weaver, John. *The Wolves of Yellowstone.* Washington, D.C.: USDI National Park Service, Natural Resources Report no. 14, 1978.

Webb, Walter Prescott. *The Great Plains.* Boston: Houghton Mifflin, 1936.

Wentworth, Edward Norris. *America's Sheep Trails: History, Personalities.* Ames: Iowa State College Press, 1948.

Wickens, James F. *Colorado in the Great Depression.* New York: Garland, 1979.

Wiebe, Robert H. *The Search for Order: 1877–1920.* New York: Hill and Wang, 1967.

Wishart, David J. *The Fur Trade of the American West, 1807–1840: A Geographical Synthesis.* Lincoln: University of Nebraska Press, 1979.

Worster, Donald. *Dust Bowl: The Southern Plains in the 1930s.* New York: Oxford University Press, 1982.

Wright, William H. *The Grizzly Bear.* Lincoln: University of Nebraska Press, 1977.

Yaffee, Steven Lewis. *Prohibitive Policy: Implementing the Federal Endangered Species Act.* Cambridge: Massachusetts Institute of Technology Press, 1982.

Young, Stanley P., and Edward A. Goldman. *The Wolves of North America.* Washington, D.C.: American Wildlife Institute, 1944.

ARTICLES

Adams, Charles C. "The Conservation of Predatory Mammals." *Journal of Mammalogy* 6, 1, February 1925.

———. "Rational Predatory Animal Control." In "Symposium on Predatory Animal Control." *Journal of Mammalogy* 11, 3, August 1930.

Adams, Charles C., Joseph Dixon, and Edmund Heller. "Supplementary Report of the Committee on Wild Life Sanctuaries, Including Provision for Predatory Mammals." *Journal of Mammalogy* 9, 4, November 1928.

Antle, Jay. "Against Kansas's Top Dog: Coyotes, Politics, and Ecology, 1877–1970." *Kansas History: A Journal of the Central Plains* 20, 3, Autumn 1997.

Bailey, Vernon, Joseph Dixon, E. A. Goldman, Edmund Heller, and Charles C. Adams. "Report of the Committee on Wild Life Sanctuaries, Including Provision for Predatory Mammals." *Journal of Mammalogy* 9, 4, November 1928.

Belknap, Orin. "Poisoning Wolves." *Forest and Stream* 48, 9, February 27, 1897.

Bell, W. B. "Hunting Down Stock Killers." Separate no. 845, from *Yearbook of the U.S. Department of Agriculture,* 1920. Washington, D.C.: Government Printing Office, 1921.

———. "Death to the Rodents." Separate no. 845, from *Yearbook of the U.S. Department of Agriculture,* 1920. Washington, D.C.: Government Printing Office, 1921.

"Black Wolf of Louisiana Takes His Own Photograph." *Science Newsletter,* November 23, 1935.

Cahalane, Victor H. "The Evolution of Predator Control Policy in the National Parks." *Journal of Wildlife Management* 3, 3, July 1939.

Carhart, Arthur Hawthorne. "Buckskin Pay-Off." *Rocky Mountain Sportsman,* February 1939.

——. "Poisons—The Creeping Killer." *Sports Afield,* November 1959.

"The Case Against the Bounty System." *Northwest Sportsman,* February 1947.

Craighead, Frank C., Jr., and John J. Craighead. *Grizzly Bear Prehibernation and Denning Activities as Determined by Radiotracking.* Wildlife Monographs of the Wildlife Society, no. 32, November 1972.

Crandall, C. S. "Reproduction of Trees and Range Cattle." *The Forester,* magazine of the American Forestry Association, July 1901.

Davis, Tony. "Wolf Revival Spreads to Southwest." *High Country News* [Paonia, Colorado], 27, 13, July 24, 1995.

Dice, Lee R. "The Scientific Value of Predatory Mammals." *Journal of Mammalogy* 6, 1, February 1925.

Etter, Alfred G. "Inside the Control Empire." *Defenders of Wildlife News,* April–June 1968.

——."Wild Predatory Mammal Control." *Defenders of Wildlife News,* Fall 1969.

Fisher, A. K. "Predatory Animals and Injurious Rodents." *The Producer, the National Live Stock Monthly* [Denver] 1, 3, August 1919.

——. "Steel Traps, Animals and Pain." *The Farm Journal* 46, 11, November 1922.

Fryxell, F. M. "An Observation on the Hunting Methods of the Timber Wolf." *Journal of Mammalogy* 7, 3, August 1926.

——. "The Former Range of the Bison in the Rocky Mountains." *Journal of Mammalogy* 9, 2, May 1928.

Goldman, E. A. "The Predatory Mammal Problem and the Balance of Nature." *Journal of Mammalogy* 6, 1, February 1925.

——. "What to Do With the Yellowstone Elk?" *American Forests and Forest Life,* May 1927.

——. "The Coyote—Archpredator." In "Symposium on Predatory Animal Control." *Journal of Mammalogy* 11, 3, August 1930.

Graham, Frank, Jr. "Hall's Mark of Excellence: The Many Battles of Mammalogist Raymond Hall." *Audubon Magazine* 86, 4, 1984.

"The Gray Wolf." *Forest and Stream* 58, 5, February 1, 1902.

Grinnell, Hilda Wood. "Joseph Grinnell: 1877–1939." *The Condor* 42, 1, January-February 1940.

Grinnell, Joseph, and Tracy Storer. "Animal Life as an Asset of National Parks." *Science,* September 15, 1916.

Gruell, George. "The Invisible Yellowstone Wolves." *High Country News* [Paonia, Colorado] 25, 5, March 22, 1993.

Hall, E. Raymond. "Obituary, Joseph Grinnell." *The Murrelet* 20, August 10, 1939.

Henshaw, Henry Wetherbee. "The Policemen of the Air: An Account of the Biological Survey of the Department of Agriculture." *National Geographic Magazine* 19, 2, February 1908.

——. "Autobiographical Notes." *The Condor* 22, March 1920.

Howell, A. Brazier. "The Borgias of 1930." *Outdoor Life,* September 1930.

Huser, Verne. "The Wolf Returns to Yellowstone." *Defenders of Wildlife News,* January-March 1969.

Kendrick, Gregory D. "An Environmental Spokesman: Olaus J. Murie and a Democratic Defense of Wilderness." *Annals of Wyoming* 50, 2, Fall 1978.

Laufer, Jack R., and Peter T. Jenkins. "Historical and Present Status of the Grey Wolf in the Cascade Mountains of Washington." *Northwest Environmental Journal* 5, 1989.

Leopold, Aldo. Review of *The Wolves of North America*. *Journal of Forestry* 42, 12, December 1944.

Leopold, A. Starker. "Grizzlies of the Sierra Del Nido." *Pacific Discovery* 20, 1967.

Lockwood, Jeffrey. "The Death of the Super Hopper: How Early Settlers Unwittingly Drove Their Nemesis Extinct, and What It Means for Us Today." *High Country News* [Paonia, Colorado] 35, 2, February 3, 2003.

Merriam, C. Hart. "Distribution of Grizzly Bears in U.S.: The Founder of the Biological Survey—Also the Collector of America's Greatest Repository on Bear Geneology— Tells Us Some Interesting Things About a Fast-Disappearing Animal." *Outdoor Life*, Vol. 50, 6, December 1922.

Miller, Frederic W. "Colorado's Mammals." *Nature Magazine* 19, 5, May 1932.

Miller, W. N. "The Truth About the Poisoners." *Hunter Trapper Trader,* March 1929.

Monks, Vicki. "Farm Bureau vs. Nature." *Defenders Magazine,* Fall 1998.

Murie, Olaus J. "The Coyote in the Mind of Man." *The Living Wilderness* 41, 1952.

Nelson, E. W., and E. A. Goldman. "A New Wolf From Mexico." *Journal of Mammalogy* 10, 2, May 1929.

Ogilvie, Carolyn Young. "The Benjamin Young House." *CUMTUX* [Astoria, Oregon], Clatsop County Historical Society Quarterly 6, 3, Summer 1986.

Perry, Harold L. "Arizona Ranch Poisoned Without Owner's Permission." *Defenders of Wildlife News,* January-March 1970.

Petersen, Shannon. "Congress and Charismatic Megafauna: A Legislative History of the Endangered Species Act." *Environmental Law* 29, 2, Summer 1999.

Peterson, David. "Artifacts, People and History." *CUMTUX* [Astoria, Oregon], Clatsop County Historical Society Quarterly 6, 3, Summer 1986.

Pimlott, Douglas H. "Wolf Control in Canada." *Canadian Audubon Magazine,* November-December 1961.

Randall, Dick. "Wanted Dead or Alive?" *BBC Wildlife,* February 1992.

Redington, Paul G. "Policy of the U.S. Biological Survey in Regard to Predatory Mammal Control." *Journal of Mammalogy* 10, 3, August 1929.

Reed, Susan, and Bill Shaw. "Dances With Coyotes." *People,* June 15, 1992.

Robinson, Michael. "Bruce Babbitt's Secret Plan to Prevent Wolf Recovery." *Wild Forest Review,* January-February 1996.

Robinson, Weldon B. "Thallium and Compound 1080 Impregnated Stations in Coyote Control." *Journal of Wildlife Management* 12, 3, July 1948.

Roosevelt, Theodore. "A Wolf Hunt in Oklahoma." *Scribner's Magazine,* November 1905.

Satchell, Michael. "One Hunter's Epiphany." *U.S. News and World Report,* October 15, 1990.

Sibbison, Jim. "EPA and the Politics of Poison: The 1080 Story." *Defenders Magazine,* January-February 1984.

"Sierra Club Activist Threatened." *Rio Grande Sierran,* newsletter of the Rio Grande Chapter of the Sierra Club, September 1992.

Smith, Douglas W., Michael K. Phillips, and Bob Crabtree. "Interactions of Wolves and Other Wildlife in Yellowstone National Park." *Wolves of America Conference Proceedings.* Defenders of Wildlife, November 1996.

"Supplementary Report of the Committee on Wild Life Sanctuaries, Including Provision for Predatory Mammals." *Journal of Mammalogy* 9, 4, November 1928.

"Symposium on Predatory Animal Control." *Journal of Mammalogy* 11, 3, August 1930.

Taylor, Robert Lewis. "Oh, Hawk of Mercy." *The New Yorker*, April 17, 1948.

Weddle, Ferris. "The Ghostly Wolves—Did Any Survive?" *Defenders of Wildlife News,* May 1973.

Winters, S. R. "Wolfhound." *American Wildlife* 29, 1, January-February 1940.

"Wolves in Wyoming and Colorado." *Forest and Stream* 58, 9, March 1, 1902.

Young, Stanley P. "Conquering Wolfdom and Catdom." *Southwest Wilds and Waters,* January 1930.

———. "Wolf!" *The American Rifleman*, June 1944, 10–11.

———. "The Strychnine Caper." *American Forests*, June 1967.

———. "The Strychnine Onslaught." *American Forests*, July 1967.

"Young Succeeds Fisher, National Head Predatory Animal Control." *Sheep and Goat Raisers' Magazine*, March 1928.

REPORTS AND DISSERTATIONS

Bailey, Vernon. *Wolves in Relation to Stock, Game, and the National Forest Reserves.* U.S. Department of Agriculture, Forest Service, Bulletin 72, 1907.

———. *Destruction of Wolves and Coyotes: Results Obtained During 1907.* USDA Bureau of Biological Survey, Circular no. 63, April 29, 1908.

Bergman, Dave, Colleen Buchanan, Cynthia Dale, Chuck Hayes, Terry Johnson, and Wally Murphy. *Mexican Wolf Recovery: Five-Year Review, Section B, Administrative Component.* December 2004, FWS.

Cain, Stanley A., et al. Advisory Committee on Predator Control. *Predator Control— 1971: Report to the Council on Environmental Quality and the Department of the Interior.* Ann Arbor: University of Michigan, January 1972.

Curnow, Edward E. "The History of the Eradication of the Wolf in Montana." Unpublished Master of Arts thesis, University of Montana, 1969 (available from the University of Montana library).

General Accounting Office (GAO). *Wildlife Services Program.* GAO-02-138. November 2001.

McBride, Roy T. "The Mexican Wolf (*Canis lupus baileyi*): A Historical Review and Observations on Its Status and Distribution." Unpublished Progress Report to the U.S. Fish and Wildlife Service, March 1980, FWS.

New Mexico Department of Agriculture. Investigative Report, Consent Agreement and Final Order for Case no. 96-24. Animal Protection of New Mexico files.

Nunley, Gary L. "The Mexican Gray Wolf in New Mexico." Unpublished manuscript, Division of Animal Damage Control, Albuquerque, New Mexico, 1977.

Oakleaf, John K., Dan Stark, Paul Overy, and Nick Smith. *Mexican Wolf Recovery: Technical Component of the Five-Year Program Review and Assessment.* December 2004, FWS.

Texas Center for Policy Studies Monograph. *TDA's Failed Enforcement for Predator Poisons: Texas Ranchers Betrayed.* P.O. Box 2618, Austin, Texas 78768, April 1995.

Washington State Department of Game. *1974–1975 Big Game Status Report, Wolf Section,* May 1975. Wolf Haven International, Tenino, Wash.

COURT CASES

Defenders of Wildlife v. Norton (D. Oregon. 2005), Case no. 03-1348-JO.

Light v. U.S., 220 U.S. 523, 31 S.Ct. 485 (decided May 11, 1911).

Wyoming Farm Bureau Fed'n v. Babbitt, 987 F. Supp. 1349 (D. Wyo. 1997), Case no. 94-CV-286-D.

Wyoming Farm Bureau Fed'n v. Babbitt, U.S. Court of Appeals, Tenth Circuit (decided January 13, 2000), Case nos. 97-8127, 98-8000, 98-8007, 98-8008, 98-8009, 98-8011.

CONGRESSIONAL DOCUMENTS

Congressional Record—House of Representatives, December 14, 1929.

Congressional Record—House of Representatives, February 1, 1931.

Congressional Record—Senate, February 17, 1931, and February 26, 1931, 5190, 6108–6109.

"Control of Predatory Animals: Letter From the Secretary of Agriculture, Report on Investigations Made by the Department of Agriculture as to the Feasibility of a Ten-Year Cooperative Program for the Control of Predatory Animals Within the United States." 70th Congress, 2nd Session, House Document 496, January 3, 1929.

"Endangered Species Act Amendments." Report together with additional views to accompany H.R. 6133. House of Representatives, 97th Congress, 2nd Session, Report 97-567, May 17, 1982.

"Endangered Species Act of 1973." Conference report to accompany S. 1983. House of Representatives, 93rd Congress, 1st Session, Report 93-740, December 19, 1973.

Hearing before the Committee on Agriculture. House of Representatives, 71st Congress, 2nd Session, on H.R. 9599, April 29–30 and May 2, 1930.

Hearing before the Committee on Agriculture and Forestry. U.S. Senate, 71st Congress, 2nd Session, on S. 3483, May 8, 1930.

Hearing before the Committee on Agriculture and Forestry. U.S. Senate, 71st Congress, 3rd Session, on S. 3483, January 28–29, 1931.

Hearing before the House Agriculture Appropriations Committee. 60th Congress, 1st Session, February 3 and 4, 1908.

"Predatory-Animal and Rodent Control." U.S. Senate, 71st Congress, 3rd Session, Report 1565, January 26, 1931.

"Predatory Animals." Hearing before the Committee on Merchant Marine and Fisheries, Subcommittee on Fisheries and Wildlife Conservation and the Environment. House of Representatives, 93rd Congress, 1st Session, March 19–20, 1973.

"Predatory and Other Wild Animal Control." House of Representatives, 71st Congress, 3rd Session, Report 2396, January 27, 1931.

"Predatory Mammals." Hearing before the Subcommittee on Fisheries and Wildlife Conservation of the Committee on Merchant Marine and Fisheries. House of Representatives, 89th Congress, 2nd Session, February 2–3 and March 22–23, 1966.

"Predatory Mammals and Endangered Species." Hearing before the Committee on Merchant Marine and Fisheries, Subcommittee on Fisheries and Wildlife Conservation. House of Representatives, 92nd Congress, 2nd Session, March 20–21 and April 10, 1972.

"Transfer of Predator Control Activities From the Department of the Interior to the Department of Agriculture." Communication from the President of the United States. House of Representatives, 95th Congress, 1st Session, House Document 95-60, January 20, 1977.

"Wild-life Conservation." Special Committee on Conservation of Wild-life Resources. U.S. Senate, 71st Congress, 3rd Session, Report 1329, January 21, 1931.

EPHEMERA

Benjamin Young Inn. Bed and breakfast brochure. 3652 Duane Street, Astoria, OR 97103.

Defenders of Wildlife. "1080: The Case Against Poisoning Our Wildlife" (booklet), 1982.

Duncan, Phyllis, and Bill Duncan. "The Story of a Pioneer Family." Unpublished history of the Caywood clan, November 1971.

Edge, Peter. "A Determined Lady." Unpublished manuscript delivered as a talk before the Chicago Literary Club, April 10, 1989 (made available by author).

Gault, Vera. "A Brief History of Astoria, Oregon 1811–1900." 1393 Franklin Avenue, Astoria, OR 97103, 1982.

Welch, Roy. Interview with Morris Snider (audiotape), 1977.

Young, Stanley P. *The Cougar Hunt*. A Biological Survey Picture (newsreel), January 1931. Available by Dr. Steve Lacy, Footprints from the Past Museum, Salt Lake City, Utah.

Index

Page numbers in italics indicate illustrations

457